Fraser Hunter

The carnyx in Iron Age Europe:
the Deskford carnyx in its European context

MONOGRAPHIEN

des Römisch-Germanischen Zentralmuseums

Band 146, 2

Römisch-Germanisches Zentralmuseum
Leibniz-Forschungsinstitut
für Archäologie

R G Z M

National
Museums
Scotland

Römisch-Germanisches Zentralmuseum
Leibniz-Forschungsinstitut für Archäologie

and

National Museums Scotland

Fraser Hunter

THE CARNYX IN IRON AGE EUROPE: THE DESKFORD CARNYX IN ITS EUROPEAN CONTEXT

VOLUME 2

Verlag des Römisch-Germanischen Zentralmuseums   Mainz 2019

Publication supported by

MARC FITCH FUND

Redaktion: Claudia Nickel, Marie Reiter (RGZM)
Satz: Claudia Nickel (RGZM)
Umschlaggestaltung: Claudia Nickel (RGZM)

Bibliografische Information
der Deutschen Nationalbibliothek

Die Deutsche Nationalbibliothek verzeichnet diese Publikation in
der Deutschen Nationalbibliografie; detaillierte bibliografische
Daten sind im Internet über **http://dnb.d-nb.de** abrufbar.

ISBN 978-3-88467-309-6
ISSN 0171-1474

© 2019 Verlag des Römisch-Germanischen Zentralmuseums

Druck: Beltz Grafische Betriebe GmbH, Bad Langensalza
Printed in Germany.

CONTENTS

APPENDIX 1: CATALOGUE OF CARNYX DEPICTIONS

This Appendix lists, describes and where possible illustrates all carnyx depictions known to me as of 31.12.2017. The structure of the catalogue is given in **table 53**. Each entry is then given a sub-number; thus A1.1 for the stater of Tasciovanus, B1.12 for Trajan's Column (with the individual carnyces here numbered B1.12.1, B1.12.2, etc.). Each section is preceded by a summary list. I have indicated whether the item has been inspected first-hand; the details for those which were not are obviously less secure. In description of trophies, unless stated otherwise, left and right are from the reader's perspective.

Abbreviations

ABC	Cottam et al. 2010
BM	British Museum (for Iron Age coins, this refers to Hobbs 1996)
BMCRE	British Museum Coins of the Roman Empire (= Mattingly 1923 *et seq*)
BMCRR	British Museum Coins of the Roman Republic (= Grueber 1910)
BN	Bibliothèque nationale de France
CCI	Celtic Coin Index, University of Oxford; www.celticcoins.ca// (or via the PAS website; see below)
D.	diameter
Depeyrot	Depeyrot 2004a-b; 2005a-b
DT	Delestrée/Tache 2002; 2004; 2007; 2008
H.	height
L.	length
LT	de La Tour 1892
m	mass
M or Mack	Mack 1975
NMS	National Museums Scotland
PAS	Portable Antiquities Scheme; www.finds.org.uk
RIB	Collingwood/Wright 1965
RIC	Roman Imperial Coinage (= Mattingly/Sydenham 1923 *et seq*; Sutherland 1984)
RIC II²	Carradice/Buttrey 2007
RRC	Roman Republican Coinage (Crawford 1974)
SNG	Sylloge Nummorum Graecorum
VA	Van Arsdell 1989
W.	width

A	coins	B	sculpture	C	artefacts
1	Iron Age – Britain	1	Rome & environs	1	Iron Age
2	Iron Age – Gaul	2	rest of Italy	2	Hellenistic
3	Greek	3	Gaulish provinces	3	Roman military & gladiatorial equipment
4	Roman – Republic	4	German provinces	4	Roman architectural fittings & decoration
5	Roman – Imperial	5	Iberian provinces	5	Roman ceramics
6	Roman – provincial	6	African provinces		
		7	E Mediterranean provinces		
		8	non-Roman		

Tab. 53 Structure of the catalogue.

A COINS

A1 BRITISH IRON AGE COINS

Table 54 summarises the details of the British Iron Age coins showing carnyces. All examples of these coins recorded in the Celtic Coin Index up to February 2000 were examined in photos and (for those in the British Museum and some private collections) first-hand; subsequent finds have been monitored, but only included where they add significant detail.

A1.1 Tasciovanus stater

Classification: VA 1730, 1732, 1734, 1736; BM 1608-1624; Mack 154-157; ABC 2562, 2565, 2568
Distribution: mainly Essex & Hertfordshire
Gold stater of Tasciovanus (his second series), from the area north and east of the Thames centred on Essex and Hertfordshire. The reverse bears a warrior on a horse, galloping R, raising a carnyx in his R hand (**figs 204-206**). He is often helmeted (in a variety of forms) and generally wears chain mail (see Kretz 2001 for detailed variations). Around the horse is the legend TASC. Details vary from coin to coin; while Robert Van Arsdell (1989) defined four separate types, the reverses can be treated as variations on a single theme. Rainer Kretz (2001) defined three reverse types featuring a carnyx and analysed the dies; this structure is used in **table 55** and **figures 204-206**. 97 examples were recorded in the Celtic Coins Index, Oxford University up to February 2000, 26 of which had significant details of the carnyx; five further examples were noted in dealers' lists with significant detail. The British Museum specimens have been examined first-hand, others from photographs in the Celtic Coin Index or catalogues. In some cases the photographs are poor and the original would provide more detail, but as most are not in museums it has not been possible to track them down.

The carnyx
The general characteristics of the carnyx on these coins are as follows: flaring mouth, jaws recurved; straight parallel tube of three boss-defined segments, with a mouthpiece knob; no ears or crest. Half show evidence of an eye, in the form of an eye peak (a brow above the eye, which is only rarely defined itself). There are variations in the number of segments (sometimes two, perhaps four on one forgery, in one case none), and the jaw position. Kretz (2001, 240) noted that the quality of die-cutting generally improved through time. **Table 55** summarises the characteristics of each reverse type. It is unclear whether the hand masks a knob in some cases, and judgements on this are made by assuming a regular spacing of the tube segments.

Date
c. 20 BC-AD 10 (Haselgrove 1987, 95; 1996, 71)

code	VA	M	BM	ABC	issuer	metal	area	description	date
A1.1	1730-1736	154-157	1608-1624	2562, 2565, 2568	Tasciovanus	AV	Essex & Hertfordshire	warrior on horseback brandishing carnyx	c. 20 BC-AD 10
A1.2	1845	194	1625-1627	441	Tasciovanus (Sego)	AV	Kent	warrior on horseback brandishing carnyx	c. 20 BC-AD 10
A1.3	181	291	2507-2508	348	Dubnovellaunus	AE	Kent	female on horseback carrying carnyx	c. 25-1 BC
A1.4	–	–	–	354	Dubnovellaunus	AE	Kent/Hertfordshire?	warrior on horseback carrying carnyx	c. 25-1 BC
A1.5	431	301	1127-1128	387	Eppillus	AV	Kent/Hampshire?	warrior on horseback with carnyx over shoulder	c. AD 1-20
A1.6	441	306	1132	399	Eppillus	AR	Kent	warrior on horseback carrying carnyx	c. AD 1-20

Tab. 54 British Iron Age coins with carnyces.

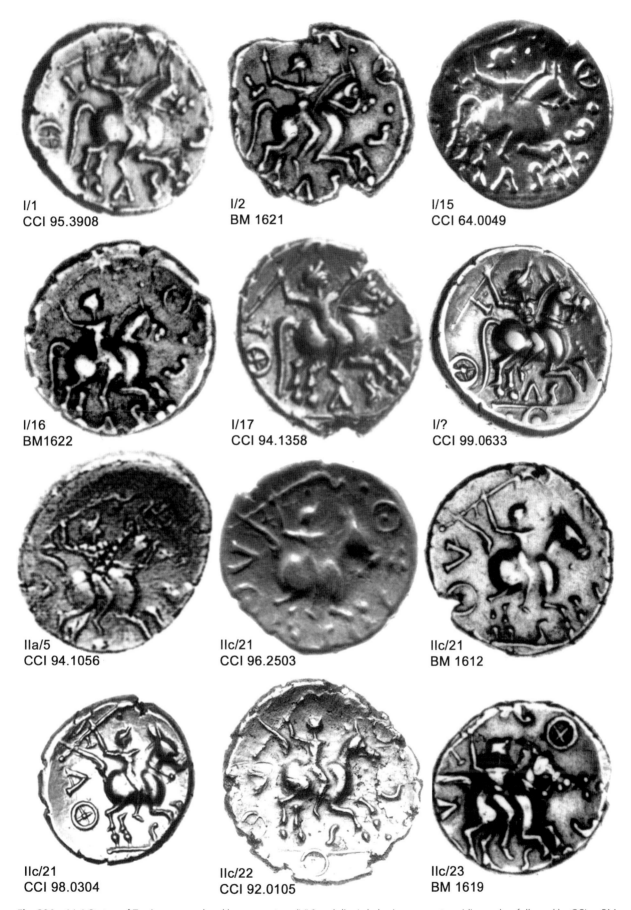

I/1
CCI 95.3908

I/2
BM 1621

I/15
CCI 64.0049

I/16
BM1622

I/17
CCI 94.1358

I/?
CCI 99.0633

IIa/5
CCI 94.1056

IIc/21
CCI 96.2503

IIc/21
BM 1612

IIc/21
CCI 98.0304

IIc/22
CCI 92.0105

IIc/23
BM 1619

Fig. 204 A1.1 Staters of Tasciovanus, ordered by reverse type (I–IV) and die. Labels give reverse type/die number followed by CCI or BM number. – (Photos British Museum, Celtic Coin Index). – Scale 3:1.

Appendix 1: Catalogue of carnyx depictions | 369

IIc/?
CCI 68.0173

IIc/21
CCI 98.0304

IId/10
CCI 96.1753

IVa/7
BM 1623

IVa/7
CCI 61.0187

IVa/7
CCI 96.2504

IVb/13
CCI 66.0100

IVb/14
BM 1611

IVb/14
CCI 83.0296

IVc/9
BM 1608

IVc/9
BM 1609

IVd/8
CCI 88.0109

Fig. 205 A1.1 Staters of Tasciovanus, ordered by reverse type (I–IV) and die. Labels give reverse type/die number followed by CCI or BM number. – (Photos British Museum, Celtic Coin Index). – Scale 3:1.

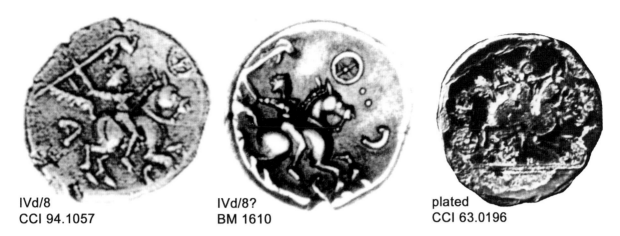

IVd/8
CCI 94.1057

IVd/8?
BM 1610

plated
CCI 63.0196

Fig. 206 A1.1 Staters of Tasciovanus, ordered by reverse type (I-IV) and die. Labels give reverse type/die number followed by CCI or BM number. – (Photos British Museum, Celtic Coin Index). – Scale 3:1.

Bibliography

Allen 1958. – Cottam et al. 2010, 128 nos 2562. 2565. 2568. – Hobbs 1996, nos 1608-1624. – Hunter 2009d, 232 f. no. 1. – Kretz 2001. – Mack 1975, 76 f. nos 154-157. – Van Arsdell 1989, nos 1730. 1732. 1734. 1736.

A1.2 Tasciovanus-Sego stater

Classification: VA 1845; BM 1625-1627; Mack 194; ABC 441

Distribution: mainly Kent

Gold stater of Tasciovanus with the additional inscription SEGO on the reverse. The reverse is very similar to the other Tasciovanus stater with a carnyx (A1.1): it shows a warrior on a horse galloping R, brandishing a carnyx in his R arm. He wears a helmet and chain mail (**fig. 207**). Only four of the six specimens recorded in the Celtic Coins Index (as at February 2000) show any significant detail (BM 1625, 1626; CCI 73.0225, 94.0315); one useful subsequent discovery has been noted (Chris Rudd List 78, 2004, lot 54). Only the BM specimens have been examined firsthand.

The significance of the SEGO inscription has been much debated. Such additional names have a variety of possible interpretations, for instance as sons or relatives of the ruler, moneyers, mints or magistrates. David Holman (1999) and Rainer Kretz (2000) have noted that the distribution of SEGO types shows a strong concentration in eastern Kent and suggest it may be linked with the acquisition of Kent by Tasciovanus. »Sego« is a Celtic word meaning strong or powerful, and would therefore be appropriate as an attribute of a conquering ruler in his new territory (*ibidem*). The term is found on other coins of Tasciovanus, and on the coins of Cunobelin and Amminus, again with a distribution concentrated in eastern Kent: Holman (1999), in noting this, suggested all are connected with Tasciovanus and his dynasty asserting their newly-established control over Kent. It has also been argued that these are issued for a relative or descendent of Tasciovanus (e. g. Cottam et al. 2010, 44), but the occurrence of SEGO on other coins makes it more likely an attribute (or location of the mint; Sills 2013) than a ruler's name.

reverse	eye	jaw recurve	segments	mouthpiece knob	notes
I	n	variable	1 or 2; 3	y	
II a	n?	variable	?	?	
II c	n	variable	3	y	die 22: first tube segment shorter
II d	n?	both	3?	?	
IV a	y	both	?	?	
IV b	variable	both	3	y	
IV c	n	both	1 or 2	?	die 9: hint of fang on lower jaw
IV d	y?	both	3?	?	

Tab. 55 Summary of carnyx characteristics on different reverse types of Tasciovanus. Reverse types and dies follow Kretz 2001.

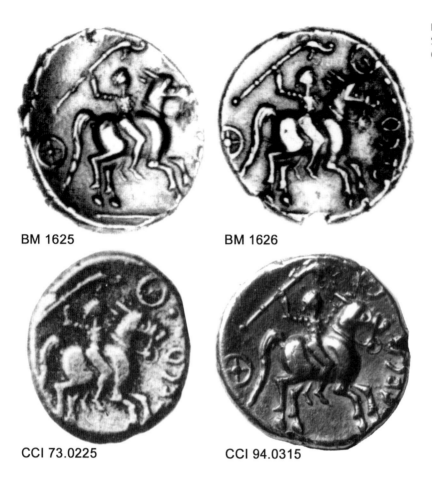

BM 1625   BM 1626

CCI 73.0225   CCI 94.0315

Fig. 207 A1.2 Staters of Tasciovanus-Sego. – (Photos British Museum, Celtic Coin Index). – Scale 3:1.

The carnyx

General characteristics are: eye peak; flared jaws, the upper recurved; three tube segments, with basal knob (where preserved), crest and ear (the latter lacking only in cases where the image is poor). The crest on BM 1625 and 1626 is rather faint, but as it appears on both specimens (which are die-linked) it is not just due to damage and should be seen as a genuine feature.

Date

c. 20 BC - AD 10 (Haselgrove 1987, 95; 1996, 71). Robert Van Arsdell (1989) suggested 10 BC - AD 10, and Cottam et al. (2010, 441) AD 5-15, assuming that Sego was a ruler following Tasciovanus, but as this is unlikely (see above) it seems safer to follow Haselgrove.

Bibliography

Allen 1958. – Cottam et al. 2010, 44 no. 441. – Hobbs 1996, nos 1625-1627. – Holman 1999. – Hunter 2009d, 233 no. 2. – Kretz 2000. – Mack 1975, no. 194. – Van Arsdell 1989, no. 1845.

A1.3 Dubnovellaunus bronze

Classification: VA 181; BM 2507-2508; Mack 291; ABC 348

Distribution: primarily Kent

The reverse shows a naked woman on horseback riding to R (not side-saddle, as Hobbs suggests, given leg profile and presence of typical saddle horns), with carnyx at an angle in R hand (**fig. 208**). Richard Hobbs suggested it was a sword, and Robert Van Arsdell equivocated, but de-

tailed examination of originals and images indicates that Derek Allen (1958, 45 and n. 1) was correct; it is a carnyx. The rider faces forward on some coins, back (towards the carnyx) on others. Her left arm is only partly visible, and probably holds the reins which are visible below the horse's mouth. The horse is standing with its R foreleg raised, as if on parade. This is a very unusual pose on British Iron Age coins, where the horse is typically in more active motion

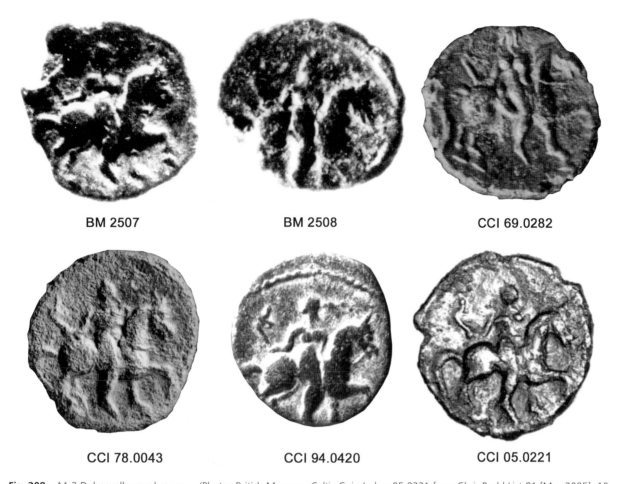

BM 2507   BM 2508   CCI 69.0282

CCI 78.0043   CCI 94.0420   CCI 05.0221

Fig. 208   A1.3 Dubnovellaunus bronze. – (Photos British Museum, Celtic Coin Index; 05.0221 from Chris Rudd List 81 [May 2005], 10 no. 21). – Scale 3:1.

(most commonly galloping, or sometimes rearing). It can be paralleled on a few issues in unaccompanied horses or winged horses which stand or walk with a markedly raised foreleg (Hobbs 1996, nos 1223-1236. 1651-1653. 1686-1687. 1987-1990. 2351-2365. 2499), but this is the only instance with a rider. (For parallel poses in a Gallo-Roman context see the horse from Neuvy-en-Sullias and a relief of Epona from Burgundy; Green 1997.)

The carnyx
The fifteen examples recorded in the Celtic Coins Index in February 2000 were scrutinised for details, and subsequent finds have been checked for significant additions. Examples in the British Museum were examined at first-hand, the others from photographs. Only the upper part of the carnyx is visible, the lower half (below the rider's arm) vanishing behind the horse. Its general characteristics are as follows: flared jaws, lower sometimes recurved; eye or eye »peak«; no tube details. The following specimens preserve significant detail: BM 2506, 2508; CCI 69.0282, 78.0043, 94.0420, 05.0221.

Date
Van Arsdell (17-10 BC) is over-precise (cf. Burnett 1989); Holman's (2000) sequence for Kent is adopted here, suggesting a bracket for Dubnovellaunus of c. 25-1 BC; this is close to Haselgrove's more general date for such coins (his phase 7) of c. 20 BC-AD 10 (Haselgrove 1987, 95; 1996, 71).

Bibliography
Allen 1958. – Cottam et al. 2010, 40 no. 348. – Hobbs 1996, nos 2507-2508. – Holman 2000, 206f. 212f. – Hunter 2009d, 235 no. 3. – Mack 1975, 291. – Van Arsdell 1989, 181.

CCI 83.0385   CCI 94.1182   Canterbury

Fig. 209 A1.4 Dubnovellaunus bronze. The Springhead example is not illustrated as it preserves no significant detail of the carnyx. – (Photos Celtic Coin Index, National Museums Scotland [94.1182], Canterbury Museum). – Scale c. 3:1.

A1.4 Dubnovellaunus bronze

Classification: ABC 354 (not present in other major catalogues); Holman (2005) DB2
Distribution: Kent/Hertfordshire
Obverse: pouncing lion L, head turned back to R; ring and pellet between head and tail with 8-point asterisk above and another below the L foreleg; 5-point star below body; pellets behind rear leg and in front of neck. Reverse: warrior on a galloping horse R, carrying a carnyx vertically in R hand, probably holding reins (visible below horse's jaw) in L. Ring and pellet in front of rider's face; pellet below horse's jaw. Below horse, DVBN. The rider is male with a bare torso; on some he appears to wear a belt, perhaps for trousers, although these are not clearly shown. He faces forward and seems to be wearing a bowl helmet with a short neck guard (**fig. 209**).

Only four specimens are known, two from Hertfordshire (Gatesbury and Duxford) and two from Kent (Canterbury and Springhead, both from excavations). The Canterbury and Duxford examples have been examined first-hand, the others from images. The distribution at present is evenly split between Hertfordshire and Kent, although on pitifully small numbers, but David Holman (2005) classed it as a Kentish type and Philip De Jersey (pers. comm.) is inclined to agree, since the obverse pentagram is much more common on Kentish coins.

The carnyx

Only the Canterbury coin preserves the full carnyx. It comes from the Cakebread Robey site (CB/R³79 context 363, find 301), and is now in Canterbury Museum. The coin is in good condition, though limited areas of corrosion obscure some details. The rider holds the carnyx about a third of the way up the cylindrical shaft, which terminates at the base just above the horse's tail in a knob; there is

clearly no continuation below the tail. The tube is plain, with a collar at the junction with the bell and another at the bell-head junction. The carnyx has no crest; a corrosion pocket obscures the rear of the head, so the presence of an ear cannot be confirmed, but it has a dot eye with a raised brow above. The jaws are defined as separate lower-relief lobes, the upper thicker towards the end, and both slightly incurved at the tip; the lower one is indistinct, both from corrosion and because it was less clearly struck. No teeth are present. Other coins are in poorer condition and add little, but CCI 94.1182 (Duxford) appears to have knobs on the shaft defining a two-segment tube.

The nature of the reverse is similar to one of Dubnovellaunus's Kentish issues (A1.3), where a female is depicted on horseback, and a silver unit of Eppillus (A1.6).

Date

Dubnovellaunus issued coins both north and south of the Thames, although there is some debate as to whether it was the same person. This was reviewed (with further references) by Holman (2000, 212), who argued the balance of evidence suggests they are the same. The dating has been reviewed above (A1.3), but in view of the uncertainties over who Dubnovellaunus was, the tighter Kentish dating should not be adopted and a broader late 1st century BC - early 1st century AD date is suggested; Colin Haselgrove (1987, 95; 1996, 71) suggested c. 20 BC - AD 10.

Bibliography

Cottam et al. 2010, 40 no. 354. – Holman 2005, fig. 2, 7. – Hunter 2009d, 235 no. 4.

Fig. 210 A1.5 Eppillus staters. –
(Photos British Museum). – Scale
3:1.

BM 1127   BM 1128

A1.5 Eppillus stater

Classification: VA 431; BM 1127-1128; Mack 301; ABC
387; Bean 2000, EPP4-1
Distribution: Kent/Hampshire
The reverse shows a warrior on a saddled horse galloping
R (**fig. 210**). The rider wears trousers and a helmet with
brow peak and cheek guards. Over his R shoulder he rests
a carnyx, held at the end in his R hand. Only two examples
are known, both in the British Museum and both from the
same die.
This type is normally seen as one of Eppillus' Kentish issues (Van Arsdell 1989, 148 f.; Hobbs 1996, 97). However, Simon Bean (2000) argued it was part of his Calleva
(Silchester) series, based on stylistic links to silver units from
the Calleva area and a find from either Wallingford, near
Silchester, Berkshire, or Watlington, Oxfordshire (Claxton
2001, 85 with references). There are strong stylistic links
to his Kentish coins, and indeed the same engraver seems
to be at work in both areas. The second find is from Sta-
ple, Kent (Evans 1864, 191; Hobbs 1996, 97 no. 1128)
and from these divergent findspots it is not possible at
present to decide which view is correct.

The carnyx
The carnyx has a straight, plain tube; the mouthpiece is
obscured by the hand. It is rather stylised, with no head

detail. The mouth is flared at about 180°, with the lower
jaw slightly recurved. The crest, defined by a single raised
line, runs from a little behind the tip of the upper jaw to
about a third of the length of the tube. It terminates in a
knob, and has a small triangular protrusion to the rear at
about half-way.

Date
Eppillus' dates are accepted as late 1st century BC-early
1st century AD (Hobbs 1996, 18 f. fig. 2), with Bean (2000,
157. 201-204 fig. 11, 5) suggesting c. 20 BC-AD 10/20,
based on a detailed argument that the fourth series of Eppillus (this stater and some related silver issues) is typologi-
cally late. As discussed above, the attribution of this stater
to Calleva rather than Kent is not certain, but his Kentish
issues can also be seen as a later phase of his reign. The
design links to the issues of other rulers suggest a date in
the first two decades AD.

Bibliography
Allen 1958. – Bean 2000, 157-162. 166. 244. – Clax-
ton 2001 (dealing with the obverse design). – Cottam et
al. 2010, 42 no. 387. – Hobbs 1996, nos 1127-1128. –
Hunter 2009d, 236 no. 5. – Mack 1975, no. 301. – Van
Arsdell 1989, no. 431.

A1.6 Eppillus silver coin

Classification: VA 441; BM 1132; Mack 306; ABC 399
Distribution: Kent
Silver unit of Eppillus, circulating in Kent. The reverse
shows a warrior galloping R with carnyx held almost vertically in R hand (**fig. 211**); prominent marks on his shoulders probably represent the shoulder plates of a chain mail

tunic, and on some specimens he wears a bowl helmet.
The British Museum specimen (BM 1132), CCI 94.0709
and 05.0222 were examined first-hand (the latter now in
NMS collections [reg. no. X.2005.10]); two other specimens in the Celtic Coins Index were examined in photographs (66.0078, 93.0727). None are certainly die-linked.

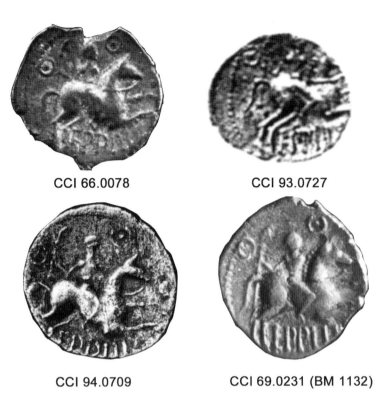

CCI 66.0078   CCI 93.0727

CCI 94.0709   CCI 69.0231 (BM 1132)

Fig. 211 A1.6 Eppillus silver coin. – (Photos Celtic Coin Index). – Scale 3:1.

The carnyx

On all examples the carnyx is worn, but its identification is clear. The head appears to be quite stylised, with a flared mouth with no recurve, a short upper jaw, and no indication of ears or crest; 94.0709 has an eye-peak, but this appears to be absent otherwise. Knob at bell-tube junction; basal knob on some but not others; apparently no other tube subdivisions, although there are hints on 93.0727. The angled line visible on the British Museum example (Allen 1958, pl. 1, 6) does not meet the tube accurately, and probably comes from defining the horse's rear leg: it is not evidence for a curved mouthpiece.

Date

Late 1st century BC - early 1st century AD (Hobbs 1996, 18 f. fig. 2). Bean (2000, 201-204) has presented a detailed argument linking Eppillus' Kentish and Calleva issues to the later part of his reign, suggesting a dating of c. 1-10/20 AD.

Bibliography

Allen 1958. – Cottam et al. 2010, 42 no. 399. – Hobbs 1996, no. 1132. – Hunter 2009d, 236 no. 6. – Mack 1975, no. 306. – Van Arsdell 1989, no. 441.

A2 GAULISH IRON AGE COINS (tabs 56-57)

A2.1 Armorican quarter stater

Classification: LT XX 6930; DT II 2049 var. (series 239/IV); Depeyrot VIII 35
Distribution: probably Calvados, Normandy
The obverse bears a head of Apollo quite close to the Greek originals, while the reverse shows a charioteer and horse, with a sword under the horse. The charioteer holds what may be a carnyx (fig. 212). The image of a charioteer holding something is a recurring one in the Armorican series, with attributes including torcs, swords and ships. Although not discussed in De Jersey's detailed study, this coin is closely related to the sword types of the Normandy group of his first phase (De Jersey 1994, 40-47). This has at least three subdivisions, the two of relevance being the »double sword type« where the charioteer holds a sword (BN 6937), and the »sword and ship« type where he holds a ship (BN 6927 f.; see also Allen 1971b). Their dating has been debated (De Jersey 1994, 44-46), but the subsequent publication of examples from the trophy of Ribemont-sur-Ancre showed that they were already current by 250 BC (Delestrée 2001, 185-187). The distribution is concentrated in the Calvados region (De Jersey 1994, map 2).

The carnyx

Ernest Muret (1889, 157) identified the object held by the charioteer as a carnyx, but this is not entirely certain from the single specimen in the BN; no other specimen is known to the writer. The coin is worn and indistinct, which makes the differentiation between the person's arm and the ?tube uncertain. There is a short straight section of tube terminating in a pellet, which then expands into a possible head, facing back toward the person, with an ear and an upturned snout; there is no defined lower jaw. Very worn features to the L of the snout may be the hair of the person or, more speculatively, a tongue, although this seems unlikely. The tube is not depicted below where the hand holds it.

It is hard to see what else this could plausibly be, as the other artefacts depicted on similar coins tend to be quite naturalistic. On balance it is accepted as a carnyx. It is a simplified version, and the position, with the head turned towards the bearer, is unusual.

Date

A closely similar quarter-stater, probably with a boat rather than a carnyx, was found at Ribemont-sur-Ancre in a secure La Tène C1 context, dated to 260-240 BC (Deles-

Fig. 212 A2.1 Armorican quarter stater. – (Photo Bibliothèque nationale de France). – Scale 3:1.

BN 6930

trée/Tache 2004, 41. 45 no. 2049; Delestrée 2001, 185-187). A slightly broader range of 270-200 BC is suggested here for the type.

Bibliography

Allen 1971b. – De Jersey 1994, 40-47. – de La Tour 1892, 4 pl. XX 6930. – de La Tour/Fischer 1992, pl. XX 6930. – Delestrée/Tache 2004, 41. 45 no. 2049 (variant). – Depeyrot 2005b, 25. 35 no. 35 (carnyx not identified). – Hunter 2009d, 236 f. no. 7. – Muret 1889, 157. – Scheers 1992a, 15.

code	LT/BN	inscription	metal	area	description	date
A2.1	XX 6930	–	AV	Calvados, Armorica	charioteer holding ?carnyx	c. 270-200 BC
A2.2	XIII 4551-4552	–	AV, AR, AE	Limousin	carnyx & part-hidden male bust	c. 200-50 BC
A2.3	DT 3421A, B		AR	Centre-west	horse with carnyx above and lyre below	c. 150-70 BC
A2.4	–	–	potin	Gué-de-Sciaux (dép. Vienne)	carnyx	c. 100-50 BC
A2.5	XVIII 5967, 5980	–	AR	E Armorica	horse and carnyces	c. 75-25 BC
A2.6	XV 5044	Dubnocov Dubnoreix	AR	Burgundy	warrior holding carnyx and standard	c. 60-54 BC
A2.7	BN 7050-7055	Belenoc	AR	Centre-west	male head (?Apollo) with carnyx & standard over shoulder	c. 60-30 BC
A2.8	XX 6398	Magurix	AE	Middle Loire	Victory holding carnyx	c. 50-1 BC

Tab. 56 Gaulish coins with carnyces.

code	LT/BN	DT	Depeyrot
A2.1	XX 6930	II 2049 var (series 239/IV)	VIII 35
A2.2	XIII 4551-4552	III 3392-3394 (series 1070)	III 34-36
A2.3		III 3421A, B (series 1083)	
A2.4	–	–	–
A2.5	XVIII 5967, 5980	II 2368-2371 (series 377)	VIII 92
A2.6	XV 5044	III 3213 (series 905/II)	IV 214
A2.7	BN 7050-7055	II 2658-2659 (series 589)	IV 125
A2.8	XX 6398	II 2670 (series 610)	V 82

Tab. 57 Correlation of major cataloguing systems.

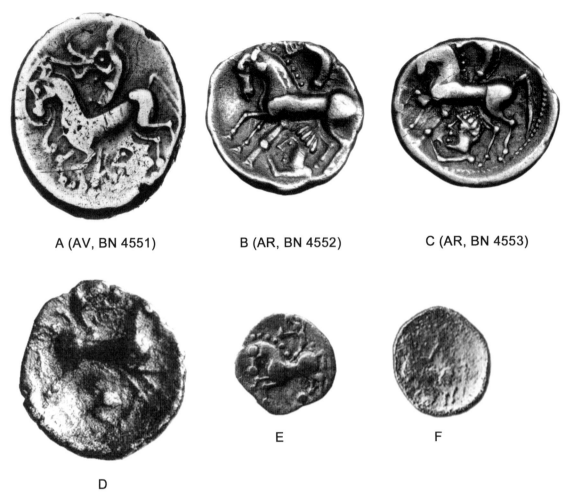

A (AV, BN 4551)   B (AR, BN 4552)   C (AR, BN 4553)

D

E

F

Fig. 213 A2.2 Stater, silver and billon units from Limousin with carnyx and male bust. Type A: gold; B-E: silver; F: billon. – (A-C photos Bibliothèque nationale de France; D Parvérie 2010, fig. 1; E Parvérie 2010, fig. 2; F Delestrée/Tache 2008, pl. XII no. DT S 3394 A). – Scale 3:1.

A2.2 Stater, silver and billon units of the Lemovices

Classification: LT XIII 4551-4552; DT III 3392-3394 (series 1070); Depeyrot III 34-36
Distribution: Limousin
This long-lived trimetallic series of coins (struck in gold, silver and billon, a copper/silver alloy) is unusual because issues share both obverse and reverse. Knowledge of the series has increased greatly in recent years, thanks to the discovery of several examples at Tintignac and the work of Marc Parvérie (2010), who noted 36 examples. Only a single gold coin is yet known (variant A), but knowledge of the silver series is much improved, with three variants (B-D) which show evidence of weight reduction over time. The three variants represent two reverse types; only a single specimen of D is published. There is also a single published example of a silver fraction (E; Parvérie 2010, fig. 2). The billon issue (F) is also rare (Delestrée/Tache 2008, 82 DT S 3394 A); Parvérie recorded two specimens, and there is a third from Gué de Sciaux (985 13 27). All

share a common iconography, with minor differences (figs 213-214).
The front shows a head derived from busts of Apollo. The reverse shows a horse facing L (except on type D, where everything faces right); behind this is a dramatic depiction of a carnyx facing L, held near-vertically by a man whose head appears under the horse. On the known stater only his head is visible (part-hidden behind the horse), the remainder of the bust lost in wear, but on the silver units his arm holds the instrument, and he may be preparing to play it. The short, stranded hairstyle identifies him as male; Parvérie (2010, 13) noted some examples may show a helmet. The carnyx and human need not necessarily be connected to the horse, which is the persistent reverse type in Gaul irrespective of what else is featured (Fischer 1991). On the stater two scroll-motifs emit from the horse's mouth, but not on the silver units. Examples in the Bibliothèque nationale (BN 4551 [type A], 4552 [B],

Fig. 214 Drawings of the carnyces on different denominations of A2.2. – (Drawings A-C Marion O'Neil; D-F Alan Braby).

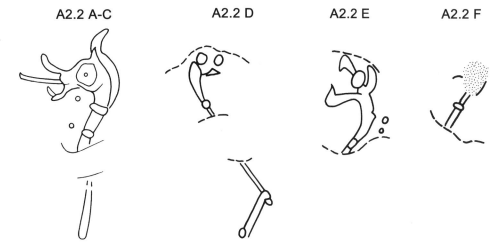

A2.2 A-C   A2.2 D   A2.2 E   A2.2 F

4553 [C]) and the Musée de Chauvigny (from Gué-de-Sciaux, 986 27 83 [234], 985 13 27 [81]) were examined first-hand, and others from photographs (Scheers 1975, no. 151 [Collection Danicourt, type B]; Allen 1990, 57 S181 [Hod Hill, C]; 1968, 45 pl. 15 no. 29; Parvérie 2010, figs 1-2 [Montignac-Charente, D; Souillac, E]; DT IV pl. XII [Barzan, F]). Further examples from Tintignac are not yet published in detail.

Parvérie (2010, 15f.) reviewed the distributional evidence, which points strongly to a Limousin source. They concentrate in the départements of Corrèze and Charent, and he suggested that they may have been struck at the Tintignac sanctuary. Of course, there is a danger that a recent find creates a bias, and another sanctuary excavation might suggest a different picture, but the idea is worth pursuing; the distribution is consistent with this, and Parvérie went on to suggest that the iconography may even evoke the ceremonies carried out at Tintignac. In contrast to many other coins from Tintignac, he noted that these ones are not mutilated.

The carnyx

The carnyx head is very detailed, well-modelled and realistic. It is dramatic and somewhat monstrous, with the eye, ear and crest very prominent, and a ferocious mouth (**fig. 214**). Catherine Homo-Lechner and Christophe Vendries (1993, 34) likened it more to a dragon than a real animal such as a boar, although BN 4551 has an upturned snout and BN 4553 a naturalistic crest.

The gold stater BN 4551 has the best-preserved head, with a raised eye in a sunken socket, a large ear and an open mouth, the upper jaw with upturned snout, the lower with a fang or tusk (others show a series of teeth along the lower jaw, while type E shows fangs or tusks in upper and lower jaws). Parvérie (2010, 16) suggested that the item projecting from the mouth is not a tongue, as usually argued, but connects to one of the volutes coming from the horse's mouth; he makes the intriguing and plausible suggestion that this might be intended to repre-

sent sound, almost an Iron Age speech bubble. A similar feature is present on the Gué-de-Sciaux silver issue (A2.4). Most specimens show a crest of varying styles, running normally from the bell to the ear; on some it runs some distance down the tube. On BN 4551 the tube is misaligned either side of the horse, with two thick sections above and a thinner part below; this is due to constraints of space, not evidence of a curved and tapering tube, as all other examples have straight cylindrical tubes. Assuming the player's hand conceals a junction (as spacing would suggest), three or four tube sections are suggested; one has a plain tube (Hod Hill). BN 4551 has junction bands with a pellet on the left edge; otherwise both bands and knobs are represented. The mouthpiece, where visible, is in line with the tube, and on one is shown as slightly flared, forming a cup; on another a knob is shown.

Date

Daphne Nash (1978b, 59f.) linked the type to the middle phase issues of her west Berry series, although noting how difficult it is to date. Given the data she provided (*ibidem* 101-104), the recorded stater weight (7.22 g) is consistent with a later 2nd- early 1st century date in this series; the heavier silver would not be incompatible with this. George Depeyrot (2004a, 7f.) argued for a 2nd century date, although his dating of metrological changes is tied to historical events, not any independent means. Parvénier (2010) presented good evidence of a weight reduction in the silver issues which indicates they were struck over some time; none come from useful contexts, but he suggested the series starts before the end of the 2nd century, with a weight reduction in the 80s or 70s BC (when he sees the »quinarius«-weight coins being struck), and a further weight reduction beyond that, finishing before the strong Roman artistic influences and later inscribed series of the mid-1st century BC. A broad range of 200-50 BC is adopted here, taking the potential start date a little earlier than other authorities suggest as these tend to be conservative.

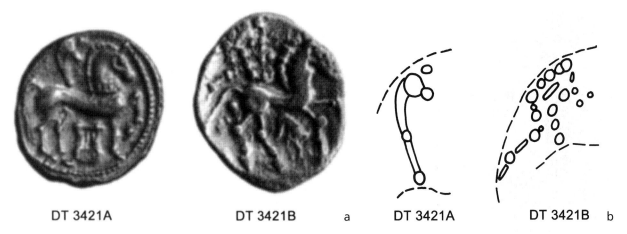

| DT 3421A | DT 3421B | a | DT 3421A | DT 3421B | b |

Fig. 215 A2.3 Silver unit from west-central France: **a** photographs of the two variants. – **b** drawings of the carnyces. – (a Delestrée/Tache 2008, pl. XX DT 3421 A-B; b drawing Alan Braby / Fraser Hunter). – Scale 3:1.

Bibliography
Allen 1980, 146 pl. 36, 554-555; 1990, 57 no. S181. – Blanchet 1971, 290. – de Lagoy 1849, 16 pl. II no. 1. – de La Tour 1892, pl. XIII 4551. – de La Tour/Fischer 1992, pl. XIII 4551. – Delestrée/Tache 2007, 114 nos 3392- 3394; 2008, 82 no. S 3394A. – Depeyrot 2004a, nos 34-36. – Homo-Lechner/Vendries 1993, 34. – Hucher 1874, 63f. – Hunter 2009d, 237 no. 8. – Muret 1889, 102. – Nash 1978a, 59f. – Parvérie 2010. – Scheers 1975, 52 pl. IX no. 152; 1992a, 10.

A2.3 Silver unit from west-central France

Classification: DT III 3421 A, B (series 1083)
Distribution: centre-west France (Limousin/Berry)
Louis-Pol Delestrée and Marcel Tache (2008, 119) provided the first publication of another silver unit from west-central France (**fig. 215**). It must be a rare type, as the two varieties they publish seem to be the only examples so far known. Both have a left-facing bust on the obverse and a horse on the reverse with a carnyx and other attributes. The style of bust is linked to types DT3362-3363, attributed to the Bituriges. The rear has a standing horse, facing right, with its left foreleg raised – the pose is reminiscent of the British coin A1.3, and suggests a scene of parade or ceremony. The published photo has hints of a decorative band around the base of its neck. A carnyx projects above the horse, leaning slightly backwards and facing right. Its tube is not continued below the horse, where there is a lyre.
3421B is markedly more stylised (and also rather lighter, suggesting it may be later, or a copy; the two coins are 13-15mm in diameter, 2.12 and 1.80g in mass). The horse is walking, again with left foreleg raised; the object below it is indistinct, and the carnyx above is barely recognisable. This is the only example of a carnyx being displayed along with another musical instrument on an Iron Age coin.

The carnyx
3421A shows the upper part of the tube leading into the expanding, curved bell; pellets define junctions between bell and tube, and at the visible base of the tube. There is a prominent pellet eye, and two elongated pellets define the mouth; there are hints of an ear, lost off the top of the flange.
3421B is much harder to recognise. The design is almost exclusively pellets, defining the tube, eye, and what is probably the mouth, though there are stray pellets in this area. The pellet-curve on the top of the head, defining the crest, runs down the bell and then curves dramatically away, behind the carnyx – an unnatural feature which suggests it was not fully understood. Lines join these pellets as they curve away, and there are hints of lines to define the mouth, but it has not been seen first-hand.

Date
Delestrée and Tache (2008, 114) placed this in the later 2nd century or first third of the 1st century BC. Although they term them »light drachmae«, the weights are consistent with the unreduced versions of A2.2; if the arguments quoted there hold water, suggesting a reduction towards the weight of a quinarius in the 80s or 70s BC (and such metrological arguments are more questionable with multiple workshops), then this would fit a date range of c. 150-70 BC.

Bibliography:
Delestrée/Tache 2008, 119.

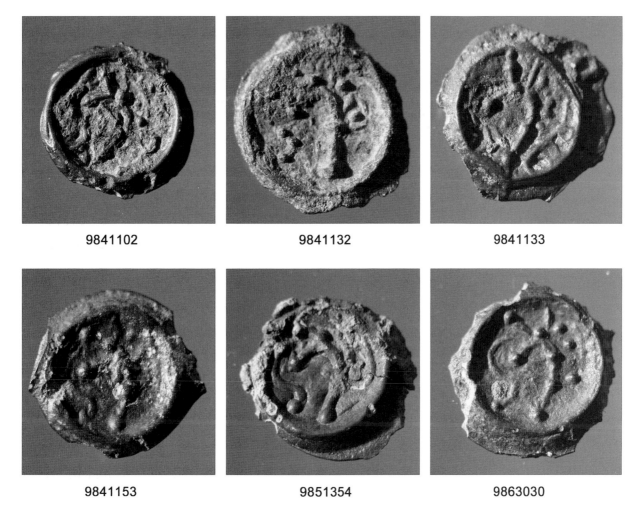

| 9841102 | 9841132 | 9841133 |

| 9841153 | 9851354 | 9863030 |

Fig. 216 A2.4 Potin coins, Gué de Sciaux. – (Photos Musée de Chauvigny, courtesy of Isabelle Bertrand). – Scale 3:1.

A2.4 Potin coin

Classification: potin »à la tête chapeautée«
Distribution: centre-west France, especially Gué-de-Sciaux (dép. Vienne)
A number of potin coins bearing a carnyx (**fig. 216**) come from the sanctuary of Gué-de-Sciaux (Antigny, Vienne); Parvérie (2010, 17) noted three further examples from the départements of Charente and Charente-Maritime and one from Corrèze, but the concentration at Gué-de-Sciaux suggests they were made there. He also noted obverse parallels to DT3209 (an Aeduan potin) and DT 3503 (a Biturigan potin).
Gué-de-Sciaux is best known as a Gallo-Roman sanctuary, originating in the Augustan period and continuing in use until the late 4th century AD (Richard 1989, 199-201; Bertrand 2007). It lay on the eastern boundary of the *civitas* of the Pictones. However, underlying this is a late La Tène sanctuary, starting perhaps in the 2nd century BC. The potins derive from a scattered hoard, disturbed by the

building of an early Augustan temple, which has not yet been studied in detail.
Three locally-produced potin types have been identified, one of which has a left-facing carnyx on the reverse. This type is styled »à la tête chapeautée« as the obverse has a head wearing what looks like a soft hat. The reverse is dominated by a carnyx facing an asymmetrical S-symbol, pointed at the end which ?emerges from the carnyx mouth, the other end terminating in a pellet. This is not the carnyx's tongue, as it is too long and not attached; was it intended to symbolise music or noise? Parvérie (2010) has suggested a similar interpretation for a curved feature more clearly connected to the carnyx mouth in type A2.2. The coins range from 14 to 17 mm in diameter and weigh from 1.67 to 3.41 g; the weight indicates this is the latest of the three types. Analysis indicates they are standard potins, with typically 71-81 % copper, 18-26 % tin and 0.3-1.8 % lead. There are eleven examples from the site (a twelfth

listed by Sarthre [2000, Annexe 2, A71], although damaged, has a different design and is analytically distinctive).

The carnyx

There are variations of detail between the various coins, but the basic form of the carnyx is constant. It is rather simplified, with the tube normally being a single straight cylinder divided from the curved expanding bell by a knob, and with a basal mouthpiece knob; on two coins the tube has two segments. A pellet-defined crest with a curving top border runs from the bell or the middle of the tube to the ears; in one case, the base of the border is extended into a decorative flourish, with two »teeth« on the outer edge. The head itself is often little-defined, with a prominent pellet eye set at the bell-jaw junction, but some have an expanded head with the eye set in this. It has one or two ears and a flared mouth (open to about 90°), typically with dots defining the ends of the linear jaws. The coins are listed as numbers 60-70 by C.-O. Sarthre (2000); their museum numbers, in the same order, are 9862799, 9841133, 9863005, 9841102, 9841121, 9841132, 9863030, 9841153, 9863043, 9851335 and 9851354.

Date

Dating evidence is vague (Sarthre 2000, 269. 274; I. Bertrand, pers. comm.): they come from a hoard (not yet studied in detail) disturbed by Augustan constructions, but this provides only a *terminus ante quem*. These potins probably predate the Gallic War: analysis shows no Roman influence on the alloy, and there is nothing Roman about the technique or the imagery. The high tin levels and weight of the earlier classes also support a pre-Gallic War date. Absolute dating is impossible, but from this argument an early-mid 1st century BC date seems appropriate. The date bracket used here is 100-50 BC, though it could be earlier.

Bibliography

Hunter 2009d, 237 no. 9. – Parvérie 2010, 17f. – Sarthre 2000, 269-277.

A2.5 Armorican silver coin

Classification: LT XVIII 5967, 5980; DT II 2368-2371 (series 377); Depeyrot VIII 92
Distribution: Eastern Armorica
Derek Allen (1965, 84) first suggested the identification of a carnyx on a northern French small silver unit (one of a series derived from the 2nd century BC coins attested in the Bridiers hoard [Creuse, Limousin], and ultimately from Emporian prototypes), with a head of Pallas Athena on the obverse and a galloping horse on the reverse with various devices around it (**fig. 217**; Allen 1965, 83f.; De Jersey 1994, 114f.). Later developments in the series move quite far from the prototype, with a wide spread of variants found in Picardy, Brittany and Hampshire. The type of relevance here is relatively early in the sequence (phase 2 in Allen's scheme), and is found in two main variants, one with the obverse head and reverse iconography facing right (Allen's type A), and the other with the orientation to the left (Allen B1). A half-unit of the first type is also known (BN 5973; Allen 1965, pl. V 12). A later variant of type A/LT 5967 was published by Delestrée and Tache (2004, nos 2370-2371), from Bazoches-les-Hautes (Eure-et-Loire), with the bust lacking the helmet and depicted in a more expressive style. The two examples illustrated have the upper carnyx only, reduced to the head alone, but two carnyces are more typical. Similar stylistic evolution is seen in the »petits billons armoricains« studied by Katherine Gruel and Alain Taccoën (1992), who commented on the diversity of this series.
Early accounts describe the devices above and below the reverse horse as a K (Muret 1889, 133); Allen (1965, 84) was the first to suggest they were stylised carnyces, and this has been followed by other scholars (e.g. Gruel/Morin 1999, 86; Delestrée/Tache 2004, 98; Brenot/Scheers 1996, 126 no. 934); it is discussed further below. The spread of provenanced specimens suggests an origin in eastern Armorica, in the Sarthe department (Brenot/Scheers 1996, 126; De Jersey 1994, map 25; Allen 1965, fig. 2).

The carnyx

The identification of the carnyx is less clear than on most coins, but on balance is plausible. The regular occurrence of a dot at the top of the vertical bar makes it unlikely to be a K, and it can be interpreted as an eye. Of the two variants, the interpretation is less convincing for LT 5967; where the die edge can be seen, the lower motif is rather short, lacking any clear sign of a tube (the upper could be hidden behind the horse). However, the variant LT 5980 is much more convincing, with most examples having long bars which can be read as tubes. This feature also makes them unlikely to be bird heads, the other possible interpretation. The tube, eye and gaping mouth make the interpretation plausible – although it is interesting that LT 5980, seen here as the more realistic, was seen by Allen as degenerate, a useful warning about the subjectivities of such analyses.
Fourteen specimens in the BN were examined (BN 5972 was unavailable) and one in the BM (Allen 1990, 57 no. 154); others were studied from photos (Musée de Bretagne [Gruel/Morin 1999, 86 nos 967-968]; Musée

Fig. 217 A2.5 Armorican silver coin, variants A, B and C. – (Photos Bibliothèque national de France; Delestrée/Tache 2004, pl. XV; British Museum; Portable Antiquities Scheme; Brenot/Scheers 1996, pl. XXXIII; Brouquier-Reddé/Gruel 2004, fig. 16, 2b). – Scale 3:1.

de Lyon [Brenot/Scheers 1996, no. 934]; Delestrée/Tache 2004, 2368-2371). The variants are as follows.

In variant A (BN 5967-5974; BM 154; DT 2368) the horse and carnyces face right. There are two carnyx symbols, above and below the horse. In each case a thick vertical line ending in a dot represents the bell, head and eye; two thinner angled lines attached to this, ending in dots, represent the mouth. The upper one always runs behind the horse's tail or rump and is very short, except in the case of BN 5971, where more of the tube is visible. The lower usually runs off the flan, but in two cases the whole motif is visible. These make it clear that only the upper part of the carnyx is represented, as the vertical bar ends in a rounded base.

Variant B has the same design, but with horse and carnyces facing left (BN 5975-5981; DT 2369; Brittany 967f. [968 is a modern cast]; Lyon 934; PAS IOW-31E7D6). The motifs consistently have longer tubes, making the identification more plausible. In some the tube is the same thickness as the jaws, but in most it is somewhat thicker. Variant C is a stylistic development of A, represented only by two coins from Bazoches-les-Hautes (Eure-et-Loire) published by Delestrée and Tache (2004, 2370f.). In both only the upper carnyx is represented, facing right and reduced to the mouth and eye pellet only.

Date

The type develops from a 2nd century BC prototype, and is early in the proposed evolutionary sequence (the second of Allen's phases). Its weight is of little help except within the series, as it is not readily related to other types (Allen 1965, 88f.). At the end of the series, the »petits billons« are post-Conquest, c. 40-10 BC (Gruel/Taccoën 1992, 180). From this, the types LT 5967/5980 are likely to belong to the first half of the 1st century BC, with developments such as DT 2370 and 2371 a little later; the range is taken here as c. 75-25 BC.

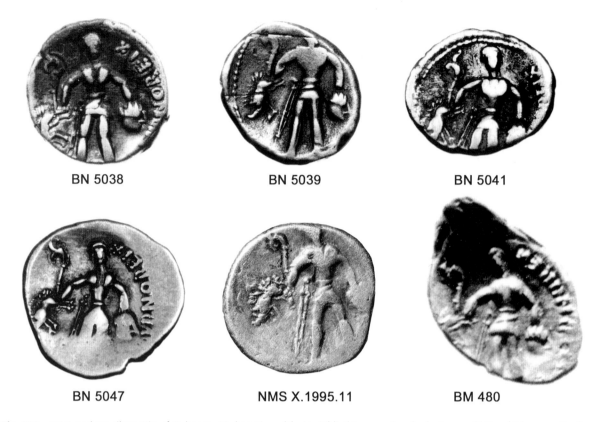

BN 5038   BN 5039   BN 5041

BN 5047   NMS X.1995.11   BM 480

Fig. 218 A2.6 Aeduan silver coin of Dubnocov/Dubnoreix. – (Photos Bibliothèque nationale de France; National Museums Scotland; British Museum). – Scale 3:1.

Bibliography
Allen 1965, esp. 84. 91 pl. V 4-11; 1990, 57 no. 154. – Brenot/Scheers 1996, no. 934. – De Jersey 1994, 114 f. – de La Tour 1892, pl. XVIII 5967. 5973. 5980. – Deles-trée/Tache 2004, 2368-2371. – Depeyrot 2005b, 7 f. 54 f. 65 no. 92. – Gruel/Morin 1999, 86. 187 nos 967-968. – Hunter 2009d, 238 f. no. 10. – Muret 1889, 133 f.

A2.6 Aeduan silver coin of Dubnocov/Dubnoreix

Classification: LT XV 5044; BN 5037-5048; DT III 3213 (series 905/II); Depeyrot IV 214
Distribution: Burgundy
The obverse bears a head and the legend DVBNOCOV; the reverse shows a warrior frontally with legs apart and the legend DVBNOREIX (**fig. 218**). The warrior wears a chain mail tunic with a belt at the waist (the shoulder pieces are very prominent); a long sword hangs from a separate belt by his R side. In his L hand he holds a severed head trophy, in his R a carnyx and boar, the latter presumably from a boar standard. On the clearest specimens he wears a knobbed bracelet on his R wrist (see picture in Colbert de Beaulieu/Fischer 1998, no. 142). Christian Goudineau and Christian Peyre (1993, 52-54) suggested he wears a torc and some form of headgear, but this is not substantiated in the specimens examined to date. In many ways the

coin epitomises an image of Gaul, bringing together many of the icons of the period. Here the carnyx is clearly linked to use in warfare, although Goudineau and Peyre (*ibidem*) pointed out that in this context the attributes are likely to be emblems of the chief's power.

The inscriptions were discussed by Jean-Baptiste Colbert de Beaulieu and Brigitte Fischer (1998, 142). Dubnoreix is another form of Dumnorix, an Aeduan chieftain referred to by Caesar (*De Bello Gallico* I.3. 9. 18-20; V.6 f.), and the warrior depicted is likely to be him. It has been suggested that Dubnocov may be his father (Hucher 1868, 28; Blanchet 1971, 408).

The carnyx

The carnyx is stylised, lacking ears and, on most specimens, eyes. However, it is instantly recognisable from the flared

Fig. 219   **a** Belenoc coin (A2.7), obverse and reverse. – **b** denarius of Caius Piso L. f. Frugi which inspired the obverse design. – (a Hucher 1868, pl. 28, 1; b Banti 1980, 400). – Scale 3:1.

and recurved mouth, crest and slightly curved two-section tube. Details of the mouthpiece are hidden by the boar standard. The crest is defined by a single line running from the upper jaw to the base of the bell. Ten examples in the BN were examined (5038f. 5041-5048) along with specimens in the BM (Allen 480-482) and NMS (X.1995.11); other examples are described from photographs (Cambridge 21; Castelin 547f.; Lyon 346). The only significant points of variation are hints of an eye peak in BN 5047, NMS X.1995.11, and the Lyon specimen; the presence of an eye on the British Museum example; and the lack of a crest on the NMS, BM and Castelin 548 specimens.

Date

The link to Dumnorix puts the coin around the time of the Gallic War, with a *terminus ante quem* of 54 BC when Dumnorix was assassinated (Colbert de Beaulieu/Fischer 1998, 240; Allen 1990, 44). The emblematic nature of the coin is appropriate to these troubled times, and a date of c. 60-54 BC seems most likely.

Bibliography

Allen 1980, pl. 22 317; 1990, 67 nos 480-482. S381f. – Blanchet 1971, 161. 407f. – Cambridge = Sylloge Nummorum Graecorum VI: The Lewis Collection in Corpus Christi College Cambridge. Part I: The Greek and Hellenistic coins (London: British Academy). – Castelin n.d., nos 547-549. – Colbert de Beaulieu/Fischer 1998, no. 142. – de Lagoy 1849, 17 pl. II no. 2. – de La Tour 1892, pl. XV 5044. – de La Tour/Fischer 1992, pl. XV 5044. – Delestrée/Tache 2007, 77 no. 3213. – Depeyrot 2004b, 116f. 160 no. 214. – Forrer 1968, 346 fig. 539. – Goudineau/Peyre 1993, 52-54. – Homo-Lechner/Vendries 1993, 34. – Hucher 1868, 28 pl. 7, 1. – Hunter 2009d, 239 no. 11. – Lyon = Brenot/Scheers 1996, no. 346. – Muret 1889, 115. – Scheers 1992a, 12.

A2.7 Silver coin inscribed Belenoc

Classification: BN 7050-7055; DT II 2658f. (series 589); Depeyrot IV 125
Distribution: centre-west of France
Silver coin, the obverse showing a male head with diadem, derived from images of Apollo, facing L with a carnyx and ?standard behind his shoulder. In front of his face is an inscription, best read as BELENOC (Colbert de Beaulieu/Fischer 1998, no. 67). An S-shaped device on his shoulder on some examples may be a bow brooch (best illustrated in Colbert de Beaulieu/Fischer 1998, 132); on Allen 31 (examined first-hand) it could be interpreted as a fantail brooch. The reverse shows a horse (cult statue?) standing on the podium of a temple (**fig. 219a**). The obverse is believed to derive from a rare Republican denarius of 67 BC, minted by Caius Piso L. f. Frugi, with obverse showing Apollo with a bow and quiver over his shoulder (**fig. 219b**; Scheers 1969, 50f.; cf. Grueber 1910, 468 no. 3815; Sydenham 1952, 145 no. 878; Crawford 1974, no. 408/1b). This series is an extensive and varied one (Crawford 1974, 419-435; Banti 1980, 173-401) but there are very few examples of this variant: in a large-scale survey Banti (1980, 400) classified it as extremely rare. The British Museum has two plated specimens which are die-linked (one illustrated in Sydenham 1952, pl. 24 no. 878); another is illustrated by Banti (1980, 400).
Opinion has been divided as to whether Apollo's attributes of bow and quiver are modified on the Gaulish coin. Simone Scheers saw them as unchanged in concept (Scheers 1969, 50f.; 1978, no. 418; Brenot/Scheers 1996, nos 856-857), as did Delestrée and Tache (2004,

145, nos 2658-2659); Colbert de Beaulieu and Fischer (1998, no. 67) tentatively identified a carnyx, while Muret (1889, 161) identified carnyx and quiver, and Derek Allen (1973) saw it as a carnyx and standard. As only part of the bow is shown on the original denarius and it has a zoomorphic appearance, it is easy to see how it could become interpreted by Gaulish die-cutters as a carnyx. The difficulty is that, because the original denarius is so scarce, it is hard to assess how far the Gaulish version deviates. The BM examples were examined first-hand and another from a photo. Here the quiver is a typical one, the conical top depicted by a stacked series of lines. This is modified on the Gaulish coins to a shaft with separated diminishing lines. Similar items are found on other Gaulish coins, and probably represent a standard, sceptre, or tree-symbol (e.g. Allen 1990, nos S197-200; de La Tour 1892, VI. 2630; XI. 3730; XLVII. 9782). The bow is less clear on the originals, although as the bust is Apollo there can be little doubt that the attributes are bow and quiver in his role as god of hunting. The BM copies have a rather poor rendition; the bow thickens as it curves, with a pellet on the curve; the string is defined only by a pellet, with two »ears« above; the other example (an official issue, given its mass of 3.80 g) has a plain bow, initially straight then curving to the tip; the details here are confused, but there is a clear string line and probably two »ears«.

While the parent denarii do not help greatly, the overall style of bow is made clearer on contemporary denarii which show Diana or Cupid with the same arrangement of quiver and bow over the shoulder; the end often has a zoomorphic quality arising from the recurve of the bow arm and the ?loose ends of the bow string (Crawford 1974, nos 372; 383; 391/2; 394/1; 407; 81-68 BC).

Similar busts of Apollo were adopted on Gaulish coinage in various areas, although without the attributes (compare de La Tour 1892, XXXIII. 8416. 8424; XXVIII. 7042. 7143; XXIX. 7363; a helmeted figure [XII. 3900] has similar ring-lets). Nothing otherwise links these coins to one another or to Apollo. However, the portrait is a distinctive one, and the question is whether the design was selected because it was known to be Apollo – was this a Gaulish god perceived as having the same properties? There was a wide range of syncretic identifications of Apollo with local deities in the Gallo-Roman period in Gaul and Germany (e.g. Jufer/Luginbühl 2001, 12. 94-96); he was clearly seen as a deity with local resonances. The depiction of a temple on the reverse provides support for a religious connection. In this case the analysis can be taken further. Apollo was frequently connected with the Gaulish deity Belenus (Green 1992a, 30 f.; Jufer/Luginbühl 2001, 28 f.). This must be the BELENOC of the coin inscription. Thus the Apollo prototype seems to have been deliberately selected. Given one of Apollo's roles in Classical mythology as god of music, the presence of the carnyx as an attribute on the Gaulish version seems highly appropriate; although we do not know if Belenus shared this role, Daniel Gricourt and Dominique Hollard (2002, 134) argued convincingly that Belenus was equated with Lug, a god with strong musical associations. The reverse provides further support for the equation. Miranda Green (1992a, 30 f.) described Belenus as a solar deity (the name means »bright« or »brilliant«), and at one of his temples (Sainte-Sabine in Burgundy) ex-voto terracottas of horses were offered; horses were closely connected with solar deities (Thevenot 1951), and with Lug in particular (Gricourt/Hollard 2002). The depiction of a cult statue of a horse in a temple on the reverse would thus make sense for Belenus, giving us a rare example of the obverse and reverse of a coin being iconographically linked (see Allen 1980, 137). Gallo-Roman inscriptions point to the cult of Belenus being centred in Cisalpine Gaul and Narbonensis, with further temples known from the Auvergne and Burgundy and inscriptions from Raetia and Noricum; Classical literary sources mention the cult in Aquitania, Noricum and northern Italy (Green 1992a, 30 f.; Jufer/Luginbühl 2001, 28 f.; Gricourt/Hollard 2002, 133 f.). Belenus' extent is broadened to Britain by the name of Cunobelin, »the hound of Belenus«, and Roman-period occurrences of versions of the name (Ross 1992, 425. 472; RIB 611. 1027; Collingwood/Wright 1991, no. 2417.9); the name also occurs in Iberia (Luján 2003, 196). The connection with the deity Belenos is interesting, as he was not primarily a martial deity, giving a non-warlike context for the use of the carnyx.

The area of origin and tribal affiliation of the coin are unclear (Scheers 1978, 100 f.; Allen 1990, 47 f.; Colbert de Beaulieu/Fischer 1998, 132). The distribution is thin and dispersed; Scheers favoured an origin in the centre-west of France, as did Daphne Nash (1978b, 256 f.), attributing it to the Pictones; more recent finds of six from Gué-de-Sciaux (Vienne) would support this (Sarthre 2000, 265 f.). Depeyrot (2004b, 96 f.) attributed it to the Bituriges, and provided a distribution map of another Belenos issue (*ibidem* 39).

The carnyx

Examples examined in the Bibliothèque nationale certainly appear more like carnyces than bows. Of the five examples seen (BN 7050, 7052-7055), three have some significant details surviving. These and examples in the British Museum (Allen 1990, 583 f.) and the Cabinet des Médailles of the Bibliothèque Royale, Brussels were examined first-hand, while specimens from Brotonne, Seine-Maritime (Scheers 1978, 100 f. no. 418), the Danicourt collection (Scheers 1975, no. 209), Lyon (Brenot/Scheers 1996, nos 856-857), Basel (Burkhardt/Stern/Helmig 1994, fig. 45 no. 176) and a series illustrated by Allen (1973) were examined from photographs (**fig. 220**). In these latter cases it is harder to assess details, especially the presence of any crest. Examples of the parent denarius were also examined in the BM and from photos.

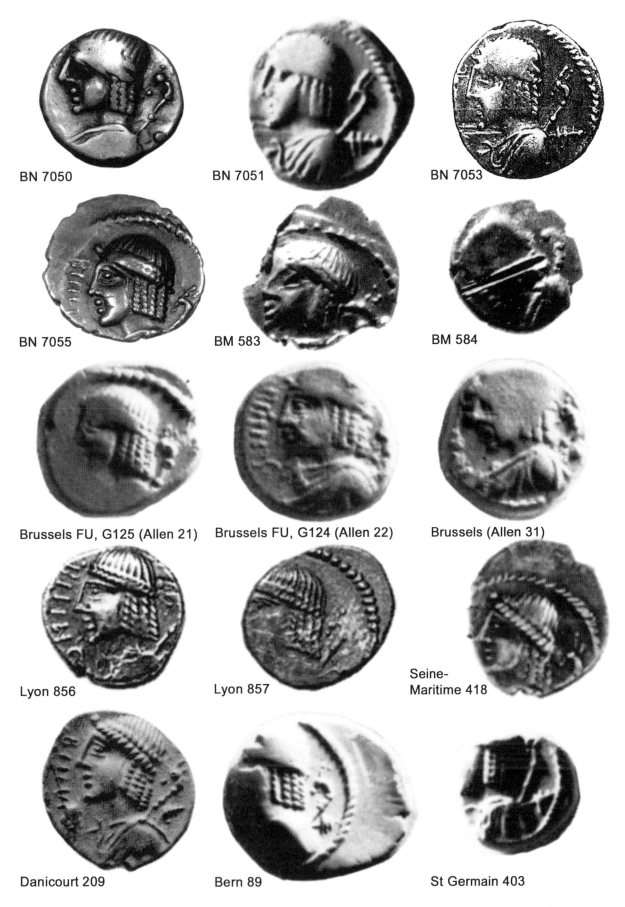

BN 7050   BN 7051   BN 7053

BN 7055   BM 583   BM 584

Brussels FU, G125 (Allen 21)   Brussels FU, G124 (Allen 22)   Brussels (Allen 31)

Lyon 856   Lyon 857

Seine-
Maritime 418

Danicourt 209   Bern 89   St Germain 403

Fig. 220   A2.7 Silver coin inscribed Belenoc. – (Photos Bibliothèque nationale de France; British Museum; Allen 1973, pl. XVI; Brenot/ Scheers 1996, pl. XXX; Scheers 1975, pl. XII; 1978, pl. XX). – Scale 3:1.

Fig. 221 A2.8 Bronze coin of Magurix. – (Photos Bibliothèque nationale de France). – Scale 3:1.

BN 6398   BN 6399

The key feature which confirms the carnyx identification is the segmented tube, an unnecessary feature for a bow. In addition the expansion of the bell and depiction of jaws rather than a string are all but impossible to see as a misconstrued bow. A single case (Allen 22) appears to have a much more typical solidly-drawn naturalistic carnyx jaw, rather than a pellet-defined one, but tantalisingly most of the image is lost off the flan edge.

The key characteristics of the carnyx are: straight segmented tube (at least two sections), ear, and highly flared jaws (at angles of 120-180°) defined by pellets or pellets and lines (with one more naturalistic case); a crest is generally absent, though found on some specimens. A pellet which terminates the head at the jaw may have been intended as the eye. Allen's (1973, 72) description of it as »goat-headed« is over-specific. He also suggested there are two variants, but this also seems over-detailed given the diversity in the depictions.

Date

The *terminus post quem* is provided by the source Republican coin which dates to 67 BC (Crawford 1974, no. 408/1b). The hoard from Vernon (Vienne), dated to 45 BC, includes over 30 examples and thus provides a *terminus ante quem* for their inception (Nash 1978b, 317f. no. 51; Hiernard et al. 1982, 27f.; Crawford 1969, 116 no. 384; the latest Roman coin is of 46-45 BC [Crawford 1974, no. 468]). Scheers (1969, 155) argued such a Romanised type is unlikely to predate the Gallic War, and quoted a find from Limésy, Rouen, where they were accompanied by coins post-dating 52 BC. However, given how heavily influenced by Rome the pre-Conquest issues were in Britain this argument seems spurious, and the type could date from the 60s BC onwards, although most common post-Conquest. It is given a mid-1st century BC date here (c. 60-30 BC).

Bibliography

Allen 1973; 1990, 47f. 70 nos 583-585. – Blanchet 1971, 104. 202. 423 pl. II, 14. – Blankhardt et al. 1994, figs 45; 283 no. 176. – Brenot/Scheers 1996, nos 856-857. – Colbert de Beaulieu/Fischer 1998, no. 67. – Depeyrot 2004b, 13. 96f. no. 125. – Hucher 1868, 24f. pl. 28, 1. – Hunter 2009d, 239f. no. 12. – Muret 1889, 161. – Scheers 1969, 50-52. 154f. pl. VI 82-83; 1975, 67 pl. XII no. 209; 1978, 100f. pl. XX no. 418.

A2.8 Bronze coin inscribed Magurix

Classification: LT XX 6398; BN 6398-6399; DT II 2670 (series 610); Depeyrot V 82
Distribution: middle Loire
The obverse bears a bust facing L with quiver over the shoulder, perhaps derived from Diana, and the legend MAGVRIX. The reverse features Victory facing L, resting on an oval shield in her L hand and holding a carnyx which faces her in her R (fig. 221).
The Marquis de Lagoy (1855, 333-335 pl. VIII no. 5) first discussed the type and identified the carnyx; Colbert de Beaulieu (1980, 22-26) provided a useful discussion of it in the context of late bronzes in the Middle Loire area. It is a rare type, with only three examples known, one of which (from Mont Beuvray) fell to pieces upon discovery. However, its reverse design links it to others from the Middle Loire area, all showing strong Roman influence.

What makes this coin of particular interest is the depiction of the carnyx in local post-conquest coinage, using what in a Roman context would be classic victory iconography, the shield and carnyx representing captured arms. This seems strange when it was presumably a potent symbol of the recent campaigns to those locals who were using the coinage. The whole series is highly Romanised (fig. 222), but some of the other reverses have Gallic overtones: those of TVRONA/DRVCCA with what may represent a standard (again with a Victory), a similar ?standard held

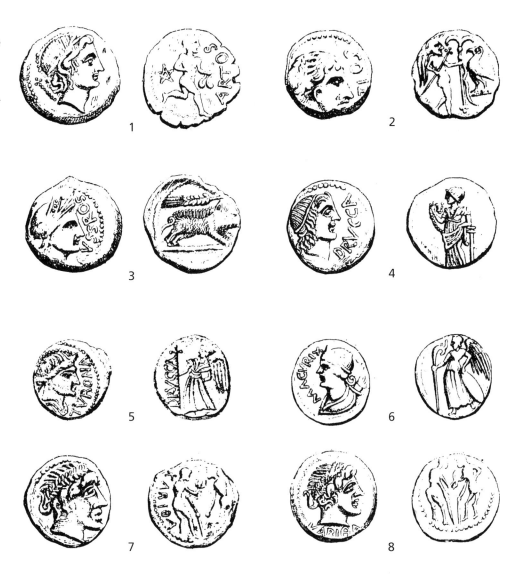

Fig. 222 Series of bronze coins from the middle Loire area related to the Magurix type. – (Colbert de Beaulieu 1980, fig. 4).

by a nude winged figure on coins of ACVTIOS, those of ACVSSROS with a running boar under an ear of corn, and perhaps that of OXOBNOS with a horseman. The rest appear entirely Roman in their iconography, although the onomastics of the legends are Celtic rather than Roman, for instance with MAGVRIX using –RIX rather than –REX (Fischer 2005, 64).

The carnyx

The two specimens in the Bibliothèque nationale were examined. Both are worn, obscuring details, and the end of the tube is lost. The carnyx is essentially similar on both, with a long straight tube, probably in three sections, no ear, and flared jaws. On BN 6398 there is an eye peak and hints of a pellet for the eye itself. There are hints of lines radiating from the bell which may be part of the crest, but wear makes this uncertain. BN 6399 is more worn, but has a clear plain crest extending from the upper jaw to the base of the bell.

Date

Simone Scheers (1980) identified Republican models for a number of coins in this series; for DRVCCA of 49-48 BC, for ACVSSROS of 63-56 BC and for ACVTIOS of 49 BC. The series clearly post-dates the Gallic War. Colbert de Beaulieu (1980) argued their wide circulation is typical of a phase of generalised relatively widespread use of Gaulish coins in the 40 years after the Gallic War, until Roman coins came into regular use. Depeyrot (2005a, 79) gave a more restricted range of 50-30 BC, but Colbert de Beaulieu's arguments are accepted here.

Bibliography

Blanchet 1971, 330. – Colbert de Beaulieu 1980, esp. 22-30. – Colbert de Beaulieu/Fischer 1998, 326. – de Lagoy 1855, 333-335 pl. VIII no. 5. – de La Tour 1892, pl. XX, 6398. – de La Tour/Fischer 1992, pl. XX, 6398. – Depeyrot 2005a, 10. 28. 79 no. 82. – Hucher 1874, 45. – Hunter 2009d, 240 no. 13. – Muret 1889, 142. – Scheers 1980 (for Republican models of related types); 1992a, 14.

A3 GREEK COIN

A3.1 Aetolian tetradrachm

Classification: BM Aetolia 4-8
Distribution: Aetolia
Silver tetradrachm of the Aetolian League, the reverse showing a personification of Aetolia sitting R on a pile of shields: most are oval La Tène style, with one round domed Macedonian one (on most variants). She rests on a spear in her R hand and has a sword in her L. Beneath the pile of shields is a carnyx, head to L and facing up. It forms the ground line of the design, with Aetolia's foot resting on the base and the spear shaft pressing against the bell (**fig. 223**).

This reverse is not simply a portrayal of Aetolia, but is a representation of the triumphal sculpture erected in Delphi by the Aetolian League to commemorate their role in vanquishing the Celts in 279-278 BC (Nachtergael 1977, 201-204; Tsangari 2007, 201; for the campaigns, Rankin 1987, 94-100). The monument itself and the wider context are discussed in detail elsewhere (B8.1). The copy is not exact: there is considerable variation in detail (Reinach 1911b, 203-206), and the coin also includes Macedonian shields, marking an Aetolian victory over the Macedonians (Nachtergael 1977, 202 f. n. 330). Dimitra Tsangari (2007, 203. 251-253) saw this as anti-Macedonian propaganda, commemorating victories over the Macedonians in 314 and around 289 BC; she argued that memories of these past feats were evoked in the context of the Aetolians' war against Demetrios of Macedonia in 239-229 BC.

Early work on the series (Reinach 1911b, 187-211; de Laix 1973) has been superseded by Tsangari's comprehensive study of Aetolian coinage (2007, esp. 37. 53. 75-81. 193. 201). Although the Aetolians struck in gold, silver and bronze, and depicted the Delphic trophy on all three, carnyces only appear on silver tetradrachms. These fall into her series 3, group II, types 16-20. 47 die combinations are recorded from 83 coins (there are also a number of modern fakes; *ibidem* 189 pl. XCVI), with 45 reverse dies and nine obverse dies known; the relatively low numbers indicate a short period of issue (Tsangari 2007, 193). The two earliest dies do not feature carnyces.

For the current study, five specimens in the British Museum (BM Aetolia 4-8), two in the Nationalmuseet Copenhagen (SNG Copenhagen 2-3), two in the Numismatic Museum Athens, and one in the coin cabinet of the Staatliche Museen zu Berlin (1873 Fox) were examined first-hand, the rest from Tsangari's photographs. These were used to construct a description of the carnyx on each die type (**tab. 58**).

The carnyx

Table 58 illustrates the minor variety in the details of the carnyx depiction, but all are variations around a basic theme. They consistently show a relatively naturalistic head with one or two ears (about a third are earless) and an eye, a slightly open mouth (closed in about a third of cases) and a segmented tube, typically in four segments, with the straight mouthpiece shown as a knob. About a third have a simple crest. A. J. Reinach (1911b, 205) saw the head as a wolf, but it would be unwise to venture an identification.

Date

Dating of the type has ranged quite widely: older authorities preferred a range of c. 279-168 BC, between the attack on Delphi and the Roman annexation of the area (e. g. Gardner 1883, 194; Reinach 1911b, 201; Grose 1979, 299); Hans-Dietrich Schultz (1997, 53) opted for 220-189 BC, while Georges Nachtergael (1977, 202 f. and Addenda) suggested a span of c. 220 BC - 146/135 BC. A more comprehensive analysis by Roger de Laix (1973) argued forcefully for a shorter and earlier period of issue. The total number of issues is small, and there are extensive die links between them, while virtually all the tetradrachm types are recorded in the Corinth hoard of c. 216 BC, providing a *terminus ante quem*. de Laix suggested they should be fitted into a period of prosperity for the Aetolians in the years c. 221-219 BC, the high denomination suggesting use in international trade (de Laix 1973, 59 f.).

More recently, Tsangari (2007, 250-253) has argued for a date of 239-229 BC, connected with the campaigns against Demetrios of Macedonia at this date; this fits the hoard evidence, the relative sequencing of the issues, and gives a context for both the inclusion of a Macedonian shield in the trophy and a broad spread of findspots, suiting the pan-Hellenic nature of the conflict. On balance, Tsangari's views seem most convincing and are preferred here.

Bibliography

Gardner 1883, 194 f. – Grose 1979, 299 no. 5401 pl. 197, 2. – de Laix 1973. – Reinach 1911b, 187-211. – Schultz 1997, 53 no. 226. – SNG Copenhagen = Sylloge Nummorum Graecorum: The Royal Collection of Coins and Medals, Danish National Museum (reprinted 1982, Sunrise Publications, W Milford). – Tsangari 2007.

Copenhagen 13,2 (die 16)

Copenhagen 13,3 (die 39)

BM 5 (die 42)

BM 4 (die 39)

BM 7 (die 11)

BM 8 (die 22)

Berlin (die 19)

Fig. 223 A3.1 Aetolian tetradrachm. – (Photos British Museum; Nationalmuseet Copenhagen; Staatliche Museen zu Berlin – Preußischer Kulturbesitz, Münzkabinett [Reinhard Saczewski]). – Scale 2:1.

die	mouth	eye	ears	crest	tube no.	mouthpiece	notes
3	open	y	2	n	?	?	
4	open	y	1?	n	4	knob	Head damaged on illustrated example
5	closed	y	2	y	4	knob	Spiky crest
6	closed	y	2	y	3?	?	?Spiky crest
7	closed	y	2	y	4	knob	Spiky crest
8	open	y	2	y	4	knob	Small ears; poorly-defined crest
9	closed	y	?	?	4?	knob	Details unclear
10	open	n?	2	y	4?	?	Spiky crest
11	closed	y	n?	?	4	knob	2 pellets on bell probably from crest; dot eye; BM 7 suggests possible single ear flattened against head
13	open	?	2	?	4	?	
16	closed	n	1	n	4	knob	
17	?	?	?	?	4	?	
18	open	?	?	?	3?	plain	
19	closed	?	n?	n	3	?	May have very small ears
20	open	y	n?	n	?	?	
21	open	y	n	y	1	?	Short crest, pointing back
22	open	y	n	y	1	?	Bell expanded and marked by knob; short crest pointing back
23	open	?	n	?	?	?	
25	open	?	n	?	1	?	
26	open	y	n	y	1	?	Small crest
27	open	y	n	?	?	?	
28	open	y	n	y	?	?	
29	open	?	2	n	4?	?	
30	open?	y	2	n	?	?	
31	open	y	n	y	?	?	
32	?	?	?	?	1	?	
33	open	y	?	n	?	?	
34	open	?	1?	?	?	?	
35	closed	?	?	?	?	?	
36	open	?	2	n	4?	?	
37	open	?	2	n	4?	knob	
39	open	n	2	n	7	knob	Double-knob at tube-bell junction
40	open	y	2	n	5	knob	
41	open	y	1?	n	?	?	
42	closed	n	2	n	5?	?	
44	open	?	2	n	?	?	
45	open	y	1	n	?	?	

Tab. 58 Characteristics of the carnyx on the reverse dies of Aetolian tetradrachms. Coins from dies 11, 16, 22, 39 and 42 were examined first-hand. Dies 1 and 2 do not show carnyces. The following dies do not preserve carnyces (at least in published illustrations): 12, 14, 15, 24, 37, 38, 43.

cat. no.	RRC ref.	date
A4.1	128	206-200 BC
A4.2	281	119 BC
A4.3	282	118 BC
A4.4	332	98 BC
A4.5	326/2	97 BC
A4.6	333	94 BC
A4.7	337/1	90 BC
A4.8	343/2	89 BC
A4.9	344/3	89 BC
A4.10	346/2	88 BC

cat. no.	RRC ref.	date
A4.11	352/1	85 BC
A4.12	366/1a	82-81 BC
A4.13	384	79 BC
A4.14	412/1	62 BC
A4.15	437	51 BC
A4.16	448	48 BC
A4.17	450/1	48 BC
A4.18	452	48-47 BC
A4.19	468	46-45 BC
A4.20	482	44-43 BC

Tab. 59 Occurrences of the carnyx on Roman Republican coins.

Fig. 224 A4.1 Denarius with Dioscuri and carnyx (RRC 128). – (Photos British Museum; Staatliche Museen zu Berlin – Preußischer Kulturbesitz, Münzkabinett [Reinhard Saczewski]). – Scale 2:1.

BM 312   BM Sydenham   BM 313

Berlin 1864/28688   Berlin Sandes

A4 ROMAN REPUBLICAN COINS (tab. 59)

A4.1 Denarius

Classification: RRC 128

The reverse shows the Dioscuri riding R, with a carnyx lying over a shield on the R, under the horses' hooves; the shield is oval with a spine (**fig. 224**). Under the ground line is the inscription ROMA. This reverse is common to a number of issues (RRC 44-132 on denarii, c. 211-190 BC), with the subject under the horses' hooves varying.

Michael Crawford offered no specific explanation of the type, but Christophe Vendries (in Homo-Lechner/Vendries 1993, 28) related it to Roman campaigns in Cisalpine Gaul in 225-218 BC (for the context see Williams 2001b, 14f.). Herbert Grueber (1910, 216) and P. Høeg Albrethsen (1987, 104 n. 9) suggested it may be of the moneyer Decia, and commemorated an ancestor, P. Decius Mus, who won a posthumous victory against Cisalpine Gauls in 295 BC in the course of the Third Samnite War (Cary/Wilson 1963, 39f.). This would explain its restoration under Trajan with the legend »DECIVS MVS« (see A5.3). While the link to the moneyer may be tentative, the Trajanic restoration does suggest this was the event being commemorated.

The carnyx

The three specimens in the British Museum and two in Berlin were examined (there are none in the BN). The basic model is consistent, with a straight or slightly curved tube in two or three segments, the end straight; the head has a flared mouth, with eye and ear. There are slight variants, notably in presence or (more often) absence of a crest,

and straight versus curved tube; the curve is probably due to space constraints.

BMCRR Italy 312 (pl. lxxxviii.6): flared mouth, eye peak, ear, crest from rear of ear down to shield (end of bell); tube curves throughout, probably to fit the available space (cf. other examples); tube has probably three segments (wear makes this uncertain) with a straight end and mouthpiece knob. The example illustrated by Crawford (1974, pl. XXIII) is of this type.

BMCRR Italy 313 & Sydenham lot 78: flared mouth, eye peak, ear, no crest; straight three-segment tube with mouthpiece knob.

Berlin 28688: flared mouth, worn eye and eye peak; ear; slight kink in tube at bell, otherwise straight, with possible tube divisions, though very worn; straight end with mouthpiece knob.

Berlin (Sandes): flared mouth, eye peak, ear; tube curves notably in upper half; segmented tube, at least two segments and possibly three (wear obscures details); straight end, no knob.

Date

206-200 BC (Crawford 1974, 207)

Bibliography

Crawford 1974, 207f. – Grueber 1910, 216. – de Lagoy 1849, 30 pl. II no. 20.

BM Italy 555   BM Italy 556   BM Italy 557   BM Italy 558

BM Italy 559   BM Italy 560   BM Italy 561   BM 1964-12-3-185

Fig. 225   A4.2 Denarius of M. Fourius (RRC 281). – (Photos British Museum). – Scale 2:1.

A4.2 Denarius of M. Fourius

Classification: RRC 281

Denarius of M. Fourius (M.FOVRI L.F PHILI). The reverse shows Roma on the R crowning a trophy with a laurel wreath. The trophy comprises tunic, ?cuirass and helmet, with sword on the L arm and rectangular shield on the R (as viewed). On either side of the trophy is a rectangular shield and a carnyx, the shields with central round bosses and lattice decoration inside a pronounced border (**fig. 225**).

Crawford (1974, 297) argued plausibly that the issue refers to the defeat of the Gaulish tribes of the Allobroges and Arverni in 121 BC and the resulting triumphs of 120 BC (Scullard 1970, 41 f.).

The carnyces

The ten examples in the British Museum were examined, of which eight preserve sufficient detail to study (BMCRR Italy 555-561, 1964-12-3-185); two examples in the Cabinet des Médailles, Brussels, were also examined. The depictions display considerable variety around their common theme: they are a good example of the variability within a type, from highly detailed (e. g. BM Italy 555) to highly stylised (e. g. BM Italy 562). The basic type is a carnyx with a flared mouth, the ends generally knobbed, eye, two ears, a variable number of tube segments (1-5), and a mouthpiece knob; some show a crest.

Date

119 BC (Crawford 1974, 297)

Bibliography

Crawford 1974, 297. – de Lagoy 1849, 20 pl. II no. 4.

A4.3 »Gaul in chariot« denarius

Classification: RRC 282/1-5

This coin type is represented by five variants which differ in their legends. They are interpreted as the work of two senior monetary magistrates (L. Licinius and Cn. Domitius)

with five junior associates. The reverse shows a naked bearded warrior in a two-horse chariot driving R; in his R hand he holds a spear over his head, ready to throw, while his L arm bears an oval shield with a criss-cross decorative

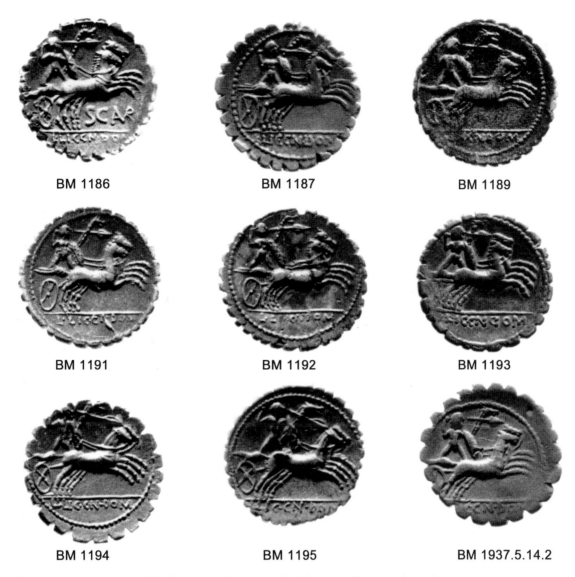

BM 1186	BM 1187	BM 1189
BM 1191	BM 1192	BM 1193
BM 1194	BM 1195	BM 1937.5.14.2

Fig. 226 A4.3 Denarius, Gaul in chariot type (RRC 282/1-5). – (Photos British Museum). – Scale 2:1.

pattern; from behind this appears a carnyx, facing R, and presumably also held in his L hand. The edge of the coin is serrated (**fig. 226**).

The type was minted in Narbo to commemorate the foundation of the colony in 118 BC. It has been argued that it represents Bituitos, the defeated ruler of the Arverni (Piggott 1952; Scullard 1970, 42), who was taken to Rome and paraded in a chariot in the triumph (Albrethsen 1987, 104). This is likely but, in the absence of an inscription, we cannot be entirely certain; it certainly represents a Gaul.

The carnyx

There are differences in the carnyx depictions used by each of the junior moneyers, mostly stemming from greater or lesser stylisation. The essential characteristics are an open mouth (not excessively flared), eye, two ears, crest, and tube defined by a series of dots. Only the upper part of the carnyx is visible; the bell is not defined from the tube except in one case (BM 1194). Specimens in the British Museum and the Cabinet des Médailles, Brussels, were examined first-hand. The following preserved significant detail: BMCRR Rome 1186f. 1189. 1191-1195, BM 1937.5.14.2, and two from Brussels (Inv. II, 53,778 and unregistered).

Date
118 BC (Crawford 1974, 71-74. 298f.)

Bibliography
Crawford 1974, 298f. – Homo-Lechner/Vendries 1993, 35.

BM Rome 1082   1083   1084   1085   1086

BM Rome 1087   1089   1090   1091   1092

BM Rome 1093   1096   1097   1099   1100

BM Rome 1102   1103   1104   1105   1106

BM Rome 1107   1108   1110   1113

BM 1928-4-14-2   1932-11-3-1   1932-11-3-2

Fig. 227   A4.4 Quinarius of T. Cloulius (RRC 332). – (Photos British Museum). – Scale 2:1.

A4.4 Quinarius of T. Cloulius

Classification: RRC 332

The reverse has Victory holding a palm branch advancing R to crown a trophy with a laurel wreath. The trophy comprises stylised tunic, helmet and perhaps armour, with an oval shield on one arm and a sword or spear on the other. At the base sits a captive, apparently bound; to the R of the trophy is a stylised carnyx, facing R (**fig. 227**).

Michael Crawford argued this type is connected to Marius's campaigns against the Cimbri and Teutones and subsequent veteran settlement. This is based both on the presence of the carnyx and the denomination: the quinarius is preferentially found in Gaul, where it was apparently favoured because of its similarity in weight to indigenous currencies (Crawford 1974, 629f.). In general its issue in quantity appears to be connected to events in Gaul which required money to be minted, such as paying troops and settling veterans. Quinarii were minted in quantity in 101 and 99-97 BC, which gives a strong chronological and geographical link to Marius's campaigns when there would be soldiers to pay and veterans to subsidise. Given this, the victory reverses were highly appropriate.

The carnyx

The carnyx is highly stylised and its base is hidden behind the trophy and the captive, but it is clearly recognisable from its straight tube, open mouth and ear. There is some variation around this basic pattern. Specimens were examined in the British Museum (BMCRR Rome 1082-1087. 1089-1093. 1096f. 1099f. 1102-1108. 1110. 1113; BM 1928-4-14-2, 1932-11-3-1, 1932-11-3-2) and the Cabinet des Médailles, Brussels (two examples). One Brussels example is markedly more naturalistic, and has two ears and an eye; the other Brussels coin has an eye peak. BMCRR 1083, 1090 and 1104 have a curving tube; on BMCRR 1085 the head and bell are thicker than the tube; the mouth is closed in about a third of cases.

Date

98 BC (Crawford 1974, 331; Mattingly 1998, 154)

Bibliography

Crawford 1974, 331f. 629f. – de Lagoy 1849, 20f. pl. II no. 6.

A4.5 Quinarius of C. Fundanius

Classification: RRC 326/2

The reverse shows Victory facing R, holding a palm branch and crowning a trophy with a laurel wreath. The trophy comprises belted tunic and horned and crested helmet, sometimes with cheekguards: it has a sub-rectangular shield on the R arm and a spear in the L (as viewed). A naked and bound barbarian kneels below it; to the R is a carnyx, upright and facing R (**fig. 228**).

Crawford linked the device to Marius's victories over the Cimbri and Teutones (Scullard 1970, 53-55. 58-60). This is noteworthy, as it and A4.4 are the first examples of the carnyx being linked to Germanic rather than Gaulish iconography in Roman coinage.

The carnyx

Specimens in the British Museum (BMCRR Rome 1696-1699. 1701-1703; BM 1920-9-7-91, 1936-10-13-64, 1949-4-3-29, 1950-10-6-355, 1950-10-6-356) and the Cabinet des Médailles, Brussels (one example) were examined. The style (and degree of stylisation) varies considerably. The recurring features of this carnyx are an open mouth, two ears, eye, a straight tube with two sections and a basal knob, although every aspect except the number of tube sections has exceptions, and one example has a crest. BM 1703 has two unequal tube segments.

Date

Michael Crawford (1974, 328) dated the issue to 101 BC, minted in Rome, but H. B. Mattingly (1998) rearranged the moneyers of this period and suggested a date of 97 BC is more likely.

Bibliography

Crawford 1974, 328 no. 326. – de Lagoy 1849, 20 pl. II no. 5.

BM Rome 1696   1697   1698   1699

BM Rome 1701   1702   1703   1920.9.7.91

BM 1936.10.13.64   1949.4.3.29   1950.10.6.355   1950.10.6.356

Fig. 228 A4.5 Quinarius of C. Fundanius (RRC 326/2). – (Photos British Museum). – Scale 2:1.

BM Rome 1076   1077   1078

BM 1928.4.14.1   1928.4.14.7   1928.4.14.9

Fig. 229 A4.6 Quinarius of C. Egnatuleius (RRC 333). – (Photos British Museum). – Scale 2:1.

BM Rome 1840   **1841**   **1950.10.6.368**

Fig. 230   A4.7 Control mark on denarius of D. Silanus (RRC 337/1). – (Photos British Museum). – Scale c. 2:1.

A4.6 Quinarius of C. Egnatuleius

Classification: RRC 333
The reverse is a variant on A4.4 and A4.5, with Victory advancing L, mounting an oval shield on a trophy comprising tunic, muscle cuirass and horned helmet, with spear on L arm and carnyx at base of trophy, to L and facing L (**fig. 229**). As with the comparable issues, this can be connected to Marius's victories over the Cimbri and Teutones.

The carnyx
The carnyx is relatively detailed given its small scale. The six examples in the British Museum (BMCRR Rome 1076-1078; BM 1928-4-14-1, 7 and 9) and single example in the Cabinet des Médailles, Brussels, were examined. The main characteristics are: flared mouth, two ears, no crest or eye, three-section tube, no basal knob.

Dating evidence
Crawford (1974, 332) dated the type to 97 BC but Mattingly (1998, 154) corrected this to 94 BC.

Bibliography
Crawford 1974, 332. 629f. – de Lagoy 1849, 21 pl. II no. 7.

A4.7 Denarius of D. Silanus (control mark)

Classification: RRC 337/1
The reverse shows Victory with palm branch in a chariot racing R. There are different variants of the series according to what lies under the horses' hooves: in variant 337/1 it is a carnyx (**fig. 230**). In others this position is taken up by a variable control mark or the legend ROMA. Hence it is unclear whether the carnyx was seen as an integral part of the composition (i. e. Victory riding down a barbarian attribute) or simply one of several possible control marks; the latter seems more likely. Crawford suggested it must be linked to Gallic campaigns, but there do not appear to be any contemporary ones, and it is more likely to relate to Roman successes in the Social War (which the revised dating would allow). This would not explain the presence of a carnyx, as the Social War was fought against Italians. Given Marius' involvement in the war in 90 BC (Scullard 1970, 68), it could have been intended as a reminder of his earlier victories against the Cimbri and Teutones, but this is highly speculative. De Lagoy (1849, 29f.) saw it as a reference to the moneyer's family history; the surname Silanus was adopted from the family Manlia, one of whose ancestors (Manlius Torquatus) defeated a Celtic leader in 361 BC (Rankin 1987, 68f.). However, in the context of other issues around this time it is much simpler to see it as a control mark similar to A4.8 and A4.9, unrelated to the Victory figure.

The carnyx
Three specimens in the British Museum (BMCRR Rome 1840f.; BM 1950-10-6-368) and one in the Cabinet des Médailles, Brussels, were examined. All show the same basic type of carnyx: flared mouth; no eye or ear; crest with defined hair, down to bell end; three-section tube, without basal knob (the Brussels example has the end squared and slightly expanded). Rome 1841 may have a fang in the jaw, but this is unclear.

Date
Crawford (1974, 336) dated the type to 91 BC, but Mattingly (1998, 154) revised this to 90 BC.

Bibliography
Crawford 1974, 336-339. – de Lagoy 1849, 29f. pl. II no. 19.

A4.8 Quinarius of M. Cato (control mark)

Classification: RRC 343/2b
The obverse of this quinarius features a head of Liber facing R, with a control mark below. Crawford (1974, 350) recorded the presence of a carnyx as a control mark in the Pontecorvo hoard, no. 858, but attempts to secure an image of this coin were in vain. It appears to be rare, as it is not recorded in Paris and was not found on specimens in BM, Berlin, Brussels or Copenhagen; thus, no details of its appearance can be provided.

Date
89 BC (Crawford 1974, 351 f.)

Bibliography
Crawford 1974, 350-352.

A4.9 Denarius of L. Titurius (control mark)

Classification: RRC 344/3
The reverse of this denarius shows Victory in a *biga*, galloping R; Crawford (1974, 356) linked the design to Roman success in the second year of the Social War. In exergue is a control mark. Ernest Babelon (1885-1886, vol. ii, 499) recorded a carnyx, but Crawford (1974, 355) did not find an example. However, one of the other marks he did not find (a prawn) was noted by the writer on a denarius in the BM (Rome 2339), suggesting Babelon was probably accurate. It is not present in the collections in the BM, Berlin, Brussels or Copenhagen, and no description can be provided.

Date
89 BC (Crawford 1974, 352)

Bibliography
Babelon 1885-1886, vol. ii, 499. – Crawford 1974, 352-356.

A4.10 Denarius of C. Censorinus (control mark)

Classification: RRC 346/2
The reverse features a horse galloping right and an inscription. It carries two control marks, one above the horse, the other in exergue (**fig. 231**). Crawford (1974, 358-360) listed the extensive control mark combinations based on the major museum collections, but omitted one illustrated by de Lagoy (1849, 31 pl. II no. 21). Given that de Lagoy is otherwise quite accurate in his depictions and descriptions, this can be accepted. The issue he illustrated has a pair of caps above the horse and a carnyx below. It fits with A4.7-4.9 and A4.11 in showing the persistence of the carnyx as an everyday icon in the years after the victories over the Cimbri and Teutones. No specimen has been located; it is not in the BM, BN, Berlin, Brussels or Copenhagen collections.

The carnyx
The carnyx faces right and down. It has a three-section tube, with knobs at the divisions and the base. A bristle-crest runs the length of the bell (which is quite vertical with the head perpendicular at the end). The head has two ears, an eye, and the mouth open to 50°. (Description taken from de Lagoy's illustration.)

Date
Crawford (1974, 357-361) dated the type to 88 BC.

Bibliography
Crawford 1974, 357-361 (the general type). – de Lagoy 1849, 31 pl. II no. 21 (the example with a carnyx).

Fig. 231 A4.10 Control mark on denarius of C. Censorinus (RRC 346/2). – (After de Lagoy 1849, pl. 2, 21). – Scale 3:1.

A4.11 Denarius of L. Iulius Bursio (control mark)

Classification: RRC 352/1

The obverse bears a male head facing R, combining attributes of Apollo (hairstyle), Mercury (wings) and Neptune (trident), with a control mark behind the head; the reverse has Victory in a *quadriga*. Babelon (1885-1886, vol. ii, 7) tabulated the control marks known to him, one of which (no. 105) is a carnyx facing left (**fig. 232**). It is represented on a coin in the BN (Ailly 10567), probably the one studied by Babelon, although his drawing is not totally accurate.

The carnyx

The coin is worn but the key features are clear. The carnyx has a straight tube with a plain end. There is a knob at the tube-bell junction (at about half the instrument's height), and the bell is rather thicker. The head has a forward-pointing ear and an open mouth (the upper jaw largely lost); if there was an eye it has been worn flat. There is no crest. A few lines around the tube are striking flaws rather than parts of the design.

Fig. 232 A4.11 Control mark on denarius of L. Iulius Bursio (RRC 352/1). – (Photo Bibliothèque nationale de France, Ailly 10567). – Scale 3:1.

Date

85 BC (Crawford 1974, 368)

Bibliography

Babelon 1885-1886, vol. ii, 6-8. – Crawford 1974, 368 f. – de Lagoy 1849, 31 pl. II no. 22.

A4.12 Denarius of C. Annius (control mark)

Classification: RRC 366/1a

Earlier versions of the issue (such as this one) were minted in Italy, later ones in Spain (see Crawford 1974, 386). The carnyx features as one of a number of control marks on the obverse, which shows a bust of a female deity facing R, with a caduceus behind her, scales in front and a control mark below (**fig. 233**). The reverse features Victory in a chariot: Crawford commented this is an appropriate type for a military issue, as these denarii were minted for the troops when the moneyer was involved in campaigns in Spain. In the aftermath of the civil war between Sulla and Marius, Annius (of the Sullan faction) commanded an army against the Marian Sertorius (Grueber 1910, 352 f.; Scullard 1970, 90). As the campaigns were thus against fellow Romans we cannot draw any connection between the events and the depiction of the carnyx: the control symbols draw on a wide range of emblems, not all military (only 8 of the 27 symbols listed by Crawford have potential military or triumphal significance).

The carnyx

Single specimens with a carnyx in the BM (BMCRR Spain 1 = 1901-4-7-23) and the BN (Ailly 4021) were examined. It lies under the bust, head to R and facing up. The Paris one is the clearer. The carnyx is rather stylised, unsurprisingly given the scale. The end of the tube is lost, but there are two (equal?) tube sections with knobbed junctions; the thicker bell turns sharply into the head, which has an upcurved ear, indications of a worn pellet eye, and a slightly open mouth, the lower jaw shorter than the upper. There is no crest.

Date

82-81 BC (Crawford 1974, 381-386)

Bibliography

Crawford 1974, 381-386. – Grueber 1910, 352 f.

BN Ailly 4021   (detail)   BM Spain 1

Fig. 233 A4.12 Control mark on denarius of C. Annius (RRC 366/1a), with detail. – (Photos Bibliothèque nationale de France; British Museum). – Scale 3:1.

A4.13 Serrated denarius of L. Papius (control mark)

Classification: RRC 384
The carnyx features as a control mark on the reverse, which shows a griffin leaping R. The carnyx lies under the griffin, with the head to the R and facing up (**fig. 234**). The obverse (head of Juno Sospita) also bears a control mark, and in general there is some link between the control marks on either side: the carnyx is paired with a sword in its scabbard (Crawford 1974, pl. LXVI. 100). A wide range of control marks was used: Crawford recorded 211 pairs, of which only around 10 have triumphal or military overtones.

The carnyx
From the collections examined, only a single example with a carnyx control mark was found, in the British Museum (BMCRR Rome 3076 = 43-1-16-890). Crawford's drawing of the carnyx does not do justice to the remarkable detail conveyed in such a small depiction; Babelon's (1885-1886, 282 no. 143) is rather better. The mouth flares at around 90°, and there is a suggestion of upper and lower fangs/tusks between a third and halfway along each jaw. An eye, single ear and crest are depicted. The crest has hints of lines to indicate spikes at the top, but is otherwise plain; it merges imperceptibly with the bell. The bell is unusually long, running to around half the object's length; below this there are two tube sections, with a straight end and basal knob for the mouthpiece.

BM 3076

Fig. 234 A4.13 Control mark on denarius of L. Papius (RRC 384). – (Photo British Museum). – Scale 3:1.

Date
79 BC (Crawford 1974, 82. 398)

Bibliography
Babelon 1885-1886, 279-282. – Crawford 1974, 82. 398 f.

A4.14 Serrated denarius of L. Roscius Fabatus (control mark)

Classification: RRC 412
The moneyer was a native of Lanuvium, near Rome, and the coin commemorates his origins, with the head of the town's goddess, Juno Sospita, on the obverse and one of her rituals on the reverse involving a girl feeding a snake (Harlan 1995, 18-22). Both sides bear control marks, fre-

Fig. 235 A4.14 Control mark on denarius of L. Roscius Fabatus (RRC 412). – (Photos British Museum; Antike Münzen 32 [28.-29.10.1996], pl. XXIV lot 483). – Scale 3:1.

BM Rome 3488   **Antike Münzen 32/483**

quently conceptually related: a vertical carnyx occurs on the reverse of some with a boar standard on the obverse (Crawford 1974, pl. lxviii, 88), both of which may be taken as symbols of Gaul. Crawford recorded 242 pairs of control marks, 15 with some military or triumphal significance.

A single specimen in the BM shows the carnyx (**fig. 235**; BMCRR Rome 3488 = 43-1-16-996); there is none in Paris. An additional specimen from a different die was examined from a photograph in an auction catalogue (Antike Münzen 32 [28.-29.10.1996], pl. XXIV lot 483).

The carnyx

The BM example is the more stylised and is poorly struck. The straight tube is defined by pellets, but while the lower five are separate, the upper three are linked by zig-zag lines before the curving bell is reached. The head is heavily

recurved but the right side is poorly formed: one ear is visible, with hints of a second, and only the lower jaw. There is no mouthpiece, although the tube pellets are closer together near the base. No ear or crest.

The Antike Münzen specimen is better formed. Seven pellets form the straight tube, with no discernible mouthpiece; this joins a bell which curves such that the flared jaws point downwards. It has two ears but no eye or crest.

Date

Crawford (1974, 83-87) suggested 64 BC, but Harlan (1995, 21) argued for 62 BC based on more recent hoard evidence and the significance of the year to the moneyer, the first time a native of his town gained the consulship.

Bibliography
Crawford 1974, 83-87. 439 f. – Harlan 1995, 18-22.

A4.15 Denarius of C. Coelius Caldus

Classification: RRC 437/2-4 and 437/4a

This denarius is a complex monument to the moneyer's ancestry. It commemorates the moneyer himself and two other relatives: C. Coelius Caldus, consul in 94 BC who is depicted on the obverse; and L. Coelius Caldus, priest of the feast of Jupiter (this follows the interpretations of Harlan [1995, 160-166] and Woytek/Zawadzka [2016]).

The first C. Coelius Caldus was a »new man« in the Roman aristocracy, the first of the family to attain the consulship. On variants RRC 437/2-3 his bust is flanked by a vexillum inscribed »HIS«, commemorating governorship of and apparently victories in Spain, and a boar standard marking victories in Gaul; on RRC 437/4 a carnyx and spear replace the boar standard. The reverse on varieties 2-4, which are the relevant ones here, has a central table with an inscription and a seated figure

BM Rome 3840   a

Fig. 236 A4.15 Denarius of C. Coelius Caldus (RRC 437): **a** A4.15.1 (RRC 437/4a obverse); BM 3840. – **b** A4.15.2 (RRC 437/2-4, reverse). – (Photos British Museum). – Scale 3:1.

Fig. 236   (continued)

BM Rome 3837   3838

BM Rome 3839   3840   b

flanked by two trophies, one of which features a carnyx. The table is that for the feast of Jupiter, with a priest preparing the *epulum*, the sacred feast. An inscription on the table relates it to L. Coelius Caldus, priest of this feast (*septemvir epulo*). The occasion was probably the celebration of the victories to which the trophies refer (Woytek/Zawadzka 2016, 151-153). That with the carnyx has been linked to a victory in Gaul over the Saluvii in 90 BC (Crawford 1974, 459; Harlan 1995, 162); the round shields and pair of spears refer to the Spanish victory alluded to on the obverse (Woytek/Zawadzka 2016, 145-148). The complexity of the design is such that most Romans would have had difficulty deciphering it (Zanker 1988, 14), but as Harlan commented it did ensure high-visibility »brand identity« for the family name.

A4.15.1 The obverse carnyx

A carnyx only appears on variant 4 (**fig. 236a**); a single example (variant 4a) was examined in the BM (BMCRR Rome 3840). The carnyx faces R, and is very stylised. It has a long plain tube with a single knob at the bell junction; the mouthpiece is lost off the flan. The bell curves through

90°; two pellets at the end define a stylised mouth, gaping at c. 180°.

A4.15.2 The reverse carnyx

Two trophies are present, their position alternating (variants a and b). One features a round shield on the L, two spears on the R and a sword across the body; it has a domed helmet. The other has a horned helmet and sword; the R arm holds an oval shield and the L a spear and carnyx (**fig. 236b**). The oval shield, horned helmet and carnyx are all recurrent identifiers of Gaul at this period. Four examples were examined in the BM, of variants 2a, 3a and 4a (BMCRR Rome 3837-3840), and one example of 2a in the Cabinet des Médailles, Brussels. In all cases the carnyx is rather stylised, and is represented by a broadly straight tube curved at the end and often with a simple crest for about a third of its length. There is sometimes a hint of an upper jaw, but no ears, eyes or construction details.

Date

52/51 BC (Crawford 1974, 83-88. 457-459; Harlan 1995, 165; Woytek 2003, 89f.)

Fig. 237 A4.16 Denarius of L. Hostilius Saserna: **a** A4.16.1 (RRC 448/1 reverse). – **b** A4.16.2 (RRC 448/3). – (Photos British Museum, Bibliothèque nationale de France). – Scale 3:1.

BM Rome 3989

BM Rome 3990

BM Rome 3993

BN Ailly 10272

a

Bibliography
Crawford 1974, 83-88. 457-459. – Evans 1991. – Harlan 1995, 160-166. – de Lagoy 1849, 32 f. pl. II nos 23-26. – Woytek/Zawadzka 2016.

A4.16 Denarius of L. Hostilius Saserna

Classification: RRC 448
L. Hostilius Saserna struck a number of denarii, all with imagery related to Caesar's Gallic War, with heads of male and female Gauls, Victory with a trophy, and a British warrior in a chariot (for which see Piggott 1952). Carnyces are present on variants 448/1 and 448/3.

A4.16.1
Variant 448/1 has a reverse with Victory running R holding a trophy over her L shoulder and a caduceus in her R hand. The trophy comprises a muscle cuirass and tunic with three palm branches behind; to R is an oval shield with elongated umbo and spine, to L a carnyx (**fig. 237a**).

The carnyx was depicted on three coins in the BM (BM-CRR 3989. 3990. 3993) and two examples in Paris (Ailly 10272 and unregistered). Only the upper part of the bell and the head are shown. The quality varies greatly, from recognisable to highly stylised (e. g. BM 3993). The jaws are typically open to c. 30°; the head has a single ear, sometimes an eye peak, but only rarely a crest (one instance).

A4.16.2
Variant 448/3 has an obverse showing a female with long unkempt hair, representing a Gaul; the unkempt hair would epitomise *Gallia Comata* or »hairy Gaul« to Roman

Fig. 237 (continued)

BM Rome 3996

BM Rome 3997

BN Ailly 10276

BN Ailly 10277   b

eyes (Homo-Lechner/Vendries 1993, 36). Behind her is a carnyx (**fig. 237b**). A similar female head is found on an issue of Caesar himself in 48-47 BC (RRC 452/3), again associated with victory imagery. The reverse of 448/3 shows Artemis, patron goddess of Massalia which Caesar captured in 49 BC during the Civil War.

The carnyx sits behind the female head on 448/3, facing R, and is a generally accurate depiction with segmented tube (in three or four sections), crest of varying form, one or two ears, an eye and a gaping mouth. Two examples in the BM and two in the BN were examined first-hand (BMCRR Rome 3996 f.; BN Ailly 10276 f.), while examples in photographs add further variety. In Classic Numismatic Group Sale 51 (15.9.99), lot 112 has a plain tube, and the crest curls up at the end to form the ear. Lot 113 has a fang in the upper jaw, and the crest appears to be superimposed on the bell: there is no separate crest, but ribbing on the bell mirrors typical crest decoration.

A copy illustrated by Babelon (1885-1886, 553), now in Paris (BN Ailly 10277) has two stylised carnyces, one in front of the female bust and one behind. The stylisation and blundered legend on the reverse indicate this is a contemporary fake (Grueber 1910, 514 n. 1). Both carnyces are very linear, with little detail; however, unlike the examples on the official issues, both have tongues. The left one has a slightly curved tube/bell, a single ear, an eye peak, and the jaw open to c. 180°, with a single dot defining the tongue. The right one is the same, but with a straight tube. The tongue is not just due to sloppy die-cutting, but is a deliberate feature (most clearly on the R one). It is interesting to speculate whether the addition of a second carnyx is deliberate, in an attempt to add significance or perhaps power to the image of Gallia.

Date
48 BC (Crawford 1974, 92. 463 f.)

Bibliography
Crawford 1974, 92. 463 f. – de Lagoy 1849, 26 pl. II no. 16.

BM Rome 3962   BM Rome 3963

Fig. 238 A4.17 Denarius of Brutus Albinus (RRC 450/1). – (Photos British Museum). – Scale 3:1.

A4.17 Denarius of Brutus Albinus

Classification: RRC 450/1
The obverse bears a helmeted head of Mars while the reverse shows crossed carnyces, facing inwards, with an oval shield above and a round shield below (**fig. 238**). Crawford linked the issue to Caesar's campaigns in Gaul, in which the moneyer was heavily involved; inter alia, he was naval commander at the siege of Massalia in 49 BC (Albrethsen 1987, 102).

The carnyces
Carnyces are the major feature of the reverse, and the space they are given means the depictions are quite detailed. They have a segmented straight tube of four to six sections, with a cup or knob for the mouthpiece, crest, eye, ear and flaring mouth. The upper tube section is typically shown expanding, as part of the bell. The heads are modelled quite three-dimensionally. Two specimens in the BM were examined first-hand (BMCRR Rome 3962 f.).

Date
48 BC (Crawford 1974, 92. 466)

Bibliography
Crawford 1974, 92. 466. – Homo-Lechner/Vendries 1993, 35. – de Lagoy 1849, 29 pl. II no. 18.

A4.18 Aureus and denarius of Caesar

Classification: RRC 452/1-2, 4-5
Series of coins minted by Caesar in 48-47 BC. In all cases the obverse bears a female head and the reverse a trophy, although details vary. Variant 3, a quinarius, does not feature a carnyx and the trophy differs slightly. In the other variants the trophy comprises a belted tunic and horned helmet, with an oval shield in the L arm and a carnyx in the R. Variants 1 and 2 (aureus and denarius respectively) additionally have an axe set upright to the R with an animal head on top (**fig. 239**). Variants 4 and 5 (both denarii) have a bearded, bound, trousered captive sitting at the base of the trophy (**fig. 240**); on some coins (e.g. BMCRR 3960) he wears a torc. The reverse clearly refers to the Gallic War: the carnyx, horned helmet, oval shield and captive are recurring features of the victory iconography of this period.

The carnyx
Eight examples in the BM (BMCRR Rome 3953-3960), six in Berlin and one in the Cabinet des Médailles, Brussels, were examined first-hand. The general features are: straight, segmented tube (two to four segments, normally three) with basal knob; crest; ears; eye; flaring mouth. Variants 4 and 5 show less detail as the carnyx is smaller, and the crest and eye are omitted on the specimens examined. One significant variant is that one specimen appears to have a fang shown in the upper jaw: the line defining the upturned snout is continued below the jaw line (Berlin Sandes). Another has a fang in the lower jaw (BM 3954). On some, the tube segments are different lengths (BM 3954; Berlin Beger Th.Br.II 558).

variant 1 (AV)

BM 3953

BM 3954

variant 2 (AR)

BM 3955

BM 3956

BM 3957

BM 3958

Berlin
(Sandes)

Berlin
(Beger, Thes.
Br. II 558)

Fig. 239 A4.18 Aureus and denarius of Caesar (RRC 452), variants 1 and 2. – (Photos British Museum; Staatliche Museen zu Berlin – Preußischer Kulturbesitz, Münzkabinett [Reinhard Saczewski]). – Scale 3:1.

Fig. 240 A4.18 Denarius of Caesar (RRC 452), variants 4 and 5. – (Photos British Museum). – Scale 3:1.

variant 4 (BM 3959)   variant 5 (BM 3960)

Date
48-47 BC (Crawford 1974, 92. 467)

Bibliography
Crawford 1974, 92. 467. – de Lagoy 1849, 21-23 pl. II nos 8-9. – Homo-Lechner/Vendries 1993, 35.

A4.19 Denarius of Caesar

Classification: RRC 468
The trophy and captives on the reverse refer to the Gallic War. The trophy comprises a belted tunic and horned helmet, with a shield, spear and carnyx on each arm (**fig. 241**). On variant 1 the shields are both oval; on variant 2, the L one is oval and the R one hexagonal, while the trophy also wears a torc. Beneath the trophy are a male and a female captive. On variant 1 the female is to the L and sits resting her head in her hand; a garment is wrapped round her lower half. The male sits on the R; he is bound, nude and bearded. On variant 2 the positions are reversed and the male kneels.

The carnyces
In the small space available the carnyx is inevitably simplified, but different dies show considerable stylistic vari-

ation. Six examples in the BM, ten in Berlin and two in the Cabinet des Médailles, Brussels, were examined first-hand. Typically the carnyx comprises a straight, plain tube, sometimes with a basal knob, two ears, an eye and a flaring mouth. Crests (in various forms) are found only on variant 2. Some depictions were rather crude, and in a number of cases the tube was omitted below the trophy's arm, or the two halves of the tube were shown at a marked angle.

Date
46-45 BC (Crawford 1974, 93. 479)

Bibliography
Crawford 1974, 93. 479. – de Lagoy 1849, 21-23 pl. II nos 10-11.

A4.20 Denarius for Caesar

Classification: RRC 482
Denarius commemorating Caesar, the obverse with the head of Venus, the reverse with a trophy inscribed to either side CAESAR/IMP. The tree trunk bears a corset-style cuirass and horned helmet, with an oval shield in the R arm, a spear in the L, a sword on the L side and crossed greaves below. Beneath the trophy are captured weapons: to the L, a chariot; to the R, an oval shield with two spears and a carnyx behind it (**fig. 242**). The type is a very rare one (Crawford 1974, 94), and is normally seen as an emis-

sion of Caesar, but there are grounds to argue it was actually struck after his death by Octavian in 43 BC. It should be seen as referring to the Gallic War; the depiction of a chariot connects it to Caesar's British campaigns (de Lagoy 1849, 25; Piggott 1952).

The carnyx
The single stylised specimen in the BM (BMCRR Spain 70) was examined first-hand, two in the BN (2808, Ailly 10901) and one in the Nationalmuseet, Copenhagen;

BM Spain 87

BM Spain 89

BM Spain 90

BM Spain 91

BM Spain 92

BM 1946.10.4.80

Berlin
(unregistered)

Berlin
(1861
B. Friedländer)

Fig. 241   A4.19 Denarius of Caesar (RRC 468). – (Photos British Museum; Staatliche Museen zu Berlin – Preußischer Kulturbesitz, Münz-kabinett [Reinhard Saczewski]). – Scale 3:1.

BM Spain 70

BN Ailly 10901
(detail under)

Picard 1957

Fig. 242   A4.20 Denarius of Caesar (RRC 482). – (Photos British Museum; Bibliothèque nationale de France; Picard 1957, pl. viii). – Scale 3:1.

further examples are illustrated by Gilbert Charles Picard (1957, pl. VIII) and Bernhard Woytek (2010, pl. 9 nos 238-240). The carnyx is rather stylised, with a plain tube (the mouthpiece hidden), ear, indication of a crest and gaping mouth; there is no eye, and on some examples crest and ears are lacking.

Date
44 BC (Crawford 1974, 94. 495) or 43 BC (Woytek 2010, 467-473)

Bibliography
Crawford 1974, 94. 495. 736. – de Lagoy 1849, 22 f. pl. II no. 12. – Woytek 2010, 467-473 pl. 9 nos 238-240.

A5 ROMAN IMPERIAL COINS

As discussed in chapter 8, there are particular difficulties in identifying carnyces on Imperial issues because the images are often less detailed than on Republican coins (**tab. 60**). See **Appendix 4**, entries A5?1-3 for other possible candidates.

code	RIC reference	date
A5.1	Civil War 131 (Galba?)	AD 68
A5.2	Galba 17 variant	AD 68
A5.3	Trajan 766	c. AD 112
A5.4	M. Aurelius and Commodus, various	AD 175-177
A5.5	Postumus 3	AD 263

Tab. 60   Carnyces on Roman Imperial coins.

A5.1 Anonymous denarius of the Civil War

Classification: RIC Civil War 131

In the troubled times of AD 68-69, with an uprising against Nero in the western provinces and then a succession of claimants to the purple in the »Year of the Four Emperors«, a series of denarii and aurei was struck. These lacked the titles of the claimant, and there has been debate over their attribution. One features on the obverse a bust of Gallia (identified by an inscription) wearing a diadem, with a ?carnyx behind (**fig. 243**); the reverse has clasped hands holding a boar standard and two ears of corn, with the legend »FIDES«. This and several others have been interpreted as coins struck in the course of the revolt on the Rhineland by Julius Civilis (Mattingly 1914, 133-135; Mattingly/Sydenham 1923, 180. 191f.). Civilis, a Batavian nobleman, was commander of an auxiliary unit on the lower Rhine. He declared ostensibly for Vespasian, rising against Vitellius' garrisons from the Rhine mouth to Vetera (Xanten) in 69. In truth it seems he wanted independence from Rome as the Batavians felt oppressed, although he portrayed himself as the saviour of an independent Gaul with the aim of creating a Gallic Empire. In 70 two leaders of the Treveri, Julius Classicus and Julius Tutor, agreed to join him; much of the Rhineland was now lost to direct Roman control, with many troops joining the rebels. However, in 70 Vespasian sent troops under Petilius Cerialis to quell the revolt, with the Batavians surrendering on favourable terms (Cary/Wilson 1963, 275-279; Tacitus, *Histories* IV.12-37. 54-80; V.14-26). A number of rare aurei and denarii which evoke Gaul rather than Rome have been linked to this event following the work of Harold Mattingly (1914; Mattingly/Sydenham 1923, 180. 191f.). Legends speak of Liberty regained, loyalty, harmony and deliverance; an issue dedicated to Mars the Deliverer is believed to celebrate the fall of the fortress at Vetera to the rebels, the reverse showing Victory with a trophy and the legend LEGION XV PRIMI[genia], the captured legion in garrison at the time (*ibidem*).

However, this attribution came under assault from Peter-Hugo Martin (1974). In a detailed study of these »anonymous coins« (of which he identifies 101 types and 36 related restorations of Augustan coins) he argued they all relate to the claims of Galba for the purple in AD 68. C. Julius Vindex, the governor of Gallia Lugdunensis rose in revolt against Nero in March, winning support from Galba (the governor of Hispania Tarraconensis) and two other Spanish provinces. Vindex was defeated in battle by the Rhineland armies in May, but on the death of Nero in June Galba was proclaimed emperor. Martin thus related the coins to the short period between March and June 68. His argument is a detailed one, and is based on a number of key points. Crucial is the similarity of many of the types to ones subsequently issued by Galba as emperor.

Fig. 243 A5.1 Anonymous Civil War denarius (RIC Civil War 131). – (Homo-Lechner/Vendries 1993, 78). – Scale 3:1.

The iconography is also significant: many relate to Hispania and Gallia (his power base), emphasise concordance between these provinces, or aim to flatter the army (the power brokers); indeed the army coins may have been intended as bribes for the Rhineland forces. Other legends (such as liberty or deliverance) reflect the desire to be rid of the tyrant Nero (Martin 1974, 64-68). Martin (1974, 87) constructed a network linking the coins by die-links, typological and other similarities. In the specific case of the Gallia coin with the carnyx, its provincial imagery can be connected to provincial personifications of Spain in Galba's series (nos 33. 88), while a coin celebrating the *concordia hispaniarum et galliarum* (no. 98) has the two personified provinces facing one another, each with attributes below; for Gallia this is a hexagonal shield (Martin 1974, 34). There are also typological similarities in hairstyle to other coins (*ibidem* 34 n. 98). The boar standard occurs also on no. 2, in the hands of Concordia. Finally, others of the provincial personifications do have clear reference to Rome, making it less likely to be espousing a separatist cause.

Martin's arguments seem coherent, consistent and well-argued, but are tacitly rejected in the revised RIC volume (Sutherland 1984, 197-215), where his corpus is widely used but his arguments are not discussed. Instead C. H. V. Sutherland continued to split the series into coins minted by Galba in Spain, by Vindex in Gaul, a »military« class perhaps struck for Vitellius in southern Gaul, and types linked to the Gallic/Batavian revolt. This disagreement makes it hard for the non-numismatist to assess, although Sutherland's position has been criticised by other numismatists (Ehrhardt 2000). Yet Martin's arguments seem plausible and well-argued, in contrast to the highly impressionistic basis of the Batavian argument. For Mattingly (1914, 134) the attribution is plausible because »The appeals are all to the love of liberty and to martial spirit, and there is a total absence of reference to the Senate, people or armies of Rome. These coins, then, form a group somewhat apart from any other and probably belong to the Gallic Revolt …«. The first edition RIC (Mattingly/Sydenham 1923, 180) followed the same line, noting »the appeal is made to Gaul, with her trumpet and her wild boar, to Liberty Regained …« and the connection to the siege of Vetera in the LEGIO XV issue. This is toned down a little in the revised RIC, but the argument remains the same.

Most of these points have been addressed by Martin, and summarised above. While the die-links provide clear connections between some of the issues, typological and stylistic similarities are inevitably more subjective. Yet the clear connections between the issues with Gaulish symbolism and those types more securely of Galba which personify Gaul and Spain show that Gaulish symbolism was not alien to Galba's coinage. This is reinforced by the rare named aureus of Galba (A5.2 below) with Gaul and Spain, the former with a carnyx, which reinforces the connections noted by Martin. Thus his arguments seem much more plausible. This leaves only the LEGIO XV issue as a fly in the ointment, but as Martin (1974, 36) noted the connection to the siege of Vetera is hypothetical. His arguments against it are equally hypothetical, but given the need to secure the loyalty of the army at this stage, there is no reason why specific army issues could not be struck. This remains problematic, but on balance the Gallia and carnyx issue fits well into the wider series of Gaulish and Spanish anonymous coins rather than a hypothetical Batavian revolt series, and it is taken here as most plausibly of Galba.

The relevant coin is represented only by a single example in the Ashmolean Museum, Oxford. As mentioned above, the obverse has the bust of Gallia and ?carnyx behind, the reverse with clasped hands holding a boar standard

and two ears of corn, with the legend »FIDES«. It is striking that the boar standard and ?carnyx are still recognised as Gaulish icons, with the ears of corn presumably marking prosperity, the clasped hands representing the alliance of the provinces, the inscription marking trust or faith. As Christophe Vendries noted (Homo-Lechner/Vendries 1993, 78), Gallia here is a very civilised lady, far from the personification of »hairy Gaul« seen in previous Roman renditions. Vendries suggested the overall theme of the obverse is taken from the denarii of L. Hostilius Saserna, with Gallia and a carnyx (A4.16.2), but here made civilised. This »civilising influence« has led to a great stylisation of the carnyx.

The carnyx

The carnyx, if such it is, is behind the bust, facing R. It comprises a long tube curving through 90° at the end, where it thickens somewhat, before flaring into an expanded (and apparently circular) mouth. There are no technical details and no strong zoomorphism; the mouth is more like a standard expanded horn mouth than an animal-like carnyx. However, the vertical position is unusual for a horn, and the design does seem to reflect that of the Saserna denarius (A4.16), suggesting a carnyx was intended. The mouthpiece end appears to be straight and undifferentiated.

Date

Martin (1974, 44-46) dated all these coins to the time of Galba's challenge to Nero in April-June 68.

Bibliography

Homo-Lechner/Vendries 1993, 78. – Martin 1974 (specifically 69 pl. 1, 5). – Mattingly 1914, 133-135. – Mattingly/Sydenham 1923, 180. 192. – Nicolas 1979, 1331 pl. XIX. – Sutherland 1984, 201-214.

A5.2 Aureus of Galba

Classification: RIC Galba 17 var.

A number of aurei and denarii of Galba feature on the reverse personifications of Gaul and Spain shaking hands (RIC Galba 15-18). They are identified by the inscription GALLIA HISPANIA. Hispania's attributes are the typical ones of a round shield, spear and short sword. Gallia normally carries a staff but on a single aureus (RIC 17 var.) from the Ponton D'Amécourt collection she carries a carnyx in her left hand, leaning on her left shoulder (**fig. 244**).

Only this single example appears to be known, and it merits detailed description. The aureus (mass 7.72 g) is now in the Berlin Münzkabinett (1909.191), acquired from the Amécourt sale via the Weber collection (no. 1089). The obverse has a laureate bust of Galba (L) on a globe, and

Fig. 244 A5.2 Aureus of Galba (RIC Galba 17 var). – (Photo Staatliche Museen zu Berlin – Preußischer Kulturbesitz, Münzkabinett). – Scale 2:1.

is inscribed GALBA IMP. It has a pellet border. The reverse bears the legend GALLIA HISPANIA round the circumference, within a pellet border. Hispania wears a knee-length tunic, the hem slightly thickened, with laddered decoration or the hanging end of a belt shown on the lap. She has a low-domed, wide-brimmed helmet and carries a round shield with round boss, a spear and a short curved sword by her left side. Gallia wears a tight-fitting thigh-length tunic with a vandyked hem, a cloak over her shoulders, and a helmet with visor, short neck-guard and cheek pieces. She wears calf-length boots and carries a carnyx at an angle in her left hand, leaning on her left shoulder. The two figures stand on a ground line.

There may have been a denarius version of this image as well, although no certain example is known to me. However, in the Bibliothèque nationale is a denarius where Gallia (with long unkempt hair) holds a straight staff (thick and square at the lower end) which has a hint of a curve at the top; this could be leading into a carnyx head, but the image is lost off the flan and I know of no other examples. The type emphasises the power base of Galba in the western provinces, and links closely to related anonymous coins of the Civil War discussed under A5.1 (Martin 1974, esp. no. 98).

The carnyx
The full length of the carnyx is shown although most of the tube is hidden behind Gallia's torso. The tube is straight and cylindrical; no junctions are shown, but the end is slightly constricted before expanding into a cupped mouthpiece. The head bends through some 140°, with the jaw open to 180°. The lower jaw is longer than the upper and is recurved to touch the tube. The head has an ear, but no eye is visible, and there is no crest.

Date
The type is dated in RIC to AD 68 and attributed to a Spanish mint.

Bibliography
Rollin/Feuardent 1887, no. 114 pl. V. – Sutherland 1984, 233 (RIC Galba 17 var.).

A5.3 Restored denarius of Trajan

Classification: RIC 766

Trajan, like several other emperors, issued a series of coins whose designs were closely based on earlier issues. Unlike his predecessors, his issues were exclusively in gold or silver and, in the case of the latter, drew solely on Republican or early Augustan prototypes, dating back as far as denarii of the later 3rd century BC; the aurei, which were less rigid copies of earlier types, mixing obverse and reverse, additionally restored those of »good« emperors. The key studies are by Harold Mattingly (1926), Holger Komnick (2001) and Bernhard Woytek (2010). A wide range of types was struck (51 denarii and 23 aurei), but only in small quantities, suggesting they were presentation pieces; Komnick (2001,

Fig. 245 A5.3 Restored denarius of Trajan (RIC 766). – (Photo Nationalmuseet Copenhagen). – Scale 3:1.

177) suggested the assumed knowledge of Roman history implies an elite, perhaps senatorial audience, to whom they may have been given as gifts. The choice of issues was of course political, notably in choosing types which recalled the past glories of the Republic and thus linked past and present glories, although the precise intended meaning of the series has been debated. Komnick (2001, 175-178) noted that positive virtues are the uniting theme, while the reverse iconography is dominated by two broad concepts: a group focussed on war, subjugation, victory and triumph; and another on the security and power of the Roman state. The overarching theme of *virtus* is seen clearly in the three earliest restored coins, all denarii of the late 3rd century BC, and all restored with inscriptions naming great heroes of the Republic: Horatius Cocles, who defended the Tiber bridge against the Etruscans under Lars Porsena in 506 BC, saving Rome; M. Furius Camillus, who won four triumphs in the early 4th century, two against other Italian peoples and two against Gauls; and Decius Mus, discussed below.

The coin under study here is represented by only three examples, one in the National Museum in Copenhagen and two recorded in sales catalogues (Woytek 2010, 510; Komnick [2001, 113] noted a further example is a post-medieval forgery). It is a restoration of RRC 128 / A4.1 (206-200 BC). The obverse has a helmeted head of Roma R with the additional legend DECIVS MVS X (the X, representing a denarius, is on the original). The reverse shows the Dioscuri mounted, charging R, trampling a crossed carnyx and oval shield; in exergue is the inscription ROMA, with Trajan's titles around the rim (IMP CAES TRAIAN AVG GER DAC P P REST). Detail is a little worn, and traces of dark corrosion survived in areas (**fig. 245**). The original issue, discussed above (A4.1), probably refers to Roman campaigns in Cisalpine Gaul. The inscription on the restored coin links it to Decius Mus, who won a posthumous victory against the Gauls at Sentinum in 295 BC in the course of the Third Samnite War (Cary/Wilson 1963, 39 f.).

The carnyx

The carnyx depiction is not particularly detailed. (The Copenhagen example was seen first-hand; its details are consistent with a second example illustrated by Woytek 2010, pl. 128 no. 803.) The straight tube has a rounded terminal and expands slightly along its length. It is split into two equal sections with a very clear narrow band between them; there are no bands to define other junctions. The head is rather worn, and the slightly uneven rear edge might hint at lost features, but there is no clear crest, ears or eye (although there is a clear brow before the snout). The jaws are open to about 30°, the upper longer than the lower. It is likely that the type had additional resonance from Trajan's campaigns against carnyx-wielding barbarians in Dacia.

Date

Varied opinions on the precise date have been expressed. Komnick (2001, 137 f.) reviewed the evidence. The titles imply a date after AD 102 (when Trajan adopted the DAC-ICVS title) and before late August 114 (when he took the title OPTIMVS), while details of the style imply it should fit later in this time span. The use of the nominative is unusual, and the only Trajanic parallels are late in this period (AD 112-114). The most plausible event for such a series is the opening of the Forum Traianum in AD 112, which was also the tenth anniversary of the first Dacian triumph (Strack 1931, 41; Komnick 2001, 138. 178). This is consistent with the more precise dating of AD 112/113 argued by Woytek (2010, 168 f.). Some of the concepts behind the Forum, such as the use of statues of earlier emperors and »great men« in a sculpture hall focussed on a statue of Trajan, echo the concepts behind the restored coinage.

Bibliography

Mattingly 1926. – Komnick 2001, 110-113. 137 f. 175-178 pl. 23, Typ 3.0. – Woytek 2010, 509 f. pl. 128 no. 803.

A5.4 Aurei, denarii and AE of Marcus Aurelius and Commodus

A series of coins minted in AD 175-177 to mark the end of the Marcomannic War bear piles of arms including a carnyx (**figs 246-247**). The series was minted jointly by Marcus Aurelius and Commodus, with the same basic reverse type used over a number of years on aurei, denarii, sestertii and apparently a semis or quadrans. The type ceased when war broke out again on the Danube in AD 178. The legends associate the coins with victories over either Germans or Sarmatians, but there are no significant differences in the equipment represented. A mixture of Roman and barbarian weapons is shown, the likely barbarian items being the carnyx, oval and hexagonal shields, scale armour, bow and axe; there are also spears, while items probably of Roman origin are the vexillum standard, tuba and ?cornu. The range of different issues can be found in **table 61**. Examples in the BM were studied first-hand.

The carnyx

Only the upper part of the instrument is shown, and the coins show a wide range of artistic qualities. Some are highly detailed, while others are so stylised that the weapons are hardly recognisable (e.g. 1603, 1636, 1657, 1664 f.), emphasising the need to study a number of examples of a type to define it. This leads to considerable variation in the depictions of the carnyx: mouths open and closed, eye or no eye, none, one or two ears and so on. On the poorer representations it would be impossible to recognise the carnyx without knowledge of the other examples, and it could equally be interpreted as a draco standard or a bow.

Further discussion is best restricted to the less stylised examples: the best depictions, 682 and 1548; and the reasonably detailed depictions 736, 740 and 1600. However, these still show considerable variation, and clearly the die-cutters had a variety of mental pictures of what a carnyx looked like. There are examples of eyes, ears, open mouths, crests and technical details such as the bell, but little consistency in their depiction. In 682 and 736 the tubes are slightly curved, the others straight; 1548 shows a differentiation between a plain bell and a pelleted tube which is otherwise lacking, and has a plain crest to about half-length. Full (visible) length crests are also present on 682 and 1600. Mouths, if depicted, are typically only slightly open.

Dating evidence

Inscriptions date the coins to AD 175-177.

Bibliography

Albrethsen 1987, 116 f. – Mattingly 1940, cxxviii, 484. 493 f. 497 f. 648. 657 f. 665. 670 f. – Mattingly/Sydenham 1930, 208 f. 239. 241. 264 f. 305-307. 309. 339.

BM 682   BM 736   BM 737   BM 738

BM 739   BM 751   BM 752   BM 740

aurei   denarii

sestertii

BM 1548   BM 1598

BM 1599   BM 1600

Fig. 246   A5.4 Aurei, denarii and sestertii of Marcus Aurelius and Commodus. – (Photos British Museum). – Scale 2:1.

BM 1601 BM 1602

BM 1603

BM 1636

BM 1657

BM 1656

BM 1658

BM 1664

BM 1665

Fig. 247 A5.4 Sestertii of Marcus Aurelius and Commodus. – (Photos British Museum). – Scale 2:1.

RIC	denomination	BMCRE	emperor	enemy	date AD
337	aureus	682	M Aurelius	Germans	175-176
338	denarius	–	M Aurelius	Germans	175-176
362	aureus	736-737	M Aurelius	Germans	176-177
363	denarius	738	M Aurelius	Germans	176-177
366	aureus	739	M Aurelius	Sarmatians	176-177
367	denarius	740	M Aurelius	Sarmatians	176-177
629	aureus	751	Commodus	Germans	177
630	aureus	752	Commodus	Sarmatians	177
633	aureus	–	Commodus	Germans	177
635	aureus	–	Commodus	Sarmatians	177
1162	sestertius	1548	M Aurelius	Germans	175-176
1184	sestertius	1596-1600	M Aurelius	Germans	176-177
1190	sestertius	1601-1605	M Aurelius	Sarmatians	176-177
1191	sestertius	–	M Aurelius	Sarmatians	176-177
1213	semis/quadrans	–	M Aurelius	Germans	177
1221	sestertius	1636	M Aurelius	Sarmatians	176-177
1569	sestertius	1655 (not seen), 1656	Commodus	Germans	177
1570	sestertius	1657-1658	Commodus	Germans	177
1576	sestertius	1664	Commodus	Sarmatians	177
1577	sestertius	1665-1666	Commodus	Sarmatians	177
Cohen 90	denarius	(queried, p. 498)	Commodus	Germans	177

Tab. 61   Range of issues of M. Aurelius and Commodus with carnyx. Cohen = H. Cohen 1880.

A5.5 Aureus of Postumus

Classification: RIC 3

An aureus of Postumus has a reverse with a trophy and two captives at its base (**fig. 248**). The trophy is a conventional type, comprising a muscle cuirass and tunic with a cloak, topped by a helmet with cheek guards and a decorative finial; below are crossed greaves, while each arm has two crossed oval shields (with round umbos), behind which are one or two spears and a carnyx. Two hairy, bearded bound captives sit at the base; on an example in the BM, they wear belted trousers and appear to have naked torsos; they may wear Phrygian caps, but this is unclear, and other examples seem to show them both with and without such caps. P. H. Webb (1933, 336) attributed this issue to the Lyon mint but this is now considered unlikely, and it was probably struck at Trier or less plausibly Cologne (Besly 1984, 230; Bourne 2001, 25 f.).

Postumus was the first emperor of the separatist Gallic Empire, seizing the western provinces (the Gauls and Germanies, Britain, Spain and for a time Raetia and northernmost Italy) from the central empire under Gallienus. He ruled from 260-269, with the separatist movement surviving his death until it was brought back into the fold by Aurelian in 274 (Salway 1981, 273-276; Bourne 2001, 10-18). The 3rd century was a general time of internal turmoil and pretenders to the purple, but it is believed this movement was stimulated by serious security concerns (Salway 1981, 271. 274; Carroll 2001, 132 f.; Bourne 2001, 11). The Germanic coalition of the Alamanni overran the frontier repeatedly in the mid 250s, even reaching northern Italy, and apparently causing the loss of the *Agri Decumantes* to the empire with the frontier in south-west Germany being withdrawn to the Rhine-Danube line (although see Wells 1999, 259 f. for cautionary remarks). Whatever the details, it is clear the German and Gaulish provinces were coming under sustained threat, and Postumus (Gallienus' lieutenant on the Rhine) rose against the central empire. His further aims are disputed, whether motivated by a separatist Gallic desire or an ambition to take the whole empire (summarised in Bourne 2001, 11. 16) but continuing problems from across the frontier focussed his attentions. His coinage has two separate issues proclaiming victory over the Germans, and he is recorded as having »driven off a horde of Germans« (Bourne 2001, 16 f.). Dating of Postumus' coinage is not easy as only a minority bear tribunal or consular titles, but one of these victory issues is probably of 260-261, the other of 262-263 (Bourne 2001, 16 f.).

The aureus issue of relevance here has no datable titles, but a detailed study of the gold of the Gallic Empire has suggested a date of AD 263 (Schulte 1983, 33 [group 6a]. 85), connecting it by die-links and typology to the other victory

Fig. 248 A5.5 Aureus of Postumus (RIC 3). – (Photos Staatliche Museen zu Berlin – Preußischer Kulturbesitz, Münzkabinett; British Museum; Schulte 1983, pl. 4). – Scale 2:1.

Berlin   BM (R10307)

Schulte 44   Schulte 46

issues. The coinage of Postumus shows a variety of triumphal issues: in many cases the mere occurrence of a Victory is likely to be conventional, but others bear titles (e. g. VICT GERM) or trophies and captives which point to a connection with actual campaigns (the full range of reverses is conveniently listed in Robertson 1978b, lxxxvii-xcv). For those aurei with specific victory iconography, Schulte's dating would connect these also to the campaigns early in Postumus' reign (RIC 39-40 of his group 3 [AD 261]; RIC 44, probably group 5 [AD 262] although it could be group 8 [AD 265]; RIC 3, 14-15, group 6a [AD 263]).

The aurei of Postumus are well-cut and well-struck, allowing iconographic study. The lower denominations are rather sloppier (Bourne 2001, 97), and the trophies correspondingly less informative (see illustrations in Bastien 1967). None of these show clear signs of carnyces, although some do have curved objects alongside the spears. These could be misunderstood carnyces, but they lack any zoomorphic characteristics to confirm this, or even any thickening at the head. The variety (from simple curves to pelleted curves and semicircles which attach the shield to the body) indicates that any original significance of the device was lost to the die-cutters, who were treating it decoratively (compare Bastien 1967, pls I, 12-14; XXXI, 150; XXXII, 156; XXXIX, 211; XLVIII-IL, 301-302).

Four relevant aurei are illustrated by Bernhard Schulte (1983, pl. 4 nos 43-46), one of which is the RIC type specimen (Webb 1933, pl. XIII, 3); another, from the Berlin collection, is illustrated by Schultz (1997, 90 no. 543). Of these, only one (Schulte 1983, no. 45) does not feature a carnyx.

This issue is of particular significance in suggesting the continuing use of the carnyx among Germanic tribes into the late 3rd century. There is nothing inherently unlikely about this, as the Marcomanni and Quadi were using it at the end of the 2nd century, but the general decline in detailed iconography in the later empire makes its continuing use hard to assess. It seems unlikely that this issue was consciously reusing earlier types, as it had been a long time since carnyces featured in trophies in this way, and it is best seen as a reflection of the use of the carnyx in the area at the time.

The carnyces

Examples in the BM and Berlin have been examined firsthand. Each arm of the trophy has a carnyx facing outwards. They are quite stylised and linear, incised as single straight strokes.

On the Berlin coin, the left carnyx is the clearest, with a snout angled slightly upwards and two ears; there is no evidence of a lower jaw, though this could have been lost, as the coin is perforated here. The right carnyx has no ear and two jaws, lightly-incised and slightly open. The »spears« are rather strangely depicted on this die; rather than the clear spearheads shown on others, we see shafts with what looks more like a baluster moulding at the top. On the BM coin (Schulte 43 = RIC pl. XIII, 3) both carnyces have heads perpendicular to the straight tube; they have two ears and very slightly open mouths, the lower jaw being quite short. A slight peck defines an eye on the right one, and less certainly on the left. The right head is triangular in overall form. The spearheads are barbed.

The other coins do not have open-mouthed carnyces, but are otherwise similar. On Schulte 44 only one carnyx is present, on the left arm, lacking an obvious ear, while Schulte 46 has two carnyces with single ears. On the BM coin the carnyces do not reappear below the shield, but they do on the Berlin coin, Schulte 44 and 46, showing a straight tube with a terminal pellet.

Date
Schulte's detailed appraisal (1983, 33-36) puts this issue into his group 6a, which he dated to AD 263.

Bibliography
Schulte 1983, 33-36. 85 pl. 4 nos 43-46. – Schultz 1997, 90 no. 543. – Webb 1933, 336 no. 3 pl. XIII no. 3.

COLONIAL AND PROVINCIAL COINS (tab. 62)

A6.1 As of the colony of Vibo Valentia, Italy

Classification: Historia Numorum (Italy) 2262
The Latin colony of Vibo Valentia was founded on the site of the earlier Greek colony of Hipponium, in Bruttium on the north coast of the »toe« of Italy, in 192 BC. It struck a limited range of asses and as fractions, each represented only by a single type, although with a variety of control marks. Among these, the asses and semis include carnyx control marks; there is no obvious theme to the marks (listed in Rutter 2001, 176). The as has a head of Jupiter on the obverse and a winged thunderbolt on the reverse, with the legend VALENTIA, a mark of value (I) to indicate it is an as, and a control mark (**fig. 249**).

The dating, in the early 2nd century BC is unexpected (recent work has argued for this early date; older scholarship suggested a longer date-bracket, into the early 1st century BC). All other uses of a carnyx as a control mark are in the period c. 90-60 BC, when the carnyx was in the popular imagination after Marius's campaigns against the Cimbri and Teutones. If these coins are correctly dated, the only plausible context at this period would be campaigns against the Cisalpine Gauls in northern Italy in 225-218 BC, an event which is perhaps marked (rather after the event) on the denarius issue A4.1 of 206-200 BC. The other option is that the dating is wrong, and they fall instead at the end of the suggested date bracket, in the early 1st century BC like the other control marks, but this seems unlikely: Prof. Suzanne Frey-Kupper, an authority on the type, kindly confirmed that the early dating is most plausible.

The carnyx
The carnyx was first recognised by de Lagoy (1849, 31). Examples in the British Museum (Poole 1873, 359f. nos 3-4) and Copenhagen (Breitenstein/Schwabacher 1981, no. 1836) were examined first-hand, others from photos (Vismari 1998, 54 nos 255-256 [Milan]; Moro 1967, no. 358 [Klagenfurt]; Troxell 1975, 474 [New York]; Sheedy 2008, no. 1125 [Australia]; SNG Germany, München 4, 1974, no. 1368). The drawbacks of the latter were obvious in comparing the descriptions of the Copenhagen example from the photo and from the specimen, the latter providing a lot of fresh detail; for instance, neither crest nor teeth were visible on the photo.

The carnyx is depicted quite naturalistically, with two ears, normally an eye, skin folds in the upper jaw, and sometimes with teeth in the lower jaw. The mouth is generally only slightly open. A series of spikes evoke the bristles of a crest on many examples. The tube has between one and three segments, with a straight base, sometimes slightly expanded as if to show a cupped mouthpiece. Examples range from highly detailed to highly stylised.

Date
A date range of 192 BC (the founding of the colony) to 89 BC (the Social War, when Rome's Italian allies rebelled) is typically quoted, but Michael Crawford (1985, 71f.) and Keith Rutter (2001, 156) argued that very few of these south Italian mints were still striking after the early 2nd century. Certainly, the limited range of coinage would support a shorter chronology. Both linked these issues to economic developments connected with the Roman need for fleets in wars against the Seleucid king Antiochus III and Philip V

code	coin	date
A6.1	As of the colony of Vibo Valentia	192-c. 150 BC
A6.2	Semis of the colony of Vibo Valentia	192-c. 150 BC
A6.3	Provincial issue of Tavium (Galatia)	late 1st-2nd century AD

Tab. 62 Colonial and provincial issues.

BM 3   BM 4   Copenhagen 1836

Munich 1368   Klagenfurt 358   ANS 474

Fig. 249 A6.1 As of Vibo Valentia (HN Italy 2262). – (Photos British Museum; Rasmus H. Nielsen, National Museum of Denmark; SNG Germany, München 4, 1974, pl. 45; Moro 1967, pl. 9; Troxell 1975, pl. 14). – Scale 2:1.

and Perseus of Macedonia in the early 2nd century, with these south Italian harbour towns providing ships.

Bibliography
Rutter 2001, 176.

A6.2 Semis of the colony of Vibo Valentia, Italy

Classification: Historia Numorum (Italy) 2263
The limited series of coins from Vibo Valentia also includes a semis with a head of Juno on the obverse and a double cornucopiae on the reverse, along with the legend VALENTIA. A carnyx is among the control marks on the reverse (**fig. 250**).

The carnyx
The depiction of the carnyx is very similar to that on A6.1. There is a range from detailed to stylised, but the best examples are depicted quite naturalistically, with skin folds in the upper jaw, two ears and some detail to the eye morphology. The mouth is generally only slightly open. Crests are rare, but on some examples are evoked by a series of spikes. The tube has two or three segments, with a straight base either rounded or ending in a knob. Examples in the British Museum (Poole 1873, 360 f. no. 16) and Copenhagen (Breitenstein/Schwabacher 1981, no. 1849) were seen first-hand, others from photos (Grose 1923, 211 no. 1777 [Cambridge/McClean]; Morcom 1995, nos 415-416; Babelon 1924, 145 no. 755 [Paris/Luynes]; Bar 2007, 30 no. 121 [Brussels]; Schultz 1993, no. 350 [Leipzig]; Vismari 1998, 56 nos 268. 270. 273 [Milan]; Troxell 1975, no. 483 [New York]; SNG Germany, München 4, nos 1378-1380).

Dating evidence
See above, A6.1

Bibliography
Rutter 2001, 176.

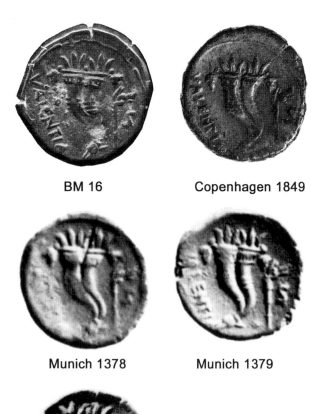

BM 16   Copenhagen 1849

Munich 1378   Munich 1379

ANS 483

Fig. 250 A6.2 Semis of Vibo Valentia (HN Italy 2263). – (Photos British Museum; Rasmus H. Nielsen, National Museum of Denmark; SNG Germany, München 4, 1974, pl. 45; Troxell 1975, pl. 14). – Scale 2:1.

Fig. 251 A6.3 Provincial issue of Tavium, Galatia. – (Photo Staatliche Museen zu Berlin – Preußischer Kulturbesitz, Münzkabinett). – Scale 3:1.

A6.3 Provincial issue of Tavium, Galatia

Roman provincial coin issued by the city of Tavium in Galatia, Asia Minor (**fig. 251**). Only a single specimen, now in the coin cabinet of the Staatliche Museen zu Berlin, has been located. It is copper alloy, weights 3.64 g, and has a slightly oval module, diameter 16-18 mm. The obverse bears the head of Zeus. On the reverse (which is struck off-centre) a pelleted border surrounds a carnyx flanked by an inscription in Greek:

ΣΕΒ ΑΣΤ
HN ΩN
TPO ΚMΩN

This transliterates as »Sebastinon Trokmon«, the civitas of the Trocmi. It was first published by Théodore-Edme Mionnet (1809, 402 no. 171), though only recognised as a carnyx by de Lagoy (1855, 334 n. 1); Friedrich Imhoof-Blumer (1908, 118) published it without illustration, and it has not yet featured in the volumes of Roman Provincial Coinage (Burnett/Amandry/Ripollès 1992; Burnett/Amandry/Carradice 1999; Amandry/Burnett 2015). Tavium was the capital of the Trocmi, the main tribe of eastern Galatia (Burnett/Amandry/Carradice 1999, 235). The importance of this coin is in suggesting the use of the carnyx in Galatia, which was named after the Galatian Celts who settled it in the 3rd and 2nd centuries BC; the Trocmi were one of the original tribes, their name surviving as a *civitas* into the Roman period and retaining a strong Celtic identity (Cunliffe 1997, 83-85; Strobel 2007). With the dismissal of the supposed carnyx carving from Pergamon (**Appendix 4**), this is the only evidence to prove that the Galatians were using carnyces.

The carnyx

The top of the head is lost and the surface is slightly uneven from corrosion and wear. Straight cylindrical tube with collar at bell-tube junction; no other clear tube divisions; conical mouthpiece. Head details mainly lost apart from a short bell and mouth open to c. 90°; both jaws are slightly sinuous, with a small rounded fang in the lower; no crest.

Dating evidence

The inscription provides no statement of date, and unfortunately the type has not yet been considered in the Roman Provincial Coinage series, but their discussion of the lettering styles of Tavium indicates a Flavian or later date for the use of Ω rather than W in the inscription. Nick Holmes, formerly the numismatic curator at NMS, kindly checked other issues of the area and said the bust of Zeus was common in the 1st and 2nd centuries AD.

Bibliography
Imhoof-Blumer 1908, 118. – de Lagoy 1855, 334 n. 1. – Mionnet 1809, 402 no. 171.

B SCULPTURE (tab. 63)

B1 ROME AND ENVIRONS

(This includes material from the cemeteries and villas adjacent to Rome.)

code	site	object	date		n
B1.1	Rome, tomb of Caecilia Metella	trophy relief on tomb	30-20 BC	×	4
B1.2	Rome, Prima Porta	cuirass statue of Augustus	20-10 BC	×	2
B1.3	Rome, Bovillae	eagle on pile of arms	AD 15-20	×	12
B1.4.1	Rome, Palace of Flavians	trophy relief	AD 90-92		3
B1.4.2	Rome, Palace of Flavians	weapons frieze	AD 90-92		1
B1.5	Castelgandolfo, Domitian's villa, reg. Lazio/I	weapons frieze	AD 83-96		1
B1.6	Rome, San Lorenzo fuori le mura	trophy capitals	AD 89-96	×	8
B1.7	Rome, Aventine	weapons frieze pillars	AD 83-105	×	23
B1.8	Rome	weapons frieze	AD 83-105		4
B1.9	Rome, Maddalena	pilaster base with trophy	AD 83-105	×	2
B1.10	Rome, Via dei Leutari	trophy capital	AD 70-96		10
B1.11.1	Rome, Trajan's Forum	relief of conquered province	AD 106-112	×	1
B1.11.2	Rome, Trajan's Forum	weapons frieze	AD 106-112		2
B1.11.3	Rome, Trajan's Forum	Great Trajanic Frieze	AD 106-112	×	3
B1.12	Rome, Trajan's Column	column	AD 108-113	×	14
B1.13.1	Tivoli, Hadrian's Villa, reg. Lazio/I	statue or column base	AD 117-125		1
B1.13.2	Tivoli, Hadrian's Villa, reg. Lazio/I	stucco trophy	AD 135-140	×	1
B1.14	Rome, Column of Marcus Aurelius	column	AD 180-192	×	4
B1.15	Rome, Portonaccio	sarcophagus	AD 175-190	×	7
B1.16	Rome, Tetrarchic arch	Victory and trophy	AD 293-304	×	4
B2.1	Isernia, reg. Molise/I	statue base	27-20 BC		4
B2.2	Isernia, reg. Molise/I	statue base	25-15 BC		2
B2.3	San Vittorino, reg. Abruzzo/I	gable	27-1 BC		1
B2.4	Alba Fucens, reg. Abruzzo/I	weapons frieze	30 BC - AD 20		1
B2.5	Scafa, reg. Abruzzo/I	weapons frieze	30 BC - AD 20		1
B2.6	Turin, reg. Piemonte/I	weapons frieze	15 BC - AD 60	×	5
B2.7	Novalesa, reg. Piemonte/I	weapons frieze	15 BC - AD 50		1
B2.8	Padova, reg. Veneto/I	weapons frieze	AD 1-30	×	1
B2.9	Como, reg. Lombardia/I	weapons frieze	AD 1-50		1
B2.10	Verona, reg. Veneto/I	pilaster base with weapons frieze	25 BC - AD 100	×	1
B2.11	Pompeii, reg. Campania/I	stucco from tomb	AD 70-79		1
B2.12	Gabii, reg. Lazio/I	cuirass statue of Domitian	AD 83-89		1
B2.13	Parma, reg. Emilia-Romagna/I	weapons frieze	AD 80-100	×	1
B2.14	Pozzuoli, reg. Campania/I	weapons frieze	AD 85-105		1

Tab. 63 Roman sculptures with carnyces. An »×« in the second-last column indicates that the monument has been seen first-hand. »n« is the number of carnyces.

code	site	object	date		n
B2.15	Benevento, reg. Campania/I	commemorative arch	AD 114-118		3
B2.16	Cumae (?), reg. Campania/I	weapons frieze	AD 119-161	×	1
B2.17	unprovenanced/I	funerary urn	AD 120-192		2
B2.18	Frascati, reg. Lazio/I	plinth with weapons frieze	AD 175-190		1
B2.19	Palermo, reg. Sicilia/I	sarcophagus	AD 175-190		4
B3.1	Narbonne, dép. Aude/F	4 weapons friezes	40 BC - AD 20	×	5
B3.2	Avignon, dép. Vaucluse/F	weapons frieze	30-20 BC	×	2
B3.3	Glanum, dép. Bouches-du-Rhône/F	commemorative arch	20 BC - AD 20	×	1
B3.4	Arc d'Orange, dép. Vaucluse/F	triumphal arch	15 BC - AD 27	×	38
B3.5	La Brague, Biot, dép. Alpes-Maritimes/F	arch/trophy	30-1 BC	×	1
B3.6	Arles, dép. Bouches-du-Rhône/F	weapons frieze	30 BC - AD 30	×	1
B3.7	Nîmes, dép. Gard/F	altar	AD 150-200	×	1
B3.8	Collias, dép. Gard/F	tombstone	AD 150-200	×	1
B4.1	Vindonissa, Kanton Aargau/CH	frieze with trophy	AD 1-100	×	1
B5.1	Mérida (theatre), com. Extremadura/E	weapons frieze	c. AD 105	×	1
B5.2	Mérida (temple), com. Extremadura /E	weapons frieze	AD 100-150	×	27
B6.1	Zian, Médenine/TN	cuirass statue	AD 40-60	×	2
B6.2	Volubilis, reg. Fès-Meknès/MA	arch	AD 216-217	×	2
B7.1	Gardun, Split-Dalmatia/HR	trophy and weapons frieze	AD 10-20		1

Tab. 63   (continued)

B1.1 Tomb of Caecilia Metella. – Via Appia, Rome

The tomb of Caecilia Metella lies just east of the Via Appia at the third milestone from Rome, situated on the edge of a lava ridge which gives it a very prominent position (**fig. 149**). The monument has been the source of extensive discussion and disagreement over its date, form, commissioner and significance: fortunately the authoritative monograph by Henrik Gerding (2002) summarised this debate and plausibly resolved many of the questions. It is the key source for this summary.

In form the tomb comprises a square podium capped by a cylindrical drum. It is made of concrete with a travertine revetment and decorative detailing in marble. There may originally have been a tumulus on top, but this cannot be demonstrated. The interior arrangements are quite complex, and it may have functioned as a shrine as well as a tomb (Gerding 2002, 92-115). Unlike most tombs on the Via Appia the monument survives in surprisingly good condition because it became church property early in its post-Roman life (certainly by the ninth century) and was subsequently converted for use as a castle in the early fourteenth century (Gerding 2002, 11-13).

The podium has now largely been stripped of its facing, but appears to have been plain. The drum has a moulding at the base (which was apparently never completed; Ger-

ding 2002, 36 f.) and an entablature at the top comprising a marble frieze of bucrania and garlands, with alternating paterae and rosettes above (*ibidem* 39). On the west side, facing the Via Appia is the dedicatory inscription carved on a substantial block of marble. It reads:

CAECILIAE / Q.CRETICI.F / METELLAE.CRASSI
(Tomb of) Caecilia Metella, daughter of Quintus Caecilius Metellus Creticus, (wife of) Crassus

Above it the frieze was interrupted by an even larger block of marble which carried a decorative scene of which only the left-hand fragment survives. This comprises a trophy and part of draped figure. The trophy presumably had a partner on the other side of the panel. The remainder has long been missing as the walls of the medieval castle are founded directly onto the broken edges (**fig. 252a**).

The trophy consists of a fringed cloak with a helmet (with cheek-pieces); on the left arm as viewed is a hexagonal shield, on the right a trilobate shield. At the base sits a bound bare-chested male barbarian, hair tousled, wearing trousers. Of the main scene all that survives is part of a draped figure, most plausibly a togate male (Gerding 2002, 59 f.). The lobed shield bears floral decoration while the hexagonal one is decorated with barbarian spolia which are best connected to Gaul (for a summary of previous views

CAECILIAE
Q·CRETICI·F
METELLAE·CRASSI

a

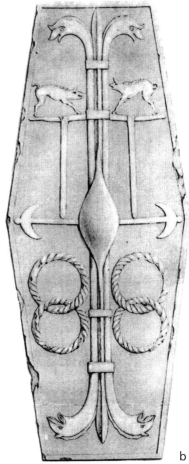

b

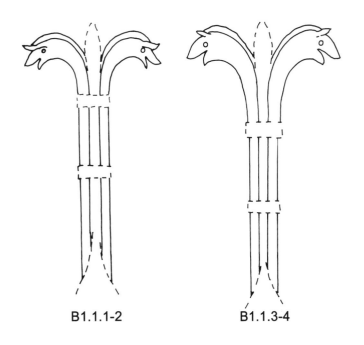

B1.1.1-2   B1.1.3-4   c

Fig. 252 B1.1 Tomb of Caecilia Metella: **a** the inscription and trophy. – **b** detail of shield in trophy. – **c** carnyces 1-4. – (a-b Azzurri 1895, pl. 1 A. C; c drawing Tanja Romankiewicz).

see Gerding 2002, 58f.). This shield has an elongated umbo with the spina comprising a bundle of weapons, a central spear with a carnyx bound on either side (**fig. 252b**). Across the middle of the shield a horizontal rib terminates in a crescent (these cannot be identified as anchors, as the device is common and purely decorative). In the upper half of the shield, each quarter has an animal standard, facing inwards: the right one is a boar, the left perhaps a wolf. Each lower quarter has two interlocked twisted penannular torcs. The shield form, carnyces, boar standards and torcs are all consistent with allusions to Gaulish victories. The lobate shield is more difficult to identify, as Gerding (2002, 59) discussed, and may have Thracian connections (Hollstein 2016, 157) or represent a sacred Roman shield type.

There are a number of points of interest about the tomb. Although it was the tomb of Caecilia Metella, it is clear that the trophy does not refer to her victories; there is more to this tomb than the commemoration of a powerful woman. She came from an important Republican family, with her father winning a triumph for pacifying Crete (hence Creticus; Gerding 2002, 68-70). She was born in the early 1st century BC, and married into the Licinii Crassi, another powerful and wealthy family which included M. Licinius Crassus who was triumvir along with Caesar and Pompey, and led the Romans to their disastrous defeat against the Parthians at Carrhae when the Roman standards were captured. His sons fought with Caesar in Gaul, and one of them (Marcus) is the most likely candidate for Caecilia's husband. Their son, also Marcus, fought initially for Antony in the civil war before turning to Octavian's side. He was governor of Macedonia and Achaea, fighting two campaigns in Moesia and Thrace against the Bastarnae and Getae and winning major victories there in 29-28 BC. He defeated the king of the Bastarnae in single combat, an exceedingly rare and prestigious feat, and was awarded a triumph in 27 BC.

If Gerding's reconstruction of the genealogy is correct, Caecilia Metella's husband died before her, and it was her son who commissioned the tomb. The tomb is redolent with political messages connected more with his situation than the commemoration of his dead mother. Much of it is speculation in the absence of substantial written evidence – M. Licinius Crassus vanishes from history after his triumph – but Gerding paints a vivid picture of the context, and in particular the politics of the period when the tomb was being built. In the early 20s BC Augustus was moving to consolidate his power. The Crassi represented one of the major potential threats to him, not least M. Licinius Crassus whose recently-won victories gave him considerable renown. In theory Crassus should have been entitled to Rome's highest triumphal honour, the *spolia opima*, for killing an enemy leader in single combat; an honour won by Romulus himself. However, he was denied it on a technicality, quite plausibly at the behest of Augustus (Gerding 2002, 118f.). Crassus' building of the

tomb for his mother can be seen as a reaction to this, a very public demonstration of his prestige. At this period, Augustus had not yet achieved his virtual monopoly on grand expressions of status, and the funding of substantial buildings or civic projects was a major arena of social competition. The tomb should be seen in this light: it was much more than a tomb. During the 1st century BC there was an increasing use of female funerals by male family members as a means to proclaim their own status: for instance, Caesar repeatedly used these occasions as a means of drawing attention to his own achievements. The creation of a monument for his mother offered Crassus the opportunity to make some very public statements about himself.

The form of the tomb was very striking. Gerding makes a strong case that, in the 1st century BC, cylindrical tombs were very strongly linked to people awarded triumphal honours (2002, 89). The fragmentary frieze emphasises this, with the surviving fragment echoing the Gallic victories of his father and uncle; the matching trophy may have evoked his own triumphs or those of his maternal grandfather. This was as much a triumphal monument as a tomb: indeed, it is possible that Crassus's *spolia opima* were displayed here, having been denied a place in the heart of Rome. Gerding argued that the internal layout of the tomb suggests it functioned as a shrine, perhaps even connected to battle-vows sworn by Crassus on campaign (Gerding 2002, 123). Thus the monument was a tomb, a triumphal monument and a religious location, all marking out the importance of Crassus and his family.

The carnyces

Since the trophy-bearing fragment is still *in situ* at some height, its examination is not straightforward. The best illustration is that published by F. Azzurri (1895, pl. 1) although it is inaccurate in detail: for instance, the animal standards are not so similar as he suggests, while the torcs are penannular rather than annular. Photographic illustrations are invariably taken at an angle and do not focus on the details of the trophy (e.g. Eisner 1986, pl. 9, 2). This study has used Azzurri's illustrations as the basis, supplemented by first-hand observation through binoculars. Photos taken during this work, albeit angled, provide a useful correction of the details of Azzurri's illustration.

The four carnyces are all but identical (**fig. 252c**). All are stylised (although not as much as Azzurri's illustration suggests), with no technical details such as tube divisions. The ends of the tubes run under the umbo and thus the mouthpieces are not visible. The heads have an eye, a single ear and an open mouth (to c. 20°). A low crest runs from the uppermost binding (about the start of the bell) to the ear.

Dating evidence

The date of the monument has been extensively debated, with opinions ranging from 67 BC-AD 14 (Gerding 2002,

15. 43-45 tab. III.1). Gerding compiled a range of evidence to argue cogently for a date of 30-20 BC. This is based on the inscription (contents and style), genealogy, the chronology of the building materials and techniques used.

Bibliography
Azzurri 1895. – Gerding 2002 (summarising all previous work).

B1.2 Cuirass statue of Augustus. – Prima Porta villa

(Current location: Vatican Museum, Braccia Nuovo, inv. no. 2290)

The statue of Augustus from the villa of Prima Porta is one of the best-known and most-debated artworks from the Classical world (**fig. 253a**). It was found in 1863 in the ruins of the villa of Livia, Augustus' wife, and presents a striking and complex portrayal of Augustus and his aims. As John Pollini (1995, 263f.) stated, the sculpture had a multitude of messages from simple to highly complex, only some of which we can decipher today. Many aspects remain contentious, and what follows is (as far as possible) a consensus view with key points of debate highlighted. It is based primarily on the work of Pollini (1978; 1995), Diana Kleiner (1992, 63-67), Niels Hannestad (1988, 50-56), Paul Zanker (1988, 188-192), Walther Amelung (1903, 19-28) and Andreas Alföldi (1937).

The over-life-size marble statue shows Augustus standing in »contrapposto«, with the weight on one leg, his right arm outstretched in the classic *adlocutio* pose of the orator addressing the crowd, the left arm by his side originally holding a cylindrical shaft, perhaps a sceptre or spear. He is in military garb, wearing a muscle cuirass with a military cloak (*paludamentum*) tied round his waist; his feet are bare. By his right leg is a Cupid on a dolphin, which provides structural support. The breastplate bears a complex decorative programme which is considered below. The dolphin may refer to his victories at Actium, while the Cupid, as son of Venus, refers to his supposed ancestry as a descendant of Venus; it has been argued to have the face of Gaius, his grandson and intended heir. The rear is less well finished, implying it was intended to stand in a niche; on the right shoulder is a trophy with a carnyx (**fig. 253c**). The statue is most plausibly a private copy (for Livia) of an official version in bronze. The attributes Augustus once held have been much debated, as has the significance of the bare feet; traditionally these should imply divinity and thus that it was a posthumous statue. However, a private statue need not be bound by the constraints of one in the public sphere, where the idea of emperors being divine was a highly sensitive topic. In any case, as Kleiner (1992, 67) noted, he is depicted barefoot on coinage of around 31 BC; it thus gives no help to the dating. In the context of this statue, they probably refer to his heroic status (Pollini 1978, 17f.).

The breastplate carries a number of scenes. On the shoulder-flaps are sphinxes, representing wisdom and prophe-cies (and thus the future). The uppermost part of the plate has depictions of celestial deities: in the centre, Caelus, god of the sky, with Sol in his chariot to the left and two female deities to the right, one carrying the other. One is best interpreted as Aurora, the dawn; the other may be a personification (Kleiner 1992, 65), Venus (Hannestad 1988, 56) or Luna (Zanker 1988, 191f.), the latter perhaps most plausible to balance Sol. The main scene, in the centre of the breastplate, depicts the return of captured Roman standards by the Parthians in 20 BC, a diplomatic success which Augustus hailed as a major victory. The standards had been lost by the *triumvir* Crassus in 53 BC, when he was defeated and killed with much of his army at the battle of Carrhae; this was seen as a major blow to Rome's pride, with further defeats in subsequent years adding to the injury. On the breastplate the standards are returned by a Parthian, perhaps the king, Phraates IV, himself. They are received by a figure in military dress with a dog at his feet. His identity has been much debated: a personification of the Roman army, Tiberius, Mars, Augustus or Romulus have been suggested, the first two being most likely. On either side are dejected personifications of captured provinces, probably Hispania to the left and Gallia to the right; they are discussed further below. At the bottom is Tellus, the earth goddess, with children and cornucopiae as symbols of abundance. To the left is Apollo riding a griffin, to the right Diana on a stag.

The iconography is complex and detailed, but in broad terms it defines Augustus' vision of the dawning of a »Golden Age«, a new and peaceful world order, watched over by the gods of the heavens. It contains references to the past (in the return of the standards, the conquest of provinces, and the deities Apollo and Diana who assisted him in the Civil War), the present (with the return of the Golden Age), and the future (the Golden Age, with Tellus and the children symbolising new fertility); Gaius, as his intended heir, also falls into this category.

Of most interest here are the trophy on the back and the two personified provinces on the front. These have been much debated, especially the provinces. That on the right, with boar standard and carnyx, her sword scabbard empty as a symbol she has been disarmed, is most plausibly interpreted as Gallia (**fig. 253b**). That on the left is seen as Hispania with eagle-hilted sword and fringed cloak. Augustus in his *Res Gestae* specifically mentioned the recovery of standards from Gallia, Hispania and Dalmatia (Hannestad

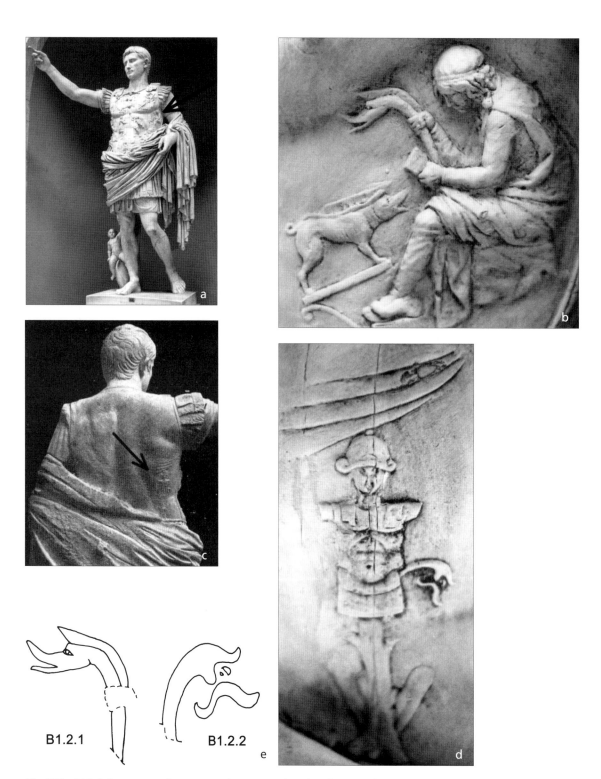

Fig. 253 B1.2 Cuirass statue of Augustus, Prima Porta: **a** front (see **fig. 146a** for a larger view). – **b** detail of Gallia with boar standard and carnyx. – **c** rear, with trophy indicated. – **d** detail of trophy on rear (from cast in Museo delle Civilta Romana). – **e** carnyces 1-2. – (a-b. d photos Fraser Hunter; c Woelcke 1911, fig. 7; e drawing Tanja Romankiewicz).

1988, 54), and it is likely these personifications provide a thematic link to the Parthian standards. There have been other views. Most divergent has been Alföldi (1937), who saw the left figure as Germania (arguing the sword was not specifically Spanish, and the cloak more appropriate for a northerner), and the right one as Dacia: rather than a carnyx, he identified the item as an animal-headed standard, known in Dacia from later coinage. While a different style from the one on the reverse, this does not mean it cannot be a carnyx, and the link with the boar standard (unknown in the iconography of Dacia) makes it certain that Gaul, not Dacia, was intended. Zanker (1988, 189) read considerable significance into the empty sword sheath on the right and the full one on the left: for him, the empty scabbard was a disarmed province, »the conquered Gallic tribes in the West, especially in Spain«, while the armed figure, »despondent but not yet disarmed … could represent the tributary peoples serving as buffer states in the East or in Germany«. There is of course endless scope for creativity, but given the iconography (especially of the right figure) and the connection to the recovery of standards, it seems most likely that Hispania and Gallia are represented.

The carnyces

The carnyces were examined on the original and in more detail on a cast in the Museo delle Civilta Romana (**fig. 253b. d-e**). The right personification depicts a seated female facing left, holding a carnyx (1) and an empty sword scabbard, with a boar standard facing her at her feet. Of the carnyx (which faces left), the upper tube, bell and head are visible. The tube is cylindrical, with Gallia's hand obscuring any junction. A plain crest runs Mohican-like to the eye; the head (at 90° to the tube) has an eye with prominent eyebrow and a slightly open mouth, the upper jaw longer and flared. There is no ear.

The trophy on the rear comprises a muscle cuirass and helmet. The helmet is a high bowl with a knob on top, a brim terminating in volutes, and cheek-pieces. There are ?greaves behind the trunk. The arms are short and stubby, with no shields; a carnyx (2) pokes out of the right side,

from behind the bottom of the cuirass. Part of a wing (implying a Victory figure) appears over the trophy, but was never completed. This carnyx is near horizontal, sloping slightly up and facing down and back, the head turned through 160°. The tube, bell and head are plain, with an eye and ear only on the head; the mouth is open to 90°, with the jaw tips recurved.

Dating evidence

The return of the Parthian standards provides a *terminus post quem* of 20 BC. Much then hinges on whether the statue is posthumous or not but, as discussed above, there are no strong grounds for this. Pollini (1978, 15-20) provided a detailed and rational assessment. The iconography supports a date preceding Augustus' later campaigns, in Illyricum (AD 6-9) and Germany (7 BC), of which there is no mention; the »Golden Age« iconography starts from c. 17 BC, and his connections with Apollo and Diana fade in his later reign; they do not appear in coinage after 9 BC. Thus a date bracket of 20-10 BC is most likely. Kleiner (1992, 67) made the case for this as a later marble copy of an original of this date; she dated the copy to the reign of Tiberius (c. AD 15), seeing him as the hero on the breastplate, but this seems unnecessarily convoluted on current evidence and the earlier date is preferred here.

Bibliography

Alföldi 1937. – Amelung 1903, 19-28. – Hannestad 1988, 50-56. – Kleiner 1992, 63-67. – Pollini 1978; 1995. – Zanker 1988, 188-192.

B1.3 Lid of funerary urn showing eagle with pile of arms. – Bovillae

(Current location: Madrid, Prado Museum, inv. no. 225E)
A remarkable marble group of an eagle clutching a thunderbolt perched on a pile of arms, now in Madrid, was found between 1645 and 1648 in a villa at Bovillae, on the via Appia some 15 km south-east of Rome. It was long misleadingly known as the »apotheosis of Claudius« owing to a bust placed on the eagle in the seventeenth century. Even if the bust represented on early drawings is Roman, it was not originally part of it, and has been removed. This restoration work also confirmed that the eagle, although made separately, was a primary part of the composition (**fig. 254a**). Stephan Schröder has provided an authoritative study (Schröder 2004, 470-481 no. 206; conveniently summarised in English in Schröder/García López/Gómez García n. d., 87-90).

The pile of over 70 visible arms is a form of trophy, typical of battlefield monuments; the eagle perching on top is the messenger of Jupiter, who ordained the victory. It contains a mixture of material which Schröder split into the following categories:

- Northern barbarians: the oval shields, although also used by Romans, have a disproportionate amount of »barbarian« decoration – notably carnyces, wolf and boar standards. He argued that the crescent (moon?) and star decoration were also linked to barbarians. Hexagonal shields show a similar pattern. A carnyx appears once on its own as well as on shield decorations.
- Eastern barbarians: mythical items like the pelta shield and griffin decoration, but also double-quivers (for bow and arrows) and Phrygian helmets.
- Hellenistic material: a Macedonian domed round shield with starburst decoration, and Hellenistic-style cuirasses.
- Generic material: muscle cuirasses, round shields, various helmets, swords, daggers, greaves and cylindrical quivers.
- Ships: stern, prow, oars and anchor.

There has been a long debate over the monument's date, with recent analysis favouring the Hadrianic period (e. g.

Fig. 254 B1.3 Lid of funerary urn, Bovillae: **a** general view. – **b** detail of left side with carnyces 6-7. – **c** detail of right side with carnyx 12. – **d** drawing of scenes with carnyces marked. – **e** carnyces 1-12. – (a-d adapted from Schröder/García López/Gómez García n. d., figs 8-11. 42; e drawing Alan Braby).

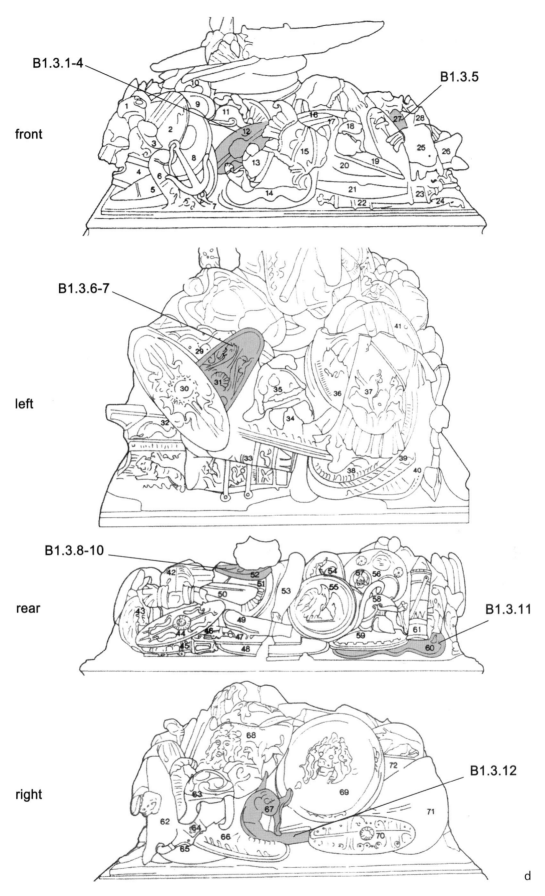

front

left

rear

right

B1.3.1-4

B1.3.5

B1.3.6-7

B1.3.8-10

B1.3.11

B1.3.12

d

Fig. 254 (continued)

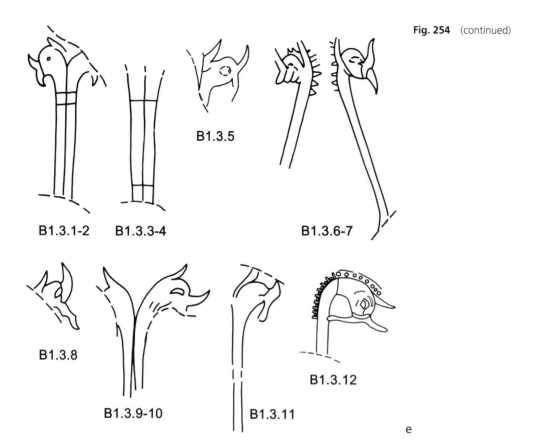

Fig. 254 (continued)

B1.3.1-2   B1.3.3-4

B1.3.5

B1.3.6-7

B1.3.8

B1.3.9-10   B1.3.11

B1.3.12

e

Polito 1998, 207-209). Schröder carefully dismissed the arguments for this and proposed an Augustan date. This is relevant to interpretation of the iconography. The mixture of eastern and northern barbarians, land and sea victories is found on other Augustan monuments, and he made good stylistic arguments for this date. The iconography is carefully constructed; the decoration on items such as shields continues the messages conveyed by the objects, with barbarian items or sea themes, in contrast to the randomly Classical decoration often found on trophy items. In the northern barbarian material, the viewer is reminded of Augustus' successes in France and Spain. The eastern material might evoke victory over the Parthians, or over Mark Antony, whose power base lay in the east. This victory is also surely implied by the ship parts and marine iconography, evoking the battle of Actium.

From the findspot, Schröder was able to take the analysis further. Inscribed lead pipes showed that the estate belonged to the Valerii Messallae family. In the Augustan period, one of the main men in the Imperial circle belonged to this family: Marcus Valerius Messalla Corvinus (64 BC - AD 13). He was a long-term supporter of Octavian/Augustus, commanded a naval squadron at Actium and was responsible for the conquest of Aquitania, for which he was awarded a triumph in 27 BC. The monument thus commemorates his own achievements as well as those of Augustus. Recent conservation has shown that the sculpture is a lid: it has a border on the underside to fit over an urn. This

suggests it was for a massive funerary urn. Messalla Corvinus' tomb was celebrated in antiquity, and Schröder made the convincing suggestion that this was the lid for it; the imagery of victory over barbarians would not only mark the deceased's achievements and link them to those of the imperial house, but could also symbolise a victory over death.

The carnyces

Twelve carnyces are present, primarily as shield decoration, once as an object. One item which Schröder identified as a carnyx (his no. 3) is a duck-headed ship part. Details are given in **Appendix 2** (**tab. 78**). The depictions are quite consistent, with cylindrical tubes, the mouthpieces hidden, single forward-pointing ears, eyes and flared mouths. Technical details are rare; there is the occasional junction shown. A crest is only shown on the (larger) representation of a carnyx, not the shield decorations (**fig. 254b-e**).

B1.3.1-4: oval shield with a central lion's head; the spina is formed of pairs of back-to-back carnyces, the heads of the lower pair obscured.

B1.3.5: hexagonal shield, largely hidden behind oval shield and muscle cuirass. At the top is a boar standard and below this the head and upper bell of a carnyx, facing right; it was clearly seen as a background piece, as in places it is weakly defined.

B1.3.6-7: oval shield crossed (and largely concealed) behind another; tip lost. Central rosette boss and tapering spina. The halves of the shield are decorated with outwards-fac-

ing carnyces, done in a mixture of incision and relief-work. B1.3.8-10: on top of the weapon pile, and now largely concealed by restored globes in the eagle's claws, is an oval shield. It has a central rosette boss with paired carnyces flanking the longitudinal spina; only three are depicted, the fourth being concealed by other objects.
B1.3.11: figure-of-eight shield with central belly, lying at base of pile; little is exposed, but a carnyx is lightly and loosely incised in its bottom right corner, facing out.
B1.3.12: carnyx lying horizontally, facing upwards, protruding from behind oval shield.

Dating evidence

The evidence for a late Augustan/early Tiberian date and a link to Marcus Valerius Messalla Corvinus, who died in

AD 13, summarised above, seems entirely convincing. It is supported by two specific pieces of weapon iconography. The pile includes two examples (14, 60) of the unusual figure-of-eight shield with a central belly which is otherwise exceedingly rare, but is represented on the (Augustan) tomb of Caecilia Metella (**fig. 252a**). There is also an unusual sword with an openwork rectangular hilt, paralleled on the Augustan arch at Pola (Polito 1998, 55 [type F] figs 80-81). This all supports Schröder's dating of AD 15-20, which is accepted here.

Bibliography

Polito 1998, 207-209. – Schröder 2004, 470-481 no. 206. – Schröder/García López/Gómez García n. d., 87-90.

B1.4 Palace of the Flavians. – Palatine, Rome

The Palatine was used as a home for the emperors intermittently since the days of Augustus, but it was Domitian who instigated a massive building project, modifying the very form of the hill to create a palatial complex with massive public areas, private residences and a series of gardens (**fig. 255**). The complex looked both north to the Forum and south to the Circus Maximus, so that the emperor was in the eyes of his people. Paul Zanker (2002) provided a valuable summary. The public part of this complex, the *Domus Flavia*, consisted of a series of enormous halls, ornately and expensively decorated with colourful marbles

and rich carvings. They were a wonder of the age, celebrated in literature of the time. The interior of the massive northern hall (known today as the Aula Regia) has been reconstructed as a series of 16 projections with the intervening niches holding colossal statues (Durry 1922, 304f.). The architectural iconography evoked Domitian's double-triumph celebrated over the Chatti and the Dacians in AD 89: he campaigned against the Germanic Chatti on the middle Rhine, and a coalition of Danubian Germans (Suebi, Quadi and Marcomanni), Sarmatians and Dacians, from AD 83 into the 90s (Cary/Wilson 1963, 285-288; Bennett

Fig. 255 Plan of the palace of the Flavians on the Palatine. Public areas are shaded light grey, with the carnyx sculpture deriving most probably from the so-called Aula Regia. – (Modified from Coarelli 2007, fig. 41).

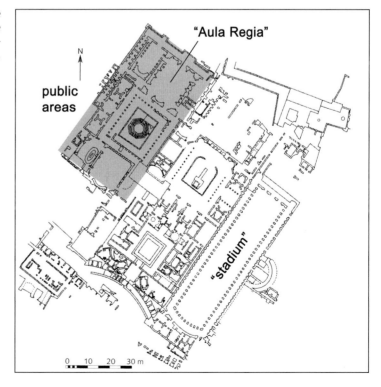

2001, 28-31). The decoration can be dated to c. AD 90-92 (Durry 1922, 315; von Blanckenhagen 1940, 68f.).

A few fragments of the decoration still survive. Depictions of weaponry and trophies are recorded on column bases (Zanker 2002, fig. 15), blocks projecting from the column tops to support an architrave, and friezes, probably from this architrave; carnyces are known in the frieze and the projecting blocks (Stefan 2005, 456).

B1.4.1 Architectural frieze with trophies. – Palatine

(Current location: Rome, Palazzo Farnesi [A-B]; Rome, Palatino, Magazzini del Criptoportico 379583 [C]; fragments also in Naples)

Among the sculptural fragments preserved in the Palazzo Farnesi are three marble blocks with Victories crowning trophies which include carnyces from 18th-century excavations (fig. 256). These are illustrated and discussed by Marcel Durry (1922), Paul Couissin (1928b, 72-74) and Peter-Heinrich von Blanckenhagen (1940, 64f. 68f.), the sources for what follows. The primary publication is that of Durry, who discussed the relevant fragments (A-C) along with fragments of another trophy (D, furry cloak and hat) probably from the same architectural setting; indeed D may be the missing part of B. Durry (1935) subsequently published two further blocks (E-F) in the National Museum in Naples, but could not illustrate them as they were almost inaccessible. Couissin (1928b, 72 n. 6) referred to a further fragment, presumably that illustrated by von Blanckenhagen (1940, pl. 32 no. 88), again a projecting block with Victory crowning a trophy; only the basal pile of arms is preserved, featuring oval, hexagonal and peltate shields, a quiver and part of a ?cuirass.

The fragments are projecting blocks from the tops of columns which carried a frieze with architrave. The front faces are decorated with Victories crowning trophies, while the sides bear images of griffins, candelabrae and Arimaspi. The two main fragments (A and B) are mirror images. Damage to the blocks means the upper parts are missing and some surface detail has been lost. The trophy scene on A is 0.28m high and 0.40m wide; on B, 0.28m × 0.35m; on C, 0.26m × 0.44m (Durry 1922, 306 n. 1). Fragment E is described as similar to B, and also features a carnyx; fragment F shows few details.

The more complete fragments show a winged Victory crowning a trophy. On fragment A, Victory faces R; her upper body, arms and head are lost. Of the trophy itself little survives bar traces of the crossed shields from the arms (oval, one with squared ends; central rib and dot-defined edge-binding) and shafts perhaps from spears. At the base is a pile of arms arranged around a conical furry hat. It mostly consists of shields (round, oval and oval with squared ends, all with Classical ornament); in the absence of primary examination not all the other items can be identified, but they include an axe, the end of a quiver, a handle or the top of a bow, and a carnyx facing the Victory.

Fragment B is a mirror image, the trophy again damaged but with oval shields (one squared off) on the arms and a furry hat with shields (oval, perhaps squared off, and one peltate) arranged around it. There is also a helmet (ornamented with a griffin), axes, a sword hilt and, facing R, a carnyx; in low relief on the L is the curved blade of a Dacian falx (Durry 1922, 311; clearer in Couissin 1928b, fig. 1 than on the photos). Durry also discussed barbed spearheads (1922, 312), although these are not obvious on the published photos.

Fragment C was published in more detail by Eugenio Polito (2009); the photo in Durry does not show the carnyx and he does not mention it, but it is clear in Polito's image. In contrast to A and B, the pile of arms is arranged around an Attic helmet, with a variety of shields (oval, oval squared, round, and peltate), a quiver and sword hilts. It was found in excavations by Pietro Rosa, whereas A and B come from Bianchini's excavations. The carnyx faces right at the back of the image. Polito suggested it differed in style from the others, but the similarity in size indicates they come from the same setting.

Durry (1922, 315) rightly suggested the mixture of Dacian and German weapons reflected Domitian's victories over these two people. The oval shields are normal barbarian gear among both Germans and Dacians, but curved swords are a clear Dacian type, and both axes and archery gear are connected in iconography with Dacians and Sarmatians (see chapter 9). Furry hats were connected in the Roman mind to cold northern climes and at this date were typically used to represent Germans. The carnyces are probably intended as German, since they occur in Domitian's earlier German propaganda (e.g. B2.12), but as they occur with Dacians in Trajan's later campaigns we cannot be dogmatic. Durry argued the scenes also include Roman and fantastic weapons. In the former he sees the hilt guard of the sword as a gladius, although with so little showing this is unclear; the form of the quiver, with its conical top, is more Classical than the normal Dacian type (compare the open quivers seen on Trajan's Column; Lepper/Frere 1988, pls II-III). He grouped the shields and helmets as fantastical weapons, but most of the shields are entirely acceptable barbarian forms, albeit with Classical motifs. As with the base of Trajan's Column (B1.12), it is clear that the Roman artists may have followed the form of barbarian weapons quite accurately but often decorated them with motifs familiar from their own repertoire. Only the pelta is a conventional type for trophies, while the helmet, although not entirely clear, looks to be a variant of the Attic type, another conventional form.

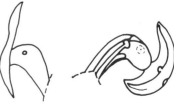

Fig. 256 B1.4.1 Architectural frieze with trophies: **a** fragment A. – **b** fragment B. – **c** fragment C. – **d** carnyces 1-2. – (a-b Durry 1922; c Sailko/Creative Commons 3.0; d drawing Tanja Romankiewicz).

B1.4.1.1-2

In his 1935 paper, Durry suggested the northern barbarian elements relate to victories in Britain rather than Germany, because he now considered these items as Celtic; this is a tantalising suggestion, but given the other evidence of iconography related to Domitian's double-triumph, a link to Germans seems far more plausible.

The carnyces

The carnyces are simplified and rather monstrous, with the emphasis very much on the huge jaws in A-B. On both, only the bell and head are visible. Details are not clear on the published illustrations, although a closer view published by Patrizio Pensabene (1979, fig. 11) provides more details of B.

Carnyx 1 (fragment A): head and part of bell, facing L. Dot-defined eye but otherwise apparently no anatomical details on the rather bulbous head; mouth opened wide to c. 180°, the lower tip of the jaw recurved.

Carnyx 2 (fragment B): more of the tube/bell is visible, turning through 90° into the head, which faces R; no junctions are depicted. A narrow plain crest runs the full visible length of the bell/tube, stopping where the head turns. The bell is decorated with two visible ribs with slightly ex-panded rounded terminals. There appears to be a triangular ear against the head, and a simple eye (with drilled pupil) on the bulbous head; again the jaw is wide open, the ends recurved.

Carnyx 3 (fragment E): no published illustration has been found.

Carnyx 4 (fragment C): head and part of bell, facing R. Broken crest, two ears, flared mouth much smaller than in the others, the visible upper tip recurved; the carnyx is generally less prominent in the scene.

Dating evidence

The decoration of the building has been dated to c. AD 90-92, which is consistent with the history of Domitian's campaigns on the Rhine, Danube and Dacia (Durry 1922, 315; Couissin 1928b, 72; von Blanckenhagen 1940, 68 f.).

Bibliography

Couissin 1928b, 72-74 (he confuses the fragment letters in the caption to figs 1-2). – Durry 1922; 1935. – Pensabene 1979, fig. 11. – Picard 1957, 352 f. – Polito 2009. – von Blanckenhagen 1940, esp. 64 f. 68 f. pl. 17, 52-53.

B1.4.2 Weapons frieze. – Palatine

(Currently lost)
Lucia Guerrini (1971, 93 pl. XLII, 2) published an illustration of a fragmentary marble weapons frieze by Pier Leone Ghezzi (1674-1755) who compiled a series of illustrations of ancient sculpture, many of them from excavations in Rome in the period 1720-1750 (**fig. 257**). This particular fragment came from excavations on the Palatine, probably in 1734; it is now lost. The preceding item illustrated also came from the Palatine, its location corresponding to the Palace of the Flavians; Guerrini drew parallels between this piece and another find from this location. Since trium-

Fig. 257 B1.4.2 Weapons frieze from the palace of the Flavians. – (a Guerrini 1971, pl. XLII, 2; b drawing Tanja Romankiewicz).

phal ornament is known to have featured in this building, it is likely that this fragment too is of Domitianic date.

The frieze features a truncated trophy on the left (muscle cuirass and bowl helmet with cheek guards) and a tunic cuirass on the right. Between them is an array of shields, all with Classical decoration: oval, round, hexagonal and pelta. From among the shields emerge various items of equipment: a long sword in its scabbard, a pair of greaves, an Attic helmet, spears, tubae and a carnyx.

The carnyx
The carnyx lies at the right hand end of the frieze by the lower border, facing downwards. Only the upper tube, bell and head are shown. The drawing in general appears to be reasonably accurate – there are no glaring anach-

ronisms or impossible features – so it can be taken as a reasonably good record. The bell curves smoothly into a naturalistic head; there is no crest, but it has an ear and a well-defined eye. The mouth is wide open, curving beyond 180° with the jaw tips strongly recurved.

Dating evidence
Given that the fragment comes from the Palatine, most likely from the Palace of the Flavians, it is likely that this too was part of the architectural decoration of the palace, which was constructed in AD 90-92.

Bibliography
Guerrini 1971.

B1.5 Weapons frieze fragment. – Domitian's villa, Castelgandolfo

(Current location: Castelgandolfo, Antiquarium della Villa Barberini)

Two fragments of marble weapons frieze, one now lost, have been recorded since 1764 at the villa of Castelgandolfo. This was Domitian's villa and they presumably come from some triumphal ornament within this complex; although the exact findspot is not known, P. Liverani (1989, 13 f.) noted that the material in the collection derives from the area of the villa. They are first illustrated by Giovanni Battista Piranesi (1764, pl. XXI; **fig. 258a**). The now-lost fragment (*ibidem* fig. IIc) shows part of a scale armour cuirass, while the surviving fragment (*ibidem* fig. III) shows round and oval shields (one with an elongated umbo), a sword scabbard and part of a tunic among other unidentified fragmentary objects. Emerging from behind a shield, facing R, is a carnyx.

The carnyx
The block has only been seen from published photos (**fig. 258b**) and the Piranesi illustration (1764, pl. XXI fig. III). Reproductions of this (e. g. Liverani 1989, fig. 1.0; Speciale 1979, fig. 48) do not do justice to the detail of the original, which is on a far larger scale and contains considerable subtlety. Where other aspects of Piranesi's engraving can be compared to published photos it is accurate, and it is used as the basis for discussion here. The surviving fragment itself has not been seen.

Only the top of the tube, bell and part of the mouth are preserved; the head has broken off (**fig. 258c**). There is a flat raised band at the tube-bell junction; Piranesi's illustrations suggest a bipartite junction, with a lower-relief section below the raised upper one. The bell expands slightly as it curves. A crest gradually tapers up from the upper part of the tube. It is plain on the tube section but on the bell is decorated with a marginal border (itself channelled over most of its length) with pendant raised arcading linked by raised ribs to the bell. The head is entirely lost, but the attachment scars of the upper jaw and part of the lower jaw survive.

Dating evidence
Although A. Tempesta (1992, 333 f.) attributed the frieze to Trajan's Forum this is clearly flawed given its findspot (clearly stated by Piranesi as »Frammento d'antichi trofei nell'istessa villa«, fragment of ancient trophy from the same villa). This strongly points to a Domitianic date; Eugenio Polito, while commenting on its resemblance to Trajanic art, attributed it to the Flavian period, most probably the reign of Domitian (AD 83-96), with close parallels to the »Trophies of Marius«.

Bibliography
Liverani 1989, 13 f. fig. 1.0. – Piranesi 1764, pl. XXI. – Polito 1998, 192. – Tempesta 1992, 333 f. fig. 23 n. 194 f. – von Hesberg in: Speciale 1979, 107 f.

B1.6 Trophy capitals. – S. Lorenzo fuori le mura, Rome

The aisles of the choir in the early Christian church of San Lorenzo fuori le mura (Rome) are supported on antique

columns (**fig. 259a**). Most have Corinthian capitals, but the first two, most visible from the nave, are a pair of mar-

Fig. 258 B1.5 Weapons frieze fragment, Domitian's villa of Castelgandolfo: **a** weapons frieze fragments. – **b** surviving block with carnyx. – **c** the carnyx. – (a Piranesi 1764, pl. XXI; reproduced from Liverani 1989, fig. 1.0; b Polito 1998, fig 127; c drawing Tanja Romankiewicz).

ble trophy capitals. They are closely similar, with small but significant differences. Here they are labelled as L and R (left/right as viewed from the nave), the faces numbered 1-4 clockwise from the one facing the nave.

The basic design model has acanthus leaves around the base, with a trophy on each face, flanked by Victories at the corners of the block. Each trophy consists of a muscle cuirass, horned helmet and greaves, with a furry hat below the cuirass. The trophy has two overlapping oval shields on each arm, behind which is a carnyx, one or two spears and a vexillum standard. The two capitals differ in detail:

left (fig. 259b)	right (fig. 259c)
Hellenistic cuirass with gorgoneion	muscle cuirass
alternating faces have hexagonal shields (decorated with interlocked circles & crescents)	all oval shields (ornate tendril designs)
	one face replaces carnyx with falx

The differences are significant; they are found in Domitianic propaganda, the hexagonal shield symbolising his German campaigns, the falx his Dacian ones (see chapter 9). This suggests the capitals are linked to his double-triumph of AD 89.

It is uncertain what building the capitals derived from, but along with the ten Corinithian capitals in the chancel and their elegant columns they form a consistent group. The assemblage formed the core of the 6th-century eastern basilica built around the tomb of St Lawrence, the two trophy capitals at the front serving to mark the tomb's position (Krautheimer/Frankl/Corbett 1959, 51. 124f.; Beny/Gunn 1981, 102-104; see also Hansen 2003, 79-81). The trophy capitals were frequently illustrated by

B1.7 Weapon pillars from an *armilustrium*. – Aventine, Rome

(Current location: Florence, Uffizi, inv. nos 1914-59, 1914-72)

Preserved in the Uffizi in Florence are two tall square-sectioned marble pillars with all four faces covered with weapons friezes (**fig. 260a**). They have plain borders on all edges, and would originally have had separate capitals and bases. Jan Willem Crous (1933) provided an authoritative study. They were found on the north-west corner of the Aventine Hill in Rome prior to the fifteenth century,

Renaissance and later artists (eg Krautheimer/Frankl/Corbett 1959, n. 3; Campbell 2004, 644. 726).

The carnyces

At least eight carnyces are present (faces L2 and R4 are hard to view owing to the morphology of the church). All are the same basic design. They have no technical detail and show some naturalistic modelling to the head, with single ears and dot-decorated bar crests running from the gaping mouth to where the tube curved less strongly (assumed to be the base of the bell). One lacks the crest. The tubes run behind the tube, but are cylindrical where visible. Not all could be recorded in detail when the church was visited, owing to a funeral. **Figure 259d** conveys the details of the ones which could be sketched.

Dating evidence

Eugen von Mercklin (1962, 266) described them as later 2nd century, but this seems to be no more than an art-historical value-judgement; no grounds are presented for it. The differences between the capitals suggest they were intended to evoke Germans and Dacians; the most likely context is Domitian's double triumph of AD 89, giving a likely date bracket of AD 89-96.

Bibliography

Campbell 2004, nos 237. 272. – von Mercklin 1962, 264-266 no. 629a-b figs 1224-1225.

Fig. 259 B1.6 Trophy capitals, S. Lorenzo fuori le mura, Rome: **a** the capitals in the church. – **b** the left capital. – **c** the right capital. – **d** the visible carnyces. – (a Beny/Gunn 1981, 90; b-c von Mercklin 1962, figs 1224-1225; d drawing Alan Braby).

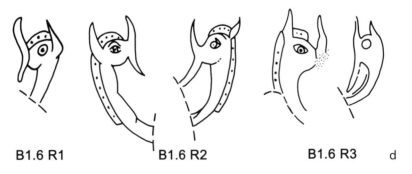

B1.6 R1   B1.6 R2   B1.6 R3   d

Fig. 259   (continued)

and were brought to Florence in 1588 after their owner became Duke of Tuscany (Crous 1933, 72). Other fragments may also have been found, but the only evidence is a somewhat confused late 16th-century depiction (Crous 1933, 16 f. 33). Crous argued they derive from the *armilustrium*, a poorly-known sacred building comprising a cloistered rectangular open space within which the ceremony of purifying the army's weapons took place before and after the campaigning season, on March 19th and October 19th (Crous 1933, 33 f. 60-72; Ogilvie 1969, 96). Here the weapons were purified and then stored; the friezes are a representation of the original weapons hung on pillars.

The pillars are single shafts of marble, 3.20 m high, 0.32-0.35 m wide and 0.30-0.32 m deep, tapering slightly to the top. There are no trophies: each face is a densely-packed weapons frieze with no real order or pattern, although they are more crammed at the base. Crous (1933, 4-6) identified some 1450 weapons of 106 different types. One face of each pillar is close to the wall in the Uffizi, making access difficult; Crous did not catalogue these faces in detail (although he did illustrate a sixteenth-century engraving of parts of them; fig. 8 f.), but otherwise presented an object-by-object listing of the material (Crous 1933, 73-106). The objects are represented at different scales to fit into the frieze; thus ship parts are reduced in size while helmets are enlarged. What is striking is its diversity, with Roman, barbarian and conventional items, naval and terrestrial. Most of the material is Roman, but some is certainly or probably barbarian: carnyces, draco standards (unlikely to be Roman at this date), hexagonal shields, archery equipment, probably the animal standards, and the horned and fur-covered helmets (the latter used as a barbarian type in iconography [chapter 9], although some Roman helmets were fur-covered; van Enckevort/Willems 1994, 127. 135).

The carnyces

23 carnyces are represented, seventeen illustrated by Crous (his 4-164 is a wolf standard, not a carnyx) and six on the pillar backs (one shown in Crous 1933, fig. 8). They are given a running number sequence here, following Crous' order for consistency: **Appendix 2** (**tab. 79**) provides a concordance and details.

The carnyces are all very similar in style, although differing considerably in decorative detail (**fig. 260**): many of the crest designs are unique, and the same decoration is never found more than three times. The lower tube is generally hidden, although in the two where more is visible (18, 23) it is plain and cylindrical, with no junctions. There is a decorated collar at the tube-bell junction, only lacking on 22, and a decorated crest typically running from this collar to the ear (only three lack the crest, although some have longer or shorter ones). One bell is decorated with triangles. Only rarely is there any sign of a bell-head junction (?18, 20): the head is treated quite naturalistically with musculature and bone structure under the jaw and around the eyes, and sometimes skin folds under the chin. The ears have a natural shape, while the eyes are typically almond-shaped with (on many) a circular pupil. Three have a particularly small ear (10, 11 and 16) and one a noticeably large eye (20). Mouths are typically wide open and hollowed to enhance the effect, with the jaw tips recurved in about half the examples; two show nostrils on the upper jaw (13-14).

Dating evidence

Crous (1933, 8 f.) drew stylistic parallels to other late Flavian monuments, notably the Farnesi reliefs from Domitian's Palace (Durry 1922), although others have argued for a Trajanic date (summarised in Coulston 1991, 111 n. 16). Stylistically it is hard to differentiate Domitianic and Trajanic works (Hannestad 1988, 148); in this instance, Jon Coulston noted the lack of similarity to the reliefs on the base of Trajan's Column, which would support a Domitianic date (AD 81-96), probably some time after his first German campaigns in 83. Polito (1998, 204-207) largely concurred, although suggesting a very early 2nd-century date is feasible; it is taken as AD 83-105 here.

Bibliography

Coulston 1991, 101. 111 n. 16. – Crous 1933. – Polito 1998, 204-207.

B1.8 Weapons frieze. – Rome

(Current location: Rome, Villa Albani, inv. no. 125)
In the sculpture collections held at Villa Albani is a rectangular marble panel (1.72 m L. 0.79 m H.) with a lunette containing a weapons frieze, published in detail by H.-U. Cain (1989). Its form is unusual, as the frieze is contained within a semicircular field springing from the tops of two capitals; the remaining two corners of the panel have sea snakes chasing dolphins (**fig. 261a**). Presumably the panel sat over a doorway, forming an arched top. There is a second similar panel from the same collection (Bol 1989, no. 126), and a third now in Munich, from Villa Aldobrandini in Rome (Cain 1989, 390). Given the unusual shape, all three probably came from the same building; the exact provenance is not known, but was probably in Rome.

The panel has been extensively restored and heavily cleaned. The composition centres on a muscle cuirass,

Fig. 260 B1.7 Weapons frieze pillars from the *armilustrium*, Aventine, Rome: **a** the pillars. – **b** carnyx 1. – **c** carnyx 12. – **d** carnyx 15. – **e** the carnyces. – (a-d photos Fraser Hunter; e drawing Tanja Romankiewicz).

with objects arranged around this: shields (hexagonal, oval, domed round, pelta and legionary), bows and a quiver, spears, helmets (Roman and other), a curved horn, S-shaped horn, eagle standard, standard with phalerae, and a sword. This includes a mixture of Roman, barbarian and conventional material (e.g. the pelta shields). The certainly barbarian weaponry comprises the oval and hexagonal shields, probably the bow and quiver, and the

horns. The curved horn could either be a Roman cornu or a barbarian instrument; the tube does not curve significantly below the bell, suggesting the latter, and the horn on frieze 126 is clearly of this form. Carnyces appear as decoration on the hexagonal shield. The second frieze (Bol 1989, no. 126) is of the same basic form: apart from objects represented on 125, it includes a much clearer curved horn, a tuba, greaves, and a double-headed axe.

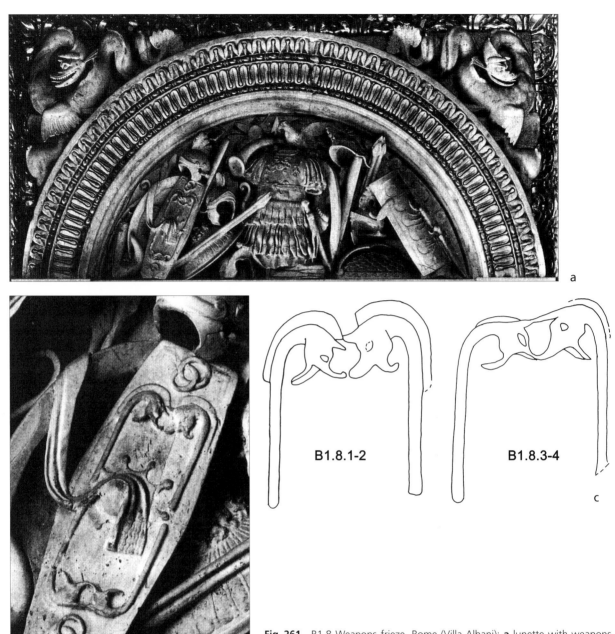

Fig. 261 B1.8 Weapons frieze, Rome (Villa Albani): **a** lunette with weapons frieze. – **b** detail of shield with carnyces. – **c** carnyces 1-4. – (a-b Cain 1989, pls 222-223; c drawing Tanja Romankiewicz).

The friezes are probably late Flavian or early Trajanic, which could make the weaponry either Germanic or Dacian. Parallels can be found for shields with carnyces and torcs in Trajanic monuments (Trajan's Column and the Great Trajanic Frieze; B1.11.3, B1.12), while bows and arrows are more common in Dacian than Germanic settings, but the horns are more typically Germanic (see chapter 10).

The carnyces

Carnyces feature as decoration on a hexagonal shield, the right half of which (including much of two carnyces) is restored (**fig. 261b-c**). The shield has a double raised band around the rim and a conical boss, its rim shaped as a ten-point star with the tips rounded. At top and bottom are interlocked torc pairs, while opposed carnyces fill each half. These have straight cylindrical tubes, the mouthpiece ends squared off (a restored one is rounded). There appear to be no junctions on the tubes or bells, which expand only slightly; the heads turn through 180° to face back towards the boss. A plain crest runs from the base of the bell (just below where the tube starts to bend) to just behind the ear. The heads are stylised, with single ears, eye peaks and eyes (which are apparently simple circles) and flared mouths (open to about 120°, the ends recurved).

Dating evidence

Cain (1989) reviewed the dating evidence, which is purely stylistic. While a Flavian origin has been suggested, he argued on the basis of a series of art-historical parallels for a Trajanic date. Polito (1998, 197 f.) noted the style is very different from the monuments of Trajan's Forum, and sug-gested an early Trajanic or late Flavian date fits best (AD 83-105).

Bibliography

Cain 1989. – Polito 1998, 197 f.

B1.9 Pilaster base with trophy. – Maddalena (near Pantheon), Rome

(Current location: Vatican Museum, Sala a Croce Greca, inv. no. 574a)

Well-preserved cuboidal marble pilaster base (1.13 m H. 0.72 m W. 0.64 m T.), with part of the border and upper left corner damaged (**fig. 262a**). The front face shows a trophy relief within a moulded border (lacking at the base). One side (probably the left) once had a relief of Mars and Rhea Silva attached, but this was removed after its discovery in or before 1777 and is now displayed separately in the Vatican in the Museo Pio Clementino Cortile Ottagono. The block was published by Georg Lippold (1936, 178 f. no. 574a), but the link to the Mars scene was not then realised (for this see Pietrangeli 1987, 146 no. 574A; 1988, 157 no. 1; Andreae et al. 1998, 20 pl. 220; Spinola 1999, 286 no. 31). The cast on display in the Museo del Civiltà Romana has restored the detached panel to the side of the trophy.

The relief shows a trophy crowned with a horned helmet with cheek guards and transverse crest, and wearing a cloak. On each arm is a hexagonal shield with two spears behind. The left shield is smaller and slightly more rounded; both have round umbos, and both are decorated. The left shield's decoration includes annular twisted torcs; the right has interlocked rings which may be torcs. At the base is a pile of arms. There are superimposed shields to left and right: on the left, hexagonal and ?oval, both decorated; on the right, an oval shield with a pelta shield in front, two more shields (peltate and oval?) partly visible at the rear of the pile. On the left, behind the shields are a carnyx and variant vexillum standard (attached to the pole at the side rather than the top), with part of an unidentified feature between the carnyx and shield. Between the shield groups lie an S-shaped horn, furry helmet, tuba and two groups of spears, one bound. Behind and right of the right shield pile are a tunic-clad cuirass, sword handle, axe, vexillum standard, animal standard (probably a wolf) and carnyx. Lippold failed to identify the carnyces, describing them as »dragon heads on sticks«.

The shape and size suggest the block functioned as a pilaster base in a wider composition; compare the blocks of similar dimensions from Diocletian's *Arcus Novus* (B1.16). Lippold argued the selection of the weapons was probably conventional, without any certain relationships with a particular defeated people, but the combination of distinctive items (carnyx, animal standard, S-shaped horn, furry helmet and horned helmet) point to a Germanic origin. It is argued below to be of Domitianic date, and can be seen as part of the commemorative programme for his Germanic victories, adorning an unknown building or arch.

The carnyces

The left carnyx faces right (**fig. 262b**); only the upper tube, bell and head are shown, without any tube divisions or joints. The tube tapers slightly. A crest runs the whole visible length to the ear, represented as a thin band by the tube and a broader outer band with transverse lines to define bristles. The pricked ear is slightly hollowed, and the eye is well defined. The mouth flares to about 110°, with the upper lip running behind the standard and the lower recurved; there are no teeth, but some lip definition is given.

More of the right-hand carnyx is visible (**fig. 262c**). It too faces right, with only the lowest part of the tube concealed. There is a marked band at the tube-bell junction, with the tube plain and cylindrical below the band (partly obscured by the flag, below which it is slightly misaligned). The bell is markedly broader than the tube and expands into the head with curved lines under the chin reflecting its shape. The crest runs from the bell base to the ear; again it is bipartite, the lower thinner band having widely-spaced transverse incisions, the upper broader band more narrowly-spaced ones. Two ears are shown, the nearer hollowed for naturalism, the other in flat relief. The eye is naturalistic, with the pupils depicted and the eyebrow well defined. The mouth (lacking tongue or teeth) opens to c. 120°, with the lower lip markedly more recurved than the upper.

Dating evidence

Lippold drew parallels to the columns of Trajan and Marcus Aurelius, especially the latter, but this seems unlikely. While the Aurelian column does feature much of the material shown here, including carnyces, other earlier monuments provide better parallels for a wider range of the material, as discussed below. Opinions have varied on the dating of the Mars and Rhea Silva panel. Andreae et al. (1998, pl. 220 caption) dated it to between the late Antonine period and the early 3rd century. In this they followed

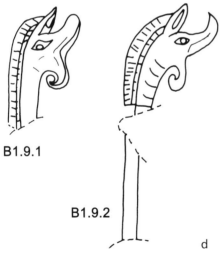

B1.9.1

B1.9.2

d

Fig. 262 B1.9 Pilaster base with trophy, Maddalena, Rome: **a** surviving front face, on display in Vatican Museums. – **b-c** details from cast in Museo delle Civilta Romana. – **d** carnyces 1-2. – (a-c photos Fraser Hunter; d drawing Tanja Romankiewicz).

Cornelius Vermeule (1957, 293 f.) who saw such images as derived from a lost sculpture group of late Hadrianic date. Walther Amelung (1908, 88 no. 36) dismissed it as »schlechte späte Arbeit«. However, others have preferred an earlier date: in discussing the mythological figures, the authors of the LIMC (II [1984] 550 no. 395a; VII [1994] 617 no. 9) suggested a date around AD 100. This is much more consistent with the weapon iconography, which has strong late Flavian parallels (a view supported by G. Spinola [1999, 286]). The furry hat is a recurring icon in Domitianic propaganda referring to Germany (e. g. on the Farnesi and Mérida theatre fragments and a range of cuirass statues; B1.4.1; B5.1; Gergel 1988, 11-16 figs 2. 6. 10; 1994, 199-203). The S-shaped horn is an unusual item, paralleled only on a group of material of late Flavian - early Trajanic date (the Uffizi pillars [B1.7], Mérida theatre frieze [B5.1]), a relief from Capua (Polito 1998, 204-207) and one from the Villa Albani (Cain 1989, pl. 226). Horned helmets are paralleled in a Domitianic context on the Uffizi pillars (Crous 1933, 80 f. type 24), the Gabii statue (B2.12) and on coins of AD 85 marking Domitian's campaigns against the Chatti (Gergel 1988, 13 fig. 4). There is nothing in the iconography to relate to Trajan's Dacian campaigns. These parallels suggest a date bracket of c. AD 83-105, most probably Domitianic.

Bibliography
Andreae et al. 1998, 20 pl. 220. – Lippold 1936, 178 f. – Spinola 1999, 286 no. 31.

B1.10 Decorated capital. – Via dei Leutari, Rome

(Current location: Rome, Capitoline Museum Tabularium)
A marble column capital decorated with Victories and trophies was found on the Via dei Leutari in the Campus Martius in 1562. Eugen von Mercklin (1927; 1962, 263 no. 625) published it in some detail (**fig. 263a-d**). The capital has a trophy on each face and Victories (mostly lost) on the corners. Each trophy has a muscle cuirass with Gorgon's head and plain bowl helmet with cheek-pieces, with crossed pairs of oval and hexagonal shields on the arms. Behind the shields are spears, vexillum standards and carnyces; the latter also feature on the shield decorations.

It has been speculated, on no particularly strong grounds, that this could have been the capital of a column which supported a colossal statue of Domitian; parts of such a statue were found in the same street (von Mercklin 1962, 263).

The carnyces
The ten carnyces are very simply depicted, with plain tubes, sometimes curving, and gaping mouths (**fig. 263e**). They lack technical details but often show quite naturalistic treatment of the eyes. In one case, perhaps two, there are ears depicted, and one of these also has a crest. Published photos are not very detailed and the object is impossible to examine as currently displayed, but others certainly lack crest and ears.

Dating evidence
On stylistic grounds von Mercklin dated it to the Flavian period (AD 70-96). It would suit Domitian's iconography following his German victories.

Bibliography
von Mercklin 1927; 1962, 263 no. 625 figs 1216-1220.

Fig. 263 B1.10 Decorated capital, Via dei Leutari, Rome: **a-d** views of the capital. – **e** the carnyces (drawn from photographs). – (a-d von Mercklin 1962, figs 1216. 1218-1220. 9, 12; e drawing Alan Braby).

Fig. 263 (continued)

Fig. 263 (continued)

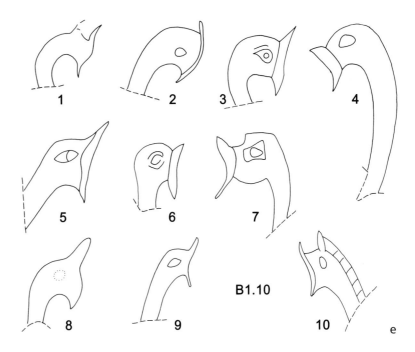

B1.11 Trajan's Forum, Rome

Trajan's Forum was one of the grandest building projects in Rome, the culmination to the development of the complex of fora which had built up over several centuries (**fig. 264**). Funded from the spoils of Trajan's Dacian Wars, one function was as an expression of the power of Rome over the barbarians and a celebration of victory. This was conveyed in the sculptural programme which adorned it, part of a series of messages and symbolism integral to the whole architectural complex. The Forum has seen extended study over the centuries, now summarised authoritatively by James Packer (1994; 1997; 2001; 2008); this account draws largely on his work.

Trajan's Dacian Wars of AD 101-102 and 105-106 marked the subjugation of an enemy who had proved problematic since the 80s and the annexation of their territory to Rome (for the wars see Lepper/Frere 1988, 36-41). The Forum complex was adorned with reminders of the conflict.

- A triple triumphal arch forming the entrance to the complex was crowned by victory sculptures, its design incorporating defeated Dacian figures.
- Throughout the complex, Dacian figures were used as supports; inscriptions (and gilt bronze groups of military standards) commemorated the legions who had fought in the campaigns, and proclaimed »EX MAN-VBIIS« – »from the spoils«, the funding source.

- The central basilica building (the Basilica Ulpia), on its southern façade had a frieze of captured Dacian weapons.
- The northern façade of the Basilica was probably the location of a narrative frieze, the Great Trajanic Frieze.
- Within a courtyard adjacent to the Basilica, on the central axis of the Forum, lay Trajan's Column, with its pedestal reliefs of captured Dacian spoils and frieze telling the story of the wars.

The only *in situ* element with carvings is the Column, which is dealt with in a separate entry owing to its complexity (B1.12). Of the other elements, we know of carnyces probably from the Basilica's southern and northern friezes and one of the triumphal arches. These will be dealt with in turn below. There are thousands of uncatalogued sculptural fragments from the Forum (Packer 1997, 287 fig. 144; 2001, xviii) and it is possible that further carnyx fragments lurk among this little-known material.

Dating evidence
The construction of the Forum took place in the period AD 106/107-112 (Packer 2001, 4).

B1.11.1 Keystone of arch with figure of grieving Dacia. – Probably from triumphal arch, Forum of Trajan

(Current location: Palazzo dei Conservatori, Rome)
Three triumphal arches (a central one and two smaller lateral ones) marked the entrance to the complex. The central arch has not been excavated, but is known from numismatic evidence and casual finds; one of the lateral arches has been excavated (Packer 1994, 178f.; 1997, 85-

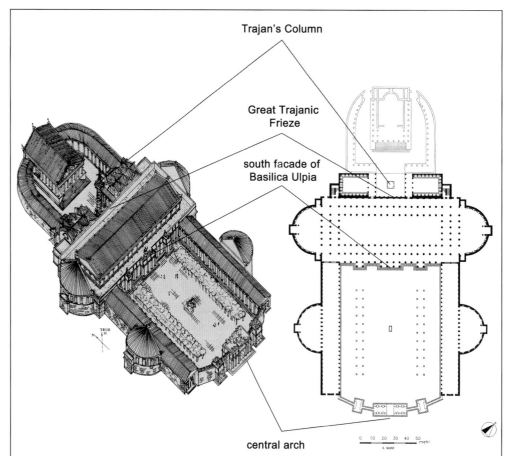

Fig. 264 B1.11 Trajan's Forum and Column. Angled view & plan, with likely locations of carnyx sculpture marked. – (Modified from Packer 2001, 3 and fig. 149A).

Trajan's Column

Great Trajanic Frieze

south facade of Basilica Ulpia

central arch

Fig. 265 B1.11.1 Keystone of arch with figure of grieving Dacia: **a** overall view. – **b** detail of the carnyx. – **c** drawing of the carnyx. – (a-b photos Fraser Hunter; c drawing Tanja Romankiewicz).

91. 415-417; 2001, 54-59). The central arch was crowned by (?gilt bronze) statues of the victorious Trajan in a chariot, flanked (inter alia) by trophies of captured arms. Its design incorporated reliefs of captive Dacians and images of victorious generals; statues of defeated, dejected Dacians were used on pedestals as architectural supports. The lateral arches probably also featured chariot groups, standards and reliefs of Dacians.

A marble keystone now in the Palazzo dei Conservatori has been argued to derive from an arch in the Forum, perhaps the central triumphal arch; its style certainly connects it to the art of the complex (Packer 1997, 377; Jones 1926, 17 f. no. 6), although Alexandre Stefan (2005, 454) argued for a Domitianic date, and the attribution to Trajan's Forum is not entirely clear-cut. The relief panel shows a grieving woman R, probably a personification of Dacia, seated on a pile of shields, her head on her L hand (both restored). Behind her are two oval shields, an axe, two spears and a carnyx (**fig. 265**).

The carnyx

The carnyx faces L. Most of the cylindrical tube (36 mm D.) is obscured, with the bell expanding only slightly (to 46 mm D.). A flat band (18 mm broad) marks the tube-bell junction; the bell-head junction is ornamented with a triple circumferential moulding. The head has a slightly raised circular eye with dished central pupil, a single forward-pointing ear, and mouth open to 180° with upturned snout and a single fang/tusk on the lower jaw. The crest runs from the forehead back to just below the

Fig. 265   (continued)

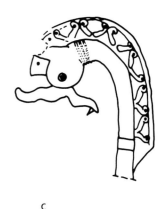

c

bell-tube junction, starting at an angle at the base. It has a raised outer border, and is decorated by opposed half S-curls, the curls at the top defined by drill-holes. This carnyx shows an understanding of technical features like the junction pieces, but the head tends towards naturalism, much like the ones on the Column; the crest decoration is also a variant of that found on the Column (B1.12).

Bibliography

Jones 1926, 17 f. no. 6. – Packer 1997, 377.

B1.11.2 Fragments of weapons frieze. – Southern façade of Basilica Ulpia?

(Current location: Trajan's Market, inv. no. 399, 436)
Considerable quantities of marble fragments from a series of panels bearing weapons friezes are known from the Forum, largely uncatalogued (**fig. 266a**; Packer 1997, 59 fig. 144) although progress is being made (Ungaro/Milella 1995; Ungaro 1994; 1995; Ungaro/Milella/Lalle 1995; Ungaro/Messa 1989). The style and subject matter is closely similar to that of the Column's pedestal, but in

higher relief (Ungaro/Messa 1989). Their location has been debated, but James Packer argued they would fit best on the south side of the Basilica Ulpia: **figure 266b** shows his reconstruction of their likely original impact. Others have placed them on the pedestal of an equestrian statue of Trajan in the centre of the courtyard (Meneghini 2001, fig. 5). Two of the fragments published to date feature carnyces.

B1.11.2.1 Inv. 436

This fragment (930 mm × 650 mm × 200 mm) preserves no original edges. It features a carnyx overlying two overlapping shields, one oval and one round, each with scale decoration; a quiver and part of a bow are also depicted (**fig. 267a-b**). The initial publication (Ungaro/Messa 1989, fig. 11) misidentified it as a dragon-headed club, but subsequent publications correctly identified it.

The carnyx

The upper tube, bell and head of the carnyx are preserved. Published photos indicate a ribbed bell and upper tube

with bands at the tube-bell and bell-head junctions. A crest (with top and bottom borders, decorated with saltire and bar motifs) runs the full visible length of the bell and tube, stopping on the forehead. There is a single ear, a round eye and a mouth open at about 120°. The lower jaw has a single fang; the jaw edges are serrated to indicate rows of smaller teeth.

Bibliography

Ungaro/Messa 1989, fig. 11. – Ungaro/Milella 1995, 172 f. – Ungaro/Milella/Lalle 1995, fig. 8.

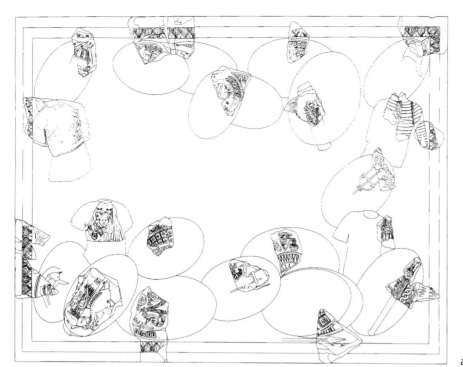

Fig. 266 B1.11.2 Weapons panel fragments from the Basilica Ulpia, Trajan's Forum: **a** reconstructed panel. – **b** reconstruction of the south façade of the Basilica Ulpia. – (a Ungaro/Milella 1995, 138; b Packer 2001, fig. 159).

a

b

B1.11.2.2 Inv. 399

Fragment 399 is illustrated only in small-scale drawings of a reconstructed panel, and thus details are not certain. It includes part of the edge moulding, with what is interpreted as part of a carnyx overlying an oval shield (fig. 267c).

The carnyx

The upper tube and lower bell of the carnyx are shown. A decorated crest is shown running the full visible length, apparently with a saltire and bar design as on B1.11.2.1. Only a small portion of the carnyx is preserved.

Bibliography

Ungaro/Milella 1995, 138. – Ungaro/Milella/Lalle 1995, fig. 9.

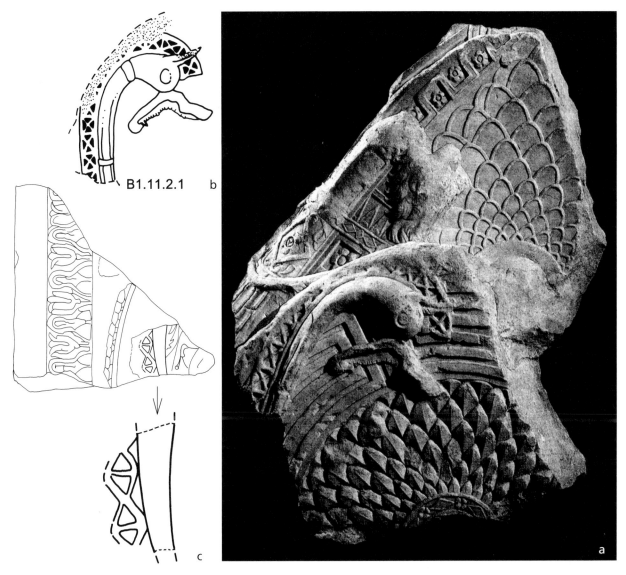

Fig. 267 Weapons panel fragments with carnyces: **a** B1.11.2.1 (fragment 436). – **b** drawing of carnyx. – **c** B1.11.2.2 (fragment 399), with detail. – (a Ungaro/Milella 1995, 173; b drawing Tanja Romankiewicz; c redrawn by Alan Braby from Ungaro/Milella 1995, 138).

B1.11.3 The Great Trajanic Frieze

(Current location: Arch of Constantine, Rome, middle passageway)

The surviving panels of the Great Trajanic Frieze are built into the middle passageway of the 4th-century Arch of Constantine. This eclectic arch was built with spolia from earlier monuments, some with the portraits recarved in Constantinian style. It has been plausibly argued that the selection of the monuments for reuse conveyed a deliberate message, as those chosen were from the »good emperors« of the 2nd century with whom Constantine wished to be associated (Kleiner 1992, 444f. 454f.).

Eight marble slabs survive today in the Arch of Constantine; the original frieze would have been over twice this length. Most make up a battle scene between Romans and Da-cians; on the left is a scene of the Emperor entering Rome (*adventus*). The origin and dating of the panels has seen extended debate (summarised in Leander Touati 1987, 91-95; see also Stefan 2005, 472-477, arguing for a Domitianic date), but they are now generally held to come from Trajan's Forum. Their position within the Forum has also been debated, but Packer's authoritative study provides the most likely answer. He saw the Frieze positioned on the attic of the northern façade of the Basilica Ulpia, opposite the Column (Packer 1994, 168f.; 2001, 198). In this position he argued it would serve to amplify and emphasise individual scenes from the Column, which was hard to »read« because of its spiral format (Packer 1994, 168f.; 1997, 113-115. 445; 2001, 72. 198 fig. 165, here **fig. 268a**).

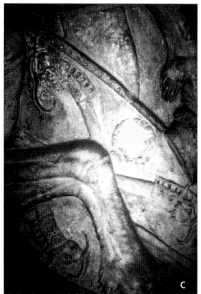

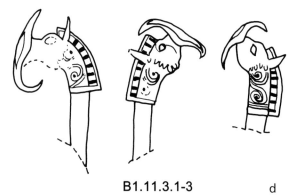

B1.11.3.1-3

d

Fig. 268 B1.11.3 Great Trajanic Frieze: **a** likely relationship of the Frieze to the Column. – **b** combat scene with carnyces on shield, bottom right. – **c** detail of fallen shield with carnyces. – **d** the carnyces. – (a Packer 2001, fig. 165; b Leander Touati 1987, pl. 3; c photo Kristian Göransson; d drawing Tanja Romankiewicz).

Carnyces feature as shield ornament in a panel (slab VI) of a combat scene in which Trajan (his features later recarved as Constantine) on horseback tramples a fallen Dacian (**fig. 268b**). Others flee or beg for mercy; one has abandoned his shield in the R corner, and it is on this which the carnyces feature (**fig. 268c**; Leander Touati 1987, 22 f. pls 3; 13, 1; Kleiner 1992, 221 fig. 185). They were incorrectly identified in the main publication as »dragon heads on poles« (Leander Touati 1987, 51).

The carnyces

The oval shield, partly obscured by a horse, has a raised border with dot decoration, and a central spine with recurved ends in the form of raptor heads, possibly eagles. It is decorated with three carnyces (**fig. 268d**) and a twisted-hoop torc with zoomorphic (?lion-head) terminals grasping a joining ring. The three carnyces are arranged irregularly rather than symmetrically for compositional reasons, to make them more visible. All are closely similar. Only the upper parts are visible, and the head angle varies from near-straight (c. 20°) to 90°, again for compositional reasons. The tube, where visible, is slightly conical and plain. A raised band marks the junction with the bell, which is rather short, squat, and bears flat-band tendril decoration based around two drilled holes. The bell-head junction is marked by a fringe of hair; the heads are naturalistically modelled with musculature, vertical ear, eye (often with prominent brow), and gaping mouth open to 180° with the ends markedly curved back. The crest (running from bell base to forehead) is decorated with a series of vertical rectangular incisions, creating the effect of bristles.

Bibliography

Kleiner 1992, 220-223. 444-455. – Leander Touati 1987, esp. 22-24 pls 3; 13, 1.

B1.12 Trajan's Column. – Forum of Trajan, Rome

Trajan's Column lies in the heart of Trajan's Forum in Rome (**fig. 143**). The column sits on a substantial rectangular pedestal and is topped by a platform which once supported a statue of Trajan. It is decorated with a spiral frieze telling the story of Trajan's Dacian Wars (of AD 101-102 and 105-106); an internal staircase gives access to the top. The pedestal contains a chamber with antechamber, and is carved externally with Dacian spolia. An inscription over the doorway records the dedication of the Column to Trajan in AD 113; it says (somewhat opaquely) that the column marks the height of the material which was cleared to make the Forum. (The account here draws primarily on Lepper/Frere 1988; Coulston 1990; Kleiner 1992, 212-220; Claridge 1993; Packer 1994; 1997; 2001).

The Column had three main functions. The first was as a marker. As the inscription indicates, it was a mark of height connected with Trajan's Forum; part of the Quirinal hill had to be cut away to accommodate the grandiose building project, and from the summit visitors could admire the expanse of the new construction in the heart of the city. It also acted as an axis-marker for the whole Forum development. The second was as a tomb (and shrine) for Trajan, and later his wife; the third was as a commemoration of the great events of Trajan's campaigns in Dacia. This victory symbolism was carried not just by the Column but by other friezes within the Forum complex, including one facing the Column (B1.11.3). Although it now stands isolated, this gives a misleading impression of how it was originally experienced (**figs 264; 268a**).

There is some debate over whether the Column was always intended by Trajan as his burial place; prior to his death the room within the pedestal may have been a votive chamber or contained a display of captured weapons. More problematic has been the question of the frieze. The inscription makes no mention of the Dacian Wars, yet the sculpture is the most prominent part of the Column: this, the tight timescales for completing the whole project in the period c. 108-113, and some other problems have led to disquiet over its place in the sequence. It has been argued (e. g. Claridge 1993) that the Column was conceived as a plain monument to mark the building of Trajan's Forum. The captured arms on the pedestal commemorated the Dacian Wars because booty from these paid for the Forum. After Trajan's death it was used as his burial place with, some 10-15 years later, the frieze being commissioned by Hadrian to commemorate Trajan, both as an act of pietas and a way of reinforcing his connections with his adoptive father.

Others are less convinced. Frank Lepper and Shepperd Frere (1988, 19-26) viewed the Column as a unitary concept, and James Packer argued that the whole Forum complex was a grand scheme in which the various elements integrated to tell a range of stories (summarised most conveniently in Packer 1994). While accepting that the construction may not have been finished until after Trajan's death, he saw the design as unitary; for instance, parallels between the Column reliefs and those elsewhere in the complex suggest they were part of an overall concept. For current purposes the details are largely irrelevant as carnyces feature only on the pedestal, which commentators agree was an integral part of the design, and not on the frieze.

While the Column's frieze has seen extended discussion and debate from historians, art historians and archaeologists, the pedestal has been rather neglected because it is not part of the main narrative of the wars. Yet the pedestal carving is of strikingly high quality (Claridge 1993, 11-13): »… a still-life study in stone of captured weaponry« (Coulston 1989, 34). At the top corners sit four eagles holding garlands, while the moulding at the base of the column is carved as a victor's laurel wreath. The sides of the pedestal, between top and bottom mouldings, are occupied by the sculptured frieze. The SE side with the door has an inscribed panel supported by two Victories above it. The rest of the four sides are taken up with Dacian and Sarmatian weapons and armour. (Sarmatian weapons appear because a Sarmatian tribe, the Roxolani, assisted the Dacians in the first war, providing the heavily armoured cavalry represented in scenes xxxi and xxxvii; see Lepper/Frere 1988, 78-80; Tacitus, *Histories* I.79.) Jon Coulston (1990, 294) commented that the pedestal reliefs broke away from standard weapons friezes in their accurate representation of barbarian equipment and absence of Roman items.

There has been debate over which items are Dacian and which Sarmatian. This can partly be resolved by comparison with the reliefs on the frieze itself. Some items are found with Dacians alone, notably curved battle-scythes (falces) and dragon standards (dracones), while scale armour and conical helmets of »Spangenhelme« type (Feugère 1994, 147) are worn by Sarmatians. Similar helmets are worn by Roman auxiliary archers (e.g. scene lxx), but these are invented figure-types developed from the spolia on the base (Bishop/Coulston 2006, 4). Other material is harder to assign. The Phrygian-style helmets (Feugère 1994, 30-32) are barbarian, although whether actually used in the Dacian Wars or simply a stock artistic type is unclear. There are two occurrences of an unusual lamellar armour, unattested in use on the frieze, which presumably was a barbarian type. The long swords could be Dacian or Sarmatian; their style is unlike Roman ones. Where Dacians are shown with swords on the frieze they tend to be short ones, while Sarmatians have long ones, but the Dacian leader Decebalus carries a long sword in scene xciii. There are similar mismatches between pedestal and frieze in a number of cases: some weaponry shown on the base does not feature in Dacian hands in the frieze (such as helmets, chain mail and carnyces). This arises at least in part from artistic convention, with Dacians being depicted unarmoured to make them more recognisable (Lepper/Frere 1988, 272); the Great Trajanic Frieze uses similar iconography (Leander Touati 1987, 42). Thus, for chain mail, we cannot be sure whether it was intended to represent Roman or barbarian material. This has misled some authors. Ortwin Gamber (1964) took the Column depictions literally, seeing the Dacians as being rather simply equipped and attributing most of the weaponry to Sarmatians. He provided a detailed genealogy for the various elements, arguing much of it was acquired from the steppe-peoples. However, his wide-ranging and eclectic approach is very much that of the armour enthusiast, and is rather uncritical in its use of the sources. Given that the Column sculptors were not creating an armour manual but a piece of propaganda, it is unwise to place over-much reliance on the detail.

Other items are shown on the frieze in both Dacian and Roman hands: bows and arrows, oval shields and vexillum standards. Some assistance in interpretation comes from the trophy scene separating the two wars (scene lxxviii). This has nothing distinctively Roman in it, but does feature oval shields, *dracones*, vexillum standards, spears, conical helmets, *falces*, scale armour, axes, arrows in quivers and long swords. Thus in the internal vocabulary of the Column these items are best interpreted as barbarian. To this should probably be added the battering ram on the SE face. This would at first sight seem more a piece of Classical military gear, but Dacians are shown using one on scene xxxii. They may have acquired the habit from contact with the Hellenistic world, or from Rome itself: in an earlier treaty with Decebalus, Domitian had supplied Roman military technology to the new client kingdom (Lepper/Frere 1988, 37. 80). This leaves only the tubae, normally seen as a Roman instrument, to explain away. Given that no other certainly Roman items appear, it may be that this (fairly simple) instrument type was also used by the Dacians. This must remain speculative, but we can perhaps modify Coulston's view slightly to state that there is nothing which must be Roman in the pedestal friezes.

The carnyces are best connected with Dacians rather than Sarmatians in this case: neither group uses them on the frieze, but elsewhere in the Forum the carnyx is connected with Dacians (notably on an arch keystone, B1.11.1).

Considerable detail was invested in the depictions, although some of this was artistic rather than technical. Classical motifs were used widely to adorn the Dacian weaponry: these can only be seen as space-fillers familiar to the artist, rather than any attempt to depict reality. Examples include rosettes, acanthus ornament, lion heads, laurel wreaths, peltae, sphinxes, and ?Mars carrying a trophy. Similarly some Dacian shields on the frieze carry Roman devices (Coulston 1989, 33 f.). However, the technical details are generally accurate (Bishop/Coulston 2006, 4). This mix-and-match approach has implications for the carnyx depictions.

The carnyces

Carnyces occur only on the pedestal reliefs, on all sides. The monument was examined first-hand from the surrounding plaza and from the cast in the Victoria & Albert Museum, London. This is one of the series of casts made for Napoleon III in the 1860s and acquired by the V&A in 1864 (reg. no. 1864-128; see Lepper/Frere 1988, 1; Coulston 1990, 291). The casts now offer substantially more detail than the original Column, thanks to the effects of modern pollution (Coulston 1989, 31).

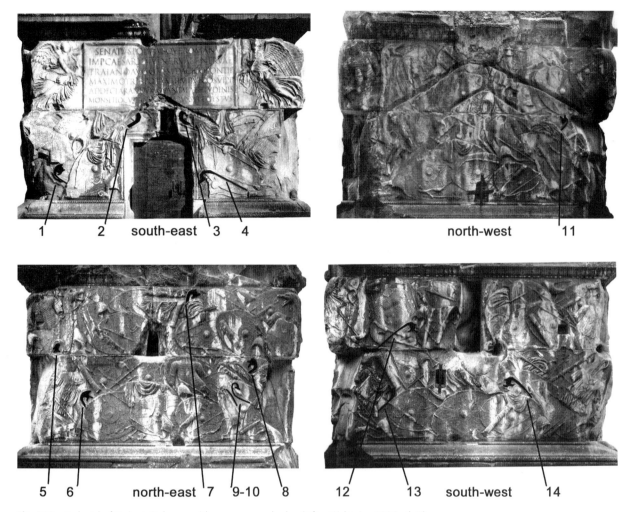

Fig. 269 Pedestal of Trajan's Column, with carnyces marked. – (After Cichorius 1896, pl. III).

Although there is considerable variety among the carnyces, a lot is likely to arise for artistic rather than technical reasons: the depictions can be seen as variants of a common theme. The key characteristics of carnyces on Trajan's Column are as follows. The tube is straight and near-cylindrical, expanding slightly towards the top; the cupped mouthpiece is in line with the tube. The tube is segmental, typically in two parts. The bell curves smoothly into the head, which has ears, eyes and a markedly flared mouth. A crest normally runs from the bell base or the very top of the tube onto the forehead. The crest and bell are always decorated. The head curves round dramatically, but this is likely to be constrained by the available space rather than reflecting a genuine feature or (for instance) a flexible, organic bell.

The artists have conveyed the basic sense of a carnyx, including a wide range of technical details such as the segmented tube and the bell-head junction, while the bell often has a supporting band at mid-point, much like the Kappel carnyx (**fig. 106**). This degree of technical detail does suggest they had genuine carnyces to work from.

However, the naturalistic training of the Roman artist took over: in the modelling they became truly zoomorphic, with fleshy lips, musculature and sometimes hair on the head. There are also artistic concerns in spacing, especially with the head position (seen clearly in 9-10, where they are fitted onto shield decoration). The decorative motifs used have no significance in terms of understanding how the instruments looked as they are general space-filling ones which recur in other contexts: for instance, pelta friezes also occur on helmet crests. Thus, while confirming details of the overall structure of carnyces (most usefully the detail of the mouthpiece end) they are not technical drawings, but artistic interpretations.

The individual depictions are summarised in **Appendix 2** (**tab. 80**). **Figure 269** shows their location on the pedestal, while they are illustrated in **figures 270-271**.

Dating evidence

While the date of the frieze has been debated, the pedestal reliefs are accepted as part of the original form of the Column, constructed in AD 108-113.

Fig. 270 Details of carnyces on Trajan's Column (from cast in V&A Museum). – (Photos Fraser Hunter).

Bibliography
Cichorius 1896; 1900. – Claridge 1993. – Coulston 1989;
1990. – Gamber 1964. – Kleiner 1992, 212-220. – Lep-
per/Frere 1988. – Packer 1994; 1997; 2001.

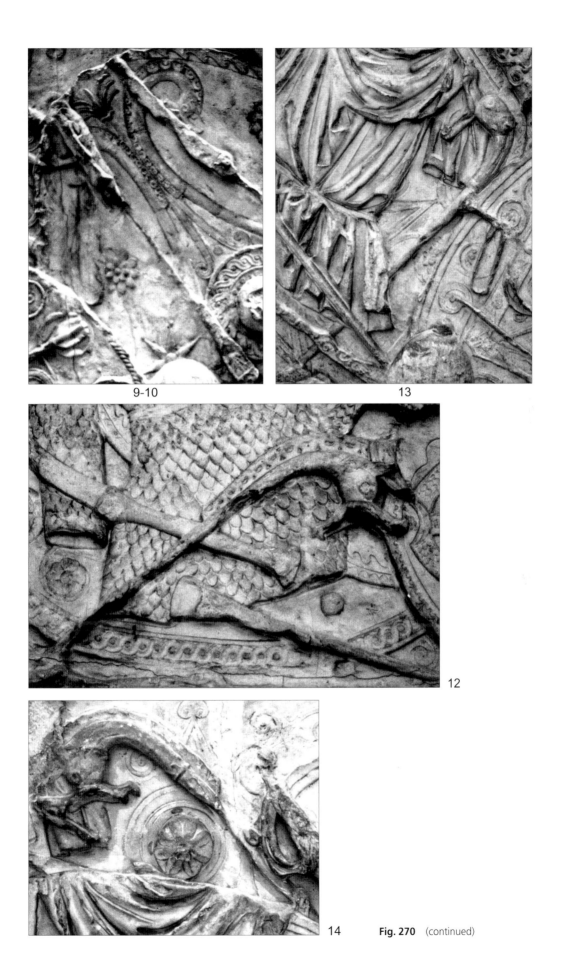

9-10

13

12

14   **Fig. 270** (continued)

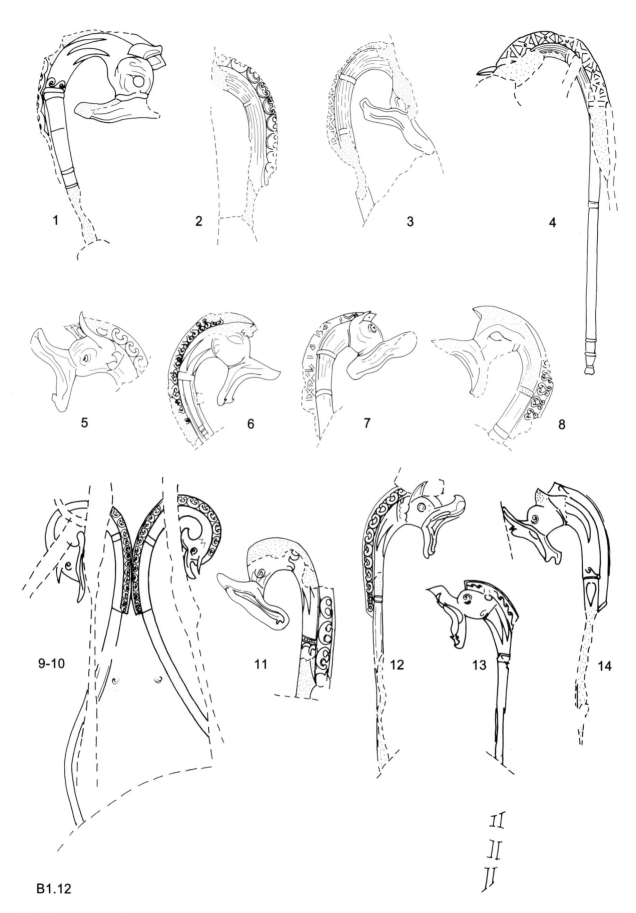

B1.12

Fig. 271 Drawings of carnyces on Trajan's Column. – (Drawing Tanja Romankiewicz).

B1.13 Hadrian's Villa

Hadrian ordered the building of a magnificent villa complex some 30 km NE of Rome, near Tivoli. Among the rich and varied sculptural decoration, two trophies with carnyces are recorded.

B1.13.1 Statue or column base. – Hadrian's Villa, Tivoli

(Current location: lost)

There are antiquarian records of a decorated base, now lost but recorded by Agostino Penna in the early 19th century (**fig. 272**). I have not seen this source, but the image is reproduced by Pierre Gusman (1904, 243. 250 fig. 408) and discussed by Gilbert Charles Picard (1957, 420) and Jutta Pinkerneil (1983, 118).

The cuboidal base (size not given) has mouldings top and bottom and a flat top to take a statue or column. Only one face seems to be carved. This shows a trophy with a bound male captive standing below it. The trophy has a bowl helmet with cheekpieces and a standard muscle cuirass, with the belt from a sword scabbard slung over it. The arms have crossed oval and hexagonal shields, with spears and a range of standards behind – a vexillum, an eagle and a hand with an imago below. The captive is bearded and wears baggy trousers, a long tunic and a cloak. In front of him is a hat, identified by Picard as an Armenian tiara. At the base of the trophy is a pile of weaponry: oval shields, bow and quiver of arrows, animal-hilted sword, single-edged axe, falx, spears, sword, and a carnyx.

Much of the iconography ties in perfectly to that of Trajan's Dacian War: the captive, the falx, the carnyx and the single-edged axe. The archery equipment could be read as a reference either to Dacia or areas further east (where the tiara leads), suggesting a commemoration of Trajan's final victories in the east against the Parthians. The context indicates that Hadrian was honouring the victories of his predecessor, either with an appropriate piece of architecture or as the base for an honorific statue.

The carnyx

The carnyx is known only from a small-scale engraving, but the amount of detail conveyed in this suggests it was a detailed depiction, not dissimilar to the detailed Trajanic images from his Column and Forum. The lower part of the tube is hidden, but the upper part includes at least one tube junction plus a junction with the bell. Tube and bell are shown as cylindrical, only expanding when the head starts. A vandyked pattern decorates the bell. The head, bent through c. 45°, has a slightly open mouth; an ear is indicated, slightly out of position, and a crest runs from the top of the head down to around the bell base.

Dating evidence

Gusman (1904, 15-17) recorded brick stamps of the early 120s and a few of the 130s, but the base could have been brought in rather than being integral to the design, if it was for a statue rather than a column. It is likely to have been erected while Trajan's successes were still fresh, and when Hadrian had a political need to commemorate them, so a date early in Hadrian's reign, c. AD 117-125, is most likely.

Bibliography

Gusman 1904, 243. 250 fig. 408. – Picard 1957, 420. – Pinkerneil 1983, 118.

Fig. 272   B1.13.1 Statue or column base, Hadrian's Villa, Tivoli. – (Gusman 1904, fig. 408).

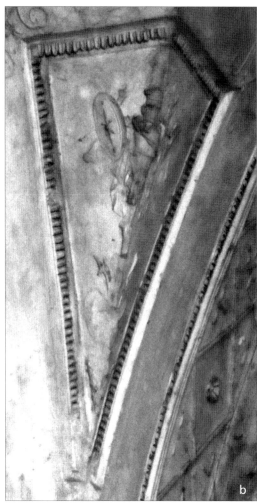

B1.13.2 Stucco with trophy. – Hadrian's Villa, Tivoli, bath complex

A large vaulted room at the south end of the *frigidarium* in the Grand Baths at Tivoli preserves part of its stucco decoration (**fig. 273a**). Two of the vault springers (in the SW and NW corners) are decorated with trophies within a frame; the NW one features a carnyx. The stucco decoration has been discussed in general in the literature, but the trophies do not appear to have been discussed (Wadsworth 1924, 61-63 pl. XVII, 2; Wirth 1929, 141 pl. 6; 1968, 70-72 fig. 31; Mielsch 1975, 85f. 166f. no. K107).

SW trophy: damaged helmet with ring-knob; plain muscle cuirass and cloak; oval and hexagonal shield on left arm (as viewed); two hexagonal shields on right arm, one with thunderbolt decoration, one with hooked lines. At the base are two oval shields, two tubae, a pelta shield and a furry helmet.

NW trophy: damaged horned helmet; plain muscle cuirass with cloak; on left arm, oval shield an sword in scabbard; on right arm, unusual bowed U-shaped shield with a

Fig. 273 B1.13.2 Stucco with trophy, Grand Baths, Hadrian's Villa, Tivoli: **a** surviving stucco decoration. – **b** detail of trophy. – **c** the carnyx. – (a Wirth 1929, pl. 26; b photo Fraser Hunter; c drawing Alan Braby).

draco standard behind it. At the base are two oval shields, a sword in a scabbard, a carnyx and a tuba.

The draco and carnyx are typical of Trajanic iconography concerning the Dacians, and this is the likely intention here. The furry helmet and the horned helmet are more often associated with Domitian's campaigns against the Germans (e.g. B1.4.1, B1.9, B5.1); their depiction here shows the iconography was current for a generation after its main occurrence in the late 80s/early 90s. Hadrian spent time on the German frontier in AD 121-122 (Birley 1997, 113f.), which might explain the German connection, or it may simply represent reuse of an earlier iconographic model.

The carnyx

The carnyx faces left from the left side of the base (**fig. 273b-c**). Only the upper (slightly curved) tube and bell and the head are visible; they are stylised and angular. A crest runs the full visible length with a series of indents to give the effect of bristles. It has a single ear, an eye and a gaping mouth (open to c. 135°).

Dating evidence

The evidence for building sequence and stylistic arguments are argued to put the stucco late in Hadrian's reign, perhaps even after his death; c. AD 135-140 (Mielsch 1975, 86. 167; Wirth 1968, 71 f.).

Bibliography

Mielsch 1975, 85 f. 166 f. no. K107. – Wadsworth 1924, 61-63 pl. XVII, 2. – Wirth 1929, 141 pl. 6; 1968, 70-72 fig. 31.

B1.14 Column of Marcus Aurelius

The Column of Marcus Aurelius still stands *in situ* in the Piazza Colonna in Rome, west of the modern via del Corso and the ancient via Flaminia (**fig. 274a**). It lay on the Campus Martius within a colonnaded space facing the via Flaminia with a temple of the divine Marcus at the other end; nearby was the (plain) Column of Antoninus Pius (Brilliant 2002, 501 f.; Kleiner 1992, 295; Ferris 2009). The frieze on the column tells the story of the struggles against Sarmatians and Germans in the Marcomannic Wars on the Danube, a series of campaigns conducted by Marcus Aurelius between AD 167 and 180 (see Birley 1987, 148 f. 155-179. 183. 189 f. 206-210. 249-255). The idea of a column with spiral frieze drew heavily on Trajan's Column, as did much of the general iconography, but the detail is substantially different in both content and style. For instance, it is noticeable that the treatment of the barbarians is much more violent on the Aurelian than the Trajanic column (Kleiner 1992, 300; Ferris 2000, 88-98; 2009, 130). It also learned technically from some of the problems of Trajan's Column: to make it more visible there are fewer spirals, the figures are in higher relief, and there is a more marked use of vertical correspondences to make key points rather than relying on historical narrative (Kleiner 1992, 295; Brilliant 2002, 500). There is some debate over its dating, but it is generally seen as an act of *pietas* by Commodus to commemorate the campaigns of his father after the latter's death in 180.

The pedestal is now plain, but early engravings of two sides show one decorated with Victories bearing garlands, the other with barbarians submitting to the emperor (Petersen/von Domaszewski/Calderini 1896, 4 f. 9; Kleiner 1992, 300 f.; Scheid/Huet 2000, figs 138-141). The carnyces feature in trophies flanking a scene of Victory inscribing a shield (**fig. 274b**). Like Trajan's Column, this scene probably divides two campaigns, in this case between the first foreign campaign of AD 173-175 and the second campaign of AD 177-180 (Morris 1952, 40; the early years of the conflict, spent expelling the barbarians from the empire, were unlikely to be marked as victorious campaigns). Carnyces do not feature in active service.

Study of the Column is more difficult than that of Trajan's Column: not only is the frieze difficult to inspect in detail *in situ*, but it has seen less study than the earlier column. There is no series of casts; the available photographs are all taken *in situ*, and the curve of the column (and greater depth of relief than on Trajan's Column) means the views are liable to distortion. Jas Elsner (2000, 255-259) has discussed the biases of perception which arise from this; as the illustrations in the basic publication by

Fig. 274 B1.14 Column of Marcus Aurelius: **a** the Column. – **b** the Victory scene. – **c** the carnyces. – (a photo Fraser Hunter; b Depeyrot 2010, 240; c drawing Tanja Romankiewicz).

Fig. 274 (continued)

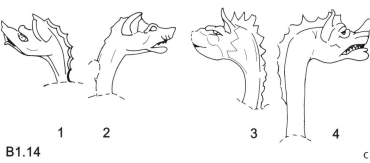

1 **2** **3** **4**

B1.14

c

E. Petersen, A. von Domaszewski and G. Calderini (1896) demonstrate, objects can look very different (or show very different details) from different perspectives. In the current case, while the monument has been examined first-hand through binoculars, this is a poor substitute for detailed autopsy of the carvings. The main source used here was Petersen/von Domaszewski/Calderini (1896), supplemented by C. Caprino et al. (1955). The former is encyclopaedic in its coverage, much like Conrad Cichorius's (1896; 1900) plates of Trajan's Column, and the overlap between plates allows some assessment of objects from different angles; for all the caveats, it provides a good source to work from. The Victory scene separates scenes LV and LVI. It shows Victory facing R, writing on a shield; she is flanked by trophies. That on the L comprises a furry hat and furry cloak, with a brooch on its R shoulder. At the base are a hexagonal and three oval shields. The left arm has a crossed round and oval shield; behind it (from L) are a double-axe, carnyx, lituus or tuba, and spear. Below the shields are four square-ended shafts, although they cannot be lined

up directly with the items above. The right arm has two crossed oval shields with (from L) a spear, carnyx and axe of uncertain form. Victory's wing partly obscures the area below the shield, but there are at least two shafts.

The right trophy comprises a tunic and fringed cloak with an Attic helmet with ring finial, cheekguards, modelled ears and face mask. Five oval shields and a domed helmet lie at the base. The left arm has a round and oval shield; behind (from L) are spear, carnyx, double-axe and tuba. The cloak conceals the area below the shields. The right arm has crossed hexagonal shields, with behind (from L) a tuba, double-axe, carnyx and spear.

The carnyces

Each arm of each trophy bears a carnyx (**fig. 274c**). These are clearly carnyces rather than draco standards. The crests are typical for the former but not the latter, and the tubes are shown as cylindrical and solid, with straight shafts and squared ends below the shields; there is no hint of the drapery which would be expected with a draco standard.

All four carnyces are variations around a theme. The heads are remarkably zoomorphic with musculature and skin folds, teeth, in one case nostrils, prominent brows, well-modelled eyes and hollowed ears. Although all have a spiky crest, they look more like wolves than boars. The mouths are only slightly open, and the heads are roughly perpendicular to the cylindrical tube. No junctions are shown. They are numbered from left to right in **figure 274c**.

Dating evidence

There has been some debate over the date of the Column, but the current consensus dating is to the reign of Commodus, AD 180-192 (Brilliant 2002, 501).

Bibliography

Brilliant 2002. – Caprino et al. 1955, pl. XXXV. – Kleiner 1992, 295-301. – Morris 1952. – Petersen/von Domaszewski/Calderini 1896, pls 63-65 (also partly visible on pl. 71). – Scheid/Huet 2000.

B1.15 Sarcophagus with battle scenes. – Portonaccio, Rome

(Current location: Museo Nazionale Romano, inv. no. 112327)

The Portonaccio sarcophagus is the finest of a series of late Antonine battle sarcophagi ornamented with scenes of combat between Romans and barbarians (**fig. 148**; Koch/Sichtermann 1982, 90-92). They relate to the Marcomannic Wars, and presumably held high-ranking officers who had fought (and often died) in these conflicts; there are close stylistic parallels to the Column of Marcus Aurelius (Kleiner 1992, 301). As Per Gustaf Hamberg

(1945, 172) rightly said, they »may be regarded as a private triumphal monument« at a time when the emperor had a monopoly on more public expressions of victory. The following account draws primarily on the studies by Hamberg (1945, 176-179), Diana Kleiner (1992, 301), L. Musso (1985) and first-hand study of the piece.

Portonaccio lies on the Via Tiburtina outside Rome. The marble sarcophagus is decorated on three sides, with a decorated lid. The front has the main battle scene, with the deceased depicted as the commander leading his

Fig. 275   B1.15 Portonaccio sarcophagus with battle scenes: **a** left trophy. – **b** right trophy. – **c** detail of carnyces in left trophy. – **d** detail of carnyces in right trophy. – **e** the carnyces. – (a-d photos Fraser Hunter; e drawing Tanja Romankiewicz).

Fig. 275 (continued)

forces against the barbarians. He is on horseback, raising his spear to strike a barbarian. In the midst of the melée he is distinguished by his greater size, plumed helmet and muscle cuirass. His portrait has not been completed, suggesting the piece was a stock one waiting to be commissioned which was required more rapidly than was thought (although Hamberg [1945, 176] saw it as later deliberate damage). The scene is flanked by trophies which harbour the carnyces of prime interest here (**fig. 275a-b**). On the left side, Roman soldiers lead two bound male barbarian captives across a pontoon bridge (Musso 1985, 179); the right side shows two barbarians standing in front of a pile of hexagonal and oval shields pleading for clemency from a Roman commander while his troops look on (Musso 1985, 178). The front of the lid has three scenes. In the centre is the marriage of the deceased; to the left, his wife bathes their first child (other interpretations are possible), while on the right the deceased sits on a curule chair receiving the submission of barbarians.

The main battle scene appears a complex mass of bodies, but there are patterns within it (Hamberg 1945, 173 pl. 40). The Romans are visually dominant although they are outnumbered, forming a compact group in the upper part of the frieze. To simplify matters for viewers the protagonists are standardised, and would doubtless originally have been coloured differently. The Romans are armoured, with helmets and either lorica segmentata or scale armour; they wield swords or spears, and carry oval shields. The barbarians wear no armour; they fight only with spears (as far as can be seen), and carry hexagonal or oval hide-shaped shields. Both sides have infantry and cavalry. The Romans hold a series of standards at the top of the scene: from the left, draco, vexillum, aquila, house-shaped, and boar, the latter perhaps a captured barbarian standard as one features in the left trophy. The barbarians appear to be Germans rather than Sarmatians: there are no distinctive Sarmatian items, such as scale armour or archery equipment (with the caveat of the ?quivers on the trophies).

The two trophies differ in detail. Both are defined on two levels: the main foreground element, which is very three-dimensional, with further equipment defined in low relief on the background. The left-hand trophy comprises a belted tunic with a cloak tied round the shoulders; it is capped by a domed helmet with cheekpieces, the bowl topped with vertical laurel wreath around a recumbent lion. In front stands a barbarian couple, with a bowl helmet behind their legs. The arm on the left has an oval shield with a circular hole cut in each terminal. Behind it is a carnyx and another broken item. The right arm bears a round shield with Medusa device; over it hangs an eagle-hilted sword in its scabbard, and behind it a carnyx and another broken item. In the background are two more carnyces, a tuba, curved horn, animal (?boar) standard, spears, some nondescript slightly curved shafts, and another oval shield; on the very corner is either a quiver or a scabbard. This material can all be classed as barbarian with the exception of the tuba, eagle-hilted sword, round shield and helmet.

The right trophy is made up of a cloak topped by a shallow bowl helmet with cheek-pieces and face mask; a decorative device on top is lost. Again a barbarian couple stand at the foot, with a griffin-protome helmet between them; the man's hair is in a Suebian knot, while the woman's right breast is bare. On the left arm is a hexagonal shield (cut-outs top and bottom make it hide-shaped); behind are an oval hide-shaped shield, two carnyces, a ?double-headed axe and a broken shaft. The right arm has an oval shield, its ends bilobate, with a carnyx and some broken shafts. Behind lie a tuba, spears, a double-headed axe and some poorly-defined curved objects; a motif on the very corner may either be a quiver or a scabbard. Apart from the helmet, tuba and axe, all this could be barbarian.

This is a virtuoso piece of sculpture, with much of the relief so deeply undercut it is almost detached; this has made it vulnerable, with a number of the items in the trophies missing large fragments. The artist was an inventive one, which should make us cautious in the interpretation of detail. Classical decoration has been lavished on the shields in the trophies, and they are also unusual shapes; hide-shaped shields are known, at least in the British Iron Age (Stead 1991c, 11-21), but we cannot be sure that this is not just artistic licence, especially with the strange forms of the oval shields. Equally there may be structural reasons for some of the forms: the highly-bent heads of most of the carnyces allowed them to be supported against the tube or other items, making them stronger.

The carnyces

The left trophy has two carnyces in the foreground (1-2) and two in the back (3-4); the right trophy has three in the foreground (5-7; **fig. 257c-e**). Numbers run from left to right. All bar no. 3 are similar in character, with cylindrical tubes and bells leading into highly recurved heads (probably to allow the mouth to be supported against the tube for strength); 6 has a sinuous S-curve to the bell and head. A saw-tooth (or similar) crest runs up the bell and head of all except 5. The heads are simple, with eyes but no ears and wide-open mouths. While straight pole/tube sections are shown below the trophies, it is unclear which belong to carnyces; however, there is no indication of a curved mouthpiece section. Carnyx 3 (on the background) differs in having a head perpendicular to the tube, a more markedly expanded bell and a less gaping mouth: in many ways this is a more typical carnyx, and the unusual shapes of the others probably owe more to artistry than reality.

Dating evidence

This series of sarcophagi are dated to the late Antonine period by their iconography and style (notably their connections to the Column of Marcus Aurelius); for the type as a whole, Guntram Koch and Hellmut Sichtermann (1982, 90-92) suggested a date range of c. AD 160-200. Kleiner (1992, 301f.) gave a date of 180-190 for Portonaccio, making it directly comparable to the Column, but given that the wars were underway in the mid 170s it is felt that the dating bracket should be extended, and range of AD 175-190 is taken here.

Bibliography

Hamberg 1945, 176-179. – Kleiner 1992, 301. – Musso 1985.

B1.16 Column base with Victory and trophy from Tetrarchic arch

(Current location: Boboli Gardens, Florence)
In the Boboli Gardens in Florence are preserved two decorated marble pedestals. Since the sixteenth century they have supported monumental statues of Dacians taken from Trajan's Forum, but they were intended for columns from a Tetrarchic arch in Rome, generally identified as the *Arcus Novus* of Diocletian. This was a commemorative arch erected across the Via Lata either in AD 293/294 (on the occasion of Diocletian's tenth anniversary, and marking the formation of the Tetrarchy) or in AD 303/304 (marking the Tetrarchy's tenth anniversary and Diocletian's twentieth). Heinz Kähler (1936), Diana Kleiner (1992, 409-413), Sandro de Maria (1988, 312-314) and Dale Kinney (1997, 129-133) summarised the material; the more recent works also provide good resumés of arguments over these much-debated pieces. There has been disagreement over whether the reliefs are related to the arch; what date they were; whether they were reused, or recarved from

earlier pieces; while Johannes Sieveking (1937) suggested that one relief (not the one bearing the carnyx) was a Renaissance copy. For the debate, see the references above; it is accepted here that the pedestals are both original (as subsequent scholars have mostly accepted), though they could have been touched up or more substantially recarved as well as repaired in the Renaissance. The question of their date is explored below.

The remains of the arch itself were demolished in 1491. Fragments were subsequently rediscovered and dispersed, the two pedestals being transported to Florence in 1785. These pedestals are carved on three sides, and would have supported free-standing columns. Two sides are decorated with triumphal iconography (Victory; Roman soldiers and prisoners), the third bearing one of the Dioscuri, probably as symbolic echoes of the twin Augusti under the Tetrarchic system. The bases probably flanked the central bay of the arch; Kähler (1936, 4 f.) argued they are reversed as they now stand, with the Dioscuri originally on facing sides of the passage. The Victory on the left pedestal (as viewed today), with palm branch and laurel wreath, stands by a palm tree (Kleiner 1992, fig. 378). The bound male barbarian on the adjacent face is being pushed towards the Victory by a Roman soldier. He wears trousers held by a decorated belt, laced shoes, is bare-chested, wears a furry hat, a furry cloak fastened by a rosette brooch, and is bearded. The sword has been removed from his scabbard. The attributes mark him as a northern barbarian. Kähler (1936, 17) saw his costume as marking a prince or noble in contrast to the other barbarians.

The second pedestal, of most interest here, also has a central Victory, standing frontally and facing to her L, her R arm with a palm branch, her L round the shoulders of the adjacent trophy, adjusting a shield (**fig. 276a**). The trophy comprises a belted scale cuirass with pteryges and skirt, and an Attic helmet; a sword belt runs across it. Each arm has two shields (hexagonal and oval), with an axe and curved horn (»Celtic lituus«) behind the L one (as viewed) and two spears angled behind the right one; below the cuirass are greaves. Carnyces appear as shield ornaments on the right shield (as viewed; **fig. 276b**). A kneeling male captive is chained to the trophy, trousered and bare-chested. The outside face has another bearded barbarian, arms bound, wearing a furry hat, belted tunic, cloak and shoes without laces, being pushed towards the Victory by a Roman soldier. Again the barbarians are of northern type.

Interpretation is complicated by the demolition of the monument and by the fact that, in typical late Antique tradition, it reused spolia from earlier monuments. This was often not just expedient reuse, but deliberate evocation of earlier times. For instance, the Arch of Constantine (AD 315/316) used only spolia from the monuments of »good« emperors, such as Trajan or Hadrian (Kleiner 1992, 461). With the Arcus Novus too there may have

been a symbolism to the reuse. It has been argued that most came from Claudius's British Victory arch (Barrett 1991), which lay about 150 m away; there is also a figural panel probably of mid-2nd century date and perhaps pieces from a Claudian *Ara Pietatis Augustae* (Kleiner 1992, 412 f.). Claudius was seen as a good emperor, and thus an appropriate target for reuse. A British connection would have additional symbolic resonance because of the success of Constantius Chlorus, one of the Tetrarchs, in recovering Britain from the separatist movement of Carausius and Allectus in 296 (or recovering northern Gaul by 293, if the earlier dating of the inscription is preferred). Kleiner (1992, 413. 422 f.) suggested a scene on the near-contemporary Arch of Galerius in Salonica may refer to the same event. The evidence for British associations is far from clear, though; Kinney (1997, 132) dismissed the Claudian connections, as other authorities have argued that the styles of the reused pieces are 2nd century.

Although an inscription was found with the monument, there is debate over its date, discussed below; here iconographic parallels for both the earlier and later date are considered. There is also some debate over the date of the pedestals – are they Diocletianic or are they too reused? This impacts on the interpretation of the carnyces. It is unlikely that they symbolise Constantius Chlorus' British campaign in 296-297 as this was essentially a civil war, not a war against barbarians, although he did campaign against barbarians in the Netherlands before his British trip (Erdrich 2003, 12; Willems 1984, 273). The dating of the arch is too early for any reference to his Pictish campaigns in 306 (Salway 1981, 306-311. 317-319). However, there could have been a conscious echo of Claudius' conquests in the use of the carnyx. While the full decoration of the Claudian arch is unknown, it is known to have included battle scenes and freestanding trophies (Barrett 1991, figs 1-2 pl. 1B); these may have included carnyces, which are known from southern British Iron Age coins of the early 1st century AD (A1.1-1.6). The carnyces could thus be a subtle cross-reference to Claudius' British victories. This is nothing but a highly speculative suggestion, although Diocletian's adoption of the title *Britannicus Maximus* in 285 may point to actions in Britain, otherwise unattested (Salway 1981, 287).

Another possibility would be a reference to Maximian's earlier campaigns in Gaul against the Alamanni or Diocletian's successes against the same group in Raetia in 286-288 (Schutz 1985, 44). The presence of northern-type barbarians on both bases supports a connection with these campaigns, and the equipment (scale armour, axe, curved horn) is that found in the iconography of the Marcomannic Wars, relating to the same general area (chapter 9). This German context seems the most convincing one. Given that the carnyces are minor elements in the design (shield decoration rather than independent attributes) their significance may be decorative rather than sym-

Fig. 276 B1.16 Column base from Tetrarchic arch: **a** general view. – **b** detail of shield. – **c** carnyces 1-4. – (a-b photos Fraser Hunter; c drawing Tanja Romankiewicz).

bolic; they are found as shield decoration on a number of older sculptures which could have served as models (e.g. Trajan's Column, Great Trajanic Frieze; B1.12, 1.11.3). However, continuing use among Germanic tribes might be supported by the late-3rd-century aureus of Postumus (A5.5).

The second base also shows a German captive, but the Victory with palm tree is clearly not a reference to north European vegetation. It might mark military victories in the east, perhaps Galerius' campaigns against the Persians in 296-298 (for which see Cary/Wilson 1963, 331; Kleiner 1992, 418). However, Kähler (1936, 22) noted the absence of eastern captives (at least on the surviving bases) or an eastern trophy, and suggested this symbolised instead a diplomatic rather than a military victory. He connected it to Diocletian's installation of a client king in Armenia in 286 which led to territorial gains from the Persians without the need for conflict, and for which he took the title *Persicus Maximus*. If the earlier dating of the arch is accepted, this seems plausible.

The carnyces

Carnyces feature as shield decoration on the oval shield on the right (as viewed; **fig. 276b-c**). This has a central Medusa head. In each quarter of the shield are two plain interlocked rings, probably representing torcs (based on clearer examples elsewhere; e.g. tomb of Caecilia Metella; B1.1). The shield has a central spine: at the ends this is a straight bar terminating in a teardrop motif, but nearer the centre it is overlain by back-to-back carnyx pairs (Kähler 1936, 5).

Part of the tube, bell and head of the carnyces are shown; the mouthpiece is not visible. The tube and bell are cylindrical, the head curving through 160-180° to face back towards the middle of the shield. There is no crest. On the top left one the head is lost behind the cuirass. The top right one has a plain tube; the head is quite naturalistic, with a forward-pointing ear and a bulbous eye; the mouth is closed. On both the lower two a band marks the tube-bell junction a little above the midpoint of its visible length. Both have naturalistic heads with single ears and slightly bulbous eyes; the mouths are slightly open (about 30°), with one or two fangs showing (top jaw on L, both jaws on R).

Dating evidence

One of the fragments plausibly connected with the arch shows a woman writing on a shield »VOTIS X ET XX« (Kleiner 1992, fig. 376). In its current form it is a pastiche of several original fragments, but casts of the fragments have been arranged into a plausible reconstruction (Kinney 1997, fig. 6). It is likely that they are reused from an earlier (mid-2nd century?) monument, with some heads and shield inscription being recarved (although Buttrey [1983, 379f.] argued strongly against this). The inscrip-

tion is typically late Roman, celebrating one anniversary and anticipating another. In this case there are two possible dates. It could mark the decennalia of Diocletian in 293/294 and anticipate his vicennalia in 303/304 (thus also celebrating the founding of the Tetrarchy); or it could mark the decennalia of the Tetrarchy (which he founded in 293) and either mark his own vicennalia or anticipate that of the system, thus dating to 303. Opinion is divided (e.g. Kleiner 1992, 413; Brilliant 1974, 266). T. V. Buttrey (1983) argued strongly that the earlier date is epigraphically correct, the later one misunderstanding the working of *vota* inscriptions, though he did not discuss the possibility that it was intended to mark both Diocletian's anniversary and the Tetrarchy's rather than anticipating future anniversaries. The later date would correlate with Diocletian himself visiting Rome (Kleiner 1992, 400), a suitable occasion for such a monument. This would also allow it to post-date Constantius Chlorus' British campaigns (explaining the reuse of the Claudian arch) and Galerius' Persian campaigns (perhaps alluded to in the palm tree). Yet the iconography would also fit the earlier date, as noted above, with the recovery of part of the rebel area, campaigns against Germans and diplomatic gains in the east. Where there is such disagreement among specialists, it is impossible for an outsider to be certain.

A further problem is whether the reliefs are Diocletianic at all, or whether they too have been reused. For Kleiner (1992, 409) they are contemporary with the arch. In contrast Cornelius Vermeule (1960, 26) suggested (rather tentatively) they may be reused from a late Severan or late Antonine monument, while Sieveking (1937) argued that one base was a Renaissance copy and the other something of a hotch-potch of fragments. De Maria (1988, 197f. 313) noted that the link to the *Arcus Novus* is inferential, and supported a late 3rd-century date instead. Brilliant (1982) suggested they were taken from a monument for Gallienus to be reused in the Diocletianic arch, but that they were deliberately archaising, evoking the styles of Marcus Aurelius. Kleiner (1992, 412) noted that a link with a lost arch of Aurelian has been argued, but she felt the Diocletian connection is more assured, although this need not rule out the fragments being reused in this context. Indeed, the side-panels of the base have clearly been cut down, with the Roman soldiers and the horses of the Dioscuri truncated; Kleiner (1992, 409) linked this to its insertion in its current, modern setting, although Kähler (1936, 4) argued that the design spread onto a second block, built into the arch's structure. The verdict can only be based on artistic assessments of style, always a tentative basis. Kleiner saw the style as being late rather than early Empire, and thus even if the pedestals were reused it is unlikely that they were more than a century old. On balance Kleiner's view that they were Diocletianic is preferred here, largely for economy of hypothesis; instead of requiring the hypothesis of an unknown 3rd-century monument we can take these as the contemporary contribution to the *Arcus Novus*.

Bibliography
Brilliant 1982. – Kähler 1936. – Kinney 1997, 129-133. – Kleiner 1992, 409-413. – De Maria 1988, 197-203. 312-314 (with summary of previous literature).

B2 ITALY

B2.1 Statue base of M. Nonius Gallus. – Isernia (reg. Molise / I)

(Current location: Isernia Museum)
Isernia (ancient Aesernia) has produced a number of early Augustan sculptures, two of which are relevant to the current study (B2.1, B2.2). Both monuments can be dated to the period 27-20 BC and relate to high-ranking equestrians winning glory by their exploits in the Augustan expansion on the northern frontier. The first is a limestone statue base, 0.72 m H. 0.59 m W. 0.42 m T., with reliefs on three faces (its main publication is by Heinrich Fuhrmann [1949, 46-65]). An inscription on the main face reads:

ATTALVS NONI M S
Attalus Noni M(arci) S(ervus)
Attalus, slave of Marcus Nonius [erected this memorial]

The subject of the dedication (who probably features on the relief as the general and the sacrificing figure) has been plausibly identified with M. Nonius Gallus, recorded also on a statue base at Isernia (CIL IX 2642; Fuhrmann 1949, 59 f.). Cassius Dio (51, 20) recorded that he suppressed a revolt of the Treveri in 29 BC, and this trophy monument probably records his victories. The slave's name suggests he was Gaulish, and may well have been captured by Nonius in this campaign.

The main face has three registers (**fig. 277**). The lowest has the attributes of Fortuna and Nemesis, a wheel, rudder and globe. Above is a *suovetaurilia* scene, which Inez Scott Ryberg (1955, 34 f.) interpreted as the lustration (or ritual cleansing) of Nonius' army after the campaign, in honour

Fig. 277 B2.1 Statue base of M. Nonius Gallus, Isernia: **a** front. – **b** angled view of left side. – **c** right side. – **d** details of carnyces. – (a-c Diebner 1979, fig. 27; d drawing Tanja Romankiewicz).

Fig. 277 (continued)

of Mars; Nonius himself is making the sacrifice. The uppermost register shows Nemesis and Fortuna, with globe, wheel and ?rudder; a Victory leads a horse towards them. This scene has been much-debated (Fuhrmann 1949, 63; Felleti Maj 1977, 254f.; Ronke 1987, 94-96): it may symbolise Nonius' equestrian rank, or refer to an *ovatio* to mark his victories, when he would have been mounted (the nature of any triumph which he was awarded is not known). Most likely is that it reflects war booty being offered to the goddesses; the Treveri were noted for their cavalry. As Gilbert Charles Picard commented, the rather fatalistic depiction of Fortuna and Nemesis presents an interesting contrast to the concern in later triumphal art with Victory and *virtus*; it is probably connected to the fate of Attalus himself, transplanted by war from northern Gaul to Italy, but as a valued house-slave rather than being sent to the arena.

The two sides are closely similar. The upper register features Fortuna's cornucopiae and globe. The lower features a trophy scene. By the trophy stands a Roman general (with cuirass, *paludamentum* and sword), who reaches his right hand towards a kneeling, bound, naked, hairy,

bearded barbarian. This may allude to the capture of Attalus, the donor, whose name is probably a Latinised Celtic one (Fuhrmann 1949, 64). The trophy comprises a corset-type cuirass with gorgon-head medallion (the photo in Diebner 1979, fig. 31 indicates the left side features a belted tunic and cloak, not a cuirass). It is topped with a horned helmet; on the right side this also has a wheel finial. The short arms of the trophy support two crossed spears with a third item angled across them. Fuhrmann (1949, 48. 50 n. 1) interpreted the item in the left arm (as viewed) as either an animal standard or a carnyx, and the right item as a long-handled axe. Sylvia Diebner (1979, 136-139 cat. Is 27) did not recognise the carnyx, describing it as a stake with an animal head, but on the better-preserved right side the identification is clear (Picard 1957, 245-247). Analysis of the photos in Fuhrmann and Diebner (which are lit from different angles) suggests all four items are carnyces. Unusually, there are no shields in the trophy.

The carnyces

Not all details are clear from the photos, but all appear to be quite simply depicted (**tab. 64**). The full length of the instrument is shown, with a straight tube and squared end. There are no technical details such as tube junctions, and no crest, but all have one or two ears, a head turned through 90-120°, and a mouth open to about 45°; #2 seems to have an upturned snout, and #4 may have a closed mouth (**fig. 277d**).

Dating evidence

Picard (1957, 234) dated the base to 29-28 BC following Gallus' Treveran victories; in reality 29 BC is the *terminus post quem*. The presence of the laurel branches on the altar has been linked to Augustus' use of such symbolism from 27 BC, which seems plausible (Diebner 1979, 139). A date bracket of 27-20 BC should cover the likely range; the chances are that it was erected while the victory was still fresh, a year or two afterwards.

Bibliography

Diebner 1979, 136-139 (cat. Is 27) fig. 27a-c. – Felletti Maj 1977, 254-256. – Fuhrmann 1949, 45-65. – Holliday 2002, 178f. – Picard 1957, 234. 245-247. – Ronke 1987, 94-96. 708 no. 126. – Ryberg 1955, 34f.

no.	location	notes	illustration
1	L side, L carnyx	Identity much clearer in Diebner 1979	F pl. 12; D fig. 31
2	L side, R carnyx	Small ear and lower jaw show in Fellmann illustration, upturned snout visible in Diebner's illustration	F pl. 12; D fig. 31
3	R side, L carnyx	2 ears and hint of eye; short lower jaw	F pl. 13; D fig. 27
4	R side, R carnyx	Lower jaw unclear; mouth perhaps closed	F pl. 13; D fig. 27

Tab. 64 Characteristics of the carnyces on B2.1 and correlation with published illustrations. F = Fuhrmann 1949; D = Diebner 1979.

B2.2 Funerary statue base of C. Septumuleius Obola. – Isernia (reg. Molise / I)

(Current location: Isernia Museum)

Isernia has produced a number of early Augustan statue bases with doric weapons friezes which probably once supported equestrian statues (Polito 1998, 137). One, of C. Septumuleius Obola, features a carnyx (**fig. 278**). The base is a rectangular limestone block 1.78 m L. 0.69 m W. 0.98 m H. with a doric frieze around the top and an inscription on one narrow face (Diebner 1979, 146-148). The metopes feature a weapons frieze and hunting scenes. Eugenio Polito (1998, 181 n. 93) categorised the weaponry as featuring a round shield, muscle cuirass, Attic helmet, greaves, spear, cornu and carnyx, the latter being the only barbarian item. The inscription (CIL IX 2668) reads:

C.SEPTVMVLEIO.C.F / TRO.OBOLAE.IIII.VIR /
EX.TESTAMEN[TO]
C(aio) Septumuleio C(ai) f(ilio) / Tro(mentina) Obolae
IIIIvir(o) / ex testament(o)

To Gaius Septumuleius Obola, son of Gaius, of the Tromentina voting tribe, quattuorvir, under the terms of his will

The carnyces

Rudolf Fellmann (1957, pl. 7, 3) provided a good image of the frieze. A pair of crossed carnyces are depicted back-to-back on one metope, in a very distorted view to respond to the available space. Their tubes are bent into an S-form; they show no technical detail, but the end flares into a cupped mouthpiece. A crest with incised hair detailing runs up the bell to the ears (one is shown on one, two on the other). They have eyes, and a gaping mouth. While distorted, the image is dramatic, and immediately recognisable.

Dating evidence

The inscription on one of the three bases provides a *terminus post quem* of 27 BC, while historical sources for the persons commemorated suggest a date range of 25-15 BC (Polito 1998, 137; Fellmann 1957, 59).

Bibliography

CIL IX 2668. – Diebner 1979, 146-148 (cat. Is 31) fig. 31a-c. – Fellmann 1957, 59 pl. 7, 3 (mistakenly attributed to another person represented on the Isernia bases). – Polito 1998, 137. 181 n. 93.

Fig. 278 B2.2 Funerary statue base of C. Septumuleius Obola, Isernia: **a-b** front and side views. – **c** detail of carnyces. – **d** drawing of carnyces. – (a-b Diebner 1979, fig. 311; c Fellmann 1957, pl. 7, 3; d drawing Alan Braby).

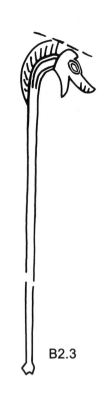

Fig. 279 B2.3 Gable stone, Amiternum (San Vittorino): **a** the stone. – **b** the carnyx. –
(a Persichetti 1912, fig. 5; b drawing Alan Braby).

B2.3

b

B2.3 Gable stone. – Amiternum /
San Vittorino (reg. Abruzzo / I)

(Current location: L'Aquila, Museo Archeologico)
Excavations were undertaken in the theatre of Amiternum
(San Vittorino, some 10 km NW of L'Aquila in the Abruzzo
region) from 1878-1880. The first two seasons of small-
scale work exposed some of the walls, with the 1880
season opening up the building's plan. In 1879 the excavator reported the discovery of a pyramidal stone 1.18 m
high with a carnyx carved on one face (Leosini 1879). This
remarkable limestone sculpture preserves a detailed and
near life-size picture of the instrument (**fig. 279**). A. Leosini stated that one face is unfinished, and was presumably not intended to be seen. There is some damage to
the base and top, and the stone broke while it was being
transported. A face adjacent to the relief has an enigmatic
inscription (CIL IX 4189):

RIIGVP
(the final letter seems to be a ligature of V and P)

Unfortunately there is no published illustration to clarify
the character or regularity of the lettering; it may represent marks connected with the building process.
Leosini correctly identified the carnyx, drawing parallels to
Republican coins and the Prima Porta statue. It was illustrated by N. Persichetti (1912, 306 fig. 5), quoted by Heinrich Fuhrmann (1949, 50 n. 1), and mentioned in passing
by Simonetta Segenni (1985, 124 n. 15), who provided a
valuable summary of information on the site. Only a single
view is published, leaving some questions over its character.
Although described as a pyramid by Leosini, which would
imply it was a freestanding feature, Persichetti called it a
wedge, and Fuhrmann (1949, 50 n. 1) identified it as a gable fragment. This seems the most plausible argument, with
the carnyx lying near-horizontally and facing downwards.
Other finds from this excavation season included quantities
of architectural friezes, columns, capitals and bases (Leosini
1879), though these are not described in any detail.

Such architectural stones fall outwith the scope of Micha-
ela Fuchs' work on theatre furnishings (1987, 60 f.),
though she mentioned other sculpture from the site.
Catherine Courtois (1989, 60 n. 167. 138 f. 186) considered the building in the context of other Italian theatres,
and suggested two phases are represented as it survives.
The building technique of the auditorium (*cavea*), in *opus
quasi-reticulatum*, suggests a late Republican date, while
she argued that the *scaenae frons* (stage) is early Augustan; Frank Sear (2006, 83) concurred that the mix of building styles fits a late Republican / early Augustan date. An
Augustan date is widely quoted (e. g. Fuchs 1987, 61; Segenni 1985, 128 with further references).

The carnyx
The carnyx takes up almost the full length of the block,
though there is plenty of blank space around it. It has
a straight cylindrical tube with a gently expanding bell.
There is no clear sign of tube divisions on the photograph,
but there is some decoration on the bell in the form of
two parallel lines, and a clear step in the relief between
the bell and head. The head is slender, with a double-out-
lined incised oval eye and tapering jaws, the upper with
incisions representing teeth. Persichetti described it as a
goose, but it looks more like a wolf. A crest starts on the
bell and expands as it comes towards the head, with incisions representing hairs; it runs to the edge of the block,
and stops at what seems to be a small ear, though the details are not entirely clear. At the bottom of the tube, the
most exciting feature is the clear depiction of a mouthpiece, as a boss aligned on the tube with an indent in the
base to mark the cup.

Dating evidence

Although the theatre was long-lived and could have been refurbished several times, the suggested early Augustan date for the stage, the main portion carrying decoration, provides a likely context. This finds support from the style. The depiction of an isolated weapon is reminiscent of blocks from La Brague and some of the Narbonne reliefs (France), the friezes from Kyzikos (Turkey) and S. Agnese, Rome, and blocks from Doric friezes such as those from Gaeta (Lazio/I); Polito (1998, 135f. 149f. 161f.) has suggested dates in the later 1st century BC for these. Of course, this is far from certain; for instance, there are parallels from the eastern Empire for isolated items in friezes apparently of 2nd-century date (Polito 1998, 215-217), and indeed on the Hadrianeum in Rome, though these are more ornate (Kleiner 1992, 283-285; Sapelli 1999, 32. 36. 56. 60. 62. 64. 80f.). However, the combination of the theatre's date and the presence of local stylistic parallels in Italy and France indicate an early Augustan date is most likely (c. 30-1 BC). Courtois (1989, 138) suggested that Augustan veterans settled in the town (though it was not a colony); this seems to be based on reliefs from a funerary monument of Augustan date featuring a triumphal procession and gladiator scenes (Rocchetti 1958). Fragments of other tombs of this general date with depictions of weaponry are also known in the neighbouring area (e.g. Persichetti 1912, fig. 7; Segennie 1985, 200. 213 no. 44.5.1. pl. XLVII, 1). While speculative, this would provide a context for the carnyx depiction on a major public monument such as the theatre.

Bibliography

CIL IX 4189. – Leosini 1879. – Fuhrmann 1949, 50 n. 1. – Persichetti 1912, 306 fig. 5. – Sear 2006, 150f. – Segenni 1985, 124 n. 15.

B2.4 Weapons frieze, probably from a funerary monument. – Alba Fucens (reg. Abruzzo/I)

(Current location: Avezzano, Antiquarium Comunale)
Five blocks from a weapons frieze are known from the colony of Alba Fucens, in the Apennines east of Rome. The exact findspot is unknown. Only one block (of breccia) is illustrated by Polito (**fig. 280**). The left side and lower edge are damaged, but two angled oval shields with squared ends can be recognised. Behind are a spear tip and carnyx; damage inhibits identification of the items in front. From Polito's analysis (1998, 187 n. 305f.), the other blocks feature round and oval shields, muscle cuirass, pseudo-Attic helmets, greaves, spears and tuba. He suggested it comes from the architrave of a funerary monument.

The carnyx

This description is drawn from the image in Polito (1998, fig. 107). The carnyx lies almost horizontally along the top edge of the frieze, pointing left and facing down (as oriented in the photo). The lower part of its tube is hid-

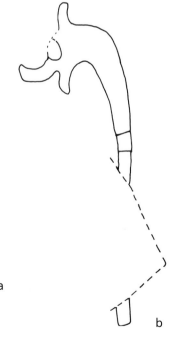

Fig. 280 B2.4 Weapons frieze, Alba Fucens: **a** the stone. – **b** the carnyx. – (a Polito 1998, fig. 107; b drawing Tanja Romankiewicz).

Fig. 281 B2.5 Weapons frieze, Scafa:
a the stone. – **b** the carnyx. – (a Russo
1981, fig. 1; b drawing Tanja Romankiewicz).

den behind a shield, although it appears to continue beyond it, with a plain straight end. There appears to be a
band at the tube-bell junction. The head (at c. 150° to the
tube) has an eye, ear and mouth open to 80°, the jaw tips
slightly recurved. There is no crest.

Dating evidence
Polito dated the frieze to the end of the Republic or first
years of the Empire on the basis of style and iconography,

although without discussing it in detail: it is taken here
as c. 30 BC-AD 20. He discussed and dismissed previous
suggestions of an Antonine or late Republican date, accepting the latter is possible but dismissing the reasoning
behind it, which relies on an unproven connection with an
excavated monument from the site (1998, 187 n. 307).

Bibliography
Polito 1998, 169 fig. 107.

B2.5 Weapons frieze, probably from a tomb. – Scafa (reg. Abruzzo / I)

(Current location: Chieti, Museo Archeologico Nazionale;
inv. no. 10007)
Severina Russo (1981) published three sculptured blocks
with a weapons frieze from Scafa in Abruzzo, central Italy.
She argued convincingly that they derive from a single
monument: they were found in the same area (albeit at
different dates), are of the same local limestone and similar dimensions, and there are close stylistic links between
them. The largest is a typical frieze of overlapping weapons, while the other two bear simpler groups of weapons:
it is likely they come from different places on the structure,
perhaps the larger block on the front and the simpler ones
on the sides. The two small blocks in particular are in very
flat relief (**fig. 281**).
Russo (1981, 30 f.) argued the structure was most probably a funerary monument. The details of the find circumstances are poor, but she felt the frieze was insufficiently
grand and sizeable for a public monument. This is not necessarily the case, but more telling are her locational arguments: the find comes from near a Roman road outside
the town in an area which has produced funerary inscriptions. A funerary use seems most likely.

The block with the carnyx (1.00 m L. 0.59 m H. 0.30 m T.)
shows an angled oval shield with flattened ends and a
hemispherical boss, decorated with three interlocked circles. Over it lies a long sword in its scabbard with a suspension belt; behind to the right is a fringed cloak, and
to the left a carnyx. Its partner block features a flat round
shield with an Attic helmet. The longer weapons frieze
features shields (oval, legionary and perhaps round); Attic helmets, one with a remarkably large feather crest; a
spear with a triangular head; a tuba; a muscle cuirass; a
lamellar arm guard; three standards with phalerae; and
a sword. This is a typical mix of barbarian, Roman and
conventional items, although with few barbarian items.
Only the carnyx is clearly non-Roman, but the long sword,
oval shields and helmets with volutes and rosette finials
are most likely barbarian. The block with the carnyx was
probably intended to feature only barbarian weaponry:
the shield, sword, carnyx and cloak would all be most at
home in a barbarian context. Some of the items are probably gladiatorial (the arm guard and, Polito suggested, the
helmet with feather crest), perhaps referring to gladiatorial games sponsored by the deceased.

The carnyx

Only the bell and head of the carnyx are shown. It lies angled up to the left, facing right. The bell runs into the head with no division, although the musculature of the jaw is shown running onto the bell. A crest runs the visible length of the bell to the ears, increasing in height; it is decorated with a plain border and a series of rectangular recesses. The head has two ears, an eye with ?pupil and prominent brow, and a fearsome tooth-lined mouth (open to c. 40°) with two pronounced fangs.

Dating evidence

Valerio Cianfarani (1973) dated the reliefs to the later 1st century AD, but Russo (1981, 31 f.) argued they must be earlier for stylistic reasons, suggesting a date of c. 50 BC - AD 50; she felt they fell most plausibly into the first decades of the 1st century AD. Polito (1998, 162-166) did not analyse the dating of the monument in detail, but put it a little before the Trasacco friezes which he dated to the end of the 1st century BC or the first quarter of the 1st century AD. A bracket for this frieze of c. 30 BC - AD 20 seems plausible.

Bibliography

Cianfarani 1973. – Polito 1998, 162-166. – Russo 1981.

B2.6 Weapons frieze. – Turin (reg. Piemonte / I)

(Current location: Turin, Museo di Antichità, inv. no. 581) Turin museum houses five marble blocks and one fragment bearing weapons friezes which feature five carnyces. Their exact findspot is unknown, but they are presumably from the immediate locale; Patricia Hagenweiler (2003, 106) said they may have been found near the Mercato di Porta Palazzo, in the area of the Roman cemetery. Goffredo Bendinelli (1933) interpreted them along with other fragments (a trophy and some decorative elements) as part of a triumphal arch. This was dismissed as unproven and unlikely by Sandro De Maria (1988, 338 f.) in his comprehensive treatment of honorific arches in Italy. He argued the fragments which Bendinelli links together are not stylistically related (especially the trophy; Bendinelli 1933, fig. 12) and felt the frieze more plausibly derives from another architectural form, probably a tomb or portico. Hagenweiler (2003, 153 f.) preferred to restore them to an arch, not least on account of their decorative wealth compared to other weapons friezes, but this could be explained by the wealth of the benefactor rather than any functional difference.

The six blocks were well illustrated and described by Bendinelli, and subsequently by Hagenweiler (2003, 106-109). De Maria queried their integrity as a monument on the basis of variations in size and style, but only Bendinelli's fragmentary block F stands out from the rest. This is poorly illustrated, but appears to lack the characteristic decorated lower border, while the scale of the cuirass is markedly different from those on the other blocks. It is also substantially thinner (at 70-75 mm), and its fragmentary nature points to a rather different history: it will not be considered further here. The other five blocks are closely related stylistically.

Study is not helped by different authors using the same letter codes for different blocks; table 65 provides a concordance. Here, the letter codes of Mario Torelli (2003) will be used, for consistency with the illustrations (fig. 282). Torelli also provided a useful discussion of the material's history: blocks C and E, which are thinner, have clearly been reworked in post-Medieval times, as Baroque mouldings are carved on the ends (Torelli 2003, 151 fig. 129). The dimensions are otherwise closely consistent, with intact thicknesses of 220-240 mm and heights of around 450 mm; length varies from 0.80 to 1.75 m. Two of the blocks (A and E) have weaponry on one short side as well, showing that they are corners.

The blocks portray a wide range of material, summarised in table 66 for each block to emphasise the similarities. This includes conventional items (the cuirasses, pelta and round shields) and Roman objects (the tubae, legionary shields, greaves, and perhaps the short swords). Some are gladiatorial (the greaves and arm guards, curved short sword, and helmets with griffin terminals and feathers). Others represent barbarians, predominantly northern ones: the hexagonal shields, fur-covered helmets, horned helmets, curved trumpets, and carnyces. The Phrygian hel-

Tab. 65 B2.6, correlation of frieze numbering between major published sources.

Torelli 2003	Bandinelli 1933	Hagenweiler n. d.	Dütschke 1880
A	D	D	9
B	E	E	9
C	A	B	14
D	C	C	9
E	B	A	6

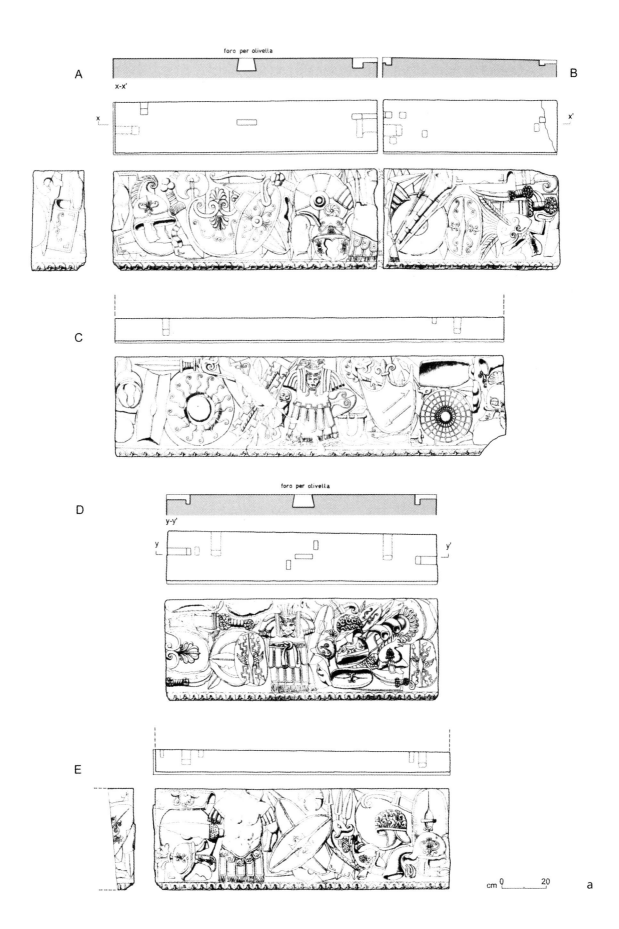

foro per olivella

A x-x' B

x x'

C

foro per olivella

D y-y'

y y'

E

cm 0 20 a

b

c

Fig. 282 B2.6 Weapons frieze, Turin: **a** drawing of the surviving stones. – **b** photo of the blocks. – **c** carnyces 1-5. – (a-b Torelli 2003, figs 130-131; c drawing Tanja Romankiewicz).

equipment	A/B	C	D	E	notes
cuirass A	×			×	muscle, with pteryges & flaps
cuirass B		×	×		plate armour with shoulder guards, 2 rows of flaps
greaves	×	×	×	×	
arm guard				×	
shield – oval	×	×	×	×	
shield – hexagonal	×	×			
shield – legionary	×	×		×	
shield – round	×	×	×	×	
shield – pelta	×	×	×		
sword – short	×	×		×	some in scabbards
sword – curved	×		×		short
spear	×	×	×	×	
double axe	×				
carnyx	×	×	×	×	
tuba	×				
curved trumpet		×	×	×	»Celtic lituus«
helmet – domed		×	×	×	some with crests
helmet – fur cover			×	×	domed
helmet – feathers/horns	×				domed
helmet – Phrygian	×				
helmet – griffin protome			×	×	
bow	×		×		
arrow	×	×			
quiver	×				
ship components			×	×	

Tab. 66 Arms and armour on the various blocks of the Turin frieze (B2.6).

mets and archery gear have eastern connections, and the frieze is an eclectic composition drawn from a wide contemporary repertoire; as on B2.5, the gladiatorial equipment would evoke games sponsored by the deceased.

Their date has been much debated. A late Augustan – Tiberian date is accepted by most recent authors, which would link the equipment to events in Gaul and Germany; the latter would be consistent with the fur-covered helmet. However, Torelli has made an ingenious link in the story. Analysis has shown that the marble was imported from Greece or Asia Minor, suggesting considerable investment in the friezes (Torelli 2003, 152). Very few other inscriptions or sculpture from Turin used a similar stone. Torelli analysed them epigraphically to see if any can be connected to the friezes, and came up with a good candidate: a fragmentary inscription, honorific or funerary (CIL V 7165; Torelli 2003, 156). Torelli's detailed autopsy and excursus is quite hypothetical in places, but he made a strong case that the slab tells of an anonymous local senator who received military honours under Claudius during the invasion of Britain (developing a suggestion made by Ritterling 1924, 1250. 1666 note; see also Birley 2005, 276). The inscription, with Torelli's expansions, runs as follows; the translation is from Birley, with additions:

...] O [?.. / ..]T.AB.TI.CLAVD[... / ...]EA.CLASSICA.VAL[... / ...]ORT.AMICORVM.[... / ...]SPITIVM.CVM.LEG.V[... / ...] VLA.ARGENT.AE[... / ...] P [?... / ...] O [... (or C, or G)

... donis militaribus dona]to ab Tiberio Claud[io Caesare Augusto Germanico... / ...coronis aur]ea classica val[lari ... / ... ex coh]ortem amicorum [Ti. Claudi Caesaris Aug? / ...ho]spitium cum legione V[IIII... / ...tab]ula argentea ae[... / ...] P [...

[unknown honorand] decorated with military decorations by Tiberius Claudius Caesar Augustus Germanicus (for the British expedition?), with crowns, a gold one, a naval one, a rampart one, ... (received into) the cohort of friends (of Claudius?... He concluded ...) a pact of hospitality with the Ninth (?) Legion ... a silver tablet ...

There are, of course, many uncertainties. The inscription is not closely provenanced; CIL records it only as from the Piemonte region, though Torelli made a case for it being Turin itself. It is the only known inscription of relevance and of the same stone; we have no idea of the unknown inscriptions. Yet, on current evidence, the case is a plausible one; Torelli argued that, at this date in Turin, there were relatively few families of this stature (indeed, he tried to pin down the person involved). The wealth seen in the imported marble and the scale of the monument, plus the styles it was evoking, are consistent with a wealthy and upwardly mobile person of this class. If this fascinating theory is correct, it would suggest a date around the middle of the 1st century AD, and a link to the conquest of Britain, with the weapons friezes evoking his military career, perhaps specifically his time in Britain. The art-historical arguments for an earlier date are not compelling, since different authorities have expressed widely differing views (summarised in Hagenweiler 2003, 106 n. 577, and varying from Augustan to Trajanic).

A little less speculatively, Torelli asked architectural colleagues to consider the reconstruction of the monument. The presence of two corners in the surviving pieces suggests a quadrilateral plinth; three blocks of a similar scale and a related border frieze, with channelled decoration, may also be connected, perhaps forming a plinth for an honorific statue or a funerary altar (Torelli 2003, 166 fig. 133; Museum Inv. 690).

The carnyces

The carnyces are very similar in style (**fig. 282c**). There are five in total: 1-3 on block C, 4 on E and 5 on A; C and E have not been seen first-hand, and their description relies on photographs. They are characterised by highly recurved heads, turned to point back down the tube; exaggerated wide-open mouths with the tips curled back

and the mouths hollowed for effect; almond-shaped eyes; wave-like crests (except on 4); and no ears. The bell-tube junction is marked by a two-band fitting.

Dating evidence

Polito (1998, 169) summarised the previous views on the dating (see also Hagenweiler 2003, 106 n. 577). Bendinelli (1933) believed the sculpture was Flavian (especially from numismatic parallels between the trophy and one featured on Domitian's coinage), but was torn because he interpreted them as derived from an Augustan-Julio-Claudian arch. He thus constructed a model of a Julio-Claudian arch which was redecorated in the Flavian period. De Maria rightly cast doubt on this convoluted scheme; he preferred a date in the middle of the 1st century AD for the reliefs, although without giving any detailed reasoning for it. Polito dismissed this, arguing from stylistic parallels for a date at the end of the 1st century BC and the first decades of the 1st century AD; this is consistent with Hegenweiler (n. d., 109), who saw them as Augustan. Torelli (2003) makes a good case for a Claudian connection; to cover this possibility, a broad range of 15 BC-AD 60 is taken here.

Bibliography

Bendinelli 1933. – De Maria 1988, 338f. pl. 113. – Dütschke 1880, 5-9. – Hagenweiler 2003, 106-109. – Polito 1998, 169. – Torelli 2003.

B2.7 Weapons frieze. – Abbey of Novalesa, near Susa (reg. Piemonte / I)

(Current location: Abbey of Novalesa)
Carlo Carducci (1982, 126-129 fig. 1) published a marble fragment of weapons frieze from the Abbey of Novalesa in Piemonte, which had been reused as an upright in a door. He attributed it to the nearby town of Susa, a major Roman centre, and saw it as part of an honorific arch. However, as argued elsewhere (chapter 8), weapons friezes are more often associated with funerary contexts, and his link to an arch has been dismissed (Mercando 1993, 103; Fogliato 1992, 44 f.). Indeed, Carducci published fragments of another block with weaponry found at the Abbey itself (1982, 129-134 fig. 4), which tends to suggest that these are fragments of funerary monuments in the area.

The block shows a row of shields (legionary and pelta) and a muscle cuirass with other material behind: the carnyx, a hexagonal shield, spears, a sword and what may be a pair of greaves (**fig. 283**).

The carnyx

The carnyx faces left, and is only shown from the bell upwards. No junctions are visible. The expanding bell curves into the head, which has a single ear and an eye with

drilled pupil. The crest (running the full visible length, and stopping on the top of the head) is decorated with incised diagonal lines to evoke hair. The mouth is open to about 60°, with the jaw tips recurved (the upper is lost). The modelling is very zoomorphic, with musculature and other anatomical features defined.

Dating evidence

Date estimates vary from Augustan to mid-1st century AD (Hagenweiler 2003, 148 n. 857). Stylistic parallels to the Turin reliefs (B2.6) are regularly quoted; these are also geographically close. A similar range of c. 15 BC-AD 50 is suggested here for the Novalesa relief.

Bibliography

Carducci 1982, 126-129 fig. 1. – Fogliato 1992, 44 f. – Hagenweiler 2003, 148. – Mercando 1993, 103.

Fig. 283 B2.7 Weapons frieze, Abbey of Novalesa, Susa: **a** the stone. – **b** the carnyx. – (a Mercando 1993, fig. 127; b drawing Alan Braby).

Fig. 284 B2.8 Weapons frieze, Padova: **a** overall view. – **b** detail. – **c** the carnyx. – (a-b Tosi 1992, 1 f.; c drawing Tanja Romankiewicz).

B2.8 Weapons frieze. – Padova (reg. Veneto / I)

(Current location: Padova, Museo Civico Archeologico, inv. no. 150)

A limestone architrave block from Padova bears decorative mouldings on the lower (recessed) half while the upper (projecting) part carries a weapons frieze (Tosi 1992). The left part is damaged but the remainder comprises a greave, spears, a muscle cuirass, hexagonal and pelta shields, a wheel, and a carnyx. Its length is 1.60 m and its height 0.66 m; it is now relatively thin, and has clearly been cut down (**fig. 284**).

G. Tosi argued (1992, 161) it was unlikely to come from a tomb because it is too large and too architecturally elaborate for this area's traditions. Neither of these holds water, as such friezes (as architraves or other components of complex funerary monuments) are quite acceptable parts of funerary monuments. Its findspot, away from the ancient urban centre, is also consistent with a tomb. Tosi indulged in some convoluted arguments over its significance (Tosi 1992, 162-164), arguing the presence of a Greek-style cuirass along with Gallic weaponry links to events in Padova's early history in the 4th-3rd centuries BC when they fought against the Gauls and also (according to Livy) repelled a Spartan naval expedition. In fact the cuirass is conventional, and this is a typical frieze with a mixture of weapons, the barbarian components being the carnyx, wheel (symbolising chariots), hexagonal shield, and the unusual spear; Polito (1998, 56. 169; 2012) argued this was an Iberian type.

The carnyx

Inclusions in the limestone mean that there is little fine detail and it is also clear the sculptor did not aspire to this, as there are plentiful claw-chisel marks. The mouthpiece is obscured, but the plain tube expands gradually into the bell and head, curving through c. 130°; no junctions are shown. A crest runs along the bell to the ear, with incised vertical double-bars evoking spiky bristles, and a marginal line at the outer edge. The head has two forward-pointing ears (hollowed for definition), a bossed eye, and a mouth (also slightly hollowed) open to 180°.

Dating evidence

Tosi's discussion of the dating is convoluted, as the supposed connection to the Spartan expedition confuses matters. Stylistically Polito noted strong parallels with the unusual mouldings on the arch of Pola, suggesting a date in the first few decades AD (c. AD 1-30). The dating of the Pola arch is itself debated, but Kleiner's assessment (1992, 111 f.) concurred with a late Augustan-early Tiberian date. The iconography would fit this context well, with the carnyx representing Gauls and the spear Iberians, and thus marking Augustus' success in these areas.

Bibliography

Bosio et al. 1981, 278 fig. 152. – Polito 1998, 169. – Tosi 1992.

B2.9 Weapons frieze. – Como (reg. Lombardia / I)

(Current location: Como, Civico Museo Archeologico Giovio, inv. no. L 411)

A rectangular marble block of unknown provenance from the Como area preserves part of a weapons frieze with a mixture of material (**fig. 285**). A trophy (with muscle cuirass and sword) supports pairs of hexagonal shields; the remainder of the frieze comprises round, curved rectangular and hexagonal shields, a muscle cuirass, greaves,

b

Fig. 285 B2.9 Weapons frieze, Como: **a** the stone. – **b** the carnyx. – (a Rossignani/Sacchi 1993, pl. 28, 2; b drawing Alan Braby).

spears, a bow and quiver (with conical top), and, on the right of the scene, a fragmentary carnyx, emerging from behind a round shield, facing right, with the edge of the head broken off.

The carnyx
The lower tube is hidden; there are no obvious technical features on the visible portion. A crest starts around the base of the bell and runs the full visible length to the fracture; tufts of hair are defined by rectangular hole. The head has a single visible ear, an eye, and a highly flared lower jaw, the upper one being lost.

Dating evidence
Maria Pia Rossignani and Furio Sacchi (1993, 132 f.) discussed stylistic parallels for the dating, and suggested the frieze most likely dates to the early 1st century AD.

Bibliography
Rossignani/Sacchi 1993, 131-134 pls 28, 2; 36, 2.

B2.10 Pilaster base with weapons frieze. – Verona (reg. Veneto / I)

(Current location: Verona, Museo Archeologico, inv. no. 22687)
Two rectangular limestone pilaster bases on display in the Museo Archeologico in Verona (nos 22687 and 22683) feature weapons friezes. The only published reference so far traced illustrates one of the bases (Marconi 1937, 144 fig. 100) but provides no further information. The bases are near-identical cuboids about 0.7 m high with a moulded plinth and capital on three sides, and carving on the front. Differences between the two are very minor: 22683 has a leaf frieze in the basal mouldings whereas 22687 is plain, and their weapons friezes are slightly different. They bear similar traces of reuse, with a T-shaped groove carved into one side and the mouldings trimmed to accommodate it. On 22683 the mouldings on the left side have been trimmed; on 22687 it is the right side, with only the rear part of the mouldings trimmed. The T here has a curving vertical bar. Both are made in the same limestone, its coarse structure giving the surface a very cracked appearance.

The two friezes have the same basic structure, and differ only in detail. The focal element is a round shield with crossed spears behind it, points downwards, flanked by hexagonal shields with oval bosses, with a double axe and muscle cuirass above, and a helmet below flanked by greaves. The bowl helmet, with brim and cheekpieces, is seen from the front on 22687, but from the side on 22683. **Table 67** shows the differences between the two. It is a mixture of Classical/conventional pieces (cuirass, round shield, pelta shield) and barbarian items: the carnyx,

probably the hexagonal shields and the archery gear, a mixture implying both eastern and northern barbarians. The most likely context is as part of an ornate funerary monument.

The carnyx
22687 has a vertical carnyx, facing left, in the bottom left corner (**fig. 286**). It is unusual in showing all of the instrument, with a slight curve at the bottom into a squared mouthpiece; evidence of a curve is otherwise very rare indeed. However, it must be noted that the carving shows no technical knowledge of the instrument: tube and bell are plain, with no junctions, there is no crest, and the head is treated naturalistically, with a raised ridge round a slightly sunken eye with a raised pupil. The mouth is slightly open, and there is a single prominent forward-pointing ear.

Dating evidence
It seems there has been no discussion of this piece, which is absent from both general surveys of the area's sculpture and of weapons friezes (Dütschke 1880; Hagenweiler 2003; Polito 1998). The range of weaponry is not distinctive enough to offer much help. The style is straightforward, with no unnecessary decoration of objects nor much overlapping; in this it is most reminiscent of friezes such as Alba Fucens and Scafa (B2.4-5), Narbonne and Avignon (B3.1-2), Chiusi, Teramo or the basilica of S. Agnese, Rome (Polito 1998, figs 93. 96. 100). However, the dates for these (from Polito) range from late 1st century BC

22687 only	shared	22683 only
open quiver with arrows	round shield	quiver with closed conical lid
curved rectangular shield	crossed spears	gladius
tuba	2 hexagonal shields	pelta shield
bow	muscle cuirass	
carnyx	double axe	
	bowl helmet	
	pair of greaves	

Tab. 67 Weaponry in the two Verona weapon panels (B2.10).

Fig. 286 B2.10 Pilaster base with weapons frieze, Verona: **a** general view. – **b-c** the carnyx. – (a-b photos Fraser Hunter; c drawing Alan Braby).

(or even earlier) to the early 2nd century AD! In truth, the dating of this piece cannot currently be narrowed down beyond c. 25 BC-AD 100.

Bibliography
Marconi 1937, 144 fig. 100.

B2.11 Tomb stucco of Victory with carnyx. – Pompeii (reg. Campania/I)

(Current location: destroyed)
François Mazois (1824, pl. XXVI, 1) illustrated a Victory on a globe holding a carnyx from Pompeii. Misleadingly, this was subsequently published by Edmond Saglio (1887) and Salomon Reinach (1922, 145 no. 5) as a painting, but Mazois (1824, 44) made clear it was a stucco relief. His description and illustrations (*ibidem* 37. 44f. pls XIV. XV. XVIII. XXIV. XXVI) give the setting soon after discovery, with Valentin Kockel (1983, 90-96) providing a thorough modern analysis. It comes from a tomb excavated in 1813

in the cemetery outside the western gate, lining the road to Herculaneum (**fig. 287a-b**; tomb 20 on the south side of the Via dei Sepolcri; Toynbee 1971, fig. 11; La Porta et al. 1983, 222; Kockel 1983, facing p. 212). The tomb is that of C. Calventius Quietus, and comprises a funerary altar on a stepped podium surrounded by a low enclosure wall (6.10m × 6.46m) which is gabled at the rear and bears short square pillars with pyramidal caps. The tomb is marble with the wall of masonry covered with stucco (**fig. 287c**). The inscription reads:

C.CALVENTIO.QVIETO / AVGVSTALI /
HVIC.OB.MVNIFICENT.DECVRIONVM /
DECRETO.ET.POPVLI.CONSESV.BISELLI /
HONOR.DATVS.EST
(CIL X 1026)

For Gaius Calventius Quietus, Augustalis. To this
man, on account of his generosity, by the decree
of the decurions and with the consent of the people, an honorific chair was given

Quietus was an *augustalis*, a role connected with the Imperial cult which enabled him to gain prestige from act-
ing as a benefactor (Hornblower/Spawforth 1996, 215).
Most *augustales* were freedmen. Below the inscription is
a depiction of a *bisellium*, a double-seat awarded to high-
ranking officials for use on public occasions such as the
theatre (Ramsay 1875; Holliday 2002, 192f.).

Mazois noted that no actual burial was found in the excavations and suggested it was a cenotaph, although Joce-
lyn Toynbee (1971, 124f.) commented that there could
have been an urn buried below the monument. Kockel's
analysis (1983, 97) indicated this area was for burials
rather than cenotaphs and argued the burial lies below
the altar, which was not removed. This seems logical.

The altar is highly decorated, while the gable bears flying Victories holding a blank panel and the raised pillars
on the enclosure wall have stucco reliefs. Those illustrated
are Oedipus and the sphinx, Theseus resting, a female
torch-bearer and two Victories. Mazois noted that he
drew the reliefs soon after the discovery, before the rains
and frosts detached them. The Victories are on the corner pillars, facing the street. They stand on globes; one
holds a carnyx, the other a vexillum standard (**fig. 287c.
e**). There is some inconsistency in their positioning: in the
more detailed view (pl. XXIV), the carnyx is on the left pillar, but on the general view (pl. XVIII) they are reversed.
The stuccos are lost; although Toynbee discussed them in

the present tense, they are absent in the photos in Kockel
(1983, pl. 23a; here **fig. 287d**), and Prof Lawrence Keppie
has confirmed this (pers. comm. 2004).

The choice of iconography is unusual. The tomb is Vespasianic in date (see below), and the figure of Victory on
a globe finds coin parallels of the Civil War and early in
Vespasian's reign (Kockel 1983, 92), evoking a theme used
earlier by Augustus. Yet the specific source is unclear: Victory holding a carnyx is otherwise unparalleled in Roman
iconography, and the carnyx was not a major propaganda
motif at this time. The nearest occurrences are coins of
the Civil War and Galba (A5.1-2), a rare and thus unlikely
source, and possible carnyces on coins of AD 79 (A5?1-
2) marking campaigns in Britain. The carnyces are highly
stylised, suggesting there was a memory in Italy of such
things but little contemporary knowledge of how they
were meant to look. It is unlikely they relate to the career
of the deceased; it would be exceptional for a freedman
to have a military career. The depiction thus remains enigmatic – could it be a reflection of current events, in the
ongoing campaigns in Britain? Kockel (1983, 96f.) noted
how the tomb bears conspicuous signs of loyalty to the
Flavian dynasty in its decoration, so a desire to reflect current events is not impossible, while its arguably unfinished
nature (see below) could imply a date of AD 78-79, consistent with the Agricolan campaigns. This is the only contemporary context for carnyx use, but in the absence of
any official propaganda prototypes it is exceedingly hard
to argue, and despite the lack of parallels we cannot rule it
out as a rarely-used stock motif. It remains puzzling.

The carnyx

The carnyx is of a rather unusual form (**fig. 287e-f**),
but Roger Ling (*in litt* 7.3.1994) indicated that Mazois's
drawings were normally quite accurate. Victory holds the
carnyx, the mouthpiece towards the left, the head up to
the right, facing left. The tube is sinuous and slightly taper-

Fig. 287 B2.11 Tomb stucco of Victory
with carnyx, Pompeii: **a** general view; the
tomb is the first altar on the right side. –
b plan (tomb 20). – **c** condition as found;
an arrow indicates the relevant stucco. –
d modern condition. – **e** the carnyx scene
as found. – **f** detail of the carnyx. – (a Mazois 1824, pl. xiv; b Kockel 1983, fig. 11;
c Mazois 1824, pl. xxiv, 1; d Kockel 1983,
pl. 23; e Mazois 1824, pl. xxvi, 1; f drawing Tanja Romankiewicz).

a

Fig. 287 (continued)

ing; it curves more markedly at the base, where there is a cupped mouthpiece. There is no crest or ear, but the head does have an eye and bends through 270° to face back against the tube, with the mouth wide open to c. 180°.

Dating evidence
Kockel (1983, 96 f.) provided a detailed discussion of the dating. The structure appears to be of two phases, with the altar later than the enclosure; the whole structure may have been renovated and the decoration renewed in the second phase. Both phases date to the last years of Pompeii, based on a number of criteria. There are epigraphic references to the deceased and his ?son in the years after AD 50; the unweathered nature of the inscription and decoration imply it was quite fresh when buried, while the space at the bottom of the inscription suggests it may have been unfinished, with the name of the erector of the monument (the son?) still to be added. Detailed architectural and stylistic comparisons with neighbouring tombs provide correlations and suggest this one was late in the sequence. Of key importance here is the use of decorative motifs (such as Victory on a globe, or the *corona civica* wreaths on the altar sides) which are paralleled only in the Vespasianic readoption of Augustan motifs. From this Kockel argued persuasively for a date of AD 70-79.

Bibliography
Kockel 1983, 90-97. – Mazois 1824, 37. 44 f. pls XIV. XV. XVIII. XXIV. XXVI. – Reinach 1922, 145 no. 5. – Saglio 1887. – Toynbee 1971, 124 f.

B2.12 Cuirass statue. – Osteria dell'Osa / Gabii (reg. Lazio / I)

(Current location: Auch, Musée des Jacobins)
Christophe Vendries (1999, fig. 17) illustrated a trophy scene with a carnyx from a marble cuirass statue found at Gabii (modern Osteria dell'Osa) in Latium. It is restored with the head of Trajan, but is of late Flavian date (fig. 288a; Vermeule 1960, 46 no. 100). Richard Gergel (1994, 199 fig. 12, 12), Vendries (1999, 388) and Alexandre Stefan (2005, 451) interpreted it as a statue of Domitian, although differing in their views of the victories commemorated.

The statue has not been seen first-hand, and this description is taken from photos kindly provided by Christophe Vendries (fig. 288). The body of the trophy comprises a cloak, topped with a horned fur-covered helmet. Each arm bears a hexagonal shield, one with a round umbo, one elongated; there may be a second, rectangular shield behind on the L arm. Behind these are animal standards (boars?) and spears. At the base of the trophy is a pile of arms, largely obscured by two kneeling bound male captives. Both are bare-chested and wear trousers, the R one also with a cloak; he is bearded, but this is not so clear on the L. Behind them are two hexagonal shields on the L, and an oval shield, cloak and carnyx on the R.

Fig. 288 B2.12 Cuirass statue, Gabii: **a** general view. – **b** the trophy scene. – **c** detail of carnyx. – **d** the carnyx. – (a-c photos Christophe Vendries; d drawing Tanja Romankiewicz).

The carnyx
The carnyx appears from behind the back of the R prisoner, and is presumably meant to be stuck in the pile of arms. It has a plain cylindrical tube, slightly curving as it rises and merges into the cylindrical bell. No junctions or other technical details are shown. A plain crest runs from about where the bell starts to just behind the ear. The head is curved through 160°, pointing towards the ground (perhaps a deliberate artistic device to indicate dejection or defeat). Details of the head are not clear on the picture, but it has an ear and perhaps an eye; the mouth is open to about 70°.

Dating evidence
Dated stylistically by Cornelius Vermeule (1960, 46) to late Flavian or Trajanic times; Gergel (1994, 199) and Vendries

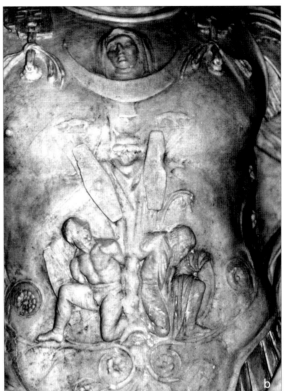

Fig. 288   (continued)

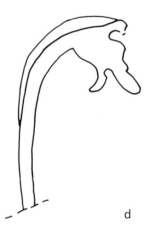

d

(1999, 388) connected this iconographic type with Domitian's German campaigns (against the Chatti) in AD 83 (Cary/Wilson 1963, 285-288). Stefan (2005, 451) argued that the differences in attire between the prisoners mean that two different barbarian groups are symbolised, and identified the right one as a Dacian, connecting it to the victories over the Dacians and Germans in AD 85 and the double triumph of 89. The iconography does not seem distinctive enough to be certain about this, and a date of c. AD 83-89 is used.

Bibliography
Vendries 1999, 388 no. 17. – Vermeule 1960, 46 no. 100.

B2.13 Weapons frieze from a tomb. – Parma (reg. Emilia-Romagna / I)

(Current location: Parma, Museo Nazionale d'Antichità, inv. no. S38, S44, S45)
Three marble blocks and a fragment from a weapons frieze preserved in the museum in Parma are described by Hans Dütschke (1882, 357 f. nos 859-862) and Patricia Hagenweiler (2003, 12-14); Dütschke's catalogue numbers are used to refer to them. Two of them join (859-860; **fig. 289a**); the third fragment (not figured here) is illus-

trated by Polito (1998, fig. 141). All bar the fragment have low-relief marginal borders at top and bottom; 861 is the right-hand end of the frieze, with part of another decorative panel on the perpendicular face showing a griffin with one paw on a krater. The blocks are some 460 mm T. and 875 mm H.; 859-860 combined are c. 1750 mm L., while 861 is 1210 mm. They entered the museum in 1809, and were found in a secondary context built into the ponte

Fig. 289 B2.13 Weapons frieze, Parma: **a** the blocks. – **b** scene with carnyx. – **c** the carnyx. – (a-b photos Fraser Hunter; c drawing Alan Braby).

c

Caprazucca, immediately south-west of the Roman town (a later source puts the discovery near the church of S. Sepolcro, but the earlier source is generally accurate; Rossignani 1975, 22 pl. II). The findspot lies near the forum, and it has been suggested the blocks came from a monumental structure at the entrance (Tempesta 1992, 329), or less prescriptively an uncertain honorific or commemorative monument (Rossignani 1975, 75; Hagenweiler 2003, 154 f.). However, the griffin iconography is more typical for a funerary context (Dütschke 1882, 358 n. 1) and they probably derive from an ornate tomb. A considerable range of blocks is known from the river near the bridge, from several different buildings and monuments (Rossignani 1975, 22).

The main element of the frieze is a row of overlapping shields of various types with a range of weaponry protruding from behind them or positioned at their base. The following material is represented: carnyx (misidentified by Dütschke as an eagle-handled sword); shields (round, legionary, oval, hexagonal, pelta); spears; helmets with crest and cheekguards; vexillum standards; swords in their scabbards; curved dagger, perhaps a gladiatorial *sica*; wheel; greaves; quiver and a bundle of arrows; muscle cuirasses;

dolabra. One oval and one hexagonal shield feature torcs in their decoration.

The crescentic pelta shield in front of the carnyx has a trophy scene, with a muscle cuirass, bowl helmet (lacking cheek pieces), and paired crossed hexagonal shields on the arms. At the base are two captives; to the left a seated naked woman with in front of her a helmet and ?sword. To the right is an indistinct standing figure, facing L.

The sculpture's likely Flavian date and the equipment represented suggest a connection to the Flavian campaigns in Britain or Germany.

The carnyx

The carnyx appears from behind a pelta shield about the middle of the larger block, angled slightly to the right and facing right (**fig. 289b-c**). The bell and head are visible above the shield, and the end of the tube below it. It is rather crude: the bell is notably thick, with no tube details. A crest comprising five back-pointing saw teeth runs from the visible base of the bell onto the head, stopping just short of the mouth. There is no ear, and the eye is a simple small round bulge; below it is a larger bulge, of no obvious function. The mouth is shown as if slightly angled

Fig. 290 B2.14 Weapons frieze, Pozzuoli: **a** the surviving fragment. – **b** the carnyx. – (a photo Margaret Robb; b drawing Alan Braby).

b

to the viewer, and is slightly hollowed; the jaws are open to c. 180° with the tips slightly recurved. The end of the tube and mouthpiece are shown in flat relief with no real detail, but the mouthpiece is straight and squared with a slight lip.

Dating evidence
A wide variety of dates, from Augustan to 2nd century AD, has been proposed. Hagenweiler (2003, 14) drew stylistic parallels to the Pula frieze of Augustan date, whereas

Polito (1998, 200 f.) found Flavian parallels for the trophy, helmet and griffin, supported by late 1st - 2nd century parallels for the general decorative style. Polito's view is followed here, and a late Flavian date (AD 80-100) is likely.

Bibliography
Hagenweiler 2003, 12-14. – Polito 1998, 200 f. figs 140-141. – Rossignani 1975, 22. 74-76. – Tempesta 1992, 329 fig. 15.

B2.14 Weapons frieze. – Pozzuoli / Puteoli, Rione Terra (reg. Campania / I)

(Current location: Pozzuoli, Museo Archeologico, inv. no. 292827)
Excavations in the heart of Pozzuoli (ancient Puteoli), in the area known as Rione Terre, uncovered a small fragment of a marble weapons frieze (fig. 290). Its near-square form indicates it has been reused, but the publications found so far give no find circumstances. The fragment has a plain border on one side and two decorated friezes (egg-and-dart and floral) on the other. The main frieze features a gladiatorial helmet decorated with a triton, a cloak, the arm of a cuirass, oval shields, a round shield seen from the rear, barbed and unbarbed spears, a boar standard and a carnyx.

The carnyx
Only the bell and head are visible, emerging from behind the boar standard and facing right. There is a pronounced moulding at the bell-head junction, and a simple bar crest running up the bell to the ears, both of which are broken. The head is simply carved, with a naturalistic eye and flared mouth, the tip of the lower jaw broken.

Dating evidence
Fausto Zevi (2009, 264) drew parallels to the friezes from the Uffizi and Capua, and from this suggested a late Flavian or early Trajanic date (c. AD 85-105).

Bibliography
Zevi 2009, 264. (I am grateful to Prof. Lawrence Keppie for drawing my attention to this find and for images of it.)

B2.15 Arch of Trajan. – Benevento (reg. Campania / I)

(Current location: *in situ*)

On the northern edge of the town of Benvento lies a monumental arch dedicated to Trajan which bears a magnificent series of decorated marble reliefs (**fig. 291a**). The arch is single-bayed, with four relief panels on each side, an encircling frieze above this and an attic with an inscription flanked by two further panels on each side. The sides are generally referred to as »city« and »country«, depending on where they face. The passage is flanked by friezes with another decorative panel above in the soffit of the arch. Trajan's titles in the inscription date the arch to AD 114, but this may be the foundation date; Hadrian's portrait has been recognised in the attic friezes, and it is likely that the arch was completed under him both as an act of *pietas* and to associate him with Trajan in people's minds (Kleiner 1992, 228 f.). The studies of the arch used as the basis for this summary are Ian Richmond (1969, 229-238), Mario Rotili (1972), Niels Hannestad (1988, 177-186) and Diana Kleiner (1992, 224-229).

The arch commemorates Trajan's achievements, both empire-wide and local. The passage reliefs refer specifically to local events. In one Trajan makes a sacrifice, marking the opening of the extension of the Via Appia (the Via Traiana) from Benevento to Brindisi in 109; the arch lies on the edge of the town, where the road departed for Brindisi. In the other Trajan distributes food supplies (*alimenta*) to needy families, a widespread policy of his but one of particular relevance locally as Benevento was a distribution centre.

The other panels commemorate the range of activities which Trajan undertook to benefit the empire. There is debate over some individual scenes (summarised in the references above) but the details are not of central importance here. One major theme is the campaigns in Germany and Dacia: there are depictions of Trajan's entry to Rome in AD 99 after pacifying the German frontier, his Dacian triumph in AD 107 (on the encircling frieze), Trajan's reception by the Dacian gods, his vanquishing of Dacia personified, and his return from the Dacian wars; the river gods Euphrates and Danube refer to the Dacian campaigns and to those in Parthia, in progress when the arch was under construction. It is notable that actual combats are not shown; rather it is the symbolic events around these, and Trajan's role in securing the empire. Other scenes depict the reorganisation of the army and the restoration of army discipline, the foundation of colonies, the building of harbours (notably that of Ostia), and the distribution of food (or arguably the growth of agriculture). Hannestad (1988, 177) aptly described it as an »illustrated catalogue of the Emperor's contribution to the welfare of Rome«.

The panel of main concern here is that in the soffit of the arch (**fig. 291b**). Within an outer border of coffers with rosettes and an inner one of spolia, Trajan in military dress

(muscle cuirass and *paludamentum*) is crowned with a laurel wreath by Victory. The inner border includes three carnyces. The relief has only been seen in pictures (notably Rotili 1972, pl. XXI, 2), and thus the details have not been confirmed first-hand, but as a minimum the following weaponry is represented:

- Shield: oval; hexagonal; figure of eight; pelta; ?round
- Helmet: Phrygian; high-domed with cheek guards and a decorative ring on top; fur-covered
- Sword: long sword in scabbard; falx; perhaps bird-hilted sword (only the ?hilt is visible)
- Axe (single-edged)
- Spear
- Muscle cuirass
- Clothing (cloak)
- Standard: draco (1); animal (1); vexillum
- Other: carnyx (3); bow; quiver

Some of this very diverse range of material is conventional or Roman (the pelta and figure-of-eight shields, the muscle cuirasses, the vexillum standards), but most is barbarian. The shields (oval and hexagonal) are quite generic, but the other weaponry includes both Dacian/Sarmatian and Germanic material, as Kleiner (1992, 227) argued. The frieze thus commemorates Trajan's Germanic and Dacian campaigns, as also reflected in his titles in the inscription (for his German campaigns on the Rhine and perhaps the Danube, see Bennett 2001, 43-52). Of the equipment, the single examples of a draco standard and falx are clearly Dacian, while Phrygian-style helmets are also known on the base of Trajan's Column and bows and arrows would be more typical for Dacians than Germans. The fur-covered helmet is normally a Germanic type (compare the example in the Farnesi trophies; B1.4.1) and animal standards are unrepresented in Dacian iconography but occur in Germanic (chapter 9). Thus the equipment supports both Germanic and Dacian victories being commemorated. The corollary of this is that we cannot be sure whether in this context the carnyces were seen as Dacian or Germanic, as they were in use by both groups.

The carnyces

Three carnyces are depicted on the border relief. Without first-hand examination details are inevitably uncertain (**fig. 291c**).

Carnyx 1: top border, about the middle of the bottom edge, facing down. Upper part of slender cylindrical tube, swelling rapidly into a bulbous head with the mouth open to 180°, the jaw tips recurved (especially the upper). It appears to have a crest on the head and bell; no further details visible.

Carnyx 2: top edge of top border, just above and right of carnyx 1, facing down. Cylindrical tube with the bell expanding more gradually than 1 and 3. Mouth open to

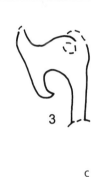

Fig. 291 B2.15 Arch of Trajan, Benevento: **a** general view. – **b** detail of soffit panel with carnyx locations marked. – **c** carnyces. – (a-b Rotili 1972, frontis. pl. 2; c drawing Tanja Romankiewicz).

180°, jaw tips apparently damaged; crest on head and bell, where it may end in a knob; no other details visible.

Carnyx 3: outer edge of left-hand border, about level with Trajan's knee. It faces left, with only the upper tube, bell and head visible. It appears to have a cylindrical tube with a short bell curving rapidly into the head. The mouth is open to 180° with the ends recurved; it may have an ear and there is a hint of an eye, but no crest.

Dating evidence
The inscription is dated to AD 114, while it is generally accepted that the arch was completed in the early years of Hadrian's reign, giving a dating bracket of AD 114-118.

Bibliography
Hannestad 1988, 177-186. – Kleiner 1992, 224-229. – Richmond 1969, 229-238. – Rotili 1972.

B2.16 Weapons frieze bordering an inscription – ?Cumae (reg. Campania / I)

(Current location: Berlin, Pergamonmuseum, inv. no. SR 958)
Two fragments of a marble weapons frieze, now in the Pergamonmuseum, were purchased in 1829 in Naples, and attributed to Cumae (Anon. 1891, no. 958; Reinach 1912, 36; Picard 1957, pl. XIV; Polito 1998, 209-211). The two fragments do not join but are clearly from the same sculpture. The larger fragment is 0.43 m H. 0.90 m L. 0.09 m T.; the smaller survives to 0.365 m H. 0.38 m L. 0.09 m T. (**fig. 292**). The larger fragment preserves the complete height, but both ends are broken; the smaller fragment lacks the lower border, but preserves an original square edge on its right hand side. As this edge lacks a border, it was probably one panel within a larger composition.

Fig. 292 B2.16 Weapons frieze, Cumae?: **a** fragment with inscription and trophy. – **b** larger frieze fragment. – **c** the carnyx. – (a-b photos Fraser Hunter; c drawing Tanja Romankiewicz).

The blocks have a narrow border top and bottom with a moulding bearing stylised vegetal decoration between this and the recessed frieze. The frieze is worked in deep three-dimensional relief, with some items incised on the background. The top border of the right fragment bears part of an inscription: »...DIA AVG«, expanded by Theodor Mommsen as *(Mati)dia Aug(usta)*, Trajan's niece (Anon. 1891, no. 958). Polito (1998, 209-211) suggested *Concordia Aug* as an alternative, seeing this as a likely Hadrianic form since *Concordia Exercitum* or *Militum* is

found on Hadrianic coinage. However, Roger Tomlin (pers. comm.) could find no instance of *Concordia Aug* prior to the sole reign of Caracalla; he confirmed that *Matidia Augusta* is the most likely restoration. It must be the final part of a longer inscription, not least because the top serifs are missing and were presumably on the block above. Thus the frieze was part of the border decoration of a large Imperial inscription.

The frieze comprises a mass of weaponry within which are a couple of focal points: in the left fragment, a standing female figure, Roma or Virtus (Anon. 1891, no. 958); and on the right fragment, a trophy with two bound captives at its base. The trophy comprises a muscle cuirass and flaps, with a crested helmet (with cheek guards) above and two crossed hexagonal shields on each arm. Behind each shield is a pair of spears; other equipment on the arms includes a carnyx, tuba, pelta shield and »Celtic lituus«. A crested helmet lies at the foot of the trophy. To the right is a bound bare-chested male barbarian, standing or kneeling (his legs are lost), who wears a cloak and trousers held by a belt; on the left is a seated naked barbarian, his back to the viewer and his hands tied behind his back. Both have lost their heads. The other material on the frieze is a mix of Classical, conventional and barbarian types. The following objects are present.

- Shields: hexagonal, oval (some curved, most flat; some with flattened ends), round and pelta; most of the hexagonal shields have round umbos but one is elongated
- Weaponry: spears (kite and barbed; individually, in pairs tucked behind shield handgrips, and in a bundle); short swords in scabbards with belts; quiver
- Armour: muscle cuirass; greaves; lamellar arm and hand guard
- Helmets: Attic; standard bearer's, with furry cover and long trailing hair
- Standards: eagle; Roman with phalerae; wolf/dog
- Music: curved horns (»Celtic litui«); carnyx; tubae
- Ship equipment: stern, prow and anchor
- Wheels

(One feature at the left edge of the right fragment was not identified.)

The barbarians are of northern type, and this is supported by the equipment: the curved trumpet is most typically found in Germanic representations (see chapter 10), and animal standards tend to be Gaulish or Germanic (see **Appendix 5**). The wheel generally has British connotations (see chapter 9 and **Appendix 5**). The carnyx would be quite at home in this milieu. Only the single quiver points to eastern barbarians. There is a lot of Roman material (notably the eagle and disc standards, the lamellar arm guard and greaves) along with conventional items like muscle cuirasses and pelta shields, while the helmets are Roman types. The inclusion of nautical spolia is quite unusual, suggesting a desire to symbolise widespread or universal victories.

The piece's late Trajanic-Antonine dating (from the inscription; see below) suggests a number of potential contexts. In the absence of clearly Dacian material or significant quantities of eastern items it is unlikely to refer to Trajan's Dacian or Parthian wars. As all (bar his earliest) iconography evokes the Dacian campaigns, this suggests a Trajanic date is unlikely. Under Hadrian and Antoninus Pius, the most likely campaigns to be commemorated are ones in Britain (see **tab. 45**): the barbarian types are inappropriate for other major events in their reigns, notably the Jewish Revolt under Hadrian or Pius' Mauretanian War. For Hadrian, his *exercitus Britannicus* is marked on coins (Robertson 1975, 368), as is Antoninus Pius' reconquest of southern Scotland. This latter may be seen as more fitting for triumphal art, as it involved conquest rather than consolidation, and was marked on coins (Robertson 1975, 369) and local monuments (Keppie 1998, 49-56), although there are no surviving sculptural monuments outside Britain. The northern barbarian iconography is appropriate for Britain, and in this context the wheel might be significant as it appears to be a symbol of Britain. A fanciful reading could even connect the ship's parts to campaigns involving a naval element, either in the transport of troops or forays up the Scottish east coast. However, this is heading towards a strong risk of over-interpretation: none of the iconography can be specifically localised, and the inscription is a poor basis for detailed chronological correlations.

The carnyx

The carnyx appears from behind the right arm of the trophy, facing downwards; only the curving bell and head are visible (**fig. 292c**). The crest runs the full visible length, up to the forward-pointing ear; it is decorated with a series of vertical lines, each partition then being further decorated with a short vertical incision. The outer edge of the crest is a series of conjoined curves, giving it a wavy appearance. The head is anatomical rather than technical: there are no visible junctions, with a line at around the bell-head junction being musculature at the rear of the jaw. There is an eye with a drilled pupil, while the mouth is open at about 60°, with the ends then recurving back.

Dating evidence

Dating evidence comes from the inscription, best interpreted as referring to Matidia, Trajan's niece. She was granted the title Augusta on her mother's death in AD 112 and was deified on her death in AD 119 by Hadrian (Hornblower/Spawforth 1996, 937); this is the likely *terminus post quem*, which fits also with the lack of classically Trajanic material. She is honoured as Antoninus Pius' (adopted) great aunt (e.g. CIL X 3833), and a group of inscriptions to her of this date are known from Campania (CIL X 4744-4747); thus the Cumae relief fits readily into a local context. This evidence allows for a date range spanning the late reign of Trajan to the reign of Antoninus Pius, AD 119-161. A suitable occasion might be Antoninus Pius' second imperial acclamation of AD 143 after his Scottish victories, but this must remain hypothetical.

Bibliography
Anon. 1891, no. 958. – Polito 1998, 209-211. – Reinach 1912, 36.

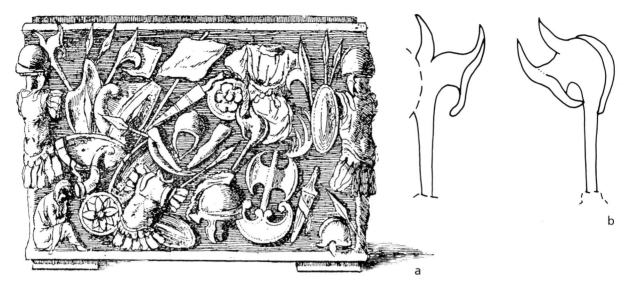

Fig. 293   B2.17 Funerary urn with weapons frieze: **a** the urn. – **b** the carnyces. – (a Lovatelli 1900, fig. 4; b drawing Tanja Romankiewicz).

B2.17 Funerary urn with weapons frieze. – Italy

(Current location: lost)

Rectangular marble funerary urn, the decoration including trophies and a panel of weaponry. The urn is illustrated by Ersilia Caetoni Lovatelli (1900, 260f.) in describing a related find from Villamagna; her account is taken from the Comte de Caylus (1759, 236f.), the primary source. As might be expected given its vintage it does not provide as full a description as might be desired, but the engravings appear to be accurate (**fig. 293**). Caylus came across it by accident in Paris (presumably in someone's collection, although this is not specified); such urns are most common in Italy and were probably made in Rome (Polito 1998, 222). It was not intact but the form could be reconstructed; it lacks the lid and any inscription, and only the two long faces are illustrated. One bears vegetal ornament with birds, the other weaponry. At each corner is a trophy comprising a muscle cuirass, an Attic helmet, and oval shields with elongated umbos. The weaponry face has spears and a carnyx behind the visible arms, with a grieving female captive seated at the base of the left trophy. Most of the items in the engraving are quite recognisable. They comprise shields (oval, hexagonal, round and pelta), another carnyx, vexillum standards, helmets (Attic, one with a crest), spears, greaves, short swords, a muscle cuirass, a tunic cuirass, a double-axe and a cornucopiae. The weaponry is thus rather conventional, with only the captive, the oval and hexagonal shields and the carnyces being clearly barbarian. This is insufficient to suggest who might be represented: it would be consistent with Gauls, Germans or Dacians. The urn is 0.30m high, and 0.49m × 0.43m in plan.

The carnyces

The overall form of the two carnyces is clear although details are uncertain from the engraving. The first lies behind the visible arm of the left trophy; it is angled upwards to the left slightly, and faces right. A slightly tapering tube, ear, eye peak and mouth open to 180° are shown. The second lies just right of the middle, facing left and angled up to the right. It has a near cylindrical tube with the bell expanding quite markedly. A simple crest runs the length of the bell to the ear; there is a possible eye peak, and the mouth is open to c. 180°, the tips slightly recurved.

Dating evidence

Such urns with weaponry are relatively rare but are typically of late 1st-early 2nd century date. There are two close parallels. A cylindrical one now in Bologna is dated by its inscription to the Hadrianic period (Sinn 1987, no. 552). The other, closer parallel is more debated; Friederike Sinn (1987, no. 94) interpreted it as early 1st century AD but Polito (1998, 222) saw parallels to late Antonine battle sarcophagi. This epitomises the problems of subjectivity in dating these items, but for consistency Polito's dating is followed here, expanded somewhat to encompass both parallels (AD 120-192).

Bibliography

Caylus 1759, 236f. pl. LXII. – Lovatelli 1900, 260f.

B2.18 Base with weapons frieze. – ?Frascati / Tusculum (reg. Lazio / I)

(Current location: Frascati, Palazzo Vescovile)
Marble pilaster base decorated on three sides (0.73 m H. 0.60 m W. 0.57 m T.). The front shows Victory inscribing a shield resting on a trophy, with captives beneath: a male wearing trousers, a child, and a woman with her head covered. The right has a frieze of arms, discussed below. The left side shows a soldier, with a horse behind, leading a bound captive male barbarian, bearded and trousered, with a naked torso and cloak. Its provenance is not recorded but is probably from Tusculum, the Roman precursor to Frascati, the source of most of the material in this collection; Martin Spannagel (1979, 359) argued it is not the kind of high-quality piece which would have been purchased and exchanged.

The weapons frieze comprises an angled muscle cuirass with oval shields in front, a cloak draped over their edge and a quiver hanging from them (fig. 294). In the lower left corner is a battering ram (an unusual feature) and axe, while behind the cuirass are an oval shield with a sword in its scabbard hanging from it, a vexillum standard, a barbed spear or arrow and a carnyx head facing up / left; a draco standard, now damaged, runs along the top.

The item is the base for a column; Spannagel (1979, 357) argued it is too small for a major public monument like an arch, but could have flanked a doorway or come from a private tomb. The iconography is official in character – there is no admixture of gladiatorial or mythical material – and it is best seen as coming from an official structure.

The carnyx
This description relies on published photographs. Only the upper bell and head are visible, with a crest decorated with triangles running the full visible length. The head (turned through 120°) has an eye, ?ear, and mouth open to c. 60°.

Dating evidence
Eugene Polito and Martin Spannagel both noted resemblances to material from Trajan's Forum, but Polito argued plausibly that it fits better in the Antonine period, on the basis of the style, the iconographic sources for scenes on the other faces, and details of the cuirass. The mixture of material – draco, carnyx, archery, axe – is consistent with the iconography of both the Dacian and Marcommanic Wars, but the barbarians are depicted as northern rather than Dacian, with no (surviving) evidence of Phrygian caps. Against this, the battering ram, a most unusual feature, is attested in connection with Dacians on the »Trophies of Marius«, or in use by Dacians on Trajan's Column, scene xxxii (Grisanti 1977, 49-51 pls XXII. XXVII; Lepper/Frere 1988, 80 pl. XXIV). Given the rarity of ram depictions, more weight should be put on the connection to northern barbarians, making a link to the Marcomannic War most likely; a date range of c. AD 175-190 is adopted here.

Bibliography
Polito 1998, 202 f. fig. 144. – Spannagel 1979, 348-377.

Fig. 294 B2.18 Base with weapons frieze, Frascati: **a** the sculpture. – **b** the carnyx. – (a Polito 1998, fig. 144; b drawing Tanja Romankiewicz).

B2.19 Sarcophagus front. – Palermo (reg. Sicilia / I)

(Current location: Palermo, Museo Archeologico Regionale, inv. no. 739/90)

The front of a small marble sarcophagus in the museum in Palermo bears a battle scene which places it in the group of late Antonine group battle sarcophagi connected with the Marcomannic Wars (Koch/Sichtermann 1982, 90-92; Kleiner 1992, 301). The battle friezes on these sarcophagi show some variation (Hamberg 1945, 172-186); this one is closely similar in overall composition to the Portonaccio sarcophagus (B1.15) but the battle scene is less complex, in part because the available relief field is narrower. It has not been seen first-hand, so some details are not certain, but Vincenzo Tusa (2005, 76f. pls CXXII-CXXVIII) provides a useful guide. Its precise provenance is not known.

The sarcophagus shows a battle scene flanked by trophies (**fig. 295a**). A Roman cavalry force is in the process of routing a group of barbarians. The Romans wear bowl helmets with a raised circumference, ring-finial and cheek-flaps, similar to those on Portonaccio; they wear scale armour, carry oval shields and fight with short sword and lance. Vexillum standards are visible in the background. The barbarians, both infantry and cavalry, are unarmoured and without helmets; they carry oval shields and fight with spears and short swords. The deceased is shown leading his troops in the middle of the composition, gesturing with his right arm as he rides down a barbarian. He is distinguished from the other Romans by being bare-headed and unarmed; he wears a muscle cuirass and cloak. Per Gustaf Hamberg (1945, 175) saw the barbarians as including both »standard Gallic types« and more Germanic individuals (probably on account of the near-nudity of some), but this appears over-complex and all can be seen as Germanic barbarians.

The two flanking trophies differ in detail and are very similar to those on Portonaccio (**fig. 295b-c**). That on the left is a belted tunic with a cloak tied over the shoulders, crowned by a helmet with cheek-pieces. In front stand a barbarian couple, with a Phrygian helmet between them. Each arm carries an oval shield. Behind this on the left (as viewed) are two opposed carnyces (#1-2) and a tuba; on

the right are tuba, carnyx (#3) and vexillum standard. The right trophy also comprises a belted tunic and cloak tied round the shoulders, but the helmet has a face-mask as well as cheek-pieces, and is crowned with a ring and two horns. A barbarian couple stand in front, the woman with her right breast bare; between them is a helmet as worn by the Romans. The left arm bears an oval shield, behind which is a vexillum standard, carnyx (#4) and what may be a falx. The right arm has a hide-shaped hexagonal shield, behind which is a spear and what may be a falx and an axe, both broken.

Both trophies are a mixture of Roman and barbarian equipment, predominantly the latter. The falx, although mostly associated with Trajan's Dacian campaigns, is also found in late Antonine iconography connected with the Marcomannic Wars; for instance, it appears on the small Ludovisi battle sarcophagus (Andreae 1956, no. 5). The single-edged axe also appears in the iconography of this period (see **Appendix 5**).

The carnyces

The left trophy has three carnyces (#1-3), the right one (#4). All are similar and rather stylised, with no technical details such as junctions: they have simple eyes, with incised lines running back from these onto the bell (**fig. 295d**). They lack ears and two have no crests. Carnyx 2 is heavily worn, and carnyx 4 has lost much of the bell and tube.

Dating evidence

The series is dated by stylistic comparisons to the late Antonine period, c. 160-200 (Koch/Sichtermann 1982, 90-92; Kleiner 1992, 301f.); the close similarities of this example to Portonaccio suggest a similar date of c. AD 175-190.

Bibliography

Andreae 1956, no. 9. – Hamberg 1945, 175f. pl. 39. – Picard 1957, 445 pl. XXIII. – Tusa 2005, 76f. pls CXXII-CXXVIII.

B3 GAULISH PROVINCES

B3.1 Weapons friezes from tombs, Narbonne (dép. Aude / F)

(Current location: Narbonne, Musée Lapidaire)

The Musée Lapidaire in Narbonne houses one of the finest collections of Roman sculpture in France with over 1700 pieces, the vast majority from the demolition of the town

ramparts. When these were constructed in the 16th century there was a deliberate policy of reusing Roman stonework for ornamental effect. Demolition started in 1869, producing a huge array of sculpture (Espérandieu 1907,

Fig. 295 B2.19 Sarcophagus, Palermo:
a general view. – **b** left trophy. – **c** right trophy. – **d** carnyces. – (a-c Tusa 1995, pls CXII. CXXVI-CXXVII; d drawing Tanja Romankiewicz / Fraser Hunter).

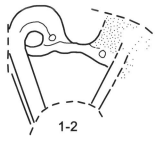

1-2   3   4   d

355-359); the illustrations published by Émile Espérandieu and Yves Solier (1986, fig. 10) give an indication of the appearance of the ramparts, dotted with sculpted fragments. There was a systematic bias to the reuse: the vast majority of surviving material is made of local stone, with marble fragments presumably being consigned to the furnaces to make lime (Hallier 1988, 109).

The origin of this material has been debated, but much of it clearly came from funerary monuments outside the Roman town. While it is hard to be dogmatic about the origins of the simpler architectural ornaments, the figural friezes are typical of funerary monuments (e. g. Widemann/Leblanc 1982), while some inscriptions support a funerary origin (e. g. Leblanc/Dodinet/Widemann 1980, 197; Espérandieu 1907, 428 no. 702). There has been more debate over the fragments of weapons friezes, with a persistent desire to link them to one or more postulated triumphal arches (e. g. Gayraud 1981, 282 f.). However, this cannot be sustained (Küpper-Böhm 1996, 167 f. 173 f.; Polito 1998, 171). These are not trophies but friezes of arms. While similar friezes do occur as minor elements on some triumphal arches, the total lack of trophies (a much more typical triumphal element) points strongly to a connection with tombs. One of the pieces has the remains of an inscription best seen as funerary, while the form can be paralleled in other tomb monuments. The Doric frieze with alternating weapons and bucrania is found in early Augustan graves, while a weapons frieze is seen vividly in the reconstructed tomb of L. Poblicius in Köln (Precht 1965, pls 1. 17-18). Poblicius was a veteran of Legio V Alauda, and it seems that weapons friezes were a typical attribute of soldiers' tombs: M. Janon (1986, 118) drew parallels to the votive deposition of weapons in a sanctuary at the end of a campaign or on leaving the army, while Annette Küpper-Böhm (1996, 173 f.) reviewed a range of interpretations, from general symbols of the deceased's good character through emblems of victory to specific military links; see further discussion in chapter 8. In the case of Narbonne, founded in 118 BC and subsequently turned into a colony for veterans of Caesar's Legio X (Rivet 1988, 74. 134), it is no surprise that so many weapons friezes are known. None of the material can be convincingly linked to a triumphal arch.

The main problem with studying the material is that the monuments have been reduced to their constituent blocks, and the sheer quantity has rather daunted scholars. Promising advances using early computer matching techniques made it possible to reconstruct partly a number of monuments, including figural scenes and weapons friezes (Leblanc/Dodinet/Widemann 1980; Leblanc/Widemann 1981; Widemann/Leblanc 1982; see also critique by Janon 1985, and response by Widemann/Leblanc 1985). Unfortunately these publications only present interim accounts of the work; no final report was produced. Most relevant here is the work of Leblanc and colleagues (1980)

on the weapons friezes. They studied 109 blocks, resolving 89 of them into 20 groupings; unfortunately the interim publication only presents 37 blocks, none including carnyces. In several cases they were able to show that different groupings followed the same basic design, implying they were different parts of a frieze from the same tomb, either from different sides or different heights.

Carnyces are found on four limestone blocks. Two (Espérandieu 1907, nos 691. 701) are closely similar in style and are probably from the same tomb. The others are not particularly close in style or composition, suggesting they came from separate monuments. The use of carnyces would be very appropriate for veterans of Caesar's Gallic Wars: it is quite evocative to think that these came from the tombs of people who saw the carnyx in battle. The weaponry depicted otherwise is a mixture of Roman, Gaulish, gladiatorial and conventional types. On the Roman side there are legionary shields and helmets, greaves, tubae and cornus. Gaulish equipment is represented by carnyces, oval and hexagonal shields (with elongated umbos and central ribs), boar standards, Gallic helmets, and arguably spears (singly or in bundles). Chain mail cuirasses are probably also Gaulish, given that these were legionary veterans rather than auxiliaries. Conventional and gladiatorial items include muscle cuirasses, belted tunic cuirasses, round shields (both flat and domed), pelta shields, curved swords, Phrygian helmets and double-axes. Swords could be either Roman or Gaulish. Given that both the deceased and much of the audience had first-hand experience of combat, we might expect a fair degree of accuracy in the depictions – or at least no outlandish errors. The style is not as naturalistic as is found in many Italian weapons friezes, with a preference for bold outlines and some slightly odd perspective views, and the depictions are somewhat stylised: there is not a great amount of technical detail on the objects. However, the overall effect was presumably one with which the veterans were content.

Little survives of one carnyx (B3.1.3), but the others are variations on a theme: there is a consistent picture of flared mouth and zoomorphic head, made naturalistic by modelling the musculature; given the relative naturalism of surviving French carnyces (chapter 7) this effect is not inappropriate. There are no technical details such as junctions. Crests tend to be long and jaws recurved, with no teeth. One example (B3.1.4.2) is unusual in having a decorated head.

Dating

It seems likely that most of this material dates to the late 1st century BC and early 1st century AD. Various styles are represented among the weapons friezes, some more stylised, others more detailed, but this could arise from different workshops as easily as different dates. Study of the foliated scrolls concluded that, while there were a very few later 1st century AD examples, most could be dated between 40 BC and 20 AD (Hallier 1988); an Augustan-Tiberian date is normally quoted for the weapons friezes (e.g. Anon. 1987, 110 f.). Polito (1998, 170-174) has suggested a stylistic subdivision and attempted a more precise dating, but this seems over-precise without more evidence, and 40 BC-AD 20 is taken here as the likely date range.

B3.1.1 Espérandieu 691

Damaged block from a weapons frieze, with plain upper architrave and lower border; both edges lost (fig. 296). The objects are arranged around a tunic cuirass with a cloak over the shoulders, held by a disc-shaped rosette brooch. On the L are a Gaulish helmet and carnyx; on the R, a pelta shield (with circular boss) overlain by two double-axes flanking a sheathed sword. This block joins to a second, illustrated by Émile Espérandieu (1907, 424). Details of this one are not so clear, but it features (from L) a pelta shield overlain by a sheathed sword and belt, and a shield of unclear form (or perhaps a pair of lamellar arm guards) overlain by another sheathed sword (?bird-headed) and a ?spear. The style of the carnyx is very similar to that on B3.1.2, and they probably come from the same monument. Overall L. of the two joining blocks 1.60 m, 0.74 m H., 0.55 m T.

The carnyx
The top of the tube, bell and head of the carnyx appear from behind the cuirass (fig. 300, 1); they are similar to B3.1.2. No junctions are shown. A crest runs the full visible length of the tube, stopping at the single forward-

Fig. 296 B3.1.1 Weapons frieze, Narbonne (Espérandieu 691). – (Photo Fraser Hunter).

pointing ear. It has an outer border and is decorated with a series of rectangular cut-outs to defined the tufts of the crest, as on B3.1.2. The ear is hollowed; the eye has a prominent brow, with bulbous eye and drill-defined pupil. The jaw is open to about 120°, with the lower jaw then recurving back to touch the bell; the upper is slightly thicker, its tip lost. The sculpture is deep-carved to create a three-dimensional feel, with the ear and jaw hollowed and some undercutting around the top of the head.

Bibliography
Espérandieu 1907, no. 691. – Homo-Lechner/Vendries 1993, 78.

B3.1.2 Espérandieu 701

(Inv. no. 949)
Top left corner of a block (fig. 297). From the left, it shows a chain mail cuirass overlying two spears, a crested helmet, carnyx, and crescentic shield overlying a double-axe and what may be a cornu; over the shield are the remains of a bird-hilted sword with sword belt. The carnyx is very similar to that on B3.1.1, and they are probably from the same monument. The surviving dimensions of the block are 0.58 m H. 0.70 m W. c. 0.45 m T.

The carnyx
The surface relief is in good condition, with some damage to the crest near the base and the top, the jaw and the lower part of the tube. The carnyx faces right, the lower tube lost off the broken edge (fig. 300, 2). There are no technical details of joins on the tube, whose diameter varies from 40 mm at the base to 57 mm on the

Fig. 297 B3.1.2 Weapons frieze, Narbonne (Espérandieu 701). – (Photo Fraser Hunter).

midpoint of the bell and 87 mm behind the ear. The crest runs the full visible length, stopping just beyond the ear. It is decorated with rectangular cut-outs which define a series of blocky tufts, with a plain border. The crest appears to narrow towards the base, although damage makes this uncertain. The head is quite naturalistic, with single ear, eye and flaring jaw. The pointed ear leans forward, and is defined from the head by a partial cut-away at its base. The eye has a prominent brow ridge and a drilled pupil. The mouth is open to about 140°, with no sign of any teeth; the lower jaw is straight, the upper slightly recurved. The whole has a very three-dimensional feel, with the relief surfaces being rounded, the whole tube being slightly undercut, and the mouth slightly hollowed internally. Overall L. 460 mm.

Bibliography
Espérandieu 1907, no. 701.

B3.1.3 Espérandieu 723

(Inv. no. 985)
Block with weapons frieze: from the L, part of carnyx, oval shield with elongated umbo and central rib, crossed greaves, part of second similar oval shield (fig. 298). Dimensions 0.58 m H. 1.17 m L. c. 0.45 m T.

The carnyx
Most of this carnyx lay on another, lost block. It faces L; all that is preserved is part of the bell and crest, and the rear underside of the head with the innermost part of the mouth, showing that the jaws were open (fig. 300, 3). Its surface is flat rather than curved. There is no internal detail or decoration; the tapering start of the crest is preserved, around the base of the bell. The upper part of the tube is worn away. The block has been reworked slightly when it was reused, with the top edge of the relief being lost and a rebated channel carved all round the sculpted face. Surviving L 230 mm, W 180 mm; relief depth 30 mm. Tube D. minimum 58 mm, maximum 111 mm. The crest is a maximum of 16 mm H.

Bibliography
Espérandieu 1907, no. 723.

Fig. 298 B3.1.3 Weapons frieze, Narbonne (Espérandieu 723). – (Photo Fraser Hunter).

Fig. 299 B3.1.4 Weapons frieze, Narbonne (museum inv. no. 740). – (Photo Fraser Hunter).

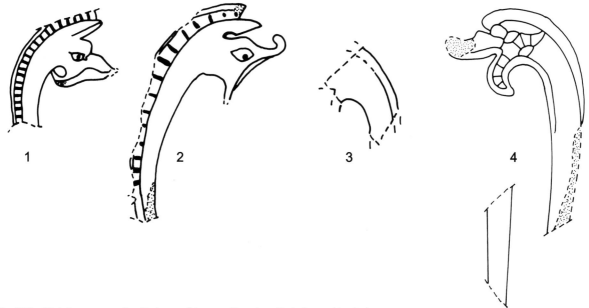

Fig. 300 B3.1 Carnyces on the Narbonne friezes. – (Drawings Tanja Romankiewicz).

B3.1.4 Museum inv. no. 740

Rectangular block with the remains of a rounded moulding at the top margin (**fig. 299**). It shows, from the left, a round shield with Medusa head flanked by two carnyces, and two crossed griffin-headed pelta shields, with only one terminal of the rearmost showing. Overall 1.12 m L. 0.44 m H. 0.36 m T. The carnyces lean outwards from the shield, facing in towards it.

The carnyces
Of the left-hand carnyx, only part of the tube is preserved with no technical details. Most of the right-hand carnyx is visible, although the tube runs off the block at the bottom; it may have continued onto another block, but given the shields are complete it is likely that this was its full extent, with the end not being defined (**fig. 300, 4**). Overall L. 440 mm. The tube (minimum D. 35 mm) is slightly damaged at the base; it is straight initially but curves gently as the bell expands. No junctions are shown. The plain crest rises up gradually from the probable base of the bell (where the curve starts); its maximum width is 20 mm. A border line on the inside of the bell, presumably for artistic effect, is continued to form the lip of the jaws. The head is decorated with incised lines, creating a series of scales; within this is a clear eye, the pupil indicated by a slight indentation; there is no certain ear, unless it is intended to be the rather squashed zone above the eye, within the line of the head. The mouth is slightly open (c. 50°) with the jaws flared, the upper jaw damaged where it runs onto the top border. There are no teeth, but the lips are clearly defined from the head by a border. The upper jaw has a bulge on its upper surface; it was debated whether this could be the eye, but one of the »scales« on the head is a more likely candidate, and this presumably is a fold in the jaw.

Bibliography
Unpublished.

B3.2 Weapons frieze from a tomb, Avignon (dép. Bouches-du-Rhône / F)

(Current location: Musée Lapidaire, Avignon, inv. no. I11) Émile Espérandieu (vol. I, no. 236) published a rectangular limestone block from Avignon, carved on two opposed long faces: both feature weaponry, one with crossed carnyces (**fig. 301a**). Other similar (but unifacial) blocks with weaponry in the museum, all from excavations in the rue Géline, are probably from the same monument (*ibidem* no. 234). This was the area of the forum, but the blocks were reused in a late Roman fortification wall (Gagnière / Granier 1986, 100-102). Over 80 fragments of sculptured stone were recovered from the excavations, including a series decorated with captives and trophies. These feature swords (short, curved), greaves, helmets, shields (oval, pelta, figure of eight), spears, and a boar standard. The curved sword and figure-of-eight shield are unusual features which Polito (1998, 43. 55. 170) saw as

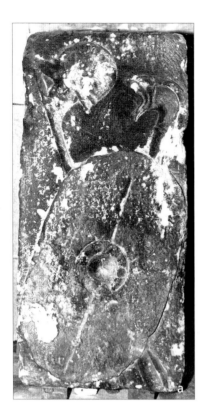

Fig. 301 B3.2 Weapons frieze from tomb, Avignon: **a** overall view. – **b** detail of mouthpiece and head. – **c** the carnyces. – (a photo Musée Calvet d'Avignon, cliché André Guerrand / Alban Rudelin; b photo Fraser Hunter; c drawing Alan Braby / Tanja Romankiewicz).

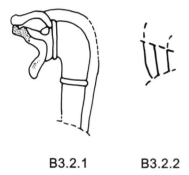

B3.2.1　　　　**B3.2.2**

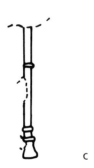

c

infrequent attributes for western or perhaps Balkan barbarians. One block features a figure (?Victory) leading a horse, while two others show captives.

These blocks are often attributed to a triumphal arch (Espérandieu 1901, 171; Gagnière/Granier 1986, 102). However, a reappraisal of the material by Küpper-Böhm

(1996, 161 f.) dismissed this, not least on account of the lack of any arch fragments in the extensive assemblage. Other fragments of sculpture and inscriptions recovered in the excavation are from funerary monuments (Gagnière/Granier 1986, 102), which is the most likely explanation of the current fragment.

The block under review here features an oval shield with round boss and central rib, with crossed carnyces behind it and a bowl helmet above (as currently displayed). The head of the lower carnyx runs onto another (lost) block, suggesting the block (0.93 m L. 0.45 m H. 0.61 m T.) should be in landscape rather than portrait format. The opposite face has a round shield and plumed helmet. In places the relief is very worn, and the stone is highly friable.

The carnyces

The carnyces are crossed behind an oval shield (**fig. 301b-c**). Of carnyx 1 (head at the top as displayed) only the bell and head are visible on this block; the rear of the bell is damaged. Carnyx 2, which appears at either end of the shield, lacks its head which was on an adjacent block. The key significance of this sculpture is that it provides the most detailed representation of a mouthpiece which we possess. As a result, a detailed description is provided.

Carnyx 1: a cylindrical tube (40 mm D.) emerges from behind the shield; at the tube-bell junction is a narrow ring, extending some 5 mm beyond the tube edge. The bell is short, squat and flared, tightly angled through 90° into the head; it has a diameter of 65 mm at the narrow ring which marks the head-bell junction. The bell is 108 mm

H. and 70 mm W. A plain crest is present on the tube, but damage obscures where it starts; it runs to the ear. The head is quite stylised, with the long ear flopping forward to touch the upper jaw, a bulbous eye and a mouth open at about 70°. The lips are fleshy, a double-raised moulding with a bulge to accommodate a tusk on the upper jaw (although no tusk is present on the lower jaw).

Carnyx 2: the lower tube and mouthpiece appear on one side of the shield, the upper tube on the other; the missing head lay on another block. Its overall surviving length is 948 mm. The upper tube expands slightly from 35-38 mm, with a plain crest along all its short visible length. The crest increases in height (from 5-15 mm) as it goes higher up the tube. At the other end is a uniquely detailed depiction of a mouthpiece (**fig. 188a**; partly overlapped by the neck-guard and cheekpiece of the helmet). The cylindrical tube shows a ring junction, another very short section of tube (20 mm), and then another ring-junction before a mouthpiece. The mouthpiece is straight, slightly expanded and cup-shaped, the blowing end flat (perpendicular to the tube) and the margins slightly rounded. The junction rings imply the mouthpiece was removable. The maximum mouthpiece D. is 25 mm, and its length (to the ring) 27 mm (here D. is 18 mm); where it runs behind the shield, D. 24 mm. The rings are 6-7 mm D and project some 3-4 mm.

Dating evidence

General parallels with the arches of Orange and Carpentras have been used to suggest a date in the early 1st century AD (Gagnière/Granier 1986, 102). However, Polito (1998, 170) noted close similarities between the capitals in the assemblage and those on the mausoleum of the Julii at Glanum, pointing to an early Augustan date (c. 30-20 BC). This would fit the late Republican/early Augustan parallels he noted for the unusual figure-of-eight shield and curved sword.

Bibliography

Espérandieu 1907, 171 no. 236. – Gagnière/Granier 1986, 100-102. – Polito 1998, 169f. 187 n. 319.

B3.3 Commemorative arch, Saint-Rémy-de-Provence / Glanum (dép. Bouches-du-Rhône / F)

(Current location: *in situ*)

The commemorative arch at Glanum lies on the road into the town from the north, positioned on the edge of the *pomerium*, the town's sacred boundary, as at Orange (B3.4). It stands only some 15 m from another remarkable monument, the »Monument of the Julii«, a tower tomb dating to 30-20 BC which commemorates a prominent local family granted citizenship by Caesar (**fig. 302a**; Rolland 1969; Kleiner 1992, 112 f.). The monograph by Henri Rolland (1977) provides an authoritative account. It is a single bay arch, the upper levels largely lost including all of the attic and any inscription; its current gabled appearance is due to later restoration. Both faces had flying Victories over the arch. Each of the piers bears a limestone panel of relief decoration on its two main faces. Originally these were trophies with pairs of captives and other figures at the base, similar to those at Orange, but in subsequent damage most of the trophies were lost, leaving the captives as the main surviving feature. The south-eastern face has pairs of male and female captives at the base of trophies. Visible items of material culture are shields (oval and hexagonal), spears and a sword scabbard. The reliefs on the north-western face are more varied. The left-hand panel has a bound male captive and a (partly-preserved) Roman with his hand on the captive's shoulder; it represents victor and vanquished. The rounded ends of two shields and a fur-covered helmet are also shown. The right panel has a bound male captive, nude apart from a cloak, and a draped female seated on a pile of arms including a carnyx (Rolland 1977, 32-37 pls 6-7. 22-25). This is described more fully below.

Detailed comparative study of the iconography has shown that the two faces of the monument tell very different stories, with deliberate contrasts between them (Gros 1981, 159-164; Clavel-Lévèque/Lévèque 1982, 683-698; Küpper-Böhm 1996, 80-85). The two trophy scenes show not pairs of captives, but captive and captor. The right scene has been interpreted as Roma seated on arms, rather than a captive Gaul; the left scene is not barbarian and Roman, but barbarian and Romanised Gaul, who wears not a toga but a fringed cloak (*sagum*) in the manner of a toga. His hand on the captive's shoulder has been seen

Fig. 302 B3.3 Commemorative arch, Glanum: **a** the arch and mausoleum. – **b** detail of the SW panel. – **c** the carnyx. – (a photo Fraser Hunter; b Rolland 1977, pl. 25; c drawing Tanja Romankiewicz).

Fig. 302   (continued)

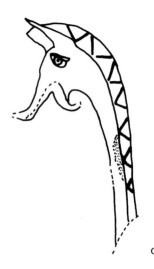

c

0   0,50   1m

b

not as a symbol of conquest but of leading the defeated to a better way of life. The other side shows only captives. This may seem speculative from quite fragmentary material, but other elements of the design support this: for instance, the Victories carry military standards on the side with only captives, but palm branches and laurel wreaths on the other; the garlands on the «Romanised« side have ripe fruit, while on the »barbarian« side it is mostly unripe. On approaching the town, one sees the benefits of Roman rule; on leaving it, the dangers of opposition and the futility of resistance.

The range of material culture fits depictions of Gauls at this time, although the fur helmet on one side is an interesting hint of a connection to campaigns in Germany.

The carnyx

The female on the south-west panel sits on a pile of arms (**fig. 302b**). Apart from the carnyx, this includes four hexagonal shields, swords in their scabbards, a helmet with volutes or ram-like horns, tubae, a saddle and a bundle of pointed items, perhaps more swords.

The carnyx is upside down against the left edge of the panel, emerging from behind the captive's cloak (which obscures the lowest part of the tube). No junctions are visible on the tube or bell (**fig. 302c**). The lower tube

is rather damaged in places. A crest runs the full visible length to just beyond the ear, increasing in height as it goes; it is decorated with incised triangles. The head has a forward-pointing ear, an eye (depicted in detail with iris, pupil and an eyebrow above), and a mouth open to about 45° with the jaw ends recurved. The mouth (which is hollowed for definition) has no teeth. The image in Rolland (1977, pl. 25) does not do it justice; the depiction is better than he shows.

Dating evidence

Past views on the dating of the arch (summarised in Rolland 1977, 43-45) have been highly divergent, but Rolland's analysis placed the monument in the Augustan period. He saw it as earlier than the arches of Orange and Carpentras and preferred a date of around 20 BC. Pierre Gros (1979, 82 f.) disagreed, feeling this was influenced by the spatial link to the Monument of the Julii which was taken (even if subconsciously) to imply a chronological link as well. He drew detailed architectural comparisons to suggest a later date of c. AD 10-20, part of a flourishing of arch construction in the area during the peaceful times between the subjugation of the Alpes Maritimae and the uprising of Sacrovir in AD 21 (which had in any case relatively little impact in the south). Gros (1979, 56) criticised the desire to connect arches directly with military campaigns, arguing many have not a specific but a wider symbolism; this point was taken up as well by Rolland (1977, 39. 46), who saw Glanum as commemorating the conquest of Gaul and marking the power of Rome, although it was not contemporary with the actual campaigns.

Küpper-Böhm (1996, 79-80) followed Gros, drawing attention in particular to the close similarities in architectural detailing to Orange, and placing Glanum around AD 10, slightly earlier than Orange. However, the dating of Orange is itself contentious, and a more general issue is a de-

sire for precise dating which is simply not reliably achievable. Architectural and art historians often claim dates which seem to the archaeological eye excessively precise without necessarily being accurate. In the absence of epigraphic or textual references to the monument, a broader date of 20 BC - AD 20 is preferred here, encompassing the main options.

Bibliography

Clavel-Lévêque/Lévêque 1982, 683-698. – Gros 1979; 1981. – Küpper-Böhm 1996, 77-85. – Rolland 1977.

B3.4 Commemorative arch, Orange (dép. Vaucluse/F)

(Current location: *in situ*)

The magnificent commemorative arch of Orange stands at the north gate of the Roman town (**fig. 141**). It is an architecturally innovative structure, a triple arch with a double attic (see further discussion under dating). An inscription in bronze letters (now lost) stood on the lower attic over the central arch. To either side were panels with naval spoils while below these, over the smaller side arches, were panels with Gaulish spoils: three of the four survive (**fig. 303a**). A small and fragmentary battle frieze runs round the monument below the lower attic, while the centre of the upper attic bears (on both the north and south sides) battle scenes between Romans and barbarians, a writhing mass of bodies similar to that on the tomb of the Julii at Saint-Rémy (Kleiner 1992, 112 f.). The short sides (east and west) were each decorated with three trophies, of which only four now survive (**fig. 303c**); above these on the lower attic were tritons. The upper attic makes up three statue bases, presumably for triumphal bronze statues. The arch has been the subject of a detailed study by Robert Amy et al. (1962), and their numbering is used here: clockwise

from the western panel on the north side, the panels and trophies are consecutively numbered I-VI.

The symbolism is complex, with the representation of victories on both land and sea. It is unclear whether the sea battles are generic or specific (e. g. referring to the battle of Actium). The land battles commemorate victories against Gauls (and arguably Germans); depending on the preferred date, they may refer either to the long-term pacification of Gaul after Augustus' reform of the Gallic provinces in 16-10 BC or the aftermath of the uprising of Florus and Sacrovir in AD 21; the latter is the conventional view.

The weaponry depicted has been thoroughly analysed by Amy et al. (1962, 77-88). The panel depictions are innovative as they represent not piles but expanses of weaponry, and it is argued these may be the representation of the original weapons mounted on wooden backdrops (*ibidem* 78). There are some differences between the representations on the panels and those on the upper attic friezes, emphasising the dangers of relying on this material as an unbiased source for weaponry. For example, Roman

Fig. 303 B3.4 Details of weaponry and trophies on the Arc d'Orange: **a** N side panel II. – **b** detail (N side panel IIe). – **c** E side trophy IIIa. – **d** S side panel IVa. – (Photos Fraser Hunter).

Fig. 303 (continued)

shields are only found on the attic friezes, while the helmet styles are different on different parts of the monument (*ibidem* 83 f.).

Carnyces feature on the panels and trophy scenes (**figs 303-304**). These feature a range of weaponry: shields (both oval and hexagonal, all decorated); helmets in a variety of forms (Amy et al. 1962, pl. 43); either severed heads or parade masks; gladii and bird-handled curved swords, a general Mediterranean type; spears; boar standards; Roman vexilla; carnyces; saddles and horse harness; and clothing, notably cloaks and breeches. Amy et al. (1962, 85) commented specifically on the Gallo-Roman rather than Gaulish nature of much of the weaponry, notably the swords (short gladius type rather than long late La Tène weapons) and the shields with Roman-style decoration (although the latter may simply represent space-fillers on the part of the sculptors; the interpretative weight put on the shield decoration [e. g. Amy et al. 1962, 83 f.] is probably unwise).

The carnyces

Orange is the most carnyx-intense monument in the Roman world, with 37 carnyces in eleven groups (**fig. 304**). The monument has been examined first-hand, but given the logistical difficulties of seeing the sculpture close-up the following analysis uses the illustrations from Amy et al.

(1962, esp. pl. 44) supplemented by personal observation. This is not ideal: although the work of Amy et al. is authoritative, they themselves commented on the need for a more detailed study of the carnyx depictions.

The carnyces occur in groups or bundles, and are described following the notation of Amy et al. (1962), with a panel letter and a letter code. (The only exception is their IIc, which conflated three separate groups, here renumbered IIc-e.) Within these groups individual carnyces are described in order from left to right and top to bottom. Details are provided in **Appendix 2 (tab. 81)**. Because of the overlapping arrangement of weapons, none of the carnyces reveals their mouthpiece, and technical details are in short supply. The cylindrical or near-cylindrical tubes are all plain, with the bell often elaborated with a decorated crest. The heads are simple but effective, with flaring mouths, eyes and ears. Some are depicted in three-quarter view, giving a more three-dimensional perspective than normal. They are naturalistically zoomorphic, probably a reflection of the Classical training of the sculptors, although the known carnyx fragments from France are relatively naturalistic (chapter 7). There is some diversity in the heads, and some look quite bird-like (e. g. IIa), but most are difficult to attribute to a particular animal.

North-west panel: in relatively poor condition, especially its eastern half.

Ia, 1-4: Towards the top right corner, four carnyces (angled upwards to the right) appear from behind a cloak, overlying a shield. They face left. The lower two are represented only by fragments of their tubes where they appear from behind the cloak (they are assumed to be carnyces from the spatial relation to the intact examples above). The other two are fairly stylised, the lower (2) slightly overlapping the upper.

Ib, 5-8: At about the same height but near the left edge is a further group of ?four carnyces in profile; the left two (5-6) are represented only by shaft fragments. More of the tube is represented but the mouthpiece is again hidden. They face left and lean diagonally up to the left. Both the surviving ones are rather battered, but some head details are visible; neither has a crest.

North-east panel: generally good condition, with five groups of carnyces scattered across it.
IIa, 9-11: On the top margin, just left of centre, is a bundle of three carnyces, angled upwards to the right, facing right; they are depicted in an angled perspective rather than in profile. 10 has a wide-open mouth gaping at view-

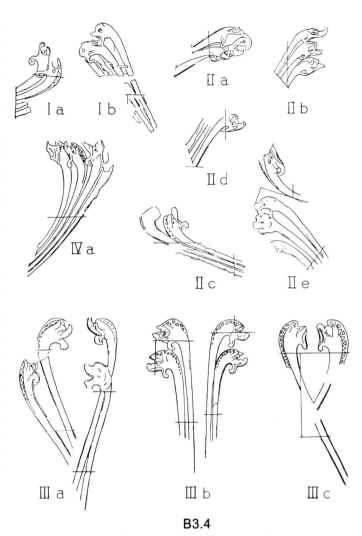

Fig. 304 B3.4 Carnyces on the Arc d'Orange. – (After Amy et al. 1962, pl. 44).

ers, while 11 appears to have an unusual, rather hooked mouth, perhaps intended to represent a bird of prey, although it could arise from damage to the lips of a gaping mouth. It is the rearmost, with only the head and part of the tube clearly visible.

IIb, 12-14: In the top right corner of the panel is a group of three carnyces, angled slightly to the right and facing right. All are depicted in profile, with gaping jaws, the lower one recurved back against the tube. The uppermost is markedly thinner than the others.

IIc, 15-17: Almost against the left-hand edge of the panel, lying slightly clockwise of horizontal, and facing up/right, is a bundle of three carnyces. The lowermost (17) is visible only as a fragment of tube; most of the middle one is visible, but damaged such that little detail can be made out; the uppermost (15) is well-preserved, and has a decorated crest.

IId, 18-20: Just left of the panel centre a bundle of three carnyces appears from behind a shield, angled upwards to the right and facing right. The upper two are poorly preserved, although parts of 18 survive as an incised line on the background, indicating they were originally depicted with some depth. Only 20 is well-preserved, although the head details are not entirely clear.

IIe, 21-24 (**fig. 303b**): Immediately above the arch on the right is a group of three carnyces lying against it (angling slightly up to the left) and facing down/left, with a fourth lying in the same plane but facing up/right above them. More of the tubes of the lower three is visible; the upper one is more concealed behind a shield. Details are not clear from the available imagery, but the upper one (21) has a crest while the lower ones do not. The lower three are progressively less well preserved, with much of the surface of 23 and 24 lost.

East trophies: the eastern side has three trophies separated by pilasters. All are similar in concept though differing in detail. The trophy comprises a belted tunic and cloak, with a sword slung over it and a helmet or hat on top. At the base are two prisoners (both male and female) in varying poses. Pairs of crossed oval or hexagonal shields stand on the arms, with weaponry behind: carnyces, boar and vexillum standards and bundles of spears. All the scenes are worn at the base but in good condition further up.

IIIa, 25-28 (**fig. 303c**): the left hand trophy has a pair of carnyces behind each arm, leaning outwards but facing inwards. All are essentially similar. Most of the tubes are shown, but not the mouthpieces; there are no technical details depicted. The head of one on the right (28) is lost in later damage.

IIIb, 29-32: the central trophy has pairs of carnyces behind each arm, vertical and facing outwards, They are closely similar to one another and to IIIa: the crests bear reserved triangular wave decoration created by cutting out opposing triangles; the ears point forward; the eyes (with drilled pupils) have prominent brow ridges; the gaping mouths are hollowed for definition, with the lower jaws recurved more markedly than the upper.

IIIc, 33-34: the right-hand trophy has a pair of facing crossed carnyces behind the left arm. They are essentially the same as those on IIIa-b.

South-east panel: well-preserved panel with a single group of carnyces.
IVa, 35-38 (**fig. 303d**): in the top right corner are a group of four carnyces, angled upwards to right and facing left. They are depicted at an angle, which emphasises the gaping mouths. Of the fourth (to the right) only the tube is

preserved, but the others all have sunken eyes with a very prominent brow, forward-pointing ear, and crest with reserved triangular wave. The lower jaws are recurved.

Dating evidence

Since the seminal study of Amy et al. (1962) the arch of Orange has normally been dated to the Tiberian period, specifically to AD 26-27 (or more cautiously 20-27) on the basis of a reconstruction of the lost inscription (using the holes for the bronze letters). This is insecure, as several reconstructions are possible (Anderson 1987, 162-166; Kleiner 1989, 204), although the survey of architectural details supported an early 1st century AD date (Gros 1979). However, there has been considerable debate because the form of the arch appears architecturally innovative, with its triple arch and double attic. Some scholars see this as impossibly early, and argue for a much later date: notably J. C. Anderson (1987), who argued it has its best parallels in the early 3rd century AD and tried to put it into a Severan context, marking the starting point of his British expeditions. Apart from the rather contrived nature of this »event«, there are, as Fred Kleiner (1998) pointed out, good grounds for arguing Orange merely seems unusual because so few arches survive; he quoted parallels for a number of the supposedly precocious features.

Küpper-Böhm (1996, 86-109) took a different approach to reconciling the evidence, arguing for three building phases: the first, with the triple-arch structure and trophies, in the early 1st century AD; the second representing a change of plan, with the inscription changed and a narrow second attic added (with the inscription giving a terminus ante quem of AD 27, if correctly reconstructed); and a third, much later phase with an enlarged second attic replacing the phase two construction. This would explain some of the stylistic differences between the different parts of the building; Küpper-Böhm argued for an early 2nd century date for the third phase, around the time of Hadrian, although parallels between the battle scene on this attic and late Antonine battle sarcophagi might support a later 2nd century date. Kleiner (1998, 611 f.), however, cautioned against such a radical rephasing of the monument, and is doubtful in particular over the division into two early phases rather than one.

Fortunately, the carnyces are all on the first phase of the structure. It is thus reasonable to accept that this bit of the arch falls into the same late Augustan/Tiberian period as other victory monuments in southern France (Gros 1979; Kleiner 1989, 204-206). The dating to AD 20-27 is related to commemoration of the subjugation of the revolt led by Julius Florus of the Treveri and Julius Sacrovir of the Aedui (Tacitus, *Annals* III.40-47). However, this dating is by no means certain and may be over-precise, especially given the arguments over reconstructing the inscription. Polito (1998, 152) doubted the Sacrovir connection and suggested instead a commemoration of Germanicus' campaigns in Gaul and Germany, with a wider theme of complete domination of land and sea. Gans (2003) drew attention to discrepancies in the dating of the southern French arches compared to those of Spain, which are consistently dated rather earlier. He argued for an earlier dating of the French examples, bringing them into line with the Spanish ones and providing a more convincing context for the French ones. He saw the major changes in Gaul coming with Augustus' subjugation of the Alpes Maritimae in 15 BC, reordering of the Gallic provinces in 16-13 BC, and the consecration of the great altar of the Three Gauls at Lyon in 12 BC. On this interpretation, Orange (and the other arches) would mark the final subjuga-

tion of Gaul; he interpreted the symbolism of the Prima Porta statue in the same light. This could be reconciled with Küpper-Böhm's phasing, with phase 1 reflecting this earlier Augustan phase (though she would not date it so early) and phase 2 the commemoration of the Sacrovir revolt in AD 27.

Whether Gans is right or not, his contribution warns of the danger of over-precise dating of monuments in the absence of convincing epigraphic information, and a broader dating of c. 15 BC - AD 27 is preferred here.

Bibliography

Amy et al. 1962. – Anderson 1987. – Gans 2003. – Kleiner 1998. – Küpper-Böhm 1996, 86-109.

B3.5 Weapons frieze blocks from tomb, La Brague, Biot (dép. Alpes-Maritimes / F)

(Current location: Antibes Museum)

In 1901, twelve large sculpted limestone blocks and one smaller one were found in a vineyard at la Brague, near Biot, a little to the north of Antibes. Three were uncarved, the rest bearing reliefs of weaponry (eight blocks) or architectural ornament (two). They were formerly on open display outside the museum, but most regrettably were vandalised in recent years (the museum's records of the event are poor). Most could be cleaned up, but the one with the carnyx was damaged beyond repair; a large part of it was chipped off, and these fragments were not apparently kept. We are reliant on old photos for interpretation (fig. 305).

The find was made on a small hillock just north of the Roman road running from Antibes along the coast to

Nice. As well as the blocks, there were some structural remains and finds, including pottery, coins and querns, but the structures were not sufficiently massive to explain the blocks, and it seems the sculpture was not *in situ*. An early 18th-century account records remains in the area, but these had vanished before any record was made of them (Donnadieu / Couissin 1931, 87).

Most of the items depicted are Gaulish: a carnyx, a boar standard, a torc, horned helmets, oval shields with central ribs (the umbo is missing in all cases), long swords and spears. There are also cuirasses with epaulettes and a pelta shield, both conventional types. Two of the blocks have mouldings suggesting they flanked a doorway, and one of the blocks was probably a lintel. From this, Robert Laurent and Charles Dugas (1907, pl. IV) plausibly recon-

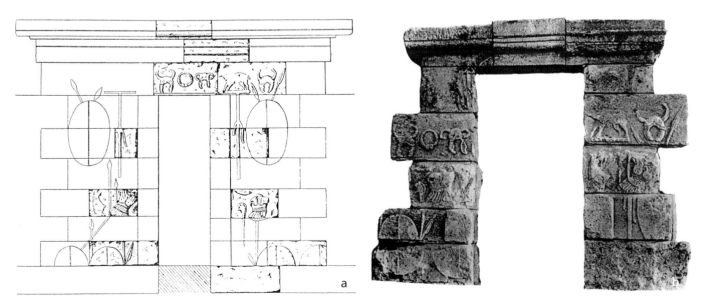

Fig. 305 B3.5 Weapons frieze blocks, La Brague, Biot: **a-b** two possible reconstructions. – **c** the carnyx block. – **d** the carnyx. – (a Laurent / Dugas 1907, pl. IV; b Dor de la Souchère 1988, pl. VII; c Espérandieu 1907, 29; d drawing Tanja Romankiewicz).

Fig. 305 (continued)

c   d

structed the fragments as a gateway in a larger structure, rather than, for instance, a triumphal arch (**fig. 305a**). While it has problems in the details (such as the truncation of the shields in the lowest level) this reconstruction is certainly better than more recent attempts to recreate a »monument« (Dor de la Souchère 1988, pl. VII), where blocks are clearly mismatched (**fig. 305b**). As Laurent and Dugas (1907, 67) noted, the arrangement of weapons is unusual, being neither a pile of arms nor a trophy. Parts (such as block 1) have some similarities to weapons friezes, as for instance at Narbonne (B3.1), but much of the design was clearly more than one block high, implying a more substantial pictorial composition than these tomb friezes. The nature of the structure itself is unknown: it has been seen as a triumphal monument (e. g. Donnadieu/Couissin 1931; Dugand 1970, 145-172; cf. Picard 1959, 150-152), but is much more likely to be a tomb for a military figure (Burnand 1975, 109 f.; Rivet 1988, 240; Küpper-Böhm 1996, 160 f.). The few coins recorded are insufficient to resolve the chronology: there are three of Tiberian-Claudian date, while five of the later empire (AD 244-321) may provide a context for reuse. The location is a striking one on a prominent hillock by the main road, and the blocks probably derive from a mortuary structure on the hill.

The carnyx

No information can now be gleaned from first-hand study, as all that survives is the right hand edge of the crest; this account is derived from published accounts (Laurent/Dugas 1907, 51. 58-60 pl. II; Espérandieu 1907, no. 24; Donnadieu/Couissin 1931, 94 f.; Polito 1998, fig. 113). The carnyx appears on the left side of a block (0.88 m L. 0.56 m H. 0.50 m T.). At top left are fragments of a garland; below this is the head and bell of the carnyx. To the right is a cuirass with epaulettes, belt and skirt; the right-hand area appears to be damaged (**fig. 305c**).

The carnyx faces left. Only the head and bell were present; an attempt to turn one of the stray shafts from another block into a tube is unconvincing as the alignment is not close enough (Dor de la Souchère 1988, pl. VII). A plain crest runs the full visible length of the bell and onto the top of the head. Details of the head and mouth are indistinct on the available pictures, but the best reconstruction is an ear which starts vertically and then angles forward, almost continuing the crest line. It has a round bulging eye; a vertical line immediately behind, running between pupil and ear, might define the back of the eye. The jaws seem to be damaged, though the likely line of a sinuous lower jaw can be traced. The form is reminiscent of the Avignon carnyx (B3.2). Laurent and Dugas (1907, 58-60) described it as a poorly-modelled example, deformed, with the mouth poorly depicted and no junctions shown.

Dating evidence

Laurent and Dugas (1907, 67 f.) argued that this structure should predate monuments such as Orange and Saint-Rémy, based on the items represented (although their arguments here are rather contradictory) and the style (neither trophy nor pile of arms). They proposed an Augustan date, which Espérandieu (1907, 32) supported on stylistic grounds; Picard (1959, 151 f.) preferred a later 1st century BC date, earlier than the other southern French monuments on stylistic grounds, and linked to a veteran of Caesar. Espérandieu noted and rightly dismissed views which linked the monument to conflict between the forces of Otho and Vitellius in AD 69. Donnadieu and Couissin (1931) related it to the campaigns of Q. Opimius against the Ligurians and other local tribes in 154 BC (Rivet 1988, 32-35), which would make it very early in the history of trophies, but the evidence is weak (Picard 1959, 150-152). Given the general prevalence of such monuments in southern Gaul, a late 1st century BC - early 1st century AD date is more likely. The style, with well-spaced equipment, is strongly reminiscent of weapons friezes from Kyzikos, Turkey (here around trophies) and S. Agnese, Rome, dated by Polito (1998, 149f. 161f.) to the third and fourth quarters of the 1st century BC respectively; this would fit the parallel to the Avignon carnyx, from a monument dated by Polito to c. 30-20 BC. A bracket of c. 30-1 BC is thus proposed for the Biot sculpture.

Bibliography
Donnadieu/Couissin 1931. – Dugand 1970, 145-172 (a rather derivative source). – Espérandieu 1907, no. 24. – Küpper-Böhm 1996, 160f. – Laurent/Dugas 1907. – Picard 1959, 150-152. – Polito 1998, 170. – Rivet 1988, 240.

B3.6 Weapons frieze, Arles (dép. Bouches-du-Rhône/F)

(Current location: Musée d'Arles FAN.92.00.382)
A local stone block from a weapons frieze was found reused in the remains of the late Roman rampart of Arles (**fig. 306a**). It has preserved most of its shape apart from a significant slice taken from the top right corner, presumably to create a rebate to lock the stones together in the later wall. There is some damage to the right edge and top left long edge, and small amounts elsewhere, but otherwise the condition is good. The weaponry represented is: oval shields; axe (type unclear); bundles of spears; sword in scabbard, with belt; carnyx; and an unidentified fragment running off the edge of the block near the shield pair.

The town walls of Arles contained considerable quantities of reused Roman stone, and large amounts were found on several occasions; the precise findspot is not specified. A number of stones with weapons friezes, soldiers or combat scenes are known from Arles from at least three different findspots (Espérandieu I 155-159; XII 7956; Küpper-Böhm 1996, pl. 34, 3-4). Küpper-Böhm's analysis (1996, 63. 67. 146f. 149) recognises one piece as part of a triumphal arch probably of Antonine date. However, the stone under review cannot be attributed to it, and the other blocks most likely derive from grave memorials.

Of the other weapons frieze fragments, Espérandieu I 157 does not readily match the carnyx piece as it is confined to a single row of stones with a defined lower border, whereas the latter seems to have been part of a taller composition. Espérandieu XII 7956 is a much closer match; the style is similar (including the same shield decoration), and it too clearly ran onto a second row of blocks. It depicts oval shields, spear bundles, helmets with volute decoration, a vexillum standard, a sword hilt, a cloak and a parade helmet with face mask. It is likely these two pieces derive from the same monument.

Fig. 306 B3.6 Weapons frieze, Arles: **a** the block. – **b** the carnyx. – (a photo Musée départemental Arles antique © Jean-Luc Maby / Lionel Roux; b drawing Alan Braby).

b

a

The carnyx

The carnyx was not identified by Espérandieu. It is near vertical, with only the bell and head on this block, the remainder presumably on the row below (**fig. 306b**). The area nearest the edge is damaged, obscuring some details, and the mouth is also slightly damaged. The bell expands smoothly into the head, which is in higher relief, with a curved chin line marking this. There is a forward-pointing sinuous ear, near-parallel to the bell, and a low plain crest which ends as the head turns. The mouth is open at about 70°, with the upper jaw longer than the lower one and the interior slightly hollowed for a three-dimensional effect. An upper lip is defined at the rear of the mouth, but not elsewhere. The eye has a central pupil, drilled at a slight angle to give it a forward-looking appearance; a short curved line behind the pupil defines the back of the eye.

Dating evidence

Dating of the Arles weapons friezes and related items has varied (Küpper-Böhm 1996, 149), but there seems to have been no stylistic discussion of the current fragment. The temptation is to date it with the bulk of the southern French material, i.e. late Augustan-Tiberian. The fly in the ointment is the weapons frieze from the arch, whose architectural detailing suggests a later 2nd-century date, showing the idea was still current then (Küpper-Böhm 1996, 150f.). However, published photos suggest it is in flatter relief than this piece (and indeed many of the southern French weapons friezes); thus the broad date range of c. 30 BC-AD 30 is used for the current fragment.

Bibliography

Espérandieu IX (1925), 6715.

B3.7 Altar to Jupiter Heliopolitanus and Nemausus, Nîmes (dép. Gard / F)

(Current location: Nîmes, Musée Archéologique, inv. no. GD 2)

Limestone altar to Jupiter Heliopolitanus and Nemausus, found in 1752 »in the basin of the fountain« in the spring sanctuary at Nîmes. Carved on three sides, with an inscription on the front face, a carnyx and oval shield on the right face (as viewed), and a depiction of Jupiter Heliopolitanus on the left (**fig. 307a-b**); the rear is plain, although the mouldings at top and bottom continue. The top of the altar is roughly chiselled and may once have held a statue. Its dimensions are 0.89 m H. 0.48 m W. 0.37 m T. The inscription runs as follows:

I.O.M.HELIOPOLITAN / ET.NEMAVSO / C.IVLIVS.TIB.FIL.
FAB / TIBERINVS.P.P.DOMO / BERYTO.VOTUM.SOLVIT
I(ovi) O(ptimo) M(aximo) Heliopolitan(o) / et Nemauso /
C Iulius Tib(erius) fil(ius) Fab(ia tribu) / Tiberinus p(rimus)
p(ilus) domo / Beryto votum solvit

To Jupiter Heliopolitanus, best and greatest, and Nemausus, Gaius Julius Tiberinus, son of Tiberius, of the Fabian voting tribe, primus pilus (chief centurion), native of Beirut, fulfilled his vow

(Espérandieu 1907, no. 431; Duval 1983; CIL XII 3072)

Nemausus was the local spring deity of Nîmes, who gave his name to the town and whose sanctuary was a major feature of the area (Bromwich 1993, 93. 101-103). Jupiter Heliopolitanus was an amalgamation of Jupiter and the Syrian deity Hadad, whose cult centre was at Heliopolis (modern Baalbek, in Lebanon; Adkins/Adkins 1996, 122). He is depicted within an arched niche on the left side on the altar, standing frontally, clad in oriental garments; on his head (now damaged) is the *calathus*, wickerwork head-gear with an expanded flat top; his raised right hand holds a whip, while his left hand holds what appears to be three stalks of corn. The panels on his clothing are decorated with thunderbolts and sun symbols. At his feet, Espérandieu identified an animal as possibly a lion. In fact he is flanked by two animals which iconographic parallels suggest are bulls (Dussaud 1903, 24; Espérandieu 1907, no. 50; Turcan 1972, 111; Henig 1978, 228 no. 351).

The right face has a diagonal oval shield with a crossed carnyx behind (**fig. 307c**). The shield, with round umbo, has a spina ending in outward-facing crescents; it has a border decorated with rectangular blocks. The carnyx is described below. The inscription and the sculpture are made to a high standard.

The altar is a fascinating one, showing a soldier with both links to his homelands (in his worship of an eastern deity) and to the country he was living in (or passing through), in the dedication to a local deity. Why do a carnyx and oval shield feature on the altar? The evidence (discussed below) points to a late 2nd century date, well after any campaigns in Gaul, and at a time when there is no real reason for a legionary centurion to be in the area. Had he retired to Nîmes, or was he passing through en route elsewhere? – the Rhône valley was a major transport route throughout the Roman period. Does the iconography have a connection to the soldier's (otherwise unknown) career, for instance on the British or German frontiers? This is very speculative; it is more plausible that the images symbolise the local deity Nemausus (Turcan 1972, 211; Homo-Lechner/Vendries 1993, 78f.). This would give the altar a pleasing symmetry, with both deities represented. The iconography is unique among the Nîmes sculpture, which does includes a range of other inscriptions to Nemausus

Fig. 307 B3.7 Altar to Jupiter Heliopolitanus and Nemausus, Nîmes: **a** angled view of inscription and carnyx. – **b** carving of Jupiter Heliopolitanus. – **c** detail of carnyx and shield. – **d** the carnyx. – (a-c photos Fraser Hunter; d drawing Tanja Romankiewicz).

(Jufer/Luginbühl 2001, 56), but the funerary altar from Collias (B3.8) provides support for the cult use of the carnyx in this area in the later 2nd century. This seems by far the most likely explanation.

The carnyx

The carnyx lies behind the shield. At top left the bell and head are visible; to bottom right the base of the tube runs to the edge of the basal moulding (**fig. 307d**). The mouthpiece is not defined, and no junctions are shown. The gaping mouth is open to about 140°, with the tips recurved; there are no teeth. The head has an eye with pupil, and a very well-defined erect ear, shown naturalistically with a flap of skin. The crest runs the full visible length of the bell, stopping vertically just in front of the ear. It has a marginal border, the main field decorated with a row of isosceles triangles, their bases against the bell. The lower end of the tube has no technical details visible; it is very slightly tapered.

Dating evidence

This altar is of interest both from its iconography and its date: Vendries suggested a date of around AD 200 (Homo-Lechner/Vendries 1993, 78f.). This is at such variance with the other southern French inscriptions that it was checked with Dr Roger Tomlin (Oxford University) and Prof. Lawrence Keppie (University of Glasgow). Both broadly agreed, based on the style of the lettering, with Prof. Keppie feeling it cannot be much earlier than AD 200, and Dr Tomlin suggesting it is unlikely to be as late as AD 200 but is reasonably Antonine; a compromise dating to the late 2nd century AD seems appropriate. This would fit with the increased occurrence of eastern deities in the western empire from the later 2nd century AD onwards.

Bibliography

CIL XII 3072. – Dussaud 1903, 353-355. – Duval 1983. – Espérandieu 1907, no. 431. – Homo-Lechner/Vendries 1993, 78f. – Turcan 1972, 109-111.

B3.8 Funerary altar, Combe de l'Ermitage, Collias (dép. Gard/F)

(Current location: hermitage of Notre-Dame-de-Laval) Limestone funerary altar with mouldings around the base and top, and two framed panels on the front; published by Émile Espérandieu (1928, no. 7628) and Michel Christol, Jean-Luc Fiches and Dominique Rabay (2007, 18 fig. 11), from whom certain details are taken, as at the time of my visit the stone had fallen forwards and was almost inaccessible (**fig. 308a**). The upper panel, recessed within a moulded frame, bears the inscription:

D M / Q . COSC . FIRMINI / ANN . XXII . M . III / JULIA
FIRMINA / MATER
D(iis) M(anibus) / Q(uinti) Cosc(onii) Firmini / ann(orum)
XXII m(ensium) III / Julia Firmina mater
To the gods of the shades and to Quintus Cosconius
Firminus, (aged) 22 years and 3 months, Julia Firmina, his
mother (put this up).
(CIL XII 2976)

The lower panel, framed with a vegetal scroll, features a carnyx; the letters »D M« flank the image, although not mentioned in CIL. The altar has been reused as a building stone. The flanking bolsters on the top have been chiselled off, and the top edge moulding removed on one side to give a straight edge. A socket was cut into the centre of the top, and a socket or clamp hole on one edge of the base.

Combe de l'Ermitage lies less than 20 km NE of Nîmes, by a limestone spring; the Roman evidence from the site has recently been synthesised (Christol/Fiches/Rabay 2007). A

Fig. 308 B3.8 Funerary altar, Combe de l'Ermitage, Collias: **a** the altar. – **b** the carnyx. – (a Christol/Fiches/Rabay 2007, fig. 11; b drawing Alan Braby).

Gallo-Greek inscription indicates activity by at least 50 BC, while analysis of inscriptions and sculpture suggests activity from the later 1st century BC to the early 3rd century AD. Although its main role was as a cult site, the presence of a number of funerary altars, like this one, suggests a settlement of some distinction nearby. Of the range of deities attested, Christol and colleagues argued that Jupiter had primacy; he is represented by an altar erected by two local communities and a further altar with a wheel symbol, as well as another altar in the nearby area. The other main deities are likely to be the mother goddesses *andoounnabo*, probably meaning the goddesses »of the source down below«. Other inscriptions include both local deities (Aramo) and Classical deities equated with local ones (Mars Budenicus, Sulevia [L]edennica Minerva); some can be localised from toponymic evidence, indicating that the Collias temple was drawing in deities from up to 20 km away to the south and east. It was a place of more than local importance. Nothing is known of its architecture beyond an inscription recording the gift of a portico, but this in itself implies a monumental presence. An interesting feature of the site is the number of inscriptions which have a pillar-like form; Christol, Fiches and Rabay (2007, 28) linked this to a local tradition of pillar stones since the 5th century BC.

Such use of a carnyx on a gravestone is unparalleled, but along with the altar to Jupiter Heliopolitanus and Nemausus from nearby Nimes (B3.7), it points to a cult use of the carnyx in this area.

The carnyx

Attempts to study the stone were thwarted to an extent by its current state, lying face-down and immovable. However, the lower part of the sculptured face was not entirely flush with the ground, and it proved possible to assess the carnyx (**fig. 308b**). This forms the basis of its description along with the image published by Christol, Fiches and Rabay, which is much clearer than that of Espérandieu.

The carnyx is the sole feature of the lower panel. It is placed vertically and faces left, with a straight, plain tube and a slightly expanded mouthpiece. The tube-bell junction is defined by a transverse hollow groove; the bell is slightly wider than the tube. No other technical details of joints are given. A low crest runs from just below the junction to the ears; both ears are shown as ovals with hollowed oval centres (thus showing the inside of both, which is a surprising perspective). There is an eye peak and an incised eye with pupil. The mouth is open to 90°; the lower jaw is bent through a further 90°, while the sinuous form of the upper one implies a tusk; single fangs are placed about half way along both upper and lower jaws. The eye and cheek have sustained limited damage.

Dating evidence

The vine-scroll ornament was studied as part of Gilles Sauron's analysis of such friezes on funerary sculpture in the Nîmes area; he dated it to the later 2nd century AD (Sauron 1983, 99-101 no. XIII.04).

Bibliography

Christol / Fiches / Rabay 2007. – CIL XII 2976. – Espérandieu 1928, 7628. – Sauron 1983, 99-101.

B4 GERMAN PROVINCES

B4.1 Fragment of trophy relief, Windisch / Vindonissa (Kanton Aargau / CH)

(Current location: Vindonissa Museum, inv. no. 34:5938) From the legionary fortress at Vindonissa in Germania Superior comes a fragment of a limestone relief with a trophy (**fig. 309a**; Bossert 1999, 40 f. no. 29). All that survives is the top left corner (0.31 m × 0.22 m), with the edge-moulding and part of the weaponry from the left arm (as viewed): two angled shields, probably both hexagonal, with a spear behind each; a carnyx in between; and the knobbed horn from a horned helmet crowning the trophy. Martin Bossert suggested it may have come from a triumphal frieze on the *via principalis* within the fortress along with other fragments known from the area (*ibidem* nos 27-28).

The carnyx

The carnyx faces right, with the lower tube concealed behind the shields (**fig. 309b**). It is recognisable, but not particularly detailed – there are no tube junctions, ears or crest, and the thickness is constant throughout, with no expansion. The section is markedly rounded. The head turns through about 90° to the tube. There is a simple incised dot-eye, with the mouth open to 90°. The upper jaw continues the line of the head, with an incised line marking its start; its end is lost, but a scar on the surface shows that it tapered to a rounded tip, with a pronounced step near the head. The lower jaw is rather thinner and shorter, with a slight curve at the tip.

Fig. 309 B4.1 Fragment of trophy relief, Vindonissa: **a** the fragment. – **b** detail of the carnyx. – **c** the carnyx. – (a-b photos Kantonsarchäologie Aargau/Vindonissa Museum; c drawing Alan Braby).

Dating evidence

Bossert (1999, 40f.) drew parallels to reliefs from Mainz which are arguably connected to the construction of the fortress under the Flavians, although they have also been dated to Neronian times. In an extended and largely inconclusive art-historical discussion, on precious little evidence, a pre-Flavian date is tentatively suggested. This seems ambitiously accurate for such a small fragment, and a broader 1st century AD date is suggested here.

Bibliography

Bossert 1999, 40f. no. 29.

B5 IBERIAN PROVINCES

B5.1 Weapons panel, Mérida, theatre (com. Extremadura / E)

(Current location: Mérida, Theatre Museum)
A series of marble fragments showing weaponry found in the theatre at Mérida in the province of Lusitania was published in valuable detail by Fabiola Salcedo Garces (1983), with subsequent commentary by Eugenio Polito (1998, 205-207) in his wider study of weapons friezes. Sixteen small fragments are known, which Salcedo Garces reconstructed into a rectangular plaque (c. 1.2 m × 0.8 m) showing a pile of arms (fig. 310a). Few of the fragments join, and it could be a more conventional, if rather narrow, running frieze, but the presence of pieces with no borders supports derivation from a panel. Salcedo Garces thought they were found in early, poorly-recorded sondages in the area of the peristyle, but Walter Trillmich (1993, 116f.) showed the first discoveries are recorded in the central area of the theatre's lower seating, where he has identified a sanctuary of the imperial cult constructed under Trajan; parts of three rows of seats in the Augustan theatre were removed to create a recessed space for Imperial statues and an altar (fig. 310b).

Inspection of fragments on display in the museum has revealed additional details and objects; table 68 lists the identifications from Salcedo Garces with additions and

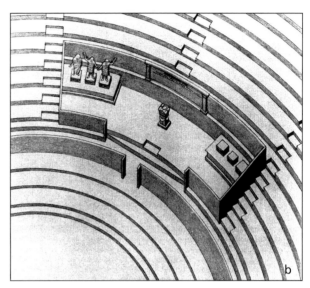

Fig. 310 B5.1 Weapons panel, Mérida, theatre: **a** possible reconstruction of the weapons panel. – **b** proposed setting in sanctuary area. – **c** the fragment. – **d** the carnyx. – (a. c Salcedo Garces 1983, 256. 275; b Trillmich 1993, 122; d drawing Tanja Romankiewicz).

reference	object	notes
I/1	hexagonal shield	dot-decorated border; further objects to the left are unidentifiable
I/2	either patera or round shield with raised rim	border with oak leaf and acorn decoration, centre with vine. Plain area of border indicates a lost object once overlay it
I/3	oval shield	
I/3a	hexagonal shield	vegetal scroll decoration; plain border
I/4	pelta shield showing chariot race	Cupid driving pair of horses in circus, with meta to left; on left, a second Cupid encourages them; no chariot visible
I/5	hexagonal shield	vegetal scroll, bipartite border
I/6	helmet	cheek pieces & short neck-guard; crest with vegetal scroll; bowl with laurel wreath
I/6a	shield fragment?	
I/7	sword	scabbard decorated with vegetal scroll
II/8	helmet cheekpiece	
II/9	muscle cuirass and sword belt with empty scabbard	
II/10	greave	decorated with Victory holding wreath & vegetal scroll
II/10a	hexagonal or rectangular shield	end only, with rosette decoration and plain border
II/11	hexagonal shield	ribbon decoration, bipartite plain border
II/12	oval shield	running lion decoration
II/13, 14, 15	oval shields	dot-decorated borders
II/16	oval shield	decorated with vertical lines and volutes
II/16a	shaft	unidentified
III/17	pelta shield	decorated with head of Jupiter Ammon flanked by eagle and acanthus
III/17a	animal standard	probably a wolf (from face and claws); overlies 17; fragmentary
III/17b	unidentified	straight border
III/17c	drapery	
III/18	cornu fragment?	with 20
III/19	catapult	lion head on corner
III/20	cornu fragment?	with 18
III/21	oval shield?	
III/22	zoomorphic terminal	standard or sword hilt; dog?
III/22a	blade – spear?	
III/23	oval or hexagonal shield	vegetal scroll decoration
IV/24	helmet plume	
IV/25	oval shield	winged thunderbolt decoration
IV/25a	unidentified	overlying 25 are a ring of studs defining supports for a circular object around a central stub with drill hole
IV/26	pelta shield	triton with rudder, blowing shell; dolphin in front
IV/27	spearhead	
IV/27a	oval shield	plain with plain border
IV/27b	unidentified	object with incised pelta ornament
IV/27c	oval shield?	
IV/27d	part of 27c?	perhaps figural protome
IV/28	pair of shafts	
V/29	fur helmet	
V/30	shield	interior of convex shield
V/31-33	shields	type unspecified; vegetal scroll decoration on 32, 33
VI/34	muscle cuirass	with griffins flanking acanthus plant
VI/35	spearhead	
VI/36	hexagonal shield	bipartite border
VI/36a	hexagonal shield	plain border only

reference	object	notes
VII/37	muscle cuirass	with gorgon's head
VII/38	hexagonal shield	bipartite border, vegetal scroll
VIII/39	ship's prow?	basal panel with dolphin decoration
VIII/40, a&b	hexagonal or rectangular shields	
IX/41	pelta shield	not a horn, as published; note flat relief and remains of griffin-head terminal. Decorated with crouching panther and vegetal scroll
IX /42	hexagonal or rectangular shield	dot-decorated border
IX /42a	shield?	form unclear; zoomorphic decoration
IX /42b	shaft	unidentified
IX /42c	oval shield	dot-defined border only
IX /43	hexagonal shield	vegetal decoration, bipartite border
IX /43a	shield	overlies 43; form unclear
IX /43b	unidentified	three components of a broken, uncertain object
IX/44-5	oval shields	
X/46	pair of shafts	
X/47	legionary shield?	
X/47a	hexagonal shield?	dot-defined border, vegetal scroll
X/47b	scabbard?	
X/48	vexillum standard	
X/48a	blade, probably spear	
X/49	carnyx	
X/49a	legionary shield	decorated with bucranium
X/49b	unidentified	decorated with curved radiating lines
X/49c	unidentified	stubs only
XI/53	muscle cuirass	
XI/53a	unidentified	object decorated with bird (flamingo?) overlies 53
XII/50	oval shield	marine scene
XII/50a	bow	
XII/51	hexagonal shield	
XII/52	legionary shield?	with thunderbolt
XII-XVI	shield bases	oval and hexagonal

Tab. 68   Weaponry on the Mérida theatre frieze (B5.1), after Salcedo Garces (1983) with additions; fragment and object numbers follow him, with additions as a, b, c etc. Fragments V, XI, XII, XIV-XVI were not seen first-hand.

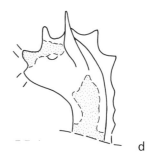

Fig. 310   (continued)

revisions. The frieze features shields (round, oval, hexagonal, legionary and pelta), muscle cuirasses, greaves, helmets (Attic, hemispherical with crest, and fur-covered), sword, spears, ballista, bow, perhaps a ship's prow, vexillum standard, animal standard, cornu and carnyx. The key modifications from Salcedo Garces' work are as follows. The »axe« (item 20) cannot be substantiated from the surviving fragments, and is more likely (with 18) to be part of a cornu. The »curved horn« (41), interpreted as similar to those on the Uffizi pillars (Crous 1933, 104f. type 105) is more plausibly the end of a pelta shield. There is an animal standard (17a), probably a wolf.

The theatre was built under Agrippa's instructions in 16-15 BC (Almagro 1959, 49-62; for current dating, Durán Cabello 2004, 126; Trillmich 2004, 278), but the style of the panel is late Flavian or Trajanic (Polito 1998, 205-207, arguing for a late Flavian date; Trillmich 1993, 117 and note 31). Reconstruction as a panel makes it very similar to ones known from Trajan's Market in Rome (B1.11.2). The iconography is wide-ranging and universalising, mostly with fairly conventional weaponry, although the ship's prow and catapult are more unusual inclusions. Among the barbarian items, northern barbarians (at this date probably Germans) are evoked by the carnyx, wolf standard, furry hat and hexagonal shields; the bow is likely to have eastern connotations.

The carnyx

The carnyx appears on Salcedo Garces' fragment X, with only the head and part of the bell surviving; its surface is rather worn (fig. 310c-d). The bell is thick and the head anatomically modelled with low-relief musculature and an incised eye; no junctions are shown. It has a saw-tooth crest, lower towards the base, with an incised line marking its base, and forward-pointing ear. The mouth is broken; the surviving portion is open to about 90°, and the lack of traces on adjacent pieces of sculpture suggests it may have recurved back through 180°.

Dating evidence

The Julio-Claudian dating proposed by Salcedo Garces (1983) has been dismissed; there is agreement that the style of the cornice is late Flavian or early Trajanic (Wegner 1961, 271; Trillmich 1993, 117 and note 31; Polito 1998, 205f.). Trillmich's identification of a Trajanic imperial sanctuary in the theatre's *cavea* and his tracing of fragments of this panel to excavations in this area makes it likely that it was displayed here, and supports an early Trajanic date. An inscription connected with the sanctuary states it was erected 130 years after the colony's foundation in 25 BC (Trillmich 1990; 2004), giving a date around AD 105.

Bibliography
Nogales Basarrate 2007, 468-471; 2011, 421f. – Polito 1998, 205-207. 228 n. 85. – Salcedo Garces 1983. – Trillmich 1993, 117 pl. V.

B5.2 Weapons frieze, Mérida, Temple of Mars (com. Extremadura / E)

(Current location: built into a shrine, the Hornito de Santa Eulalia; one block in Mérida Museum)
Ornamented marble architectural blocks from the Temple of Mars in Mérida survive through reuse in the shrine of the Hornito (little oven) de Santa Eulalia, a chapel constructed in 1612 and dedicated to an early Christian martyr of Mérida who was burnt to death in an oven (fig. 311a-b). The provenance is given by the reused inscription, although the precise location of the temple is unknown (see Edmondson 2007, 563-567 for discussion):

MARTI SACRVM / VETILLA PACVLI
Dedicated to Mars by Vetilla, wife of Paculus
(CIL II 468; Almagro 1959, 44)

Walter Trillmich (in Trillmich et al. 1993, 294f.) summarised scholarship around the inscription. The donor, Domitia Vetilla, is named in full along with her husband L. Roscius Paculus on an inscription from Vercelli (CIL V 6657); he has been equated with a suffect consul of AD 133 or 136, though the evidence is disputed. The surviving elements comprise two Corinthian capitals, five blocks of architrave with a weapons frieze carved on the underside (soffit), and parts of a projecting cornice. Trillmich noted that spolia may have been taken from different parts of the town to make the shrine (Trillmich et al. 1993, 294), although the surviving components could all have been part of the same building. Curiously, this fascinating set of material has never been fully studied. There is no detailed architectural assessment, no published measurements, and while Maria del Pilar Leon Alonso (1970) prepared a useful general assessment, this lacks the necessary detail for full iconographical analysis. She numbered the blocks according to their orientation in the shrine today; here they are numbered 1-5, working anticlockwise from the north-east (figs 311c; 312-316; for correlation, see below). A sixth block, taken to Mérida museum after the Civil War, is heavily worn from later use as a stair (fig. 318; Leon Alonso 1970, 181f.), and there must have been further blocks from this structure.
Each block is an architrave with decorated soffit. The architrave has a frieze of nine alternating Medusa heads and plant motifs, with half-motifs at the ends (except on 2 and

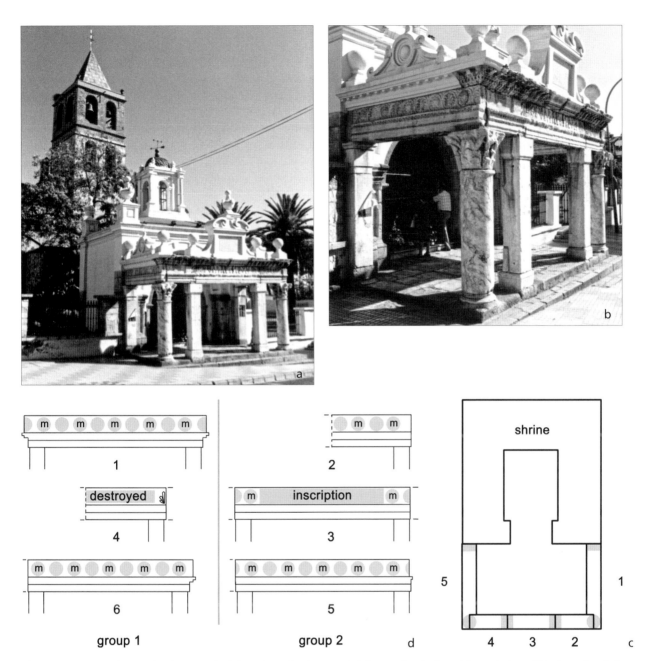

Fig. 311 B5.2 Mérida, temple of Mars: **a-b** shrine of Hornito de Santa Eulalia. – **c** sketch plan with numbering of blocks. – **d** stylistic grouping of blocks (schematic). »m« indicates Medusa medallion. – (Images Fraser Hunter).

6); below this, the decorative mouldings feature an upper plant-derived frieze and a lower egg-and-dart frieze. The Medusa-and-plant frieze is only present on the outer face; the inner faces are rougher and cut more deeply to create a ledge which would take structural elements of the building. The blocks fall into two different styles.

- Blocks 1, 4 and 6 have unframed motifs, and the decorative borders on the vertical face have slightly different spacings and designs from the others. All three have different plants; on block 1, all the plants are the same, but on block 6 the outer and inner plants form matching pairs.

- Blocks 2, 3 and 5 have frames round the motifs, forming medallions which are bound together, with leaves above and below the joint. The plants alternate between medallions. There are slight differences in the Medusa heads, with either volutes (3, 5) or snakes (2) under her chin.

Block 1 (DE) is complete with projecting mouldings at both ends, so it must have formed one end or side of the original structure, with columns at either end. The half-medallions at the ends were trimmed off when it was reused. Leon Alonso (1970, 183) argued the difference was because the frieze was a 17th-century copy, but there are no grounds for believing this, given that it is consistent with blocks 4 and 6, and there is no sign of differential weathering.

Block 2 (DFa) has been neatly cut down at a boundary between two medallions. Four alternating medallions are preserved. Its surviving original vertical end and column placement indicate another architrave butted against it.

Block 3 (DF) is complete; the soffit is central to blank areas for columns at either end. It ends neatly in half-medallions of plants, and has the inscription centred in the architrave, flanked by Medusa medallions. It could form a complete end of a structure, but the straight edges make it more likely that further architraves attached to either side, forming a front at least three bays wide.

Block 4 (DFb) represents the end of a shortened block with a placement for a column on the underside and a half palmette (with no frame) at the end, its looping leaves differing in style from the other plants. The rest of the frieze has been removed by a later inscription. Its straight edge indicates another block butted against it.

Block 5 (DO) is complete. It was supported on two columns and has nine medallions with half-medallions at the edges. On the visible end, the medallion and other mouldings run round the corner; the other end must have butted against another architrave. The corner does not project in the way that block 1 does.

Block 6 (museum) preserves its full length. It is much more worn than the others, especially on its outer side. It ends in full, not half medallions. The exposed top shows structural details from fastening; the rear corners are facetted at 45° with clamp holes on the upper surface, and there is a shallow roughened area on the upper surface. Mouldings at one end imply this was an original corner.

We are thus left with two different stylistic groups which cannot be put into the same facade without obvious mismatches (as the building's current appearance shows). It is likely that they formed different components of the structure. Block 3, with the inscription, must be the central piece; the iconography, with Victory inscribing a shield, supports this. Its straight edges suggest it had an architrave either side, implying a three-bay structure as a minimum; block 5 would match it, forming a corner. Either option would make a facade substantially larger than that represented by block 1, which preserves both ends and is from an altogether smaller construction. This may suggest an inner and outer precinct, or two sides of a peristyle. Leon Alonso (1970, 197) drew parallels to a temple at Brescia which has a projecting porch extending from the portico (Benoit 1911, 406 fig. 310, XV); while this provides more scope for shorter lengths and corners, the inconsistencies noted above suggest this would not work.

Corners preserved on blocks 1, 5 and 6 confirm that the outer face today was the original outer face. With this information, we can see that the orientation of the central medallions in these friezes differs; 3, 5 and 6 were orientated for viewing from one direction, 1 from the other.

This may simply be accidental but it suggests different elements of the one building. Block 6 was stylistically linked to block 1; this inconsistency might relate to accessible and inaccessible parts of the building, affecting how the frieze was viewed, but this is going beyond what the evidence can sustain without more detailed study. The close stylistic links indicate all came from the one building; for instance, 1 and 5 share the same pattern of roundel designs. **Figure 311d** summarises the state of play; it is to be hoped that a full architectural study will be undertaken of this intriguing monument.

The weapons friezes

Leon Alfonso's publication and accompanying illustrations do not provide sufficient detail for study. While the current work cannot emulate Jan Willem Crous's comprehensive study of the Uffizi pillars (B1.7), it is worth summarising the results of extended first-hand inspection. Each frieze is structured around three roundels, one in the centre and one at each end, containing a variety of devices (**tab. 69**). Over 500 items are depicted in the friezes, and the weaponry represented is diverse; **table 70** provides detailed identifications for the well-preserved blocks 1-5 (numbered as per **figs 312-316**) while **table 71** summarises this, using the classifications in **table 44**, with the addition of a column for mythological material. It covers the typical range: generic Classical weaponry; mythical weapons; gladiatorial weapons; and those linked to barbarians. The generic Classical material dominates, although among this are some unusual items such as a battering ram and a basket of artillery bolts. It is notable that there are no nautical items. The admixture of some gladiatorial material is typical of private commissions, as noted elsewhere (chapter 8); it includes a number of curved swords or daggers, including one with a zoomorphic hilt. These are clearly differentiated from three examples of the falx in the friezes and two further examples in a trophy. Whereas other eastern barbarian items, such as archery gear and Phrygian helmets, became generic, as argued in chapter 9, the falx remained a symbol of the Dacians. In this light, the draco is probably best seen as a reference to Dacian campaigns. Among northern barbarian material, apart from the carnyx we may note horned helmets, boar and wolf standards and furry hats.

Walter Trillmich (in Trillmich et al. 1993, 295) suggested the frieze was heavily influenced by the earlier Mérida theatre frieze. This may be part of the background, but it is far more eclectic; its closest similarities lie with friezes on the pillars from the *armilustrium* in Rome (B1.7) and from Capua (Polito 1998, 204-207). This suggests the aim was to symbolise the totality of martial equipment, appropriately for a temple of Mars, although the lack of nautical material in contrast to the other two examples is noteworthy. Thus the carnyces are likely to be present as representatives of generic northern barbarian equipment rather than connected to specific campaigns, but this can still potentially inform us about the dating.

Decoration on the items uses conventional Classical motifs such as thunderbolts, dolphins and so forth. A few items merit individual note, though they cannot be pursued in detail here. An unusual spear has concave sides like a holly leaf; there is a similar spear on a relief from Padova (B2.8), and as it also features on some Iberian early Imperial coins, Polito (1998, 56) argued it was a Spanish form. Two of the swords seem clearly to be ring-pommel forms. There is also a series of circular items, varying in detail but all with dished profiles and often a central boss of some form, which it has not yet proved possible to identify.

On block 1, the trophy has a bowl helmet with cheek pieces; belted tunic and cloak. On each arm, a small oval shield crosses over larger one, with two spears. To L is a kneeling bound captive in eastern gear (Phrygian cap, belted tunic, tight trousers); to R, a seated bound captive, ?hairy, belted tunic, tight trousers; it is unclear if he is wearing a hat. On block 5, the trophy has a bowl helmet with cheekpieces, scale armour, belt and fringed cloak; there are crossed oval shields and a falx on each arm, and greaves on the trunk. A barbarian to either side, seated on a rock, is bound, with a nude torso and baggy trousers; the head is lost on both, but there is no indications of hats.

The carnyces

27 carnyces are present on the friezes (**fig. 317**). They show no real technical details; only two have realistic band junctions at the tube-bell junctions, and most show a clear desire on the part of the artist for naturalistic zoomorphic modelling in the detailed eyes, prominent brows, lipped mouths, depictions of hair tufts at the head-bell junction in many cases, and even a nostril on one upper jaw. Several different styles of crest are shown, and the tubes are often curved to fit the available space; some are cylindrical, others conical. Only carnyx 1 is shown in full; it has a straight tube and plain end (**fig. 317a**). Details are summarised in **table 82**.

Dating evidence

Trillmich's interpretation of the inscription, discussed above, suggests a late Hadrianic - early Antonine date. This would fit the decoration in Polito's view, and was Leon Alonso's verdict. However, there are grounds to pause. Trillmich noted the epigraphic evidence was disputed, rely-

ing as it does on linking several inscriptions. One may also query whether the inscription is primary or a re-dedication: the Marqués de Valdeflores, who visited the site in 1752-1753, recorded that »the surface of the rectangle over which the letters extend is not smooth and polished, as is most of the frieze« (unpublished archive, translated and quoted in Edmondson 2007, 566); he suggested it was all covered in sheet metal, but it could as readily reflect removal of part of the carving, or indeed an earlier inscription which was inappropriate to changing circumstance (a dedication for Domitian, for instance). Leon Alonso's stylistic judgements are rather quickfire and loosely argued, and it is worrying that she dated the Corinthian capitals to the mid-2nd century when Jose Luis de la Barrera Anton's more detailed assessment of capitals from Mérida (1984, 34 f. 82) put them as Flavian. This latter author also quoted an unpublished assessment of the weapons friezes as late Flavian - Trajanic. Can the iconography add anything?

As a private commission it will be more of a mixture than patterns in official art. Having said that, the falx is overwhelmingly associated in sculpture with Domitian and Trajan (**Appendix 5**), and this would also be a plausible context for the draco. The horned helmet, carnyx and furry hats/helmets are consistent features of the German iconography of Domitian (and Trajan, to a lesser degree; see chapter 9). This all suggests a late 1st-early 2nd century date, or at least an inspiration of this date, accepting that a private commission could show something of a timelag. From the weaponry side, the only things against this early dating are two examples of ring-pommel swords. These are a typical mid-2nd/early 3rd-century type, but Marcin Biborski's (1994) analysis emphasised the large number of unstratified examples, especially from within the empire, with many dated examples coming from Barbaricum. The earliest known examples date to the first decades of the 2nd century, so a date anywhere in the earlier 2nd century is feasible.

The upshot of this is to suggest a broadening of the date range, to the first half of the 2nd century rather than specifically seeing it as Hadrianic or Antonine, which seems unduly precise given the number of caveats.

Bibliography

Edmondson 2007, 563-567. – Leon Alonso 1970. – Nogales Basaratte 2007, 422; 2011, 469 f. – Polito 1998, 219. 231 n. 177-179. – Trillmich et al. 1993, fig. 130 pls 64-65 (more detailed pictures of certain parts). – Wegner 1957, pl. 9a.

Tab. 69 Medallion details for the various friezes in the Mérida temple. For 1, 3, 5 and 6, left and right are orientated to either side of the central trophy. The orientation of fragments 2 and 4 is not known.

frieze	left	centre	right
1	eagle and snake	trophy	Pegasus
2	round shield	?	?
3	round shield	Victory inscribing shield	griffin and ?laurel tree
4	?	?	round shield
5	eagle and snake under tree	trophy	Pegasus drinking
6	round shield	eagle and hare	round shield

shrine

A

left

A′ B

B′ road

a

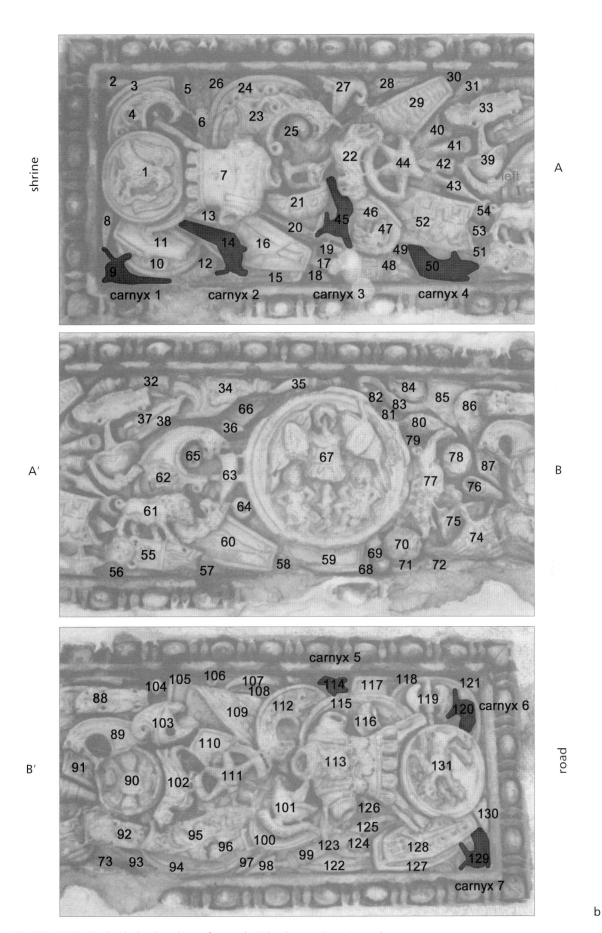

Fig. 312 B5.2 Mérida, block 1 (numbers refer to **tab. 70**). – (Images Fraser Hunter).

A

A′   B

B′

a

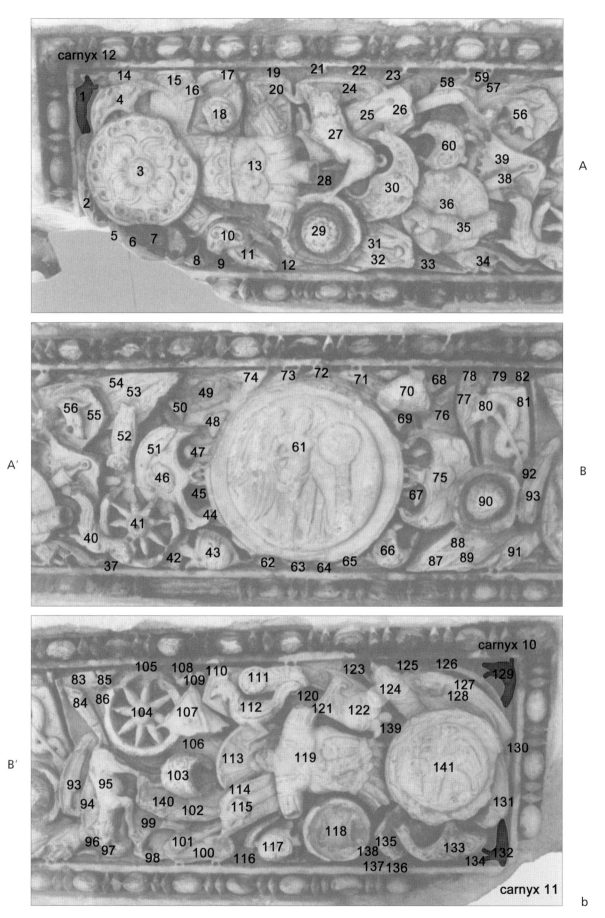

Fig. 313 B5.2 Mérida, block 3 (numbers refer to **tab. 70**). – (Images Fraser Hunter).

shrine

A

A'

B

B'

road

a

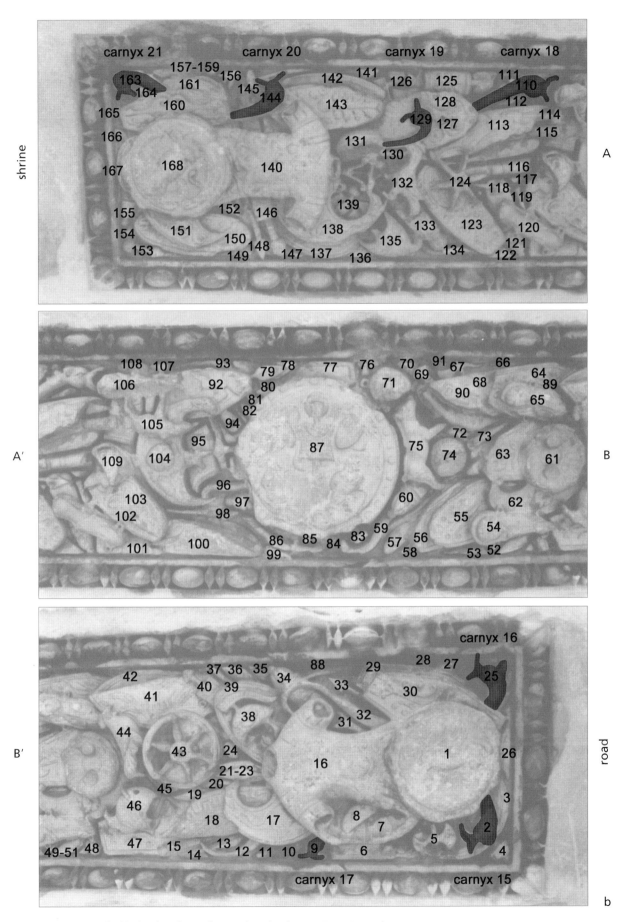

Fig. 314 B5.2 Mérida, block 5 (numbers refer to **tab. 70**). – (Images Fraser Hunter).

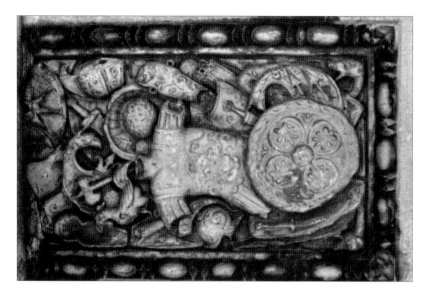

Fig. 315 B5.2 Mérida, block 2 (numbers refer to **tab. 70**). – (Images Fraser Hunter).

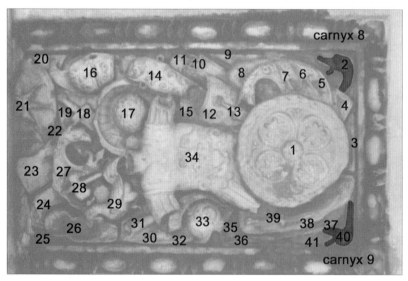

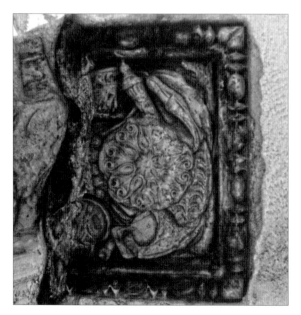
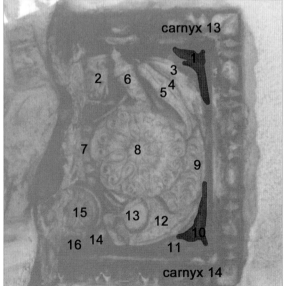

Fig. 316 B5.2 Mérida, block 4 (numbers refer to **tab. 70**). – (Images Fraser Hunter).

Fig. 317 B5.2 Mérida: **a** carnyces 1 and 2. – **b** carnyces 1-27. – (a photo Fraser Hunter; b drawings Alan Braby).

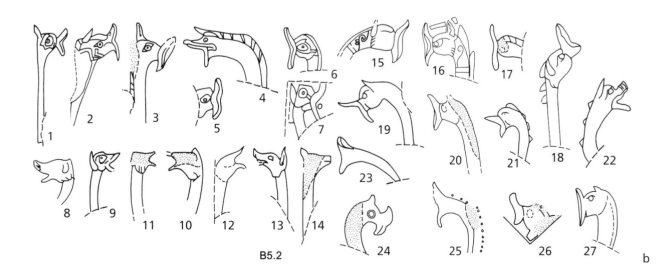

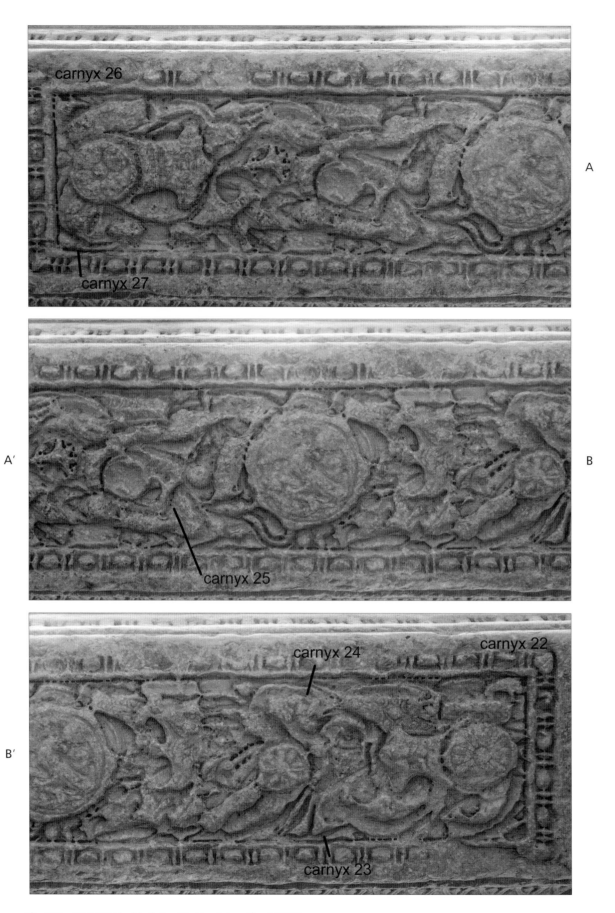

carnyx 26

carnyx 27

A

A'

carnyx 25

B

carnyx 24

carnyx 22

B'

carnyx 23

Fig. 318 B5.2 Mérida, block 6. – (Archivo Fotográfico MNAR).

frieze	no.	identification	decoration/notes
1	1	medallion	eagle grasping snake
1	2	quiver	conical lid
1	3	oval shield with squared ends	plain
1	4	pelta shield	vegetal scroll; griffin terminals
1	5	spearhead	
1	6	blade?	
1	7	muscle cuirass	pteryges flank medallion 1
1	8	spear	
1	9	carnyx #1	
1	10	oval shield	series of bosses with central holes
1	11	hexagonal shield	diamond umbo
1	12	?end of plain oval shield	
1	13	tuba	band at end
1	14	carnyx #2	
1	15	hexagonal shield	mostly hidden
1	16	hexagonal shield	no umbo; decorative bands parallel to outline
1	17	sword hilt	
1	18	barbed spear or arrow	
1	19	barbed spear or arrow	
1	20	spear	
1	21	bowl helmet	no fittings; decorated
1	22	cockerel standard	
1	23	pelta shield	griffin terminals; vegetal decoration
1	24	pelta shield?	circle and dot decoration
1	25	double axe	
1	26	?legionary shield	rectangular edge only
1	27	Phrygian helmet	
1	28	unidentified	
1	29	hexagonal shield	wave decoration
1	30	spear	
1	31	quiver	conical lid
1	32	laminar arm guard	
1	33	greave	inside view
1	34	legionary shield	pelta and eagle on wreath
1	35	curved dagger	
1	36	barbed spear	
1	37	gladius or dagger	
1	38	hexagonal shield	plain
1	39	Attic helmet	
1	40	tuba	band below mouth
1	41	tuba	band below mouth
1	42	tuba	band below mouth
1	43	spear	
1	44	wheel	
1	45	carnyx #3	
1	46	spear	
1	47	oval shield	lion-head decoration
1	48	basket with bolt heads	
1	49	spear	
1	50	carnyx #4	

frieze	no.	identification	decoration/notes
1	51	?spear	
1	52	legionary shield	dolphin and meander
1	53	spear	
1	54	tuba	band below mouth
1	55	greave	Medusa
1	56	spear	
1	57	spear	
1	58	spear	
1	59	hexagonal shield	plain
1	60	hexagonal shield	diamond umbo
1	61	boar standard	
1	62	pelta shield	griffins and Medusa head
1	63	dolabra	
1	64	ring	unidentified
1	65	double axe	
1	66	?shield	part only visible
1	67	trophy	
1	68	?hexagonal shield	
1	69	sword hilt	
1	70	human face	parade helmet?
1	71	hexagonal shield	end only
1	72	gladius	
1	73	?spear with midrib	
1	74	Phrygian helmet	decorated
1	75	?hexagonal shield	plain
1	76	tuba	2 bands
1	77	boar standard	lacks visible means of support
1	78	unidentified	spherical object, surface lost
1	79	tuba	
1	80	quiver	conical lid
1	81	unidentified	
1	82	sword hilt	
1	83	bow	
1	84	eagle head	purpose unidentified
1	85	hexagonal shield	
1	86	oval shield	leaf decoration
1	87	hexagonal shield	paired volutes
1	88	greave	mask at top
1	89	pelta shield	griffin terminals; plain
1	90	curved oval shield	inside view
1	91	hexagonal shield	
1	92	greave	
1	93	oval shield	
1	94	oval shield	
1	95	legionary shield	vegetal decoration
1	96	sword	
1	97	spear	
1	98	barbed spear	
1	99	quiver	conical lid
1	100	oval shield	
1	101	Attic helmet	with crest

frieze	no.	identification	decoration/notes
1	102	cockerel standard	support not shown
1	103	gladiator helmet	Phrygian style, with face mask
1	104	hilt	
1	105	hexagonal shield	
1	106	tuba	
1	107	curved sword	zoomorphic hilt
1	108	spear?	
1	109	legionary shield	oval umbo; scale decoration
1	110	hexagonal shield	plain
1	111	wheel	
1	112	pelta shield	griffin terminals; tendril decoration
1	113	muscle cuirass	Gorgon head
1	114	carnyx #5	
1	115	round shield	
1	116	sword hilt	eagle or griffin terminal
1	117	hexagonal shield	
1	118	round shield	
1	119	double axe	
1	120	carnyx #6	
1	121	sword hilt	
1	122	oval shield	
1	123	oval shield	
1	124	arrow	
1	125	bow	
1	126	tuba	
1	127	hexagonal shield	
1	128	hexagonal shield	trident with volutes from shaft
1	129	carnyx #7	
1	130	spear	
1	131	medallion	Pegasus
1	132	oval shield	
2	1	round shield	laurel wreath rim; central rosette circled by acanthus leaves in medallions
2	2	carnyx #8	
2	3	shield	hexagonal or rectangular; mostly hidden
2	4	hexagonal shield	crescent
2	5	pelta shield	griffin terminals; tendril decoration
2	6	barbed arrow	
2	7	barbed arrow	
2	8	oval shield	fleur-de-lys
2	9	unidentified	marginal feature
2	10	quiver	open cylindrical form
2	11	?oval shield	
2	12	legionary shield	thunderbolt, volute
2	13	sword	ring-pommel form
2	14	greave	human mask at top
2	15	oval shield	volutes
2	16	gladiator helmet	with peak and face mask; vegetal decoration
2	17	furry hat	unusual dished profile with central boss and raised edges; perhaps overlying a round shield
2	18	sword	
2	19	oval shield	

frieze	no.	identification	decoration/notes
2	20	unidentified	mostly hidden
2	21	wheel	
2	22	legionary shield	inside view
2	23	vexillum standard	
2	24	oval shield	paired volutes
2	25	spear	
2	26	greave	
2	27	pelta shield	griffin terminals; central fleur de lys; scorpions
2	28	double axe	
2	29	cockerel standard	support not shown
2	30	hexagonal shield	
2	31	tuba	
2	32	bow	
2	33	Attic helmet	decorated with hybrid griffin with marine tail
2	34	muscle cuirass	
2	35	?hexagonal shield	
2	36	spear	
2	37	oval shield	
2	38	oval shield	
2	39	falx	
2	40	carnyx #9	
2	41	oval shield	
3	1	carnyx #12	
3	2	hexagonal shield	crescents and circles
3	3	medallion	round shield, double dished profile, leaves spring from central rosette with flanking lyre pattern
3	4	pelta shield	no griffin terminals; dolphins
3	5	round shield	
3	6	oval shield	
3	7	gladius in scabbard	
3	8	hexagonal shield	
3	9	?pelta shield	
3	10	Attic helmet	volute on side; crest
3	11	quiver	cylindrical
3	12	?hexagonal shield	
3	13	muscle cuirass	Gorgon head; ribbons around belt
3	14	?rectangular or hexagonal shield	
3	15	hexagonal shield	very distorted
3	16	gladius in scabbard	
3	17	hexagonal shield	
3	18	Phrygian helmet	ram head decoration
3	19	hexagonal shield	leaf pairs
3	20	dolabra	
3	21	spear	
3	22	spear	
3	23	spear	
3	24	greave	
3	25	gladius	
3	26	legionary shield	?thunderbolt
3	27	boar standard	support not shown

frieze	no.	identification	decoration/notes
3	28	spear	
3	29	?furry hat	unusual circular object with raised brim
3	30	pelta shield	griffin terminals; lion head and tendril scroll
3	31	gladius in scabbard	
3	32	hexagonal shield	dolphins
3	33	?spear	large blade
3	34	bow case with bow and arrows	
3	35	manica	armour for hand and arm
3	36	round shield	dished profile
3	37	spear	
3	38	sword	ring-pommel form
3	39	vexillum standard	
3	40	cockerel standard	
3	41	wheel	
3	42	hexagonal shield	
3	43	helmet	central device (form unclear); laurel wreath; defined brim
3	44	tuba	
3	45	spear	
3	46	pelta shield	no griffin terminals; tendrils and panther head
3	47	unidentified	
3	48	unidentified	
3	49	helmet	very worn
3	50	?bow terminal	bird head
3	51	spear	
3	52	greave	human mask at top
3	53	spear	
3	54	curved oval shield	?winged thunderbolt
3	55	hexagonal shield	tendrils and crescents
3	56	draco	
3	57	?round shield	
3	58	hexagonal shield	
3	59	spear	
3	60	helmet	horns; vegetal decoration
3	61	medallion	Victory inscribing shield supported pedestal
3	62	spear	
3	63	spear	
3	64	spear	
3	65	arrow	
3	66	helmet	bowl form with cheekpieces; broken device on top
3	67	?sword hilt	
3	68	spear	
3	69	tuba	
3	70	helmet	very worn; type unclear
3	71	eagle-hilted sword	
3	72	unidentified	fragments only
3	73	unidentified	fragments only
3	74	unidentified	fragments only
3	75	pelta shield	griffin terminals; Gorgon, dolphin
3	76	?hexagonal shield	
3	77	hexagonal shield	

frieze	no.	identification	decoration/notes
3	78	?oval shield	
3	79	?oval shield	
3	80	draco	
3	81	hexagonal shield	
3	82	?spear	
3	83	hexagonal shield	inside view
3	84	quiver	conical lid
3	85	?dolabra	
3	86	hexagonal shield	
3	87	curved oval shield	wreath
3	88	arrow	large
3	89	arrow	large
3	90	?furry hat	unusual circular object with raised brim
3	91	bow case with bow and arrows	
3	92	oval shield	
3	93	curved knife	
3	94	oval shield	
3	95	wolf standard	support not shown
3	96	spear	
3	97	spear	
3	98	oval shield	
3	99	pelta shield	tendril decoration; unclear if griffin terminals
3	100	greave	
3	101	tuba	
3	102	hexagonal shield	dolphins
3	103	helmet	horns; vegetal decoration
3	104	wheel	
3	105	round shield	
3	106		number not used
3	107	vexillum standard	
3	108	spear	
3	109	double axe	
3	110	hexagonal shield	
3	111	greave	
3	112	cockerel standard	support not shown
3	113	round shield	dished profile
3	114	legionary shield	winged thunderbolt
3	115	battering ram	
3	116	spear	
3	117	Attic helmet	with crest
3	118	unusual round object	cf 4/15; perhaps the rear view of a domed round shield
3	119	muscle cuirass	eagle
3	120	shaft	
3	121	legionary shield	thunderbolt
3	122	Phrygian helmet	
3	123	bow	
3	124	quiver	cylindrical
3	125	spear	
3	126	oval shield	
3	127	hexagonal shield	

frieze	no.	identification	decoration/notes
3	128	falx	
3	129	carnyx #10	
3	130	spear	very small
3	131	oval shield	crescents
3	132	carnyx #11	
3	133	pelta shield	griffin terminals; tendril decoration
3	134	oval shield	
3	135	hexagonal shield	trident
3	136	spear	
3	137	spear	
3	138	tuba	
3	139	?sword hilt	
3	140	spear	
3	141	medallion	griffin and laurel tree
4	1	carnyx #13	
4	2	oval shield	leaf pairs
4	3	oval shield	
4	4	hexagonal shield	plain
4	5	curved dagger or sword	
4	6	quiver	conical lid
4	7	muscle cuirass	lappets and skirt only
4	8	medallion	round shield ; profile has two concentric dishes; lyre pattern around central rosette
4	9	oval shield	stylised tree
4	10	carnyx #14	
4	11	barbed spear	size suggests spear rather than arrow
4	12	pelta shield	griffin terminals
4	13	hexagonal shield	plain
4	14	tuba	
4	15	unidentified	strange round device with complex profile; perhaps rear view of shield
4	16	unidentified	fragments only
5	1	medallion	Pegasus drinking
5	2	carnyx #15	
5	3	round shield	plain double border
5	4	sword hilt	decorated
5	5	double axe	
5	6	?rectangular or hexagonal shield	misshapen
5	7	round shield	dished; scalloped decoration
5	8	sword hilt	eagle hilt
5	9	carnyx #17	
5	10	spear	
5	11	spear	
5	12	falx blade	
5	13	spear	
5	14	barbed ?arrow	
5	15	tuba	banded
5	16	muscle cuirass	eagle above; below, figures flanking vegetal stem
5	17	pelta shield	turtle?
5	18	curved oval shield	circular boss; laurel wreath surround; meander
5	19	spear	

frieze	no.	identification	decoration/notes
5	20	spear	
5	21	spear	
5	22	spear	
5	23	spear	
5	24	sword hilt	
5	25	carnyx #16	
5	26	unidentified	
5	27	spear	
5	28	spear	
5	29	hexagonal shield	
5	30	hexagonal shield	trident and crescent
5	31	tuba	2 bands
5	32	bow	decorated arm; bird's head terminal
5	33	arrow	
5	34	quiver	conical lid
5	35	spear	
5	36	spear	
5	37	shaft	
5	38	Attic helmet	with crest
5	39	oval shield	
5	40	gladius	
5	41	curved oval shield	ribbons and bucranium
5	42	oval shield	
5	43	wheel	
5	44	cockerel standard	support not shown
5	45	hexagonal shield	
5	46	gladiator helmet	with peak and face mask
5	47	hexagonal shield	paired volutes and eagle heads
5	48	sword hilt	
5	49	spear	
5	50	spear	
5	51	spear	
5	52	shaft	
5	53	spear	
5	54	greave	human mask at top
5	55	oval shield	volutes and crescents
5	56	hexagonal shield	
5	57	eagle-hilted sword	
5	58	spear	
5	59	bow	tendrils
5	60	quiver	conical lid
5	61	unidentified	round object, dished profile, leaves round rim, two opposed circles on rim inner edge
5	62	pelta shield	tendrils; no griffin terminals
5	63	hexagonal shield	double axe decoration
5	64	hexagonal shield	
5	65	greave	human mask at top
5	66	spear	
5	67	dolabra	
5	68	curved oval shield	meander and tendril
5	69	sword hilt	

frieze	no.	identification	decoration/notes
5	70	spear	
5	71	helmet visor	attachment ring at top
5	72	?double axe	
5	73	tuba	
5	74	furry hat	
5	75	boar standard	support not shown
5	76	unidentified	
5	77	hexagonal shield	plain
5	78	spear	
5	79	spear	
5	80	spear	
5	81	spear	
5	82	spear	
5	83	sword hilt	
5	84	shaft	
5	85	shaft	
5	86	curved dagger	gladiatorial?
5	87	trophy	
5	88	round shield	underlies 32-34
5	89	spear	over 64
5	90	spear with wavy edge	over 68
5	91	spear	
5	92	hexagonal shield	griffin
5	93	oval shield	
5	94	tuba	
5	95	vexillum standard	
5	96	bow	
5	97	quiver	cylindrical
5	98	arrow	
5	99	spear	
5	100	curved oval shield	thunderbolt
5	101	bow case with bow and arrows	
5	102	gladius or dagger	
5	103	oval shield	crescent
5	104	pelta shield	griffin terminals; human mask
5	105	boar standard	support not shown
5	106	greave	mask at top
5	107	sword hilt	
5	108	hexagonal shield	
5	109	?Phrygian helmet	
5	110	carnyx #18	
5	111	?spear	
5	112	?tuba	
5	113	legionary shield	flying eagle
5	114	spear	
5	115	tuba	
5	116	tuba	banded
5	117	spear	
5	118	arrow	
5	119	shaft	

frieze	no.	identification	decoration/notes
5	120	greave	
5	121	empty scabbard	
5	122	spear	
5	123	hexagonal shield	paired volutes
5	124	wheel	
5	125	?quiver	
5	126	sword hilt	
5	127	oval shield	vegetal tendrils and rosettes
5	128	?	lion decoration overlapping 127
5	129	carnyx #19	
5	130	spear	
5	131	fur helmet	
5	132	cockerel standard	with support
5	133	quiver	conical lid
5	134	bow	
5	135	Phrygian helmet	
5	136	spear	
5	137	?pelta shield rim	
5	138	pelta shield	griffin terminals; dolphin
5	139	sword	
5	140	muscle cuirass	winged Gorgon; 2 tritons; ?military standard
5	141	spear	
5	142	oval shield	
5	143	oval shield	vegetal decoration
5	144	carnyx #20	
5	145	bow	
5	146	sword	animal pommel
5	147	spear	
5	148	arrow	
5	149	?tuba	
5	150	oval shield	trident
5	151	pelta shield	tendril scroll; no griffin terminals
5	152	spear	
5	153	gladius or dagger	
5	154	?bow terminal	
5	155	quiver	cylindrical
5	156	arrow	
5	157	spear	
5	158	spear	
5	159	spear	
5	160	hexagonal shield	trident, dolphins
5	161	oval shield	
5	162		number not used
5	163	carnyx #21	
5	164	spear	
5	165	spear	
5	166	spear	
5	167	round shield	
5	168	medallion	eagle and snake under tree

Tab. 70 Identifications of weaponry in the well-preserved blocks 1-5 of the Mérida temple frieze (B5.2).

Classical/conventional	gladiatorial	mythical	N barbarian	E barbarian
muscle cuirasses	helmets	pelta shield	carnyx	draco
round shields	greaves	double axe	furry helmet/hat	falx
conical-lid quivers	arm guards		wheel?	bow/bow case/open quiver
legionary shield	curved swords/daggers		boar standard	Phrygian helmet
eagle-hilted swords			wolf standard?	arrows?
oval shield			horned helmet?	
basket of bolt heads			hexagonal shield?	
dolabra				
parade helmet*				
gladius				
battering ram				
tuba				
vexilla				
cockerel standard				
curved oval ?legionary shield				
helmets				

Tab. 71 Range of material in the Mérida temple of Mars friezes. Items marked * could also be seen as gladiatorial; those marked ? could be conventional rather than barbarian.

B6 AFRICAN PROVINCES

B6.1 Cuirass statue, Zian (Médenine / TN)

(Current location: Paris, Louvre, inv. no. Cat. MA 1825 [Inv. MNC 934])

Torso of a marble cuirass statue found in excavations in the forum of Zian (ancient Zitha), Tunisia (the province of Tripolitania) by E. Pellissier and donated to the Louvre in 1887 (**fig. 319a**). The site lies a few kilometres from the Mediterranean coast; the limited excavations concentrated on the forum.

The torso stands 1.06 m high. The head (separately carved) is missing and the limbs are lost. The muscle cuirass is partly covered by a cloak (*paludamentum*) fastened at the right shoulder, but the visible design shows two Victories standing on foliage flanking an object with a tripod base, probably a candelabrum. Below the cuirass are two rows of pteryges. The higher-relief decoration is rather worn, although the scenes can be identified. On the lower row a series of pteryges are adorned with shields, helmets and in two cases carnyces. The relevant pieces (from left to right as viewed) are:

- Central round shield flanked by hexagonal shields (one is damaged, and may be oval)
- Hexagonal shield, helmet and carnyx (= 1)
- Central round shield flanked by two hexagonal shields
- Hexagonal shield, helmet and carnyx (= 2)
- Helmet with pelta shield below and hexagonal shield above
- Central round shield with two oval shields behind

The round shields and helmets are Classical types. The shields have raised centres and a bossed umbo. The helmets are crested, and have neck flaps and cheek guards. The hexagonal and oval shields were probably intended as barbarian types, with an elongated umbo and spina. Where the surface detail is better preserved they are decorated with loose scrollwork and irregular arcading along the edges inside the rim.

The carnyces

The two flaps with carnyces are mirror images (**fig. 319b-d**). Each has an angled hexagonal shield with crested helmet below and carnyx rising from behind the shield. Carnyx 1 faces right, while carnyx 2 faces left. On the second flap there is a hint of an oval shield crossed behind the hexagonal one, below the carnyx, defined by faint incised lines. This flap shows more surface detail.

Both carnyces are similar in style. Little of the tube is visible, and it does not emerge below the shield (in 1 it would be obscured by the helmet). The tube starts straight but curves rapidly into the bell, with little expansion. No technical details such as tube junctions are shown. Each carnyx has a single ear, no crest, an eye peak and eye. The jaws gape at c. 180°; the lower one has a slight kink in it, while the upper is only partially defined as it was obscured behind a pteryx from the upper row. No teeth are shown.

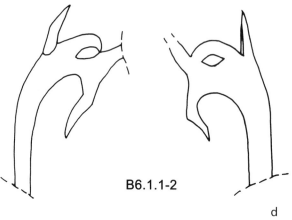

B6.1.1-2

Fig. 319 B6.1 Cuirass statue, Zian: **a** overall view. – **b-c** details of individual lappets. – **d** the carnyces. – (a photo Louvre/RMN, Pierre and Maurice Chuseville; b-c photos Louvre/RMN, Christophe Piccinelli-Dassaud; d drawing Tanja Romankiewicz).

Dating evidence

On stylistic grounds Klaus Stemmer (1978, 28) suggested an early Imperial date, perhaps Claudian; the excavations at Zian revealed that the forum started in the Claudian period, but saw little subsequent development, although the site continued in use (Mattingly 1995, 132). A mid-1st century AD date (AD 40-60) seems most likely.

Bibliography

Stemmer 1978, 28. – Vermeule 1960, 53.

B6.2 Arch of Caracalla, Volubilis (reg. Fès-Meknès / MA)

(Current location: *in situ*)

At the main crossroads in the city of Volubilis in Mauretania Tingitana (today Morocco), an honorific arch was erected to Caracalla and his mother by the procurator, M. Aurellius Sebastenus (**fig. 320a**). In the inscription Caracalla bears the titles *Parthicus maximus* (from his father's victories in Parthia, commemorated in AD 199) and *Britannicus maximus* (adopted during the campaigns in Scotland in AD 210). The surviving decoration includes references to both these victories. Most striking is a damascened bronze drapery fragment from a statue, plausibly argued to be from the figure of Caracalla driving a six-horse chariot which surmounted the arch and is mentioned in its dedicatory inscription (Boube-Piccot 1966, 278). This technically complex and detailed fragment shows two captives flanking a trophy (ornamented muscle cuirass, oval and hexagonal shields, spears, and horned helmet with rosette finial); below is a weapons frieze. Christiane Boube-Piccot's analysis (1966; 1969, 87-103) and Stuart Piggott's (1968) synthesis identified them by their dress as a Parthian and a Briton, the latter a Caledonian or Maetae complete with tartan trews (**fig. 320b**).

Four blocks depicting weaponry are known from the arch (Domergue 1966, 212 pl. XVII; Boube-Piccot 1966, 242-246 pls XXIII-XXV). These were part of a relatively restrained decorative scheme based around single limestone blocks or motifs, little of which was returned to the arch when it was restored. The decoration falls into sets and plausible attempts have been made to reconstruct it, aided by antiquarian drawings (**fig. 320c**; Domergue 1966; Riße 2001, 53-57). Flanking the arch were Victories on one side and large hexagonal shields with medallions on the other. On the attic, the inscription was flanked by a weaponry

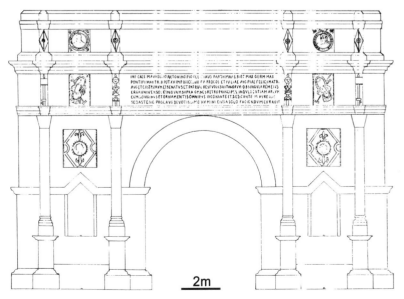

Fig. 320 B6.2 Arch of Caracalla, Volubilis: **a** general view. – **b** Caledonian and Parthian captives on bronze drapery. – **c** reconstruction of decoration. – (a photo Fraser Hunter; b Piggott 1968, fig. 1; c Domergue 1966, pl. XII).

Fig. 321 B6.2 Arch of Caracalla: **a** block 1. – **b** detail of carnyx. – **c** block 3. – **d** detail of possible carnyx. – **e** the carnyces. – (a-d photos Fraser Hunter; e drawing Alan Braby).

block and probably by blocks with military standards, with vegetal ornament at the ends of the attic. Above this was a series of medallions showing the four seasons, interspersed with eight lozenge-shaped shields.

Claude Domergue recorded four blocks with weapons friezes, one only represented by a single fragment which is now apparently lost. The three surviving blocks are re-strained and self-contained compositions based around a muscle cuirass with only a little other material.

Block 1 (1.14 m × 1.08 m). Crossed muscle cuirass and oval shield decorated with ?capricorn; behind, carnyx and spear (**fig. 321a-b**; Boube-Piccot 1966, pl. XXIII).

Block 2 (1.57 m × 1.0 m). Trophy arrangement of muscle cuirass with short sword hung from a baldric to the side, crowned with a domed helmet with cheekpieces and Phry-gian-style protome; feathers are attached to the helmet's sides. Traces of an oval shield. Angled below is an unusual item identified by Boube-Piccot as a kind of two-pointed pickaxe »appropriate for fortification works«; its identifica-tion is uncertain. Much of the surface is damaged and the left side of the block is lost (Boube-Piccot 1966, pl. XXIV).

Block 3 (1.52 m × 1.03 m). Angled muscle cuirass overly-ing a decorated oval shield. Top left are a spear and an item Boube-Piccot identified as a carnyx with another shaft (lacking its head) below the arm; top right, the shaft of an unidentified object, its head lost in damage; bottom right is a double-headed axe (**fig. 321c-d**; Boube-Piccot 1966, pl. XXV).

Much of the weaponry is Roman or conventional. The Phrygian-style helmet and double-axe probably evoke the Parthian campaigns. As Boube-Piccot noted (1966, 246), only the carnyx recalls British (Caledonian) equipment. This relief provides evidence for the continued use of the carnyx in Scotland in the early 3rd century AD, or at least the perception that it was an appropriate thing for Cale-donians to be using.

The carnyces

Of the two items claimed as carnyces by Boube-Piccot, that on block 1 can be readily accepted; although the head is damaged and mostly lost, traces of the ear and jaw are preserved. The item on block 3 is much less certain. As it survives it is simply a shaft with an amorphous curved end. It is notably smaller than that on block 1, although scales need not be consistent between blocks, and all head de-tails have been lost. It resembles a club, but this would be very unusual in a weapons frieze, being more typical of a hunting or Bacchic scene. On surviving evidence, given the presence of one carnyx in the decoration, the most likely interpretation is that this too was a carnyx. Both are rather stylised (**fig. 321e**).

Carnyx 1 (on block 1): slightly curved tube with no techni-cal details, swelling into the bell and head (set at 90°). No crest. Stub of protruding ear survives, but the rest of the head is damaged (the decorated portion has spalled off) and the mouth area is almost entirely lost; only a trace of the start of the lower jaw is visible.

?Carnyx 2 (on block 3): long cylindrical tube, with no junc-tions, which turns through c. 110° into the ?head. The up-per surface has spalled off and the area of the ?mouth is damaged, so no technical details are visible, but there is no trace of crest or ear on the stone surface.

Dating evidence

The inscription dates the dedication of the arch between Caracalla taking his fourth consulate on 10 December 216 and his death on 8 April 217 (Boube-Piccot 1966, 242-244; Lenoir 1984, 241-247).

Bibliography

Boube-Piccot 1966, 242-246 pls XXIII-XXV. – Domergue 1966. – Piggott 1968. – Riße 2001, 52-57.

B7 EASTERN PROVINCES

B7.1 Weapons frieze bordering inscription, Gardun / Tilurium (Split-Dalmatia / HR)

(Current location: Split, Archaeological Museum, inv. no. D 129)

From Gardun (ancient Tilurium) in Dalmatia come two marble fragments of separate blocks from a substantial of-ficial monument. The inscription, probably over two lines, spanned several blocks and was set within a frame with pelta-like vegetal scrollwork at the ends. Only the final let-ter O from the top line and a leaf stop are preserved. The inscription was flanked by a trophy at either end, with a weapons frieze running underneath it. The two surviving fragments come from different ends of the monument. The one of relevance here preserves the end of the inscrip-tion, part of the weapons frieze, and a trophy (**fig. 322a**); on its side is a garlanded bucranium. It is 1.04 m H. 1.36 m L. 0.24 m T. The smaller fragment preserves the bottom left part of the inscription frame, part of the weapons frieze and very worn remains of the other trophy; it is not illustrated here (see Sanader / Tončinić 2009, fig. 2; Libren-jak 2010; Cambi 2013, fig. 5).

The trophy (**fig. 322b**) comprises a muscle cuirass decorated with a pair of dolphins on the shoulders (the head is lost, but surviving traces suggest the neck-guard of a helmet or the splayed flap of a bonnet). A cloak hangs behind it. The arms support crossed oval and hexagonal shields with round bosses. Behind the trophy's right arm two pairs of spears flank a tuba, with crossed oval shields below, the front one decorated with a stylised thunderbolt. On its left arm the spear pairs flank a carnyx, with crossed oval and hexagonal shields below; the latter is decorated with two torcs and four small crescents. At the foot of the trophy two seated barbarians are chained to the trunk. The man on the left is identified by his costume

(notably the conical hat) as an eastern-style barbarian, perhaps a local (Cambi 2013, 13); he sits on rocks, wears a loose tunic gathered by a brooch on his right shoulder, is bare-legged and has notably ornate openwork shoes. To the right is a bound bare-chested barbarian, his baggy trousers tied at the ankles, with similar shoes. This attire suggests a northern barbarian (»un ›Galate‹ de type pergaménien«; Picard 1957, 252), although there are suggestions of headgear, which would be atypical for a northerner but more typical for a local; the head is badly damaged, and without first-hand inspection it is impossible to be sure (see further below). He sits on a bundle of cloth, perhaps his cloak. The frieze under the inscription

Fig. 322 B7.2 Weapons frieze, Gardun: **a** main fragment. – **b** detail of trophy. – **c** detail of carnyx. – **d** the carnyx. – (a-c photos John Cruse; d drawing Tanja Romankiewicz).

is primarily a series of shields (round, oval and legionary) along with Hellenistic-style muscle cuirasses, double-axe, spear and single-edged sword.

Tilurium was the fortress of Legio VII from the Balkan revolt of AD 6-9 (or perhaps a decade or two before) until around AD 50-60, when it moved to Moesia (see Sanader/Tončinić 2010, 45-47, for discussion of dating evidence). This sculpture is normally argued to commemorate the suppression of this major revolt in Dalmatia and Pannonia (e.g. Cambi 2013, 13; for the revolt see Wilkes 1969, 69-79). Polito noted that in the absence of most of the inscription the relief cannot be closely dated, and on stylistic grounds saw it as late Augustan-Julio-Claudian. A potential later context would be the awarding of the legion's titles *Claudia Pia Fidelis* in AD 42 for its loyalty after a revolt in Dacia (Keppie 1984, 208). However, it is far more likely that such a substantial monument was erected to commemorate these Balkan campaigns: »of all the wars waged abroad, second only to the Punic Wars in gravity« (Suetonius, *Tiberius* 16). The triumph was delayed owing to the Varus disaster, and was finally celebrated jointly by Tiberius and Germanicus in AD 12 (Wilkes 1969, 76); a date in the second decade of the 1st century AD seems by far the most plausible for this sculpture.

The monument would have been an impressive one. Nenad Cambi proposed a dramatic but highly speculative reconstruction as a trophy, with the inscription forming part of a base eight metres long (see Sanader/Tončinić 2009, fig. 3; Cambi 2013, figs 7-8). This is a lot to build on a single surviving letter, but it would have been a substantial official monument, the decoration on the surviving side showing it was freestanding.

It is hard to assess the iconographic programme when we know that half of it is missing. Clearly two different barbarian groups are marked by the two figures. The commemoration of the Dalmatian revolt explains the local barbarian figure. If the other figure is indeed a northern barbarian, this would fit the presence of carnyx and torc, and suggest the theme went beyond local events to broader ones. However, the identification is not certain; the two different barbarians might plausibly represent the two peoples involved in the revolt, Dalmatians and Panonnians (Ivčević 2010; Cambi 2013, 14). In this case, the carnyx would relate to notions of universal victory, a theme found in other Augustan and Tiberian propaganda. The carnyx and torc in propaganda of this time generally relate to Gaul (see chapter 9).

The carnyx
The carnyx is upright and faces right (**fig. 322c-d**). The depiction is very stylised, with no technical details such as tube junctions. The head is rather duck-like, with an elongated eye, two ears, and the mouth only slightly open (c. 15°), although its ends are damaged. There is no crest.

Dating evidence
See discussion above; AD 10-20, in the context of commemorating the suppression of the Dalmatian-Pannonian revolt, seems by far the most likely.

Bibliography
Cambi et al. 1973, 8f. – Librenjak 2010. – Picard 1957, 252f. pl. XII. – Polito 1998, 155f. fig. 89. – Sanader/Tončinić 2009, 199f. – Cambi 2013.

B8 NON-ROMAN SCULPTURE

B8.1 Base of a statue of Aetolia with captured weaponry, Delphi (Phocis/GR)

(Current location: Delphi, Museum)

From the temple of Apollo at Delphi come two sculpted limestone blocks which formed the base for a statue of the personification of a triumphant Aetolia (**fig. 323**). The base comprises depictions of the captured weaponry from the Celtic invasions of Greece in 279-278 BC. A. J. Reinach's (1911a) study of the fragments remains fundamental and is the main source for what follows as the pieces have not been seen by the writer; it is supplemented by more recent discussions by Britta Rabe (2008, 119-121), Lionel Pernet (2013, 22-25) and Serge Lewuillon (2017, 235), and by photos of the original kindly taken for me by Margaret Clift.

The monument was erected to commemorate the role of the Aetolians in repulsing the attacks of migrant Celts under the leadership of Brennos. They plundered their way through northern Greece, culminating in an attempt to attack Delphi, home of the oracle of Apollo and thus to wealthy treasuries. Resistance was led by the Aetolian League (who controlled Delphi at that point) with the help of other Greek groups. From as early as the 1st century BC there was confusion over whether Delphi was actually sacked, but it seems most likely that it was not and the Celts were defeated, supposedly following divine intervention from Apollo (Nachtergael 1977, 94f. 124; Rankin 1987, 97-99; Scott 2014, 170-172; for possible motives behind the various versions see Williams 2001b, 165-

Fig. 323 B8.1 Delphi, statue base of Aetolia; specific items annotated: **a-e** views of the base. – **f** reconstruction. – (a-e photos Margaret Clift; f Courby 1927, fig. 236).

168; Champion 1996, 315-319). The campaign actually involved several actions (summarised in Reinach 1911a, 227-239; Rankin 1987, 88-100; Freeman 2006, 31-38), another crucial one being the Celtic sack of Kallion (Callium), part of a diversionary tactic to draw the Aetolians away from Delphi. This entered the annals as an act of savage brutality, with the slaughter of innocents and tales of cannibalism: much of this may be stereotypical views of barbarians rather than reality, but it clearly had a major impact on the psyche of the Greeks. The subsequent crushing defeat of the Celtic groups was viewed as vengeance for this act.

The repulse of the Celts was seen as a major event: for Polybius (2.35.7) it was on a par with the defeat of the Persians in the 5th century BC, and Pausanias (X.19.5) saw it as the greatest foreign threat to Greece. Most of the Greek states tried to extract some political capital from their role (Nachtergael 1977, 175f.), but it was the Aetolians, as the main players in the events, who made fullest use of it. They erected a trophy in Thermos, the capital of the confederation (the base of this has been found, featuring a pile of weapons but no carnyx; Rabe 2008, 121-123 pl. 36, 1-2), and a series of monuments at Delphi. Subsequently they reinstigated the *Soteria*, the festival of salvation, at the site in 245 BC. Delphi, believed by the Greeks to be the centre of the world, was renowned as an oracle and was the site of the first temple founded by Apollo (Andronikos 1976, 5-7; Mee/Spawforth 2001, 302-314; Scott 2014); it developed into a major and wealthy sanctuary of the god, with city states from across Greece competing to have the grandest representation here. We are fortunate that Pausanias, writing in the 2nd century AD, left a detailed description of the remains; excavations have confirmed and augmented this. There were four main Aetolian monuments (Flacelière 1937, 108f.; Nachtergael 1977; Jacquemin 1985; Champion 1996, 319f.):

- Celtic arms fixed to the architrave of the temple of Apollo, matching the Persian shields hung there by the Athenians after the battle of Marathon (a frieze block from this temple preserves the outline of an oval shield with traces of clamps to hold it; Amandry 1978, fig. 7).
- A statue group showing Aetolian strategists along with Apollo, Athena and Artemis.
- A statue of the commander of the confederation, Eurydamus.
- The statue of Aetolia personified.

It has been argued convincingly that captured arms were also displayed in the portico to the west of the temple, where Pierre Amandry (1978) identified remains of a dedicatory inscription and traces of wooden struts to hold the weapons. Anne Jacquemin (1985, notes 7. 10) revised Amandry's dating of the structure and placing of certain elements, although the basic interpretation still holds; the arms were displayed in an existing structure, not one erected for the purpose (see also Bommelaer 1991, 219f.). Pausanias' passage describing the figure of Aetolia states:

>»There is a trophy, erected by the Aetolians, together with an image of an armed woman, no doubt representing Aetolia. These offerings were dedicated by the Aetolians after they had chastised the Gauls for their cruelty to the Callians.«

(Pausanias X.18.7)

The text implies this lay near the south-west corner of the terrace of the temple of Apollo, and this is confirmed by the surviving remains (Jacquemin 1985, 28. 30; Bommelaer 1991, 223). Reinach (1911a, 180-187. 240) and Fernand Courby (1927, 288-291) described two blocks forming the base of the monument; only the larger has a detailed findspot, coming from the terrace excavations near the south-west angle.

The surviving remains comprise two limestone blocks which, when fitted together, form an ellipse in plan. The larger (1.09 m × 0.74 m, and 0.98 m H.) is intact, the smaller (0.51 m × 0.40 m) fragmentary; when joined they are 1.60 m × 0.75 m. This sat on a hexagonal plinth, probably of two stepped tiers. On top of the base are fittings for a bronze statue of Aetolia around twice life-size; from this the orientation of the base is known. The settings for the statue suit the pose on Aetolian silver coins (see A3.1). Picard (1957, 94f.) assumed there was both a trophy and a statue, but it seems clear that Aetolia sits on the trophy.

The elliptical form comes from the Celtic oval shields which comprise it. These are depicted lying flat in a stack, with two superimposed ones at the top, the remaining three slightly angled from the horizontal and separated by other items, mostly textile. The shields define four registers, here lettered A-D from the top. Reinach (1911a) provided the most thorough identifications, partly updated in places by Rabe (2008, 121-123) and Pernet (2013, 23). The workmanship is rather crude and it is likely to be the product of a local workman, perhaps unused to carving such items as there is little evidence of a tradition of trophy representation at this early date (Reinach 1911a, 205f.; Nachtergael 1977, 204). The right side has a vertical area of later damage; the left shows more wear than the right. Identification is not straightforward owing to this wear and to the crudeness of the carving, especially in the absence of first-hand inspection under good light. Few of Reinach's interpretations can be dismissed – he seems to have had the benefit of first-hand inspection, at a time when the monument was less eroded – but not all are certain. Textiles (shown with folds, some with clear fringes) are the dominant element. Numbers refer to **figure 323**.

Register A is predominantly textile, but the rear shows a rectangular item with a boss towards its stepped right end (1) overlying another item with a boss (2; right edge lost in damaged area). These probably represent the shoulder piece of Greek-style armour (Rabe 2008, 119; Pernet 2013, 23 n. 21) rather than a belt, as Reinach suggested. Register B has most of the weaponry. The left side has the two ?carnyces (3-4); the corrugated item below them is probably the fringe of a cloak. On the right side this register tapers away, and seems to contain only textile; a narrow cylindrical item protruding at an angle is probably just tight-folded cloth (5).

Register C is predominantly textile, but the left end of the left side has what Reinach identified as part of a greave (6). A fringed cloak on the right side overlapped into register D. Beyond this Reinach identified what may be a piece of rolled textile with straps around it, suggested to be a bandolier (7), but not clearly visible on images available to me.

Register D featured what Reinach identified as a complete greave (8). On the rear a perforated cylindrical item (9) pokes out at an angle. Reinach saw this as a wheel hub, with the wheel inserted as a separate piece into the hole, but there is no other evidence of multiple components on the sculpture, and there was no reason not to carve it directly into the stone. The wheel hub interpretation thus seems unlikely; it may represent a rolled-up piece of textile. The right side includes a conical helmet with ?triangular cheekpiece and knobbed top (10), of Montefortino type (Polito 1998, 91; Rabe suggested a second helmet was present on the left side, but this is not visible to me). Pernet (2013, 25) argued the base was modelled from spolia, given the absence of other artistic representations to copy, and this is plausible. Less certain is attribution of all the material as Celtic (cf. Pernet 2013, 25): the greaves and armour are not typical Celtic material, and the sculpture seems to mix both Celtic and Greek weaponry.

Reinach (1911a, 232) argued that this monument commemorated the wider events of the time, not specifically the defence of Delphi, as the Aetolians played the greatest roles in the other parts of the campaign, especially the reaction to the sack of Kallion. He based this partly on the text of Pausanias and partly on the relief, arguing that the wheel (dismissed here) and bandolier (?) are more appropriate to the sack of the Celtic supply train at Heraclea than the assault on Delphi, as chariots would be impractical in the mountain passes.

The statue was not only represented on coinage, but sculptural copies were made. Picard recognised a fragmentary statue from Corinth as a representation of this monument, but on the copy there are no carnyces (Johnson 1931, 21f.; for the reinterpretation, see Picard 1932, 44; Flacelière 1937, 109 n. 2).

The carnyces

On the left side are two facing items with curved near-perpendicular ends, interpreted by Reinach as carnyces. Pernet (2013, fig. 6) has proposed a reconstruction based on photographs but it looks unconvincing to my eyes, and such reconstructions are hazardous in the absence of detailed autopsy. No such illustration is proposed here; the eye can be tempted to see details it wants. Their condition is poor – they are worn and in places damaged. At some angles the left one can be interpreted as swelling into a bell before turning through a right angle, with a possible flared mouth below. At other angles the »head« seems unduly swollen at the bell and thin at the »mouth«.

The right one is more plausible, with a near-straight parallel tube (the end is not clear), curving into a slightly downturned ?head, potentially with an ear; but the »mouth«, near-straight, is asymmetrical to the likely »head«, on my preferred reconstruction. Neither shows any trace of a crest.

If one was starting from scratch, on the basis of evidence available to me I would not have recognised a carnyx here. Yet Reinach's observations require a response. He was absolutely assured in his identification, and saw it in a better condition; other of his identifications can be challenged, but in these cases he presented more arguments, suggesting he was less certain. The items certainly appear different from the folded textiles which dominate the sculpture otherwise. There is also circumstantial support: while the coins depicting this sculpture (A3.1) do not show great detail, the presence of a carnyx at the base suggests the instrument was present on the monument.

The sculpture requires first-hand autopsy under varying light conditions, but on balance they are retained on Reinach's testimony, with caveats; the overall form of a tube with a perpendicular »head« and possible »mouth« is plausible, but the devil lies in the detail, and this cannot be reconstructed from second-hand sources.

Dating evidence

There has been no detailed discussion of the sculpture's dating, but the monuments must have been erected after the defeat of the Celts, most probably reasonably quickly. A date within a generation (278-250 BC) is likely, most probably within a few years of the event; a decree issued on Cos in spring 278 indicates that captured arms were already on display at Delphi by then (Amandry 1978, 579). Picard (1927, 60) suggested a date of around 275 for the monument, and it has to predate the coins (A3.1) of 239-229 BC.

Bibliography

Courby 1927, 288-291. – Jacquemin 1985. – Lewuillon 2017, 235. – Nachtergael 1977, 201-204. – Pernet 2013, 22-25. – Picard 1957, 94f. – Polito 1998, 91 and n. 104. – Rabe 2008, 121-123. 178 no. 34 pls 34-35. – Reinach 1911a. – Scott 2014, 172.

B8.2 Gateway to Buddhist stupa, Sanchi (Madhya Pradesh / India)

(Current location: *in situ*)

In the centre of India, between the towns of Bhilsa and Bhopal, lies the Buddhist monastic complex of Sanchi, established in the 3rd century BC as part of the westerly spread of Buddhism from the middle Ganges (Fergusson 1868, 87; Shaw 2000). Central to this is the Great Stupa (Fergusson 1868, 87 pls I-II), comprising a platform mound some 35 m in diameter supporting a near-hemispherical stone dome 12 m high; its flat top was capped by a balcony with umbrellas. A stupa was a ritual tumulus built over a sacred relic of the Buddha or another holy person (Thapar 2003, 263-266). Around the mound is a stone railing with four monumental gateways; and on the decoration of one of the pillars of the northern gateway are the furthest-flung carnyces yet known (fig. 324a).

The description of the site is taken from the work of James Fergusson (1868, 87 f.), Walter Kaufmann (1981, 62-65) and Debala Mitra (2003). The pillars of the gateways (which mimic earlier wooden forms) are highly ornamented on every available surface with scenes from the life of Buddha. The one of interest here shows worshippers at a stupa, much like Sanchi itself, of domed form with a ritual platform on top shaded by umbrellas with garlands, and surrounded by three enclosures at various levels. Winged mythical beings (Garudas) and human at-

tendants bring garlands to adorn the stupa; below, two rows of men are taking part in ceremonies (fig. 324b). In the upper row are six men, three (perhaps four) bearing offerings, one with his hands in a position of prayer and one carrying a standard. Standing slightly in front of them is a twirling dancer. The lower row consists of musicians: from the left, two trumpeters playing what seem to be carnyces, a man in a conical hat playing a double-flute, three drummers with various shapes of drums, and a man playing a waist-level portable string instrument, perhaps a small harp. The figures all wear a long, close-fitting tunic, belted at the waist, with long sleeves; they also wear short cloaks and calf-length boots. Some wear conical hats, others close-fitting bowl caps with ?flowers (or fur); some have their short hair uncovered. All are clean-shaven apart from one with a beard and one with a possible moustache.

A number of authors have commented on this scene (Fergusson 1868, 121 f.; Marcel-Dubois 1937, 38 f.; Kaufmann 1981, 62-65). All noted that the figures differ from any others shown at Sanchi, and that the trumpets are unique in the representational repertoire of ancient India. To take the figures first, their costume (rather over-dressed for the local climate) suggests they are from northern or north-western India, perhaps from the foothills of the

Fig. 324 B8.1 Gateway to stupa, Sanchi: **a** stupa and gateway. – **b** panel with musicians. – **c** detail of carnyx players. – **d** the carnyces. – (a-c photos Carsten Hermann; d drawing Tanja Romankiewicz).

Himalayas; Fergusson made a connection to figures in sculpture from the monastery at Takht-i-Bahi in the North-West Frontier Province of Pakistan. They were certainly intended to be seen as incomers or travellers come to worship at the shrine.

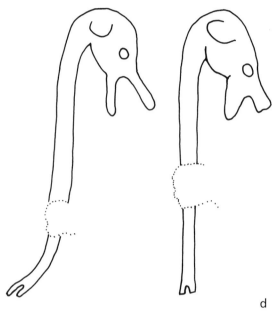

Fig. 324 (continued)

The instruments have also occasioned some comment, as they are unlike any others known in India. Both Claudie Marcel-Dubois and Walter Kaufmann noted the resemblance to carnyces. Marcel-Dubois was more tentative in her interpretation, comparing the curved form to that of the Roman lituus, borrowed from the Celtic carnyx. She quoted the Gundestrup cauldron as a close parallel but offered no interpretation. Kaufmann saw a stronger connection, noting similarities to the carnyx (for which he drew on Behn's 1954 monograph) and illustrating the Gundestrup scene as a comparison. He noted that the chronology of the two is closely similar, and despite the spatial separation mused as to how far one could consider connections between them. He then speculated on these trumpets as the forerunners of the S-shaped horns still played in the Himalayan region today.

As discussed below, the identification as a carnyx seems sound. The authorities quoted above have found no local contemporary instruments of this form. Connections to Europe are also less strained than it may seem. History provides some of the links with the trailblazer being Alexander the Great, who reached the Indus around the Swat Valley, in the area where some would put the Sanchi »northerners«. The successor Graeco-Bactrian kingdoms retained connections back to the Mediterranean-focussed Hellenistic world where Celtic mercenaries were widely used (Kaul 1995, 23). Thus the Greek connection provides one possible link to India. But contacts were wider than this, especially in the last centuries BC and 1st century AD. The »Silk Road« provided connections across the Middle East to India and beyond to China, from around the 2nd century BC (Milleker 2000, 11-23; Miller 1969, 119-148). The Gundestrup cauldron and other examples of south-east European metalwork are argued to show connections to India in their iconography (Taylor 1992; C1.1), although the details and nature of these contacts have been questioned (Kaul 1995, 22-25).

The Sanchi foreigners do not look like our Classical picture of Celts, but therein lies part of the problem – our picture is Classical and stereotypical. We are likely in any case to be very wrong in trying to label groups when looking for connections. Tim Taylor (1992, 70) speculated on the role of itinerant artisans (metalsmiths, musicians and ritual specialists) as an agency of cultural contact, a group separate from settled societies who could move between cultures. This may be what we see in the itinerant musicians at Sanchi. The idea of the itinerant bard found in literature describing Celts (Homo-Lechner/Vendries 1993, 32) may hold the key to a wider model, with musicians as a likely vector of cultural contacts. This is discussed in more detail in chapter 11.

This evidence of east-west connections indicates there is nothing impossible about western items appearing in India. How exactly the carnyx reached the area will remain a mystery, but it opens up fascinating possibilities. The fact that the bearers do not appear as »classic Celts« should cause no concern – what we may suggest is not a historical-ethnic model which requires »peoples« as vectors, but one where groups with particular skills (be they musicians, metal-workers or religious specialists) could move between communities over substantial areas, and in the process create connections and carry material and ideas as we see fossilised in stone on the Sanchi stupa.

The carnyces

The carnyx players are on the left of the relief, walking to the right as they play (**fig. 324b-c**; the right-hand one is shown in mid-stride with his legs crossed). It is a highly significant relief for carnyx studies as it is one of the very few instances of the instrument in use, but first we should consider the identification. The instruments are slightly stylised – there is no detail shown on the tubes – but there seems little doubt that they are carnyces (**fig. 324d**). They have a long cylindrical tube, curved sharply through 170° into a zoomorphic head with an open mouth (to 60°). The heads seem quite plain, with a simple circular eye and an ear flat against the head; there is no crest. However, the depiction is entirely consistent with many of the carnyces known from the Classical world; if found on a Roman frieze, they would have occasioned no surprise.

Both players have their heads bent well back to play the instrument. The left hand holds the instrument a little below its middle while the right holds the mouthpiece to the lips. In the left-hand example the base of the tube is slightly curved to the player's lips, with a plain mouthpiece shown. The instrument on the right has a straight tube, the mouthpiece depicted as if an angled cut had been made across the tube. Rather frustratingly, these embody the two alternatives as to how the mouthpiece functioned! It should perhaps warn us of the dangers both of using iconography and of trying to impose single solutions on the data; this is discussed further in chapter 10.

Dating evidence

Fergusson (1868, 89-91) discussed the evidence of inscriptions from the stupa to suggest a 1st century AD date. Marcel-Dubois (1937, 37) gave the relief a 1st century AD date and Kaufmann (1981, 62-64 captions) a 1st century BC one, both without further discussion. Milleker (2000, 131 f.) provided a more detailed summary. The core of the stupa may have been founded by Ashoka, the Mauryan ruler who adopted Buddhism in the 3rd century BC and built many stupas with the zeal of the convert. It was enlarged by the Shunga dynasty in the 2nd-1st century BC, with the gateways built in the first half of the 1st century BC.

Bibliography

Fergusson 1868, 121 f. – Kaufmann 1981, 62-65. – Marcel-Dubois 1937, 38 f. – Milleker 2000, 131 f.

C ARTEFACTS (tab. 72)

C1 IRON AGE

code	site	object	date	current location		n
C1	Iron Age					
C1.1	Gundestrup (Nordjyl-land/DK)	cauldron	150-1 BC	Denmark, Nationalmuseet C6562-6576	×	4
C1.2	Bouy (dép. Marne/F)	pendant	120-75 BC	Châlons-sur-Marne. Service Régional de l'Archéologie INC 9/213	×	1
C1.3	Kondoros (Békés county/H)	statuette	150-1 BC	Herman Otto Museum, Mis-kolc HOM 2007.22.1		1
C2	Hellenistic					
C2.1	Hermopolis Magna (Minya governorate/ Egypt)	perfume flask	250-150 BC	Musée de Limoges E351c		1
C2.2	Unprovenanced (Egypt)	perfume flask	250-150 BC	Alexandria, Graeco-Roman Museum 23958		1
C2.3	Old Nisa (Akhal Vilayet/Turk-menistan)	ivory rhyton	150-50 BC	?		1
C3	Roman military & gladiatorial					
C3.1	Pompeii (reg. Campa-nia/I)	gladiator's helmet (*mur-millo*)	20 BC - AD 14	Naples, Museo Nazionale 5674	×	4
C3.2	Herculaneum (reg. Campania/I)	gladiator's helmet (*pro-vocator*)	AD 1-79	Naples, Museo Nazionale 5670	×	3
C3.3.1	Vindonissa (Argo-vie/CH)	scabbard mount	AD 22-23	Vindonissa Museum V 90.4	×	2
C3.3.2	Vindonissa (Argo-vie/CH)	scabbard mount	AD 22-23	Vindonissa Museum KAA 416,1	×	2
C3.3.3	Vindonissa (Argo-vie/CH)	scabbard mount	AD 22-23	Vindonissa Museum 23:311		2
C3.3.4	Baden (Aargau/CH)	scabbard mount	AD 22-23	Baden, Historisches Museum 1458 (RGZM cast 32253a)	×	2
C3.3.5	Valkenburg (Lim-burg/NL)	scabbard mount	AD 20-30	Leiden, Rijksmuseum van Oudheden H1991/9.3679	×	2
C3.3.6	Ptuj/Poetovio (Podravska regija/SL)	scabbard mount	AD 20-30	Maribor, Pokrajinski Muzej (RGZM cast 33818)	×	2
C3.4	Xanten-Wardt (Kr. We-sel/D)	parade helmet	AD 40-47	Bonn, LVR-LandesMuseum 86.0070	×	2
C3.5	Niederbieber (Lkr. Neu-wied/D)	decorated disc from standard	AD 1-100	Bonn, LVR-LandesMuseum 77.0131	×	1
C4	Architectural fittings and decoration					
C4.1	Pompeii, Villa of Mys-teries (reg. Campa-nia/I)	wall painting	80-50 BC	*In situ*	×	1
C4.2.1	Rome/I	terracotta antefix	30-20 BC	Bonn, Akademisches Kunst-museum D161	×	1

code	site	object	date	current location		n
C4.2.2-3	Rome?/I	terracotta antefix	30-20 BC	Rome, Museo Nazionale		1
C4.2.4	Rome?/I	terracotta antefix	30-20 BC	Rome, Antiquarium Comunale		1
C4.3.1	?/I	Campana plaque	29-25 BC	British Museum 1805.7-3.314	×	1
C4.3.2	Ostia (Roma/I)	Campana plaque	29-25 BC	Ostia Antiquarium 3413		1
C4.4.1	Ostia (Roma/I)	Campana plaque	AD 83-85	Ostia Antiquarium 13272		2
C4.4.2	Rome, via di Grotta-perfetta/I	Campana plaque	AD 83-85	Rome, Museo Nazionale	×	2
C4.5.1	Unprovenanced	glass plaque with trophy	50 BC - AD 30	New York, Metropolitan Museum 17.194.359	×	1
C4.5.2	Rome?/I	glass plaque with trophy	50 BC - AD 30	University of Pennsylvania 29-128-1219		1
C4.5.3	Unprovenanced	glass plaque with trophy	50 BC - AD 30	?		1
C5	Ceramics					
C5.1	Unprovenanced	lamp with trophy	50 BC - AD 50	Paris, Bibliothèque nationale 5299	×	2

Tab. 72 Depictions of carnyces on artefacts. An »×« in the second-last column indicates that the item has been seen first-hand. »n« is the number of carnyces.

C1.1 Decorated cauldron, Gundestrup (Nordjylland / DK)

(Current location: Copenhagen, Nationalmuseet, inv. no. C6562-6576)

The Gundestrup cauldron is one of the most illustrated and most debated of Iron Age antiquities: »probably no other surviving relic of European craftsmanship, with the exception of Stonehenge, has occasioned so much publication and dispute« (Megaw 1970, 131). For the carnyx connoisseur it is the quintessential piece, the best depiction of a carnyx in use; and yet views on its origins and date have been widely divergent.

The cauldron was found on 28 May 1891 during peat-cutting in the bog of Rævemosen (»Fox Bog«) near the hamlet of Gundestrup in northern Jutland. It had been dismantled prior to deposition, with the decorated plates which formed the wall removed and placed within the bowl of the cauldron. The find was rapidly reported to the National Museum in Copenhagen, and has been a centre-piece of their displays ever since. Shortly afterwards a profile of the peat from within a metre of the findspot was removed for palynological analysis. Analysis suggested that the bog had been firm rather than watery at the time of deposition, implying the vessel was simply placed on the firm peat surface, where it gradually became overgrown by vegetation which subsequently formed more peat (Benner Larsen 1987, 394 f.; Kaul 1999, 195 f.). This has been queried in more recent reappraisal of the archives, the findspot and the condition of the iron rim (Nielsen et al. 2005, 45. 50-52); it is more likely that the vessel was

placed in a pit, perhaps a pre-existing peat-digging, the anaerobic environment allowing the iron rim to survive. There is no indication of settlement in the immediate vicinity. Tim Taylor (1992, 66) suggested that the object was deliberately hidden with the intent of recovery, but this seems excessively pragmatic. Flemming Kaul (1999, 196) quoted other Danish examples of high-status metalwork which were placed on the surface of dry bogs rather than buried, and saw these as deliberate offerings, while there are plentiful examples of valued objects and bog bodies being placed in pits in bogs (Nielsen et al. 2005, 51). The dismantling of the object could have as much to do with its ritual »death« as attempts at concealment.

The cauldron consists of a hemispherical base (0.69 m D. 0.21 m H.) hammered from a single sheet of silver, and originally 13 decorated plaques (of which 12 were found) some 0.20 m high (**fig. 132c**). These were soldered to the top of the bowl to form a double-skinned wall, held by an iron rim with a tubular silver cover. Seven surviving and one missing square plaques formed the outside skin, each with a frontal bust of a male or female figure with various subsidiary attributes; five rectangular plaques with more complex compositions make up the inside skin. The decoration is high-relief repoussé with details chased in from the front and gilding applied selectively to highlight particular areas; the eyes of the busts were inlaid with glass. The plates do not join directly to one another but were soldered to a framework, probably of silver. Two fragments of the silver rim-tube survive, with traces of the iron rim within. There are no surviving handles, but diametrically-opposed holes mark their likely position. A beautifully decorated disc with a bull-fight scene is soldered over a slightly off-centre hole in the base of the bowl which formed at a point of weakness, but it is likely that the disc originally served some other purpose, perhaps a horse phalera (Taylor 1992, 69) or crowning a lid (Benner Larsen 1987, 400-403). This and other evidence of wear indicate that the cauldron had an extended use-life.

Stylistic analysis allows the plates to be split into four groups (Kaul 1999, fig. 30). This correlates with analysis of punch-marks which showed that three different sets of punches had been used (Benner Larsen 1987; of the two plates without punch-marks, one constitutes the fourth group). Subsequent work on a broader range of toolmarks has refined this, with four groups of tools for the plates more firmly identified. This has also shown the complexity of the working practices, for the most ornate plate, the Bull Plate, has at least three sets of tools used on it, and arguably five or six (Nielsen et al. 2005, 9-14). Latest results of a range of analytical techniques show reasonable correlations between groupings based on different techniques, but also discrepancies which indicate that the craft-workers involved were working closely together, with some mixing of materials (Nielsen et al. 2005, 42-45).

Views on the cauldron's origin and date have been widely divergent (conveniently summarised in Benner Larsen 1987, tab. 1; Kaul 1999, 201-207). Ignoring the more wilfully variant opinions, scholars have fallen into two camps: those who prefer a west Celtic (Gaulish) origin, and those who see it as south-east European, essentially Thracian (some steer a complicated middle course; Falkenstein 2004). The Celticists (notably Klindt-Jensen 1950, 119-152; 1959; 1979; most comprehensively Hachmann 1990) have seen in the decoration, the attributes (such as carnyces and shields) and the symbolism clear reflections of Celtic life and beliefs, with parallels pointing to a Gaulish origin. Some have even read a version of the Irish epic »Táin Bó Cuailnge« into it (Olmsted 1979, esp. 211-228). In contrast, those who favour a south-east European origin have pointed to stylistic and symbolic parallels in that area (e. g. Powell 1971; Megaw 1970, 131 f.; Megaw/Megaw 2001, 174-176; Bergquist/Taylor 1987; Taylor 1992; Kaul 1991b; 1993; 1995). There is an extended and highly detailed debate over the topic, but the balance of evidence now points strongly to the south-east European school. As Flemming Kaul (1995) usefully summarised, none of the supposedly western Celtic attributes are exclusive to this area (those which may be termed »Celtic« are very much pan-Celtic, and most are shared with south-east Europe); some attributes (such as costume) and stylistic features (such as the treatment of the animal pelts and incidental features such as the style of shoe; Bergquist/Taylor 1987, 18) point strongly to south-east Europe; and, most per-suasively, there was no tradition of repoussé sheet silver work in the Celtic areas while there was a thriving one in south-east Europe over several centuries (e. g. Fol 1989; Kaul 1995, 12). The weight of the pieces is argued to represent logical multiples of Persian coinage, a weight standard common in Thrace (Taylor 1992, 69, although note the caveats of Kaul 1995, 23 f.). Even R. Hachmann's (1990) detailed analysis cannot sway the argument; as Kaul's critique demonstrated (1995, 2-7), while his analyses are valuable and rigorous, the appraisal of the various arguments is biased. Manufacture of the cauldron in the lower Danube (north-west Bulgaria or south-west Romania) is the most likely scenario.

Scientific analysis has added some evidence for the origins of different components. The iron of the rim is non-Danish (Nielsen et al. 2005, 45), while the isotopic signature of the tin used for solder matches Cornish sources (*ibidem* 38). More controversial are the results of lead isotope analysis (*ibidem* 29-40). These are successful at ruling out various sources (Anatolia, east Mediterranean, Britain, and most west Mediterranean and central European sources), but are less successful at confirming provenance. The authors note the lack of analyses for ores and artefacts in much of central Europe, but then overlook this in focussing very much on the small datasets available (looking at Celtic coinage in Brittany and the middle Rhine), even though there are also matches to eastern Alpine sources. They are successful in isolating batches of silver within the cauldron, and suggest the results indicate varying degrees of mixing from two sources, but their conclusion that these sources were from northern France and western Germany must be treated with considerable suspicion; there is, for instance, no comparative evidence from the eastern Celtic area or any Thracian metalwork. The technique has considerable potential, but more data are needed before too much weight is put on the results.

As Flemming Kaul (1993, 46 f.; 1995, 24 f.) noted, even if the south-east origin is accepted, the very debate highlights the problem – that Gundestrup represents an amalgam of styles. While the techniques match Thracian ones, cauldrons are much more of a Celtic idea (although the only parallels for repoussé silver sheet vessel plates come from the Săliştea hoard in Romania; **fig. 120**; Gschwandtler 1981, 225. 228f.; Spânu 2010, figs 4-5), and many of the design elements are at home in a Celtic milieu. As Terence Powell (1971, 184) wrote, it »is part-Celtic in context but never La Tène in style«. The depictions of torcs epitomise the problem, as they include both Celtic (twisted and knobbed) and non-Celtic styles (Kaul 1993, 44; 1995, 2; Kaul/Martens 1995, 114-120). Tim Taylor (1992) highlighted the diversity of stylistic sources utilised and drew attention to connections as far afield as India in both the pose of some scenes (although Kaul [1995, 23] questioned the significance of some aspects) and the depiction of elephants. These latter are somewhat misunderstood representations derived from copies rather than primary observation.

As noted, the lower Danube in north-west Bulgaria and south-west Romania seems the most likely production area of the cauldron. Both Bergquist and Taylor (1987, 19-22) and Kaul (1993; 1995) used a combination of archaeological and historical sources to identify a mixed Thracian – Celtic milieu in this very area which would provide an appropriate setting for the creation of such a piece. Celts are recorded as invaders in the 4th century BC and migrants to settle in the 3rd; sources talk of the Celtic Scordisci settling around Belgrade and it is argued they interacted with one of the dominant Thracian tribes, the Triballi, creating an archaeologically distinctive group with elements of both Thracian and Celtic material culture. The Scordisci are recorded as a troublesome headache to the Romans until the area was annexed during the 1st century BC (Kaul 1993, 40; 1995, 25 f.).

This historical ballet of cultures may make pleasant stories, but it is worth querying what lies behind it. It is a very culture-historical approach, with monolithic cultural entities forming blocks and arrows on maps of Europe, giving rise to hybrids which smack more of rose cultivation than human interaction. Such explanations leave so many unanswered questions. How many people? Both men and women? What did they bring? Why did they move? What happened when they tried to settle in someone else's land? Who then farmed the land, fought the wars, made the decisions? What language did they speak? This ties into the general question of these large proto-historical units in the European Iron Age, which is considered in more detail in chapter 9. While the anointed area of the lower Danube is likely to be the source of the cauldron, the very act of interaction would create a social situation which cannot be so easily categorised as a »cultural co-existence between a Celtic and a Thracian tribe« (Kaul 1993, 46). These »hyphen-cultures« (see also Romano-British, Gallo-Roman, Gallo-Belgic, Celto-Ligurian, Thraco-Getic and so on) are beloved of archaeologists but they simplify the complex social circumstances behind them. In situations where people were moving around, apparently on a large scale, these interactions are something which requires detailed exploration, not simplistic labelling, and we must remember these are shorthand rather than reality.

Tim Taylor (1992) took some steps towards dismantling these ethnic blocks in his analysis of the cauldron. In noting the connections to the east he emphasised the variety of influences which make up its iconography, and suggested the agency of specialist (and highly mobile) metalworkers, akin to modern Romany groups, who moved among these cultural groups. This idea of the mobile specialist is an appealing one, although it is less successful in explaining the emergence and relative conservatism of particular stylistic traditions, but it reinforces the point that there was contact and influence over long distances

during the Iron Age. Kaul (1995, 22), in reviewing Taylor's ideas, noted that another potential mechanism was the existing network of Greek-speaking elites which spanned the area from Macedonia to the Indus Valley in the wake of Alexander the Great's campaigns.

While our understanding of the interaction of Iron Age peoples in south-east Europe may still be theoretically naïve, it seems this area is the best candidate for the origin of the cauldron, using local metalworking traditions but drawing on influences from a much wider area. What then took it to Denmark? The agency of the Cimbri, a Germanic tribe from in or around Jutland, is often invoked (e.g. Bergquist/Taylor 1987, 22; Megaw/Megaw 2001, 176; Kaul 1993, 48 f.; 1995, 28 f.). According to Classical sources, large numbers of them left their homelands in 120 BC and went on an extensive migration into south-east Europe and subsequently southern France, defeating Roman armies on a number of occasions and posing a major threat to the safety of the Republic before being defeated by the forces of Marius in 102-101 BC (Kaul/Martens 1995, fig. 1; Scullard 1970, 53-56. 59 f.; for Roman coins minted to celebrate, see A4.4-4.6). The Cimbri were in the lower Danube area between 118 and 113 BC, and Kaul (1993, 48) suggested they may have allied with the Scordisci to harry the Romans, the cauldron perhaps representing a symbol of their alliance which made it back to the homelands. The findspot in Jutland is generally seen as lying within the Cimbri's heartlands (Kaul 1995, 28 f.; Kaul/Martens 1995, 151 f.).

While plausible, such specific historical solutions are utterly unprovable with the archaeological data which we have. The cauldron cannot be tightly dated, and may indeed post-date the Cimbric migration (see below). Even if it did not, it would be a bold scholar who would take the vagaries of archaeological survival and write history from it. The Gundestrup cauldron is unique today, but was it unique then? Its technology indicates craft-workers at the height of their powers – this was part of an extensive tradition, and it seems unlikely it was the only such vessel these metalsmiths made. The carnyx may serve as an example here: fragments of only around twenty survive from an original population which must have numbered thousands. Even our most dramatic and precious survivals from the past must be seen as representative of an original greater whole. If we had five more scattered cauldrons, would we still invoke the Cimbri? Plaques such as the one from Săliştea (Romania; Gschwandtler 1981, 225. 228 f.; Spânu 2010, figs 4-5) indicate they must have existed, while other metalwork of south-east European origin is widely scattered in north-west Europe, whether from Thracian auxiliaries in the Roman army or through existing Iron Age elite networks (e.g. Bergquist/Taylor 1987, 16; Allen 1971b). Turning to the scanty historical sources to explain the equally scanty archaeology is dangerous, albeit alluring. Archaeology is better explained as a pro-

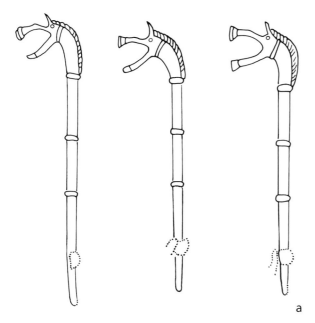

a

Fig. 325 C1.1 Carnyces on the Gundestrup cauldron: **a** plaque E. – **b** graffiti on plaque B. – (Drawings a Marion O'Neil; b Alan Braby, from Nielsen et al. 2005, fig. 16).

b

cess rather than trying to pinpoint events, and the data collated by Powell (1971, 198 f.), Kaul and Martens (1995) provide such a process: connections between Scandinavia and the Black Sea region since the Neolithic, with substantial evidence of contacts in the last few centuries BC. The Gundestrup cauldron did not need to follow on the coat-tails of the Cimbri: it moved along established axes of contact which brought other high-status metalwork from south-east Europe into Scandinavia, and which the Cimbri followed on their jaunt.

The carnyces
Plaque E – the carnyx players

The carnyx players appear on one of the inner plaques (plaque E, following the scheme of Klindt-Jensen 1950, figs 77-78; inventory number C6574; **figs 132a-b; 325a**). The scene is one of warriors, and is split into two registers, with the three carnyx players providing a visual join at the right-hand end and a giant figure (some 2.5 times human size) linking them at the other. The three carnyx players stand at the rear of a column of armed men in the lower register, marching to the left. The column comprises six men with shields and leaf-shaped spears, and a warrior at the rear of them with boar-crest helmet and sword. The shields are sub-rectangular, with circular riveted bosses. Above them, as if balanced on their spear tips, is a long stem with roots and vegetation, perhaps a stylised tree, separating the two registers. At the left a dog on its hind legs confronts them at the feet of the giant pigtailed figure who is dipping a human in a vat or bucket. The upper register has four cavalrymen riding to the right, each with an ornate helmet (from left to right, with crest, horns, boar and bird); two of them carry spears. The horses are harnessed, with reins, saddles and leather harness with

circular phalerae; their tails are braided. The riders wear spurs. Ahead of them, above the carnyces and facing right, is a ram-horned snake.

As with all the Gundestrup iconography, there have been highly divergent interpretations. Given the uncertainty over the cultural milieu in which it was created and the inherent uncertainty in interpreting symbolism in a pre-historic period, there seems little point in trying to assess these various efforts. The plaque clearly shows warriors; equally clearly, they are not in battle but on the march, probably taking part in some ceremony. The figure at the left could be priest or god, and could be either drowning captives or revitalising the dead; such entirely opposed interpretations show something of the problems (Kaul 1999, 200 f.). The ram-horned snake, an unnatural creature, points to the presence of the divine, and the most plausible interpretation of Gundestrup's iconography generally is as religious scenes, but the detail evades us. The plaques probably form a narrative, but as we cannot even be sure what order they were originally in it is largely futile to speculate. For present purposes what matters is that the carnyces are carried in a context which can be summarised as both martial and ritual.

Gundestrup gives us our most detailed depiction of a carnyx being played. The technical detail implies it was done by craftworkers familiar with the instrument (Kaul 1995, 8), although the sketch discussed below suggests not all involved were entirely au fait with carnyces. Yet the depiction is detailed and realistic. John Kenny, the musician who plays the reconstruction carnyx, has commented that the players show a classic brass embouchure (pers. comm.), and a similar level of detail is seen in the instruments themselves. The tubes comprise three equally-sized cylindrical sections with higher-relief joining knobs, rounded at the edges and defined by impressed lines top and bottom. There is a shorter mouthpiece tube and a bell which curves into a head with gaping jaws and a demarcated and slightly upturned snout; the tip of the lower jaw is similarly defined by an impressed groove, but tapers rather than expanding. Just before the snout, a slight bump in each upper jaw marks the fold of the lip round the tusk (which is not itself shown). An eye (defined by a punched ring) and a forward-pointing ear are depicted, while a crest of forward-pointing bristles runs from the base of the crest (above the knob) to the ear. A band marks the bell-head junction; it is defined by two impressed lines, and does not project beyond the bell edges. The bristle crest indicates the animals are boars. The players (in tight-fitting long-sleeved tunics and belted knee-length trousers) play the carnyces vertically, their left hands steadying the instrument at the first knob; only one arm is shown. There is no pronounced curve or knob at the end to indicate a complex mouthpiece, and it seems the end of the tube was either curved under or cut at an angle, creating a mouthpiece on the side of the tube. When first studying this from pictures I convinced myself I could justify a slight curve on the end, making the instrument more playable, but having examined the object first-hand this cannot be sustained. When the rear of the plaque is examined, it is clear that each end terminates in a curve rather than a straight line, but it does not curve beyond the vertical line of the tube, with the players' mouths jutting forward slightly to meet it.

Plaque B – the artists' sketchbook

One of the most remarkable results of the recent technical analysis was the observation that the rear of some plaques had been used as a sketchbook by the artists to try out and discuss designs. One of these (plaque B, number C6572) showed a standing human figure holding an animal-headed horn, with another version of the head of the horn below (**figs 132d; 325b**; Nielsen et al. 2005, 17-20).

The figure (only 44 mm high) faces left, with an open-legged stance, and is shown in outline with a line to indicate the hair and a misplaced, angled eye. Anatomical detail is lacking but the short hair suggests a male is represented. The uneven line of the back may indicate costume, such as a billowing cloak or tunic. The left arm curves down to the hip, while the right holds the horn just beyond its midpoint. This is shown with a gently curved cylindrical tube (and no defined mouthpiece) expanding into a zoomorphic head with an open, slightly flared mouth pointing upwards and a lentoid eye on the top of the head. The body is decorated with vertical hatching. Below the player's elbow is a sketch of the head, very similar in form but with the lower jaw less flared.

Erling Benner Larsen, who spotted the graffito, commented (in Nielsen et al. 2005, 18) that »this instrument looks quite different from the relatively much longer instruments played by the three carnyx blowers«, suggesting it may have been an animal horn with a metal bell – but is it so different? It seems quite a coincidence to have two zoomorphic-headed instruments on the one cauldron. I suggest what we are seeing is people unfamiliar with the carnyx experimenting with how it should look. Indeed, the fact that what is shown is essentially just the

bell and head suggests they may have had a dismantled carnyx to work from as a model – which would explain the accuracy of the main depiction. It is interesting that all the graffiti are found on plaques of toolset II, whereas the carnyx plaque is of toolset I, reinforcing again the evidence for creative dialogue between the artisans. Serge Lewuillon's argument (2017, 239f.) that this represents a significantly earlier depiction on a plaque which was reworked later lacks any convincing supportive argument.

Dating evidence

The widely varying views on the cauldron's origin are matched by disputes over its age (summarised in Benner Larsen 1987, tab. 1, to which add most notably Hachmann's [1990] suggestion of an Augustan date). The datable artefacts depicted (shields, spurs, helmets) could best be fitted into a date-bracket of late 2nd - 1st century BC (Kaul 1999, 201; Klindt-Jensen 1959); the discovery of a roundel in similar style from the Augustan fortress of Oberaden (D), abandoned c. 8 BC, shows that the style was still in circulation then with no appreciable Roman influence (von Schnurbein 1986; Kühlborn 1992, 149 pls 35. 76). Thracian silver-working flourished in the 2nd - 1st century BC (Bergquist/Taylor 1987, 13-16).

Scientific analysis provides some further evidence. Analysis of the glass inlays suggested a date range of 2nd century BC - 1st century AD (Nielsen et al. 2005, 40-42), although with the caveat that this dates the glass, not its use for inlay. A series of radiocarbon dates has also been obtained, but are highly divergent. One on carbon in the iron rim has been dismissed as methodologically unsound; of the two sets of dates on beeswax (which was used to support the rear of the silver during working), one set gives ranges of AD 1-400, another set of 6th - 3rd century BC (Nielsen et al. 2005, 46-50. 57)! There is clearly an unresolved methodological issue here, and it would be foolish to take one set of dates over another. In balancing these conflicting possibilities, a broad date range of c. 150-1 BC is taken here.

Bibliography (selective)

Benner Larsen 1987. – Bergquist/Taylor 1987. – Falkenstein 2004. – Hachmann 1990. – Klindt-Jensen 1950; 1959; 1979. – Kaul 1991a; 1991b; 1995; 1999. – Megaw 1970, 131f. – Megaw/Megaw 2001, 174-176. – Nielsen et al. 2005. – Powell 1971. – Taylor 1992.

C1.2 Carnyx pendant, Bouy »La Voie de Vadenay« (dép. Marne / F)

(Current location: Châlons-sur-Marne, Service Régional de l'Archéologie, inv. no. INC 9/213)

A tiny copper-alloy pendant (27 mm L.) in the form of the bell and head of a carnyx was found during excavation in 1975 of a cemetery at Bouy (»La Voie de Vadenay«), Marne, from »tombe 9« (**figs 131; 326a**). The site is not fully published, although there are summaries (Frézouls 1977, 405 f.; Flouest/Stead 1977, 73 f., with the best plan; Chossenot 1997, 341). Christophe Vendries, in bringing the pendant to wider notice, was able to draw on further information from the excavators (Homo-Lechner/Vendries 1993, 37; Vendries 1999, 370). The cemetery comprised 30 inhumation tombs largely of middle La Tène date and 15 cremation burials of late La Tène date. There was also a large bipartite rectangular enclosure and ten smaller square ones. Tomb 9, where the pendant was found, was the richest in the whole cemetery. The abundant and partly cremated grave goods were scattered across much of the pit. They included eleven pots, remains of around ten brooches, two bracelets and some glass beads badly deformed by heat, an iron knife and »fork«, and about ten pendants including an axe, animals, the carnyx, and three potin and bronze wheels (some figured in Frézouls 1977, 406 fig. 18). There were also iron fittings, probably from a casket. The excavators dated the tomb to the start of the 1st century BC based on the presence of a bronze La Tène III Nauheim brooch associated with the remains of La Tène II brooches; see discussion below under dating. Jean-Loup Flouest and Ian Stead (1977, 73 f.), who also worked on the site, suggested the enclosures are La Tène III in date, with any associated cremation burials being shallow and thus lost to erosion. However, they doubted whether »tombe 9« (a large rectangular pit just south of one of the small enclosures) was really a tomb. In a letter to the author, Ian Stead wrote:

»… ›Tombe 9‹, excavated by the French before we arrived, was a remarkable deposit outside one of the enclosures. A rich collection of artefacts, and it included calcined bones, but I suspect it was not a grave. Certainly it was different from the other graves at Bouy, and the other cremations I have seen in Champagne. The bones were scattered throughout the filling of the pit, along with sherds from at least 12 pots. A ›normal‹ burial would have had complete pots, or at least bases on the floor of the grave, and the bones would be in a heap or in one of the pots. And ›tombe 9‹ included three wheel pendants, more at home in a temple context than a grave.«

Michel Chossenot (1997, 341) interpreted the large enclosure as a Hallstatt cult enclosure, while accepting the smaller ones as La Tène III. This earlier ritual activity on the site would provide a context for later offerings such as the unusual assemblage of »tombe 9«.

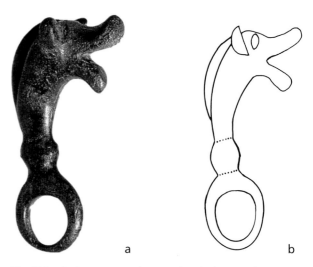

a   b

Fig. 326 C1.2 Bouy pendant. – (a Clodoré/Vendries 2002, fig. 71; b drawing Marion O'Neil).

The carnyx

The cast copper-alloy pendant comprises the head and bell of a carnyx, terminating at the bell-tube junction knob; below this is a suspension ring, worn from use (**fig. 326**). The crest and slightly upturned snout imply a boar is represented. The mouth flares, with no teeth or tongue; two forward-pointing ears; an eye is visible on the right side (Clodoré/Vendries 2002, fig. 71, and especially Kruta/Lička/Cession-Louppe 2006, 233) but not the left (Homo-Lechner/Vendries 1993, 37), suggesting the latter was preferentially worn in use. (I have only seen the object on display, and close autopsy was not possible.) The crest rises smoothly from the knob, reaching its maximum where the bell curves most, and then curves gently down to terminate at the ears. A clear knob marks the bell-tube junction. 27 mm L. 19 mm W. 9 mm T. mass 3.13 g.

Dating evidence

The excavators dated the tomb to the start of the 1st century BC based on the presence of a bronze La Tène III Nauheim brooch associated with the remains of La Tène II brooches; but the chronology of Nauheim brooches starts c. 120 BC (Striewe 1996), and this slightly earlier date would fit the presence of La Tène II brooches as well; a bracket of c. 120-75 BC is taken here.

Bibliography

Chossenot 1997, 341. – Clodoré/Vendries 2002, fig. 71. – Flouest/Stead 1977, 73 f. (with best plan). – Frézouls 1977, 405 f. – Homo-Lechner/Vendries 1993, 37. – Vendries 1999, 370.

C1.3 Carnyx player statuette, Kondoros (Békés county / H)

(Current location: Miskolc, Herman Otto Museum, inv. no. HOM 2007.22.1)

In 2003 the Herman Otto Museum acquired two bronze statuettes from a private collector. One is a pendant of a large-eared dog, the other a masturbating carnyx player; both are quite schematic in treatment, but capture the essence of the subject. The objects were said to have been found »in the vicinity of Kondoros« about 1950 during the construction of an irrigation channel, and had entered a local teacher's collection; after his death, they had been bought by the person who then sold them to the museum. This account draws heavily on the researches of János Veres (2009); he has considered the issue at length, concluding there are no strong grounds to doubt either provenance or authenticity. (I am grateful to János for details, photographs and valuable discussions.) Iron Age activity is known in the vicinity, and the style and subject matter are consistent with other bronze figurines especially from oppida, where nude figures and musicians are attested (Veros 2009, 234-241). Analysis of the alloys was entirely consistent with an Iron Age date (bronze with a trace of antimony).

The naked figure stands contrapposto, the left foot slightly forward of the right, which is on tiptoe; it conveys a sense of movement (**fig. 130**). He is naked, his hair depicted as an incised chequerboard pattern, with simple dot eyes; modelling is generally simple, but with details such as creasing behind the knees and over the right buttock. His left hand grasps his erect penis while his right holds the carnyx, which leans forward off the vertical. The elbow sticks out at right angles, the hand holding the tube against the mouth in an underhand grip. The statuette does not stand unaided, but shows no obvious signs of attachment. Overall 98 mm H. human 71 mm H. carnyx 48 mm L. (68 % human height).

The image is one of virility, and the nudity of the player could fit either a martial or ritual context; indeed, there need be no hard line between the two. Such statuettes are likely to have had a cult role, perhaps as offerings in a shrine.

The carnyx

The instrument is rather stylised, with a slightly sinuous tube expanding smoothly before turning through 90° into a zoomorphic head with gaping jaws and two dot eyes (**fig. 327**). Veros (2009, 242 f.) suggested it may be a bird or, more likely, a snake, perhaps deliberately simplified to its essentials to evoke the stylised, shape-shifting »dragons« found in various areas of Celtic art. The player's hand obscures the mouthpiece, which is slightly angled to the tube. It is held in one hand only (the right), the weight of the tube resting on the ball of the palm. There are no tech-

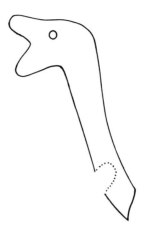

Fig. 327 C1.3 Carnyx from statuette, Kondoros. – (Drawing Marion O'Neil).

nical details such as tube junctions, and no ears or crest (which would be consistent with identification as a snake).

Dating evidence

The style of both the human and the dog acquired with it is quite simple. A range of human and animal depictions is known in Hungary from the early Iron Age onwards, but the closest parallels for both lie in late Iron Age oppida sites (e. g. Déchelette 1914, figs 565. 568; Veres 2009). The obvious parallel for the human is the bronze statuette of an ithyphallic horn player from the oppidum of Stradonice in the Czech Republic (**fig. 195d**; Clodoré/Vendries 2002, 113 f. fig. 82; Megaw 1991, 644 f.), dated to the 2nd - 1st century BC. This is a reasonable date for the Kondoros piece.

Bibliography

Veres 2009.

C2 HELLENISTIC DEPICTIONS

C2.1 Terracotta perfume flasks, El Ashmunein / Hermopolis Magna (Minya governorate / Egypt)

(Current location: one in Musée de Limoges, E 351c; the current whereabouts of a second, in Collection Fouquet in 1921, are unknown)

Two terracotta perfume flasks, probably from the same mould, are known, in the form of Eros with Celtic accoutrements (fig. 328). One, published by P. Perdrizet (1921, 142 f. no. 379 pl. XCIII), is now lost, but a second was recently discovered in the Musée de Limoges by Kevin Parachaud in the course of his doctoral work; I am grateful to him for details of this and permission to refer to it. The Perdrizet example is known only from a single photograph taken from the front, and details are not clear; it was 165 mm H. The Limoges example is slightly smaller as it survives (134 mm H.) but better photos are available; it was apparently found in a grave.

Eros stands on a lotus flower, walking to the R. He is nude, wears a buffer-ended torc and carries an oval shield on his L arm and a carnyx in his R. His hair is straggly, as in depictions of Celts. The carnyx is held upside down, with the head to the ground; Eros holds it to his lips to play it in this position. This could indicate disrespect for a vanquished enemy, but seems more likely to be part of the tradition of the playful Eros.

a　　　　　　b

c　　　d

Fig. 328　C2.1 Terracotta perfume flask, Hermopolis Magna: **a-b** the lost flask. – **c** the Limoges flask. – **d** the carnyx. – (a Perdrizet 1921, pl. XCIII; b drawing Alan Braby; c photo Kevin Parachaud; d drawing Tanja Romankiewicz).

In Ptolemaic Egypt the Celts had rather a mixed press. This is one of a number of Egyptian terracottas with Celts: some show them as heroic warriors, one has a Celt being trampled by an elephant, and others show Cupids or the Egyptian god Bes with Celtic weaponry (Perdrizet 1921, 141-143; Picard 1927; Mollard-Besques 1963, pl. 150b. d. f; Hausmann 1984; Dunand 1990, 61 cat. 104; Bailey 1995). Don Bailey (1995) outlined the rather schizophrenic view of the Celts in Ptolemaic Egypt: as in much of the Hellenic world, they were seen as feared enemies (the Bes figures reflect a tradition that he was responsible for defeating them; Picard 1927, 54), but they were also extensively used as mercenaries. Ptolemy II Philadelphos had problems with his 4000-strong force revolting, and trapped them on an island where they killed one another or died of starvation; for this he was hailed as a great victor. However, in other actions they proved to be the heroes of the day, winning battles for the Ptolemaic armies. Thus some of the terracottas show the defeat of the Celts, while others represent them as heroic warriors.

There is a terracotta of Eros with a Celtic shield in the Louvre, holding a trumpet to his lips, but the bulk of the instrument is broken and its form is unclear. This is a terracotta rather than a flask, and is dated by Dunand (1990, 61 no. 104) to the Roman period.

The carnyx

The head of the Limoges example is unfortunately damaged, while details are not fully visible on the Perdrizet photograph. The carnyx has a near-closed mouth (perhaps because it is upside down), an ear, and perhaps an eye. There is no crest (**fig. 328d**). The tube tapers somewhat, and has probably three junction bands (damage in the lower tube prevents certainty) defining three segments. The end is straight.

Dating evidence

Celts were being used as mercenaries in the Greek world in 277 BC, within two years of the attack on Delphi (Hannestad 1993, 19). They were still in use as late as the early 1st century BC (Bailey 1995, 2), but most of the terracottas seem to be of early 3rd-late 2nd century BC date (e.g. Besques 1992, 104 no. D4501; Leyenaar-Plaisier 1979, 281 no. 730; Bailey 1995). This is similar to the general date-bracket of c. 250-150 BC suggested by Ulrich Hausmann (1984) for Erotes with Celtic equipment in Alexandrian art, although there was a continuing terracotta tradition into the Roman period, and some authors date figures of Eros with Celtic equipment into the early centuries AD (e.g. Dunand 1990, 61 no. 104; Fischer 1994, 290f. no. 670; 386 no. 992), without an explicit rationale. These seem to be mostly terracotta figures rather than flasks, as here, and the earlier dating seems most appropriate.

Bibliography

Bailey 1995. – Hausmann 1984, 285. – Perdrizet 1921, 142 no. 379 pl. XCIII.

C2.2 Terracotta perfume flask (alabastron), Egypt (unprovenanced)

(Current location: Alexandria, Graeco-Roman Museum, inv. no. 23958)

An unprovenanced Ptolemaic terracotta perfume flask (alabastron) from Egypt carries a rare depiction of the carnyx from the Hellenistic world. Dorothy Burr Thompson (1964, 314f. 317f.) and Ulrich Hausmann (1984, 285f.) described and illustrated it, although the published illustrations are too poor to assess details (**fig. 329a**). The vessel has four decorative zones. The upper has intercrossing bands with medallions (a typical Alexandrian motif); the second one bears a scene of fighting Erotes on one side and a festival scene on the other; the third has garlands; and the fourth, at the base, bears acanthus ornament.

The main interest here is with the central zone. This features a pair of fighting Erotes, both with swords, the left with a round shield, the right with a foreshortened oval one. On the right an Eros plays a carnyx, while on the left one holds a wine amphora. The festival scene on the reverse features a priest, an Isis priestess and a dancing figure of the god Bes. Thompson and Hausmann linked the iconography to Classical accounts of Celts fighting at feasts, a habit Hausmann suggested would be known from mercenaries serving in Egypt. However, other interpretations are possible: for instance, the Erotes with round and oval shields could symbolise conflict between Greeks and Celts (Reinach 1911b, 98), and the significance of Bes as defeater of the Celts has been noted (Picard 1927). Erotes occurred regularly in Ptolemaic art with the attributes of Celts (Hausmann 1984), and indicate familiarity with »alien« Celtic habits. This probably arose from the Egyptian use of them as mercenaries, as Egypt avoided the Celtic invasions and migrations which plagued Greece and Asia Minor.

The carnyx

Unfortunately the published photographs located so far barely allow the carnyx to be distinguished (**fig. 329b**). It is played by an Eros walking left, held at an angle to the vertical; this and its small size are presumably to fit it into the field. The tube is straight but the mouthpiece is obscured and the head is in shadow, although an ear can be seen. There are hints of two lines on the tube which may indicate segments.

a

b

Fig. 329   C2.2 Terracotta perfume flask: **a** the flask; the carnyx appears in the bottom right image. – **b** the carnyx (details are very unclear). – (a Thompson 1964, fig. 8; b drawing Alan Braby).

Marie-Dominique Nenna and Merwatte Seif el-Din (2000, 38f.) were more circumspect about precise dating, and noted that the tradition of faience vessels ran through the 2nd century BC and probably into the 1st; the form falls into their alabastron type 8.2 (*ibidem* fig. 11). Hausmann's wider review of Eros iconography suggested a date bracket of late 3rd-early 2nd century BC. This is consistent with the evidence for Celtic contact with the Hellenistic world and for Celtic mercenaries serving in Egypt (Bailey 1995). A date range of c. 250-100 BC is taken here.

Dating evidence
Hausmann (1984, 285. 288f.) suggested the vessel's form parallels 3rd-century BC faience types, although

Bibliography
Hausmann 1984, 285f. – Thompson 1964, 314f. 317f.

C2.3 Ivory rhyton, Old Nisa (Akhal Vilayet / Turkmenistan)

(Current location: not known)
In 1948, excavations in the Parthian town of Old Nisa revealed an assemblage of some 50 ivory rhytons in a courtyard building referred to as the Square House. In its final phase in the late 1st century AD it was a storehouse, but previously it had been a banqueting hall, and the rhytons are likely to relate to this. They show strong Hellenistic influence in their decoration, and Niccolò Manassero (2013) recognised a carnyx on one of them.
The engraved band around the rhyton's mouth shows the selection, pursuit and ultimate sacrifice of a goat by satyrs (**fig. 330a-b**). The carnyx is played by an elderly satyr while a younger one attempts unsuccessfully to catch the goat which is standing on a pile of rocks. Manassero (2013) argued for deliberate iconographic evocations of

Pergamene depictions of Gauls, though this is not certain, and the comic mocking of Celts and Celtic material is found in other Hellenistic contexts, as noted above.
The discovery of such items in a Parthian area might occasion some surprise, but there was strong interaction between the Parthian and Hellenistic worlds. Old Nisa was founded by the Parthian king Mithridates I or Mithridates II in the 2nd century BC, with Hellenistic craftsmen working at the site (Manassero 2013, 69f.). The rhytons could either be imports from the Hellenistic world or made on site.
Manassero (2013) discussed the find in considerable detail, arguing strongly for a Pergamene connection and seeking to link the sacrifice scene to the cult of Cybele, with the Celtic carnyx forming a visual pun on the two meanings of the word γαλλος in Greek as a Gaul or a

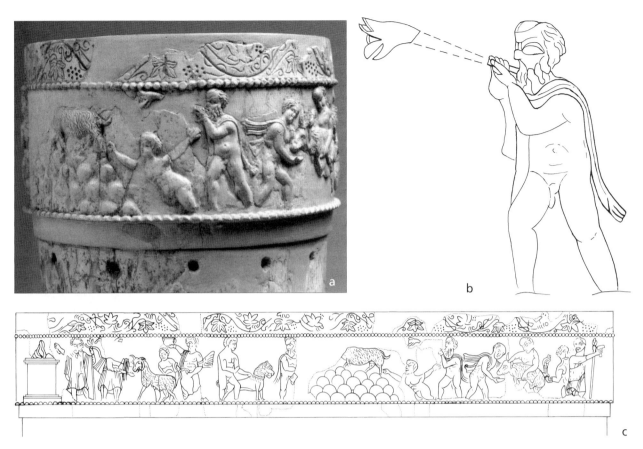

Fig. 330 C2.3 Ivory rhyton from Old Nisa: **a** detail of mouth. – **b** unrolled view of scene. – **c** the carnyx player. – (a Manassero 2013, fig. 2; b drawing Marion O'Neil after Manassero 2013, fig. 1; c drawing Marion O'Neil).

eunuch priest of Cybele. Both arguments are interesting but speculative, and not of direct relevance to the topic in hand; this rhyton provides another instance of the carnyx in a Hellenistic context, and shows just how far this Hellenistic influence could stretch.

The carnyx

A satyr holds the carnyx to his lips and blows into the straight tube (**fig. 330c**). The 20° angle it is held at reflects the available space on the frieze rather than a realistic depiction of how such instruments were played. The middle portion of the tube is lost; the head is naturalistically zoomorphic with a bird-like hooked beak, lidded eyes and two ears.

Dating evidence

The last phase of the building, when the rhytons were deposited, dated to the late 1st century AD, but Manassero (2013, 61. 79) argued they objects were linked to the foundation phase of the city, late 2nd - early 1st century BC.

Bibliography

Manassero 2013.

C3 ROMAN MILITARY AND GLADIATORIAL EQUIPMENT

C3.1 Decorated *murmillo* gladiator helmet, Pompeii (reg. Campania / I)

(Current location: Naples, Museo Archeologico Nazionale, inv. no. 5674)

Excavations of the gladiator's barracks in Pompeii in 1766-1767 produced a remarkable range of gladiatorial equipment including decorated helmets (Junkelmann 2000a, 38 f.). Sadly the nature of the excavation means that the details are not at all clear, and there has been persistent confusion over whether some came from Pompeii or Herculaneum (see C3.2), but they appear to represent material in use at the time of the city's destruction in AD 79.

The building, the quadriporticus behind the theatre, had been converted for gladiatorial use after the earlier barracks were damaged in the earthquake of AD 62 (Jacobelli 2003, 48. 65f.). One of the helmets includes representations of carnyces. The helmets are in embossed bronze, but Marcus Junkelmann (2000a, 38-43) argued convincingly that they were for use in combat rather than parade: technically they are strong and show modifications suggesting practical use, while a relief from Pompeii itself shows a gladiator fighting while wearing a decorated helmet.

By the late Augustan-early Imperial period gladiatorial equipment was highly standardised, with different types of gladiators having very specific equipment. This helmet with its angular crest is typical of a *murmillo*, a heavily-armoured gladiator who fought with a version of standard legionary equipment: a large curved shield, a gladius, a greave on his left leg and an arm protector on his right arm (Junkelmann 2000a, 44. 48-51).

The iconography of such helmets was often relevant to gladiatorial combat. Junkelmann (2000b, 85) listed the main themes as gladiatorial, military, theatrical, mythological, non-specific animals, and bucolic. The latter two are standard space-fillers, but the gladiatorial and military scenes were of specific significance while the deities represented were carefully chosen, such as Mars Ultor (Zanker 1988, fig. 218), Hercules (Junkelmann 2000a, figs 24. 58) or Venus (the lover of Mars; Junkelmann 2000a, fig. 38). In both C3.1 and C3.2, triumph is the linking theme. Both show scenes of victory, with trophies, captives and spolia; the parallel was to victory in the amphitheatre. C3.1 draws on mainstream Augustan state iconography, with references to the return of the Parthian standards, the battle of Actium, and probably Augustus' German campaigns.

The bowl of the helmet is decorated with embossed and incised designs running in a frieze round it (**fig. 154a-b**).

The overall theme is the glorification of Rome. In the centre is a depiction of Roma in armour, carrying a *parazonium* and leaning on a spear: her right foot rests on a ship's prow, most probably a reference to the battle of Actium (Zanker 1988, 82-85). On either side are barbarians carrying standards, one arm outstretched in supplication. The one on the left is identified as a Parthian by his hat; that on the right is probably also a Parthian, as his hairstyle is more formal than is normal for northern barbarians (it may be a cap, but this is not clear). This commemorates the return in 20 BC of the standards lost to the Parthians by Crassus at Carrhae in 53 BC, a major moment in Augustus' reign and a key motif in his propaganda (Zanker 1988, 185-192). To either side are Victories erecting trophies; the scenes differ only in detail and may be described together. The trophy is made up of a corset-style cuirass over a tunic, topped with a fur-covered helmet; this Hellenistic style of corset is typical of the late Republican and Augustan period (Polito 1998, 46f.). On either arm are pairs of hexagonal shields which the Victories are adjusting. Behind each arm is a carnyx and two or three spears. At the base is a pile of arms: hexagonal and round shields, swords, and helmets (Attic on the left, fur-covered on the right). The plume holders are decorated to represent greaves. The Victories stand on the edge of the trophy: towards the centre is a bound captive, male to the left (with trousers and a cloak, hairy but beardless), female to the right (with a long dress, a cloak and uncovered long hair). The weaponry and costume marks them out as northern barbarians, with the furry helmet suggesting a specifically Germanic origin. Junkelmann (2000b, 171) recorded decoration on the brim of Minerva stabbing the giant Pallas and Priapus in a theatrical mask; the brim also has a punched inscription »MCP«.

Fig. 331 C3.1 Carnyces on the helmet of a *murmillo*, Pompeii: **a** right side. – **b** left side. – **c** the carnyces. – (a photo Fraser Hunter; b Junkelmann 2000b, fig. 121; c drawing Tanja Romankiewicz).

Fig. 331 (continued)

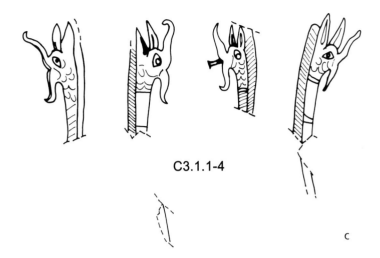

C3.1.1-4

c

The carnyces

The carnyces are numbered 1-4 from the left (**figs 179c; 331**). All are similar in character, with minor differences. They show the top of the tube, bell and head with junction-pieces marked by single or double incised lines (only 1 lacks any junctions); the crest runs the full visible length of the tube to the ears, and is decorated (except on 1) with forward-pointed incised lines to represent bristles. The head is quite naturalistic, with the two ears being hollowed to give them some depth, and the eye having the iris and pupil shown. The mouth is wide open (140-160°); in one case (3) a tongue is shown. In all cases the head is decorated with incised scales, while on 1 and 3 the tube and bell are decorated with spiral-twisting lines.

Dating evidence

The helmet's dating is not entirely certain, although the eruption of Vesuvius in AD 79 provides a *terminus ante quem* and gladiatorial use of these barracks post-dates AD 62 (Jacobelli 2003, 48. 65 f.). However, this tight bracket dates the use, not manufacture. Junkelmann (2000b, 171. 177) dated it to the third quarter of the 1st century AD on typological grounds. His work indicated that the fitting of fixed visors (as on both C3.1 and C3.2) was a feature of the late Augustan-early Imperial period, in the very early 1st century AD, while he quoted parallels on Flavian-period reliefs (Junkelmann 2000a, 38; 2000b, 61-64). For Junkelmann, the *murmillo* helmet was state of the art in the Flavian period. However, this date rests almost entirely on assumed sequences of typological development with few fixed points. Other authors have preferred the earlier end of this spectrum in discussing the iconography. Comparing it to southern French sculpture, R. Amy et al. (1962, 85 n. 43) suggested a late Augustan date while Henri Rolland (1977) opted for a date around 20 BC given the reference to the return of the Parthian standards. Donald Strong (1928) also proposed an Augustan date, as did Paul Zanker (1988, 275) for another

helmet from the site. The German triumph of Germanicus in AD 17 has also been cited as the event portrayed (Fiego n.d., 41).

There are strong grounds for an Augustan date. The reference to the return of the Parthian standards in 20 BC was commonplace in Augustan art, and the figure of Roma with her foot on a ship's prow can be seen as a reference to the battle of Actium in 31 BC (e.g. Zanker 1988, 82-85. 185-192). The trophies and their equipment and captives can only be seen as northern barbarians, either Gaulish or Germanic (probably the latter, given the furry helmets); this would be appropriate at a range of dates as these areas were the focus of active campaigning in the late Augustan-Flavian period, but the Actium and Parthian references do seem distinctively Augustan. This leaves a difficulty with Junkelmann's substantially later dating. The detailed grounds for this are primarily typological (summarised in Junkelmann 2000b, 50 f. 54 f. 61-64). He attempted to date the various Pompeii helmets to within a quarter of a century using this scheme, with all being dated in the second or third quarter of the century (Junkelmann 2000b, 165-180). This carries a number of inherent dangers, not least the rigidity of the typology (which is inherently questionable since the Pompeii find has several different types of helmet deposited together). There is also the likelihood, especially with more decorative items, that there was considerable variation from helmet to helmet arising from maker's or commissioner's whim rather than any linear typological development. It is felt here that while the typology may work in classificatory terms, its chronological validity has not been demonstrated, and the art-historical dating of the decoration (where possible) provides a better basis. Thus a late Augustan date for C3.1 is accepted here (c. 20 BC-AD 14).

Bibliography

Ensoli/La Rocca 2000, 591 no. 286. – Junkelmann 2000b, 171. – Ulbert 1969, 104 f.

C3.2 Helmet of a *provocator*, Herculaneum (reg. Campania / I)

(Current location: Naples, Museo Archeologico Nazionale, inv. no. 5670)

A second decorated gladiatorial helmet is often stated to come from the same find, though the early records are rather garbled; archival research has indicated it in fact comes from Herculaneum, where a range of gladiatorial equipment was also recovered (Hoffmann-Schmipf/Melillo/Schwab 2011, 15).

This helmet is that of a *provocator*, who fought with a straight sword and used a legionary-type or a blunted-oval shield, single greave and arm guard; they also had armour for the upper chest, uniquely for gladiators, and fought against opponents of the same type (Junkelmann 2000a, 37. 57-59). The helmet is a version of the standard military Weisenau (or Imperial Gallic) type, with the addition of visors; they had no crest or brim, unlike most other gladiatorial helmets (*ibidem*).

Marcus Junkelmann (2000b, 176 f.) provided a basic description of the helmet, and Bernd Hoffmann-Schimpf, Luigia Melillo and Roland Schwab (2011) published a detailed technical account, although the iconography has seen less detailed treatment. It lacks its visors and parts of the brow-guard and the plate below this, but is otherwise in good condition, though it has seen some restoration (**fig. 332**; Hoffmann-Schimpf/Melillo/Schwab 2011, fig. 15). The bowl is ornamented all over with embossed and incised decoration, mixing mythological and triumphal scenes, with a trophy flanked by the Dioscuri and a range of Roman, conventional and northern barbarian weaponry. In the centre is Jupiter's eagle with outstretched wings, holding a laurel wreath in its beak and clutching a thunderbolt in its claws. Around it is a frieze comprising a central trophy surrounded by a weapons frieze. The vertical portion of the neck-guard is ribbed, with a punched inscription reading »EX OFFICINA L MENI NATA«, »from the workshop of Lucius Maenius Natalis« (Hoffmann-Schmipf/Melillo/Schwab 2011, 23). The wide horizontal part of the neck-guard is decorated with depictions of a

Fig. 332   C3.2 Helmet of a *provocator*, Herculaneum: **a** left side. – **b** front view. – **c** right side. – **d** rear. – **e** the carnyces. – (a-d Hoffmann-Schimpf/Melillo/Schwab 2011, figs 1a; 22b-d; e drawing Tanja Romankiewicz).

a

b

Fig. 332 (continued)

c

d

provocator helmet and two arm guards. On the left side, below the brow-band, is the head of Oceanus between two dolphins and two Cupids riding sea-monsters.

It is the trophy and weapons frieze which are of concern here. The trophy is an odd one: it comprises a cloak crowned with a bearded male head which was interpreted as Priapus or more plausibly Jupiter, perhaps Jupiter Feretrius, traditional receiver of trophies and booty (Hoffmann-Schimpf/Melillo/Schwab 2011; Adkins/Adkins 1996, 121). On the arms are crossed hexagonal shields, with further shields (hexagonal, round and pelta) and a fur-covered helmet at the base. To either side are the Dioscuri (?), one with a standard topped with a hand, the other now restored with a sword but perhaps originally also holding a standard (Junkelmann 2000b, 177).

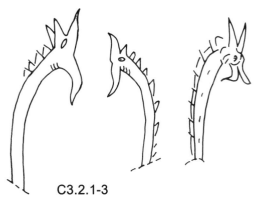

C3.2.1-3

e

The weapons frieze runs round the rest of the bowl, and can be divided into seven groups. Running anti-clockwise from the trophy these are as follows.

- Crossed hexagonal shields with three spears and a carnyx (1) behind.
- Muscle cuirass with torc (disguising a plume holder), in front of crossed hexagonal shields; behind, round shields, spears and a vexillum standard.
- Two crossed shields (one hexagonal, one oval) with spears behind.
- Muscle cuirass with torc in front of a round shield flanked by two pelta shields. Behind are three hexagonal shields, spears, a tuba and two carnyces (2-3).
- Crossed hexagonal shields.
- Muscle cuirass (now with a torc, restored on the model of the other side) in front of crossed oval shields with a round shield, spears and a vexillum standard behind.
- Crossed shields (restored, but the base of a hexagonal one is original) with a hybrid standard of a vexillum topped by an animal, perhaps a bull.

This helmet mixes the mythological and triumphal, but unlike the *murmillo* helmet it has no clear iconographic link to particular events. The carnyces and hexagonal shields point to northern barbarians, the fur-covered helmet suggesting it relates most probably to German campaigns.

The carnyces

Carnyces 1-2 are near-identical, with curving tube, sawtooth crest, two ears, eye and gaping mouth. Carnyx 3 differs, with the head curved more downwards, the mouth less open and the crest a different style (**fig. 332e**). All are rather crude, linear and stylised compared to those on the *murmillo* helmet; there are none of the attempts at three-dimensional modelling or technical detail. No junctions are shown. All have small incised lines around the chin to evoke skin folds or hair tufts.

Dating evidence

The *provocator* helmet developed from the military Weisenau type which was introduced in the Augustan period, but Junkelmann saw the decoration on the Pompeiian examples as marking a deviation from the military prototypes (Junkelmann 2000b, 54f.). As discussed under C3.1, he argued for a date of AD 50-75 on typological grounds, but this is far from certain. Unlike C3.1, the iconographic references are not specific enough to offer a tighter dating, and a broader date range (AD 1-79) needs to be accepted.

Bibliography

Junkelmann 2000b, 176f. – Hoffmann-Schmipf/Melillo/Schwab 2011.

C3.3.1-6 Decorated mouth plates from sword scabbards

In late Augustan and early Imperial times there was a habit of decorating weapons, especially swords, shields and helmets, often with propaganda motifs or mythological scenes (Künzl 1988b, 541). Among this is a series of decorated sword scabbards which include a scene of trophies with carnyces. These are known primarily from Switzerland, best illustrated by the complete sword found with its scabbard and belt in the legionary fortress at Vindonissa (**fig. 155**). Six are currently known: three from Vindonissa (CH; Germania Superior) and single finds from Baden (CH; Germania Superior), Ptuj (SL; Pannonia Inferior) and Valkenburg (NL; Germania Inferior). All are rectangular copper-alloy plates with an embossed design from the mouth of a sword scabbard: their breadth, and the intact Vindonissa scabbard, shows they came from legionary *gladii* scabbards. They were stamped out: all appear to have come from the same model. The key works are by Ernst Künzl (1988b; 1994; 1996) and Eckardt Deschler-Erb (1996; 1998); they are also discussed by Christian Miks (2007, 246f. pl. 190).

The intact Vindonissa scabbard has three plates on it: the mouth plate, a central long rectangular plate with a thunderbolt, and a basal triangular plate with two fields, the upper with a cavalryman spearing a barbarian (naked bar either trousers or a belt, and carrying a hexagonal shield),

the lower with a trophy (of muscle cuirass, cloak, sword, greaves, horned helmet, hexagonal shields with spears behind, and a helmet at the base). There is one similar triangular plaque known, also from Vindonissa (Künzl 1996, 457 M27 pl. 48, 4). The mouth plate shows a kneeling male barbarian, body facing to the right and head turned to the left, between two trophies. He is bound and naked, hairy and bearded, with both hair and beard having well-defined broad strands; Deschler-Erb (1996, 24) and Künzl (1996, 411) saw him as a Gaul. Each trophy comprises an oval shield decorated with a thunderbolt, with carnyx and spear behind; the right one also has a sword; at the foot is a domed helmet, the cheek-pieces decorated with scrollwork. Elsewhere in the scene are individual motifs of hands pointing downwards, daggers and spearheads. The plate is die-stamped and is made from a single sheet of copper alloy, folded to shape and fastened (?soldered) at the rear. Views on the iconography are summarised by Deschler-Erb (1996, 25). Some have argued the motifs are general ones appropriate to the frontier, but Künzl (1996, 411f.) proposed a specific and seductive interpretation. He saw the disembodied right hands as a symbol of broken oaths or a betrayal of trust; with this, the concentrated find-spots, and the general dating (see below) he linked them to the quelling of the revolt of Julius Sacrovir and the Aedui in

AD 21 (Tacitus, *Annals* III.40-47). The legion based at Vindonissa at this time, Legio XIII, played the major role in this action, and these plaques can be seen almost as military honours. All the findspots have connections with the subsequent moves of Legio XIII, supporting this link, and it is near-certain they were made at Vindonissa. (The intact scabbard was found in a later 1st century context, showing it had a life of some 40-50 years and ended up in the hands of a different legion; Deschler-Erb 1996, 27 f.)

This interpretation is a plausible one, although the iconography itself is rather stylised. Three generations after the conquest, were the Aedui still stereotypical naked hairy Gauls? Tacitus' account indicates a range of armour:

> »... one-fifth were equipped like Roman soldiers, the rest with hunters' spears, knives, and other such arms. There was also a party of slaves training to be gladiators. Completely encased in iron in the national fashion, they were too clumsy for offensive purposes but impregnable in defence.«

It seems the images used a standard and well-recognised iconographic stereotype. This does not therefore constitute firm evidence of carnyx use in Gaul persisting at this period.

The carnyces

In the left trophy, the carnyx is angled up to the right and faces left; the right one is on the left side of the trophy, vertical and facing right. Both are stylised and not always well-struck, but combining the different plaques provides a better overall picture: the one from Valkenburg is the clearest (**fig. 333**). They have a cylindrical tube with no junctions, curving smoothly through 140-160° into the head. There are no ears, crest or eyes (except on the Baden left example, where an eye appears to have been punched in subsequently; there is also a hint of an eye on the Ptuj example). The mouth is open to 90° with the jaw tips recurved. In several instances the left carnyx is better struck and thus clearer. The hints of a crest on the Baden example are probably a striking flaw.

Dating evidence

Künzl (1988b) dated the general flourishing of such decorated weaponry to the Augustan-Tiberian period. In some instances the iconography provides a precise dating: for instance, the »sword of Tiberius« from Mainz refers to Germanicus' German triumph in AD 17 (*ibidem* 543). In the case of these scabbard mounts, Künzl's arguments about their iconographic context suggest a date shortly after the Sacrovir uprising of AD 21. This is confirmed by the belt plate with a bust of Tiberius found with the intact Vindonissa scabbard (Deschler-Erb 1996, 24 f.). Künzl (1996, 409 f.) narrowed the date range further by drawing parallels with the plaque and numismatic depictions with a similar globe and cornucopiae motif which are found only on Tiberius' coins of AD 23. This suggests a dating of AD 22-23 for this set of mounts.

Bibliography

Deschler-Erb 1996; 1998. – Künzl 1988b; 1994; 1996.

C3.3.1 Vindonissa (Aargau/CH), legionary camp barracks, 1990

(Current location: Vindonissa Museum, inv. no. V 90.4)

Main references
Deschler-Erb 1996; 1998. – Künzl 1996, 458 M 35 pls 42, 1-3; 53, 6. – Miks 2007, 761 f. pl. 190, A790.

C3.3.2 Vindonissa (Aargau/CH), Schutthügel-Ost 1855

(Current location: Vindonissa Museum, inv. no. KAA 416,1)

Main references
Unz/Deschler-Erb 1997, 62 no. 2398 pl. 79. – Künzl 1996, 456 M18 pl. 48, 5. – Miks 2007, 908 f. pl. 190. B328,64.

C3.3.3 Vindonissa (Aargau/CH), Schutthügel-Ost 1923

(Current location: Vindonissa Museum, inv, no. 23:311)

Main references
Unz/Deschler-Erb 1997, 62 no. 2399 pl. 79. – Künzl 1996, 456 M19 pl. 48, 6. – Miks 2007, 909 pl. 190. B328,65.

C3.3.4 Baden (Aargau/CH)

(Current location: Baden, Historisches Museum, inv. no. 1458; cast in RGZM, 32253a)

Main references
Künzl 1988b, fig. 221d; 1994, fig. 17; 1996, 453 M1 pl. 53, 1. – Miks 2007, 780 f. pl. 190. B18,6.

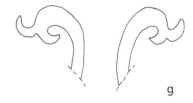

Fig. 333 C3.3 Scabbard plates with barbarian and trophy: **a** C3.3.1 Vindonissa. – **b** C3.3.2 Vindonissa. – **c** C3.3.3 Vindonissa. – **d** C3.3.4 Baden. – **e** C3.3.5 Valkenburg. – **f** C3.3.6 Ptuj. – **g** the carnyces. – (a-c photos Kantonsarchäologie Aargau/Vindonissa Museum; d. f Künzl 1996, pl. 53; e photo National Museum of Antiquities, Leiden; g drawing Tanja Romankiewicz).

C3.3.5 Valkenburg (prov. Limburg/NL)

(Current location: Leiden, Rijksmuseum van Oudheden, inv. no. H 1991/9.3679)

Main references
Künzl 1996, 458 M39 pl. 53, 3-5. – Miks 2007, 886 pl. 190, B300,4.

C3.3.6 Ptuj/Poetovio (Podravska regija/SLO)

(Current location: Maribor, Pokrajinski Muzej; cast in RGZM, 33818)

Main references
Künzl 1988b, fig. 221e; 1996, 455 M11 pl. 53, 2. – Miks 2007, 861 pl. 190, B230,1.

C3.4 Decorated cavalry helmet, Xanten-Wardt (Kr. Wesel/D)

(Current location: Bonn, LVR-LandesMuseum, inv. no. 86.0070)

This magnificent iron helmet with silver-gilt decorative overlay came from the collection of material which included a wealth of 1st century militaria, found in gravel extraction in an old branch of the Rhine at Xanten (fig. 334a; Schalles/Schreiter 1993). The motives behind the deposit are not clear. Schalles (1994) suggested there are likely to be several mechanisms at work, including the accumulation of casual losses from river traffic and troop movement, and the loss of plunder following the Batavian Revolt when the garrison was besieged. One should add the likelihood of a series of votive deposits (a persistent habit in this locale, given the presence of several pieces of Bronze Age metalwork and a late La Tène sword: Weber 1993; Schalles/Schreiter 1993, 199). So many fine helmets were deposited intact along the frontier in rivers and pits that it is hard to believe all were casual losses or unfortunate accidents, and they may relate to ceremonies at the end of a soldier's service (van Enckevort/Willems 1994, 128-134).

This example is a cavalry helmet of Weiler type (Feugère 1994, 104-110), with cheek-pieces and narrow neckguard. Their distribution (*ibidem* 109) concentrates strongly in the Rhineland and points to manufacture in this area. It is covered with an embossed silver sheet, gilt in places, which depicts a head of hair (in rows) with an olive wreath, fronted with a portrait medallion. The cheek pieces are decorated to represent a beard, and the neck guard has a vegetal scroll with hunting cupids. (For full description see von Prittwitz und Gaffron 1993.)

The feature of interest here is the portrait medallion (fig. 334b). This shows an emperor, most likely Tiberius or Claudius, in a muscle cuirass. Around him is a frieze of weapons paired symmetrically. From the base they comprise a pelta shield, a greave, two overlapping round shields with spears behind, a muscle cuirass, two crossed hexagonal shields, a carnyx, a helmet and an unclear item at the top. Only the hexagonal shields and the carnyx are barbarian equipment.

The helmet is particularly interesting because it is lop-sided, not from damage but in manufacture, and Hans-Hoyer von Prittwitz und Gaffron argued plausibly that this was a commissioned piece for a soldier with a deformity, whose head angled over to the left. This implies that the piece must have been specially commissioned, and thus that the iconography had a personal relevance. It is likely that such hel-

Fig. 334 C3.4 Decorated cavalry helmet, Xanten-Wardt: **a** general view. – **b** bust and roundel on front. – **c** the carnyces. – (a-b von Prittwitz und Gaffron 1993, pls 37. 39; c drawing Tanja Romankiewicz).

mets with wreaths reflected honours won (Feugère 1994, 109) rather than simply being decorative. Von Prittwitz und Gaffron linked the olive wreath to triumphal iconography, to the recipient of a small triumph (*ovatio*) or the organiser of a major one. He argued the helmet thus symbolises the victory (in the triumphant emperor and the frieze of Roman and barbarian weapons) and the peaceful outcome (seen in the vegetation and cupids on the neck guard). The stylistic dating evidence (see below) suggests a date in the 40s AD, for which the historically attested triumphs or *ovationes* are Caligula's campaigning in lower Germany and advance to the Channel coast in 40, Claudius' British triumph in 43 or Aulus Plautius' *ovatio* after his British victories in 47. From this the carnyx and hexagonal shields relate to either Germanic or British barbarians.

The carnyces

The two carnyces are stylised but recognisable by their flaring mouths, although they do not seem to have been correctly identified previously: von Prittwitz und Gaffron only described them as »ein Signalhorn«. They emerge from behind the crossed hexagonal shields, and thus only the upper part is visible (**fig. 334c**). Each faces outwards, and the right one is rather damaged. No technical details are shown, nor do they have eyes, ears or a crest, but the mouth has clearly-defined lips, open to 180°, slightly hollowed and with the tips flaring slightly backwards.

Dating evidence

Von Prittwitz und Gaffron summarised the dating evidence. The bust is not easily identified but is probably either Tiberius or Claudius, while this style of hair in rows of curls is stylistically dated to the 40s AD, supporting a Claudian date.

Bibliography

Feugère 1994, 104-110. – von Prittwitz und Gaffron 1993.

C3.5 Disc from a standard, Niederbieber (Lkr. Neuwied/D)

(Current location: Bonn, LVR-LandesMuseum, inv. no. 77.0131)

Silver disc from a standard, partly gilt and decorated in repoussé with the figure of a victorious Roman commander standing on a barbarian and a pile of arms (**fig. 335a**). The disc has spawned an extensive literature and debate: the summary by Ernst Künzl (1988b, 564f.) is the main source used here, supplemented by Hans-Hoyer von Prittwitz und Gaffron (2007, 131f.). The disc (190mm D.) was found in the fort of Niederbieber in Germania Superior along with a standard-spear and a silver plaque inscribed »COH V[…]« (Lindenschmit 1858, Heft VII pl. 5; Töpfer 2011, 418-420). This is interpreted as the remains of the standard of the *cohors VII Raetorum equitata*, who had been stationed since the reign of Domitian (c. AD 90) in the fort of Koblenz-Niederberg and came to the assistance of the garrison of Niederbieber during the Frankish raids of AD 259-260 in which they perished; the standard was found with a skeleton, presumably the *imaginifer* (Künzl 1988c, 564).

There has been considerable debate over the identity of the beardless commander depicted (Künzl 1988c, 564f.; von Prittwitz und Gaffron 2007, 131f.). Some authorities have recognised a 3rd-century general such as Saloninus, son of Gallienus, but the style does not readily fit a 3rd-century date and is more appropriate for the 1st century AD. Künzl suggested a connection to Domitian, but Augustus, Tiberius and Caligula have also been argued; the portrait is not a particularly diagnostic one. Künzl argued that Caligula is an unlikely candidate as his northern campaigns were insufficiently impressive to justify keeping his image

for so long. With both Caligula and Domitian there is the difficulty of *damnatio memoriae*: would their images have survived in use for two centuries? Of course, our failure to recognise the figure could have been a concern in Roman times as well. Tiberius is the other most likely candidate, as his German campaigns (or those waged on his behalf) were substantial.

The disc shows the Roman commander in muscle cuirass and *paludamentum*, holding sword and spear, standing on a bearded ?naked barbarian and a pile of arms. The weaponry comprises (from the left) three spears, carnyx, oval shield, cloak, barbarian, pile of oval shields, bowl helmet with brow, cheek-pieces, neck-guard and volute decoration, spear, »Celtic lituus«, tuba, two single-edged axes and a curved sword. The barbarian, carnyx and »Celtic lituus« are all typical of northern barbarians, and it presumably represents German campaigns under Augustus, Tiberius or Domitian. From the data in **table 47** and **Appendix 5** on the occurrence of axes, curved swords and »litui« a late Flavian association would fit the evidence best.

The carnyx

The carnyx is on the left of the disc, lying horizontally to the left and facing up. Only the head, bell and upper tube are depicted; none have any technical detail (**fig. 335b**). The tube is a thin cylinder, the bell expanding slightly before it swells at the head. This has no crest or ear, but does have an eye peak and a flaring mouth open to 180° with the tips curved back and then curved forward again.

Fig. 335 C3.5 Standard disc, Niederbieber: **a** the disc. – **b** the carnyx. – (a photo LVR-Landes-Museum Bonn; b drawing Tanja Romankiewicz).

b

a

Dating evidence

The iconography suggests a 1st century date, most probably in the reign of Domitian, but an earlier date (most plausibly Tiberian) cannot be ruled out.

Bibliography

Künzl 1988c, 564 f. – Töpfer 2011, 418-420 cat. A1.1-3. – von Prittwitz und Gaffron 2007, 131 f.

C4 ROMAN ARCHITECTURAL FITTINGS

C4.1 Wall painting, Pompeii, Villa of the Mysteries (reg. Campania / I)

Eugenio Polito (1998, 127-129) discussed a frieze in the atrium in the Villa of the Mysteries near Pompeii which has never been published in detail. He noted the presence of a carnyx along with an oval shield as the sole representatives of western barbarian equipment. The bulk of the frieze is helmets and shields of Hellenistic type, along with greaves, swords, lances and muscle cuirasses. Some of the helmet types are otherwise rare in Roman art, notably the pseudo-Corinthian and Phrygian ones, both of Greek derivation.

The frieze was part of the decoration of the two pilasters between the atrium and the peristyle (**fig. 336a**; Mazzo-leni/Pappalardo 2005, 103). Their decoration was in two main zones, a lower part imitating a wall inlaid with semi-precious marbles, and an upper part with (presumably) a figural scene surrounded by a weapons frieze. The upper scenes have been removed, leaving the frieze behind, though on both the top half is entirely destroyed.

The carnyx

The carnyx is on the right-hand side of the left pilaster on leaving the room. It is crossed by an oval shield, concealing its base, and overlies another oval shield (**fig. 336b-c**). The instrument is outlined in a red-brown line and infilled

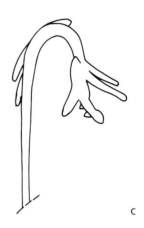

Fig. 336 C4.1 Wall painting, Villa of the Mysteries, Pompeii: **a** view of room decoration; the carnyx is arrowed. – **b** the carnyx scene. – **c** the carnyx. – (a Mazzoleni/Pappalardo 2005, 103; b photo Margaret Robb; c drawing Tanja Romankiewicz).

with buff paint. It is depicted as a cylindrical tube with no junctions, swelling very slightly at the bell and recurving through 180°. The mouth is open to c. 90°, and there seems to be a single fang in the upper jaw. It has two long, thin ears and appears to have a dot eye, while a few thin, elongated backward-pointing triangles define a rather sparse crest, starting only where the tube turns through 180° and running about a third of the visible tube length. (I am grateful to Prof. Lawrence Keppie and Margaret Robb for seeking out the frieze and taking the photographs on which this description is based; it could not be closely approached when I visited.)

Date
Polito's discussion of the date connected the painting to refurbishment of the villa after Sulla's foundation of a colony at Pompeii, with a likely bracket of c. 80-50 BC.

Bibliography
Polito 1998, 127-129.

C4.2 Terracotta antefixes, Rome/I

A series of terracotta antefixes show a variant of Augustus' Actium trophy (**fig. 337**). The original trophy is long vanished but it is depicted on Augustan coinage (RIC Augustus 265), and comprised naval spolia erected on a mast: a trophy with spears and a hexagonal shield in its arms, a rudder and anchor crossed beneath it, and a prow at the base. The antefixes subtly alter this: the anchor is either absent or replaced by a carnyx; the helmet style is changed to a bowl with brim, cheek-pieces and rosette or circle on the top; the cuirass style is simplified; and two dolphins now flank the prow, from which a vexillum standard flies (Picard 1957, 256f.; Woelcke 1911, 152-157). P. Pensabene and M. R. S. Di Mino (1983, 309f.) defined two variants: one has a torc on the trophy's neck but no carnyx (type 234, 1), the other a carnyx but no torc (234, 2; their account omits the carnyx). Harald Mielsch

Fig. 337 C4.2 Terracotta antefix, Rome: **a** C4.2.1 Bonn. – **b** C4.2.2 Rome (Gorga collection). – **c** C4.2.4 Rome. – **d** detail of carnyx on Bonn antefix. – **e** the carnyx. – (a. d photos Fraser Hunter courtesy of Akademisches Kunstmuseum Bonn; b Ceccarini 1999, 117 fig. 10; c Anselmino 1977, pl. XI, 51; e drawing Tanja Romankiewicz).

(1971, 24), followed by L. Anselmino (1977, 110), Pensabene and Di Mino (1983, 309 f.), interpreted the device as a *cheniscus*, the goose-headed stern of a ship, but Gilbert Charles Picard (1957, 256 f.) and Karl Woelcke (1911, 153) saw it as a carnyx; examination of the Bonn example and published photos of other specimens confirms the carnyx identification.

Picard interpreted the changes as a desire to move away from the specificity of Actium imagery towards a more general reminder of Augustus' power and the implication of universal victory, a general theme in Augustan propaganda. Here the carnyx evokes victories in Gaul, as seen in the southern French triumphal arches. Most of these antefixes lack findspots, but provenanced examples are all from Rome. Picard attributed them to the temple of Apollo Palatine (*ibidem* 269), which was dedicated to the victory at Actium, but this seems unlikely because of the use of multiple matrices (as single building projects tended to use consistent matrices) and their small size compared to known examples from this temple (0.22 m compared to 0.39 m; Hölscher 1985, 94-96; 1988, 369 cat. 201; Carettoni 1988, cat. 127-129; Coarelli 1968, 196 f.). F. Coarelli (1968, 197) observed that known examples all appeared in museum collections around the same time, and speculated about a single chance find which became dispersed, perhaps from construction work in the Tiber around 1875. Tonio Hölscher (1985, 94-96; 1988, 369) suggested instead a model in a more precious material, perhaps marble, which acted as a prototype for the widespread transmission of the type to private buildings. The Actium antefix is one of a number of antefixes with Augustan propaganda, some of which are known to come from private dwellings. This is an important indicator of the spread of Augustan propaganda to the private sphere, with individuals choosing these architectural decorations to show loyalty to the emperor and subscription to his policies (Hölscher 1985, 94-96; Zanker 1988, 82-85. 265-274).

Unfortunately, many examples are not published in detail or illustrated. Coarelli (1968, 206 f. n. 25) drew much of the evidence together, and this was augmented by Anselmino (1977, 110). **Table 73** summarises the known

finds. Three of the four known to feature carnyces have published illustrations.

The carnyx

The Bonn antefix has been viewed first-hand, but poor modelling and wear (especially to the right of the mast) mean that some of the details are not entirely clear (**fig. 337d-e**); this description draws also on published illustrations of the other examples. Since the details elsewhere on the antefix are well-modelled, only fairly clear indicators of the carnyx's form have been accepted as genuine.

The carnyx slopes down from the left, its head turned back through 150° and facing upwards. The long straight cylindrical tube tapers at the end to a rounded point. No tube junctions are visible. There is no crest and no clear eye; there is an ear, and the mouth is open to c. 90°; it has no teeth or tongue. Antefix overall 215 mm H. 154 mm W. 95 mm surviving T.

Date

Actian imagery must post-date the battle in 31 BC, and was falling from fashion by around 20 BC to be replaced by the iconography of the return of the Parthian standards (Picard 1957, 273). A bracket of 30-20 BC seems valid.

C4.2.1 Bonn, Akademisches Kunstmuseum (inv. no. D161)

Bibliography
Mielsch 1971, 24 f. 48 fig. 33 no. 35. – Picard 1957, 257. 269 pl. XI. – Woelcke 1911, 152-157 pl. VIII. – Coarelli 1968, 196. – Hölscher 1985, fig. 8. – Zanker 1988, fig. 65.

C4.2.2 Rome, Museo Nazionale Romano (inv. no. 262604)

Bibliography
Pensabene/Di Mino 1983, 309 f. no. 964. pl. 143. – Ceccarini 1999, 117 fig. 10.

C4.2.3 Rome, Museo Nazionale Romano (inv. no. 311143)

Bibliography
Pensabene/Di Mino 1983, 309 f. no. 965.

C4.2.4 Rome, Antiquarium Comunale (inv. no. 4374)

Bibliography
Anselmino 1977, 109 no. 133 pl. XI, 51. – Coarelli 1968, n. 25 fig. 8.

C4.3-4 Campana plaques, Ostia and Rome (Roma/I)

A series of terracotta plaques manufactured in Rome and the surrounding area includes examples with reliefs of trophies, prisoners and triumphal scenes. They are known as Campana plaques after the first scholar to collect and publish them, Giovanni Pietro Campana (1852; Sarti 2001, esp. 76-80; 2002). This summary draws primarily on

museum	inv. no.	carnyx?	reference	illustration	provenance/ notes
Rome, Museo Nazionale Romano	4509	no	Pensabene/Di Mino 1983, 309 f. no. 958; Coarelli 1968, n.25	Pensabene/Di Mino 1983, pl. 143; Coarelli 1968, fig. 5	Rome, Tiber
	11189	no	*ibidem* no. 959		
	11139	no	*ibidem* no. 960		
	262605	no	*ibidem* no. 961		Gorga collection 8135
	4511	no	*ibidem* no. 962; Coarelli 1968, n. 25	Coarelli 1968, fig. 6	Rome, Tiber
	262606	no	*ibidem* no. 963		
	262604	yes C4.2.2	*ibidem* no. 964	**fig. 337b**	Gorga collection 8124
	311143	yes C4.2.3	*ibidem* no. 965		
Rome, Antiquarium of Museo Nazionale Romano	Gorga collection 8162	?	Anselmino 1977, 110		
	Gorga collection 8163	?	Anselmino 1977, 110		
Rome, Antiquarium Comunale	4305	no	Anselmino 1977, 109 no. 132; Coarelli 1968, n. 25	Coarelli 1968, fig. 7	
	4374	yes C4.2.4	Anselmino 1977, 109 no. 133	**fig. 337c**	
	18788	?	*ibidem* no. 134		Rome, via Gallia
Louvre	CP3949	?	Anselmino 1977, 109		Rome
Bonn, Akademisches Kunstmuseum	D161	yes C4.2.1	see below	**fig. 337a**	Rome
Philadelphia, University Museum	256	no	Mielsch 1971, 48; Coarelli 1968, 196	Woelcke 1911, fig. 4	Rome

Tab. 73   Antefixes with Actium imagery. Note the confusion on several counts, notably with the Gorga Collection; part was published by Pensabene/Di Mino 1983, but Anselmino 1977 referred to further examples which appear to be unpublished; these do not feature in a later catalogue of the Gorga collection (Ceccarini 1999). Additionally, the item illustrated as no. 4374 in Coarelli (1968, fig. 8) is not the same as the antefix published with this number by Anselmino (1977, 109 no. 133; further complicated because her image cross-reference is misplaced). This latter item is illustrated by Hölscher 1988, cat. 201 as Inv. 4511 but this must be an error as 4511 has no carnyx. Anselmino is taken as the authority (despite the confusion in image numbering) because this is the published catalogue.

the synthetic work of Stefano Tortorella (1981a; 1981b), developed with more recent publications by Maria Josè Strazzulla (1991; 1993), Carla Martini (1996) and Anne Viola Siebert (2011), and Tortorella's work specifically on triumphal imagery (in La Rocca/Tortorella 2008, 126-129. 194 f.; Tortorella 2008).

The Classical world had a long tradition of decorative architectural ceramics, used especially to ornament temples. Campana plaques were mould-formed rectangular plaques intended to be mounted in series to create friezes. They were figural reliefs, developed from earlier traditions of purely decorative schemes, and are primarily a phenomenon of the late Republican and early Imperial pe-

riod: the earliest well-dated examples fall into the second quarter of the 1st century BC, but they flourished in the Augustan-Julio-Claudian period, with production continuing on a small scale into the 2nd century AD (Tortorella 1981a, 61-68; 1981b, 218-223; Siebert 2011, 22-24). Over thirty stamps are known, almost all of late Republican, Augustan or Julio-Claudian date (Tortorella 1981a, 68). While they saw use on temples, as was typical for architectural terracottas, they were also used extensively on public buildings and especially on private houses, villas and tombs (Tortorella 1981a, 62-65 figs 1-3; 1981b, 219). Their use concentrated in Rome and a 50 km radius in the surrounding area; only small numbers are known elsewhere in Italy. Many of these further-flung examples are local products, but there are also suggestions of the export of plaques or perhaps of matrices (Tortorella 1981b, 223f.). The decoration draws on themes current in other media: for instance, many show classic Augustan iconography (Strazzulla 1991; e.g. Campana 1852, pl. XX, with Apollo and Hercules contesting the Delphic tripod; pl. VIII with fishing cupids riding dolphins). Originally they would be painted, although this rarely survives.

Tortorella identified two main series of plaques, one Augustan (C4.3), one Flavian (C4.4). In both cases, stamps or decorative details which link different designs suggest they were intended to form a frieze showing a series of elements of the triumphal procession.

C4.3 Campana plaque

A number of Augustan-period plaques are known which feature a trophy flanked by two prisoners, sometimes guarded by captors. Stamps and iconographic details indicate at least three different matrices, one of which certainly features a carnyx, one of which may have, and one which did not.

The certain example is on plaques from the workshop of Marcus Antonius Epaphra. Tortorella (2008, 308f.) catalogued five, of which two show carnyces: one from Ostia and one (unprovenanced) now in the British Museum (fig. 338a-b). Combining fragments from Ostia gives overall dimensions as 410mm wide by 320mm tall, with a decorative border at the top and plain basal border. The plaque shows a trophy flanked by two barbarians, each guarded by a Roman. On the left is a Roman soldier, wearing a cuirass, tunic, cloak, boots, and a sword by his right side. His right hand holds a rope which binds the right wrist of the captive standing to the right. The barbarian is hairy and bearded, and wears trousers and a fringed cloak in a V at the front, draped over his left shoulder. His torso is bare; he wears a torc. To the right of the trophy, a bound male barbarian is nude apart from a fringed cloak; he is held captive by a togate male. In the centre, a gnarled tree trunk bears a trophy. A fringed cloak is draped over it, topped by a bowl helmet with cheekpieces and a ring on the peak. The right arm as viewed has a single oval shield with two vexilla behind it. The left arm bears an unusual hexagonal shield, its ends expanded, with a spear to the right and a carnyx to the left. Neither protrudes below the shield. It is stamped M . ANTON / EPAPHRA, Marcus Antonius Epaphra.

A similar scene is found on plaques stamped OCTAVI (Tortorella 2008, 309). An unprovenanced example, now in the Museo Nazionale in Rome shows two prisoners, very similar to the Epaphra ones but without guardians (La Rocca/Tortorella 2008, 194 II.3.5); there is a further fragment in the Museo delle Terme in Rome (inv. 4337; von Rohden/Winnefeld 1911, 132 fig. 247). Tortorella (ibidem) discussed the close iconographic similarity to the Epaphra pieces, but neither of the published examples preserves a carnyx. He noted (in La Rocca/Tortorella 2008, 126) that OCTAVI stamps and stylistic details link a series of plaques connected to triumph, and argued that these were scenes in a frieze (fig. 338c): two northern barbarian captives on a cart in a triumphal procession (Campana 1852, pl. XC; von Rohden/Winnefeld 1911, 132f. pls LXXIII; LXXXVII 1); a bull being led to sacrifice; and the trophy scene.

The final variant is seen on an unprovenanced plaque now in the Musée Fol, Geneva. It is complete. The trophy has a cloak with a fringe and a helmet with ring design, oval and hexagonal shields, spears, an eagle-hilted sword, and an unidentified curved item, perhaps a further eagle-hilted sword (von Rohden/Winnefeld 1911, 131f. LXXX-VII 2; Tortorella 2008, 309). There is no carnyx.

The carnyx
Only the upper part of the carnyx is visible (fig. 338d). Its mouth is open to 60°, with a fang on the lower jaw only and no tongue; eye, two ears, no crest. The bell/tube junction is represented by a band defined by two incised grooves. No other tube subdivisions are shown on the visible part of the tube.

Dating evidence
Strazzulla (1991; 1993) saw the plaques as primarily an Augustan phenomenon, while Picard (1957, 284f.) drew parallels to the Augustan and Tiberian arches of southern France, suggesting a date in the early decades of the 1st century AD (c. AD 1-25). The weaponry (carnyx, hexagonal shields) and the costume and appearance of the captives supports a connection to northern barbarians: at this date these are most likely Gauls or Germans, the torc suggesting the former. The name on one stamp, M. Antonius Epaphra, indicates he was a freedman of Marc Antony; thus his workshop is likely to have flourished in the later 1st century BC (Helbig 1972, 124). Tortorella (2007; 2008; La Rocca/Tortorella 2008, 194) supported the Augustan date, but argued the triumphal iconography relates to a specific event – Augustus' triumph of 29 BC, which included various Gaulish and Germanic peoples alongside Dalmatians, Pannonians and others. The link to other triumphal imagery makes this highly plausible, and a date range of c. 29-25 BC is adopted here.

Fig. 338 C4.3 Augustan Campana plaques: **a** C4.3.1 British Museum D626. – **b** C4.3.2 (right), Ostia. – **c** reconstruction of overall scene. – **d** the carnyx. – (a photo British Museum; b La Rocca/Tortorella 2008, 194 II.3.4; c Tortorella 2008, fig. 1; d drawing Tanja Romankiewicz).

C4.3.1 Uncertain findspot (Townley collection)

(Current location: British Museum, inv. no. 1805.7-3.314 [Terracotta D626])
About a third of the scene on the right side is missing. 305 mm H. 275 mm W. as it survives (**fig. 338a**).

Bibliography
CIL XV 2542. – Tortorella 2008, 308 no. 2.1.1. – von Rohden/Winnefeld 1911, 131f. pl. LXXV 2. – Walters 1903, 406f. no. D626.

C4.3.2 Campana plaque, Ostia (Roma/I)

(Current location: Ostia Antiquarium, inv. no. 3413)
3413 preserves the complete size, but lacks the top right and parts of the bottom left corner; a further fragment (18735) preserves the right hand side of the scene (**fig. 338b**).

Bibliography
Helbig 1972, 123f. no. 3150. – La Rocca/Tortorella 2008, 194 II.3.4. – Tortorella 1981a, fig. 11; 2008, 308f. nos 2.1.2-3.

C4.4 Campana plaques, Rome and Ostia

Two examples are known of another plaque with a trophy and prisoners, a near-complete one from a cemetery near Rome and a fragment from Ostia which conveniently illustrates the missing part (**fig. 339a-b**). A central tree trunk is bedecked with a muscle cuirass, sheathed sword, fringed cloak, and bowl helmet with peak knob, curved horns and cheek pieces. The left arm (as viewed) has two crossed hexagonal shields, the front one decorated with buffer-terminal torcs and crescents. Behind this are a spear and carnyx, facing left. The right arm has a single hexagonal shield with two spears to the left and a carnyx to the right. At the foot of the trophy is a pile of arms: a wheel, a helmet and a domed circular shield. A grieving female, veiled, sits on the shield. To the right is a bound male barbarian wearing shoes, trousers and a fringed (furry?) cloak, with a thin band in his hair. A stamp reads VALES (both VALES and VALENTI[S] are known from this workshop; cf. CIL XV.1, 2552-3; Tortorella 1981b, 228; 2008, 306f. 309).
Although the flourishing of Campana plaques is rather earlier, there are a few other examples of Flavian date or slightly later. Of note here is a plaque featuring Victory with a date palm and a pile of arms, which commemorates the Jewish victories of Vespasian and Titus (La Rocca/Tortorella 2008, 195 II.3.6).

The carnyces
Carnyx 1 (to the left, facing left) has the upper tube, bell and head preserved (**fig. 339c**). The cylindrical tube meets the bell at a junction defined by two incised lines. A crest runs from the bell base to just in front of the pointed ear, where it ends in a quiff. The lower part of the crest is plain but the upper part has vertical incised lines to define bristles. There is a sunken eye; the mouth opens to about 90°, with the upper jaw slightly recurved.
Carnyx 2 faces right. The cylindrical tube emerges from behind a shield; there is a trace of a band at the bell junction. A crest with incised bristles runs the full visible length of the tube to the two ears. It has a naturalistic eye and a wide-open mouth, the tips curved in different directions.

Dating evidence
The iconography of the figures is closely similar to sestertii of Domitian celebrating his triumph over the Chatti in AD 83 (Carradice/Buttrey 2007, Domitian 397; La Rocca/Tortorella 2008, 195 II.3.5 bis). Thus a date of c. AD 83-85 is most likely.

C4.4.1 Ostia

(Current location: Ostia Antiquarium, inv. no. 13272)
Left corner of plaque only.

Bibliography
Tortorella 1981a, 68 fig. 9; 2008, 309 no. 2.4.2.

C4.4.2 Rome, cemetery of via di Grottaperfetta, tomb 74

(Current location: Rome, Museo Nazionale Romano, unregistered)
Complete apart from left corner. 310 mm H. 420 mm W.

Bibliography
La Rocca/Tortorella 2008, 195 II.3.5 bis. – Tortorella 2008, 309 no. 2.4.1.

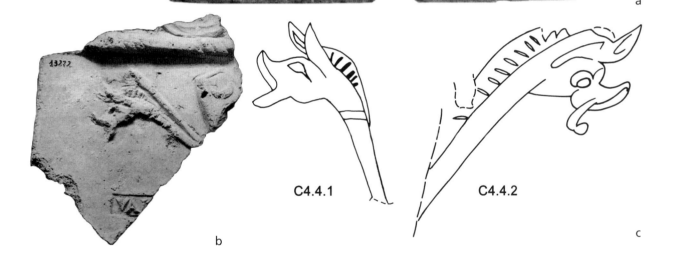

Fig. 339 C4.4 Flavian Campana plaque: **a** C4.4.2 Rome, via di Grottaperfetta. – **b** C4.4.1 Ostia. – **c** the carnyces. – (a La Rocca/Tortorella 2008, 195 II.3.5 bis; b Tortorella 1981, fig. 9; c drawing Tanja Romankiewicz / Alan Braby).

a

C4.4.1

C4.4.2

b

c

C4.5 Glass plaques with trophy, one ?from Rome/I, others unprovenanced

A series of mould-formed glass plaques carry a range of subjects including trophy reliefs (**fig. 340**), much like the terracotta plaques (C4.3-4). These were presumably intended as small-scale ornamentation, probably for furniture (Whitehouse 1997, 13; the Pennsylvania fragment is only 75 mm high and 5 mm thick). Wilhelm Froehner (1903, 69-72) listed a series from the Gréau collection: apart from trophies, subjects include piles of arms, tri-tons, lion heads, mythological scenes and vegetal ornament. They are made in a sandwich technique, with a core of white (transparent or opaque), clear or blue-green glass coated on both sides in blue (again, transparent or opaque; information from Froehner, *ibidem*).

These plaques have not received much detailed attention. Froehner (1903, 69-72 pl. LII) catalogued four with trophies or weaponry. Using his numbering, they are as follows:

Fig. 340 C4.5 Glass plaques with trophy: **a** C.4.5.1. – **b** C.4.5.2. – **c** the carnyx. – (a photo Chris Lightfoot / Metropolitan Museum of Art, New York; b photo University of Pennsylvania Museum of Archaeology & Anthropology; c drawing Tanja Romankiewicz).

C4.5.1

C4.5.2

469 Pile of arms: animal standard, shields (round, oval, oval with flattened ends, the latter decorated with a boar standard), bowl helmets, spears, quiver
470 Trophy of Gaulish arms
471 Trophy of Gaulish arms
472 Trophy of Gaulish arms

470-472 are fragments of plaques from the same mould, with 471 and 472 including the portion with a carnyx; 472, the largest fragment, was examined first-hand in the Metropolitan Museum of Art, New York (where 469 is also held). Another fragment now in the collections of the University of Pennsylvania Museum of Archaeology and Anthropology (Fleming 1999, 141) was examined from photographs, while a fragment of the left side in the British Museum (GR 1976.10-2.33) was examined first-hand. A further fragment is in the Louvre (Arveiller-Dulong/Nenna 2011, no. 672). All seem to be from the same mould; at least four plaques are represented by the surviving fragments. Together the fragments give a better picture of the overall form.

The composition centres on a trophy of a belted tunic and helmet. The helmet (with cheekpieces and face mask) has ram's horns and a decorative ring and dot finial; this finds parallels in Augustan iconography in Gaul (e. g. Amy et al. 1962, pl. 43). The tunic appears to be furry. From the belt hangs a long sword. On the left (little of which is visible on

472) is an oval shield decorated with stars and crescents; behind it is a vertical spear and a crossed vexillum (to the right) and boar standard (to the left). Below survives (on the BM example) the head of a young ?male captive. The right arm also has an oval shield, decorated with a bucranium within two concentric circles and two pairs of interlocked rings (best interpreted as torcs) above and below. Vertically behind the shield is a spear; to the left, a vexillum with spear tip; to the right, a boar standard, in mirror image of the other arm. Below are a female captive and a carnyx, the latter probably in a (missing) pile of arms at the base. Froehner (1903, 70) saw the weaponry as Gallic and read it as an allusion to the Gallic War. The allusions are definitely Gallic, given the combination of carnyx and boar standard, while the oval shield with torcs would suit this as well (only the quiver on 469 is inconsistent, as archery equipment is very unusual in the north-west provinces). However, as discussed in the dating section, it need not be restricted to the time of the Gallic War. A different style of plaque, known only in a single fragment, may have a similar theme; it appears to be a battle scene showing ?Gauls and an oval shield (Whitehouse 1997, 21 no. 10).

The carnyx
The carnyx is presumably inserted in a pile of arms at the base of the trophy; it is angled upwards to the right, and

faces left (**fig. 340c**). The depiction shows little technical detail: no tube junctions are shown. The cylindrical tube and bell are undifferentiated, and the bell expands only slightly as it curves into the head (which is at c. 150° to the tube). A plain crest runs from about the start of the curve to behind the ear. The head has a single ear, eye (with prominent eyebrow), and mouth open to about 60°, with the snout upturned.

Dating evidence
Froehner (1903, 70) linked the iconography to the Gallic War. However, while definitely Gallic, it need not be so specifically dated. This imagery persisted beyond the time of Caesar (for instance, the tomb of Caecilia Metella in Rome, dated to early Augustan times, has all these elements bar the oval shield; B1.1). The plaques are also closely related in concept and iconography to the terracotta Campana plaques, and a similar date may be suspected. The latter have a floruit in the late Republic and early Empire (Tortorella 1981, 61-68), and the Gallic iconography would be at home in a Caesarean, Augustan or Tiberian context. Thus a date range of c. 50 BC-AD 30 may be suggested.

C4.5.1 New York, Metropolitan Museum of Art, inv. no. 17.194.359 (Gift of J Pierpont Morgan 1917; formerly Gréau Collection 472)

C4.5.2 University of Pennsylvania Museum of Archaeology & Anthropology, inv. no. 29-128-1219 (Maxwell Sommerville Collection, ?from Rome)

C4.5.3 The current location of the other fragments listed by Froehner (1903, 69-71 esp. no. 471) is unknown.

Bibliography
Fleming 1999, 141. – Froehner 1903, 69-71 pl. 52.

C5 ROMAN NON-ARCHITECTURAL CERAMICS

C5.1 Oil lamp, unprovenanced

(Current location: Paris, Bibliothèque nationale, inv. no. 5299)
Ceramic lamp in yellow-brown fabric with traces of a brown slip; handle-less; anchor-shaped nozzle flanked by curled volutes. Rim incised with four concentric circles. The central concave medallion bears a scene of a trophy with helmet, cuirass and a pair of greaves (**fig. 341a**). On each arm are crossed oval and hexagonal shields, with a carnyx angled behind on the outside. The oval shields (which are foremost) have oval umbos and elongated spinae with decorative branches. One has pairs of curls flanking the umbo. Similar decorative spinae are visible on the rear shields. 110 mm L. 80 mm D. 33 mm H.
Hellmann (1987, 16) dated the lamp on typological grounds to the late 1st century BC or, at the very latest, early 1st century AD. Although a few other lamps with trophies are known (e.g. Hellmann 1987, no. 205; Bailey 1980, 50f. Q965; 1988, Q2396; Leibundgut 1977, 170 no. 230) none are like this, and Hellmann argued for its derivation from Caesarean depictions of Gaulish trophies on late Republican coins (e. g. A4.18-4.20). Its findspot is unknown: it was acquired in 1802 from the sale of the collection of Citizen Julliot, which had formerly been in the Cabinet of the Duc de Chaunes (Hellmann 1987, ix).

The carnyces
Only the upper portion of each carnyx is visible; the rest is hidden behind the shields with no continuation of the tube below (**fig. 341b-c**). Both have prominent spiked crests, ears, bulging eyes and open mouths.
Left carnyx: only the curved bell and head are visible, facing right, with a crest starting part-way up the bell and running to the short, stubby, triangular ear. The crest comprises five angled spikes, the tips curved slightly forwards. The head has a bulging, raised eye and a rather distorted mouth, with the upper jaw tapered at the end (perhaps representing a fold over a tusk?) and the lower jaw, at 90°, much attenuated. There are no clear technical details apart from a moulded line running from the ear to the lower jaw, defining the head; this appears anatomical

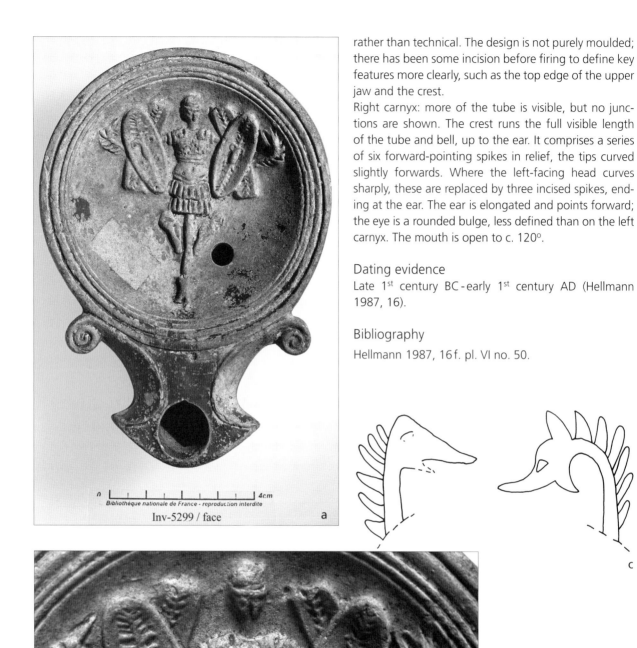

rather than technical. The design is not purely moulded; there has been some incision before firing to define key features more clearly, such as the top edge of the upper jaw and the crest.

Right carnyx: more of the tube is visible, but no junctions are shown. The crest runs the full visible length of the tube and bell, up to the ear. It comprises a series of six forward-pointing spikes in relief, the tips curved slightly forwards. Where the left-facing head curves sharply, these are replaced by three incised spikes, ending at the ear. The ear is elongated and points forward; the eye is a rounded bulge, less defined than on the left carnyx. The mouth is open to c. 120°.

Dating evidence
Late 1st century BC - early 1st century AD (Hellmann 1987, 16).

Bibliography
Hellmann 1987, 16 f. pl. VI no. 50.

Fig. 341 C5.1 Oil lamp: **a** overall view. – **b** detail of trophy. – **c** the carnyces. – (a-b photos Bibliothèque nationale de France; c drawing Tanja Romankiewicz).

APPENDIX 2: DETAILS OF CARNYX DEPICTIONS

Tables 74-84 summarise and codify the evidence which can be extracted from carnyx depictions for the appearance of the instrument. For Roman sculptures with multiple carnyces, these are summarised in **table 77** and detailed in **tables 78-82** (these latter vary in their format, as they are tailored to the individual monuments). Coding used in the tables is as follows.

Italicised entries have not been seen first-hand

no	number of carnyces depicted
survival mhcbt	presence of **m**outh, **h**ead, **c**rest, **b**ell, and **t**ube
*+-~	intact, damaged/partial, absent, variable
angle	how far the head bends round from the vertical line of the tube, measured to a line which bisects the mouth
eye	peak = eyebrow peak visible but no clear eye defined
ears	number given
mouth	angle is coded: 1, less than 30°; 2, 30-90°; 3, >90°
crest	runs to bell base unless there is a *, which implies a variant; details in notes
sections	number of tube sections: + implies this is a minimum number
tube form	I straight, C curved, S sinuous
tube diameter	ll cylindrical, V conical
end	I straight, J curved
?	uncertain feature; ~ variable occurrence (where there are multiple examples); y yes; n no

code	coin	no	survival mhcbt	angle	eye	ear	mouth	teeth	crest y/n	crest form	junctions	sections	tube form	tube D	end	mouthpiece	notes
A1.1	ABC 2562, 2565, 2568	1	**-**	60-110	~	0	2-3	?on 1	n		knob	3~	I	II	I	knob	
A1.2	ABC 441	1	*****	80-100	peak	1	2-3		y	plain	knob	3	I	II	I	knob	
A1.3	ABC 348	1	**-*+	90-100	y	0	2		n		n	?	I	II			
A1.4	ABC 354	1	++-**	120	y	?	2?		n		knob	1-2	I	II	I	knob	
A1.5	ABC 387	1	****+	100	n	0	3		y	plain	n	1	I	II	I		
A1.6	ABC 399	1	+*-**	90?	n~	0	3?		n		knob	1~	I	II	I	knob	
A2.1	LT XX 6930	1	**-*+	90	n	1	?		n		knob	?	I	II	I		
A2.2	LT XIII 4551-4552	1	*****+	110-120	y	1	2	y	y	plain, pellet	knob, band	3-4	I	II	I	cup, knob	tongue
A2.3	DT 3421 A, B	1	**~*+	90	y	1?	2		~*	pellet	knob	2+	I	II			crest runs to mid-tube
A2.4	Gué de Sciaux	1	*****	120	y	1-2	2		y	pellet	knob	1-2	C	II	I	knob	tube curves slightly
A2.5	LT XVIII 5967	2	**-*+	120	y	0	2		n		n	1	I	II			
A2.6	LT XV 5044	1	****+	60-110	n~	0	3		y~	plain	knob	2+	S	II			
A2.7	BN 7050-7055	1	**~*+	90-110	?	1	3		n~	plain	knob	2+	I	II			
A2.8	LT XX 6398	1	*****+	120-140	~	0	3		y	plain	knob	3?	I	II			

Tab. 74 Characteristics of carnyces on Iron Age coins.

code	reference	no	survival mhcbt	angle	eye	ear	mouth	teeth	crest y/n	crest form	junctions	sections	tube form	tube D	end	mouthpiece	notes
A4.1	RRC 128	1	*****	80	peak	1	2		~	plain	knob	2-3	I C	II	I	knob	
A4.2	RRC 281	2	*****	60-90	y	1-2	2-3		~*	plain	knob	1-5	I	II	I	knob	some crests start on tube
A4.3	RRC 282/1-5	1	****+	70-90	y~	2~	1		y~	plain	pellet-defined tube	4-6	I	II			crest runs full visible length
A4.4	RRC 332	1	****+	70-80	~	1~	1		n		knob	1	I	II	I		stylised
A4.5	RRC 326/2	1	**-**	80-90	y	1-2	1		n~		knob	2~	I	II	I	knob	very variable
A4.6	RRC 333	1	**-**	80-90	n	2	2		n		knob	3	I	II	I	plain	
A4.7	RRC 337/1	1	*****	90	n	n	2		y	bristle	knob	3	I	II	I	plain	
A4.10	*RRC 346/2*	*1*	*****+*	*90*	*y*	*2*	*2*		*y*	*bristle*	*knob*	*3*	*I*	*II*	*I*	*knob*	
A4.11	RRC 352/1	1	+*-**	90	?	1	3		n	plain	knob	1	I	II	I	plain	

code	reference	no	survival mhcbt	angle	eye	ear	mouth	teeth	crest y/n	crest form	junc- tions	sec- tions	tube form	tube D	end	mouth- piece	notes
A4.12	RRC 366/1a	1	**-*+	120	y	1	3		n		knob	2	l	l	l	knob	fairly stylised
A4.13	RRC 384	1	*****	100	y	1	2	?	y	bristle	knob	2	l	V	l	knob	very detailed; long bell
A4.14	RRC 412	1	**-**	160-180	n	0-2	2		n		pellet tube		l	ll	l	plain	
A4.15.1	RRC 437/4a	1	**-*+	90	n	n	3		n		knob	1	l	ll			very stylised
A4.15.2	RRC 437/2-4	1	****+	60	n	n	1		y	plain		1	l	ll			
A4.16.1	RRC 448/1	1	**-*+	90	~	1	1		n~				l	ll			
A4.16.2	RRC 448/3	1	*****	90-100	y	1-2	2	~	y	pellet/ spike	knob	3-4	l	ll	l	knob	variable
A4.17	RRC 450/1	2	*****	130	y	1	3		y*	pellets	band	4-6	l	V	l	cup/ knob	crest on upper tube; upper tube flares
A4.18	RRC 452	1	*****	90-110	y~	2	2	~	y~	pellets	knob	2-4	l	ll	l	knob/ ?cup	some variants less de- tailed, lack eye/crest
A4.19	RRC 468	2	**~++	90-110	y~	2	3		n~	plain	–	1	l	ll	l	plain/ knob	simplified
A4.20	RRC 482	1	****+	120	n	1	3		y	spikes	–	1	l	ll	l		
A5.1	*RIC Civil War 131*	*1*	**-**	*90*	*n*	*n*	*3*		*n*			*1*	*l*	*ll*	*l*	*plain*	*not very zoomorphic*
A5.2	RIC Galba 17 var	1	**-*+	140	n	1	3		n		n	1	l	ll	l	cup	
A5.3	RIC 766	1	**-**	60	n	0	1		n		band	2?	l	V	l	plain	
A5.4	RIC var	1	**~-*+	100-130	~	0-2	1		n~	plain	– or pel- let tube		S l	ll			very variable
A5.5	RIC 3	2	**-*+	90	n~	0-2	1		n		–	1	l	ll			linear
A6.1	Vibo Valentia as	1	*****	70-90	y	2	1	~	y~	spikes/ dots	knob	1-3	l	ll	l	plain/ ex- panded	
A6.2	Vibo Valentia semis	1	*****	80-90	y	2	1		~	spikes	knob	2-3	l	ll	l	plain/ knob	
A6.3	Tavium	1	*+-**	120	?	?	2	y	n		knob	3	l	ll	l	knob	

Tab. 75 Characteristics of carnyces on Roman coins.

code	site/name	no	survival mhcbt	angle	eye	ear	mouth	teeth	crest y/n	crest form	junctions	sections	tube form	tube D	end	mouthpiece	notes
A3.1	Aetolian coin	1	*****	70-90	~	0-2	1		n~	plain	knob	1, 3-7	I	II	I	knob/plain	
B8.1	Delphi base	1	?	?	?	?	?	?	?	?	?	?	?	?	?	?	
B8.2	Sanchi stupa	2	**-**	170	y	0	2		n		n	1	I	II	I J	angled?	
C2.1	Hermopolis Magna terracotta	1	**-**	80	?	1	1		n		band	3?	I	II	I	angled cut?	
C2.2	Egyptian alabastron	1	?+-+*	?	?	1	?		n		?	?	I	?	I	?	
C2.3	Old Nisa rhyton	1	**-*+	80	y	2	1		n		?	?	I	?	I	?	

Tab. 76 Characteristics of carnyces on Hellenistic and Indian material.

code	site	no	survival mhcbt	angle	eye	ear	mouth	teeth	crest y/n	crest form	junctions	sections	tube form	tube D	end	mouthpiece	notes
B1.1	Caecilia Metella	4	****+	140	y	1	1		y	plain	n	1	I	II			
B1.2.1	Prima Porta	1	*****+	90	y	0	1		y	plain	n	1	I	II			
B1.2.2	Prima Porta	1	**-*+	160	y	1	2		n		n	1	I	II			
B1.3	Bovillae	12	varying	60-180	y	1	3		n~	various	band, line	1-2	I	IIV			see **tab. 78**
B1.4.1	Palace of Flavians	3	**~*-	50-90	y	0-1	3		~*		n		I	II			stylised; one with crest full visible length, & ribbed bell; prominent mouths
B1.4.2	Palace of Flavians	1	**-*+	110	y	1	3		n		n						
B1.5	Castelgandolfo	1	+-+++	?	?	?	?		y	arcade & ribs	band, bipartite?	?		II			
B1.6	San Lorenzo	8	****+	120	y	1	3		y	plain, dot-decorated	n		I C	II			

code	site	no	survival mhcbt	angle	eye	ear	mouth	teeth	crest y/n	crest form	junctions	sections	tube form	tube D	end	mouthpiece	notes
B1.7	Aventine	23	*****+	90-190	y	1	3		y	various	collar, varied	1	I	=			naturalistic; see **tab. 79**
B1.8	Rome	4	*****	180	y	1	3		y	plain	n	1	I	=	I	plain squared	
B1.9	Maddalena	2	*****+	90-110	y	1-2	3		y	bristles	band	1	I	=			musculature, skin folds; 2-bar crest
B1.10	Via de' Leutari	10	**~*+	70	y	1~	3		n~	plain	n	1	I C	V			
B1.11.1	Trajan's Forum	1	*****+	170	y	1	3	y	y	S-curls	collar, band	?	I	=			
B1.11.2	Trajan's Forum	2	**+++	180	y	1	3	y	y	XIXI	band	?	I	//			bell ribbed
B1.11.3	Trajan's Forum	3	*****+	20-70	y	1	3		y	bristles	band	1	I	V			naturalistic e. g. hair fringe; bell decorated
B1.12	Trajan's Column	14	*****+	110-270	y	1	3	y~	y	various	collar, band, groove	1-2	I S	=		cup	naturalistic e. g. hair fringe, musculature; bell decorated; see **tab. 80** for details
B1.13.1	Tivoli	1	*****+	45	y	1	1		y	plain	band	2+	I	//			
B1.13.2	Tivoli	1	*****+	80	y	1	3		y	bristles	n	1	I	=			
B1.14	Column of M. Aurelius	4	*****+	80	y	1	1	y	y	saw tooth	?	?	I S	=	I	plain squared	naturalistic
B1.15	Portonaccio	7	++**+	110-230	y	0	3~		y~	saw tooth	band	1?	I S	=	I	?	
B1.16	Tetrarchic arch	4	**-*+	160-180	y	1	1	y	n		band	1	I	=			canine appearance
B2.1	Isernia	4	**-**	120	?	1	2		n		n	1	I	//	I	plain	
B2.2	Isernia	2	******	variant	y	2	3		y	bristles	n	1	I S	=	I	cup	
B2.3	San Vittorino	1	*****	160	y	1	2	y	y	bristles	n	1	I	=	I	cup	bell decorated
B2.4	Alba Fucens	1	**-*+	150	y	1	2		n		band	?	I	=	I	plain, squared	
B2.5	Scafa	1	***+-	110	y	2	2	y	y	bristles	?	?	I				
B2.6	Turin	5	***++	170-190	y	0	3		y~	wave	band	1?	I	=			
B2.7	Novalesa	1	****-	100	y	1	2		y	bristles	?	?	I				naturalistic
B2.8	Padova	1	******	140	y	2	3		y	bristles	n?	1	I	=	I	squared	
B2.9	Como	1	+***+	100	y	1	3		y	bristles	?	?	?	//			
B2.10	Verona	1	**-**	90	y	1	1		n		n	1	I	=	J	angled cut	

code	site	no	survival mhcbt	angle	eye	ear	mouth	teeth	crest y/n	crest form	junctions	sections	tube form	tube D	end	mouthpiece	notes
B2.11	Pompeii	1	**-**	270	y	0	3		n		n	1	S	V	J	cup	
B2.12	Gabii	1	****+	160	peak	1	2		y	plain	n	1	I	V			
B2.13	Parma	1	****+	80	y	0	3		y	saw tooth	?		-	II	-	squared with lip	
B2.14	Pozzuoli	1	****-	90	y	2	3		y	plain	?	?	?				
B2.15	Benevento	3	****+	50-120	y~	0-1	3		y~	plain	n	1	I	II			very stylised
B2.16	Cumae(?)	1	****-	100	y	1	2		y	corrugated	?						
B2.17	unprovenanced	2	**~*+	110-150	?	1	3		~	plain	n?	1?	I	V			drawing not detailed
B2.18	Frascati	1	*+++-	120	y	1?	2		y	zig-zag	?						
B2.19	Palermo	4	**-*+	140-180	y	0	3		n~	plain	?band	?	I	II			
B3.1	Narbonne	5	****+	120-160	y	0-1	2-3		y	plain, bristles	n	1	I C	II			one with decorated head
B3.2	Avignon	2	**-*+	100	y	1	2	lip fold	y*	plain	collar	?	I	V	-	cup	unusual; crest onto tube
B3.3	Glanum	1	+****+	160	y	1	2		y*	zig-zag	n	1	I	II			crest full visible length
B3.4	Orange	38	*****+	90-150	y	1	3		~	various	n	1	I C	II			some bird-like; see tab. 81
B3.5	La Brague	1	+***-	90	y	1?	2		y	plain	?						
B3.6	Arles	1	**++-	60	y	1	2		y	plain	?						
B3.7	Nîmes	1	**+++	90	y	1	3		y	zig-zag	?						
B3.8	Collias	1	*****	80	y	2	2	y	y	plain	band	1	I	II		cup	
B4.1	Vindonissa	1	+*-*+	90	y	0	2		n		?				-		
B5.1	Mérida theatre	1	++++-	?	y	1	3		y	saw tooth	?						
B5.2	Mérida temple	27	**~*+	70-160	y	0-1	1-3		~	various	n or band at bell	1?	I C	II V	-	plain	see tab. 82
B6.1	Zian	2	**-*+	90-110	y	1	3		n		n	1	I	II			
B6.2	Volubilis	2	++-*+	90-110	?	0-1	?		n		n	1	I C	II			
B7.2	Gardun	1	**-*+	90	y	2	1		n		band	?	I	V			

Tab. 77 Characteristics of carnyces on Roman sculpture.

no	S	tube	bell	crest	head	notes
1	12	cylindrical	band junction with tube	no	dot eye	
2	12	cylindrical	band junction with tube	no	damaged	
3	12	slight flare before bell; two segments shown	line at tube junction	no	hidden	
4	12	slight flare before bell; two segments shown	line at tube junction	no	hidden	
5	28	n/a	barely visible	no	eye defined as slight bulge with incised tear ducts	no technical details
6	31	slightly tapered; lower part incised, not relief, and weakly defined; plain	no junctions shown	bristles or triangles; slightly enlarged towards base. Runs onto top of head	low-relief eye; a few dots mark its extent. Skin folds shown	jaw damaged; lower tube end not defined
7	31	slightly tapered, fading at base; line continued as decorative scroll; plain	double line at bell-head junction	bristles or triangles	raised eye with incised tear ducts; skin folds shown. Ear poorly defined	lower end not defined
8	52	n/a	n/a	?	faint ear, elongated eye; sinuous jaws	solitary
9	52	slightly flared tube; plain	no junctions shown	no	lost & restored; ear visible	
10	52	slightly flared tube; plain	no junctions shown; couple of decorative lines on bell	no	elongated incised eye	globe obscures details
11	60	cylindrical (stylised)	no junctions shown	no	simple eye	
12	67	only very top shown	long bell; lines at junction with tube and head	upper portion bar with drill-holes; lower, individual strands with drill-holes between	very 3D eye (with eyebrow) and mouth	lots of musculature

Tab. 78 Characteristics of carnyces on the Bovillae sculpture, B1.3. S = reference number from Schröder 2004, 470-481 no. 206.

pillar / side	Crous 1933 (illus. no)	carnyx no	collar	bell	crest	head	notes
RIGHT (59)							
front	1, 12	1	decorated band; broad central band of raised sub-square motifs flanked by narrower herringbone strips		collar to ear; narrow rectangular round-ended hollows, reserved areas bearing incised vertical line; top border	plain eye, eyebrow; mouth open to 180°	some damage to tube
	3, 135	2	broad central band with drilled dots, flanked by dual incised lines	skin folds shown under chin	collar to ear; forward-pointing teardrop-shaped hollows, top border	mouth open to 180°	
right	4, 184	3	bipartite moulding	decorated with triangles developed from junction, with vertical incised lines near base	bell to head, stopping short of ear; decorated with arcading; top mirrors this in corrugated effect	small ear; eye with sunken pupil; mouth open to 180°, tips recurved	
	5, 196	4	tripartite moulding		collar to top of head; drilled circles separated by half-length vertical lines	mouth open to 180°, jaw tips recurved	
	6, 238	5	bipartite moulding		collar ?to mouth; forward-slanting incised lines, top border	small ear, mouth open to 90°, jaw tips strongly recurved	
	6, 269	6	bipartite moulding	skin folds under chin	start obscured; runs round to mouth; recessed forward-slanting rectangles, ends rounded	mouth open to 180°, jaw tips recurved; incised lines on outside of mouth	
back	Pigh. 363r (Crous 1933, fig. 8)	7	broad band with three pairs of lines	some skin folds	collar to just ahead of eye; hollowed curvilinear bars and incised lines mirroring them	mouth open to 120°, jaw tips recurved	
	–	8	?		full extent lost; runs onto top of head; narrow arch-shaped hollows inside continuous incised square frames; top border	mouth lost	badly damaged, with most of tube, head and mouth lost or damaged
	–	9	tripartite moulding	skin folds	collar to ear; lower plain border, series of drilled holes separated by curved lines	mouth open to c. 140°	

Appendix 2: Details of carnyx depictions

pillar / side	Crous 1933 (illus, no)	carnyx no	collar	bell	crest	head	notes
left	7, 293	10	not defined (not visible?)	?skin folds	runs full visible length to ear; vertical drilled round-ended rectangles	small ear, not projecting beyond head; mouth open to 180°, jaw tips recurved	head damaged
	9, 338	11	plain band	skin folds	just above collar to top of head; vertical drilled round-ended rectangles, top border	small ear, barely projecting beyond head; little moulding around eye, pupil drilled; mouth open to 130°, tips recurved	
LEFT (72)							
front	10, 388	12	flat band with three narrow ridges	skin folds	just below collar to behind ear, where it runs into border; vertical drilled round-ended rectangles separated by incised lines, top border	mouth open to 110°, tips highly recurved	
	11, 465	13	decorated with drilled circles		top of tube (full visible length) at least to behind ear (where it runs into edge); wave-shaped, with (in upper part) semi-circles with central dots in hollows	mouth open to 140°, with jaw tips recurved; incised line on upper may represent nostril	
	12, 526	14	raised ridge with paired drill-holes on the margins, joined by incised lines, giving knobbed effect		collar to ear; wave motif, ring- and dot motifs in hollows above	mouth open to 120°, jaw tips strongly recurved; drilled nostril hole on upper jaw; mouth slightly angled, strongly hollowed	
right	13, 557	15	tripartite moulding, central one broader, band of drilled holes below		start damaged; runs from collar to mouth; pointed-wave shape with drill-holes	mouth open to 180°, jaw tips recurved	
	14, 602	16	decorated with drilled circles		middle of bell to mouth; low wave with drilled circles	very small ear, not projecting beyond head; mouth open to 180°	
	15, 638	17	stepped bipartite collar, thicker towards top		none	mouth open to 110°, tips slightly recurved	worn
back	–	18	obscured behind flag	two transverse lines may be skin folds or bell-head junction	obscured but runs at least on bell and to ear; vertical lines, top border	mouth open to 120°	lots of tube shown – plain, cylindrical, no further junctions
	–	19			none	mouth open to 90°	head only visible

pillar / side	Crous 1933 (illus, no)	carnyx no	collar	bell	crest	head	notes
left	–	20	tube not visible	bipartite ridge at bell-head junction	none	very large eye; mouth open to 120°, tips strongly recurved (upper broken)	
	17, 718	21	?	?	wave-shape; extent unclear	details unclear	head badly damaged, all detail lost
	17, 734	22	none		only runs from ear to mouth (owing to proximity of border), in low wave	mouth open to 120° (upper jaw tip broken)	
	18, 754	23	stepped bipartite collar, wider portion to top	skin fold	collar to just behind ear; forward-pointing wave pattern, top and bottom borders (upper plain, lower with vertical lines)	more bent than others, bending through c. 180°; mouth open to 110°	lots of plain cylindrical tube visible, with no other junctions

Tab. 79 Characteristics of carnyces on the *armilustrium* pillars (B1.7).

no	side	survival mhcbt	eye	ear	jaw °	teeth	head °	crest	bell-head join	tube segs/D	tube junctions	mouth-piece	head decor	bell decor/D	crest decor	notes
1	front	+*+*	plain	y	180	–	180	tube top : >ear	n	2+; upper slightly conical; D 27-35	flanged band	-	n	triangles, running wave (D 35-51.5)	peltae (E)	
2	front	--+++	-	-	-	-	-	-	-	-; D 31	-	-	-	ribbed, collar; D 35.5	peltae (E)	
3	front	*++*+	-	-	180	n	210	tube top :?	band & ?decor	-; D 27.5	flat band	–	–	ribbed, collar; D 28.5-40	saltires & bars	
4	front	-++**	-	y		-	120	?tube top : >ear	-	2, slightly conical (lower, 25-28; upper 30 at base, top lost)	band, collar	straight, cup; L 65. Short collar/section at junction, L 39.5, D 28	–	ribbed; D 38.5 in middle	saltires & bars	L 970
5	right	**++-	rim & pupil	y	120	1 lower	-	? : >ear	band & wave/hair	-	-	-	n	?wave or hair fringe at top; D 44 at base	peltae (C)	

no	side	survival mhcbt	eye	ear	jaw°	teeth	head°	crest	bell-head join	tube segs/D	tube junctions	mouth-piece	head decor	bell decor/D	crest decor	notes
6	right	*+**-	damaged	y	120	2 lower	140	bell base :>ear	hair	–	–	–	hair	triangles, ribbing, collar; D 33.5-54	lyres	
7	right	*****-	raised, pupil	y	180	n	120	tube top :>ear	plain band	–	flat band	–	n	ribbed, collar	saltires & bars	
8	right	+++*+	flat, pupil	–	120	1 lower	130	bell base: >ear	plain band	–; D 35.5	plain band	–	?n	triangles (2 sets), collar; D 35.5-55.5	lyres	
9	right	*****+	pupil	y	180	n	270	bell base: >ear	n	2; D 26-28	groove	–	n	collar	peltae (C)	on shield; curved to fit space
10	right	*****+	sunken	y	180	1 lower	270	bell base: >ear	hair	1+; D 23.5-26	groove	–	hair	decorated collar with wave motifs	peltae (C)	on shield; curved to fit space
11	rear	*+**+	peak	–	180	1 lower	140	tube : ?	hair?	–; D 28	ornate band at bell, tripartite band, centre with vertical lines, waves below	–	hair?	triangles; D 28-43	peltae (E)	
12	left	*****+	sunken	y	100	1 fang & row	120	tube top : ?ear	band & ?hair	2; lower D 25, upper 28	collar	straight	hair	triangles; D 37-54	peltae (C)	L 800; very worn helmet cheekpiece lying between crest and ear confused earlier scholars
13	left	**+*+	spiral, pupil	–	120	2 lower, 1 upper	110	? : >ear	groove	1; D varies from 21-29	ribbed collar	–	hair	triangles; D 31.5-52	wave	
14	left	**+*+	spiral with pupil	y	180	1 lower, ?1 upper	120	upper tube : ?	band, ?hair	1, slightly conical; D 26-29.5	(tube is decorated)	–	hair?	triangles; wave; D 40-54.5	wave	

Tab. 80 Characteristics of carnyces on Trajan's Column. Survival uses standard coding. In other columns: –, does not survive; n, not present. E-type peltas have a central strut, while C-type peltas do not; the curved rear is always towards the instrument. Head angles are measured by extending the line of the tube and measuring the deviation between this and a line drawn through the centre of the head and mouth. Crest extent given as »start:stop«; > means beyond. Key dimensions are in millimetres.

	survival mhcbt	eye	ear	jaw/recurve	crest/decoration	notes
1	****+	y	1	110°, y	n	
2	****+	y	1	90°, y	y; triangles	
3	----+	–	–	–	–	fragment only
4	----+	–	–	–	–	fragment only
5	----+	–	–	–	–	fragment only
6	----+	–	–	–	–	fragment only
7	+*-*+	y	y?	90°, y	n	
8	**-*+	y	y?	90°	n	
9	++-*+	?	?	?	n?	damaged; angled
10	**-*+	y	?	gaping	n?	angled
11	++--+	?	?	hooked?	n?	head damaged? Angled
12	**-*+	y	1	130°, y lower	n	
13	**-*+	y	1	130°, y lower	n	
14	**-*+	y	1	180°, y lower	n	
15	****+	y	1	90°	y; triangles	
16	++?++	?	?	?	y?	surface damaged
17	----+	–	–	–	–	only lower tube survives
18	-+--+	–	–	–	–	upper parts incised in background
19	----+	–	–	–	–	badly damaged
20	**-*+	y	1	180°, y?	n	
21	****+	y	1	180°, y lower	y; ?triangles	
22	**-*+	y	?1	90°	n	
23	++-*+	?	?	?	n	surface of head very worn
24	---++	–	–	–	n	badly damaged
25	+***+	y	1	110°, y	y; relief triangular wave	
26	****+	y	1	90°, y	y; relief triangular wave	
27	****+	y	1	90°, y	y; ?relief triangular wave	
28	---++	–	–	–	–	head damaged
29	****+	y	1	90°, y lower	y; relief triangular wave	
30	****+	y	1	100°, y lower	y; relief triangular wave	
31	****+	y	1	90°, y lower	y; relief triangular wave	
32	****+	y	1	90°, y lower	y; relief triangular wave	
33	****+	y	1	140°	y; relief triangular wave	
34	****+	y	1	140°	y; relief triangular wave	
35	****+	y	1	90°, y lower	y; relief triangular wave	angled
36	****+	y	1	110°, y lower	y; relief triangular wave	angled
37	**-*+	y	1	90°, y lower	?	angled
38	---++	–	–	–	–	angled

Tab. 81 Characteristics of the carnyces on the Arc d'Orange (B3.4).

block	no.	tube	crest	bell	head	mouth	notes
1	1	cylindrical, plain; end simply squared off	no	plain		c. 90°	
1	2	conical, plain	bar with angled incisions	vandyked band at head junction		c. 135°; nostril shown	tube damaged
1	3	cylindrical, plain	bar with angled incisions	plain		c. 180°	
1	4	plain	full visible length; angled relief tufts	highly curved		c. 90°	
1	5	?	?	?	incised almond eye, drilled pupil	180°	head only
1	6	?	plain bar	vandyked junction	modelling around eye; no ear	c. 160°	paired with #7
1	7	top only; cylindrical	plain bar; stops at ear	vandyked junction		c. 135°	
2	8	?	no	hairy junction	damaged	60°	paired with 9
2	9	slightly conical, plain	no	narrow		60°	
3	10	cylindrical, slight curve, plain	no	barely expands; hairy junction	?	?	badly damaged; paired with 11
3	11	cylindrical, slight curve, plain	no	barely expands; hairy junction	?	c. 90°	badly damaged
3	12	conical, plain	no	?hairy junction	?	c. 90°	damaged
4	13	cylindrical, plain	no	curved boundary	plain eye	c. 20	worn; lower jaw lost; ear well-modelled
4	14	cylindrical, plain	no	?	?	c. 20°	paired with 13; very worn
5	15	bar at bell junction	low bar on tube and bell	hairy junction; decorated with tendril		180°	damage to head; paired with 16
5	16	bar at bell junction	2 angled spikes, and 2 detached spikes beyond ear	hairy junction; decorated with tendril	pupil to front of eye	180°	
5	17	?	bar with angled incisions	no detail	no ear	180°	damaged
5	18	cylindrical, plain	3 spikes	hairy junction		c. 120°	
5	19	cylindrical, curved, plain	no	plain, no junction		c. 120°	
5	20	cylindrical, sl curved, plain	no	hairy junction	less modelled	c. 135°	
5	21	cylindrical, plain	triangles	no junction		c. 90°	worn
6	22	conical, plain, very curved	triangles	no junction	skin folds on upper jaw	c. 60°	worn
6	23	conical, plain, very curved	no	Plain	ear presses on jaw	c. 160°	pair of 24
6	24	thick, curved	?	?		c. 180°	worn
6	25	conical, plain, curved	drill holes from lost crest	?	no ear?	180°	very worn
6	26	?	hints only	plain?	no visible ear	160°	protrudes from corner; only head visible
6	27	thick	possible low bar	hairy junction	worn ear	180°	very worn

Tab. 82 Details of the carnyces on the blocks from the Temple of Mars, Mérida (B5.2).

Tab. 83 Characteristics of carnyces on Iron Age artefacts.

code	object	no	survival mhcbt	angle	eye	ear	mouth	teeth	crest y/n	crest form	junctions	sections	tube form	tube D	end	mouthpiece	notes
C1.1.1-3	Gundestrup cauldron	3	*****	90-110	y	1	2	tusk fold	y	bristles	knob	3	I	II	I	rounded/angled?	
C1.1.4	Gundestrup cauldron graffiti	2	**-++	?	y	n	1		n		n	?	?	?			
C1.2	Bouy pendant	1	****-	100	y	2	2		y	plain	knob	?	I				
C1.3	Kondoros figurine	1	**-**	70	y	0	2		n		n	1	C	V	J	?	

Tab. 84 Characteristics of the carnyces on Roman artefacts.

code	object	no	survival mhcbt	angle	eye	ear	mouth	teeth	crest y/n	crest form	junctions	sections	tube form	tube D	end	mouthpiece	notes
C3.1	gladiator's helmet, Pompeii	4	****+	90-110	y	2	3		y	bristles	bands / lines	?	I	II			crest onto upper tube; tongue on one; scales on head; spiral twist tube decoration on two
C3.2.1-2	gladiator's helmet, Herculaneum	2	****+	90-160	y	1-2	3		y	saw tooth	n	?	C	II			quite crude; crest onto tube; skin folds & hair tufts
C3.2.3	gladiator's helmet, Herculaneum	1	*****+	160	y	2	1		y	saw tooth, bristle	n	?	I	II			quite crude; crest onto tube, hair tufts
C3.3	scabbard mounts	2	**-*+	140-170	n~	0	2		n		n		C	II			stylised
C3.4	parade helmet, Xanten-Wardt	2	**-*+	70	n	0	3		n		n		I	?			stylised
C3.5	standard disc, Niederbieber	1	**-*+	150	peak	0	3		n		n		?	II?			
C4.1	wall painting, Pompeii	1	*****+	180	y	2	2		y	lobes	n	1	I	II			irregular crest lobes onto tube
C4.2	terracotta antefix	1	*+-**	150	?	1	2		n		band?	1?	I	II	I	plain	
C4.3	terracotta plaque	1	**-*+	90	y	2	2	y	n		band	?	I	II			
C4.4	terracotta plaque	1	*****+	70-90	y	1	2		y	bristles	band	?	I	II			
C4.5	glass plaque	1	**~*+	170	y	1	2		y~	plain	n	?	I	II?			
C5.1	lamp	2	****+	90-170	y	1	1-2		y	spikes	n	?	I	II			crest onto tube

APPENDIX 3: UNCERTAIN CARNYCES

A number of carnyces or carnyx depictions have been noted or claimed in the literature, but are difficult to prove on current evidence. They are summarised in **table 85** and discussed below. The same categories are used as in the main catalogue, but with a »?« before the subdividing number.

code	object	date
A1?1	British Iron Age minim (VA 153)	late 1st century BC
A4?1	control mark on denarius of L. Piso Frugi (RRC 340)	90 BC
A5?1	aurei & denarii of Titus (RIC II¹ 1-2, 11, 17 = RIC II² 1, 29-31, 48-49)	AD 79
A5?2	aurei & denarii of Titus (RIC II¹ 21 = RIC II² 100-105)	AD 80
A5?3	bronze medallion of Hadrian (RIC 643)	AD 123-128
B1?1	weapons frieze, ?Rome	?
B2?1	weapons frieze, Todi (prov. Perugia/I)	c. 40 BC
B4?1	weapons frieze, Augst (Kanton Basel-Landschaft/CH)	AD 75-100
C?1	intaglio	3rd - 1st century BC

Tab. 85 Possible carnyx depictions which cannot be proved on current evidence.

A1 BRITISH IRON AGE COIN

A1?1 South-east silver minim (VA 153; ABC 255)

This has been described as showing a warrior with spear or carnyx (Van Arsdell 1989, 95 no. 153; Mack 1975, no. 316e). Only one example is known, from Kent (CCI 61.0162). It depicts a rider R carrying something in their R hand; the coin is very worn in its upper half and any attributes are not visible (Philip De Jersey, pers. comm. 1.8.02). Until clearer examples appear this cannot be included in the carnyx record, although it could well be a silver denomination related to the other south-east types. Illustrated in Mack 1975, pl. XXX no. 316e; Cottam et al. 2010, 37 no. 255; discussed in Hunter 2009, 246.

A4 ROMAN REPUBLICAN COIN

A4?1 Denarius of L. Piso Frugi (RRC 340)

Among the extensive control marks of this series, Michael Crawford illustrated a curious design with a triple-forked end (Crawford 1974, 340-344 pl. LXX, 5). This could be seen as a highly-stylised gaping-jawed carnyx with single ear, but it is too stylised to have any real confidence in this identification. It is in the collection of the Bibliothèque nationale in Paris (A6313) but has not been seen first-hand (**fig. 342**).

Fig. 342 A4?1 Control mark on RRC 340. – (After Crawford 1974, pl. LXX, 5).

A5 ROMAN IMPERIAL COINS

A5?1 Aureus and denarius of Titus

(RIC II[1] Titus 1-2. 5. 11. 17 = RIC II[2] Titus 1. 29-31. 48-49; BMCRE Titus 1-3. 5. 14-15. 30-32)

Several issues of Titus in AD 79 bear a reverse of a captive kneeling R in front of a trophy, a motif continued from issues of Vespasian for Titus earlier in 79 (RIC II[1] Vespasian 208). The design is found on both aurei and denarii (**fig. 343**). The trophy comprises a muscle cuirass and tunic, helmet, sword across body with scabbard to R, round shield on R arm and two crossed objects on L (as viewed). The captive is male, bound and naked apart from a cloak over his back. On some he is clearly bearded. The type plausibly refers to Agricola's campaigns in north Britain (Mattingly 1930, xli; Cody 2003, 111).

The objects held in the L arm are usually described as »crossed swords(?)« (BMCRE II, Titus 1; Robertson 1962, 254 f. Titus 1 & 7). Most are simply straight lines (sometimes with knobbed terminals) which could be intended as either swords or spears (BMCRE II, Titus 31 & 32). Others are clearly crossed spears (e. g. Robertson 1962, pl. 44, 1; Brussels, Cabinet des Médailles, Inv II, 62.724). One example in the BM combines a sword (?) and a curved item (1939-6-8-1; top left in **fig. 343**). The degree of stylisation and the size of the design make it impossible to be certain about the identification. The ?sword is depicted as a straight line with lobes at the base. The object crossing it curves at the end (although it does not significantly thicken); a slightly offset line continues the shaft/tube beyond this curve, and may be intended as an ear. However, it is most likely that it is simply a poorly-cut die.

Fig. 343 A5?1 Aurei (lower) and denarii of Titus (RIC 1-2, 5, 11, 17). – (Photos British Museum). – Scale 3:1.

A5?2 Aureus and denarius of Titus

(RIC II[1] Titus 21 = RIC II[2] Titus 100-105; BMCRE Titus 36-41)

Aurei and denarii of Titus of AD 80 bear a trophy with a captive seated either side, a female in a long dress and a bound nude bearded male (**fig. 344**). The trophy comprises a cuirass and tunic, sometimes with a cloak, helmet, and shield on each arm with a curved object emerging from behind. The shields are sometimes oval, sometimes hexagonal; occasionally greaves are shown below the tunic. The issue has been linked to a victory in Britain (Mattingly 1930, lxxii; Cody 2003, 111 f.), which at this date would be connected with Agricola's consolidation of his conquest of southern Scotland.

Could the curved objects be a carnyces? As with the other Titus issue (A5x1), the small size and degree of stylisation make it impossible to say. Details on some coins hint at identification as a carnyx – a thickened »head« turned through 90° (BM 40; Mazzini 1957, 228 no. 307), and tentative snouts (BM 37) or ears (Antike Münzen Auktion XXXII, 28-29.10.1996, lot 604 [Frank Sternberg AG, Zürich]). They are too indistinct for any assurance, and must be rejected on current evidence.

Fig. 344 A5?2 Aureus (top left) and denarii of Titus (RIC 21). – (Photos British Museum). – Scale 3:1.

A5?3 Bronze medallion of Hadrian

A rare bronze medallion of Hadrian of AD 119-138 (his third consulship) has a pile of arms on the reverse (**fig. 345**). The type is first mentioned in Henry Cohen's second volume (1882, 145 no. 469), without illustration; he described »cinq trompettes gauloises« among a pile of arms in a coin from M. Rollin's collection. Francesco Gnecchi (1912, 17 no. 65) described the same coin as »Ammasso di armi«, again without illustration. A worn

Fig. 345 A5?3 Bronze medallion of Hadrian. – (After Strack 1933, pl. XVI no. 443). – Scale 1:1.

specimen from the Weifert Collection in Belgrade was depicted by Paul Strack (1933, pl. XVI, 443), and he recorded a specimen in the Trau collection in Vienna. This was sold in 1935 (Trau 1935, 33 lot 1219; »Haufen gallischer Waffen«), but not illustrated. Mazzini (1957, vol. 2, 91 pl. XXXII no. 469) illustrated the same coin as Strack. Thus at least two different examples have so far been recorded; none has yet been traced in a public collection.

The design is strongly reminiscent of the weaponry on coins of Marcus Aurelius and Commodus (A5.4). Arranged around a ?scale cuirass are hexagonal and oval shields, spears, an axe, tuba, vexillum standard, Phrygian-style helmet and what Cohen and Mazzini identified as five carnyces. There are in fact four objects, the left clearly a spear on Strack's illustration, the right probably a spear on Mazzini's illustration, and the third item amorphous. The identification of the second item from left as a carnyx is not impossible but neither is it certain. It shows a shaft with a curved expanded end and hints of a complex/zoomorphic terminal; this could be read as an ear and upturned snout, the mouth closed, while an optimist might see hints of a crest on the Strack example, but a pessimist would see only wear and die flaws.

It has not yet been possible to examine a specimen. However, the judgement in RIC (Hadrian 643) gives cause for concern – »A curious coin«, with no further comment. The implication seems to be that it could be a forgery, which could explain the resemblance to late Antonine examples; a similar Trajanic issue with a pile of arms has been shown to be a forgery (see **Appendix 4**). At present the jury is out both on the presence of a carnyx and the authenticity of the coin. If genuine, the Phrygian helmet and axe suggest an eastern connection, perhaps to Hadrian's campaign against the Roxolani in AD 118 or a reminder of Trajan's victories – this material was in use among such Sarmatian groups, and the carnyx featured along with Sarmatian material in Dacian war propaganda (**tab. 47**). The carnyx might link to his British campaigns, giving the weaponry a more universal character representing a series of victories in his reign, but the type is too uncertain for any confidence in it at present.

B ROMAN SCULPTURE

B1?1 Weapons frieze, ?Rome/I

Among the depictions of Roman antiquities in the British royal collection is a 17th-century pen-and-ink drawing of a lost weapons frieze (**fig. 346**). It is square, with crossed shields and a series of items behind, very similar to the reliefs known from the Hadrianeum, though Ian Campbell (2004, 823 no. 318), who published the drawing, argued it is not from this find but from a similar setting. He identified the weaponry as a figure-of eight (ancile) shield, an oval shield, griffin-pommel swords, arrows and a carnyx; there are also sword scabbards. It is hard to be sure from a copy such as this, but the »carnyx«, while having an open mouth and zoomorphic head, is similar in scale to the griffin-pommel swords. Another item pokes out of the left edge of the design, and it is tempting, in combination with the arrows, to see these as bow-tips. Without the original panel to examine, it must remain in the realms of uncertainty.

B2?1 Weapons frieze, Todi (prov. Perugia/I)

Eugenio Polito (1998, 132 f.) described a weapons frieze on the Doric cornice of the plaza foundations of a sanctuary at Todi in Perugia. He argued the form of the cornice suggests a date around 40 BC. Sadly he noted that the condition of the frieze is bad, making interpretation difficult without more detailed study: he noted possible carnyces crossed behind a pelta shield, but they could equally be greaves. No other barbarian weaponry is recorded on the frieze. Given this, it must remain in the uncertain class until examined first-hand or published more fully.

B4?1 Weapons friezes, Augst and Kaiseraugst (Kanton Basel-Landschaft/CH)

Claudia Bossert-Radtke (1992, 61-68 pls 27-31) published a series of blocks with weapons friezes, and identified two carnyces on them. There are problems with both identifications: one is plausible but irresolvable, while the other should be dismissed. The blocks in question are her catalogue numbers 41a and 41c. 41a and b were found in

Fig. 346 B1?1 Drawing of a lost weapons frieze, ?Rome. – (Campbell 2004, 823 no. 318).

Fig. 347 B4?1 Weapons frieze, Kaiseraugst. – (Bossert-Radtke 1992, pl. 29).

digging a canal in Kaiseraugst in 1932. Both derive from the one weapons frieze. 41b bears overlapping round and oval shields with spear shafts. 41a is a corner block. One face has a bound male captive in front of a pile of arms, and is probably part of a trophy. The adjacent decorated face has a pelta shield with parts of other, less well-preserved shields behind bearing similar decoration (**fig. 347**). A sword belt hangs over them, and a belt or ribbon over another area. To the left, overlapping the pelta shield in a badly-damaged area, Bossert-Radtke (1992, 61) saw the outline of a carnyx. However, from close inspection this cannot be sustained. The outline can be traced clearly, and tapers as it curves towards the terminal; the terminal itself is squared off; and it is clear (from the continuous surface of the underlying shield) that there are neither ears nor crest. The surviving ornament (a marginal incised line and a central incised line) is more consistent with a shield than a carnyx. It is best interpreted as part of a second pelta shield overlying the first, and should be dismissed. (It is worth noting, on the other face, a tantalising slightly coni-

Fig. 348 B4?1 Weapons frieze, Augst. –
(Bossert-Radtke 1992, pl. 30).

cal tube which may be a musical instrument [either tuba or carnyx], but the crucial elements are lost.)

The other piece (Bossert-Radtke 1992, 62 f. pl. 30) is impossible to resolve. It is a block with a weapons frieze found in Augst, probably in the temple area in the Grienmatt, around 1800 and subsequently lost. Only a single contemporary illustration survives (**fig. 348**). This shows on the right a round shield, apparently with a man standing on it (but perhaps a pair of greaves, as Bossert-Radtke argued), and a cloak behind. Thus it seems likely to be a trophy. To the left is a rudder, in front of which is a zoomorphic item. The head and neck of this do look like a carnyx, with a single eye, open mouth with recurved lower lip (the upper is lost) and a cylindrical tube. There is no ear or crest. However, the »tube« then curves back as if it was an animal. It may be a zoomorphic ship's prow, or a draco standard with the »sock« billowing out. Alternatively, the artist misunderstood it: if he was unfamiliar with a carnyx he may have tried to convert it into something comprehensible. He described it as »un cheval marin«, implying he saw it as an animal, and in his account specifically commented on the indistinct attributes and how hard it was to resolve them in his sketch (Bossert-Radtke 1992, 62). Thus it is quite likely he could not fully make out what he was looking at. Interpretation as a carnyx is thus plausible but, on the available evidence, not certain.

Bossert-Radtke (1992, 65 f.) argued 41a-c are likely to derive from the one monument. On stylistic grounds she proposed a Flavian date, drawing parallels to the Uffizi pillars among others, and contrasting this to the flat-relief of Trajan's Column.

C ARTEFACTS

C?1 Intaglio

A glass paste intaglio now in the Staatliche Münzsammlung in Munich shows a trophy with muscle cuirass and slightly flared bowl helmet, with an oval shield on each arm with elongated umbo and spina (Brandt/Schmidt 1970, 226 no. 2134 pl. 185). Behind these are spears, a tuba and what the authors called a possible carnyx (**fig. 349**). This is not at all clear from the published photo, and without first-hand inspection must remain uncertain. The authors (*ibidem* 81) gave all such intaglios a broad 3rd- 1st century BC date.

Fig. 349 C?1 Munich intaglio. – (Brandt/Schmidt 1970, pl. 185).

APPENDIX 4: FALSAE

A number of items have crept, or in some cases leapt, into the literature and put down roots. Several have been corrected previously but often the misidentification persists. They are tabulated below and discussed in the order of the main catalogue. A particular problem has been the graphic restoration of poorly-preserved monuments which has led to the insertion of carnyces in illustrations even if not claimed as such in the text. The identification of falsae is not always easy. Given the sparsity of surviving carnyces, there is a danger that the iconography creates an interpretative straightjacket, with a circularity of argument over how a carnyx should look. Since our view of the appearance of a carnyx is largely defined by depictions in iconographic sources, themselves subject to various representational biases and working within their own tradition of what a carnyx should look like, objects which do not fit the stereotype risk being rejected even if they are simply variants. This is very hard to guard against, but each example has been considered in detail, with rejection on one or more of three grounds.

- Misidentification: the »carnyx« is actually another item. This applies to a number of the coins, which show draco standards rather than carnyces.
- Lack of key characteristics, in particular zoomorphism.
- Technical infeasibility. This is the main argument against the two most persistent carnyx claimants, from Pergamon and Castiglione delle Stiviere. They have not been rejected lightly, but it is felt that both fail to satisfy on one or more key points.

It is of course likely that further work and other researchers will view this differently, and given the diversity observed in surviving carnyces variety is not inherently improbable. However, in the context of this study all the material listed in **table 86** merits outright rejection from the corpus. The rationale is given below.

ARTEFACTS

Le Mans (dép. Sarthe / F)

The Museum of Le Mans have confirmed (*in litt.* 17.8.92) that the »carnyx fragment« mentioned by Stuart Piggott (1959, 22), following Eugène Hucher (1874, 63), is not a carnyx. Hucher described it as: »un minime fragment recourbé, en bronze, d'un instrument qui peut avoir été un carnyx de petite dimension« (a very small fragment of curved bronze from an instrument which could have been a carnyx of small dimensions). Its true identification is not known.

Castiglione delle Stiviere (prov. Mantua / I)

Another supposed carnyx must regrettably be struck from the record. Raffaele De Marinis (1987, 184-186; 1990, 123; 1997) identified fragments from a 3rd century BC grave at Castiglione delle Stiviere, north Italy, as a carnyx, and this has since been taken up by other writers (e.g. Megaw 1991, 645-647; Bonini 1998, 94). De Marinis (1997) provided a valuable full publication of the burial in which he outlined the details of his reconstruction (here **fig. 124a**). It comprises a conical mouth with vegetal repoussé orna- ment, a bird head in two halves with similar decoration (including an eye motif), and a tapering conical tube.

Sadly, the identification cannot be sustained, as there are flaws which make the reconstruction unfeasible. The »tube« tapers much more sharply than any other known example, either actual or depicted, and one end is angled rather than square, indicating it was intended to fix at an angle rather than straight. It is also very narrow and very short. The conical shape of the »mouth« is unparalleled in any realistic de-

Artefacts
Le Mans (dép. Sarthe/F)
Castiglione delle Stiviere (prov. Mantua/I)
River Malbork (Pomorskie/POL)
Folly Lane (Hertfordshire/UK)

A1 British Iron Age coins

VA 423, 510/1	Verica silver minim
BM 306-328 / VA 1476-5	Whaddon Chase stater
BM 1724-1727 / VA 1750	Tasciovanus bronze
BM 1629-1637, 1647-1649 / VA 1780, 1786	Tasciovanus Ricon stater and quarter stater
BM 1698-1701 / VA 1892	Tascio-Rues bronze

A2 Gaulish coins

BN 4581-4584	Armorican gold and silver coins
BN 7777-7782	Parisi gold coin
BN 8054-8080	Belgic bronze
BN 8453-8457	?Ambiani bronze
BN 10254-10255	Belgic gold
Scheers 40	Belgic gold

A4 Roman Republican coins

RRC 443	Caesar
RRC 460/1-2	Q. Metellius
Semis with Jupiter in quadriga and carnyx	

A5 Roman Imperial coins

BMCRE II, p409n	Domitian quadrans
RIC 267, 295, 303, 329	Domitian bronze
RIC 601	Commodus denarius
BMCRE 555-7	Severus sestertius
Various	Severus, Caracalla and Geta aurei and denarii
RIC 921	Probus antoninianus

B Classical sculpture
»Trophies of Marius«, Rome/I
Column of Antoninus Pius, Rome/I
Porta Argentariorum, Rome/I
Trophy of La Turbie (dép. Alpes-Maritimes/F)
Arch of Carpentras (dép. Vaucluse/F)
Trophy monument of St-Bertrand-de-Comminges (dép. Haute-Garonne/F)
Pergamon frieze (İzmir/TR)
Funerary altar, Falerii Novi (prov. Viterbo/I)

C Artefacts
Stradonice statuette (okr. Beroun/CZ)
Gavalou/Trichoneion plaque (Aetolia-Acarnania/GR)

Tab. 86 Objects and depictions which have been falsely claimed as carnyces.

piction; carnyces are shown with two separate jaws, not a single cone. Its repoussé decoration would point backwards in use, showing the toolmarks on the underside (De Marinis [1997, 133] argued strongly against this point, but Venceslas Kruta [2013, 44 f.] raised similar objections). Additionally, its edge is stepped as if to provide a seating or firm base for attachment, rather than the edge of a mouth.

To understand this material we must look at the other contents of the grave. It was found in 1914 and the contents rapidly dispersed (Atti della R. Accademia dei Lincei, Serie Quinta; Notizie degli scavi di antichità XII/9, 1915, 302 f.; Menotti 1998). Some of the material was studied by Paul Jacobsthal (1944, 110. 145 f. 203 f. pls 201. 257), but the assemblage as a whole was largely unknown until De Marinis (1997) provided a full description and discussion. There are a number of other bird-related items, including a plate with a pair of feet and a pair of articulated model wings, another highly unusual find. De Marinis incorporated this into a bird figurine, arguing that discrepancies in size between this and the »carnyx« pointed to two rather than one items; he suggested this bird was a standard or cult statue (1997, 158-160). This leaves us with a remarkable burial containing two unique objects. Applying Occam's Razor, it seems better to attempt to rationalise these as a single bird statue.

Figure 124b gives the writer's first attempt at a reconstruction, and **figure 124c** that of Venceslas Kruta which developed from this; he has proposed a rather more elegant freestanding sculpture in the form of a crane. The components are redrawn from De Marinis (1997), except the wings which are from photos taken during a study visit, when the rivet holes were noted (they are not shown in De Marinis 1997, fig. 14). The wings would have been positioned as if flapping: the »arm« (De Marinis 1997, fig. 14, 4) is a structural element originally attached to the wing which would fit inside the body to fix it at an angle. The head remains thus, albeit now lacking a terminal to its beak; a decorative curved piece may be the neck (Hunter) or more plausibly tail (Kruta), while the »tube« is most probably a leg, tapering to fit into a plate which depicts a bird's feet; the angled end now makes sense, with an angled leg meeting the hypothetical body (a flaw in Kruta's reconstruction). The movable wings do indeed seem too small as they survive, but rivet holes at the edges suggest there was a second set of feathers, probably in a lost organic material. (While other pieces have modern rivet holes from mounting, these are noted by De Marinis to be randomly scattered; this set are consistently placed and appeared to this writer to be ancient.) The body is assumed to be organic, and the »mouth« becomes a base. This carries echoes of the raven on the Ciumeşti helmet (Rusu 1969; Megaw 1970, no. 211), and could come from a helmet, standard or cult figure. (For interpretation as part of a helmet, see also Grassi 1991, 107; Menotti 1998, 132; while it may seem cumbersome in this role, the decorated helmets in the Tintignac find show this was not a material concern; Maniquet 2008, fig. 22, 24.)

The detailed reconstruction is of course uncertain, but there is little doubt that it is not a carnyx. However, this intriguing and important bird figurine merits wider attention in its own right, especially given its assured and elegant decoration (Kruta in: Chieco Bianchi 1988, 306), which Vincent and Ruth Megaw (2001, 198) noted as akin to the British Torrs-Witham-Wandsworth style.

River Nogat, Malbork (Pomorskie / POL)

The complete lack of zoomorphism means the curved horn from the River Malbork in Poland cannot be a carnyx, despite confused descriptions which call it one (Malinowski 1981, 268 f. pl. 10). It is a horn of the Caprington-Saalburg type (see chapter 10; **fig. 200c**).

Folly Lane (Hertfordshire / UK)

Among the finds from the rich mid-1st-century AD burial at Folly Lane were two joining fragments of cylindrical cast tube. In discussing interpretations, Jennifer Foster (1999, 155 f.) raised the possibility that they could come from the tube of a carnyx. At the time, no cast tubes were known; now, with the cast carnyx from Tintignac (chapter 7), they must be reconsidered. There are several cylinder fragments from the burial, but the two best-preserved ones are a maximum of 77 mm long and 24 mm in diameter; one of them is intact. They splay slightly at one end, while the other has a circumferential rib and then chamfers to fit inside the lower end of the next element. The problem with seeing them as carnyx fittings is their small size – the Tintignac elements, in contrast, are 200-285 mm long (Maniquet 2008, 309 f.) and have evidence of junction rings to secure the fittings, which are not attested at Folly Lane. Such small tubes seem unfeasible for a carnyx, and the other options suggested by Foster (another form of instrument or a furniture fitting) should be preferred.

A1 BRITISH IRON AGE COINS

Verica silver minim

(VA 423/510-1; ABC 1280; **fig. 350**)
Descriptions of this coin have been rather varied. While Robert Van Arsdell catalogued it as two separate types (Van Arsdell 1989, nos 423; 510-1), Simon Bean (2000, 246. 251 VERC2-8) identified this as the result of a flawed die leading to apparently different obverses. Van Arsdell's obverse description is in any case wrong in both entries; he identified a mounted warrior on 510-1 and a wreath on 423 when it is actually inscribed VIRIC within a beaded border. Of relevance here is the reverse. This shows a boar with devices above and below. Van Arsdell read these alternately as ?vestigial EPP above/ring below (VA 423) and ?C above/O below (VA 510-1). To Bean (2000, 246 VERC2-8), however, it was ring below, carnyx above.

Dr Philip De Jersey kindly reviewed the available illustrations in the CCI (pers. comm. 1.8.2002) and confirmed that most are clearly C above, O below; this »CO« inscription is found on other minims of Verica (e. g. Bean 2000, VERC2-5 to –8) as a contraction of the more usual »COMF« or »COMMIF«, »son of Commius«. A number of examples differ from this, and he sent images of CCI

Fig. 350 Silver minim of Verica (VA 423/510-1). – (Photo Celtic Coin Index). – Scale 2:1.

85.0024 and 91.0592 for inspection. It is these which presumably gave rise to the carnyx attribution. In both, a straight featureless line joins the bottom of the C at around 45°, resulting in a hook-shape with some similarities to a carnyx, with curving »bell« and flaring »mouth«. However, even allowing for the very small field available to the die-cutter (a mere 8 mm diameter), it is unlikely to be a carnyx. The degree of curvature is far greater than on any other carnyces on Celtic coins; only on some of the later Roman depictions is such a curve found (e. g. Portonaccio sarcophagus; B1.15). In its native milieu, such unfamiliarity is unlikely. There are in truth no diagnostic carnyx features: the »flaring mouth« is actually the squared serif of the C with no depiction of jaws, and there are no other details such as tube segments, eyes or ears. Given the quality of die-engraving on 91.0592, where the boar's pelt is depicted with tufts of hair, the crest shows detailed spikes and the bifurcated trotter is shown, it was clearly within their ability even on a small die to indicate relevant details.

Dr De Jersey suggested that the altered motif may arise from a die flaw (as on some obverse dies), which was then incorporated into the motif when it was copied, filling up a blank space in the design. This is possible: on 91.0592 the line is very much an adjunct, and may be a flaw; on 85.0024 it is more integral, although the outline of the lower serif of the C is still visible. However, even on this latter which is the most carnyx-like (and which is more poorly cut), the shape and lack of any realistic detail argues against it as a carnyx. There are no grounds for thinking that a carnyx was in the die-cutter's mind as he was engraving (Hunter 2009, 246).

Whaddon Chase stater

(VA 1476-5; ABC 2433; **fig. 351**)
Robert Van Arsdell (1994) argued that one die variant of the Whaddon Chase type of stater (VA 1476) includes a representation of a carnyx. The motif on most coins of the

series is a marginal border of pellets around the flan with an oval »ring and pellet« design partly overlapping this. Van Arsdell argued that on one die this is modified into a »tube« formed of a curving line of pellets with a »head«

Fig. 351 Whaddon Chase stater, with detail to right. – (Van Arsdell 1994, fig. 1; 1995, fig. 2). – Scale 1:1.

represented by a complex ellipse at the end. In this Van Arsdell saw an eye, snout and mouth. This identification has already been questioned (Hunter 1994), primarily because the motif has none of the characteristic features of a carnyx: the tube is curved and the design of the »head« does not clearly show any of the features which Van Arsdell can see in it – there is no clear crest, ear or gaping mouth. It was also argued that Van Arsdell's concentration on the depiction of the eye and resulting parallels with Deskford was misplaced, as in the overall scheme of a carnyx the eye was not a dominant feature – it merely dominates the Deskford example because only a fragment survives.

In reply, Van Arsdell (1995) rejected these arguments. He argued again that there are clear features of the head in the elliptical design, and that the tube is close enough to straight. Yet to this writer's eye even his enhanced and enlarged image of the ellipse fails to reveal any features which might reasonably be seen as parts of a head. Comparison with genuine examples of carnyces shows just how far from this the Whaddon Chase stater is. In arguing the tube tends to straightness by applying a straight-line fit, he misunderstands the nature of such fits. Any curve can have a straight line fitted to it, and depending on the degree of curvature and the arc represented it will be a better or worse fit. However, observation of the closeness of fit will reveal not the random scatter expected when a line is fitted to an approximately linear set of data but a clear trend, with points being sequentially under, over and then under the fitted line. This is exactly what can be seen in Van Arsdell's (1995) figure 2 (middle). The line is clearly a curve.

Van Arsdell also appeared to misunderstand the nature of classification, in arguing that the criteria proposed for identifying a carnyx in Hunter (1994) would fail to identify obvious carnyces such as the Trinovantian stater (A1.1). Yet it was clearly stated that an image should fulfil some or all of these criteria. This is a polythetic, not a monothetic, classification: almost no images will have all the features, but all share some characteristics of the »idealised« carnyx. The Trinovantian stater has a long straight segmented tube, mouthpiece and flared jaws, which securely identify it. The Whaddon Chase stater by contrast has none of these features, and must be dismissed as a carnyx (Hunter 2009, 246 f.).

Andrew Fitzpatrick (*in litt.*, 2.4.96) suggested a much more plausible explanation for the motif. He noted the ellipse is likely to be simply two superimposed oval and pellet motifs: there are traces of this on the other specimen illustrated in Van Arsdell (1989), pl. 40. This could arise from the recutting of worn reverse dies, with a failure to cut the motif in exactly the same place. It is notable that other, supposedly later coins such as VA 1493-1 again show the simple oval and pellet overlying the pellet-defined border. The motif is far better seen as such an accidental by-product of coin production than a unique and uncharacteristic carnyx depiction which requires tortuous logic and the bending of criteria to make it fit.

Tasciovanus bronze

(VA 1750; ABC 2676; Mack 171; BM 1724-1727; **fig. 352**) A bronze coin of Tasciovanus features a mail-clad cavalryman riding R, carrying on oval shield in his L arm and raising what Richard Hobbs (1996, 121) and Robert Van Arsdell (1989, 375) saw as a carnyx in his R arm, an identification repeated by Cottam et al. (2010, 131 no. 2676). The reverse design is closely similar to the Tasciovanus stater (A1.1), and this has encouraged the identification as a carnyx, although Allen (1958, 44 n. 3) noted that the head details are unclear and it could be a long spear, while Mack (1975, 79) identified it as a sword.

The identification of the item in the rider's R hand as a carnyx cannot be supported. Very few specimens preserve head details (**tab. 87**), but the best-preserved one (94.1372, now in a private collection) has been examined first-hand, and it is clear that it is a spear, not a carnyx (**fig. 352**). This allows the »knobs« on some shafts to be seen as the start of spearheads rather than carnyx tube junctions; none has any head details to gainsay this interpretation (Hunter 2009, 247).

Fig. 352 Tasciovanus bronze (CCI 94.1372, VA 1750). – (Photo National Museums Scotland). – Not to scale.

no.	details
BM 1725	straight featureless shaft. Head runs off flan.
CCI 71.0027	only upper half survives; head too worn. Knob near end of shaft – spearhead.
CCI 73.0252	worn, base lost. Knob near end of shaft – spearhead
CCI 90.0377	base and upper end lost. Straight featureless shaft.
CCI 90.0422	badly corroded, but appears straight and featureless.
CCI 94.1372	clearly a spear – straight featureless shaft with leaf-shaped pointed head.

Tab. 87 Characteristics of Tasciovanus bronze VA 1750. BM: British Museum; CCI: Celtic Coins Index.

Tasciovanus Ricon stater

(VA 1780, 1786; ABC 2580, 2601; BM 1629-1637. 1647-1649; Mack 184-185; **fig. 353**)
On the obverse of certain staters and quarter staters of Tasciovanus, the inscription is framed by a box with devices behind it. Chris Rudd has interpreted this as stylised trophy, with the curved »hockey-stick« symbols in each quarter being carnyces (Chris Rudd List 84, 2005, no. 46; *ibidem* 65, 2002, no. 99). The box could represent a hide-shaped shield with a spear behind it, but the other symbols do not fit easily into this interpretation. The vertical bars are clearly not spears, as they end in pellet terminals,

and alternate ones have pelleted shafts. The four curved items never have carnyx attributes, such as a mouth, nor any details such as a crest or segmented tube. The trophy identification cannot be sustained; it is simply a stylised wreath (Hunter 2009, 247).

Fig. 353 Tasciovanus Ricon stater (ABC 2601 / VA 1786). – (After Cottam et al. 2010, 129 no. 2601). – Scale 1:1.

Tascio-Rues AE

(VA 1892; ABC 2754; **fig. 354**)
The reverse of a bronze of Tasciovanus with the inscription RVII has been interpreted as a warrior with carnyx (Hobbs 1996, 120) or spear/carnyx (Van Arsdell 1989, 392). In contrast Allen (1958, 46 f.) saw it correctly as a warrior with short sword; Philip De Jersey (pers. comm. 1.8.2002) confirmed that none of the images in CCI at that date include a carnyx. The type is illustrated here by an example which has been examined first-hand, courtesy of Mr G. Cottam (see Hunter 2009, 247).

Fig. 354 Tasciovanus-Rues bronze (VA 1892) (not to scale). – (Photo National Museums Scotland).

A2 GAULISH COINS

Armorican gold and silver coin

(LT XIV 4581; BN 4581-4584; DT II 2101; Depeyrot VIII 103-104; **fig. 355**)
Among the extensive Armorican series are coins with a human-headed horse riding R with a charioteer raising an S-shaped object to his mouth (de La Tour 1892, pl. XIV). It has a broad mouth with a raised ridge, and curls to terminate in a pellet. Eugène Hucher (1868, 10 pl. 6, 2), Ernest

Fig. 355 Armorican gold coin. – (Hucher 1868, pl. 6, 2). – Scale c. 2:1.

Muret (1889, 103) and George Depeyrot (2005b, 72. 81) called it a carnyx, but it has none of the characteristic features: indeed, as depicted it could not function as a musical instrument, and is more likely to be a drinking horn (Hunter 2009, 247).

Gold coin of Parisi

(LT XXXI 7777-7782; BN 7777-7782; DT I 83; **fig. 356**)
Hucher (1868, 18 pl. 75, 1) illustrated a Parisian stater with the reverse showing a horse L with a number of other devices: a net-like symbol above it, a snake-like line rising from its mouth, a rosette under and a curved item above its hind quarters. He suggested this last item is a carnyx but it has none of the characteristic features and should be dismissed. The motif is found on other coins (e.g. Brenot/Scheers 1996, nos 755-756) and may represent a stylised charioteer (Hunter 2009, 247).

Fig. 356 Gold coin of the Parisi. – (Hucher 1868, pl. 75, 1). – Scale 2:1.

Bronze coin, Belgic Gaul

(LT XXXII 8054; BN 8054-8080; DT I 595)
The reverse of this coin shows a lion with a dolphin under. Allen (1995) described it as »dolphin (or dolphin-headed carnyx)«, but there is no reason for this additional complication – other authorities did not hesitate to call it a dolphin (e. g. Muret 1889, 186; Scheers 1978, 146; 1983, 633), the sinuous body, forked tail and asymmetrical fins being inconsistent with a carnyx but quite consistent with a dolphin (see esp. Scheers 1978, pl. XXV, 695; 1983, pl. XIX, 523; Allen 1995, pl. II, 67; Hunter 2009, 248).

Bronze coin, Belgic Gaul (Ambiani?)

(LT XXXIII 8456; BN 8453-8457; DT I 467; Scheers 1983 type 80c)
Person on horseback holding a curved object in their L hand which curves over their head, expanding gradually in width and terminating in a circle with a defined hollow to indicate this is open. Muret (1889, 194) identified it as a carnyx but it lacks characteristic features, although it is a musical instrument. It is not being played as the man's mouth is shown, but is held in the L hand while his R hand holds the horse. Such a highly curved instrument is probably a small curved horn of the C-shaped type known from the relief of the Dying Gaul and (on a larger scale) the Loughnashade trumpets (**fig. 195a**; chapter 10; Hunter 2009, 242).

Gold coin, Belgic Gaul

(BN 10254-10255; Scheers 1983 type 3 III b)
Gold half and quarter staters show a person squatting on the back of a horse, playing a curved horn. Both Muret (1889, 246f.) and Scheers (1983, 229) called it a carnyx but this is wrong as there is no hint of zoomorphism in the terminal. It is instead a detailed depiction of the instrument known as the »Celtic lituus« (**fig. 195c**; chapter 10; Hunter 2009, 242).

Gold coin, Belgic Gaul

(Scheers 1983 type 40; **fig. 357**)
The reverse shows a warrior holding a round shield in his R arm and what Blanchet (1971, 396f.) and Scheers (1983, 467f.) described as an upside-down carnyx in his L. Although the drawing is rather stylised, it shows a curved object terminating in a rectangle with a saltire design. This geometric terminal argues strongly against the carnyx identification. A similar motif is found on other coins

Fig. 357 Belgic gold coin (Scheers type 40). – (Blanchet 1905, fig. 413). – Scale 1:1.

where it shows no sign of being a carnyx (e.g. Scheers 1983, 443f. pl. X, 257; Brenot/Scheers 1996, nos 945 & G12). It is more likely to be a standard (*ibidem* 128; Hunter 2009, 248).

A4 ROMAN REPUBLICAN COINS

Caesar

(RRC 443; **fig 358**)
The reverse of RRC 443, a denarius of Caesar struck in 49-48 BC (Crawford 1974, 161), is sometimes misinterpreted as an elephant trampling a carnyx (e.g. Albrethsen 1987, 105 fig. 8A). In fact the curved zoomorphic item rearing against the elephant is a dragon or a snake, as Crawford noted. Examination of a range of specimens confirmed that the beast has an entirely curved body and a closed mouth; there is nothing about this to encourage identification as a carnyx (see also Woytek 2003, 121-123; Woods 2009).

Fig. 358 RRC 443 Denarius of Caesar with elephant trampling a snake. – (Photo British Museum, R.8822). – Scale 2:1.

Q. Metellius

(RRC 460/1-2)
Aurei and denarii minted by Q. Metellius show on the reverse a curule chair with scales balanced on a cornucopiae, a corn ear to L and another item to the R. This second item has been seen as a carnyx head (Babelon 1885-1886, 135; Grueber 1910, 571), although Michael Crawford (1974, 472) described it as a dragon head. Examination of two examples in the British Museum indicated this is unlikely to be a carnyx; instead, a gemstone parallel suggests it is a hand plucking something, perhaps an ear of corn (Schlüter/Platz-Horster/Zazoff 1975, no. 1652). This would make more sense in the context of the reverse.

Semis with Jupiter and carnyx

The Marquis de Lagoy (1849, 28 note 1) referred to »an uncertain semis with carnyx and Jupiter on quadriga« published by Andrea Morellio (1734, vol. 1, 476; vol. 2, Roma tab. 2, XIV; see **fig. 359**). This shows a clean-shaven bust of ?Apollo with laurel wreath on the obverse, inscribed S; the reverse has a nude bearded male in quadriga R, with the reins in his right hand and the carnyx in his left; in exergue, ROMA. The type is not attested in any major catalogues, suggesting it is either a fake or an engraver's misidentification of an unclear coin;

Fig. 359 Semis with »Jupiter and carnyx«. – (Morellio 1734, vol. 2, Roma tab. 2, XIV). – Not to scale.

I am grateful to Richard Abdy of the British Museum for discussion of this point.

A5 ROMAN IMPERIAL COINS

Quadrans of Domitian

(BMCRE II, p. 409n)
In discussing the undated bronzes of Domitian, BMCRE II, 409 n. describes a quadrans with »dragon-trumpet« in Vienna. Letters to the Münzkabinett in the Kunsthistorisches Museum elicited no response, but Dr Johan van Heesch of the Cabinet des Médailles in Brussels, who has been through the relevant material, had no memory of such a coin; it is also omitted from the revised edition of RIC II (Carradice/Buttrey 2007), and must be considered false.

Dupondius and As of Domitian

(BMCRE 311. 351 f. 357, & pp 377. 383; RIC II[1] 267. 295. 303. 329 = RIC II[2] 296. 372. 386. 481; **fig. 360**)
Dupondii and asses minted for Domitian in AD 85-86 as part of the celebrations for his German victories include types with the reverse showing an arrangement of arms on the back. This was described by Harold Mattingly (1930, 373) as »Oblong shields crossed over crossed spears and trumpets, and vexillum upright«. From behind the weapons on either side two zoomorphic-headed objects emerge horizontally and curve sharply upwards such that the heads face back along the shafts. These have been seen by some writers as carnyces (Mazzini 1957, 260 nos 536-537; Albrethsen 1987, 115 fig. 18; Stefan 2005, 480 fig. 212). Six examples were examined first-hand in the British Museum, casting doubt on identification as a carnyx.
The important point to note is how detailed the depictions on the best examples are (**fig. 360**), with the folds of the vexillum and the crescent which tops it shown, the ornament on the shield, and even the technical detail of the tuba mouthpiece which expands, contracts before the mouthpiece and then forms a cup as known from extant

Fig. 360 Dupondii of Domitian with weaponry. – (Photos British Museum [left]: Staatliche Museen zu Berlin – Preußischer Kulturbesitz, Münzkabinett). – Scale c. 1:1.

Gallo-Roman examples (e. g. Homo-Lechner/Vendries 1993, 80 f. 83 f.). In other words the depictions are detailed and accurate. In contrast, the »carnyces« are not good representations. The mouths are closed, there is no crest, and most tellingly the junction to the »tube« makes it look more like a zoomorphic terminal than an integral part of the bell. Unlike other objects, the ends of the »tube« do not appear on the far side of the shield, making it much shorter than a carnyx should be. For all these reasons it is felt that this is not a carnyx representation and should be dismissed from the record. Its true nature remains unclear, but it may be that the two terminals are part of a single object, perhaps a recurved bow.

Forged sestertius of Trajan

A sestertius of Trajan with a pile of arms on the reverse is recorded in BMCRE III, 216. The only known example is in Naples Museum, who kindly provided a photo (**fig. 361**). Paul Strack (1931, pl. VIII no. 453) illustrated a cast, which is clearer in certain details. It is plausible that a rather stylised carnyx is intended. (Strack identified it as a bow, but this appears to be a confusion with the bow shown below it.) A cuirass sits on a groundline in front of a pile of oval and hexagonal shields; arranged around it (clockwise from L) are a bow and full quiver; a *vexillum*; a helmet (domed, with neckguard, visor and cheek-guards) on a spear; a ?carnyx; a bow; two spears; and a further quiver. This curious and unique issue is a forgery. Detailed

Fig. 361 Forged sestertius of Trajan. – (Photo Soprintendenza Archeologica delle province di Napoli e Caserta). – Scale 2:1.

analysis by Bernhard Woytek showed that its observe die-matches three sestertii which all have Fortuna Redux on the reverse, and the pile of arms has been created by judi-cious re-carving of this design (Woytek 2010, 550 f. cat. no. X11 pl. 136).

Denarius of Commodus

(BMCRE M. Aurelius 640; RIC M. Aurelius 601)
In the description of this coin Mattingly (1940, 477) recorded the reverse as showing Commodus with a trophy to R, with at its base »shield, carnyx(?) and spear(?)«. The caution is justifiable – from inspection of the coin in the British Museum, the attributes emerging from behind the shield are simply too small and too stylised to identify. This example should be dismissed from the carnyx record.

Sestertius of Severus

(BMCRE Wars of Succession 555-557)
A sestertius of Severus with trophy and captives was struck to commemorate his victories over Arabs and Adiabenians who had fought for his rival Pescennius and then sought sanctuary with the Parthians. The captives are typical eastern barbarians, but Harod Mattingly (BMCRE V, 137) identified »dragon-trumpets (?)« in the trophy. The question-mark is well merited; on the published illustration there is no sign of any carnyx.

Aurei and denarii of Severus, Caracalla and Geta

(BMCRE Severan wars of succession 206-213; Severus 105-113. 228. 234-239. 256-259. 383-387. 391-394)
In describing an aureus of Caracalla of AD 196-198, the reverse showing Caracalla with a trophy, Mattingly (1950, 53) commented in the notes that »… what look like bands hanging at the sides may perhaps be dragon trumpets.« The type is also known on denarii (Mattingly/Sydenham 1936, 213). Similar trophies occurs with Minerva on another of Caracalla's coins (BMCRE 105-113), with Geta the young prince (BMCRE 228. 234-239), and on a trophy from the Parthian campaigns (BMCRE 256-259. 383-387. 391-394). In each case Mattingly identified »dragon-trumpets(?)«. These have only been examined from illustrations. On the Caracalla 206-213 type there may be zoomorphic-headed items (although they are not certain), but if so they are draco standards given the depiction of the »bands« as flowing tails which must be some form of fabric (for draco standards see Coulston 1991). On the other issues there is no clear zoomorphism and the »tails« are simply the edges of the cloak behind the trophy.

Antoninianus of Probus

(RIC 921)
The online catalogue of McMaster University's coin collection identifies a carnyx on an antoninianus of Probus. This coin shows the emperor (on the left) holding an object and facing Jupiter, who presents a globe. On the McMaster coin, the attribute held by Probus is identified as a carnyx (see reference below), and this seems outwardly possible. However, examination of the 26 examples in the British Museum shows that he actually holds an eagle-tipped sceptre, the eagle facing R, its wings partly raised and one foot pointing forward; the staff is sometimes beaded, and the head sometimes facing forward, sometimes curved back. On poorly-cut or worn examples, there can be a superficial similarity to a carnyx, but this is clearly incorrect. For the identification, see: http://tapor1.mcmaster.ca/~coin/search.php?coinId=629; accessed 6.9.2010.

B CLASSICAL SCULPTURE

»Trophies of Marius«, Rome / I

Two monumental free-standing marble trophies now stand at the top of the steps on the Piazza del Campidoglio, on the Capitoline Hill in Rome (**fig. 362a**). Originally from a triumphal monument of Domitian celebrating his German and Dacian campaigns, they were moved to a nymphaeum built by Severus Alexander on the Esquiline in 226, and then in 1590 shifted to their present position. It has been argued they are Trajanic rather than Domitianic: however, although the art styles of the two periods are very similar, an inscription on the base shows they were quarried under Domitian (Claridge 1998, 235. 297-299; Grisanti 1977, 49. 56-60; Stefan 2005, 456-464).

The left trophy is a fur cloak and helmet with oval and hexagonal shields on the arms and a range of weaponry, including a muscle cuirass, a Hellenistic helmet, a battering ram, bows and arrows and the scabbard of a long sword. Winged genii (now largely lost) assemble the trophy. On the reverse are round and oval shields at the base, and bundles of quivers on the backs of the arms. The right trophy has a scale armour cuirass and cloak, with hexagonal shields and an empty sword scabbard. A bound female barbarian stands at the base, surrounded by an array of weaponry: oval and hexagonal shields, bows and quivers of arrows. Again two winged genii are present. On the back are round and hexagonal shields, and bundles of quivers on the arms. They are discussed and illustrated by Giovanna Tedeschi Grisanti (1977, 49-51 pls XXII. XXVII). The weaponry certainly includes typical Germanic items for the Flavian period (the fur cloak and hexagonal shields); the archery equipment is more unusual in this context and may be Dacian, as may the battering ram (which Dacians are shown using on Trajan's Column in scene xxxii; Lepper/Frere 1988, 80 pl. XXIV).

The item of interest here is on the left trophy, immediately right of the central helmet. It survives today as a cylindrical tube, curving to the left at the top; here the original surface is missing and the end totally lost, but the start of the mouth is preserved. Grisanti (1977, 49 f.) described it as »a type of horn«, and on Luigi Canina's (1836) etching it is shown as a carnyx (Grisanti 1977, pl. XXIII; the illustration was reversed by Canina's publisher but is restored in **fig. 362b**). While this would be quite at home on a Domitianic monument, as it survives today there is insufficient to confirm this identification and we must turn to the earlier illustrations, as presented by Grisanti (1977, pls XXIII-XXVI). There are four important illustrations of the monument: those of Francisco de Ollando in 1539-1540, Giovanni Battista Piranesi in 1761, A. M. Garnaud

Fig. 362 The »Trophies of Marius«: **a** as they survive today. – **b** imaginative reconstruction by Canina in 1836, restoring a carnyx. – (a photo Fraser Hunter; b Grisanti 1977, pl. XXIII, 1; image reversed to match reality).

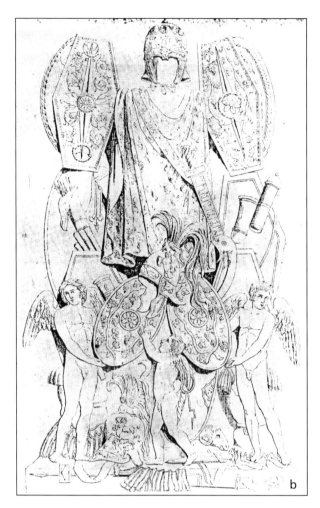

b

Fig. 362 (continued)

around 1821, and Canina in 1836; in addition, Salomon Reinach (1909, 290) published a drawing of it. All are reasonably accurate in general, but vary rather on points of detail and in how much graphical restoration they do. De Ollando, Piranesi and Garnaud all stay close to what is visible today, and we can see over time the gradual loss of certain elements. Most of the side genii, parts of the right lower shield and the central helmet were lost between 1539-1540 and 1761; there has been some subsequent damage, but Piranesi's illustration is closely similar to what survives today.

Table 88 summarises the depictions of the animal-headed element. It is clear that earlier representations do not show it as a carnyx: it has a closed mouth, and its bird-like head and sinuous form are more likely to be the end of a bow, as seen flanking the captive in the right hand trophy. The animal head was still present in Piranesi's 1761 illustration, but lost by the time of Garnaud's around 1821 when it assumed its present form. Thus Canina's depiction of a carnyx head in 1836 can only be an artistic restoration. It is noticeable that his drawing is the most »restored«, with the genii being complete, a sword being placed in the scabbard and the helmet on top being restored. From this it is clear that his illustration cannot be trusted. On the evidence we have the item in this trophy was a bow, not a carnyx.

artist	date	depiction
Francisco de Ollanda	1539-1540	bird head, closed hooked beak, sinuous neck
Piranesi	1761	smaller, more curved ?bird head, sinuous neck
Garnaud	c. 1821	tube curved at end; head lost
Canina	1836	carnyx, with eye and mouth open to 180°; tube less sinuous
Reinach	1909	small curved bird head

Tab. 88 Depictions of the »carnyx« on the »Trophies of Marius«.

Column of Antoninus Pius, Rome / I

In publishing the surviving base of the Column of Antoninus Pius, Lise Vogel (1973, 33) identified »a curved object ending in a griffin's head« and »an object in the form of a lion's (?) head« among weaponry on the apotheosis relief as »probably versions of the *carnyx* or war trumpet, used by many barbarian tribes and frequently appearing on Roman trophies«. Examination of a cast of the base in the RGZM indicates this is unsustainable. The »curved object« is a recurved bow with animal head tips, while the »lion head« is most likely the hilt of a sword: details are obscured by Roma's foot, but the head is too small for a carnyx, the mouth closed and the head highly naturalistic, as animal-hilted swords are.

Porta Argentariorum, Rome / I

The Arch of the Argentarii is a private monument of Severan date erected in AD 204 in the Forum Boarium, the ancient cattle market (**fig. 363a**). It was probably erected by one of the guilds connected with the trade: the inscription mentions *argentari* and *negotiantes*, silversmiths and merchants. The arch is published in detail by D. E. L. Haynes and P. E. D. Hirst (1939) and Massimo Pallottino (1946), and synthesised by Diana Kleiner (1992, 334-337). One face includes a panel of two Roman soldiers and two captive Parthians with a weapons frieze below (**fig. 363b**). In discussing this frieze, only part of which survives, Haynes and Hirst (1939, 37 f.) identified from right to left a tuba and axe crossed in front of a circular shield, a sword in its scabbard, a tunic, the head of a double-headed axe

Fig. 363 Porta Argentariorum, Rome:
a general view. – **b** panel with supposed carnyx in lower frieze. – **c** detail of frieze. – (Photos Fraser Hunter).

and the top of a carnyx above a helmet (**fig. 363c**). By contrast Pallottino (1946, 96) identified a tuba and cornu, a third unidentifiable instrument, a tunic cuirass, a wheel, an Asiatic helmet in the form of a Phrygian cap, a carnyx, a quiver, an oval shield and the shaft of an unidentified weapon. Polito (1998, 199) did not provide a detailed analysis, but commented specifically on the tunic and the cornu.

This wide diversity of interpretations arises from the poor state of preservation of the frieze. It was examined firsthand on three occasions in varying light conditions. From this it was clear that there is no carnyx present. The de-

tails are not certain in its worn condition, but I read the frieze (from the right) as crossed tuba and cornu; ???; tunic; spearhead emerging above L shoulder; double axe and Phrygian helmet below this; bow and quiver to L; ?oval shield with something (?rudder or ?sword) overlying it. There are further unrecognisable features in the bottom right corner and at the left side of the frieze, but the carnyx can be firmly dismissed. The curved tip of the bow and the head of the spear do look like a carnyx head, but the resulting »head« is very poorly defined, and once they are recognised for what they are (and the line of the bow in particular is spotted) the carnyx identification crumbles.

Trophy of the Alps, La Turbie (dép. Alpes-Maritimes / F)

The trophy of the Alps at La Turbie was erected as a victory monument to commemorate Augustus' successful campaigns against the Alpine tribes in 25 and 16-14 BC which resulted in their subjugation and the safeguarding of the Po Valley and the coastal route to Gaul and Spain. The inscription dates the dedication of the monument to 7-6 BC. The trophy had two square podia (the lower with an inscription flanked by trophy reliefs), a circular colonnade and a conical roof. Its core survived from reuse as a fortification, and the monument was restored after extensive excavations in the 1930s. Some 3000 marble fragments from the original structure were found, and the excavator, Jules Formigé, went to considerable lengths to reconstruct the monument's appearance. The excavation monograph details the results (Formigé 1949; summary also in Bromwich 1993, 270-275), although reassessment suggests it is open to question in details, especially of decoration (S. Binninger, pers. comm.).

While the basic outline of the monument is secure, the details are not always so certain. Of key interest here is

the west face of the first podium. This bore the inscription commemorating the Alpine victories, and Formigé interpreted fragments of trophy sculptures as deriving from two flanking trophy reliefs with barbarian prisoners (1949, 52-54). His reconstruction was heavily influenced by the surviving imagery of the Carpentras and Orange arches (Formigé 1949, 52 f.). Examination indicates the placing and interpretation of fragments is conjectural in many cases. Of the two trophies, that to the right of the inscription is better preserved (Formigé 1949, fig. 51). It is restored with a carnyx behind each arm and another beside the left shield; all these are entirely conjectural (the single original fragment in one is an undiagnostic shaft fragment that could come from a spear). Formigé (1949, 53) specifically mentioned »une trompe« fixed to the tree trunk, but this is probably his interpretation of the fragments of what may be a curved horn, which he reconstructs as a pair of horns based on the west face of the Carpentras arch.

Arch of Carpentras (dép. Vaucluse / F)

The honorific arch of Carpentras in southern France features a pair of captives flanking a trophy on its ends. Illustrations often show the trophies with carnyces (e. g. Espérandieu 1907, vol. I, 243; Reinach 1909, 98), but examination of the monument confirmed that these are graphic restorations for which there is no evidence on

the original. Each of the four captives is accompanied by an attribute. On the east face is a German captive with a curved item by his feet, but detailed examination indicates quite clearly this is not a carnyx; the most likely interpretation is as a helmet.

Trophy of St-Bertrand-de-Comminges (dép. Haute-Garonne / F)

Like Carpentras, graphic restorations of this highly fragmentary monument often feature carnyces (e. g. Picard

1957, facing p. 272; Gans 2003, fig. 2), but there is no evidence for this (as seen in Gans 2003, fig. 1).

Weapons frieze, Pergamon (İzmir / TR)

The balustrade of the Temple of Athena Nikephoros from Pergamon included a striking and innovative weapons frieze (Droysen 1885; Jaeckel 1965; Polito 1998, 91-95). This featured a range of Hellenistic and Galatian equipment from the various battles fought by the kings of Pergamon. It was erected by Eumenes II (197-160 BC), probably around 183 BC if a restored inscription can be trusted, and commemorated the victories of the Attalid dynasty over Galatians and Hellenistic enemies (the Seleucid king Antiochus Hierax or Philip V of Macedon). It is most plausible a general statement of the dynasty's victories rather than a reference to a specific event (as Polito discussed; for the historical background see Davis/Kraay 1973, 250-256).

The bulk of the material is clearly Hellenistic: to the Galatians can be attributed chain mail shirts, oval shields, arguably chariot components, and even more arguably the trumpets. The straight trumpets with segmented construction indicated by rings are said by Peter Jaeckel to be unlike Greek examples (1965, 113), which lack rings, and he supported Couissin's view of these as Celtic (Couissin 1927, 77 fig. 136). It is argued elsewhere (chapter 10) that the evidence for straight trumpets in Iron Age Europe is sparse, and the Pergamon reliefs are not sufficiently clear to sway the evidence.

The item of main concern here is a bull-headed item on one of the friezes (**fig. 364a**) which is regularly identified as a kind of carnyx (e. g. Powell 1980, 129; Moscati et al. 1991, 335; Polito 1998, 59), or at least a trumpet (Droysen 1885, 113). Paul Couissin (1927, 303-4) suggested it was a battering ram, a possibility rejected by Hans Droysen (1885, 113) on the grounds that it was technically unfeasible given its shape and construction. Subsequent scholars have varied in their views: Jaeckel (1965, 113f.) shared Droysen's doubts, while it was summarily dismissed as a carnyx by Woelcke (1911, 228 n. 105); Vendries (1999, 374 n. 36) thought it was a battering ram; Pernet (2013, 30) suggested it was a standard.

Examination of the original in the Pergamonmuseum in Berlin suggests to this writer it is not a carnyx. The depictions on the friezes are generally very life-like but the »carnyx« looks nothing like other carvings of carnyces. Although it has an open mouth (and thus could be played), the neck (»bell«) is very thick and shows no signs of tapering (**fig. 364b-c**). The extreme naturalism may just arise from Hellenistic artistic conventions, but there are no technical details to indicate construction; by contrast, the trumpet has junctions depicted, while a wheel shows such minutiae as pegs to hold the spokes in the felloe (Jaeckel 1965, 113f. fig. 57). Here the »carnyx«

a

Fig. 364 Block from a weapons frieze, Pergamon: **a** the block. – **b-c** details of the supposed carnyx. – (a Powell 1980, fig. 99; b-c photos Fraser Hunter).

Fig. 364 (continued)

looks so like a bull that we might think of some piece of equipment covered in a bull's hide, a thought supported by the hair-like texture of the head which is also found on another largely-hidden object in the lower left corner – perhaps part of the same object such as a battering ram. The carnyx connection should be dismissed.

Grave altar, Falerii Novi (prov. Viterbo / I)

Eugenio Polito (1991) provided a full description of this Tiberian-Claudian marble grave altar, found during excavations in Falerii Novi (some 50 km N of Rome) in 1821-30 and now at Sanssouci in Berlin (Hüneke 2000, 294. 297). The altar has a hollowed top to receive the ashes; among a range of decoration, the weapons frieze on the front is of concern here. The panel of arms, symmetrically arranged around a scale armour cuirass with pteryges, contains a range of weaponry: shields (peltate, round, oval and hexagonal); vexillum standards crowned with eagles; spears; swords; helmets; tubae; and ship parts (*akrostolia*) (fig. 365a-b).

Fig. 365 Grave altar, Falerii Novi: **a** general view. – **b** detail of weapons frieze. – **c** detail of two bird-headed items. – (Photos Fraser Hunter).

Five animal-headed items in the weapons frieze were identified by Polito as probably carnyces. Following first-hand inspection and much agonising, this identification must be rejected. All have a bird's head with a closed raptor-like beak, either hooked or straight, a pointed ear and a pronounced eye (**fig. 365c**). They were clearly conceived together, albeit implemented with varying degrees of stylisation, but are likely to represent different items. Two have a sinuous shaft, strongly suggesting they are bow tips; the other two curve into a straight shaft, and might be zoomorphic handles. The cause of the agonising is the signs of crests on two or three of them, which suggests a carnyx. However, what rules them out is their silence; the closed mouths are entirely inconsistent with carnyces. While closed mouths are sometimes found on coin specimens, they are unknown on sculpture (albeit occasional examples are barely open; e. g. one of the Prima Porta carnyces, or those on the column of Marcus Aurelius; B1.2, B1.14). They are depicted with naturalistic zoomorphism, suggesting the sculptor has simply taken a motif or object and used it decoratively, but there is nothing to support a carnyx identification.

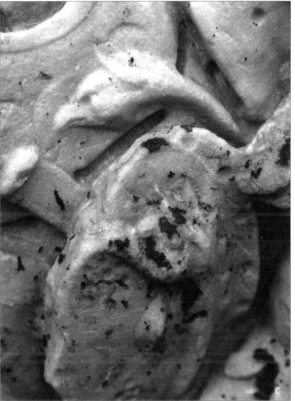

Fig. 365   (continued)

C ARTEFACTS

Stradonice figurine (okr. Beroun / CZ)

The figurine of a musician from Stradonice oppidum in the Czech Republic (Pič 1906, 66f. pl. XX, 33; Clodoré/Vendries 2002, 113f. fig. 82; Megaw 1991, 644f.) has been described as a carnyx player (Hada 1988, no. 166). Examination of the original confirmed there is no hint of zoomorphism, and some other form of bronze aerophone is represented (see chapter 10; **fig. 195d**).

Gavalou / Trichoneion plaque (Aetolia-Acarnania / GR)

A sheet silver plaque found in a grave at Gavalou, ancient Trichoneion, in Aetolia, shows a combat scene, with two riders either side of an infantry soldier, and a fallen soldier below one cavalryman (Rabe 2008, 83f. 189 no. 76 pl. 19, 3). It predates the 2nd century BC (based on the date of an overlying grave). To the left stands Nike with a palm branch. To the right is a trophy with armour, helmet, greaves, a domed round shield, and a sheathed sword hanging from what Britta Rabe (2008, 84) identified as »ein Blashorn mit zoomorpher Mündung« (**fig. 366**). This is not a carnyx, given the highly unusual form: the »tube« is formed by the horizontal arm of the trophy, with a swan's neck curve into the »head«. To the immediate right of the trophy is a flowing coil of vegetation with coiled ends; rather than representing a horn, it is more plausible that it represents a similarly ornate vegetal terminal to the organic elements of the trophy, plausibly a flower. Rabe notes that the warriors cannot be differentiated by their costumes; this scene represents combat between Greeks, not between Greeks and barbarians.

a

b

Fig. 366 Silver plaque, Gavalou/Trichoneion (Aetolia-Acarnania/ GR): **a** general view (L. 220 mm). – **b** detail of trophy. – (Rabe 2008, pl. 19, 3).

APPENDIX 5: BARBARIAN MATERIAL CULTURE IN ROMAN ICONOGRAPHY

Tables 89-96 list the occurrences known to the writer of key items of barbarian material culture in Roman triumphal art which are drawn on in the analysis in chapter 9. This covers torcs (**tab. 89**), chariots and chariot parts (**tab. 90**), the falx (**tab. 91**), single-bladed axes (**tab. 92**), draco standards (**tab. 93**), animal standards (**tab. 94**), armour (**tab. 95**) and fur hats or helmets (**tab. 96**).

object	image type	place/code	period	date	area/group	event	notes	reference
coin	attribute			211-208 BC	Cisalpine Gaul?			RRC 91
coin	attribute			113-112 BC	Cisalpine Gaul	Combat versus Gauls, 361 BC (moneyer's ancestor)		RRC 295
vessel handle	barbarian	Herculaneum (prov. Campania/I)		late C2 BC?	Gauls?			Stefanelli 1990, 277 figs 70. 192-193
coin	control mark			90 BC		references moneyer's ancestor		RRC 337/1
coin	control mark			81 BC		control mark		RRC 378
coin	control mark			79 BC		control mark		RRC 384
coin	control mark			67 BC		control mark		RRC 408
coin	attribute			65 BC		references moneyer's ancestor		RRC 411
coin	control mark			62 BC		control mark		RRC 412
intaglio	barbarian			50-1 BC	Gaul?		?torc	Schlüter/Platz-Horster/Zazoff 1975, no. 335
tomb of Caecilia Metella	trophy	Rome, Via Appia/I	early Augustan	30-20 BC	Gaul	Gallic War		B1.1
trophy monument	trophy	St Bertrand de Comminges (dép. Haute-Garonne/F)	early Augustan	30-20 BC	Gaul, Spain & Actium			Gans 2003; Walter 1993, nos 89-92
terracotta plaque	trophy & captive	Campana plaque	Augustus	29-25 BC	Gaul/German	Augustus' campaigns		C4.3
statue base of M. Cominius Pansa	weapons frieze	Isernia (reg. Molise/I)	Augustus	25-20 BC				Polito 1998, 137
glass plaque	trophy, captive & pile of arms			50 BC - AD 25	Gaul		shield decoration	C4.5
arch	trophies & piles of arms	Orange (dép. Vaucluse/F)	Augustus-Tiberius	50 BC - AD 25	Gaul & Germany		shield decoration	B3.4
frieze	combat	Mantua (from Rome/I)	Augustan?		Gauls?			Strong 1961, fig. 41
cameo	trophy & captives	Gemma Augustea	Augustan		Illyrians, other	debated		Kleiner 1992, 69-72; Zanker 1988, 230-232; Picard 1957, 305-308

object	image type	place/code	period	date	area/group	event	notes	reference
inscription with trophy & weapons frieze	trophy & weapons frieze	Gardun (Split-Dalmatia/HR)		AD 10-20	Illyria	suppression of Balkan revolt		B7.1
tomb block	weapons frieze	Pescina (prov. L'Aquila/I)		AD 1-30			shield decoration	Polito 1998, 166 f.
grave altar	pile of arms	Falerii Novi (prov. Viterbo/I)	Julio-Claudian	AD 14-54				Polito 1991; **fig. 365**
tomb with combat scene	combat	Bartringen (Luxembourg)	late Tiberian	AD 25-40	Rhine frontier			Krier 2003; **fig. 172g**
tomb block	weapons frieze	Rome, Pietra di Papa/I	early Julio-Claudian	AD 35-50				Polito 1998, 167
frieze	battle scene	Rome, Tiber/I	Claudian?		?	?	shield decoration; fragment only	La Rocca/Tortorella 2008, 174 II.1.6
gladiator's helmet	weapons frieze	Herculaneum (prov. Campania/I)		AD 1-79				C3.2
terracotta plaque	trophy	Campana plaque	Domitian	AD 83-85	Germany/ Chatti?	Caledonian link?	shield decoration	C4.4
pedestal base	trophy & pile of arms	Rome, Maddalena/I	Domitian	AD 83-105	Germany	Domitian's campaigns verus Chatti?	shield decoration	B1.9
antefix of German prince	barbarian	Vindonissa (Kanton Aargau/CH)	Flavian?	late C1 AD	Germany		neckband	Speidel 2000, fig. 2
frieze	weapons frieze	Trieste (reg. Friuli-Venezia Giulia/I)		C1 AD				Verzár-Bass 2003, 143-145 cat. RP6-8
tomb frieze	weapons frieze	Parma (reg. Emilia Romagna/I)	late Flavian	AD 80-100			shield decoration	B2.13
cuirass statue	trophy	Rome/I		c. 100 AD	Germany/ Chatti		shield decoration	Schröder 1993, cat. 42
relief	Roma seated on pile of arms	Rome, Villa Albani/I		early C2 AD?			shield decoration	Bol 1989, 22-25 no. 1
column	pile of arms	Rome, Trajan's Column/I	Trajan	AD 108-113	Dacia	Dacian Wars	shield decoration	B1.12
cuirass statue	barbarian	Pula (Istria/HR)	?Hadrian					Stemmer 1978, III 23; Vermeule 1960, 172

object	image type	place/code	period	date	area/group	event	notes	reference
distance slab	barbarian	Summerston (Glasgow/UK)	A. Pius	AD 140-142	Scotland	conquest of southern Scotland	?torc on one barbarian (from first-hand inspection; not in published sources)	Keppie/Arnold 1984, no. 137
balteus fittings	combat	Gela (Sicilia/I)		C2?				Ortiz 1994, no. 233
battle sarcophagus	combat	Rome, Ammendola/I	late Antonine	AD 150-170	Gauls	historical battles versus Gauls		Reinach 1968, 205; Jones 1926, 74f.; Andreae 1956, no. 3
battle sarcophagus	combat	Bergsten coll'n/?Italy	late Antonine					Christies South Kensington 21.4.1999, lot 192
battle sarcophagus	combat	Rome, Via Tiburtina/I	late Antonine		Gauls	historical battles versus Gauls		Bertinetti/de Lachenal/Palma 1985, 268-270; Andreae 1956, no. 4
battle sarcophagus	combat	Rome, Villa Doria Pamphilj/I	late Antonine		Gauls	historical battles versus Gauls		Calza et al. 1977, no. 232; Andreae 1956, no. 8
battle sarcophagus	combat	Rome, Giustiniani/I	late Antonine		Gauls	historical	not certain; details not clear	Reinach 1968, 260; Andreae 1956, no. 14
block	Victory & pile of arms	Durrës/Dyrrachium (Durrës county/AL)	late Antonine	AD 161-192		?Marcomannic war	shield decoration	Polito 1998, 212f.
sarcophagus fragment?	combat	La Granja/E		late C2?	Gauls			Reinach 1912, 191; Bienkowski 1908, pl. IIb
block	weapons frieze	St-Cyr-sur-Mer/Tauroentum (dép. Var/F)					torc on cuirass	Espérandieu I 46
torso	barbarian	now in Rhode Island/USA						Ridgway 1972, 92f. 209
relief	barbarian	British Museum						BM G&R 1958 2-13 1
terracotta figurine	barbarian	Vindonissa (Kanton Aargau/CH)						Simonett 1947, pl. 42a

object	image type	place/code	period	date	area/group	event	notes	reference
statuette	barbarian	British Museum						Walters 1899, no. 819; Stead n. d., no. 113
portrait	young man with torc	Bologna (reg. Emilia-Romagna/I)						Vitali/Minarini 2001

Tab. 89 Depictions of torcs in Roman triumphal art.

object	image type	place/code	period	date	area/group	event	motif	reference
coin	attribute			209-208 BC	?Cisalpine Gaul	?campaigns in Cisalpine Gaul	wheel	RRC 79
coin	warrior			118 BC	Transalpine Gaul	conquest of Transalpine Gaul	chariot	RRC 282
coin	warrior			48 BC	Britain	Caesar's British invasion	chariot	RRC 448/2
coin	trophy			44 BC	?Britain	Caesar's British invasion	chariot	RRC 482
tomb block	weapons frieze	Padova (reg. Veneto/I)		AD 1-30			wheel	B2.8
coin	triumphal arch	RIC Claudius 98, 114	Claudius	AD 41-50	?Germany	?Drusus' campaigns	wheel	BMC 121-123, 188
funerary urn lid	weaponry	Rome, Museo Gregoriano/I	Claudius			invasion of Britain?	wheel	Sinn 1991, no. 143
wall paintings, *schola armaturarum*	trophies	Pompeii (reg. Campania/I)		AD 1-79?		Julio-Claudian or Flavian activities in Britain?	chariot	Jacobelli 2003, 68; Picard 1957, 221 f.; Richmond 1963
terracotta plaque	trophy		Domitian	AD 83-85	Germany/Chatti?	possible Caledonian link?	wheel	C4.4
pillars	weapons frieze	Rome, *armilustrium*/I	late Flavian	AD 80-100		universalising	wheel	B1.7
funerary urn of L. Arruntius Anthus	weaponry	Louvre	late Flavian			Agricola in N Britain?	wheel	Sinn 1987, no. 432
tomb frieze	weapons frieze	Parma (reg. Emilia-Romagna/I)	late Flavian	AD 80-100		Agricola in N Britain?	wheel	B2.13

object	image type	place/code	period	date	area/group	event	motif	reference
frieze	weapons frieze	Capua (reg. Campania/I)	late Flavian - early Trajanic	AD 80-100		universalising	wheel	Polito 1998, 205
funerary urn	trophy	Villamagna (prov. Chieti/I)	Trajan-Hadrian	AD 96-138		Hadrianic activities in Britain?	chariot	Sinn 1987, 115 no. 94; Lovatelli 1900
funerary urn of Hermippus	pile of arms	Bologna (reg. Emilia-Romagna/I)	Hadrian			Hadrianic activities in Britain?	wheel	Sinn 1987, no. 552; Brizzolara 1986, 75 f.
inscription with frieze	trophy & weapons frieze	Cumae (reg. Campania/I)		AD 119-150		Hadrian or A. Pius in Britain?	wheel	B2.16
decorated pillars	weapons frieze	Merida, temple of Mars (com. Extremadura/E)		AD 100-150		universalising	chariot, wheel	B5.2
frieze	weapons frieze	Nemi (reg. Lazio/I)		late C2 - early C3		generic Roman victory	wheel	Polito 2003
ivory object	spoliae	British Museum					chariot	BM GR 1873.8-20.654, 655

Tab. 90 Depictions of chariots in Roman triumphal art.

object	image type	place/code	period	date	area/group	event	notes	reference
cavalry tombstone	cavalryman riding down foe	Mainz-Zahlbach (D)	Flavian	AD 70-75	Germans		sica	Schleiermacher 1984, no. 20
architectural frieze	trophy	Rome, Palace of Flavians/I	Domitian	AD 90-92	Germany & Dacia	Domitian's campaigns		B1.4
trophy capital	trophy	Rome, S. Lorenzo/I	Flavian	AD 89-96	Germans/Dacians	Domitian's German/Dacian triumph		B1.6
standard disc	general, pile of arms & captive	Niederbieber (Lkr. Neuwied/D)		AD 1-100		German campaigns of Augustus/Tiberius or Domitian	curved sword	C3.5
coin	captive		Trajan	AD 103-111	Dacia	Dacian Wars		BMC Trajan 145-149. 175-184
coin	trophy		Trajan	AD 103-111	Dacia	Dacian Wars		BMC Trajan 250f. 355-370
coin	standing captive & weapons		Trajan	AD 103-111	Dacia	Dacian Wars		BMC Trajan 381-384

object	image type	place/code	period	date	area/group	event	notes	reference
coin	captive seated on pile of arms		Trajan	AD 103-111	Dacia	Dacian Wars		BMC Trajan 385-389
coin	captive seated on pile of arms		Trajan	AD 103-111	Dacia	Dacian Wars		BMC Trajan 390-394
coin	trophy, captive & pile of arms		Trajan	AD 104-111	Dacia	Dacian Wars		BMC Trajan 785-792. 887f. 928f.
coin	Victory & trophy		Trajan	AD 104-111	Dacia	Dacian Wars		BMC Trajan 817-821. 897f. 941
coin	Pax burning arms		Trajan	AD 104-111	Dacia	Dacian Wars		BMC Trajan 892
coin	trophy		Trajan	AD 104-111	Dacia	Dacian Wars		BMC Trajan 905-910
coin	captive seated on pile of arms		Trajan	AD 104-111	Dacia	Dacian Wars		BMC Trajan p195
coin	weaponry		Trajan	AD 104-111	Dacia	Dacian Wars		BMC Trajan 948
coin	weaponry		Trajan	AD 104-111	Dacia	Dacian Wars		BMC Trajan 949-953
historical reliefs	combat scenes	Rome, Great Trajanic Frieze/I	Trajan	AD 106-112	Dacia	Dacian Wars		B1.11.3
column	pile of arms	Rome, Trajan's Column/I	Trajan	AD 108-113	Dacia	Dacian Wars		B1.12
frieze	weapons frieze	currently in Potsdam/D	Trajan	AD 108-117	Dacia	Dacian Wars		Polito 1991
trophy monument	weapons frieze	Adamklissi (jud. Dobrogea/RO)	Trajan	AD 109	lower Danube	warfare on lower Danube		Polito 1998, 212; Richmond 1982, 50. 52
honorary arch	weapons frieze	Benevento (reg. Campania/I)	Trajan	AD 114-118	Dacia & Germany	Trajan's successes in Dacia & Germany		B2.15
plaque	pile of arms	Gârla Mare (jud. Mehedinti/RO)	Trajan	AD 105-117	Dacians	Dacian Wars		Popescu 1998, 310 no. 283; Pop 2000; **fig. 176d**
blocks	weapons frieze	Sorrento (reg. Campania/I)	late Trajan-early Hadrian	AD 110-125		?Dacian Wars		Polito 1998, 201f.
tombstone of T. Claudius Maximus	combat	Grammeni, Philippi (Macedonia/GR)	late Trajan-early Hadrian	AD 115-130	Dacian	death of Decebalus	small	Speidel 1970
statue base of Sextus Vibius Gallus	combat	Amastris (Bartin/TUR)	Trajan/Hadrian?		Dacians?		Maier 2007 argued for a late C3 date	Mendel 1966, 1155; Vermeule 1968, 412. 490

object	image type	place/code	period	date	area/group	event	notes	reference
block	trophy	Hadrian's Villa, Tivoli (reg. Lazio/I)		AD 117-125	Dacia & ?Parthia	Trajan's victories		B1.13.1
coin	personification		Hadrian	AD 118-122	Dacia			BMC Hadrian p428, p485
coin	personification		Hadrian	AD 134-138	Dacia			BMC Hadrian 1735-1746
coin	trophy		Hadrian	AD 134-138	Dacia			BMC Hadrian 784
coin	personification		A. Pius	AD 139	Dacia			BMC A. Pius p189
decorated pillars	weapons frieze	Mérida, temple of Mars (com. Extremadura/E)		AD 100-150		universalising?		B5.2
battle sarcophagus	combat	Rome, Via Portuense/Viale Gianicolense/I	mid Antonine	AD 160-180			sica	McCann 1978, no. 18
coin	Armenia & pile of arms	BMC M. Aurelius 234f. 239-241. 271-276. 298f. 365-367	M. Aurelius	AD 162-165	Armenia	Victories in Armenia		
battle sarcophagus	combat	Rome?, Ludovisi (small)/I	late Antonine	AD 170-190		Marcomannic wars		Reinach 1968, 330; Giuliano 1979-1995, vol. I/5, 49-53; Andreae 1956, no. 5
triumphal frieze	triumph, trophy & captives	Rome, Ludovisi/I	late Antonine?			?Parthian triumph of L. Verus	Stefan (2005, 448f.) argued Domitianic date	Reinach 1968, 289; Giuliano 1979-1995, cat. I/5 195-8
	trophy & captive		M. Aurelius	AD 172-174	Danube	Marcomannic War	?curved sword	BMC M. Aurelius 578-582. 595-600
battle sarcophagus	combat & trophies	Palermo (reg. Sicilia/I)	late Antonine	AD 175-190	Germans	Marcomannic Wars	falx?	B2.19
coin	Britannia		Commodus	AD 183-184	UK	victory in Britain	curved sword	BMC Commodus p796
coin	Caracalla & trophy		Severus	AD 196-198		generic reference to Caracalla's prowess	curved sword	BMC Severus 206-213. 458. 608
sculpture	weaponry	Birdoswald (Cumbria/UK)		AD 219	Dacians	auxiliary cohort of Dacians		RIB 1914; Coulston/Phillips 1988, no. 266
sculpture	weaponry	Birdoswald (Cumbria/UK)		early C3 AD	Dacians	auxiliary cohort of Dacians		RIB 1909; Coulston/Phillips 1988, no. 267
capital	trophy	Falerii (prov. Viterbo/I)						von Mercklin 1962, no. 632

Tab. 91 Depictions of the falx in Roman triumphal art.

object	image type	place/code	period	date	area/group	event	notes	reference
block	weapons frieze	Antikythara (Kythera/GR)		100-70 BC				Polito 1998, 178
block	weapons frieze	Arles (dép. Bouches-du-Rhône/F)	Augustus-Tiberius	30 BC - AD 30				Espérandieu IX 6715
column	trophies etc.	Baia (reg. Campania/I)	Augustus					Campbell 2004. no. 70 f.
standard disc	general, pile of arms & captive	Niederbieber (Lkr. Neuwied/D)		AD 1-100	Germany	German campaigns of Augustus/Tiberius or Domitian		C3.5
pillars	weapons frieze	Rome, armilustrium/I	Late Flavian - early Trajan	AD 80-100		universalising		B1.7
frieze	trophy	Rome, Palace of Flavians/I	Domitian	AD 90-92	Germany & Dacia	Domitian's campaigns		B1.4
tombstone of C. Iulius Euphrosynus	weapons frieze	San Albano Stuva (reg. Piemonte/I)		late C1				Mercando/Paci 1998, pl. LXXXIII no. 74
frieze	weapons frieze	Potsdam/D (Italian find)	Trajan	AD 108-117	Dacia	Dacian Wars		Polito 1991
column	pile of arms	Rome, Trajan's Column/I	Trajan	AD 108-113	Dacia	Dacian Wars		Poltio 1998, 192-195
arch keystone	personification & weapons	Rome, Trajan's Forum/I	Trajan	AD 106-112	Dacia	Trajan's Dacian Wars		B1.11.1
frieze	weapons frieze	Potsdam/D (an Italian find)	Trajan	AD 108-117	Dacia	Dacian Wars	?axe	Polito 1991
honorary arch	weapons frieze	Benevento (reg. Campania/I)	Trajan	AD 114-118	Dacia & Germany	Trajan's successes in Dacia & Germany		B2.15
panels	weapons frieze	Rome (in Capitoline Museum & BM)	?Trajan					Polito 1998, 145-147; Smith 1904, no. 2620
blocks	weapons frieze	Sorrento (reg. Campania/I)	late Trajan - early Hadrian	AD 110-125		?Dacian Wars		Polito 1998, 201 f.
block	trophy	Hadrian's Villa, Tivoli (reg. Lazio/I)		AD 117-125	Dacian, ?Parthian			B1.13.1
pedestal base	weapons frieze	Frascati (reg. Lazio/I)	Antonine	AD 138-192	Germans?	Marcomannic War?		B2.18
arch	weapons frieze	Reims (dép. Grand Est/F)	Antonine?					Lefèvre/Legros 1985

object	image type	place/code	period	date	area/group	event	notes	reference
frieze	weapons frieze	Rome, Hadrianeum/I	A. Pius	AD 145		personified provinces		Jones 1926, 3-14; Polito 1998, 198
coin	pile of arms		M. Aurelius	AD 175-176	Danube	Marcomannic War		BMC M. Aurelius 1548
frieze	weapons frieze	St Bertrand de Comminges (dép. Haute-Garonne/F)	?late Antonine	?AD 170-190			also gladiatorial weapons	Polito 1998, 220; Walter 1993, 85 f.
battle sarcophagus	combat & trophies	Palermo (reg. Sicilia/I)	late Antonine	AD 175-190	Germany	Marcomannic Wars	?axe	B2.19
column	combat, trophy	Rome, Column of Marcus Aurelius/I	Commodus	AD 180-192	Danube	Marcomannic War		B1.14
frieze	weapons frieze	Rome/I		C2?				Vermeule 1958, fig. 14, 200f.
pedestal base	Victory, trophy & captive	Rome, Tetrarchic Arch/I		AD 293-304	Britain/Germany?	see B1.16		B1.16
frieze	trophy & weapons frieze	Saint-Just de Valcabrère (dép. Haute-Garonne/F)				both E & W?	also gladiatorial weapons	Espérandieu XI 7665
block	weapons frieze	Bordeaux (dép. Gironde/F)		pre-C3 (re-used then)				Zieglé 2000

Tab. 92 Depictions of single-bladed axes in Roman triumphal art.

object	image type	place/code	period	date	area/group	event	notes	reference
pillars	weapons frieze	Rome, *armilustrium*/I	late Flavian - early Trajan	AD 80-100		universalising		B1.7
column	pile of arms	Rome, Trajan's Column/I	Trajan	AD 108-113	Dacia	Dacian Wars		B1.12
honorary arch	weapons frieze	Benevento (reg. Campania/I)	Trajan	AD 114-118	Dacia & Germany	Trajan's successes in Dacia & Germany		B2.15
panels	weapons frieze	Rome (Capitoline Museum, BM)	?Trajan					Polito 1998, 145-147; Smith 1904, no. 2620
stucco	trophy	Tivoli (reg. Lazio/I)	Hadrian	AD 120-138	Dacia (& Germany?)	Dacian Wars / ?Hadrian in Germany		B1.13.2
coin	personification		A. Pius	AD 139	Dacia			BMC A. Pius 1187
frieze	weapons frieze	Rome, Hadrianeum/I	A. Pius	AD 145		personified provinces		Jones 1926, 3-14; Polito 1998, 198
decorated pillars	weapons frieze	Mérida, temple of Mars (com. Extremadura/E)		AD 100-150		universalising		B5.2
frieze	weapons frieze	Bologna/unprovenanced (reg. Emilia-Romagna/I)	Antonine	AD 138-192		E & W		Polito 1998, 211
pedestal base	weapons frieze	Frascati (reg. Lazio/I)	Antonine	AD 138-192	Germans?	Marcomannic War?		B2.18
battle sarcophagus	combat	Rome, Giustiniani/I	late Antonine					Reinach 1968, 261; Andreae 1956 no. 15
column	combat, trophy	Rome, Column of Marcus Aurelius/I	Commodus	AD 180-192		Marcomannic War		B1.14
coin		BMC Severus 206-213, 458, 608	Severus	AD 196-198		generic ref to Caracalla's prowess	?draco	Caracalla & trophy
frieze	weapons frieze	Rome/I		C2?				Vermeule 1958, fig. 14, 200f.

Tab. 93 Depictions of draco standards in Roman triumphal art.

object	image type	place/code	period	date	area/group	event	animal	reference
coin	control mark			62 BC		control mark	animal	RRC 412
coin	trophy			51 BC	Gaul, Spain, East?	various victories	boar	RRC 437
tomb	trophy	Rome, tomb of Caecilia Metella/I	early Augustan	30-20 BC	Gaul	Gallic War	boar, ?wolf	B1.1
tomb?	weapons frieze	Avignon (dép. Vaucluse/F)	Augustus	30-20 BC	Gaul		boar	Espérandieu I 234
tomb	weapons frieze	Narbonne (dép. Aude/F)	Augustus	40 BC - AD 20	Gaul		boar	Espérandieu I 695
tomb	weapons frieze	Narbonne (dép. Aude/F)	Augustus	40 BC - AD 20	Gaul		boar	Espérandieu I 737
blocks	weapons frieze	Biot (dép. Alpes-Maritimes/F)	Augustus	15 BC - AD 30	Gaul	Gallic War?	boar	B3.5
cuirass statue	barbarian	Copenhagen/DK	Augustus				boar	Cadario 2004, 135 f. pl. XVIII 4
glass plaque	trophy, captive & pile of arms	Italy		50 BC - AD 25	Gaul		boar	C4.5
glass plaque	pile of arms	Italy		50 BC - AD 25			boar, animal	Froehner 1903, pl. LII, 1 no. 469
cuirass statue of Augustus	personifications, trophy	Rome, Prima Porta/I	Augustus	20-10 BC	Gaul & Spain	Augustus' campaigns, recovery of Parthian standards	boar	B1.2
cuirass statue	barbarian	Copenhagen/DK, Glyptotek (from Rome?)	Augustus		Gaul?		boar	Bienkowski 1928, 60 fig. 109; Vermeule 1960, no. 14
arch	trophies & piles of arms	Orange (dép. Vaucluse/F)	Augustus-Tiberius	25 BC - AD 25	Gaul & Germany		boar	B3.4
funerary sculpture	pile of arms	Rome, Bovillae/I	Augustus-Tiberius	AD 15-20	Gaul	Gaulish campaigns, Actium	wolf, boar	B1.3
gladiator's helmet	weapons frieze	Herculaneum (reg. Campania/I)		AD 1-79			?bull	C3.2
coin	attribute		Galba	AD 68	Spain & Gaul	evoking Spain & Gaul	boar sceptre	RIC Galba 15-18, 109, 154; BMC 170 f. 228; Mazzini 1957, pl. LVIII, p. 73
coin	attribute		Civil War/ Gallic Revolt	AD 69-70	Gaul/lower Germany	Batavian revolt	boar	RIC Civil War 132; Martin 1974, no. 2

object	image type	place/code	period	date	area/group	event	animal	reference
coin	attribute		Civil War/Gallic Revolt	AD 69-70	Gaul/lower Germany	Batavian revolt	boar	Martin 1974, no. 5; RIC Civil War 131
statue	trophy, captives & pile of arms	Gabii (reg. Lazio/I)	Domitian	AD 83-89	Germany	Domitian's campaigns versus Chatti	?boar	B2.12
pillars	weapons frieze	Rome, *armilustrium*/I	late Flavian - early Trajan	AD 80-100		universalising	boar, wolf, bull	B1.7
frieze	weapons frieze	Capua (reg. Campania/I)	late Flavian - early Trajan	AD 80-100		universalising	animal	Polito 1998, 205
pedestal base	trophy & pile of arms	Rome, Maddalena/I	Domitian	AD 83-105	Germany	?Domitian's campaigns versus Chatti	wolf	B1.9
frieze	weapons frieze	Pozzuoli (reg. Campania/I)	Flavian - Trajan	c. 85-105			boar	B2.14
frieze/panel	weapons frieze	Mérida theatre (com. Extremadura/E)	Trajan	AD 105	?Germany		wolf	B5.1
frieze	Roma seated on pile of arms	Rome, Villa Albani/I		early C2			wolf	Bol 1989, 22-25 no. 1
arch	weapons frieze	Benevento (reg. Campania/I)	Trajan	AD 114-118	Dacia & Germany	Trajan's successes in Dacia & Germany	animal	B2.15
inscription with frieze	trophy & weapons frieze	Cumae (reg. Campania/I)		AD 119-150			wolf	B2.16
decorated pillars	weapons frieze	Mérida, temple of Mars (com. Extremadura/E)		AD 100-150		universalising	boar	B5.2
funerary urn of Hermippus	pile of arms	Bologna (reg. Emilia-Romagna/I)	Hadrian				boar, bull	Sinn 1987, no. 552; Brizzolara 1986, 75 f.
block	Victory & pile of arms	Durrës/Dyrrachium (Durrës county/AL)	late Antonine	AD 161-192		?Marcomannic War	animal	Polito 1998, 212 f.
battle sarcophagus	combat	Rome, Portonaccio/I	late Antonine	AD 175-190		Marcomannic War	boar	B1.15
standing barbarian	trophy	Rome, Vatican/I		C2 AD	Gaul/Germany		boar	Lippold 1956, 33 pl. 28/605

object	image type	place/code	period	date	area/group	event	animal	reference
frieze	weapons frieze	Rome, Baths of Caracalla/I	Caracalla	AD 212–217	?Germany		boar (on shield)	Polito 1998, 199 f.
frieze	weapons frieze	Nemi (reg. Lazio/I)		late C2 - early C3	generic Roman victory		wolf (Roman? - on vexillum)	Polito 2003
relief	goddess & boar standard	Betting-les-Saint-Avold (dép. Moselle/F)			Gaul		boar	Espérandieu 4439; Moreau 1995, 24, fig. 14
relief	trophy	Rome (Museo Gregoriano Etrusco)/I					boar	Helbig 1963, 467 f. no. 603

Tab. 94 Depictions of animal standards in Roman triumphal art.

object	image type	place/code	period	date	area/group	event	armour	reference
stucco	weapons frieze	Rome, House of Augustus/I	Augustus	c. 28 BC			ring	Polito 1998, 129-131
block	weapons frieze	Falerii Novi (prov. Viterbo/I)	early Augustus	30-1 BC			scale	fig. 365
tomb block	weapons frieze	Trasacco (L'Aquila/I)		AD 1-30			scale	Polito 1998, 165 f.
cameo	triumph & captive	The Hague, library (Zuid-Holland/NL)	Claudius		UK	Claudius' British victories	scale	Reinach 1912, 427
block	weapons frieze	Castelgandolfo (reg. Lazio/I)	Domitian	AD 81-96			scale	Polito 1998, 192
»Trophies of Marius«	trophies	Rome, Capitoline/I	Domitian	AD 83-96	Germany/Dacia	Campaigns in Germany & Dacia	scale	Grisanti 1977
column	pile of arms	Rome, Trajan's Column/I	Trajan	AD 108-113	Dacia	Dacian Wars	scale, ring	B1.12
frieze	weapons frieze	Potsdam/D (Italian find)	Trajan	AD 108-117	Dacia	Dacian Wars	scale	Polito 1991
blocks	weapons frieze	Sorrento (reg. Campania/I)	late Trajan - early Hadrian	AD 110-125		?Dacian Wars	scale	Polito 1998, 201 f.
block	weapons frieze	Corinth (GR)	Trajan	AD 108-117		?Dacian wars	scale	Polito 1998, 212
panels	weapons frieze	Rome/I (Capitoline Museums & BM)	Trajan?				scale	Polito 1998, 145-147; Smith 1904, no. 2620
frieze	weapons frieze	Rome, Sant'Urbano alla Caffarella/I	Antonine	AD 138-192			scale	Polito 1998, 198 f.
coin	pile of arms		M. Aurelius	AD 175-176	Danube	Marcomannic War	scale	A5.4
gate	weapons frieze	Pisidian Antioch (Isparta prov./TR)	late Antonine	AD 160-200			scale	Robinson 1927; Polito 1998, 216 f.
silver dish	weapons frieze	Marengo (reg. Piedmont/I)	?late Antonine				ring	Mercando n. d., fig. 16
pedestal base	Victory, trophy & captive	Rome, Tetrarchic Arch/I		AD 293-304	Britain/Germany?	debated	scale	B1.16
pedestals	weaponry	Pisidian Antioch (Isparta prov./TR)	?	?			scale	Robinson 1927
block	weapons frieze	Vienne (dép. Isère/F)					ring	Espérandieu III 2643
statuette	barbarian	BM bronze 821					ring	Walters 1899, no. 821

Tab. 95 Depictions of barbarian armour in Roman triumphal art.

object	image type	place/code	period	date	event	clothing	hat/helmet	reference
triumphal frieze	trophy	Rome, temple of Apollo Sosianus/I	Augustus	c. 25 BC	Panonnian-Dalmatian triumph		hat?	Strong 1961, fig. 31; Künzl 1988a, 123 fig. 43b
arch	captives & pile of arms	Glanum (dép. Bouches-du-Rhône/F)	Augustus	20 BC - AD 20			helmet	B3.3
cuirass statue	trophy	Solin/Salona (Dalmatia/HR)	Tiberius				hat	Stemmer 1978, V 1
arch	trophies & piles of arms	Orange (dép. Vaucluse/F)	Augustus - Tiberius	15 BC - AD 27			hat	B3.4
tomb block	weapons frieze	Trasacco (L'Aquila/I)		AD 1-30			helmet	Polito 1998, 165f.; Strazzulla 2001
trophy monument	trophy	St Bertrand de Comminges (dép. Haute-Garonne/F)	early Augustan	30-20 BC		cloak		Ganz 2004; Walter 1993, nos 89-92
helmet cheekpiece	Victory & trophy	Vize (Marmara/TR)		AD 1-30	?Germany		hat	Born/Junkelmann 1997, fig. 17
tomb blocks	weapons frieze	Turin (reg. Piemonte/I)	Augustus - Claudius	AD 1-60	British conquest?		helmet	B2.6
gladiator's helmet	trophy & captives	Pompeii (reg. Campania/I)	Augustus	20 BC - AD 14	Return of Parthian standards; German/Gaulish campaigns		helmet	C3.1
gladiator's helmet	weapons frieze	Pompeii (reg. Campania/I)		AD 1-79			helmet	C3.2
cuirass statue	trophy	Gabii (reg. Lazio/I)	Domitian	AD 83-89		tunic	hat	Stemmer 1978, I 9; Gergel 1988, 14 fig. 6; 1994, 199 fig. 12.10; Vermeule 1960, I 101
cuirass statue	trophy	Civitavecchia (reg. Lazio/I)	Domitian	AD 89-96	Domitian's campaigns		hat	Stemmer 1978, V 9; Vermeule 1960, I 88; Gergel 1994, 199-203
cuirass statue	trophy	London, Hampton Court/UK	Domitian	AD 89-96	Domitian's campaigns		hat	Gergel 1988, 16 fig. 10; Vermeule 1960, I 89
cuirass statue	trophy	Princeton/USA	Domitian		Domitian's German campaigns		hat	Gergel 1988, 11-12 fig. 2a-b; Padgett 2001, 27-33 (arguing for Neronian date)

object	image type	place/code	period	date	event	clothing	hat/helmet	reference
coin	trophy & captives		Domitian	AD 85-87	Victories over Chatti	cloak		BMC Domitian 294, 325f. 361. 372. 395
coin	Victory & trophy		Domitian	AD 85	Victories over Chatti	cloak		BMC Domitian 312. 367
pillars	weapons frieze	Rome, *armilustrium*/I	Late Flavian - early Trajan	AD 80-100	universalising		helmet	B1.7
architectural frieze	trophy	Rome, Palace of Flavians/I	Domitian	AD 90-92	Domitian's campaigns	cloak	hat	B1.4
statue	trophy, captives & pile of arms	Gabii (reg. Lazio/I)	Domitian	AD 83-89	Domitian's campaigns versus Chatti		helmet	B2.12
trophies	trophies	Rome, Capitoline, »Trophies of Marius«/I	Domitian	AD 83-96	Campaigns in Germany & Dacia	cloak		Grisanti 1977
trophy capital	trophy	Rome, S. Lorenzo/I	Flavian	AD 89-96	Domitian's German/Dacian triumph		hat	B1.6
cuirass statue	trophy	Rome (now in Prado)		c. 100 AD			helmet	Schroeder 1993, cat. 42
block	weapons frieze	Torres de Maquiz (prov. Jaén/E)		C1 AD			hat?	Baena del Alcazar/Beltran Fortes 2002, no. 114
frieze	trophy	Fiesole (reg. Toscano/I)	poss. Claudian??	C1 AD			helmet?	Schumacher 1935, no. 46
frieze	trophy	Saint-Romain-en-Gal (dép. Rhône/F)		late C1 AD		tunic		Terrer et al. 2003, 314. 317-320
frieze/panel	weapons frieze	Mérida theatre (com. Extremadura/E)	Trajan	AD 105			hat	B5.1
honorary arch	weapons frieze	Benevento (reg. Campania/I)	Trajan	AD 114-118	?Trajan's successes in Dacia & Germany		helmet	B2.15
stucco	trophy	Tivoli (reg. Lazio/I)		AD 117-138			helmet	B1.13.2
battle sarcophagus	combat	Ince Blundell collection	late Antonine		Dacian War		hat	Michaelis 1882, 399; Andreae 1956, no. 2; Bienkowski 1908, pl. VIIa

object	image type	place/code	period	date	event	clothing	hat/helmet	reference
battle sarcophagus	combat	Rome, Ammendola/I	late Antonine	c. AD 150-170	historical battles versus Gauls		helmet	Reinach 1968, 205; Jones 1926, 74f.; Andreae 1956, no. 3; Bienkowski 1908, pl. IV; Krierer 1995, pl. 24
cuirass statue	trophy	Susa (reg. Piedmont/I)	early Antonine				hat?	Stemmer 1978, VIII 7; Vermeule 1960, I 151
battle sarcophagus	combat	Rome, Villa Doria Pamphilj/I	late Antonine				helmet	Reinach 1968, 247; Calza et al. 1977, no. 232; Andreae 1956, no. 8
coin	trophy & captives		M. Aurelius	AD 175-177	Marcomannic War		hat?	BMC M. Aurelius 683-685. 741. 758
sarcophagus	trophy & captives, submission	Vatican, Cortile del Belvedere/I		c. AD 180			hat	Andreae 1977, no. 501; Andreae et al. 1998, pls 264-265
battle sarcophagus	combat	Bergsten collection	late Antonine				hat	Christies South Kensington 21.4.1999, lot 192
military sarcophagus	prisoners, trophies	Rome, vicolo Malabarba/I	late Antonine				hat	Bertinetti/de Lachenal/Palma 1985, 273-279
column	combat, trophy	Rome, Column of Marcus Aurelius/I	Commodus	AD 180-192	Marcomannic War	cloak	hat	B1.14
standing barbarian	trophy	Vatican, Scala Inv. 163/I		C2 AD		cloak		Lippold 1956, 33 pl. 28/605; Bienkowski 1928, 191 f.
funerary urn	combat & trophies	Paris, Cabinet des Médailles/F	Severus (could be late Antonine)	AD 180-220			hat?	Sinn 1987, no. 701
frieze	weapons frieze	Rome, Baths of Caracalla/I	Caracalla	AD 212-217			hat	Polito 1998, 199f.
pedestal base	Victory, trophy & captive	Rome, Arch of Diocletian/I	Tetrarchy	AD 293/294 or 303/304	see **Appendix 1**, B1.16	cloak	hat	B1.16
block	weapons frieze	Saint-Romain-en-Gal (dép. Rhône/F)				tunic?		Espérandieu III 2643; Terrer et al. 2003, 315
battle sarcophagus	combat	Pisa, Campo Santo (reg. Toscano/I)					hat	Reinach 1968, 120; Bienkowski 1908, pl. VIIb
frieze	trophy	Baiae (reg.Campania/I)				cloak	helmet	Schumacher 1935, no. 49
bronze trophy	trophy	Vienna/A					helmet	Pfahl 1993, 131 f. fig. 8

Tab. 96 Depictions of fur cloaks, hats or helmets in Roman triumphal art.

Appendix 5: Barbarian material culture in Roman iconography

BIBLIOGRAPHY

ANCIENT SOURCES

C. Julius Caesar, De Bello Gallico (The Gallic War) (S. A. Handford [trans.], London 1951).

Cassius Dio, Roman History, books 50-56 (I. Scott-Kilvert [trans.], London 1987).

Diodorus Siculus (translation taken from Tierney 1960).

Eustathius Archiepiscopi Thessalonicensis, Commentarii ad Homeri Iliadem Pertinentes ad fidem codicis laurentiani editit (van der Valk 1987 for the text; translation taken from Vendries 1999, 368).

Hesychius, Lexicon (translation taken from Vendries 1999, 369).

Lucan, Pharsalia (J. D. Duff [trans.], London 1922).

Pausanias, Description of Greece (J. G. Frazer [trans.], London 1898).

Plutarch, Fall of the Roman Republic: six lives by Plutarch (R. Warner [trans.], London 1972).

Polybius, The Histories (W. R. Paton [trans.], London 1922).

Suetonius, The Twelve Caesars (R. Graves [trans.], London 1957).

Tacitus, Annals (M. Grant [trans.], The Annals of Imperial Rome, Harmondsworth 1959).

Tacitus, Germania (H. Mattingly / S. A. Handford [trans.], The Agricola and the Germania, Harmondsworth 1970).

Tacitus, Histories (K. Wellesley [trans.], Harmondsworth 1964).

ABBREVIATED REFERENCES

CIL: Corpus Inscriptionum Latinarum (Berlin).

CSIR: Corpus Signorum Imperii Romani (Corpus of Sculpture of the Roman World).

DES: Discovery and Excavation in Scotland (Edinburgh).

DNB: Dictionary of National Biography, vols 1-63 (London 1885-1900).

LIMC: Lexicon Iconographicum Mythologiae Classicae (Zürich, München, various dates).

REFERENCES

Adam 1996: A.-M. Adam, Le fibule di tipo celtico nel Trentino. Patrimonio Storico e Artistico del Trentino 19 (Trento 1996).

2006: A.-M. Adam, Dépôts d'objets métalliques du second âge du Fer dans le nord-est de l'Italie et les Alpes orientales. In: G. Bataille / J.-P. Guillaumet (eds), Les dépôts métalliques au second âge du Fer en Europe tempérée. La Collection Bibracte 11 (Glux-en-Glenne 2006) 135-145.

Adkins/Adkins 1996: L. Adkins / R. A. Adkins, Dictionary of Roman religion (New York 1996).

Adler 2003: W. Adler, Der Halsring von Männern und Göttern. Saarbrücker Beiträge zur Altertumskunde 78 (Bonn 2003).

Aitchison 1988: N. B. Aitchison, Roman wealth, native ritual: coin hoards within and beyond Roman Britain. World Archaeology 20/2, 1988, 270-284.

Albrethsen 1987: P. H. Albrethsen, Carnyx. En keltisk krigstrompet som møntmotiv og romersk sejrstrofæ. Nordisk Numismatisk Unions Medlemsblad 5, 1987, 102-123.

Alcock 1989: E. A. Alcock, Pictish stones Class I: where and how? Glasgow Archaeological Journal 15, 1988-1989 (1989), 1-21.

Alcock 1987: L. Alcock, Pictish studies: present and future. In: Small 1987, 80-92.

Alexander 2000: D. Alexander, Excavation of Neolithic pits, later prehistoric structures and a Roman temporary camp along the line of the A96 Kintore and Blackburn Bypass, Aberdeenshire. Proceedings of the Society of Antiquaries of Scotland 130, 2000, 11-75.

2003: D. Alexander, The oblong fort at Finavon, Angus: an example of the over-reliance on the appliance of science? In: Ballin Smith/Banks 2003, 44-54.

2005: D. Alexander, Redcastle, Lunan Bay, Angus: the excavation of an Iron Age timber-lined souterrain and a Pictish barrow cemetery. Proceedings of the Society of Antiquaries of Scotland 135, 2005, 41-118.

Alexandrescu 2010: C.-G. Alexandrescu, Blasmusiker und Standartenträger im römischen Heer. Untersuchungen zur Benennung, Funktion und Ikonographie. Imagines 1 (Cluj-Napoca 2010).

Alföldi 1937: A. Alföldi, Zum Panzerschmuck der Augustusstatue von Primaporta. Mitteilungen des Deutschen Archäologischen Instituts, Römische Abteilung 52, 1937, 48-63.

1956: A. Alföldi, The main aspects of political propaganda on the coinage of the Roman Republic. In: R. A. G. Carson / C. H. V. Sutherland (eds), Essays in Roman coinage presented to Harold Mattingly (Oxford 1956) 63-95.

Allason-Jones 2010: L. Allason-Jones, A tale of four paterae. Archaeologia Aeliana (Fifth Series) 39, 2010, 427-432.

Allen 1958: D. Allen, Belgic coins as illustrations of life in the late pre-Roman Iron Age of Britain. Proceedings of the Prehistoric Society 24, 1958, 43-63.

1965: D. Allen, Les pièces d'argent minces du comté de Hampshire: nouveau lien entre la Gaule Celtique et la Grande-Bretagne. Revue Numismatique 1965, 79-93.

1968: D. Allen, The Celtic coins. In: I. Richmond, Hod Hill. 2: Excavations carried out between 1951 and 1958 for the Trustees of the British Museum (London 1968) 43-57.

1971a: D. Allen, The Sark hoard. Archaeologica 103, 1971, 1-31.

1971b: D. Allen, The ship on Gaulish coins. Antiquaries Journal 51, 1971, 96-99.

1973: D. Allen, Temples or shrines on Gaulish coins. Antiquaries Journal 53, 1973, 71-74.

1980: D. Allen, The coins of the ancient Celts (Edinburgh 1980).

1990: D. Allen, Catalogue of the Celtic coins in the British Museum with supplementary material from other British collections. II: Silver Coins of North Italy, South and Central France, Switzerland and South Germany (ed. J. Kent / M. Mays) (London 1990).

1995: D. Allen, Catalogue of the Celtic coins in the British Museum with supplementary material from other British collections. III: Bronze Coins of Gaul (ed. M. Mays) (London 1995).

Allen/Anderson 1903: J. R. Allen / J. Anderson, The early Christian monuments of Scotland (Edinburgh 1903).

Almagro 1959: M. Almagro, Mérida: guide de la ville et de ses monuments (Mérida 1959).

Alt/Jud 2007: K. W. Alt / P. Jud, Die Menschenknochen aus La Tène und ihre Deutung. In: Betschart 2007, 46-59.

Amandry 1978: P. Amandry, Consécration d'armes gauloises à Delphes. Bulletin de Correspondance Héllenique 102, 1978, 571-586.

Amandry/Burnett 2015: M. Amandry / A. Burnett, Roman provincial coinage. III: Nerva, Trajan and Hadrian (AD 96-138) (London 2015).

Amelung 1903: W. Amelung, Die Sculpturen des Vaticanischen Museums I (Berlin 1903).

1908: W. Amelung, Die Sculpturen des Vaticanischen Museums II (Berlin 1908).

Amy et al. 1962: R. Amy / P.-M. Duval / J. Formigé / J.-J. Hatt / A. Piganiol / C. Picard / G.-C. Picard, L'Arc d'Orange. Gallia, Supplement 15 (Paris 1962).

Anderson 1883: J. Anderson, Scotland in pagan times: the Iron Age (Edinburgh 1883).

1885: J. Anderson, Notice of a bronze caldron found with several small kegs of butter in a moss near Kyleakin, in Skye; with notes of other caldrons of bronze found in Scotland. Proceedings of the Society of Antiquaries of Scotland 19, 1884-1885 (1885), 309-315.

1904: J. Anderson, Note on a late Celtic armlet of bronze now presented to the National Museum; with notes on the identification of two other late Celtic armlets in the museum, and on a massive bronze armlet recently found in Sutherlandshire. Proceedings of the Society of Antiquaries of Scotland 38, 1903-1904 (1904), 460-466.

Anderson/Black 1888: J. Anderson / G. F. Black, Reports on local museums in Scotland obtained through Dr R H Gunning's Jubilee Gift to the Society of Antiquaries of Scotland. Proceedings of the Society of Antiquaries of Scotland 22, 1887-1888 (1888), 332-422.

Anderson 1987: J. C. Anderson, The date of the arch at Orange. Bonner Jahrbücher 187, 1987, 159-192.

Anderson 1938: R. S. G. Anderson, A bronze bowl from the Rhinns of Galloway. Proceedings of the Society of Antiquaries of Scotland 72, 1937-1938 (1938), 137-142.

Anderson/Rees 2006: S. Anderson / A. R. Rees, The excavation of a large double-chambered souterrain at Ardownie Farm Cottages, Monifieth, Angus. Tayside and Fife Archaeological Journal 12, 2006, 14-60.

Andersson 1995: K. Andersson, Romartida guldsmide i Norden. III: Övriga smycken, teknisk analys och verkstadsgrupper (Uppsala 1995).

Andreae 1956: B. Andreae, Motivgeschichtliche Untersuchungen zu den römischen Schlachtsarkophagen (Berlin 1956).

1991: B. Andreae, The image of the Celts in Etruscan, Greek and Roman art. In: Moscati et al. 1991, 61-69.

Andreae et al. 1998: B. Andreae / K. Anger / M. G. Granino / J. Köhler / P. Liverani / G. Spinola, Bildkatalog der Skulpturen des Vatikanischen Museums. II: Museo Pio Clementino Cortile Ottagono (Berlin, New York 1998).

Andronikos 1976: M. Andronikos, Delphi (Athen 1976).

Ankner/Moreau 1995: D. Ankner / J. Moreau, Analyses physico-chimiques. In: Moreau et al. 1995, 18-19.

Anon. 1879: Banff and neighbourhood: a popular handbook, topographical, historical and archaeological (Banff 1879).

1891: Beschreibung der antiken Skulpturen im Alten Museum (Berlin 1891).

1892: Catalogue of the National Museum of Antiquities of Scotland (Edinburgh 1892).

1904: Illustrated guide to burghs of Banff and Macduff and neighbouring villages with notes on local historical ruins (Banff 1904).

1911: Palace of History: catalogue of exhibits (Glasgow 1911).

1987: Les Gladiateurs [exhibition catalogue] (Lattes 1987).

Anselmino 1977: L. Anselmino, Terrecotte architettoniche dell'Antiquarium Comunale di Roma. 1: Le Antefisse (Roma 1977).

Armbruster 2011: B. Armbruster, Les aspects technologiques. In: Maniquet et al. 2011, 88-95.

Armit 1996: I. Armit, The archaeology of Skye and the Western Isles (Edinburgh 1996).

1997: I. Armit, Celtic Scotland (London 1997).

1999: I. Armit, The abandonment of souterrains: evolution, catastrophe or dislocation? Proceedings of the Society of Antiquaries of Scotland 129, 1999, 577-596.

2003: I. Armit, Towers in the north: the brochs of Scotland (Stroud 2003).

2006: I. Armit, Anatomy of an Iron Age roundhouse: the Cnip wheelhouse excavations, Lewis (Edinburgh 2006).

2012: I. Armit, Headhunting and the body in Iron Age Europe (Cambridge 2012).

Armit/Büster forthcoming: I. Armit / L. Büster, Darkness visible: the Sculptor's Cave, Covesea, from the Bronze Age to the Picts (Edinburgh forthcoming).

Armit/Ginn 2007: I. Armit / V. Ginn, Beyond the grave: human remains from domestic contexts in Iron Age Atlantic Scotland. Proceedings of the Prehistoric Society 73, 2007, 113-134.

Armit/McKenzie 2013: I. Armit / J. McKenzie, An inherited place: Broxmouth hillfort (Edinburgh 2013).

Armit/Dunwell/Hunter in prep.: I. Armit / A. Dunwell / F. Hunter, The hill at the empire's edge: excavations on Traprain Law, 1999-2011 (in prep.).

Armit et al. 2011: I. Armit / R. Schulting / C. J. Knüsel / I. A. G. Shepherd, Death, decapitation and display? The Bronze and Iron Age human remains from the Sculptor's Cave, Covesea, northeast Scotland. Proceedings of the Prehistoric Society 77, 2011, 251-278.

Arnold-Biucchi 1981: LIMC I (1981) 432-433 s.v. Aitolia (C. Arnold-Biucchi).

Arveiller-Dulong/Nenna 2011: V. Arveiller-Dulong / M.-D. Nenna, Les verres antiques du Musée du Louvre. III: Parures, instruments et éléments d'incrustation (Paris 2011).

Ashmore 2003: P. Ashmore, Orkney burials in the first millennium AD. In: Downes/Ritchie 2003, 35-50.

Atkinson/Piggott 1955: R. J. C. Atkinson / S. Piggott, The Torrs chamfrein. Archaeologia 96, 1955, 197-235.

Azzurri 1895: F. Azzurri, Osservazioni sul fregio marmoreo del sepolcro di Cecilia Metella. Bullettino della Commissione Archeologica Comunale di Roma 23, 1895, 14-25.

Babelon 1885-1886: E. Babelon, Description historique et chronologique des monnaies de la république romaine (Paris 1885-1886; reprinted Bologna 1978).

Babelon 1924: J. Babelon, Catalogue de la collection de Luynes. Monnaies Grecques. I: Italie et Sicile (Paris 1924).

Baena del Alcázar/Beltrán Fortes 2002: L. Baena del Alcázar / J. Beltrán Fortes, Esculturas romanas de la provincia de Jaén. CSIR España I, 2 (Murcia 2002).

Bailey 1980: D. M. Bailey, A catalogue of the lamps in the British Museum. II: Roman lamps made in Italy (London 1980).

1988: D. M. Bailey, A catalogue of the lamps in the British Museum. III: Roman provincial lamps (London 1988).

1995: D. M. Bailey, A Gaul from Egypt. In: Raftery/Megaw/Rigby 1995, 1-3.

1999: D. M. Bailey, A chalcedony barbarian. In: M. Henig / D. Plantzos (eds), Classicism to Neo-classicism. Essays dedicated to Gertrud Seidmann. BAR International Series 793 (Oxford 1999) 79-81.

Baines 1976: A. Baines, Brass instruments: their history and development (London 1976).

Baitinger 2011: H. Baitinger, Waffenweihungen in griechischen Heiligtümern. Monographien des RGZM 94 (Mainz 2011).

Ballin Smith 1994: B. Ballin Smith, Howe: four millennia of Orkney prehistory (Edinburgh 1994).

Ballin Smith/Banks 2003: B. Ballin Smith / I. Banks (eds), In the shadow of the brochs: the Iron Age in Scotland (Stroud 2003).

Banti 1980: A. Banti, Corpus Nummorum Romanorum: Monetazione Republicana. 2: Aufidia-Calpurnia (Firenze 1980).

Bar 2007: M. Bar, Sylloge Nummorum Graecorum, Belgique. I: La collection de bronzes grecs de Marc Bar (Bruxelles 2007).

Baray 2017: L. Baray, Celtes, Galates et Gaulois, mercenaires de l'antiquité (Paris 2017).

Baray et al. 1994: L. Baray / S. Deffressigne / C. Leroyer / I. Villemeur, Nécropoles protohistoriques du Sénonais. Documents d'Archéologie Française 44 (Paris 1994).

Barber et al. 1989: J. Barber / P. Halstead / H. James / F. Lee, An unusual Iron Age burial at Hornish Point, South Uist. Antiquity 63, 1989, 773-778.

Barbour 1902: J. Barbour, Notice of the excavation of the camp or earthwork at Rispain in Wigtownshire. Proceedings of the Society of Antiquaries of Scotland 36, 1901-1902 (1902), 621-626.

Barclay 1993: G. J. Barclay, The excavation of pit circles at Romancamp Gate, Fochabers, Moray, 1990. Proceedings of the Society of Antiquaries of Scotland 123, 1993, 255-268.

Barclay 1922: W. Barclay, Banffshire. Cambridge County Geographies (Cambridge 1922).

Barnes 1982: B. Barnes, Man and the changing landscape (Liverpool 1982).

Barral 2003: P. Barral, Le pays de Montbéliard à l'âge du Fer (Montbéliard 2003).

2007: P. Barral (ed.), Epomanduodurum, une ville chez les séquanes: bilan de quatre années de recherche à Mandeure et Mathay (Doubs). Gallia 64, 2007, 353-434.

2009: P. Barral, Les dépôts du sanctuaire de Mandeure. In: Honegger et al. 2009, 185-195.

2015: P. Barral (ed.), Nouvelles données sur l'agglomération antique d'Epomanduodurum (Mandeure et Mathay, Doubs). Gallia 72/2, 2015, 11-142.

Barral/Jaccottey/Pichot 2007: P. Barral / L. Jaccottey / V. Pichot, L'agglomération de Mandeure (Doubs) et son territoire au second âge du Fer. In: Barral et al. 2007, 139-160.

Barral et al. 2007: P. Barral / A. Daubigney / C. Dunning / G. Kaenel / M.-J. Roulière-Lambert (eds), L'âge du Fer dans l'arc jurassien et ses marges. Dépôts, lieux sacrés et territorialité à l'âge du Fer. Actes du XXIXe colloque international de l'AFEAF; Bienne, 5-8 mai 2005 (Besançon 2007).

de la Barrera Anton 1984: J. L. de la Barrera Anton, Los Capiteles Romanos de Mérida. Monografias Emeritenses 2 (Badajoz 1984).

Barrett 1991: A. A. Barrett, Claudius' British Victory arch in Rome. Britannia 22, 1991, 1-19.

Barrett 1989: J. C. Barrett, Food, gender and metal: questions of social reproduction. In: M. L. Stig Sørensen / R. Thomas (eds), The

Bronze Age – Iron Age transition in Europe. BAR International Series 483 (Oxford 1989) 304-320.

Barrow 1989: G. S. Barrow, The tribes of north Britain revisited. Proceedings of the Society of Antiquaries of Scotland 119, 1989, 161-163.

Bartholin 1697: C. Bartholin, De tibiis veterum (Amsterdam 1697; not seen; reference from de Lagoy 1849, 15).

Bastien 1967: P. Bastien, Le monnayage de bronze de Postume. Numismatique Romaine 3 (Wetteren 1967).

Bataille 2007: G. Bataille, L'équipement du guerrier. In: Barral 2007, 382-384.

Bateson 1981: J. D. Bateson, Enamel-working in Iron Age, Roman and sub-Roman Britain. BAR British Series 93 (Oxford 1981).

Bateson/Hall 2002: D. Bateson / M. Hall, Inchyra, Perthshire. In: R. Abdy / I. Leins / J. Williams (eds), Coin hoards from Roman Britain XI. Royal Numismatic Society: Special Publication 36 (London 2002) 119-120.

Bateson/Holmes 2013: J. D. Bateson / N. M. McQ. Holmes, Roman and medieval coins found in Scotland, 2006-10. Proceedings of the Society of Antiquaries of Scotland 143, 2013, 227-263.

Bayley 1998: J. Bayley, The production of brass in antiquity with particular reference to Roman Britain. In: P. Craddock (ed.), 2000 years of zinc and brass (revised edition). British Museum: Occasional Paper 50 (London 1998) 7-26.

Bean 2000: S. C. Bean, The coinage of the Atrebates and Regni. Studies in Celtic Coinage 4 (Oxford 2000).

Beard 1911: C. Beard, Arms and armour in Banff museum. Transactions of the Banffshire Field Club 1910-1911 (1911), 4-21.

Beard 2007: M. Beard, The Roman Triumph (Cambridge, Mass. 2007).

Beazley 1947: J. D. Beazley, Etruscan vase painting (Oxford 1947).

Becker/Joachim 2016: H. Becker / H.-E. Joachim, Alter Fund mit neuer Deutung. Teile von carnyx-Trompeten aus Abentheuer. Berichte aus den LVR-LandesMuseum Bonn 01/2016 (2016), 14-18.

Behn 1912: F. Behn, Die Musik im römischen Heere. Mainzer Zeitschrift 7, 1912, 36-47.

1954: F. Behn, Musikleben im Altertum und frühen Mittelalter (Stuttgart 1954).

Beliën 2009: P. Beliën, Authorized or tolerated? Some new perspectives on the GERMANVS INDVTILLI L. series. In: van Heesch/Heeren 2009, 31-51.

Bemmann/Bemmann 1998: G. Bemmann / J. Bemmann, Der Opferplatz von Nydam. Die Funde aus den älteren Grabungen: Nydam-I und Nydam-II (Neumünster 1998).

Bendinelli 1933: G. Bendinelli, Un arco imperiale eretto in »Augusto Taurinorum« nel 1º secolo dopo Cristo. Rassegna Mensile del Municipio di Torino 11, 1933, 3-20.

Benner Larsen 1987: E. Benner Larsen, SEM-identification and documentation of tool marks and surface textures on the Gundestrup cauldron. In: J. Black (ed.), Recent advances in the conservation and analysis of artifacts (London 1987) 393-408.

Bennett 2001: J. Bennett, Trajan: optimus princeps (London ²2001).

Benoit 1911: F. Benoit, L'architecture: antiquité (Paris 1911).

Benton 1931: S. Benton, The excavation of the Sculptor's Cave, Covesea, Morayshire. Proceedings of the Society of Antiquaries of Scotland 65, 1930-1931 (1931), 177-216.

Beny/Gunn 1981: R. Beny / P. Gunn, The churches of Rome (London 1981).

Berecki 2014: S. Berecki, The coexistence and interference of the late Iron Age Transylvanian communities. In: C. N. Popa / S. Stoddart (eds), Fingerprinting the Iron Age. Approaches to identity in the European Iron Age: integrating south-eastern Europe into the debate (Oxford 2014) 11-17.

Bergquist/Taylor 1987: A. Bergquist / T. Taylor, The origin of the Gundestrup cauldron. Antiquity 61, 1987, 10-24.

Bernhard/Lenz-Bernhard 2003: H. Bernhard / G. Lenz-Bernhard, Ein keltisches Metallhorn von der Limburg. Archäologie in der Pfalz: Jahresbericht 2001 (2003), 322-328.

Bertinetti/de Lachenal/Palma 1985: M. Bertinetti / L. de Lachenal / B. Palma, Museo Nazionale Romano. I: Le sculture. Catalogo delle Sculture esposte nelle Aule delle Terme 8, 2 (Roma 1985).

Bertrand 1894: A. Bertrand, Le vase ou chaudron de Gundestrup. Revue Archéologique (Third Series) 24, 1894, 152-169.

Bertrand 2005: I. Bertrand, Au-delà des apparences … Les restes d'un sanglier-enseigne en métal dans le sanctuaire du Gué-de-Sciaux (Antigny). Le Pays Chauvinois 43, 2005, 138-142.

2007: I. Bertrand, Le Gué-de-Sciaux, Antigny (Vienne). In: Bertrand/Maguer 2007, 113-114.

Bertrand/Maguer 2007: I. Bertrand / P. Maguer (eds), De pierre et de terre: les Gaulois entre Loire et Dordogne [exhibition catalogue]. Association des Publications Chauvinoises: Mémoire 30 (Chauvigny 2007).

Besly 1984: E. Besly, The gold coinage of the Gallic Empire. Numismatic Chronicle 144, 1984, 228-233.

Besques 1992: S. Besques, Catalogue raisonné des figurines et reliefs en terre-cuite grecs, étrusques et romains. 4, 2: Époques hellénistique et romaine, cyrénaïque, Egypte ptolémaïque et romaine, Afrique du Nord et Proche-Orient (Paris 1992).

Beswick et al. 1990: P. Beswick / M. R. Megaw / J. V. S. Megaw / P. Northover, A decorated late Iron Age torc from Dinnington, South Yorkshire. Antiquaries Journal 70, 1990, 16-33.

Betschart 2007: M. Betschart (ed.), La Tène: die Untersuchung – die Fragen – die Antworten. Die Publikation zum Stand der Forschung und ihrer Geschichte (Biel 2007).

Biborski 1994: M. Biborski, Typologie und Chronologie der Ringknaufschwerter. In: H. Friesinger / J. Tejral / A. Stuppner (eds), Markomannenkriege: Ursachen und Wirkungen. Spisy Archeologického Ústavu AV ČR Brno 1 (Brno 1994) 85-97.

Bieńkowski 1908: P. R. Bieńkowski, Die Darstellungen der Gallier in der hellenistischen Kunst (Wien 1908).

1928: P. Bieńkowski, Les Celtes dans les arts mineurs gréco-romains avec des recherches iconographiques sur quelques autres peuples barbares (Cracovie 1928).

Binding 1993: U. Binding, Studien zu den figürlichen Fibeln der Frühlatènezeit. Universitätsforschungen zur prähistorischen Archäologie 16 (Bonn 1993).

Birch/Cruickshanks/McKenzie in prep.: S. Birch / G. Cruickshanks / J. McKenzie, Excavations at High Pasture Cave, Skye (Oxford in prep.).

Birley 1987: A. Birley, Marcus Aurelius: a biography (revised edition) (London 1987).

1997: A. R. Birley, Hadrian: the restless emperor (London 1997).

2005: A. R. Birley, The Roman government of Britain (Oxford 2005).

Bishop/Coulston 2006: M. C. Bishop / J. C. N. Coulston, Roman military equipment from the Punic Wars to the fall of Rome (Oxford ²2006).

Black 1893: G. F. Black, Report on the antiquities found in Scotland, and preserved in the British Museum, &c., London, and in the Museum of Science and Art, Edinburgh. Proceedings of the Society of Antiquaries of Scotland 27, 1892-1893 (1893), 347-368.

1894: G. F. Black, Descriptive catalogue of loan collections of prehistoric and other antiquities from the shires of Berwick, Roxburgh, and Selkirk. Proceedings of the Society of Antiquaries of Scotland 28, 1893-1894 (1894), 321-342.

Black/Bisset 1894: G. F. Black / J. Bisset, Catalogue of Dr Grierson's museum, Thornhill (Thornhill 1894).

Blanchet 1971: A. Blanchet, Traité des Monnaies Gauloises (Bologna 1971 [reprint of 1905 edition]).

von Blanckenhagen 1940: P.-H. von Blanckenhagen, Flavische Architektur und ihre Dekoration; untersucht am Nervaforum (Berlin 1940).

Blankenfeldt 2009: R. Blankenfeldt, Keltiske elementer i tidlig germansk kunst. In: K. M. Boe / T. Capelle / C. Fischer (eds), Tollundmandens verden. Kontinentale kontakter i tidlig jernalder (Silkeborg 2009) 140-151.

Boardman/Brown/Powell 1971: J. Boardman / M. A. Brown / T. G. E. Powell (eds), The European community in later prehistory: studies in honour of C. F. C. Hawkes (London 1971).

Bol 1989: P. C. Bol (ed.), Forschungen zur Villa Albani: Katalog der antiken Bildwerke. I: Bildwerke im Treppenaufgang und im Piano nobile des Casino (Berlin 1989).

1998: P. C. Bol (ed.), Forschungen zur Villa Albani: Katalog der antiken Bildwerke. V: In den Gärten oder auf Gebäuden aufgestellte Skulpturen sowie die Masken (Berlin 1998).

Bommelaer 2015: J.-F. Bommelaer, Guide de Delphes: le site (Paris ²2015).

Bonini 1988: A. Bonini, I Cenomani. In: Tesori della Postumia. Archeologia e storia intorno a una grande strada romana alle radice dell'Europa [exhibition catalogue Cremona] (Milano 1988) 91-96.

Boon/Lewis 1976: G. C. Boon / J. M. Lewis (eds), Welsh antiquity. Essays mainly on prehistoric topics, presented to H. N. Savory upon his retirement as Keeper of Archaeology (Cardiff 1976).

Borangic 2006: C. Borangic, Falx dacica. I. Propunere pentru o tipologie a armelor curbe dacice. Nemus I/1-2, 2006, 47-105.

Borel 1655: P. Borel, Trésor de recherches et antiquités gauloises (Paris 1655; not seen; reference in de Lagoy 1849, 15).

Born/Junkelmann 1997: H. Born / M. Junkelmann, Römische Kampf- und Turnierrüstungen. Sammlung Axel Guttmann 6 (Mainz 1997).

Bosio et al. 1981: L. Bosio / G. del Fogolari / A. M. C. Bianchi / G. B. Pellegrini / F. Sartori / M. S. Bassignano / A. Prosdocimi / B. F. Tamaro, Padova Antica: da comunità paleoveneta a città Romano-Cristiana (Padova 1981).

Bossert 1999: M. Bossert, Die figürlichen Skulpturen des Legionslagers von Vindonissa. CSIR Schweiz I, 5 = Veröffentlichungen der Gesellschaft pro Vindonissa 16 (Brugg 1999).

Bossert-Radtke 1992: C. Bossert-Radtke, Die figürlichen Rundskulpturen und Reliefs aus Augst und Kaiseraugst. Forschungen in Augst 16 (Augst 1992).

Boube-Piccot 1966: C. Boube-Piccot, Trophée damasquiné sur une statue impériale de Volubilis. Bulletin d'Archéologie Marocaine 6, 1966, 189-278.

1969: C. Boube-Piccot, Les bronzes antiques du Maroc. I: La statuaire. Études et Travaux d'Archéologie Marocaine 4 (Rabat 1969).

Boudet 1995: R. Boudet, Le sanglier-enseigne gaulois de Soulac-sur-Mer: caractères, comparaisons et rôle social. In: Moreau et al. 1995, 43-53.

Bourne 2001: R. J. Bourne, Aspects of the relationship between the Central and Gallic empires in the mid to late third century AD with special reference to coinage studies. BAR International Series 963 (Oxford 2001).

Božič 1997: D. Božič, Spätrepublikanische Bronzegefäße oder Bronzehelme? Instrumentum 5, 1997, 1. 11.

Bradley 1990: R. Bradley, The passage of arms (Cambridge 1990).

Brailsford 1975a: J. W. Brailsford, Early Celtic masterpieces from Britain in the British Museum (London 1975).

1975b: J. W. Brailsford, The Polden Hill hoard. Proceedings of the Prehistoric Society 41, 1975, 222-234.

Brandt/Schmidt 1970: E. Brandt / E. Schmidt, Antike Gemmen in deutschen Sammlungen. I: Staatliche Münzsammlung München; 2: Italische Gemmen etruskisch bis römisch-republikanisch; Italische Glaspasten vorkaiserzeitlich (München 1970).

Brandt 2001: J. Brandt, Jastorf und Latène: Kultureller Austausch und seine Auswirkungen auf soziopolitische Entwicklungen in der vorrömischen Eisenzeit. Internationale Archäologie 66 (Rahden/Westf. 2001).

Breeze/Jones/Oltean 2015: D. Breeze / R. Jones / I. Oltean (eds), Understanding Roman frontiers. A celebration for Professor Bill Hanson (Edinburgh 2015).

Breitenstein/Schwabacher 1981: N. Breitenstein / W. Schwabacher, Sylloge Nummorum Graecorum. The Royal Collection of coins and medals, Danish National Museum. 1: Italy-Sicily (reissued West Mitford NJ 1981).

Brenot/Scheers 1996: C. Brenot / S. Scheers, Musée des Beaux-Arts de Lyon: Les monnaies massaliètes et les monnaies celtiques (Leuven 1996).

Bride 2007: A.-S. Bride, Le dépôt de bracelets et anneaux en verre. In: Barral 2007, 379-382.

Briggs 2014: S. Briggs, The Torrs chamfrein or head-piece: restoring »A very curious relic of antiquity«. In: Gosden/Crawford/Ulmschneider 2014, 341-355.

Brilliant 1974: R. Brilliant, Roman art from the Republic to Constantine (London 1974).

1982: R. Brilliant, I piedistalli del giardino di Boboli: spolia in se, spolia in re. Prospettiva 31, 1982, 2-17.

2002: R. Brilliant, The column of Marcus Aurelius re-viewed. Journal of Roman Archaeology 15, 2002, 499-506.

Briner 2007: C. Briner, Chronologie et fonctionnement du site de La Tène à partir des fibules répertoriées à Neuchâtel. In: Barral et al. 2007, 367-372.

Brizzolara 1986: A. M. Brizzolara, Le sculture del Museo Civico Archeologico di Bologna: La Collezione Marsili (Bologna 1986).

Broholm/Larsen/Skjerne 1949: H. C. Broholm / W. P. Larsen / G. Skjerne, The lures of the Bronze Age. An archaeological, technical and musicological investigation (Copenhagen 1949).

Bromwich 1993: J. Bromwich, The Roman remains of southern France: a guidebook (London 1993).

Brouquier-Reddé/Gruel 2004: V. Brouquier-Reddé / K. Gruel (eds), Le sanctuaire de Mars Mullo chez les Aulerques Cénomans (Allonnes, Sarthe) Vᵉ s. av. J.-C.-IVᵉ s. apr. J.-C. État des recherches actuelles. Gallia 61, 2004, 291-396.

Brown 1878: [?] Brown, Antiquities found in Ayrshire and preserved amongst the archaeological collections of Miss Brown of Waterhaughs and Lanfine. Archaeological & Historical Collections relating to the Counties of Ayr and Wigton 1, 1878, 61-65.

Brown/Goldberg in prep.: L. Brown / M. Goldberg, Excavations at Bruthach à Tuath, Benbecula, by J. Wallace and J. G. Scott. For submission to Scottish Archaeological Internet Reports (in prep.).

Brück 1999: J. Brück, Houses, lifecycles and deposition on Middle Bronze Age settlements in southern England. Proceedings of the Prehistoric Society 65, 1999, 145-166.

Brunaux/Meniel/Poplin 1985: J. L. Brunaux / F. Meniel / F. Poplin, Gournay. I: Les fouilles sur le sanctuaire et l'oppidum (1975-1984). Revue Archéologique de Picardie: Numéro spécial 1985/4 (Amiens 1985).

Buchsenschutz/Guillaumet/Ralston 1999: O. Buchsenschutz / J.-P. Guillaumet / I. Ralston, Les remparts de Bibracte. Recherches récentes sur la Porte du Rebout et le tracé des fortifications. La Collection Bibracte 3 (Glux-en-Glenne 1999).

Budde/Nicholls 1964: L. Budde / R. Nicholls, A catalogue of the Greek and Roman sculpture in the Fitzwilliam Museum Cambridge (Cambridge 1964).

Bull 2007: S. Bull, Triumphant rider: the Lancaster Roman cavalry tombstone (Lancaster 2007).

Burkhardt/Stern/Helmig 1994: A. Burkhardt / W. B. Stern / G. Helmig, Keltische Münzen aus Basel. Numismatische Untersuchungen und Metallanalysen. Antiqua 25 (Basel 1994).

Burnand 1975: Y. Burnand, Domitii Aquenses. Une famille de chevaliers romains de la region d'Aix-en-Provence. Mausolée et domaine. Revue Archéologique de Narbonnaise, Supplément 5 (Paris 1975).

Burnett 1989: A. Burnett, Review of Van Arsdell 1989. British Numismatic Journal 59, 1989, 235-237.

Burnett/Amandry/Carradice 1999: A. Burnett / M. Amandry / I. Carradice, Roman Provincial Coinage. II: From Vespasian to Domitian (AD 69-96) (London 1999).

Burnett/Amandry/Ripollès 1992: A. Burnett / M. Amandry / P. P. Ripollès, Roman Provincial Coinage. I: From the death of Caesar to the death of Vitellius (44 BC - AD 69) (London 1992).

Burnham et al. 2005: B. C. Burnham / F. Hunter / A. P. Fitzpatrick / S. Worrell / M. W. C. Hassall / R. S. O. Tomlin, Roman Britain in 2004. Britannia 36, 2005, 383-498.

Buteux 1997: S. Buteux, Settlements at Skaill, Deerness, Orkney. BAR British Series 260 (Oxford 1997).

Buttrey 1983: T. V. Buttrey, The dates of the arches of »Diocletian« and Constantine. Historia: Zeitschrift für alte Geschichte 32, 1983, 375-383.

Cadario 2004: M. Cadario, La corazza di Alessandro: loricati di tipo ellenistico dal IV secolo a. C. al II d. C. (Milano 2004).

Cahill 2002: M. Cahill, The Dooyork hoard. Irish Arts Review, Summer 2002, 118-121.

Cain 1989: H.-U. Cain, Waffenrelief. In: Bol 1989, 388-393.

1998: H.-U. Cain, Zwei Fragmente eines Waffenfrieses. In: Bol 1998, 149-151.

Callander 1908: J. G. Callander, The early Iron Age in Scotland. Transactions of the Banffshire Field Club 1907-1908 (1908), 41-56.

1916a: J. G. Callander, Notice of a jet necklace found in a cist in a Bronze Age cemetery, discovered on Burgie Lodge farm, Morayshire, with notes on Scottish prehistoric jet ornaments. Proceedings of the Society of Antiquaries of Scotland 50, 1915-1916 (1916), 201-240.

1916b: J. G. Callander, Notices of (1) three stone cups found in a cairn in Aberdeenshire, and (2) a short cist containing a Beaker urn found at Boglehill Wood, Longniddry, East Lothian. Proceedings of the Society of Antiquaries of Scotland 50, 1915-1916 (1916), 145-151.

1918: J. G. Callander, Notice of a harp-shaped fibula found on the estate of Polmaise, Stirlingshire, and of another in the Perth Museum. Proceedings of the Society of Antiquaries of Scotland 52, 1917-1918 (1918), 26-31.

Callander/Grant 1934: J. G. Callander / W. G. Grant, The broch of Midhowe, Rousay, Orkney. Proceedings of the Society of Antiquaries of Scotland 68, 1933-1934 (1934), 444-516.

Caló Levi 1952: A. Caló Levi, Barbarians on Roman imperial coins and sculpture. Numismatic Notes and Monographs 123 (New York 1952).

Calza et al. 1977: R. Calza / M. Bonanno / G. Messineo / B. Palma / P. Pensabene, Antichità di Villa Doria Pamphilj (Roma 1977).

Cambi 2013: N. Cambi, Roman military tropaea from Dalmatia. In: M. Sanadar / A. Rendić-Miočević / D. Tončinić / I. Radman-Livaja (eds), XVII Roman Military Equipment Conference, Zagreb 2010, 24th-27th May, 2010. Proceedings of the XVIIth Roman military equipment conference: weapons and military equipment in a funerary context. Dissertationes et Monographi[a]e 7 (Zagreb 2013) 9-21.

Cambi et al. 1973: N. Cambi / I. Marović / M. Nikolanci / Ž. Rapanić, Guide to the Archaeological Museum of Split (Split 1973).

Cameron/Stones 2001: A. S. Cameron / J. A. Stones (eds), Aberdeen: an in-depth view of the city's past. Excavations at seven major sites within the medieval burgh. Society of Antiquaries of Scotland Monograph Series 19 (Edinburgh 2001).

Cameron 2002: K. Cameron, The excavation of Neolithic pits and Iron Age souterrains at Dubton Farm, Brechin, Angus. Tayside and Fife Archaeological Journal 8, 2002, 19-76.

Campana 1852: G. P. Campana, Antiche opera in plastic (Roma 1852).

Campbell/MacGillivray 2000: D. M. Campbell / T. MacGillivray, Acoustics of the carnyx. In: Hickmann/Laufs/Eichmann 2000, 357-363.

Campbell 1991: E. Campbell, Excavations of a wheelhouse and other Iron Age structures at Sollas, North Uist, by R. J. C. Atkinson in 1957. Proceedings of the Society of Antiquaries of Scotland 121, 1991, 117-173.

2000: E. Campbell, The raw, the cooked and the burnt: interpretations of food and animals in the Hebridean Iron Age. Archaeological Dialogues 7/2, 2000, 184-198.

Campbell 2004: I. Campbell, Ancient Roman topography and architecture. 1: Drawings by Francesco di Giorgio, Ligorio, Labacco, Dosio and four anonymous sixteenth-century draughtsmen (London 2004).

Campbell/Greated 1987: M. Campbell / C. Greated, The musician's guide to acoustics (London 1987).

Cannon 1988: R. D. Cannon, The Highland bagpipe and its music (Edinburgh 1988).

Caprino et al. 1955: C. Caprino / A. M. Colini / G. Gatti / M. Pallottino / P. Romanelli, La colonna di Marco Aurelio (Roma 1955).

Card/Downes 2003: N. Card / J. Downes, Mine Howe – the significance of space and place in the Iron Age. In: Downes/Ritchie 2003, 11-19.

Carducci 1982: C. Carducci, Rilievi romani nell'Abbazia della Novalesa. In: Atti del V Congresso Nazionale di Archeologia Cristiana (Roma 1982) 123-142.

Carettoni 1988: G. Carettoni, Die »Campana«-Terrakotten vom Apollo-Palatinus-Tempel. In: Kaiser Augustus und die verlorene Republik [exhibition catalogue] (Berlin 1988) 267-272.

von Carnap-Bornheim/Ilkjær 1996: C. von Carnap-Bornheim / J. Ilkjær, Illerup Ådal. 7: Die Prachtausrüstungen (Århus 1996).

Carradice 1993: I. Carradice, Coin types and Roman history: the example of Domitian. In: M. Price / A. Burnett / R. Bland (eds), Essays in honour of Robert Carson and Kenneth Jenkins (London 1993) 161-175.

Carradice/Buttrey 2007: I. A. Carradice / T. V. Buttrey, The Roman Imperial Coinage. II, 1: From AD 69 to AD 96. Vespasian to Domitian (London ²2007).

Carroll 2001: M. Carroll, Romans, Celts and Germans: the German provinces of Rome (Stroud 2001).

Carson/Kraay 1978: R. A. G. Carson / C. M. Kraay (eds), Scripta nummaria romana: essays presented to Humphrey Sutherland (London 1978).

Carter/Hunter/Smith 2010: S. Carter / F. Hunter / A. Smith, A 5th century BC Iron Age chariot burial from Newbridge, Edinburgh. Proceedings of the Prehistoric Society 76, 2010, 31-74.

Cary/Wilson 1963: M. Cary / J. Wilson, A shorter history of Rome (London 1963).

Cassillis 1911: A. K. Cassillis, The rulers of Strathspey (Inverness 1911).

Castelin n. d.: K. Castelin, Keltische Münzen. Katalog der Sammlung des Schweizerischen Landesmuseum Zürich I (Stäfa no date).

Castellvi 2003: G. Castellvi, Le captif au trophée: développement d'un thème iconographique dans l'art romain (IIe s. av. J.-C.-IVe s. ap. J.-C.). In: Peuples et territoires en Gaule méditerranéenne. Hommage à Guy Barruol. Revue Archéologique de Narbonnaise 35 (Montpellier 2003) 451-462.

Cavers 2008: G. Cavers, The later prehistory of »black holes«: regionality and the south-west Scottish Iron Age. Proceedings of the Society of Antiquaries of Scotland 138, 2008, 13-26.

Cavers/Crone 2018: G. Cavers / A. Crone, A lake dwelling in its landscape. Iron Age settlement at Cults Loch, Castle Kennedy, Dumfries & Galloway (Oxford 2018).

Caylus 1759: A. C. P. Caylus, Recueil d'Antiquités Egyptiennes, Etrusques, Grecques, Romaines et Gauloises III (Paris 1759).

Ceccarini 1999: T. Ceccarini, Le antefisse. In: M. Barbera (ed.), La Collezione Gorga (Milano 1999) 113-118.

Cédelle 2007: J.-C. Cédelle, Faciès monétaire gaulois du sanctuaire du Gué-de-Sciaux, Antigny (Vienne). In: Bertrand/Maguer 2007, 115-117.

Chalmers 1887: G. Chalmers, Caledonia: or, a historical and topographical account of north Britain from the most ancient to the present times, with a dictionary of places chorographical and philological (new edition) I (Paisley 1887).

Champion 1996: C. Champion, Polybius, Aetolia and the Gallic attack on Delphi (279 B.C.). Historia: Zeitschrift für alte Geschichte 45/3, 1996, 315-328.

Chapman/Mytum 1983: J. C. Chapman / H. C. Mytum (eds), Settlement in north Britain 1000 BC-AD 1000. BAR British Series 118 (Oxford 1983).

Chapman 1992: M. Chapman, The Celts: the construction of a myth (Basingstoke 1992).

1994: M. Chapman, Thoughts on Celtic music. In: M. Stokes (ed.), Ethnicity, identity and music: the musical construction of place (Oxford 1994) 29-44.

Chieco Bianchi et al. 1988: A. Chieco Bianchi / G. Colonna / B. D'Agostino / F. D'Andria / E. M. De Juliis / R. De Marinis / V. Kruta / M. Landolfi / F. Roncalli, Italia omnium terrarum alumna. La civiltà dei Veneti, Reti, Liguri, Celti, Piceni, Umbri, Latini, Campani e lapigi. Antica Madre 11 (Milano 1988).

Childe 1935a: V. G. Childe, The prehistory of Scotland (London 1935).

1935b: V. G. Childe, Excavation of the vitrified fort of Finavon, Angus. Proceedings of the Society of Antiquaries of Scotland 69, 1934-1935 (1935), 49-80.

1944: V. G. Childe, Arthur J. H. Edwards. Proceedings of the Society of Antiquaries of Scotland 78, 1943-1944 (1944), 150-151.

Chossenot 1997: M. Chossenot, Recherches sur La Tène Moyenne et Finale en Champagne: Étude des processus de changement. Mémoire de la Société Archéologique Champenoise 12 (Reims 1997).

Christison/Anderson 1899: D. Christison / J. Anderson, On the recently excavated fort on Castle Law, Abernethy, Perthshire. Proceedings of the Society of Antiquaries of Scotland 33, 1898-1899 (1899), 13-33.

Christison/Anderson/Ross 1905: D. Christison / J. Anderson / T. Ross, Report on the Society's excavations of forts on the Poltalloch estate, Argyll, in 1904-5. Proceedings of the Society of Antiquaries of Scotland 39, 1904-1905 (1905), 259-322.

Christol/Fiches/Rabay 2007: M. Christol / J.-L. Fiches / D. Rabay, Le sanctuaire de la Combe de l'Ermitage à Collias (Gard). Revue Archéologique Narbonnaise 40, 2007, 15-32.

Church/Nesbitt/Gilmour 2013: M. J. Church / C. Nesbitt / S. M. D. Gilmour, A special place in the saltings? Survey and excavation of an Iron Age estuarine inlet at An Dunan, Lewis, Western Isles. Proceedings of the Society of Antiquaries of Scotland 143, 2013, 157-226.

Cianfarani 1973: V. Cianfarani, Schede del Museo Nazionale di Antichità degli Abruzzo: quarta serie (Chieti 1973).

Cichorius 1896: C. Cichorius, Die Reliefs der Traianssäule. 1. Tafelband: Der Erste Dakische Krieg. Taf. I-LVII (Berlin 1896).

    1900: C. Cichorius, Die Reliefs der Traianssäule. 2. Tafelband: Der Zweite Dakische Krieg, Taf. LVIII-CXIII (Berlin 1900).

Čižmář 2002: M. Čižmář, Keltské oppidum Staré Hradisko. Archeologické Památky Střední Moravy 4 (Olomouc 2002).

Claridge 1993: A. Claridge, Hadrian's Column of Trajan. Journal of Roman Archaeology 6, 1993, 5-22.

    1998: A. Claridge, Rome: an Oxford Archaeological Guide (Oxford 1998).

Clarke 1971: D. V. Clarke, Small finds in the Atlantic province: problems of approach. Scottish Archaeological Forum 3, 1971, 22-54.

Clarke 1993: G. A. Clarke, Deskford parish: loons, lairds, preachers and teachers (Aberdeen 1993).

Clarke 1939: R. R. Clarke, The Iron Age in Norfolk and Suffolk. Archaeological Journal 96, 1939, 1-113.

Clavel-Lévèque 1983: M. Clavel-Lévèque, La domination romaine en Narbonnaise et les formes de représentation des gaulois. In: Modes de contacts et processus de transformation dans les sociétés anciennes. Collections de l'École Française de Rome 67 (Paris, Rome 1983) 607-633.

Clavel-Lévèque/Lévèque 1982: M. Clavel-Lévèque / P. Lévèque, Impérialisme et sémiologie: l'espace urbain à Glanum. Mélange de l'École Française de Rome: Antiquité 94/2, 1982, 675-698.

Claxton 2001: J. Claxton, A victory for common sense. In: R. J. Wallis / K. Lymer (eds), A permeability of boundaries? New approaches to the archaeology of art, religion and folklore. BAR International Series 936 (Oxford 2001) 85-92.

Clodoré/Leclerc 2002: T. Clodoré / A.-S. Leclerc (eds), Préhistoire de la musique. Sons et instruments de musique des âges du Bronze et du Fer en France [exhibition catalogue] (Nemours 2002).

Clodoré/Vendries 2002: T. Clodoré / C. Vendries, Le second âge du fer et la civilisation celtique (450-52 avant J.-C.). In: Clodoré/Leclerc 2002, 101-127.

Close-Brooks 1982: J. Close-Brooks, Brooch. In: Peltenburg 1982, 194-195.

    1986: J. Cose-Brooks, Cauldron chains from Bailie Knowe, Dumfriesshire. Glasgow Archaeological Journal 13, 1986, 69-73.

Coarelli 1968: F. Coarelli, Il tempio di Diana »in circo Flaminio« e alcuni problemi connessi. Dialoghi di Archeologia 2, 1968, 191-209.

    1995: F. Coarelli, Da Pergamo a Roma: I Galati nella città degli Attalidi (Roma 1995).

    2007: F. Coarelli, Rome and environs: an archaeological guide (Berkeley 2007).

Cochran-Patrick 1878: R. W. Cochran-Patrick, The Caprington horn. Archaeological & Historical Collections of Ayrshire & Wigtonshire 1, 1878, 74-75.

Cody 2003: J. M. Cody, Conquerors and conquered on Flavian coins. In: A. J. Boyle / W. J. Dominik (eds), Flavian Rome: culture, image, text (Leiden 2003) 103-123.

Colbert de Beaulieu 1980: J.-B. Colbert de Beaulieu, Le bronze d'OXOBNOS et l'ensemble des monnaies tardives de la Loire Moyenne. Revue Belge de Numismatique 126, 1980, 9-30.

Colbert de Beaulieu/Fischer 1998: J.-B. Colbert de Beaulieu / B. Fischer, Receuil des Inscriptions Gauloises (R.I.G.). IV: Les légendes monétaires. Gallia, Supplément 45 (Paris 1998).

Coleman/Hunter 2002: R. Coleman / F. Hunter, The excavation of a souterrain at Shanzie Farm, Alyth, Perthshire. Tayside and Fife Archaeological Journal 8, 2002, 77-101.

Coles 1960: J. M. Coles, Scottish Late Bronze Age metalwork: typology, distributions and chronology. Proceedings of the Society of Antiquaries of Scotland 83, 1959-1960 (1960), 16-134.

    1963: J. M. Coles, Irish Bronze Age horns and their relations with northern Europe. Proceedings of the Prehistoric Society 29, 1963, 326-356.

    1968: J. M. Coles, The 1857 Law Farm hoard. Antiquaries Journal 48, 1968, 163-174.

    1969: J. M. Coles, Scottish early Bronze Age metalwork. Proceedings of the Society of Antiquaries of Scotland 101, 1968-1969 (1969), 1-110.

    1973: J. Coles, Archaeology by experiment (London 1973).

Coles/Simpson 1968: J. M. Coles / D. D. A. Simpson (eds), Studies in ancient Europe. Essays presented to Stuart Piggott (Leicester 1968).

Collingwood 1904: W. G. Collingwood, Two bronze armlets from Thirlmere. Transactions of the Cumberland and Westmorland Antiquarian and Archaeological Society (New Series) 4, 1904, 80-84.

Collingwood/Myres 1937: R. G. Collingwood / J. N. L Myres, Roman Britain and the English settlements. The Oxford History of England 1 (Oxford ²1937).

Collingwood/Wright 1965: R. G. Collingwood / R. P. Wright, The Roman Inscriptions of Britain. I: Inscriptions on stone (Oxford 1965).

    1991: R. G. Collingwood / R. P. Wright, The Roman Inscriptions of Britain. II: Instrumentum domesticum, fascicule 2 (edited by S. S. Frere / R. S. O. Tomlin) (Stroud 1991).

Collis 1996: J. Collis, The origin and spread of the Celts. Studia Celtica 30, 1996, 17-34.

    1997: J. Collis, Celtic myths. Antiquity 71, 1997, 195-201.

    2003: J. Collis, The Celts: origins, myths & inventions (Stroud 2003).

Colquhoun/Burgess 1988: I. Colquhoun / C. B. Burgess, The swords of Britain. Prähistorische Bronzefunde IV, 5 (München 1988).

Conn 1998: S. Conn, Carnyx. In: J. Calder (ed.), Present poets (Edinburgh 1998) 6.

Connolly 1981: P. Connolly, Greece and Rome at war (London 1981).

Cook 2010: M. Cook, New light on oblong forts: excavations at Dunnideer, Aberdeenshire. Proceedings of the Society of Antiquaries of Scotland 140, 2010, 79-91.

2011: M. Cook, New evidence for the activities of Pictish potentates in Aberdeenshire: the hillforts of Strathdon. Proceedings of the Society of Antiquaries of Scotland 141, 2011, 207-229.

2013: M. Cook, Open or enclosed: settlement patterns and hillfort construction in Strathdon, Aberdeenshire, 1800 BC to AD 1000. Proceedings of the Prehistoric Society 79, 2013, 297-326.

2016: M. Cook, Prehistoric settlement patterns in the north-east of Scotland: excavations at Grantown Road, Forres 2002-2013. Scottish Archaeological Internet Report 61. www.sair.org.uk (Edinburgh 2016).

forthcoming: M. Cook, The faunal remains. In: Hunter forthcoming a.

in prep.: M. Cook, Excavations at Kintore, Aberdeenshire 2 (Edinburgh in prep.).

Cook/Dunbar 2008: M. Cook / L. Dunbar, Rituals, roundhouses and Romans: excavations at Kintore, Aberdeenshire 2000-2006 (Edinburgh 2008).

Cool 2000: H. E. M. Cool, The significance of snake jewellery hoards. Britannia 31, 2000, 29-40.

Cordiner 1780: C. Cordiner, Antiquities and scenery of the north of Scotland: in a series of letters to Thomas Pennant Esq. (London 1780).

1788: C. Cordiner, Remarkable ruins, and romantic prospects, of north Britain. With ancient monuments, and singular subjects of natural history (London 1788).

Cosma 1966: V. Cosma, Archäologische musikalische Funde in Rumänien. Beiträge zur Musikwissenschaft 8, 1966, 3-14.

Cottam et al. 2010: E. Cottam / P. De Jersey / C. Rudd / J. Sills, Ancient British coins (Aylsham 2010).

Couissin 1923: P. Couissin, Les armes figurées sur les monuments romains de la Gaule méridionale. Revue Archéologique (Fifth Series) 18, 1923, 43-79.

1927: P. Couissin, Les armes Gauloises figurées sur les monuments Grecs, Étrusques et Romains. Revue Archéologique (Fifth Series) 25, 1927, 138-176. 301-325.

1928a: P. Couissin, L'équipement de guerre des gaulois sur les monnaies romaines (2e article). Revue Numismatique 1928, 161-186.

1928b: P. Couissin, Les triomphes de Domitien. Revue Archéologique (Fifth Series) 28, 1928, 65-94.

1929: P. Couissin, Les armes gauloises figurées sur les monuments grecs, étrusques et romains: deuxième partie, les armes gauloises sur les monuments étrusques. Revue Archéologique (Fifth Series) 29, 1929, 235-280.

Coulston 1981: J. C. Coulston, A sculptured Dacian falx from Birdoswald. Archaeologia Aeliana (Fifth Series) 9, 1981, 348-351.

1989: J. C. Coulston, The value of Trajan's Column as a source for military equipment. In: C. van Driel-Murray (ed.), Roman Military Equipment: the sources of evidence. BAR International Series 476 (Oxford 1989) 31-44.

1990: J. C. N. Coulston, Three new books on Trajan's Column. Journal of Roman Archaeology 5, 1990, 290-309.

1991: J. C. N. Coulston, The »draco« standard. Journal of Roman Military Equipment Studies 2, 1991, 101-114.

2003: J. C. N. Coulston, Tacitus, Historiae I.79 and the impact of Sarmatian warfare on the Roman empire. In: C. von Carnap-Bornheim (ed.), Kontakt – Kooperation – Konflikt. Germanen und Sarmaten zwischen dem 1. und dem 4. Jahrhundert nach Christus. Schriften des Archäologischen Landesmuseums Ergänzungsreihe 1 = Veröffentlichung des Vorgeschichtlichen Seminars Marburg Sonderband 13 (Neumünster 2003) 415-433.

Coulston/Phillips 1988: J. C. Coulston / E. J. Phillips, Hadrian's Wall west of the North Tyne, and Carlisle. CSIR I, 6 Great Britain (Oxford 1988).

Courby 1927: F. Courby, Fouilles de Delphes. II: Topographie et Architecture; 2: La Terrasse du Temple (Paris 1927).

Courtois 1989: C. Courtois, Le bâtiment de scène des théâtres d'Italie et de Sicile. Archaeologia Transatlantica 8 = Publications d'Histoire de l'Art et d'Archéologie de l'Université Catholique de Louvain 65 (Louvain-le-Neuve 1989).

Cowie 1988: T. G. Cowie, Magic metal: early metalworkers in the North-East (Aberdeen 1988).

Craddock 1978: P. T. Craddock, The origins and early use of brass. Journal of Archaeological Science 5/1, 1978, 1-16.

Craddock/Cowell/Stead 2004: P. Craddock / M. Cowell / I. Stead, Britain's first brass. Antiquaries Journal 84, 2004, 339-346.

Cramond 1891: W. Cramond, The annals of Banff I (Aberdeen 1891).

1904: W. Cramond, The annals of Cullen 961-1904 (Buckie 1904).

Craw 1931: J. H. Craw, An underground building at Midhouse, Orkney; two urns found at Lintlaw, Berwickshire; and the excavation of a cairn at Drumelzier, Peeblesshire. Proceedings of the Society of Antiquaries of Scotland 65, 1930-1931 (1931), 357-372.

Crawford 1969: M. H. Crawford, Roman Republican coin hoards. Royal Numismatic Society: Special Publication 4 (London 1969).

1974: M. H. Crawford, Roman Republican coinage (Cambridge 1974).

1985: M. H. Crawford, Coinage and money under the Roman Republic. Italy and the Mediterranean Economy (London 1985).

Crawford 1949: O. G. S. Crawford, Topography of Roman Scotland north of the Antonine Wall (Cambridge 1949).

Creed 2000: J. Creed, Reconstructing the Deskford carnyx. In: Hickmann/Laufs/Eichmann 2000, 347-350.

Creighton 2000: J. Creighton, Coins and power in late Iron Age Britain (Cambridge 2000).

Cressey/Anderson 2011: M. Cressey / S. Anderson, A later prehistoric settlement and metalworking site at Seafield West, near Inverness, Highland. Scottish Archaeological Internet Report 47. www.sair.org.uk (Edinburgh 2011).

Crone 2000: B. A. Crone, Analysis of samples from Westwater and Deskford [unpublished archive report (AOC 3227)] (Edinburgh 2000).

Croom 2003: A. T. Croom, Iron. In: N. Hodgson, The Roman fort at Wallsend (Segedunum): excavations in 1997-8. Tyne and Wear Museums Archaeological Monograph 2 (Newcastle upon Tyne 2003) 217-222.

Crous 1933: J. W. Crous, Florentiner Waffenpfeiler und Armilustrium. Mitteilungen des Deutschen Archäologischen Instituts, Römische Abteilung 48, 1933, 1-119.

Cumont 1942: F. Cumont, Recherches sur le symbolisme funéraire des romains. Bibliothèque Archéologique et Historique 35 (Paris 1942).

Cunliffe, 1991: B. Cunliffe, Iron Age communities in Britain (London ³1991).

1995: B. Cunliffe, The Celtic chariot: a footnote. In: Raftery/Megaw/Rigby 1995, 31-39.

1997: B. Cunliffe, The ancient Celts (Oxford 1997).

2003: B. Cunliffe, The Celts: a very short introduction (Oxford 2003).

Curle 1946: A. O. Curle, The excavation of the »wag« or prehistoric cattle-fold at Forse, Caithness, and the relation of »wags« to brochs, and implications arising therefrom. Proceedings of the Society of Antiquaries of Scotland 80, 1945-1946 (1946), 11-25.

Curle 1940: C. L. Curle, The chronology of the early Christian monuments of Scotland. Proceedings of the Society of Antiquaries of Scotland 74, 1939-1940 (1940), 60-116.

Curle 1911: J. Curle, A Roman frontier post and its people: the fort of Newstead in the parish of Melrose (Glasgow 1911).

1932: J. Curle, An inventory of objects of Roman and provincial Roman origin found on sites in Scotland not definitely associated with Roman constructions. Proceedings of the Society of Antiquaries of Scotland 66, 1931-1932 (1932), 277-397.

Curtis/Hunter 2006: N. G. W. Curtis / F. Hunter, An unusual pair of Roman bronze vessels from Stoneywood, Aberdeen, and other Roman finds from north-east Scotland. Proceedings of the Society of Antiquaries of Scotland 136, 2006, 199-214.

Cussans 2013: J. E. M. Cussans, Animal bone. In: Armit/McKenzie 2013, 433-469.

Dannheimer/Gebhard 1993: H. Dannheimer / R. Gebhard (eds), Das keltische Jahrtausend [exhibition catalogue Rosenheim]. Ausstellungskataloge der Prähistorischen Staatssammlung München 23 (Mainz 1993).

Darblade-Audoin 2006: M.-P. Darblade-Audoin, Nouvel Espérandieu. Recueil général des sculptures sur pierre de la Gaule. II: Lyon (Paris 2006).

Davidson/Henshall 1989: J. L. Davidson / A. S. Henshall, The chambered cairns of Orkney. An inventory of the structures and their contents (Edinburgh 1989).

1991: J. L. Davidson / A. S. Henshall, The chambered cairns of Caithness. An inventory of the structures and their contents (Edinburgh 1991).

Davies/Spratling 1976: J. L. Davies / M. G. Spratling, The Seven Sisters hoard: a centenary study. In: Boon/Lewis 1976, 121-147.

Davis/Gwilt 2008: M. Davis / A. Gwilt, Material, style and identity in first century AD metalwork, with particular reference to the Seven Sisters hoard. In: Garrow/Gosden/Hill 2008, 146-184.

Davis/Kraay 1973: N. Davis / C. M. Kraay, The Hellenistic kingdoms: portrait coins and history (London 1973).

De Caro 1996: S. De Caro, The northern barbarians as seen by Rome. In: dell'Orto 1996, 25-29.

Déchelette 1914: J. Déchelette, Manuel d'archéologie préhistorique, céltique et gallo-romaine. II: Archéologie celtique ou protohistorique; 3: Second âge du Fer ou époque de La Tène (Paris 1914).

Degrassi 1947: A. Degrassi (ed.), Inscriptiones Italiae. XIII, 1: Fasti consulares et triumphales (Roma 1947).

De Jersey 1994: P. De Jersey, Coinage in Iron Age Armorica. Studies in Celtic Coinage 2 = Oxford University Committee for Archaeology: Monograph 39 (Oxford 1994).

1996: P. De Jersey, Celtic coinage in Britain. Shire Archaeology 72 (Princes Risborough 1996).

2002: P. De Jersey, AGR, and life after Cunobelin. Chris Rudd List 64, 2002, 5-8.

Delamarre 2003: X. Delamarre, Dictionnaire de la langue gauloise (Paris ²2003).

Delestrée 2001: L.-P. Delestrée, L'or du trophée laténien de Ribemont-sur-Ancre (Somme), témoin d'une bataille oubliée. Revue Numismatique 157, 2001, 175-213.

Delestrée/Tache 2002: L.-P. Delestrée / M. Tache, Nouvel Atlas des Monnaies Gauloises. I: De la Seine au Rhin (Saint-Germain-en-Laye 2002).

2004: L.-P. Delestrée / M. Tache, Nouvel Atlas des Monnaies Gauloises. II: De la Seine à la Loire moyenne (Saint-Germain-en-Laye 2004).

2007: L.-P. Delestrée / M. Tache, Nouvel Atlas des Monnaies Gauloises. III: La Celtique, du Jura et des Alpes à la façade atlantique (Saint-Germain-en-Laye 2007).

2008: L.-P. Delestrée / M. Tache, Nouvel Atlas des Monnaies Gauloises. IV: Supplément aux tomes I – II – III (Saint-Germain-en-Laye 2008).

dell'Orto 1996: L. F. dell'Orto (ed.), Roman reflections in Scandinavia [exhibition catalogue Malmö] (Roma 1996).

De Maria 1988: S. De Maria, Gli archi onorari di Roma e dell'Italia Romana. Bibliotheca Archaeologica 7 (Roma 1988).

De Marinis 1987: R. De Marinis, Il Mantovano tra invasioni galliche e romanizzazione: appunti per una ricerca. In: R. De Marinis (ed.), Gli Etruschi a nord del Po [exhibition catalogue Mantova]. Zeta Università 9 (Udine 1987) 183-187.

1990: R. De Marinis, L'età gallica in Lombardia (IV-I secolo a. C.): Risultati delle ultime ricerche e problemi aperti. In: Atti 2 Convegno Archeologico Regionale 13-14-15 Aprile 1984 (Como 1990) 93-172.

1997: R. De Marinis, La tomba gallica di Castiglione delle Stiviere (Mantova). Notizie Archeologiche Bergomensi 5, 1997, 115-177.

Demetz 2002: S. Demetz, Zur Eingliederung des Bozner Raumes in das Imperium Romanum. In: L. Dal Ri / S di Stefano (eds), Archäologie der Römerzeit in Südtirol – Beiträge und Forschungen. Forschungen zur Denkmalpflege in Südtirol 1 (Bozen 2002) 29-45.

Demierre 2012: M. Demierre, Sanglier-enseigne. In: Poux 2012, 54.

Demierre/Garcia/Poux 2012: M. Demierre / M. Garcia / M. Poux, Trophee d'armes. In: Poux 2012, 164-165.

Depeyrot 2004a: G. Depeyrot, Le numéraire celtique. III: De l'Atlantique aux Arvernes. Collection Moneta 36 (Wettern 2004).

2004b: G. Depeyrot, Le numéraire celtique. IV: Bituriges, Éduens, Séquanes, Lingons. Collection Moneta 41 (Wettern 2004).

2005a: G. Depeyrot, Le numéraire celtique. V: Le centre parisien. Collection Moneta 44 (Wettern 2005).

2005b: G. Depeyrot, Le numéraire celtique. VIII: La Gaule occidentale. Collection Moneta 47 (Wettern 2005).

2010: G. Depeyrot, La colonne de Marc Aurèle. Collection Moneta 105 (Wetteren 2010).

Deschler-Erb 1996: E. Deschler-Erb, Vindonissa: Ein Gladius mit reliefverzierter Scheide und Gürtelteilen aus dem Legionslager. Jahresbericht. Gesellschaft pro Vindonissa 1996, 13-31.

1998: E. Deschler-Erb, Vindonissa (Windisch AG – Switzerland): a gladius with a relief decorated sheath and belt pieces from the legionary camp. Arma 10, 1998, 2-5 (with correction in Arma 11/12, 1999/2000, 2).

Dhénin 1995: M. Dhénin, Le sanglier-enseigne dans la numismatique gauloise. In: Moreau et al. 1995, 28-42.

Diebner 1979: S. Diebner, Aesernia – Venafrum: Untersuchungen zu den römischen Steindenkmälern zweier Landstädte Mittelitaliens. Archaeologica 8 (Roma 1979).

Dimitrova-Milčeva 2006: A. Dimitrova-Milčeva, Die Bronzefunde aus Novae (Moesia Inferior) (Warszawa 2006).

Dobrzańska/Megaw/Poleska 2005: H. Dobrzańska / V. Megaw / P. Poleska (eds), Celts on the margin: studies in European cultural interaction 7th century BC - 1st century AD dedicated to Zenon Woźniak (Kraków 2005).

Domergue 1966: C. Domergue, L'arc de triomphe de Caracalla à Volubilis: le monument, la décoration, l'inscription. Bulletin Archéologique du Comité des Travaux Historiques et Scientifiques Années 1963-1964 (1966), 201-229.

Donnadieu/Couissin 1931: A. Donnadieu / P. Couissin, Egitna et le monument de Biot. Revue Archéologique (Fifth Series) 33, 1931, 69-101.

Dor de la Souchère 1988: R. Dor de la Souchère, Travaux pour servir à l'histoire d'Antibes (ed. P. Ginestet) (Antibes 1988).

Downes/Ritchie 2003: J. Downes / A. Ritchie (eds), Sea change: Orkney and Northern Europe in the later Iron Age AD 300-800 (Balgavies 2003).

Downey 1993: P. Downey, Lip-blown instruments of Ireland before the Norman invasion. Historical Brass Society Journal 5, 1993, 75-91.

Drack 1955: W. Drack, Ein Mittellatèneschwert mit drei Goldmarken von Böttstein (Aargua). Zeitschrift für Schweizerische Archäologie und Kunstgeschichte 15/4, 1954-1955 (1955), 193-235.

Droysen 1885: H. Droysen, Die Balustradenreliefs. In: R. Bohn, Das Heiligtum der Athena Polias Nikephoros. Altertümer von Pergamon II (Berlin 1885) 95-138.

Dugand 1970: J.-E. Dugand, De l'Aegitna de Polybe au trophée de la Brague. Recherches relatives au contexte historique, archéologique et topographique, de la première opération de conquête des Romains en Provence, dans les parages de Nice et d'Antibes. Collection Méditerranée Antique et Moderne 2 (Paris 1970).

Dunand 1990: F. Dunand, Catalogue des terres cuites gréco-romaines d'Égypte (Paris 1990).

Dungworth 1996a: D. B. Dungworth, The production of copper alloys in Iron Age Britain. Proceedings of the Prehistoric Society 62, 1996, 399-421.

1996b: D. Dungworth, Caley's »zinc decline« reconsidered. Numismatic Chronicle 156, 1996, 228-234.

1998: D. B. Dungworth, EDXRF analysis of copper alloy artefacts. In: Main 1998, 347-352.

Dunning 1991: C. Dunning, La Tène. In: Moscati et al. 1991, 366-368.

Dunwell 1999: A. Dunwell, Edin's Hall fort, broch and settlement, Berwickshire (Scottish Borders): recent fieldwork and new perceptions. Proceedings of the Society of Antiquaries of Scotland 129, 1999, 303-357.

2007: A. Dunwell, Cist burials and an Iron Age settlement at Dryburn Bridge, Innerwick, East Lothian. Scottish Internet Archaeological Report 24 (www.sair.org.uk) (Edinburgh 2007).

Dunwell/Strachan 2007: A. Dunwell / R. Strachan, Excavations at Brown Caterthun and White Caterthun hillforts, Angus 1995-1997. Tayside and Fife Archaeological Committee: Monograph 5 (Perth 2007).

Durán Cabello 2004: R.-M. Durán Cabello, El teatro y el anfiteatro de Augusta Emerita. BAR International Series 1207 (Oxford 2004).

Durry 1922: M. Durry, Les trophées Farnèse. Mélanges d'Archéologie et d'Histoire (Ecole Française de Rome) 39, fascicule IV-V, 1921-1922 (1922), 303-318.

1935: M. Durry, Les trophées Farnèse: note complémentaire. Mélanges de l'Ecole Française de Rome 52, 1935, 77-80.

Dussaud 1903: R. Dussaud, Notes de mythologie syrienne. Revue Archéologique (Fourth Series) 1, 1903, 347-382.

Dütschke 1880: H. Dütschke, Antike Bildwerke in Oberitalien. IV: Antike Bildwerke in Turin, Brescia, Verona und Mantua (Leipzig 1880).

1882: H. Dütschke, Antike Bildwerke in Oberitalien. V: Antike Bildwerke in Vicenza, Venedig, Catajo, Modena, Parma und Mailand (Leipzig 1882).

Duval 1983: A. Duval, Autel. In: L'art celtique en Gaule [exposition catalogue Marseille et al.] (Paris 1983) 195.

1987: A. Duval, Notes sur quelques objets provenant de »Gergovie« (Puy de Dôme) et conservés au Musée des Antiquités Nationales. Antiquités Nationales 18-19, 1986-1987 (1987), 211-215.

Duval 1977: P.-M. Duval, Les Celtes (Paris 1977).

1987: P.-M. Duval, Monnaies gauloises et mythes celtiques (Paris 1987).

Duvernoy 1883: C. Duvernoy, Note sur une enceinte récemment découverte à Mandeure (Doubs). Mémoire de la Société Nationale des Antiquaires de France 44, 1883, 29-44.

Earwood 1991: C. Earwood, Two early historic bog butter containers. Proceedings of the Society of Antiquaries of Scotland 121, 1991, 231-240.

Edmondson 2007: J. Edmondson, The cult of Mars Augustus and Roman imperial power at Augusta Emerita (Lusitania) in the third century A.D.: a new votive dedication. In: Nogales Basaratte/González 2007, 541-575.

Edwards/Ralston 1978: K. J. Edwards / I. Ralston, New dating and environmental evidence from Burghead fort, Moray. Proceedings of the Society of Antiquaries of Scotland 109, 1977-1978 (1978), 202-210.

Eggers 1964: H. J. Eggers, Die Kunst der Germanen in der Eisenzeit. In: H. J. Eggers / E. Will / R. Joffroy / W. Holmqvist, Kelten und Germanen in heidnischer Zeit (Zürich 1964) 5-87.

Ehrhardt 2000: C. Ehrhardt, Pseudo-Augustus, pseudo-political. In: B. Kluge / B. Weisser (eds), XII. Internationaler Numismatischer Kongress; Berlin 1997. Akten – Proceedings – Actes I (Berlin 2000) 517-520.

Eisner 1986: M. Eisner, Zur Typologie der Grabbauten im Suburbium Roms. Mitteilungen des Deutschen Archäologischen Instituts, Römische Abteilung: Ergänzungsheft 26 (Mainz 1986).

Elsner 2000: J. Elsner, Frontality in the column of Marcus Aurelius. In: Scheid/Huet 2000, 251-264.

van Enckevort/Willems 1994: H. van Enckevort / J. H. Willems, Roman cavalry helmets in ritual hoards from the Kops Plateau at Nijmegen, The Netherlands. Journal of Roman Military Equipment Studies 5, 1994, 125-137.

Engl 2008: R. Engl, Coarse stone. In: Cook/Dunbar 2008, 210-225.

Ensoli/La Rocca 2000: S. Ensoli / E. La Rocca (eds), Aurea Roma: dalla città pagana alla città cristiana [exposition catalogue] (Roma 2000).

Eogan 1983: G. Eogan, Ribbon torcs in Britain and Ireland. In: O'Connor/Clarke 1983, 87-126.

Erdrich 2003: M. Erdrich, Spel zonder grenzen? Een speurtocht naar de Limes in de late Oudheid (Nijmegen 2003).

Espérandieu 1907-1938: E. Espérandieu, Recueil général des bas-reliefs, statues et bustes de la Gaule romaine I-XI (Paris 1907-1938).

Evans 2006: D. Evans, Celtic art revealed. The South Cave weapons hoard. Current Archaeology 203, 2006, 572-577.

Evans 1864: J. Evans, The coins of the ancient Britons (London 1864).

1881: J. Evans, The ancient bronze implements, weapons, and ornaments, of Great Britain and Ireland (London 1881).

Evans 1991: R. J. Evans, The denarius issue of CALDVS IIIVIR and associated problems. The Ancient History Bulletin 5/5-6, 1991, 129-134.

Fairhurst 1971: H. Fairhurst, The wheelhouse site A' Cheardach Bheag on Drimore Machair, South Uist. Glasgow Archaeological Journal 2, 1971, 72-106.

Fähndrich 2005: S. Fähndrich, Bogenmonumente in der römischen Kunst. Ausstattung, Funktion und Bedeutung antiker Bogen- und Torbauten. Internationale Archäologie 90 (Rahden/Westf. 2005).

Falkenstein 2004: F. Falkenstein, Anmerkungen zur Herkunftsfrage des Gundestrupkessels. Prähistorische Zeitschrift 79/1, 2004, 56-88.

Farley/Hunter 2015: J. Farley / F. Hunter (eds), Celts: art and identity [exhibition catalogue] (London 2015).

Fasham 1985: P. J. Fasham, The prehistoric settlement at Winnall Down, Winchester: excavations of MARC3 Site R17 in 1976 and 1977. Hampshire Field Club and Archaeological Society: Monograph 2 (Southampton 1985).

Faust 2012: S. Faust, Schlachtenbilder der römischen Kaiserzeit. Erzählerische Darstellungskonzepte in der Reliefkunst von Traian bis Septimius Severus. Tübinger archäologische Forschungen 8 (Rahden/Westf. 2012).

Feachem 1966: R. W. Feachem, The hill-forts of northern Britain. In: Rivet 1966, 59-87.

1971: R. W. Feachem, Unfinished hill-forts. In: D. Hill / M. Jesson (eds), The Iron Age and its hill-forts. Papers presented to Sir Mortimer Wheeler on the occasion of his eightieth year at a conference held by the Southampton University Archaeological Society, 5th-7th march, 1971 (Southampton 1971) 19-39.

Fecht 1995: M. Fecht, Description et techniques de fabrication. In: Moreau et al. 1995, 11-17.

Felletti Maj 1977: B. M. Felletti Maj, La Tradizione Italica nell'Arte Romana. Archaeologica 3 (Roma 1977).

Fellmann 1957: R. Fellmann, Das Grab des Lucius Munatius Plancus bei Gaëta. Institut für Ur- und Frühgeschichte der Schweiz: Schriften 11 (Basel 1957).

Fenton 1963: A. Fenton, Early and traditional cultivating implements in Scotland. Proceedings of the Society of Antiquaries of Scotland 96, 1962-1963 (1963), 264-317.

Ferguson 1984: J. P. S. Ferguson, Directory of Scottish newspapers (Edinburgh 1984).

Fergusson 1868: J. Fergusson, Tree and serpent worship: or illustrations of mythology and art in India in the first and fourth centuries after Christ from the sculptures of the Buddhist topes at Sanchi and Amravati (London 1868).

Ferris 1994: I. Ferris, Insignificant others: images of barbarians in military art from Roman Britain. In: S. Cottam / D. Dungworth / S. Scott / J. Taylor (eds), TRAC 94: Proceedings of the fourth annual Theoretical Roman Archaeology Conference Durham 1994 (Oxford 1994) 24-31.

1997: I. Ferris, The enemy without, the enemy within: more thoughts on images of barbarians in Greek and Roman art. In: K. Meadows / C. Lemke / J. Heron (eds), TRAC 96: Proceedings of the sixth annual Theoretical Roman Archaeology Conference Sheffield 1996 (Oxford 1997) 22-28.

2000: I. M. Ferris, Enemies of Rome: barbarians through Roman eyes (Stroud 2000).

2009: I. Ferris, Hate and war. The column of Marcus Aurelius (Stroud 2009).

Feugère 1993: M. Feugère, Les armes des Romains de la république à l'antiquité tardive (Paris 1993).

1994: M. Feugère, Les casques antiques. Visages de la guerre de Mycènes à l'Antiquité tardive (Paris 1994).

Fichtl 2000: S. Fichtl, La ville celtique (Les oppida de 150 av. J.-C. à 15 ap. J.-C.) (Paris 2000).

Fiego n.d.: G. C. Fiego, Museo Nazionale di Napoli: le raccolte archeologiche (Naples no date).

Field n.d.: N. Field, Fiskerton in the Iron Age (Lincoln no date, c. 1981).

1986: N. Field, An Iron Age timber causeway at Fiskerton, Lincolnshire. Fenland Research 3, 1985-1986 (1986), 49-53.

Field/Parker Pearson 2003: N. Field / M. Parker Pearson, Fiskerton: an Iron Age timber causeway with Iron Age and Roman votive offerings: the 1981 excavations (Oxford 2003).

Field/Parker Pearson/Rylatt 2003: N. Field / M. Parker Pearson / J. Rylatt, The Fiskerton causeway: research – past, present and future. In: S. Catney / D. Start (eds), Time and tide: the archaeology of the Witham valley. Proceedings of the Witham Archaeological Seminar of December 2001 (Lincoln 2003) 16-32.

Filip 1956: J. Filip, Keltové ve Střední Europě. Monumenta Archaeologica 5 (Praha 1956).

Fischer 1991: B. Fischer, Le bestiaire des monnaies gauloises. Cahiers Numismatiques 23/110, 1991, 7-15.

2003: B. Fischer, La vie des gaulois à travers leurs monnaies. Études Celtiques 35, 2003, 25-32.

2005: B. Fischer, Celticité et romanisation des légendes monétaires gauloises. In: J. Metzler / D. Wigg-Wolf (eds), Die Kelten und Rom: neue numismatische Forschungen. Studien zu Fundmünzen der Antike 19 (Frankfurt 2005) 59-70.

Fischer 1959: F. Fischer, Der spätlatènezeitliche Depot-Fund von Kappel (Kreis Saulgau). Urkunden zur Vor- und Frühgeschichte aus Südwürttemberg-Hohenzollern 1 (Stuttgart 1959).

1981: F. Fischer, Bad Buchau-Kappel. In: K. Bittel / W. Kimmig / S. Schiek (eds), Die Kelten in Baden-Württemberg (Stuttgart 1981) 300-302.

Fischer 1994: J. Fischer, Griechisch-Römische Terrakotten aus Ägypten. Die Sammlungen Sieglin und Schreiber. Dresden, Leipzig, Stuttgart, Tübingen. Tübinger Studien zur Archäologie und Kunstgeschichte 14 (Tübingen 1994).

Fitzpatrick 1984: A. P. Fitzpatrick, The deposition of La Tène Iron Age metalwork in watery contexts in southern England. In: B. Cunliffe / D. Miles (eds), Aspects of the Iron Age in central southern Britain. Oxford University Committee for Archaeology: Monograph 2 (Oxford 1984) 178-190.

1989: A. P. Fitzpatrick, The submission of the Orkney Islands to Claudius: new evidence? Scottish Archaeological Review 6, 1989, 24-33.

1996a: A. P. Fitzpatrick, »Celtic« Iron Age Europe: the theoretical basis. In: P. Graves-Brown / S. Jones / C. Gamble (eds), Cultural identity and archaeology: the construction of European communities (London 1996) 238-255.

1996b: A. P. Fitzpatrick, Night and day: the symbolism of astral signs on later Iron Age anthropomorphic short swords. Proceedings of the Prehistoric Society 62, 1996, 373-398.

2015: A. Fitzpatrick, Review of Lejars 2013. Archaeological Journal 172, 2015, 460-462.

Fitzpatrick/Schönfelder 2014: A. Fitzpatrick / M. Schönfelder, Ascot hats: an Iron Age leaf crown helmet from Fiskerton, Lincolnshire? In: Gosden/Crawford/Ulmschneider 2014, 286-296.

Flacelière 1937: R. Flacelière, Les Aitoliens à Delphes. Contribution à l'histoire de la Grèce centrale au IIIᵉ siècle av. J.-C. Bibliothèque des Ecoles Françaises d'Athènes et de Rome 143 (Paris 1937).

Fleming 1999: S. J. Fleming, Roman Glass: reflections on cultural change (Philadelphia 1999).

Flouest/Stead 1977: J.-L. Flouest / I. M. Stead, Recherche sur des cimetières de La Tène en Champagne (1971-1976): premier bilan. Gallia 35, 1977, 59-74.

Fogliato 1992: D. Fogliato, L'arco di Augusto a Susa (Torino 1992).

Fogolari 1960: G. Fogolari, Sanzeno nella Anaunia. In: Civiltà del Ferro: Studi pubblicati nella ricorrenze cenenaria della scoperta di Villanova. Documenti e Studi 6 (Bologna 1960) 267-321.

Fol 1989: A. Fol (ed.), The Rogozen Treasure (Sofia 1989).

Formigé 1949: J. Formigé, Le Trophée des Alpes (La Turbie). Gallia, Supplément 2 (Paris 1949).

Forrer 1968: R. Forrer, Keltische Numismatik der Rhein- und Donaulande (Graz 1968 [reprint of 1908 edition]).

Forsyth 1964: J. F. Forsyth, Some notes on the bronze cauldron recovered from Loch Gamhna, Inverness-shire. Proceedings of the Society of Antiquaries of Scotland 97, 1963-1964 (1964), 249-251.

Foster 1977: J. Foster, Bronze boar figurines in Iron Age and Roman Britain. BAR British Series 39 (Oxford 1977).

1999: J. Foster, The metal finds. In: R. Niblett, The excavation of a ceremonial site at Folly Lane, Verulamium. Britannia: Monograph Series 14 (London 1999) 133-176.

Fox 1946: C. Fox, A find of the early Iron Age from Llyn Cerrig Bach, Anglesey (Cardiff 1946).

1958: C. Fox, Pattern and purpose (Cardiff 1958).

Franks 1863: A. W. Franks, Description of the plates. In: Kemble 1863, 123-217.

Fraser 1883: W. Fraser, The chiefs of Grant. I: Memoirs (Edinburgh 1883).

Freeman 2006: P. Freeman, The philosopher and the Druids. A journey among the ancient Celts (New York 2006).

Frere/Wilkes 1989: S. S. Frere / J. J. Wilkes, Strageath: excavations within the Roman fort 1973-86. Britannia: Monograph Series 9 (London 1989).

Frey 1995a: O.-H. Frey, Some comments on swords with dragonpairs. In: Raftery/Megaw/Rigby 1995, 163-175.

1995b: O.-H. Frey, Das Grab von Waldalgesheim. Eine Stilphase des keltischen Kunsthandwerks. In: H.-E. Joachim, Waldalgesheim. Das Grab einer keltischen Fürstin. Kataloge des Rheinischen Landesmuseums Bonn 3 (Bonn 1995) 159-206.

Frézouls 1977: E. Frézouls, Informations Archéologiques: circonscription de Champagne-Ardenne. Gallia 35, 1977, 389-418.

1988: E. Frézouls (ed.), Les villes antiques de la France. 2: Germanie Supérieure; 1: Besançon – Dijon – Langres – Mandeure (Strasbourg 1988).

Froehner 1903: W. Froehner, Collection Julien Gréau. Verrerie antique émaillerie et poterie appartenant à M. John Pierpont Morgan (Paris 1903).

Fuchs 1987: M. Fuchs, Untersuchungen zur Ausstattung römischer Theater in Italien und den Westprovinzen des Imperium Romanum (Mainz 1987).

Fuhrmann 1949: H. Fuhrmann, Zwei Reliefbilder aus der Geschichte Roms. Mitteilungen des Deutschen Archäologischen Instituts 2, 1949, 23-65.

Gabelmann 1973: H. Gabelmann, Römische Grabmonumente mit Reiterkampfszenen im Rheingebiet. Bonner Jahrbücher 173, 1973, 132-200.

Gagnière/Granier 1986: S. Gagnière / J. Granier, Avignon de la Préhistoire à la Papauté (Avignon 1986).

Gamber 1964: O. Gamber, Dakische und sarmatische Waffen auf den Reliefs der Traianssäule. Jahrbuch der Kunsthistorischen Sammlung Wien 60, 1964, 7-34.

Gans 2003: U.-W. Gans, Zu Datierung und Aussage augusteischer Siegesdenkmäler im gallischen und iberischen Raum. In: Noelke/ Naumann-Steckner/Schneider 2003, 149-158.

Garbsch 1978: J. Garbsch, Römische Paraderüstungen (München 1978).

Garcia/Petit 2009: J.-P. Garcia / C. Petit, Un événement hydrodynamique de haute énergie de type tsunami sur le lac de Neuchâtel pour expliquer le gisement du pont de Cornaux/Les Sauges (et celui de La Tène?). In: Honegger et al. 2009, 113-123.

Gardner 1883: P. Gardner, A catalogue of the Greek coins in the British Museum. Thessaly to Aetolia (London 1883).

Garrow 2008: D. Garrow, The space and time of Celtic art: interrogating the »Technologies of Enchantment« database. In: Garrow/Gosden/Hill 2008, 15-39.

Garrow/Gosden 2012: D. Garrow / C. Gosden, Technologies of enchantment? Exploring Celtic art: 400 BC to AD 100 (Oxford 2012).

Garrow/Gosden/Hill 2008: D. Garrow / C. Gosden / J. D. Hill (eds), Rethinking Celtic art (Oxford 2008).

Gassmann 2009: P. Gassmann, Inventaire exhaustif des datations des bois provenant du site de La Tène. In: Honegger et al. 2009, 49-55.

Gayraud 1981: M. Gayraud, Narbonne antique des origines à la fin du IIIe siècle. Revue Archéologique de Narbonnaise, Supplément 8 (Paris 1981).

Gentles 1993: D. Gentles, Vitrified forts. Current Archaeology 133, 1992 (1993), 18-20.

Gerding 2002: H. Gerding, The tomb of Caecilia Metella: tumulus, tropaeum and thymele (Lund 2002).

Gergel 1988: R. A. Gergel, A late Flavian cuirassed torso in the J. Paul Getty Museum. The J. Paul Getty Museum Journal 16, 1988, 5-24.

1994: R. A. Gergel, Costume as geographic indicator: barbarians and prisoners on cuirassed statue breastplates. In: J. L. Sebesta / L. Bonfante (eds), The world of Roman costume (Madison WI 1994) 191-209.

Gerloff 2010: S. Gerloff, Atlantic cauldrons and buckets of the late Bronze Age and early Iron Ages in western Europe. Prähistorische Bronzefunde II, 18 (Stuttgart 2010).

Gillan 1862: J. Gillan, Notes on some antiquities in the parish of Alford, Aberdeenshire. Proceedings of the Society of Antiquaries of Scotland 4, 1860-1862 (1862), 382-386.

Gillies 2002: V. Gillies, The lightning tree (Edinburgh 2002).

Ginoux 2007: N. Ginoux, Le thème symbolique de la »paire de dragons« sur les fourreaux celtiques (IVe-IIe siècles avant J.-C.). Etude iconographique et typologie. BAR International Series 1702 (Oxford 2007).

Giuliano 1979-1995: A. Giuliano (ed.), Museo Nazionale Romano. I: Le Sculture, vols 1-12 (Roma 1979-1995).

Gleirscher 2014: P. Gleirscher, Fragments of a carnyx from Leisach (Austria). In: Gosden/Crawford/Ulmschneider 2014, 113-118.

Glodariu 1965: I. Glodariu, Sarmizegetusa Dacică în timpul stăpînarii romane. Acta Musei Napocensis 2, 1965, 119-133.

Gnecchi 1912: F. Gnecchi, I medaglioni romani (Milano 1912).

Goldberg 2015: M. Goldberg, The cult of Vitiris and Ptolemy's Votadini: vernacular religion in northern Britain. In: Breeze/Jones/Oltean 2015, 196-211.

Gorget 2007: C. Gorget (ed.), Catalogue: le trésor de Neuvy et ses comparaisons. In: Gorget/Guillaumet 2007, 214-243.

Gorget/Guillaumet 2007: C. Gorget / J.-P. Guillaumet (eds), Le cheval et la danseuse: à la redécouverte du trésor de Neuvy-en-Sullias [exhibition catalogue Orléans] (Paris 2007).

Gosden/Crawford/Ulmschneider 2014: C. Gosden / S. Crawford / K. Ulmschneider (eds), Celtic art in Europe: making connections. Essays in honour of Vincent Megaw on his 80th birthday (Oxford 2014).

Goudineau/Peyre 1993: C. Goudineau / C. Peyre, Bibracte et les Eduens. A la découverte d'un peuple gaulois (Paris 1993).

Grassi 1991: M. T. Grassi, I Celti in Italia (Milano 1991).

Green/Sorrell 1968: B. Green / A. Sorrell, Prehistoric Britain (Guildford 1968).

Green 1992a: M. Green, Dictionary of Celtic myth and legend (London 1992).

1992b: M. Green, The iconography of Celtic coins. In: Mays 1992, 151-163.

1995: M. Green, Celtic goddesses (London 1995).

1996a: M. Green, Art and religion: aspects of identity in pagan Celtic Europe. Studia Celtica 30, 1996, 35-58.

1996b: M. Green, Celtic art: reading the messages (London 1996).

1997: M. Green, The symbolic horse in pagan Celtic Europe: an archaeological perspective. In: S. Davies / N. A. Jones (eds), The horse in Celtic culture: medieval Welsh perspectives (Cardiff 1997) 1-22.

Gregory 2001: R. A. Gregory, Excavations by the late G. D. B. Jones and C. M. Daniels along the Moray Firth littoral. Proceedings of the Society of Antiquaries of Scotland 131, 2001, 177-222.

Gregory/Jones 2001: R. A. Gregory / G. D. B. Jones, Survey and excavation at Tarradale, Highland. Proceedings of the Society of Antiquaries of Scotland 131, 2001, 241-266.

Greig 1970: C. Greig, Excavations at Castle Point, Troup, Banffshire. Aberdeen University Review 43, 1970, 274-283.

1971: J. C. Greig, Excavations at Cullykhan, Castle Point, Troup, Banffshire. Scottish Archaeological Forum 3, 1971, 15-21.

1972: C. Greig, Cullykhan. Current Archaeology 32, 1972, 227-231.

Greig/Greig 1989: M. K. Greig / C. Greig, Remains of a 12th-century structure and other medieval features on the Knoll of Castle Point, Troup (Cullykhan), Banff and Buchan. Proceedings of the Society of Antiquaries of Scotland 119, 1989, 279-296.

Gricourt/Hollard 2002: M. Gricourt / D. Hollard, Lugus et le cheval. Dialogues d'Histoire Ancienne 28/2, 2002, 121-166.

Grierson n.d.: T. B. Grierson, Running catalogue of the contents of my museum consisting of natural history specimens, antiquities, and objects of virtu, &c. [unpublished manuscript catalogue; original in Dumfries Museum, copy in NMS library, no date].

Griffith 1935: G. T. Griffith, The mercenaries of the Hellenistic world (Cambridge 1935).

Grisanti 1977: G. T. Grisanti, I »Trofei di Mario«: il ninfeo dell'Acqua Giulia sull'Esquilino. I Monumenti Romani 7 (Roma 1977).

Gros 1979: P. Gros, Pour une chronologie des arcs de triomphe de Gaule Narbonnaise (à propos de l'arc de Glanum). Gallia 37, 1979, 55-83.

1981: P. Gros, Note sur deux reliefs »antiques« de Glanum: le problème de la romanisation. Revue Archéologique de Narbonnaise 14, 1981, 159-172.

Grose 1788: F. Grose, Military antiquities respecting a history of the English army from the Conquest to the present time 2 (London 1788).

1801: F. Grose, Military antiquities respecting a history of the English army from the Conquest to the present time (London ²1801).

Grose 1923: S. W. Grose, Catalogue of the McClean collection of Greek coins. I: Western Europe, Magna Graecia, Sicily (Cambridge 1923).

1979: S. W. Grose, Catalogue of the McClean collection of Greek coins. II: The Greek mainland, the Aegean islands, Crete (Cambridge 1923-1929; reprinted Chicago 1979).

Grueber 1910: H. A. Grueber, Coins of the Roman Republic in the British Museum [= BMCRR] (London 1910).

Gruel/Morin 1999: K. Gruel / E. Morin, Les monnaies celtes du Musée de Bretagne (Paris 1999).

Gruel/Taccoën 1992: K. Gruel / A. Taccoën, Petit numéraire de billon émis durant et après la conquête romaine dans l'Ouest de la Gaule. In: Mays 1992, 165-188.

Gschwantler 1981: K. Gschwantler, Dakische Schatzfunde und griechisch-römische Bronzen aus dem Gebiet der Sozialistischen Republik Rumänien. In: Die Daker: Archäologische Funde aus Rumänien [exhibition catalogue Vienna] (Mainz 1981) 226-235.

1984: K. Gschwantler, Eine bronzene Eberstatuette aus Enns-Lauriacum. Alba Regia 21, 1984, 71-77.

de Guadán 1979: A. M. de Guadán, Las armas en la moneda iberica (Madrid 1979).

Guerrini 1971: L. Guerrini, Marmi antichi nei disegni di Pier Leone Ghezzi. Documenti e Riproduzioni 1 (Città del Vaticano 1971).

Guichard 1994: V. Guichard, La céramique peinte des IIᵉ et Iᵉʳ s. avant J.-C. dans le nord du Massif Central: nouvelles données. Etudes Celtiques 30, 1994, 103-136.

2003: V. Guichard, Un dernier moment de folie créatrice: le repertoire ornemental de la ceramique dans le nord-est du Massif central au IIᵉ siècle avant J.-C. In: O. Buchsenschutz / A. Bulard / M.-B. Chardenoux / N. Ginoux (eds), Décors, images et signes de l'âge du Fer européen. Revue Archéologique du Centre de la France, Supplément 24 (Tours 2003) 91-113.

2009: V. Guichard, Imaginative designs from the heart of France. Pottery from Clermont-Ferrand, about 120 BC. In: Müller 2009a, 234-237.

Guido 1978: M. Guido, The glass beads of the prehistoric and Roman periods in Britain and Ireland. Society of Antiquaries of London Research Report 35 (London 1978).

Guillaumet/Schönfelder 2007: J.-P. Guillaumet / M. Schönfelder, Feuilles, carnyx et enseignes. In: Barral 2007, 384-387.

Gunby 2000: J. Gunby, Oval shield representations on the Black Sea littoral. Oxford Journal of Archaeology 19/4, 2000, 359-365.

Gusman 1904: P. Gusman, La villa impériale de Tibur (Villa Hadriana) (Paris 1904).

Gwilt/Haselgrove 1997: A. Gwilt / C. Haselgrove (eds), Reconstructing Iron Age societies. New approaches to the British Iron Age. Oxbow Monograph 71 (Oxford 1997).

Hachmann 1990: R. Hachmann, Gundestrup-Studien. Untersuchungen zu den spätkeltischen Grundlagen der frühgermanischen Kunst. Bericht der Römisch-Germanischen Kommission 71/2, 1990, 565-903.

Hada 1998: K. Hada (ed.), Treasures of Celtic art: a European heritage [exhibition catalogue] (Tokyo 1998).

Haffner 1976: A. Haffner, Die westliche Hunsrück-Eifel-Kultur. Römisch-Germanische Forschungen 36 (Berlin 1976).

Hagenweiler 2003: P. E. G. Hagenweiler, Römische Ausstattungskunst in Oberitalien. Beihefte der Bonner Jahrbücher 54 (Mainz 2003).

Hallén 1994: Y. Hallén, The use of bone and antler at Foshigarry and Bac Mhic Connain, two Iron Age sites on North Uist, Western Isles. Proceedings of the Society of Antiquaries of Scotland 124, 1994, 189-231.

Halliday 2007: S. Halliday, The later prehistoric landscape. In: RCAHMS 2007, 79-114.

Hallier 1988: G. Hallier, Les rinceaux de Narbonne. Journal of Roman Archaeology 1, 1988, 108-109.

Hamberg 1945: P. G. Hamberg, Studies in Roman imperial art; with special reference to the state reliefs of the second century (Uppsala 1945).

Hannestad 1993: L. Hannestad, Greeks and Celts: the creation of a myth. In: P. Bilde / T. Engberg-Pedersen / L. Hannestad / J. Zahle / K. Randsborg (eds), Centre and periphery in the Hellenistic world. Studies in Hellenistic Civilization 4 (Aarhus 1993) 15-38.

Hannestad 1988: N. Hannestad, Roman art and imperial policy. Jysk Arkaeologisk Selskab: Skrifter 19 (Aarhus 1988).

2001: N. Hannestad, Rome and her enemies: warfare in imperial art. In: T. Bekker-Nielsen / L. Hannested (eds), War as a cultural and social force: essays on warfare in antiquity. Historisk-filosofiske Skrifter 22 (Copenhagen 2001) 146-154.

Hansen 2003: M. F. Hansen, The eloquence of appropriation: prolegomena to an understanding of spolia in early Christian Rome. Analecta Romana Instituti Danici, Supplementum XXXIII (Roma 2003).

Harding 1982: D. W. Harding (ed.), Later prehistoric settlement in south-east Scotland. University of Edinburgh, Department of Archaeology: Occasional Paper 8 (Edinburgh 1982).

2003: D. W. Harding, Torrs and the early La Tène ornamental style in Britain and Ireland. In: Ballin Smith/Banks 2003, 191-204.

Harlan 1995: M. Harlan, Roman Republican moneyers and their coins 63 BC - 49 BC (London 1995).

Haselgrove 1987: C. Haselgrove, Iron Age coinage in south-east England: the archaeological context. BAR British Series 174 (Oxford 1987).

1996: C. Haselgrove, Iron Age coinage: recent work. In: T. C. Champion / J. R. Collis (eds), The Iron Age in Britain and Ireland: recent trends. Recent Trends Series 4 (Sheffield 1996) 67-85.

1999: C. Haselgrove, Iron Age societies in central Britain: retrospect and prospect. In: B. Bevan (ed.), Northern exposure: interpretative devolution and the Iron Ages in Britain. Leicester Archaeology Monographs 4 (Leicester 1999) 253-278.

2016: C. Haselgrove (ed.), Cartimandua's capital? The late Iron Age royal site at Stanwick, North Yorkshire: fieldwork and analysis 1981-2011. CBA Research Report 175 (York 2016).

Haselgrove/McCullagh 2000: C. Haselgrove / R. McCullagh (eds), An Iron Age coastal community in East Lothian: the excavation of two later prehistoric enclosure complexes at Fishers Road, Port Seton, 1994-5 (Edinburgh 2000).

Haselgrove/Fitts/Turnbull 1990: C. C. Haselgrove / R. L. Pitts / P. Turnbull, Stanwick, North Yorkshire, part 1: recent research and previous archaeological investigations. Archaeological Journal 147, 1990, 1-15.

Hatherley/Murray forthcoming: C. Hatherley / R. Murray, Excavations at Culduthel, Inverness (Edinburgh forthcoming).

Hatt 1970: J.-J. Hatt, Celts and Gallo-Romans (Geneva 1970).

Hausmann 1984: U. Hausmann, Zur Eroten- und Gallier-Ikonographie in der Alexandrinischen Kunst. In: N. Bonacasa / A. di Vita (eds), Alessandria e il mondo ellenistico-romano II. Istituto di Archeologia: Studi e Materiali 5 (Roma 1984) 283-295.

Haynes/Hirst 1939: D. E. L. Haynes / P. E. D. Hirst, Porta Argentariorum (London 1939).

Heald 2001: A. Heald, Knobbed spearbutts of the British and Irish Iron Age: new examples and new thoughts. Antiquity 75, 2001, 689-696.

2003: A. Heald, Non-ferrous metalworking in Iron Age Scotland 700 BC - AD 700 [unpublished PhD thesis, University of Edinburgh 2003].

2006: A. Heald, Crucible. In: H. K. Murray / J. C. Murray, Thainstone Business Park, Inverurie, Aberdeenshire. Scottish Archaeological Internet Reports 21. www.sair.org.uk (Edinburgh 2006) 12.

Heather 1994: P. Heather, State formation in Europe in the first millennium AD. In: B. E. Crawford (ed.), Scotland in Dark Age Europe. The proceedings of a Day Conference held on 20 February 1993. St John's House Papers 5 (St Andrews 1994) 47-70.

Hébert/Péchoux 2017: O. Hébert / L. Péchoux (eds), Gaulois. Images, usages et stéréotypes. Hors-collection 06 (Autun 2017).

van Heesch/Heeren 2009: J. van Heesch / I. Heeren (eds), Coinage in the Iron Age: essays in honour of Simone Scheers (London 2009).

Heitz 2006: C. Heitz, Alles bare Münze? Fremdendarstellungen auf römischem Geld. Bonner Jahrbücher 206, 2006, 159-230.

2009: C. Heitz, Die Guten, die Bösen und die Hässlichen – nördliche »Barbaren« in der römischen Bildkunst. Schriftenreihe Antiquitates 48 (Hamburg 2009).

Helbig 1963: W. Helbig, Führer durch die öffentlichen Sammlungen klassischer Altertümer in Rom I (ed. H. Speier) (Tübingen ⁴1963).

1972: W. Helbig, Führer durch die öffentlichen Sammlungen klassischer Altertümer in Rom IV (ed. H. Speier) (Tübingen ⁴1972).

Hellmann 1987: M.-C. Hellmann, Lampes Antiques de la Bibliothèque Nationale. II: Fonds général: lampes pré-romaines et romaines (Paris 1987).

Henderson 1991: J. Henderson, Industrial specialization in late Iron Age Britain and Europe. Archaeological Journal 148, 1991, 104-148.

Henig 1978: M. Henig, A corpus of Roman engraved gemstones from British sites. BAR British Series 8 (Oxford 1978).

1995: M. Henig, The art of Roman Britain (London 1995).

Henshall 1972: A. Henshall, The chambered tombs of Scotland II (Edinburgh 1972).

Henshall/Ritchie 2001: A. S. Henshall / J. N. G. Ritchie, The chambered cairns of the central Highlands (Edinburgh 2001).

Heslop 2008: D. H. Heslop, Patterns of quern production, acquisition and deposition: a corpus of beehive querns from northern Yorkshire and southern Durham. Yorkshire Archaeological Society: Occasional Paper 5 (Leeds 2008).

Hickmann/Both/Eichmann 2006: E. Hickmann / A. A. Both / R. Eichmann (eds), Studien zur Musikarchäologie. V: Musikarchäologie im Kontext, archäologische Befunde, historische Zusammenhänge, soziokulturelle Beziehungen (Rahden/Westf. 2006).

Hickmann/Laufs/Eichmann 2000: E. Hickmann / I. Laufs / R. Eichmann (eds), Studien zur Musikarchäologie. II: Musikarchäologie früher Metallzeiten (Rahden/Westf. 2000).

Hiernard et al. 1982: J. Hiernard / D. Nony / J.-P. Bost / G. Lintz / J. Perrier, Corpus des trésors monétaires antiques de la France. I: Poitou-Charentes et Limousin (Paris 1982).

Hill 1995a: J. D. Hill, Ritual and rubbish in the Iron Age of Wessex. BAR British Series 242 (Oxford 1995).

1995b: J. D. Hill, The pre-Roman Iron Age in Britain and Ireland (ca. 800 BC to AD 100): an overview. Journal of World Prehistory 9/1, 1995, 47-98.

1997: J. D. Hill, »The end of one kind of body and the beginning of another kind of body«? Toilet instruments and »Romanisation« in southern England during the first century AD. In: Gwilt/Haselgrove 1997, 96-107.

Hingley 1992: R. Hingley, Society in Scotland from 700 BC to AD 200. Proceedings of the Society of Antiquaries of Scotland 122, 1992, 7-53.

1996: R. Hingley, Ancestors and identity in the later prehistory of Atlantic Scotland: the reuse and reinvention of Neolithic monuments and material culture. World Archaeology 28/2, 1996, 231-243.

1998: R. Hingley, Settlement and sacrifice: the later prehistoric people of Scotland (Edinburgh 1998).

Hingley et al. 1997: R. Hingley / H. L. Moore / J. E. Triscott / G. Wilson, The excavation of two later Iron Age fortified homesteads at

Aldclune, Blair Atholl, Perth & Kinross. Proceedings of the Society of Antiquaries of Scotland 127, 1997, 407-466.

Hobbs 1996: R. Hobbs, British Iron Age coins in the British Museum (London 1996).

2001: R. Hobbs, Review of Creighton 2000. Numismatic Chronicle 161, 2001, 364-368.

Höckmann 1991: U. Höckmann, Gallierdarstellungen in der etruskischen Grabkunst des 2. Jahrhunderts v. Chr. Jahrbuch des Deutschen Archäologischen Instituts 106, 1991, 199-230.

Hodder 1982: I. Hodder, Symbols in action (Cambridge 1982).

Hoffmann 2004: K. Hoffmann, Kleinfunde der römischen Kaiserzeit aus Unterfranken. Studien zur Siedlungsgeschichte und kulturellen Beziehung zwischen Germanen und Römern. Internationale Archäologie 80 (Rahden/Westf. 2004).

Hoffmann-Schimpf/Melillo/Schwab 2011: B. Hoffmann-Schimpf / L. Melillo / R. Schwab, Ein Gladiatorenhelm aus Herculaneum. Restaurierung und Archäologie 4, 2011, 15-36.

Holder 1982: P. A. Holder, The Roman army in Britain (London 1982).

Hollard 2003: D. Hollard, La voix, la lyre et l'arc: images de Lugus sonore. Cahiers Numismatiques 40/158, 2003, 13-22.

Holliday 2002: P. J. Holliday, The origins of Roman historical commemoration in the visual arts (Cambridge 2002).

Hollstein 2016: W. Hollstein, The aureus of Casca Longus (RRC 507/1). Numismatic Chronicle 2016, 155-170.

Holman 1999: D. J. Holman, SEGO and DUNO: reassessment and reinterpretation. British Numismatic Journal 69, 1999, 196-198.

2000: D. Holman, Iron Age coinage in Kent: a review of current knowledge. Archaeologia Cantiana 120, 2000, 205-233.

2005: D. Holman, Iron Age coinage and settlement in east Kent. Britannia 36, 2005, 1-54.

Holmes 1978: P. Holmes, The evolution of player-voiced aerophones prior to 500 AD [unpublished PhD thesis, Middlesex Polytechnic 1978].

1980: P. Holmes, The manufacturing technology of the Irish Bronze Age horns. In: M. Ryan (ed.), The origins of metallurgy in Atlantic Europe. Proceedings of the Fifth Atlantic Colloquium [held in] Dublin, 30th March to 4th April 1978 (Dublin 1980) 165-188.

Holmes/Coles 1981: P. Holmes / J. M. Coles, Prehistoric brass instruments. In: Megaw/Longworth 1981, 280-286.

Hölscher 1985: T. Hölscher, Denkmäler der Schlacht von Actium: Propaganda und Resonanz. Klio 67, 1985, 81-102.

1988: T. Hölscher, Historische Reliefs. In: Kaiser Augustus und die verlorene Republik [exhibition catalogue] (Berlin 1988) 351-400.

Homo-Lechner 1996: C. Homo-Lechner, Sons et instruments de musique au moyen age: archéologie musicale dans l'Europe du VIIe au XIVe siècle (Paris 1996).

2002: C. Homo-Lechner, L'archéologie musicale. In: Clodoré/Leclerc 2002, 17-22.

Homo-Lechner/Vendries 1993: C. Homo-Lechner / C. Vendries, Le carnyx et la lyre. Archéologie musicale en Gaule celtique et romaine (Besançon 1993).

Honegger et al. 2009: M. Honegger / D. Ramseyer / G. Kaenel / B. Arnold / M.-A. Kaeser (eds), Le site de La Tène: bilan des connaissances – état de la question. Actes de la Table ronde internationale de Neuchâtel. 1-3 novembre 2007. Archéologie Neuchâteloise 43 (Hauterive 2009).

Hooker 2003: J. Hooker, The meaning of the boar. Chris Rudd List 69, 2003, 2-4.

Hoppe 2009: T. Hoppe, A masterly group of carvings. Carved cult objects from Fellbach-Schmiden, 127 BC. In: Müller 2009a, 238-241.

Horn 2015: J. Horn, Tankards of the British Iron Age. Proceedings of the Prehistoric Society 81, 2015, 311-341.

Hornblower/Spawforth 1996: S. Hornblower / A. Spawforth, The Oxford Classical dictionary (Oxford 1996).

von Hornbostel/Sachs 1961: E. M. von Hornbostel / C. Sachs, Classification of musical instruments. Galpin Society Journal 14, 1961, 3-29.

Hornung/Zawadzka 2017: S. Hornung / A. Zawadzka, A little bit of history reconstructed – new evidence on the provenance of the Abentheuer carnyces and their historical context. Bonner Jahrbücher 217, 2017, 55-93.

Howard/Hodges/Pyddoke 1969: M. M. Howard / H. Hodges / E. Pyddoke, Ancient Britons (London 1969).

Hucher 1868: E. Hucher, L'art gaulois ou les gaulois d'après leurs médailles 1 (Paris 1868).

1874: E. Hucher, L'art gaulois ou les gaulois d'après leurs médailles 2 (Paris 1874).

Hughes 1972: M. J. Hughes, A technical study of opaque red glass of the Iron Age in Britain. Proceedings of the Prehistoric Society 38, 1972, 98-107.

Huie 1975: A. C. Huie, Antiquities of Banffshire. In: Commemorating the county of Banff (Keith 1975) 6-17.

Hüneke 2000: S. Hüneke, Bauten und Bildwerke im Park Sanssouci (Potsdam 2000).

Hunter 1993: F. Hunter, Four decorated antler mounts and a stone »egg« amulet from Bu Sands, Burray, Orkney. Proceedings of the Society of Antiquaries of Scotland 123, 1993, 319-336.

1994: F. Hunter, Celtic chicanery questioned. Spink Numismatic Circular 102/6, July 1994, 259.

1996: F. Hunter, Recent Roman Iron Age metalwork finds from Fife and Tayside. Tayside and Fife Archaeological Journal 2, 1996, 113-125.

1997: F. Hunter, Iron Age hoarding in Scotland and northern England. In: Gwilt/Haselgrove 1997, 108-133.

1998a: F. Hunter, Discussion of the artefact assemblage. In: Main 1998, 393-401.

1998b: F. Hunter, Copper alloy. In: Main 1998, 338-346.

1999: F. Hunter, Artefacts. In: Dunwell 1999, 332-342.

2000: F. Hunter, Reconstructing the carnyx. In: Hickmann/Laufs/Eichmann 2000, 341-345.

2001a: F. Hunter, The carnyx in Iron Age Europe. Antiquaries Journal 81, 2001, 77-108.

2001b: F. Hunter, Roman and native in Scotland: new approaches. Journal of Roman Archaeology 14, 2001, 289-309.

2001c: F. Hunter, Unpublished Roman finds from the Falkirk area. Calatria. Journal of the Falkirk Local History Society 15, 2001, 111-123.

2002: F. Hunter, Birnie: buying a peace on the northern frontier. Current Archaeology 181, 2002, 12-16.

2003: F. Hunter, Romano-British trumpet brooch. In: McGill 2003, 25-26.

2005a: F. Hunter, Rome and the creation of the Picts. In: Z. Visy (ed.), Limes XIX: proceedings of the 19th International Congress of Roman Frontier Studies (Pécs 2005) 235-244.

2005b: F. Hunter, The image of the warrior in the British Iron Age – coin iconography in context. In: C. C. Haselgrove / D. Wigg (eds), Ritual and Iron Age coinage in north-west Europe. Studien zu Fundmünzen der Antike 20 (Frankfurt 2005) 43-68.

2006a: F. Hunter, New light on massive armlets. Proceedings of the Society of Antiquaries of Scotland 136, 2006, 135-160.

2006b: F. Hunter, Art in later Iron Age society. In: C. Haselgrove (ed.), Celtes et Gauloises, l'archéologie face à l'histoire. 4: Les mutations de la fin de l'âge du Fer (Glux-en-Glenne 2006) 93-115.

2006c: F. Hunter, Recent finds from Strageath Roman fort. Tayside and Fife Archaeological Journal 12, 2006, 81-88.

2007a: F. Hunter, Beyond the edge of the Empire: Caledonians, Picts and Romans (Rosemarkie 2007).

2007b: F. Hunter, Silver for the barbarians: interpreting denarii hoards in north Britain and beyond. In: R. Hingley / S. Willis (eds), Roman finds: context and theory (Oxford 2007) 214-224.

2007c: F. Hunter, Artefacts, regions and identities in the northern British Iron Age. In: C. C. Haselgrove / T. Moore (eds), The later Iron Age in Britain and beyond (Oxford 2007) 286-296.

2008: F. Hunter, Celtic art in Roman Britain. In: Garrow/Gosden/Hill 2008, 129-145.

2009a: F. Hunter, Une oreille de carnyx découvert à La Tène. In: Honegger et al. 2009, 75-85.

2009b: F. Hunter, Miniature masterpieces: unusual Iron Age brooches from Scotland. In: G. Cooney / K. Becker / J. Coles / M. Ryan / S. Sievers (eds), Relics of old decency: archaeological studies in later prehistory. A Festschrift for Barry Raftery (Dublin 2009) 143-155.

2009c: F. Hunter, Barbarians and their equipment on Roman provincial sculpture. In: V. Gaggadis-Robin / A. Hermary / M. Reddé / C. Sintes (eds), Les ateliers de sculpture régionaux: techniques, styles et iconographie. Actes du Xe Colloque International sur l'art provincial romain (Aix-en-Provence 2009) 793-801.

2009d: F. Hunter, The carnyx and other trumpets on Celtic coins. In: van Heesch/Heeren 2009, 231-248.

2010a: F. Hunter, Beyond the frontier: interpreting late Roman Iron Age indigenous and imported material culture. In: R. Collins / L. Allason-Jones (eds), Finds from the frontier: material culture in the 4th-5th centuries. CBA Research Report 162 (York 2010) 96-109.

2010b: F. Hunter, Buried treasure: a major Iron Age gold hoard from the Stirling area. The Forth Naturalist and Historian 33, 2010, 61-64.

2010c: F. Hunter, Changing objects in changing worlds: dragonesque brooches and beaded torcs. In: S. Worrell / G. Egan /

J. Naylor / K. Leahy / M. Lewis (eds), A decade of discovery: Proceedings of the Portable Antiquities Scheme conference 2007. BAR British Series 520 (Oxford 2010) 91-107.

2011: F. Hunter, The sound of Iron Age music: reconstructing the Deskford carnyx. In: K. Staubermann (ed.), Reconstructions: recreating science and technology of the past (Edinburgh 2011) 50-58.

2014: F. Hunter, Art in context: the massive metalworking tradition of north-east Scotland. In: Gosden/Crawford/Ulmschneider 2014, 325-340.

2015a: F. Hunter, Craft in context: artefact production in later prehistoric Scotland. In: F. Hunter / I. Ralston (eds), Scotland in later prehistoric Europe (Edinburgh 2015) 225-246.

2015b: F. Hunter, The lure of silver: denarius hoards and relations across the frontier. In: Breeze/Jones/Oltean 2015, 251-269.

2016: F. Hunter, Iron Age swords and Roman soldiers in conquest-period Britain. In: X. Pauli Jensen / T. Grane (eds), Imitation and inspiration: proceedings of the 18th International Roman Military Equipment Conference, Copenhagen 2013. Journal of Roman Military Equipment Studies 17, 2016, 11-21.

2018: F. Hunter, The Blair Drummond (UK) gold torc hoard: regional styles and international connections in the later Iron Age. In: R. Schwab / P.-Y. Milcent / B. Armbruster / E. Pernicka (eds), Early Iron Age gold in Celtic Europe: society, technology and archaeometry. Proceedings of the International Congress held in Toulouse, France, 11-14 March 2015 (Rahden / Westf. 2018) 431-439.

forthcoming a: F. Hunter, Context for a carnyx: excavation of a long-lived ritual site at Leitchestown, Deskford, Moray. Archaeological Journal 176, 2019.

forthcoming b: F. Hunter, Crucibles and moulds. In: Hatherley/Murray forthcoming.

forthcoming c: F. Hunter, The glass finds and glass-working debris. In: Hatherley/Murray forthcoming.

forthcoming d: F. Hunter, The copper-alloy finds. In: Hatherley/Murray forthcoming.

in prep. a: F. Hunter, Excavations at Birnie, Moray, 1998-2011 (in prep.).

in prep. b: F. Hunter, A scattered hoard of Iron Age horse and chariot gear from Dueshill, Northumberland (for submission to Archaeologia Aeliana).

in prep. c: F. Hunter, Boss-style metalwork in Iron Age and Roman Britain (in prep.).

Hunter et al. 2015a: F. Hunter / M. Goldberg / J. Farley / I. Leins, In search of the Celts. In: Farley/Hunter 2015, 18-35.

2015b: F. Hunter / M. Goldberg / J. Farley / I. Leins, Celtic arts in the long term: continuity, change and connections. In: Farley/Hunter 2015, 260-279.

Hüssen 1983: C.-M. Hüssen, A rich late La Tène burial at Hertford Heath, Hertfordshire. British Museum Occasional Paper 44 (London 1983).

Ilkjær 2001: J. Ilkjær, Illerup Ådal. 9: Die Schilde (Århus 2001).

2002: J. Ilkjær, Illerup Ådal: archaeology as magic mirror (Højbjerg 2002).

Imhoof-Blumer 1908: F. Imhoof-Blumer, Zur griechischen und römischen Münzkunde (II. Abtheilung). Revue Suisse de Numismatique 14, 1908, 1-211 (also numbered consecutively from part I
as 114-323).

Imlach 1868: J. Imlach, History of Banff (Banff 1868).

Innes 1845: G. Innes, Parish of Deskford. New Statistical Account of
Scotland 13, 1845, 63-78.

Ireland 1992: A. Ireland, The finding of the »Clonmacnoise« gold
torcs. Proceedings of the Royal Irish Academy 92C, 1992, 123-
146.

Ireland 2008: S. Ireland, Roman Britain: a sourcebook (London
³2008).

Istenič 2009: J. Istenič, Roman military equipment and the beginnings of the Roman use of brass in Europe. In: A. W. Busch / H.-J.
Schalles (eds), Waffen in Aktion. Akten der 16. Internationalen
Roman Military Equipment Conference (ROMEC). Xanten, 13.-
16. Juni 2007. Xantener Berichte 16 (Mainz 2009) 237-242.

Ivčević 2010: S. Ivčević, Relief, tropaion. In: Radman-Livaja 2010,
106.

Iversen 2011: R. Iversen, Ellekilde – en gravplads fra yngre romersk
jernalder med fyrstegrav og cirkusbægre. Aarbøger for Nordisk
Oldkyndighed og Historie 2009 (2011), 69-120.

Jackson / Craddock 1995: R. P. J. Jackson / P. T. Craddock, The Rib-
chester hoard: a descriptive and technical study. In: Raftery / Megaw / Rigby 1995, 75-102.

Jacobelli 2003: L. Jacobelli, Gladiators at Pompeii (Roma 2003).

Jacobsthal 1944: P. Jacobsthal, Early Celtic art (Oxford 1944).

Jacquemin 1985: A. Jacquemin, Aitolia et Aristaineta: offrandes
monumentales étoliennes à Delphes au IIIᵉ s. av. J.-C. Ktema 10,
1985, 27-35.

    1999: A. Jacquemin, Offrandes monumentales à Delphes. Biblio-
    thèque des Écoles Françaises d'Athènes et de Rome 304 (Paris
    1999).

    2014: A. Jacquemin, Armes galates à Delphes: d'une illusion à
    une proposition. In: G. Alberti / C. Féliu / G. Pierrevelcin (eds),
    Transalpinare. Mélanges offerts à Anne-Marie Adam. Ausonius
    Editions: Mémoires 36 (Bordeaux 2014) 129-132.

Jaeckel 1965: P. Jaeckel, Pergamenische Waffenreliefs. Waffen- und
Kostümkunde 7/2, 1965, 94-122.

James 1999: S. James, The Atlantic Celts: ancient people or modern invention? (London 1999).

    2006: S. T. James, The impact of Steppe peoples and the Partho-
    Sasanian world on the development of Roman military equip-
    ment and dress, 1st to 3rd centuries AD. In: M. Mode / J. Tubach
    (eds), Arms and armour as indicators of cultural transfer. The
    steppes and the ancient world from Hellenistic times to the early
    Middle Ages. Nomaden und Sesshafte 4 (Wiesbaden 2006) 357-
    392.

Jankuhn 1967: H. Jankuhn, Archäologische Beobachtungen zu
Tier- und Menschenopfern bei den Germanen in der römischen
Zeit. Nachrichten der Akademie der Wissenschaften in Göttin-
gen, Philosophisch-Historische Klasse 1967/6, 118-145.

Janon 1985: M. Janon, Note préalable à l'étude des collections lapi-
daires de Narbonne. A propos de deux articles récents. Dialogues
d'Histoire Ancienne 11, 1985, 771-783.

    1986: M. Janon, Collections lapidaires de l'église Notre-Dame-
    de-Lamourguier. In: Solier 1986, 113-124.

Jardine 1865: W. Jardine, Address of the president. Transactions of
the Dumfriesshire and Galloway Natural History and Antiquarian
Society 1864-1865 (1865), 1-24.

Jarvie / Philip 1994: F. Jarvie / C. Philip, The Romans in Scotland:
activity book (Edinburgh 1994).

Jervise 1862: A. Jervise, An account of the excavation of the round
or »bee-hive« shaped house, and other underground chambers,
at West Grange of Conan, Forfarshire. Proceedings of the Society
of Antiquaries of Scotland 4, 1860-1862 (1862), 492-499.

Jeunot 2007: L. Jeunot, Les monnaies gauloises provenant de Mandeure. In: Barral 2007, 372-376.

Joass 1864: J. M. Joass, Notice of a cist and its contents in the
parish of Eddertoun, Ross-shire, recently opened. Proceedings
of the Society of Antiquaries of Scotland 5, 1862-1864 (1864),
311-315.

Jobey 1974: G. Jobey, Excavation at Boonies, Westerkirk, and the
nature of Romano-British settlement in eastern Dumfriesshire.
Proceedings of the Society of Antiquaries of Scotland 105, 1972-
1974 (1974), 119-140.

    1982: G. Jobey, The settlement at Doubstead and Romano-
    British settlement on the coastal plain between Tyne and Forth.
    Archaeologia Aeliana (Fifth Series) 10, 1982, 1-23.

Johnson 1931: F. P. Johnson, Corinth: results of excavations conducted by the American School of Classical Studies at Athens.
IX: Sculpture 1896-1923 (Cambridge MA 1931).

Johnston 1994: D. A. Johnston, Carronbridge, Dumfries & Galloway: the excavation of Bronze Age cremations, Iron Age settlements and a Roman camp. Proceedings of the Society of Antiquaries of Scotland 124, 1994, 233-291.

Joly 2007: M. Joly, Le sanctuaire gallo-romain. In: Barral 2007, 390-
395.

Jones / Keillar 2002: B. Jones / I. Keillar, »In fines borestorum«: reconstructing the archaeological landscapes of prehistoric and
proto-historic Moray. Northern Scotland 22, 2002, 1-25.

Jones / Keillar / Maude 1993: B. Jones / I. Keillar / K. Maude, The
Moray aerial survey: discovering the prehistoric and protohistoric
landscape. In: Sellar 1993, 47-74.

Jones 1926: H. S. Jones (ed.), The sculptures of the Palazzo dei
Conservatori (Oxford 1926).

Jones 1997: S. Jones, The archaeology of ethnicity. Constructing
identities in the past and present (London 1997).

Jope 1983: E. M. Jope, Torrs, Aylesford, and the Padstow hobby-
horse. In: O'Connor / Clarke 1983, 149-159.

    2000: E. M. Jope, Early Celtic art in the British Isles (Oxford
    2000).

Jud / Alt 2009: P. Jud / K. W. Alt, Les ossements humains de La Tène
et leur interprétation. In: Honegger et al. 2009, 57-63.

Jufer / Luginbühl 2001: N. Jufer / T. Luginbühl, Les dieux gaulois:
répertoire des noms de divinités celtiques connus par l'épigraphie, les texts antiques et la toponymie (Paris 2001).

Junkelmann 2000a: M. Junkelmann, Familia Gladiatoria: the heroes
of the amphitheatre. In: E. Köhne / C. Ewigleben (eds), Gladia-

tors and Caesars. The power of spectacle in ancient Rome (London 2000) 31-74.

2000b: M. Junkelmann, Das Spiel mit dem Tod: so kämpften Roms Gladiatoren (Mainz 2000).

Kaenel 2007a: G. Kaenel, L'après Vouga et l'avenir de La Tène. In: Reginelli Servais 2007, 181-183.

2007b: G. Kaenel, Autour du site de La Tène… In: Barral et al. 2007, 343-345.

2013: G. Kaenel, Prologue. In: Lejars 2013, 13-15.

Kähler 1936: H. Kähler, Zwei Sockel eines Triumphbogens im Boboligarten zu Florenz; 96. Winckelmannsprogramm der Archäologischen Gesellschaft zu Berlin (Berlin, Leipzig 1936).

1948: Paulys Real-Encyclopädie der Classischen Altertumswissenschaft: Neue Bearbeitung VII A (1948) 373-493 s. v. Triumphbogen (Ehrenbogen) (H. Kähler).

Kalser 2014: J. Kalser, Die vergessene Burg von Leisach. Von der Neuenburg zurück in die römische Zeit und zu den verschollenen Opferkultplätzen unserer Ahnen: Entdeckungen und neue Erkenntnisse (Leisach 2014).

Kaufmann 1981: W. Kaufmann, Altindien. Musikgeschichte in Bildern II, 8 (Leipzig 1981).

Kaul 1991a: F. Kaul, Gundestrupkedlen: Baggrund og billedverden (København 1991).

1991b: F. Kaul, The Gundestrup cauldron – Thracian, Celtic or both? In: F. Kaul / I. Marazov / J. Best / N. de Vries, Thracian tales on the Gundestrup cauldron. Publications of the Holland Travelling University 1 (Amsterdam 1991) 7-42.

1993: F. Kaul, The Gundestrup cauldron and the periphery of the Hellenistic world. In: P. Bilde / T. Engberg-Pedersen / L. Hannestad / J. Zahle / K. Randsborg (eds), Centre and periphery in the Hellenistic world. Studies in Hellenistic Civilization 4 (Aarhus 1993) 39-52.

1995: F. Kaul, The Gundestrup cauldron reconsidered. Acta Archaeologica 66, 1995, 1-38.

1999: Reallexikon der Germanischen Altertumskunde 13 (1999) 195-211 s. v. Gundestrup (F. Kaul).

Kaul/Martens 1995: F. Kaul / J. Martens, Southeast European influences in the early Iron Age of southern Scandinavia: Gundestrup and the Cimbri. Acta Archaeologica 66, 1995, 111-161.

Keller 1923: C. Keller, La faune de La Tène. In: Vouga 1923, 131-134.

Kemble 1863: J. Kemble, Horae ferales; or, studies in the archaeology of the northern nations (London 1863).

Kendrick 1995: J. Kendrick, Excavation of a Neolithic enclosure and an Iron Age settlement at Douglasmuir, Angus. Proceedings of the Society of Antiquaries of Scotland 125, 1995, 29-67.

Kenny 2000: J. Kenny, The reconstruction of the Deskford carnyx – an ongoing multidisciplinary project. In: Hickmann/Laufs/Eichmann 2000, 351-356.

Keppie 1983: L. Keppie, Colonisation and veteran settlement in Italy 47-14 BC (Rome 1983).

1984: L. Keppie, The making of the Roman army: from Republic to Empire (London 1984).

1998: L. Keppie, Roman inscribed and sculptured stones in the Hunterian Museum, University of Glasgow (London 1998).

Keppie/Arnold 1984: L. J. F. Keppie / B. J. Arnold, CSIR Great Britain I, 4 Scotland (Oxford 1984).

Kilbride-Jones 1935a: H. E. Kilbride-Jones, An account of the excavation of the stone circle at Loanhead of Daviot, and of the standing stones of Cullerlie, Echt, both in Aberdeenshire, on behalf of H. M. Office of Works. Proceedings of the Society of Antiquaries of Scotland 69, 1934-1935 (1935), 168-223.

1935b: H. E. Kilbride-Jones, An Aberdeenshire Iron Age miscellany. Proceedings of the Society of Antiquaries of Scotland 69, 1934-1935 (1935), 445-454.

1938: H. E. Kilbride-Jones, Glass armlets in Britain. Proceedings of the Society of Antiquaries of Scotland 72, 1937-1938 (1938), 366-395.

1980: H. E. Kilbride-Jones, Celtic craftsmanship in bronze (London 1980).

Kimmig 1977: W. Kimmig, Zu einem unerklärten latènezeitlichen Objekt aus Mandeure (Doubs) (Epomanduodurum). In: K. Stüber / A. Zürcher (eds), Festschrift Walter Drack zu seinem 60. Geburtstag. Beiträge zur Archäologie und Denkmalpflege (Zürich 1977) 77-83.

King/Soffe 2001: A. King / G. Soffe, Internal organisation and deposition at the Iron Age temple on Hayling Island, Hampshire. In: J. Collis (ed.), Society and settlement in Iron Age Europe. Actes du XVIIIe colloque de l'AFEAF, Winchester (April 1994). Sheffield Archaeological Monographs 11 (Sheffield 2001) 111-124.

Kinney 1997: D. Kinney, Spolia. Damnatio and renovatio memoriae. Memoirs of the American Academy in Rome 42, 1997, 117-148.

Klar 1966: M. E. Klar, Musikinstrumente der Römerzeit in Trier. Kurtrierisches Jahrbuch 6, 1966, 100-109.

1971: M. Klar, Musikinstrumente der Römerzeit in Bonn. Bonner Jahrbücher 171, 1971, 301-333.

Kleiner 1992: D. E. E. Kleiner, Roman sculpture (New Haven 1992).

Kleiner 1989: F. S. Kleiner, The study of Roman triumphal and honorary arches 50 years after Kähler. Journal of Roman Archaeology 2, 1989, 195-206.

1991: F. S. Kleiner, The trophy on the bridge and the Roman triumph over nature. L'Antiquité Classique 60, 1991, 182-192.

1998: F. S. Kleiner, The Roman arches of Gallia Narbonensis. Journal of Roman Archaeology 11, 1998, 610-612.

Klindt-Jensen 1950: O. Klindt-Jensen, Foreign influences in Denmark's early Iron Age (København 1950).

1959: O. Klindt-Jensen, The Gundestrup bowl: a reassessment. Antiquity 33, 1959, 161-169.

1979: O. Klindt-Jensen, Gundestrupkedelen (København 1979).

Knoepfler 2007: D. Knoepfler, De Delphes à Thermos: un témoignage épigraphique méconnu sur le trophée galate des étoliens dans leur capitale (le traité étolo-béotia). Comptes rendus des séances de l'Academie des Inscriptions et Belle-Lettres 151/3, 2007, 1216-1253.

Koch 1988: G. Koch, Roman funerary sculpture. Catalogue of the collections (Malibu 1988).

Koch/Sichtermann 1982: G. Koch / H. Sichtermann, Römische Sarkophage (München 1982).

Koch 2007: J. T. Koch, Mapping Celticity, mapping Celticization. In: C. Gosden / H. Hamerow / P. De Jersey / G. Lock (eds), Communities and connections: essays in honour of Barry Cunliffe (Oxford 2007) 263-286.

Kockel 1983: V. Kockel, Die Grabbauten vor dem Herkulaner Tor in Pompeji. Beiträge zur Erschließung hellenistischer und kaiserzeitlicher Skulptur und Architektur 1 (Mainz 1983).

Komnick 2001: H. Komnick, Die Restitutionsmünzen der frühen Kaiserzeit: Aspekte der Kaiserlegitimation (Berlin 2001).

Krämer 1985: W. Krämer, Die Grabfunde von Manching und die latènezeitlichen Flachgräber in Südbayern. Die Ausgrabungen in Manching 9 (Stuttgart 1985).

1989: W. Krämer, Das eiserne Roß von Manching. Fragmente einer mittellatènezeitlichen Pferdeplastik. Germania 67, 1989, 519-539.

Krämer/Schubert 1970: W. Krämer / F. Schubert, Die Ausgrabungen in Manching 1955-1961. Die Ausgrabungen in Manching 1 (Wiesbaden 1970).

Krautheimer/Frankl/Corbett 1959: R. Krautheimer / W. Frankl / S. Corbett, Corpus Basilicarum Christianorum Romae. II, 1: The early Christian basilicas of Rome (IV-IX Cent.) (Citta del Vaticano 1959).

Kremer 2009: G. Kremer, Das frühkaiserzeitliche Mausoleum von Bartringen (Luxemburg). Dossiers d'Archéologie du Musée National d'Histoire et d'Art XII (Luxembourg 2009).

Kretz 2000: R. Kretz, The »RICON« staters of Tasciovanus. Spink Numismatic Circular 108, 2000, 97-102.

2001: R. Kretz, Tasciovanos' second coinage staters – a first classification. Spink Numismatic Circular 109, 2001, 234-243.

Krier 2003: J. Krier, Ein neuer Reliefblock aus Bartringen und die Grabmonumente mit Reiterkampfdarstellungen an Mosel und Rhein. In: Noelke/Naumann-Steckner/Schneider 2003, 255-263.

Krierer 1990: K. R. Krierer, Zur Barbarenikonographie in der provinzialrömischen Kunst. In: M. Hainzmann / D. Kramer / E. Pochmarski (eds), Akten des 1. Internationalen Kolloquiums über Probleme des provinzialrömischen Kunstschaffens. Mitteilungen der Archäologischen Gesellschaft Steiermark 3-4 (Wien 1990) 94-103.

1995: K. R. Krierer, Sieg und Niederlage. Untersuchungen physiognomischer und mimischer Phänomene in Kampfdarstellungen der römischen Plastik. Wiener Forschungen zur Archäologie 1 (Wien 1995).

1997: K. Krierer, Der Ritt über den Barbarenschädel: Eine Notiz zu Haarknoten auf römischen Grabdenkmälern. In: B. Djurić / I. Lazar (eds), Akten des IV. Internationalen Kolloquiums über Probleme des provinzialrömischen Kunstschaffens. Situla 36 (Ljubljana 1997) 151-159.

2004: K. R. Krierer, Antike Germanenbilder. Archäologische Forschungen 11 = Österreichische Akademie der Wissenschaften, Philosophisch-Historische Klasse: Denkschriften 318 (Wien 2004).

Krüger 1972: M.-L. Krüger, Die Reliefs des Stadtgebietes von Carnuntum. 2: Die dekorativen Reliefs. CSIR Österreich I, 4 (Wien 1972).

Kruta 2013: V. Kruta, Les bronzes de Castiglione delle Stiviere: carnyx ou effigie d'un échassier? Études Celtiques 39, 2013, 41-60.

Kruta/Lička/Cession-Louppe 2006: V. Kruta / M. Lička / J. Cession-Louppe, Celtes. Belges, Boïens, Rèmes, Volques … [exposition catalogue Mariemont] (Morlanwelz 2006).

Kühlborn 1992: J.-S. Kühlborn, Das Römerlager in Oberaden. III: Die Ausgrabungen im nordwestlichen Lagerbereich und weitere Baustellenuntersuchungen der Jahre 1962-1988. Bodenaltertümer Westfalens 27 (Münster 1992).

Künzl 1988a: E. Künzl, Der römische Triumph: Siegesfeiern im antiken Rom (München 1988).

1988b: E. Künzl, Politische Propaganda auf römischen Waffen der frühen Kaiserzeit. In: Kaiser Augustus und die verlorene Republik [exhibition catalogue] (Berlin 1988) 541-545.

1988c: E. Künzl, Germanien und Rom – Katalog. In: Kaiser Augustus und die verlorene Republik [exhibition catalogue] (Berlin 1988) 552-580.

1994: E. Künzl, Dekorierte Gladii und Cingula: Eine ikonographische Statistik. Journal of Roman Military Equipment Studies 5, 1994, 33-58.

1996: E. Künzl, Gladiusdekorationen der frühen römischen Kaiserzeit: dynastische Legitimation, Victoria und Aurea Aetas. Jahrbuch des RGZM 43, 1996, 383-474.

Küpper-Böhm 1996: A. Küpper-Böhm, Die römischen Bogenmonumente der Gallia Narbonensis in ihrem urbanen Kontext. Kölner Studien zur Archäologie der römischen Provinzen 3 (Espelkamp 1996).

La Baume 1941: W. La Baume, Der altpreußische Schild aus dem Landesamt für Vorgeschichte in Königsberg (Pr). Alt-Preußen 6/1, 1941, 5-12.

Lafaye 1896: G. Lafaye, Gladiator. In: C. Daremberg / E. Saglio (eds), Dictionnaire des Antiquités Grecques et Romaines. II, 2: F-G (Paris 1896) 1563-1599.

de Lagoy 1849: R. M. de Lagoy, Recherches numismatiques sur l'armement et les instruments de guerre des Gaulois (Aix 1849).

1855: R. M. de Lagoy, Mélange de quelques médailles Arsacides et Gauloises. Revue Numismatique 1855, 326-335.

Laing/Laing 1986: L. Laing / J. Laing, Scottish and Irish metalwork and the »conspiratio barbarica«. Proceedings of the Society of Antiquaries of Scotland 116, 1986, 211-221.

de Laix 1973: R. A. de Laix, The silver coinage of the Aetolian League. Californian Studies in Classical Antiquity 6/7, 1973, 47-75.

Landskron 2005: A. Landskron, Parther und Sasaniden. Das Bild der Orientalen in der römischen Kaiserzeit. Wiener Forschungen zur Archäologie 8 (Wien 2005).

Lange 1983: G. Lange, Die menschlichen Skelettreste aus dem Oppidum von Manching. Die Ausgrabungen in Manching 7 (Wiesbaden 1983).

Lantier 1947-1966: R. Lantier, Recueil général des bas-reliefs, statues et bustes de la Gaule romaine. Supplément XII-XV (Paris 1947-1966).

La Porta et al. 1983: A. La Porta / L. García y García / J. McConnell / H. B. Van der Poel, Corpus Topographicum Pompeianum. II: Toponymy (Rome 1983).

La Rocca/Tortorella 2008: E. La Rocca / S. Tortorella (eds), Trionfi romani [exposition catalogue Rome] (Milano 2008).

de La Tour 1892: H. de La Tour, Atlas de monnaies gauloises (Paris 1892).

de La Tour/Fischer 1992: H. de La Tour / B. Fischer, Atlas de monnaies gauloises (Paris 1992).

Laurent/Dugas 1907: R. Laurent / C. Dugas, Le monument romain de Biot, Alpes-Maritimes. Revue des Études Anciennes 9, 1907, 48-68.

Lawson 1999: G. Lawson, Getting to grips with music's prehistory: experimental approaches to function, design and operational wear in excavated musical instruments. In: A. F. Harding (ed.), Experiment and design: archaeological studies in honour of John Coles (Oxford 1999) 133-138.

Lawson/Margeson 1993: G. Lawson / S. Margeson, Musical instruments. In: S. Margeson, Norwich households: the medieval and post-medieval finds from Norwich survey excavations 1971-1978. East Anglian Archaeology 58 (Norwich 1993) 211-215.

Leander Touati 1987: A.-M. Leander Touati, The Great Trajanic Frieze. The study of a monument and of the mechanisms of message transmission in Roman art. Skrifter Utgivna av Svenska Institutet i Rom: Quarto 45 (Stockholm 1987).

Lebel 1962: P. Lebel, Catalogue des collections archéologiques de Montbéliard. III: Les bronzes figurés. Annales Littéraires de l'Université de Besançon 57 (Paris 1962).

Leblanc/Widemann 1981: J. Leblanc / F. Widemann, Reconstitution de fragments de monuments démontés à l'aide de moyens informatiques: méthodes et résultats obtenus dans l'application à la collection lapidaire gallo-romaine de Narbonne. Revue Archéologique 1981-1 (New Series), 169-183.

Leblanc/Dodinet/Widemann 1980: J. Leblanc / M. Dodinet / F. Widemann, Reconstitution de monuments demontés, contribution de l'informatique à la détection de raccords de pierres. Applications aux frises de trophées de Narbonne. Revue d'Archéometrie 2, 1980, 187-197.

Leeds 1933: E. T. Leeds, Celtic ornament in the British Isles down to AD 700 (Oxford 1933).

Lefèvre/Legros 1985: F. Lefèvre / R. Legros, La porte Mars de Reims (Reims 1985).

Leibundgut 1977: A. Leibundgut, Die römischen Lampen in der Schweiz. Eine kultur- und handelsgeschichtliche Studie (Bern 1977).

Lejars 1994: T. Lejars, Gournay III: Les fourreaux d'épée. Le sanctuaire de Gournay-sur-Aronde et l'armement des Celtes de La Tène moyenne (Paris 1994).

2007a: T. Lejars, Un dépôt d'objets métalliques à Vieux Poitiers (Vienne) et les origines gauloises de l'agglomération antique. In: Bertrand/Maguer 2007, 131-132. 239-241.

2007b: T. Lejars, La Tène: les collections du Musée Schwab à Bienne (canton de Berne). In: Barral et al. 2007, 357-365.

2013: T. Lejars, La Tène: la collection Schwab (Bienne, Suisse). La Tène, un site, un mythe 3 (Lausanne 2013).

Lenoir 1984: M. Lenoir, Pour un Corpus des inscriptions latines de Maroc. Bulletin d'Archéologie Marocaine 15, 1983-1984 (1984), 225-280.

Leon Alonso 1970: M. del P. Leon Alonso, Los relieves del Templo de Marte en Mérida. Habis 1, 1970, 181-197.

Leosini 1879: A. Leosini, VIII. S. Vitterino. Notizie degli Scavi di Antichità 1879 (Roma).

Lepper/Frere 1988: F. Lepper / S. Frere, Trajan's Column. A new edition of the Cichorius plates (Gloucester 1988).

Lerche 1995: G. Lerche, Radiocarbon dates of agricultural implements in »Tools & Tillage« 1968-1995: revised calibrations and recent additions. Tools & Tillage 7/4, 1995, 172-205.

Lethbridge 1952: T. C. Lethbridge, Excavations at Kilphedir, South Uist, and the problem of brochs and wheel-houses. Proceedings of the Prehistoric Society 18, 1952, 176-193.

1953: T. C. Lethbridge, Burial of an Iron Age warrior at Snailwell. Proceedings of the Cambridge Antiquarian Society 47, 1953, 25-37.

Lewuillon 2017: S. Lewuillon, Le roman du carnyx I. Le nom de la trompe. In: Hébert/Péchoux 2017, 223-243.

Leyenaar-Plaisier 1979: P. G. Leyenaar-Plaisier, Les terres cuites grecques et romaines. Catalogue de la collection du Musée National des Antiquités à Leiden (Leiden 1979).

Liampi 1998: K. Liampi, Der makedonische Schild (Bonn 1998).

Librenjak 2010: A. Librenjak, Fragment of a relief from a tropaion. In: Radman-Livaja 2010, 107.

Lindenschmit 1858: L. Lindenschmit, Die Alterthümer unserer heidnischen Vorzeit (Mainz 1858).

Lippold 1936: G. Lippold, Die Sculpturen des Vatikanischen Museums. III, 1: Sala delle Muse. Sala Rotonda. Sala a Croce Greca (Berlin, Leipzig 1936).

1956: G. Lippold, Die Sculpturen des Vatikanischen Museums. III, 2: Ingresso. Ambulacro. Ingresso Superiore. Atrio dei Quattro Cancelli. Scala. Sala della Biga. Galleria dei Candelabri. Galleria Geografica. Nachträge (Berlin, Leipzig 1956).

Livens 1976: R. G. Livens, A Don terret from Anglesey, with a discussion of the type. In: Boon/Lewis 1976, 149-162.

Liverani 1989: P. Liverani, L'Antiquarium di Villa Barberini a Castel Gandolfo (Città del Vaticano 1989).

Liversidge 1968: J. Liversidge, Britain in the Roman Empire (London 1968).

Long/Picard 2009: L. Long / P. Picard (eds), César: le Rhône pour mémoire. Vingt ans de fouilles dans le fleuve à Arles [exposition catalogue] (Arles 2009).

Lorimer 1994: D. H. Lorimer, The human remains. In: Ballin Smith 1994, 260-263.

Lovatelli 1900: E. C. Lovatelli, Urna marmorea con rappresentanze di trofei. Bulletino della Commissione Archeologica Comunale di Roma (Fifth Series) 28, 1900, 241-265.

Lowther 2000: Metalworking remains. In: Haselgrove/McCullagh 2000, 138-140.

Luján 2003: E. R. Luján, Gaulish personal names: an update. Études Celtiques 35, 2003, 181-247.

Lund 1981: C. Lund, The archaeomusicology of Scandinavia. In: Megaw/Longworth 1981, 246-265.

1986: C. S. Lund, The bronze lurs. Second conference of the ICTM Study Group on Music Archaeology II. Kungliga Musikaliska Akademiens Skriftserie 53, 2 (Stockholm 1986).

McCann 1978: A. M. McCann, Roman sarcophagi in the Metropolitan Museum of Art (New York 1978).

McCormick 1997: F. McCormick, The faunal remains from Mills Mount. In: S. T. Driscoll / P. A. Yeoman, Excavations within Edinburgh Castle in 1988-91. Society of Antiquaries of Scotland: Monograph Series 12 (Edinburgh 1997) 201-212.

Macdonald 1918: G. Macdonald, Roman coins found in Scotland. Proceedings of the Society of Antiquaries of Scotland 52, 1917-1918 (1918), 203-276.

Macdonald 2007a: P. Macdonald, Llyn Cerrig Bach. A study of the copper alloy artefacts from the insular La Tène assemblage (Cardiff 2007).

2007b: P. Macdonald, Perspectives on insular La Tène art. In: C. Haselgrove / T. Moore (eds), The later Iron Age in Britain and beyond (Oxford 2007) 329-338.

McGill 2003: C. McGill, The excavation of a palisaded enclosure and associated structures at Ironshill East, near Inverkeilor, Angus. Tayside and Fife Archaeological Journal 9, 2003, 14-33.

MacGregor 1962: M. MacGregor, The early Iron Age metalwork hoard from Stanwick, N. R. Yorks. Proceedings of the Prehistoric Society 28, 1962, 17-57.

1976: M. MacGregor, Early Celtic art in north Britain. A study of decorative metalwork from the third century B.C. to the third century A.D. (Leicester 1976).

Macinnes 1982: L. Macinnes, Pattern and purpose: the settlement evidence. In: Harding 1982, 57-73.

1984: L. Macinnes, Brochs and the Roman occupation of lowland Scotland. Proceedings of the Society of Antiquaries of Scotland 114, 1984, 235-249.

Mack 1975: R. P. Mack, The coinage of ancient Britain (London ³1975).

MacKenzie 1900: J. B. MacKenzie, Notes on some cup-marked stones and rocks near Kenmore, and their folklore. Proceedings of the Society of Antiquaries of Scotland 34, 1899-1900 (1900), 325-334.

MacKie 1974: E. W. MacKie, Dun Mor Vaul: an Iron Age broch on Tiree (Glasgow 1974).

2016: E. W. MacKie, Brochs and the empire. The impact of Rome on Iron Age Scotland as seen in the Leckie broch excavations (Oxford 2016).

Mackreth 1996: D. F. Mackreth, The bronze brooch. In: Simpson 1996, 77.

MacLaren 1984: A. MacLaren, A Bronze Age burial cairn at Limefield, Lanarkshire. In: R. Miket / C. Burgess (eds), Between and beyond the walls: essays on the prehistory and history of North Britain in honour of George Jobey (Edinburgh 1984) 97-116.

Mahood 1919: A. E. Mahood, Banff and district (Banff 1919).

Maier 2007: C. Maier, Ein Stein aus dem kaiserlich ottomanischen Museum in Stambul: Sextus Vibius Gallus im Kampf mit den Dakern. In: E. Christof / G. Koiner / M. Lehner / E. Pochmarski (eds), ΠΟΤΝΙΑ ΘΗΡΩΝ. Festschrift für Gerda Schwarz zum 65. Geburtstag. Veröffentlichungen des Instituts für Klassische Archäologie der Karl-Franzens-Universität Graz 8 (Wien 2007) 247-260.

Maier 1998: F. Maier, Manching und Tarent: Zur Vergoldungstechnik des keltischen Kultbäumchens und hellenistischer Blattkränze. Germania 76/1, 1998, 177-216.

Main 1998: L. Main, Excavation of a timber round-house and broch at the Fairy Knowe, Buchlyvie, Stirlingshire, 1975-8. Proceedings of the Society of Antiquaries of Scotland 128, 1998, 293-417.

Malinowski 1981: T. Malinowski, Archaeology and musical instruments in Poland. In: Megaw/Longworth 1981, 266-272.

Manassero 2013: N. Manassero, Celto-Iranica: the strange case of a carnyx in Parthian Nisa. Études Celtiques 39, 2013, 61-86.

Maniquet 2005a: C. Maniquet, Les carnyx de Tintignac. Archéologia 419, 2005, 16-23.

2005b: C. Maniquet, The Tintignac Celtic warrior hoard. Minerva 16/4, 2005, 29-31.

2008a: C. Maniquet, Le dépôt cultuel du sanctuaire gaulois de Tintignac à Naves (Corrèze). Gallia 65, 2008, 273-326.

2008b: C. Maniquet, Les carnyx du dépôt cultuel du sanctuaire gaulois de Tintignac à Naves (Corrèze). In: A. A. Booth / R. Eichmann / E. Hickmann / L.-C. Koch (eds), Studien zur Musikarchäologie. VI: Herausforderungen und Ziele der Musikarchäologie; Vorträge des 5. Symposiums der Internationalen Studiengruppe Musikarchäologie im Ethnologischen Museum der Staatlichen Museen zu Berlin, 19.-23. September 2006. Orient Archäologie 22 (Rahden/Westf. 2008) 57-76.

2009a: C. Maniquet, Les guerriers gaulois de Tintignac (Limoges 2009).

2009b: C. Maniquet, Le dépôt du sanctuaire de Tintignac à Naves: de nouvelles références pour le site de La Tène. In: Honegger et al. 2009, 207-217.

2009c: C. Maniquet, Le sanctuaire gaulois de Tintignac (Corrèze). In: I. Bertrand / A. Duval / J. Gomez de Soto / P. Maguer (eds), Les Gaulois entre Loire et Dordogne. Actes du XXXIe colloque de l'AFEAF, Chauvigny, 17-20 mai 2007. Mémoire 34 (Chauvigny 2009) 121-148.

Maniquet et al. 2011: C. Maniquet / T. Lejars / B. Armbruster / M. Pernot / M. Drieux-Daguerre / P. Mora / L. Espinasse, Le carnyx et le casque-oiseau celtiques de Tintignac (Naves-Corrèze). Description et étude technologique. Aquitania 27, 2011, 63-150.

Mann/Breeze 1987: J. C. Mann / D. J. Breeze, Ptolemy, Tacitus and the tribes of north Britain. Proceedings of the Society of Antiquaries of Scotland 117, 1987, 85-91.

Mann 1925: L. McL. Mann, Note on the results of the exploration of the fort at Dunagoil. Transactions of the Buteshire Natural History Society 9, 1925, 56-60.

Marcadé/Queyrel 2003: J. Marcadé / F. Queyrel, Le gaulois blessé de Délos reconsidéré. Monuments et Mémoires de la Fondation Eugène Piot 82, 2003, 1-74.

Marcel-Dubois 1937: C. Marcel-Dubois, Notes sur les instruments de musique figurés dans l'art plastique de l'Inde ancienne. Revue des Arts Asiatiques 11, 1937, 36-49.

Marconi 1937: P. Marconi, Verona Romana (Bergamo 1937).

Marcuse 1966: S. Marcuse, Musical instruments: a comprehensive dictionary (London 1966).

1975: S. Marcuse, A survey of musical instruments (Newton Abbot 1975).

Mărghitan 1969: L. Mărghitan, Tezaurul de podoabe dacice din argint de la Săliştea (fost. Ciora, jud. Alba). Studii şi Cercetari de Istorie Veche 20, 1969, 315-327.

Marshall/Boughton 2014: M. Marshall / D. Boughton, Two late Iron Age – early Roman looped ring fittings from northern England. Later Prehistoric Finds Group Newsletter 3, 2014, 5-8.

Marszal 2000: J. R. Marszal, Ubiquitous barbarians. Representations of the Gauls at Pergamon and elsewhere. In: N. T. de Grummond / B. S. Ridgway (eds), From Pergamon to Sperlonga: sculpture and context. Hellenistic Culture & Society 34 (Berkeley 2000) 191-234.

Martin 1974: P.-H. Martin, Die anonymen Münzen des Jahres 68 nach Christus (Mainz 1974).

Martínez 1991: A. J. Martínez, Numantia. In: Moscati et al. 1991, 406-407.

Martini 1996: C. Martini, Campana plaques. In: dell'Orto 1996, 76-78.

Maryon 1971: H. Maryon, Metalwork and enamelling (New York ⁵1971).

Marzatico/Gleirscher 2004: F. Marzatico / P. Gleirscher, Guerrieri principi ed eroi fra il Danubio e il Po dalla preistoria all'alto Medioevo [exhibition catalogue] (Trento 2004).

Mathiesen 2002: T. J. Mathiesen, Book reviews. American Journal of Archaeology 106/3, 2002, 479-481.

Mattei 1991: M. Mattei, The dying Gaul. In: Moscati et al. 1991, 70-71.

Mattingly 1995: D. Mattingly, Tripolitania (London 1995).

Mattingly 1914: H. Mattingly, The coinage of the civil wars of 68-69 AD. Numismatic Chronicle (Fourth Series) 14, 1914, 110-137.

1923: H. Mattingly, Coins of the Roman Empire in the British Museum. I: Augustus to Vitellius (= BMCRE I) (London 1923).

1926: H. Mattingly, The restored coins of Trajan. Numismatic Chronicle (Fifth Series) 6, 1926, 232-278.

1930: H. Mattingly, Coins of the Roman Empire in the British Museum. II: Vespasian to Domitian (= BMCRE II) (London 1930).

1936: H. Mattingly, Coins of the Roman Empire in the British Museum. III: Nerva to Hadrian (= BMCRE III) (London 1936).

1940: H. Mattingly, Coins of the Roman Empire in the British Museum. IV: Antoninus Pius to Commodus (= BMCRE IV) (London 1940).

1950: H. Mattingly, Coins of the Roman Empire in the British Museum. V: Pertinax to Elagabalus (= BMCRE V) (London 1950).

Mattingly/Sydenham 1923: H. Mattingly / E. A. Sydenham, The Roman Imperial Coinage. I: Augustus to Vitellius (= RIC I) (London 1923).

1926: H. Mattingly / E. A. Sydenham, The Roman Imperial Coinage. II: Vespasian to Hadrian (= RIC II) (London 1926).

1930: H. Mattingly / E. A. Sydenham, The Roman Imperial Coinage. III: Antoninus Pius to Commodus (= RIC III) (London 1930).

1936: H. Mattingly / E. A. Sydenham, The Roman Imperial Coinage. IV, 1: Pertinax to Geta (= RIC IV) (London 1936).

Mattingly 1998: H. B. Mattingly, Roman Republican coinage c. 150-90 BC. In: A. Burnett / U. Wartenberg / R. Witschonke (eds), Coins of Macedonia and Rome: essays in honour of Charles Hersh (London 1998) 151-164.

Maxfield 1981: V. A. Maxfield, The military decorations of the Roman army (London 1981).

Maxwell 1983: G. S. Maxwell, Recent aerial survey in Scotland. In: G. S. Maxwell (ed.), The impact of aerial reconnaissance on archaeology. Council for British Archaeology Research Report 49 (York 1983) 27-40.

1990: G. Maxwell, A battle lost: Romans and Caledonians at Mons Graupius (Edinburgh 1990).

May 1995: A. May, Seitlich angeblasene Hörner in der antiken Darstellung. Nachtrag zur systematischen und historischen Einordnung des Middewinterhorns. Bentheimer Jahrbuch 1995, 291-297.

2000: A. May, Quergeblasene Hörner – ein Beispiel einer ethnographischen Analogie. In: Hickmann/Laufs/Eichmann 2000, 365-372.

Mays 1992: M. Mays (ed.), Celtic coinage: Britain and beyond. BAR British Series 222 (Oxford 1992).

Mazois 1824: F. Mazois, Les ruines de Pompéi (Paris 1824).

Mazzini 1957-1958: G. Mazzini, Monete Imperiali Romane 1-5 (Milano 1957-1958).

Mazzoleni/Pappalardo 2005: D. Mazzoleni / U. Pappalardo, Pompejanische Wandmalerei: Architektur und illusionistische Dekoration (München 2005).

Meduna 1961: J. Meduna, Staré Hradisko. Katalog der Funde im Museum der Stadt Boskovice. Fontes Archaeologiae Moravicae 2 (Brno 1961).

1970: J. Meduna, Staré Hradisko II. Katalog der Funde aus den Museen in Brno/Brünn, Praha/Prag, Olomouc, Plumlov und Prosějov. Fontes Archaeologiae Moravicae 5 (Brno 1970).

Mee/Spawforth 2001: C. Mee / A. Spawforth, Greece: An Oxford Archaeological Guide (Oxford 2001).

Megaw 1960: J. V. S. Megaw, Penny whistles and prehistory. Antiquity 34, 1960, 6-13.

1961: J. V. S. Megaw, Penny whistles and prehistory: further notes. Antiquity 35, 1961, 55-57.

1963: J. V. S. Megaw, A British bronze bowl of the Belgic Iron Age from Poland. Antiquaries Journal 43, 1963, 27-37.

1968: J. V. S. Megaw, Problems and non-problems in palaeoorganology: a musical miscellany. In: Coles/Simpson 1968, 333-358.

1970: J. V. S. Megaw, Art of the European Iron Age (Bath 1970).

1971: J. V. S. Megaw, The possible wrest-plank from Dùn an Fheurain. In: J. N. G. Ritchie, Iron Age finds from Dùn an Fheurain, Gallanach, Argyll. Proceedings of the Society of Antiquaries of Scotland 103, 1970-1971 (1971), 106-107.

1982: J. V. S. Megaw, The prehistoric flute – two further notes with an optimistic sound. Galpin Society Journal 35, 1982, 147-148.

1983: J. V. S. Megaw, From Transdanubia to Torrs: further notes on a gabion of the late Jonathan Oldbuck. In: O'Connor/Clarke 1983, 127-148.

1989: J. V. S. Megaw, The emperor's new clothes: the new music archaeology? In: E. Hickmann / D. W. Hughes (eds), The archaeology of early music cultures. Third International Meeting of the ICTM Study Group on Music Archaeology. Orpheus-Schriftenreihe zu Grundfragen der Musik 51 (Bonn 1989) 343-353.

1990: J. V. S. Megaw, Bone whistles and related objects. In: M. Biddle, Object and economy in medieval Winchester. Winchester Studies 7, 2: Artefacts from medieval Winchester (Oxford 1990) 718-723.

1991: J. V. S. Megaw, Music archaeology and the ancient Celts. In: Moscati et al. 1991, 643-648.

2001: J. V. S. Megaw, »Your Obedient and Humble Servant«: notes for an Antipodean antiquary. In: A. Anderson / I. Lilley / S. O'Connor (eds), Histories of old ages: essays in honour of Rhys Jones (Canberra 2001) 95-110.

Megaw/Longworth 1981: J. V. S. Megaw / I. Longworth, The archaeology of musical instruments. World Archaeology 12/3, 1981, 231-232.

Megaw/Megaw 1996: J. V. S. Megaw / M. R. Megaw, Ancient Celts and modern ethnicity. Antiquity 70, 1996, 175-181.

1998: J. V. S. Megaw / M. R. Megaw, »The mechanism of (Celtic) dreams?«: a partial response to our critics. Antiquity 72, 1998, 432-435.

2000: J. V. S. Megaw / R. Megaw, Review of Adam 1996. Germania 78, 2000, 502-507.

Megaw/Megaw 1989: R. Megaw / V. Megaw, Celtic art: from its beginnings to the Book of Kells (London 1989).

1992: R. Megaw / V. Megaw, The Celts: the first Europeans? Antiquity 66, 1992, 254-260.

1999: R. Megaw / V. Megaw, Celtic connections past and present: Celtic ethnicity ancient and modern. In: R. Black / W. Gillies / R. O'Maolalaigh (eds), Celtic connections: proceedings of the 10th International Congress of Celtic Studies. I: Language, literature, history, culture (East Linton 1999) 19-81.

2001: R. Megaw / V. Megaw, Celtic art: from its beginnings to the Book of Kells (revised & expanded edition) (London 2001).

Mendel 1966: G. Mendel, Musées Impériaux Ottomans: Catalogue des sculptures grecques, romains et byzantines (Rome, facsimile edition 1966, original publication details not given).

Meneghini 2001: R. Meneghini, Il foro di Traiano: ricostruzione architettonica e analisi strutturale. Mitteilungen des Deutschen Archäologischen Instituts, Römische Abteilung 108, 2001, 245-268.

Ménez 1990: Y. Ménez, Les sculptures gauloises de Paule (Côtes-d'Armor). Gallia 56, 1990, 357-414.

Méniel 2007: P. Méniel, Les animaux de La Tène. In: Betschart 2007, 60-65.

2016: P. Méniel, Le cheval à la Gorge Meillet. In: L. Olivier (ed.), Autopsie d'une tombe gauloise. La tombe à char de la Gorge-Meillet à Somme-Tourbe (Marne). Cahiers du Musée d'Archéologie Nationale 2 (Saint-Germain-en-Laye 2016) 269-275.

Menotti 1998: E. M. Menotti, Castiglione delle Stiviere (Mn) – Tomba. In: Tesori della Postumia. Archeologia e storia intorno a una grande strada romana alle radice dell'Europa [exhibition catalogue Cremona] (Milano 1998) 131-132.

Mercando 1993: L. Mercando, La città, le mura, le porte. In: L. Mercando (ed.), La Porta del Paradiso: un restauro a Susa. Quaderni della Soprintendenza Archeologica del Piemonte: Monografie 2 (Torino 1993) 61-136.

n.d.: L. Mercando, Museo di Antichità Torino: le collezioni (Torino no date).

Mercando/Paci 1998: L. Mercando / G. Paci, Stele funerari in Piemonte. Monumenti Antichi 57 (Roma 1998).

Mercer 2018: R. Mercer, Native and Roman on the northern frontier. Excavations and survey in a later prehistoric landscape in upper Eskdale, Dumfriesshire (Edinburgh 2018).

von Mercklin 1927: E. von Mercklin, Zwei Bruchstücke eines Trophäeonkapitells im Tabularium zu Rom. Mitteilungen des Deutschen Archäologischen Instituts, Römische Abteilung 42, 1927, 193-202.

1962: E. von Mercklin, Antike Figuralkapitelle (Berlin 1962).

Merriman 1987: N. Merriman, Value and motivation in prehistory: the evidence for »Celtic spirit«. In: I. Hodder (ed.), The archaeology of contextual meanings (Cambridge 1987) 111-116.

Meucci 1989: R. Meucci, Roman military instruments and the lituus. Galpin Society Journal 42, 1989, 85-97.

Meyer/Schreiber 2012: K.-M. Meyer / T. Schreiber, Keltendarstellungen im Archäologischen Museum der Westfälischen Wilhelms-Universität Münster. Boreas: Münstersche Beiträge zur Archäologie 35, 2012, 139-167.

Michaelis 1882: A. T. F. Michaelis, Ancient marbles in Great Britain (Cambridge 1882).

Mielsch 1971: H. Mielsch, Römische Architekturterrakotten und Wandmalereien im Akademischen Kunstmuseum Bonn (Berlin 1971).

1975: H. Mielsch, Römische Stuckreliefs. Mitteilungen des Deutschen Archäologischen Instituts, Römische Abteilung, Ergänzungsheft 21 (Heidelberg 1975).

Miket 1983: R. Miket, The Roman fort at South Shields: excavation of the defences 1977-1981 (Newcastle upon Tyne 1983).

2002: R. Miket, The souterrains of Skye. In: Ballin Smith/Banks 2003, 77-110.

Miks 2007: C. Miks, Studien zur römischen Schwertbewaffnung in der Kaiserzeit. Kölner Studien zur Archäologie der römischen Provinzen 8 (Rahden/Westf. 2007).

Milleker 2000: E. J. Milleker (ed.), The Year One: art of the ancient world east and west [exhibition catalogue] (New York 2000).

Miller 1969: J. I. Miller, The spice trade of the Roman empire (Oxford 1969).

Milnor 2002: K. Milnor, Review of Ferris 2000. Journal of Roman Studies 92, 2002, 214-215.

Mionnet 1809: T. E. Mionnet, Description de médailles antiques, grecques et romaines 4 (Paris 1809).

Mitra 2003: D. Mitra, Sanchi (New Delhi 2003).

Moitrieux/Castorio 2010: G. Moitrieux / J.-N. Castorio, Nouvel Espérandieu: Recueil général des sculptures sur pierre de la Gaule. III: Toul et la cité des Leuques (Paris 2010).

Mollard-Besques 1963: S. Mollard-Besques, Catalogue raisonné des figurines et reliefs en terre-cuite grecs et romaines. II: Myrina (Paris 1963).

Möllers/Schlüter/Sievers 2007: S. Möllers / W. Schlüter / S. Sievers (eds), Keltische Einflüsse im nördlichen Mitteleuropa während der mittleren und jüngeren vorrömischen Eisenzeit. Akten des Internationalen Kolloquiums in Osnabrück vom 29. März bis 1. April 2006. Kolloquien zur Vor- und Frühgeschichte 9 (Bonn 2007).

Morcom 1995: J. Morcom, Sylloge nummorum Graecorum. X: The John Morcom collection of western Greek bronze coins (Oxford 1995).

Moreau 1995: J. Moreau, Les enseignes militaires dans le monde celtique et leurs figurations antiques. In: Moreau et al. 1995, 20-27.

Moreau et al. 1995: J. Moreau / D. Ankner / R. Boudet / M. Dhénin / M. Fecht, Le sanglier-enseigne gaulois de Soulac-sur-Mer (Gironde). Étude de l'emblématique du sanglier dans le monde celtique (Soulac-sur-Mer 1995).

Morellio 1734: A. Morellio, Thesaurus Morellianus, sive Familiarum Romanorum numismata omnia (Amsterdam 1734) (copy accessed in BM Coins & Medals library).

Moreno 2003: P. Moreno, La battaglia di Telamone in un dipinto dall'Esquilino. In: Vitali 2003a, 283-291.

Moro 1967: G. Moro, Sylloge Nummorum Graecorum. Sammlung Dreer/Klagenfurt im Landesmuseum für Kärnten. I: Italien – Sizilien. Buchreihe des Landesmuseums für Kärnten 15 (Klagenfurt 1967).

Morris 1952: J. Morris, The dating of the column of Marcus Aurelius. Journal of the Warburg and Courtauld Institute 15, 1952, 33-47.

Moscati et al. 1991: S. Moscati / O.-H. Frey / V. Kruta / B. Raftery / M. Szabó (eds), The Celts [exhibition catalogue] (Milano 1991).

Mudie 2007: G. Mudie, Excavations on the site of a late Iron Age roundhouse and souterrain, Glen Cloy, Brodick, Isle of Arran. Scottish Archaeological Journal 29/1, 2007, 1-29.

Müller 1986: F. Müller, Der Olifant von Montvoie. Archäologie der Schweiz 10/2, 1986, 97-100.

1990: F. Müller, Der Massenfund von der Tiefenau bei Bern. Zur Deutung latènezeitlicher Sammelfunde mit Waffen. Antiqua 20 (Basel 1990).

1992: F. Müller, La Tène (canton de Neuchâtel) et Port (canton de Berne): les sites, les trouvailles et leur interprétation. In: G. Kaenel / P. Curdy (eds), L'Âge de Fer dans le Jura. Cahiers d'Archéologie Romande 57 (Lausanne 1992) 323-328.

2007: F. Müller, Les dépôts en milieu humide dans la région des Trois-Lacs (Suisse): un bilan de l'information disponible. In: Barral et al. 2007, 347-355.

2009a: F. Müller (ed.), Art of the Celts 700 BC to AD 700 (Bern, Brussels 2009).

2009b: F. Müller, Le mobilier mis au jour à l'emplacement des ponts de La Tène: offrandes, trophées, objéts funéraires? In: Honegger et al. 2009, 87-91.

Müller 2001: Reallexikon der Germanischen Altertumskunde 18 (2001) 114-118 s. v. La Tène (R. Müller).

Müller/Steuer 2011: Reallexikon der Germanischen Altertumskunde[2] 8 (2011) 411-607 s. v. Fibel und Fibeltracht (R. Müller / H. Steuer).

Müller 1892: S. Müller, Det store sølvkar fra Gundestrup i Jylland. Nordiske Fortidsminder 1, 1892, 35-61.

Mulville et al. 2003: J. Mulville / M. Parker Pearson / N. Sharples / H. Smith / A. Chamberlain, Quarters, arcs and squares: human and animal remains in the Hebridean late Iron Age. In: Downes/Ritchie 2003, 20-34.

Muret 1889: E. Muret, Catalogue des monnaies gauloises de la Bibliothèque Nationale (Paris 1889).

Murray 2002: H. Murray, Late prehistoric settlement, Berryhill, Aberdeenshire. Proceedings of the Society of Antiquaries of Scotland 132, 2002, 213-227.

Murray 2011a: J. Murray, Radiocarbon dates from peat bog finds in Shetland Museum collections, 2010/11. DES 2011, 206-207.

2011b: J. Murray, Cultivating the divine. Ritual deposition of agricultural equipment in Shetland peat bogs [unpublished M.Litt. dissertation, University of the Highlands and Islands 2011].

Murray 2007: R. Murray, Iron-masters of the Caledonians. Current Archaeology 212, 2007, 20-25.

Musso 1985: L. Musso, Sarcofago da Portonaccio con raffigurazione di scontro tra Romani e barbari. In: A. Giuliano (ed.), Museo Nazionale Romano. I, 8, 1: Le Sculture (Roma 1985) 177-188.

Nabbefeld 2008: A. Nabbefeld, Römische Schilde: Studien zu Funden und bildlichen Überlieferungen vom Ende der Republik bis in die späte Kaiserzeit. Kölner Studien zur Archäologie der römischen Provinzen 10 (Rahden/Westf. 2008).

Nachtergael 1977: G. Nachtergael, Les Galates en Grèce et les Sôtéria de Delphes. Recherches d'histoire et d'épigraphie hellénistiques. Academie Royale des Sciences des Lettres et des Beaux-Arts de Belgique. Classe des Lettres et des Sciences Morales et Politiques: Mémoires. Coll. in 8. 2; 63, 1 (Bruxelles 1977).

Nash 1975: D. Nash, The chronology of Celtic coinage in Gaul: the Arvernian »hegemony« reconsidered. Numismatic Chronicle (Seventh Series) 15, 1975, 204-218.

1978a: D. Nash, Plus ça change…: currency in Central Gaul from Julius Caesar to Nero. In: Carson/Kraay 1978, 12-31.

1978b: D. Nash, Settlement and coinage in central Gaul c. 200-50 B.C. BAR Supplementary Series 39 (Oxford 1978).

1987: D. Nash, Coinage in the Celtic world (London 1987).

de Navarro 1972: J. M. de Navarro, The finds from the site of La Tène. I: Scabbards and the swords found in them (London 1972).

Nenna/Seif el-Din 2000: M.-D. Nenna / M. Seif el-Din, La vaisselle en faïence d'époque gréco-romaine. Catalogue du Musée gréco-romain d'Alexandrie. Études Alexandrines 4 (Le Caire 2000).

Nicolas 1979: E. P. Nicolas, De Néron à Vespasien: Études et perspectives historiques suivies de l'analyse, du catalogue, et de la reproduction des monnaies »oppositionelles« connues des années 67 à 70 (Paris 1979).

Nielsen et al. 2005: S. Nielsen / J. H. Anderson / J. A. Baker / C. Christensen / J. Glastrup / P. M. Grootes / M. Hüls / A. Jouttijärvi / E. B. Larsen / H. B. Madsen / K. Müller / M.-J. Nadeau / S. Röhrs / H. Stege / Z. A. Stos / T. E. Waight, The Gundestrup cauldron: new scientific and technical investigations. Acta Archaeologica 76, 2005, 1-58.

Nierhaus 1953: R. Nierhaus, Zu den ethnographischen Angaben in Lukans Gallien-Exkurs. Bonner Jahrbücher 153, 1953, 46-62.

Noble/Gondek 2011: G. Noble / M. Gondek, Symbol stones in context: excavations at Rhynie, an undocumented Pictish power centre of the 6th-7th centuries AD? Medieval Archaeology 55, 2011, 317-321.

Noble/Sveinbjarnson 2014a: G. Noble / O. Sveinbjarnarson, Durn Hill fort. Discovery and Excavation in Scotland 2014, 25.

2014b: G. Noble / O. Sveinbjarnarson, Crathie Point promontory fort. Discovery and Excavation in Scotland 2014, 25.

Noble et al. 2016: G. Noble / M. Goldberg / A. McPherson / O. Sveinbjarnarson, (Re)discovering the Gaulcross hoard. Antiquity 90, 2016, 726-741.

Noelke/Naumann-Steckner/Schneider 2003: P. Noelke / F. Naumann-Steckner / B. Schneider (eds), Romanisation und Resistenz in Plastik, Architektur und Inschriften der Provinzen des Imperium Romanum: Neue Funde und Forschungen (Mainz 2003).

Nogales Basaratte 2007: T. Nogales Basaratte, Culto imperial in Augusto Emerita: imágenes y programas urbanos. In: Nogales Basaratte/González 2007, 447-541.

2011: T. Nogales Basaratte, Imperialismo romano: iconografía al servicio del poder. Modelos romanos, provinciales y de Augusta Emerita. Madrider Mitteilungen 52, 2011, 411-439.

Nogales Basaratte/González 2007: T. Nogales Basaratte / J. González (eds), Culto imperial: política y poder. Actas del Congreso internacional, Mérida, Museo Nacional de Arte Romano, 18-20 de mayo, 2006. Hispania antigua: Serie Arqueologica 1 (Roma 2007).

Nothdurfter 1979: J. Nothdurfter, Die Eisenfunde von Sanzeno im Nonsberg. Römisch-Germanische Forschungen 38 (Mainz 1979).

O'Connor/Clarke 1983: A. O'Connor / D. V. Clarke (eds), From the Stone Age to the »Forty-Five«. Studies presented to R. B. K. Stevenson (Edinburgh 1983).

O'Dwyer 1994: S. O'Dwyer, Coirn na hÉireann: horns of ancient Ireland (musical CD) (Dublin 1994).

1998: S. O'Dwyer, The Loughnashade trumpet – curved trumpet or carnyx? Archaeology Ireland 44, 1998, 28-29.

2000: S. O'Dwyer, Four voices of the Bronze Age horns of Ireland. In: Hickmann/Laufs/Eichmann 2000, 337-340.

2004: S. O'Dwyer, Prehistoric music of Ireland (Stroud 2004).

Ogilvie 1969: R. M. Ogilvie, The Romans and their gods in the age of Augustus (London 1969).

Oldeberg 1947: A. Oldeberg, A contribution to the history of the Scandinavian bronze lur in the Bronze and Iron Ages. Acta Archaeologica 18, 1947, 1-91.

Olmsted 1979: G. S. Olmsted, The Gundestrup cauldron. Its archaeological context, the style and iconography of its portrayed motifs, and their narration of a Gaulish version of Táin bó Cúailnge. Collections Latomus 162 (Bruxelles 1979).

Ortiz 1994: G. Ortiz, In pursuit of the absolute: art of the ancient world from the George Ortiz collection (London 1994).

Östenberg 2009: I. Östenberg, Staging the world: spoils, captives and representations in the Roman triumphal procession (Oxford 2009).

Otte 1994: M. Otte (ed.), Sons originals: préhistoire de la musique (Liège 1994).

Owen 1992: O. A. Owen, Eildon Hill North, Roxburgh, Borders. In: J. S. Rideout / O. A. Owen / E. Halpin, Hillforts of southern Scotland (Edinburgh 1992) 21-71.

Packer 1994: J. E. Packer, Trajan's Forum again: the column and the temple of Trajan in the master plan attributed to Apollodorus(?). Journal of Roman Archaeology 7, 1994, 163-182.

1997: J. E. Packer, The Forum of Trajan in Rome. A study of the monuments (Berkeley 1997).

2001: J. E. Packer, The Forum of Trajan in Rome. A study of the monuments in brief (Berkeley 2001).

2008: J. E. Packer, The column of Trajan: the topographical and cultural contexts. Journal of Roman Archaeology 21, 2008, 471-478.

Padgett 2001: J. M. Padgett (ed.), Roman sculpture in the Art Museum, Princeton University (Princeton NJ 2001).

Pallottino 1946: M. Pallottino, L'Arco degli Argentari. I Monumenti Romani 2 (Roma 1946).

Palmer-Brown/Rylatt 2002: C. Palmer-Brown / J. Rylatt, Gifts to the gods at Iron Age Fiskerton. Minerva 13/5, 2002, 37-38.

Parker Pearson 1999: M. Parker Pearson, Food, sex and death: cosmologies in the British Iron Age with particular reference to East Yorkshire. Cambridge Archaeological Journal 9/1, 1999, 43-69.

Parker Pearson/Sharples 1999: M. Parker Pearson / N. Sharples, Between land and sea: excavations at Dun Vulan, South Uist (Sheffield 1999).

Parvérie 2010: M. Parvérie, Les monnaies lémovices »au carnyx«: un état des découvertes récentes. Cahiers Numismatiques 47/185, 2010, 13-20.

Pastor Eixarch 1987: J. M. Pastor Eixarch, Las trompas de Guerra celtibericas. Celtiberia 73, 1987, 7-19.

Pau Ripollès/Abascal 2000: P. Pau Ripollès / J. M. Abascal, Monedas Hispánicas. Catálogo del Gabinete de Antigüedades II, 1 (Madrid 2000).

Pearson 1796: G. Pearson, Observations on some ancient metallic arms and utensils; with experiments to determine their composition. Philosophical Transactions 86, 1796, 395-451.

Peltenburg 1982: E. Peltenburg, Excavations at Balloch Hill, Argyll. Proceedings of the Society of Antiquaries of Scotland 112, 1982, 142-214.

Pensabene 1979: P. Pensabene, Frammenti della decorazione architettonica dalla Domus Flavia sul Palatina. In: Piranesi: nei luoghi di Piranesi, section »Orti Farnesiani: Archeologica Piranesiana« (Roma 1979) 73-83.

Pensabene/Di Mino 1983: P. Pensabene / M. R. S. Di Mino, Museo Nazionale Romano. III: Le Terrecotte; 1: Le Antefisse (Roma 1983).

Perdrizet 1921: P. Perdrizet, Les terres cuites grecques d'Egypte de la collection Fouquet (Nancy 1921).

Pernet 2013: L. Pernet, Les représentations d'armes celtiques sur les monuments de victoire aux époques hellénistique et romaine. De la statue de l'Étolie vainqueur à l'arc d'Orange: origine et mutation d'un stéréotype. In: H. Ménard / R. Plana-Mallart (eds), Contacts de cultures, constructions identitaires et stéréotypes dans l'espace méditerranéen antique (Montpellier 2013) 21-35.

Pernot 2011: M. Pernot, Étude métallurgique. In: Maniquet et al. 2011, 96-100.

Persichetti 1912: N. Persichetti, Iscrizioni e rilievi del Museo Civico Aquilano. Mitteilungen des Kaiserlich Deutschen Archäologischen Instituts, Römische Abteilung 27, 1912, 298-310.

Petersen/von Domaszewski/Calderini 1896: E. Petersen / A. von Domaszewski / G. Calderini, Die Marcus-Säule auf Piazza Colonna in Rom (München 1896).

Petrie 1833: G. Petrie, Ancient Irish trumpets. The Dublin Penny Journal 2/56, 1833, 27-30 (authorship is on the authority of Raftery 1987; the article is simply signed »P«).

von Petrikovits 1983: H. von Petrikovits, Sacramentum. In: B. Hartley / J. Wacher (eds), Rome and her northern provinces. Papers presented to Sheppard Frere in honour of his retirement from the Chair of the Archaeology of the Roman Empire, University of Oxford, 1983 (Gloucester 1983) 179-201.

Petrovszky 1993: R. Petrovszky, Studien zu römischen Bronzegefäßen mit Meisterstempeln. Kölner Studien zur Archäologie der römischen Provinzen 1 (Buch am Erlbach 1993).

Pfahl 1993: S. F. Pfahl, Das römische Bronzetropaeum von Lorch und verwandte Stücke. Fundberichte aus Baden-Württemberg 18, 1993, 117-135.

Phillips 1934: C. W. Phillips, The present state of archaeology in Lincolnshire: part II. Archaeological Journal 91, 1934, 97-187.

Phillips 1977: E. J. Phillips, Corbridge; Hadrian's Wall east of the North Tyne. CSIR Great Britain I, 1 (Oxford 1977).

Pič 1906: J. L. Pič, Le Hradischt de Stradonitz en Bohême (Leipzig 1906).

Picard 1927: C. Picard, Apollon, Bès, et les galates. Genava 5, 1927, 52-63.

Picard 1932: G. C. Picard, Review of Johnson (1931). Supplément critique au Bulletin de l'Association Guillaume Budé 4, 1932, 43-45.

1957: G. C. Picard, Les trophées romains (Paris 1957).

Pichot 1996: V. Pichot, Le sanctuaire d'Epomanduodurum (Mathay-Mandeure, Doubs) et ses antécédents celtiques [unpublished thesis, Université de Franche-Comté, Faculté des Lettres et Sciences Humaines de Besançon 1996].

Pietrangeli 1987: C. Pietrangeli, La provenienza delle sculture dei musei Vaticani I. Bollettino dei Monumenti Musei e Gallerie Pontificie 7, 1987, 115-149.

Piggott 1953: C. M. Piggott, Milton Loch crannog I: a native house of the 2nd century AD in Kirkcudbrightshire. Proceedings of the Society of Antiquaries of Scotland 87, 1952-1953 (1953), 134-152.

Piggott 1952: S. Piggott, Celtic chariots on Roman coins. Antiquity 26, 1952, 87-88.

1953: S. Piggott, Three metal-work hoards of the Roman period from southern Scotland. Proceedings of the Society of Antiquaries of Scotland 87, 1952-1953 (1953), 1-50.

1959: S. Piggott, The carnyx in early Iron Age Britain. Antiquaries Journal 39, 1959, 19-32.

1966: S. Piggott, A scheme for the Scottish Iron Age. In: Rivet 1966, 1-15.

1968: S. Piggott, An ancient Briton in North Africa. Antiquity 42, 1968, 128-130.

1970: S. Piggott, Early Celtic art (Edinburgh 1970).

1971: S. Piggott, Firedogs in Iron Age Britain and beyond. In: Boardman/Brown/Powell 1971, 243-270.

Piggott/Daniel 1951: S. Piggott / G. E. Daniel, A picture book of ancient British art (Cambridge 1951).

Piggott/Henderson 1958: S. Piggott / K. Henderson, Scotland before history (London 1958).

Pillonel/Reginelli Servais 2009: D. Pillonel / G. Reginelli Servais, Une image emblématique de La Tène: les bois mortaisés à la lumière de l'analyse technologique. In: Honegger et al. 2009, 37-47.

Pinkerneil 1983: J. Pinkerneil, Studien zu den trajanischen Dakerdarstellungen [PhD dissertation Univ. Freiburg 1983].

Piranesi 1764: G. Piranesi, Antichitá d'Albano e di Castel Gandolfo (Roma 1764).

Pitts 2002: M. Pitts, Altar of the druids. New Scientist (16.2.2002), 40-42.

Polito 1991: E. Polito, Due rilievi d'armi ritrovati. Un'ara funeraria ed un frammento di rilievo nel Castello di Sanssouci a Potsdam. Jahrbuch der Berliner Museen 33, 1991, 37-46.

1998: E. Polito, Fulgentibus Armis. Introduzione allo studio dei fregi d'armi antichi. Xenia Antiqua: Monografie 4 (Roma 1998).

2003: E. Polito, Un gruppo di lastre marmoree con raffigurazioni di armi e Muse dal teatro di Nemi. In: J. Brandt / X. Dupré i Raventós / G. Ghini (eds), Lazio e Sabina I. Atti del primo incontro di studi sul Lazio e la Sabina. Lavori e studi della Soprintendenza per i Beni Archeologici del Lazio 1 (Roma 2003) 251-258.

2009: E. Polito, Frammento di fregio con catasta d'armi dall'Aula Regia della Domus Flavia. In: F. Coarelli (ed.), Divus Vespasianus: il bimillenario dei Flavi [exposition catalogue Rome] (Milano 2009) 506.

2012: E. Polito, Augustan triumphal iconography and the Cantabrian wars: some remarks on round shields and spearheads depicted on monuments from the Iberian peninsula and Italy. Archivo Español de Arqueología 85, 2012, 141-148.

Poller in prep.: T. Poller, Excavations of hillforts and a lowland broch in Perthshire (in prep.).

Pollini 1978: J. Pollini, Studies in Augustan »historical« reliefs [unpublished PhD thesis, University of California, Berkeley 1978].

1995: J. Pollini, The Augustus from Prima Porta and the transformation of the Polykleitan heroic ideal: the rhetoric of art. In: W. G. Moon (ed.), Polykleitos, the Doryphoros, and tradition (Madison WI 1995) 262-282.

Pollock 1997: D. Pollock, The excavation of Iron Age buildings at Ironshill, Inverkeilor, Angus. Proceedings of the Society of Antiquaries of Scotland 127, 1997, 339-358.

Poole 1873: R. S. Poole, A catalogue of the Greek coins in the British Museum. I: Italy (London 1873).

Pop 2000: C. Pop, Un petit tropaeum en bronze découvert dans la Dacie romaine. In: H. Ciugudean / V. Moga (eds), Army and urban development in the Danubian provinces of the Roman Empire. Bibliotheca Musei Apulensis 15 (Alba Iulia 2000) 333-335.

Popescu 1998: G. A. Popescu, Traiano: ai confini dell'imperio (Milano 1998).

Poppi 1981: L. K. Poppi, La sépulture de Casa Selvatica à Berceto (prov. de Parme) et la limite occidentale du faciès Boïen au IIIe siècle av. n. è. Études Celtiques 18, 1981, 39-48.

Poux 2012: M. Poux, Corent: voyage au cœur d'une ville gauloise [exhibition catalogue Corent] (Paris 2012).

Powell 1971: T. G. E. Powell, From Urartu to Gundestrup: the agency of Thracian metal-work. In: Boardman/Brown/Powell 1971, 181-210.

1980: T. G. E. Powell, The Celts (London ²1980).

Precht 1975: G. Precht, Das Grabmal des Lucius Poblicius: Rekonstruktion und Aufbau (Köln 1975).

Priest/Clay/Hill 2003: V. Priest / P. Clay / J. D. Hill, Iron Age gold from Leicestershire. Current Archaeology 188, 2003, 358-362.

von Prittwitz und Gaffron 1993: H.-H. von Prittwitz und Gaffron, Der schiefe Prunkhelm. In: Schalles/Schreiter 1993, 59-63.

2007: H.-H. von Prittwitz und Gaffron, Der Kaiser ist immer und überall. Das Kaiserhaus auf Waffen und Orden. In: M. Hegewisch (ed.), Krieg und Frieden: Kelten Römer Germanen [exhibition catalogue] (Bonn 2007) 125-132.

Purser 1992: J. Purser, Scotland's music (Edinburgh 1992).

1994: J. Purser, Homecoming of the Deskford carnyx after 2000 years of silence. In: J. M. Fladmark (ed.), Cultural tourism (Aberdeen 1994) 374-384.

1996: J. Purser, Music in Dark Age Scotland. In: J. R. F. Burt (ed.), Ancestral voices: proceedings from the conferences of the Pictish Arts Society 1993-4 (Edinburgh 1996) 1-7.

1997: J. Purser, The Kilmartin sessions: the sounds of ancient Scotland (CD recording) (Kilmartin 1997).

2000: J. Purser, The sounds of ancient Scotland. In: Hickmann/Laufs/Eichmann 2000, 325-336.

Querel/Woimant 2002: P. Querel / G.-P. Woimant, Le site d'Estrées-Saint-Denis: sanctuaire et habitat. Une agglomération secondaire? Revue Archéologique de Picardie 2002, 3/4 (Amiens 2002).

Rabe 2008: B. Rabe, Tropaia. τροπή und σκύλα – Entstehung, Funktion und Bedeutung des griechischen Tropaions. Tübinger Archäologische Forschungen 5 (Rahden/Westf. 2008).

Radman-Livaja 2010: I. Radman-Livaja (ed.), Finds of the Roman military equipment in Croatia [exhibition catalogue] (Zagreb 2010).

Raftery 1983: B. Raftery, A catalogue of Irish Iron Age antiquities. Veröffentlichung des Vorgeschichtlichen Seminars Marburg: Sonderband 1 (Marburg 1983).

1984: B. Raftery, La Tène in Ireland: problems of origin and chronology. Veröffentlichung des Vorgeschichtlichen Seminars Marburg: Sonderband 2 (Marburg 1984).

1987: B. Raftery, The Loughnashade horns. Emania 2, 1987, 21-24.

1990: B. Raftery (ed.), Celtic Art (Paris 1990).

Raftery/Megaw/Rigby 1995: B. Raftery / V. Megaw / V. Rigby (eds), Sites and sights of the Iron Age. Essays on fieldwork and museum research presented to Ian Mathieson Stead. Oxbow Monograph 56 (Oxford 1995).

Ralston 1979: I. B. M. Ralston, The Iron Age: northern Britain. In: J. V. S. Megaw / D. D. A. Simpson (eds), Introduction to British prehistory. From the arrival of Homo Sapiens to the Claudian invasion (Leicester 1979) 446-501.

1980: I. Ralston, The Green Castle and the promontory forts of north-east Scotland. Scottish Archaeological Forum 10, 1980, 27-40.

1987: I. Ralston, Portknockie: promontory forts and Pictish settlement in the North-East. In: Small 1987, 15-26.

1996: I. Ralston, Recent work on the Iron Age settlement record in Scotland. In: T. C. Champion / J. R. Collis (eds), The Iron Age in Britain and Ireland: recent trends. Recent Trends Series 4 (Sheffield 1996) 133-153.

Ralston/Clarke 1978: I. B. M. Ralston / D. V. Clarke, Ancient treasures of Scotland (Aberdeen 1978).

Ralston/Inglis 1984: I. Ralston / J. Inglis, Foul hordes: the Picts in the North-East and their background (Aberdeen 1984).

Ralston/Sabine/Watt 1983: I. Ralston / K. Sabine / W. Watt, Later prehistoric settlements in north-east Scotland: a preliminary assessment. In: Chapman/Mytum 1983, 149-173.

Ramsay 1875: W. Ramsay, Sella. In: W. Smith (ed.), A dictionary of Greek and Roman antiquities (London 1875) 1014-1016.

Ramseyer 2009: D. Ramseyer, Le pont celtique de Cornaux/Les Sauges: accident ou lieu de sacrifices? In: Honegger et al. 2009, 103-111.

Rankin 1987: D. Rankin, Celts and the Classical world (London 1987).

Rapin 1993: A. Rapin, Restauration des »feuilles-oreilles« en fer du temple de Champlieu (Oise). Revue Archéologique de Picardie 1993/1/2, 199-200.

Rau 2010: A. Rau, Nydam Mose. 1: Die personengebundenen Gegenstände. Grabungen 1989-1999 (Moesgård 2010).

RCAHMS 1957: RCAHMS, An inventory of the ancient and historical monuments of Selkirkshire (Edinburgh 1957).

1971: RCAHMS, Argyll: an inventory of ancient monuments. 1: Kintyre (Edinburgh 1971).

1997: RCAHMS, Eastern Dumfriesshire: an archaeological landscape (Edinburgh 1997).

2007: RCAHMS, In the shadow of Bennachie: a field archaeology of Donside, Aberdeenshire (Edinburgh 2007).

Reddé 2003: M. Reddé, Le materiel archéologique d'Alésia ou les surprises de la chronologie absolue. In: B. Mandy / A. de Saulce (eds), Les marges de l'Armorique à l'Âge du Fer. Archéologie et histoire: culture matérielle et source écrits. Actes du XXIIIe colloque de l'Association Française pour l'Étude de l'Âge du Fer (Musée Dobré, Nantes, 13-16 mai 1999). Revue Archéologique de l'Ouest, Supplément 10 (Rennes 2003) 287-292.

Rees 1979: S. E. Rees, Agricultural implements in prehistoric and Roman Britain. BAR British Series 69 (Oxford 1979).

1983: S. E. Rees, A wooden ard-share from Dundarg, Aberdeenshire, with a note on other wooden plough pieces. Proceedings of the Society of Antiquaries of Scotland 113, 1983, 457-463.

Reginelli Servais 2007: G. Reginelli Servais, La Tène, un site, un mythe. 1: Chronique en images (1857-1923). Archéologie Neuchâteloise 39 (Neuchâtel 2007).

2009: G. Reginelli Servais, La Tène remis au jour: fouilles de 2003 et thèse en cours. In: Honegger et al. 2009, 29-35.

Reinach 1911a: A. J. Reinach, Les galates dans l'art alexandrin. Fondation Eugène Piot, Monuments et Mémoires 18, 1911, 37-115.

1911b: A. J. Reinach, Un monument Delphien: l'Étolie sur les trophées gaulois de Kallion. Journal International d'Archéologie Numismatique 13, 1911, 177-240.

Reinach 1888a: S. Reinach, Les gaulois dans l'art antique et le sarcophage de la vigne Ammendola. Revue Archéologique (Third Series) 12, 1888, 11-22.

1888b: S. Reinach, Les gaulois dans l'art antique et le sarcophage de la vigne Ammendola (deuxième article). Revue Archéologique (Third Series) 12, 1888, 273-284.

1889a: S. Reinach, Les gaulois dans l'art antique et le sarcophage de la vigne Ammendola (troisième article). Revue Archéologique (Third Series) 13, 1889, 187-203.

1889b: S. Reinach, Les gaulois dans l'art antique et le sarcophage de la vigne Ammendola (quatrième et dernier article). Revue Archéologique (Third Series) 13, 1889, 317-352.

1909: S. Reinach, Répertoire de reliefs grecs et romains. I: Les ensembles (Paris 1909).

1912: S. Reinach, Répertoire de reliefs grecs et romains. II: Afrique – Iles Britanniques (Paris 1912).

1922: S. Reinach, Répertoire de peintures grecques et romaines (Paris 1922).

1968: S. Reinach, Répertoire de reliefs grecs et romains. III: Italie – Suisse (reprinted in Rome 1968; original publication date not given).

n. d.: S. Reinach, Antiquités nationales: description raisonnée du Musée de Saint-Germain-en-Laye. Bronzes figurées de la Gaule romaine (Paris no date, c. 1894).

Reinerth 1936: H. Reinerth, Das Federseemoor als Siedlungsland des Vorzeitmenschen. Führer zur Urgeschichte 9 (Leipzig 1936).

Rennie 1984: E. B. Rennie, Excavations at Ardnadam, Cowal, Argyll, 1964-1982. Glasgow Archaeological Journal 11, 1984, 13-39.

Richard 1989: C. Richard, Gué de Sciaux (Antigny/Vienne). Une ville gallo-romaine. Fouilles d'un sanctuaire. Société de Recherches Archéologique de Chauvigny: Mémoire 4 (Chauvigny 1989).

Richmond 1963: I. A. Richmond, Review of Picard 1957. Journal of Roman Studies 53, 1963, 221-222.

1969: I. Richmond, Roman archaeology and art. Essays and studies (London 1969).

1982: I. Richmond, Trajan's army on Trajan's Column (London 1982).

Richmond/McIntyre 1936: I. A. Richmond / J. McIntyre, The Roman fort at Fendoch in Glenalmond: a preliminary note. Proceedings of the Society of Antiquaries of Scotland 70, 1935-1936 (1936), 400-406.

Ridgway 1972: B. S. Ridgway, Catalogue of the classical collection. I: Classical sculpture (Providence RI 1972).

Rieckhoff/Fichtl 2011: S. Rieckhoff / S. Fichtl, Keltenstädte aus der Luft (Stuttgart 2011).

Rigby/Freestone 1997: V. Rigby / I. Freestone, Ceramic changes in late Iron Age Britain. In: I. Freestone / D. Gaimster (eds), Pottery in the making. World ceramic traditions (London 1997) 56-61.

Rimmer 1981: J. Rimmer, An archaeo-organological survey of the Netherlands. In: Megaw/Longworth 1981, 233-245.

Riße 2001: M. Riße (ed.), Volubilis: eine römische Stadt in Marokko von der Frühzeit bis in die islamische Periode (Mainz 2001).

Ritchie 1995: A. Ritchie, Prehistoric Orkney (London 1995).

2003: A. Ritchie, Paganism among the Picts and the conversion of Orkney. In: Downes/Ritchie 2003, 3-10.

Ritterling 1924: E. Ritterling, Legio: Bestand,Verteilung und Kriegerische Betätigung der Legionen von Augustus bis Diocletian (extract from G. Wissowa / W. Kroll [ed.], Paulys Real-Encyclopädie der Classischen Altertumswissenschaft 12/1-2) (Stuttgart 1924).

Rivet 1966: A. L. F. Rivet (ed.), The Iron Age in northern Britain (Edinburgh 1966).

1988: A. L. F. Rivet, Gallia Narbonensis: southern France in Roman times (London 1988).

Robertson 1962: A. S. Robertson, Roman Imperial coins in the Hunter Coin Cabinet, University of Glasgow. I: Augustus to Nerva (Oxford 1962).

1970: A. Robertson, Roman finds from non-Roman sites in Scotland. Britannia 1, 1970, 198-226.

1975: A. S. Robertson, The Romans in north Britain: the coin evidence. In: H. Temporini (ed.), Aufstieg und Niedergang der Römischen Welt II/3, 1975, 364-426.

1978a: A. S. Robertson, The circulation of Roman coins in north Britain: the evidence of hoards and site-finds from Scotland. In: Carson/Kraay 1978, 186-216.

1978b: A. S. Robertson, Roman Imperial coins in the Hunter Coin Cabinet, University of Glasgow. IV: Valerian I to Allectus (Oxford 1978).

2000: A. S. Robertson, An inventory of Romano-British coin hoards (London 2000).

Robinson 1927: D. M. Robinson, Roman sculptures from Colonia Caesarea (Pisidian Antioch). The Art Bulletin 9, 1927, 5-56.

Rocchetti 1958: L. Rocchetti, Amiternum. Enciclopedia dell'Arte Antica Classica e Orientale I, 320 (Roma 1958).

von Rohden/Winnefeld 1911: H. von Rohden / H. Winnefeld, Die antiken Terracotten. IV: Architektonische römische Tonreliefs der Kaiserzeit (Berlin, Stuttgart 1911).

Rolland 1969: H. Rolland, Le mausolée de Glanum (Saint-Rémy-de-Provence). Gallia, Supplément 21 (Paris 1969).

1977: H. Rolland, L'Arc de Glanum. Gallia, Supplément 31 (Paris 1977).

Rollin/Feuardent 1887: Rollin / Feuardent, Collection de M. le Vicomte de Ponton d'Amécourt: Monnaies d'or romaines et byzantines, Sale Catalogue, 25-30.4.1887 (Paris 1887).

Romanelli 1942: P. Romanelli, La colonna Antonina. Rilievi fotografici eseguiti in occasione dei lavori di protezione antiaerea (Roma 1942).

Roncador 2009: R. Roncador, La »riscoperta« del carnyx di Sanzeno (Val di Non, Trentino, Itali): Storia degle studi ed inquadramento cultural. In: S. Grunwald / J. K. Koch / D. Mölders / U. Sommer / S. Wolfram (eds), ARTeFACT: Festschrift für Sabine Rieckhoff zum 65. Geburtstag. Universitätsforschungen zur prähistorischen Archäologie 172 (Bonn 2009) 547-555.

2014: R. Roncador, Celti e Reti tra V e I sec. a. C.: contesto culturale e progetto di ricerca »Karnyx di Sanzeno«. In: R. Roncador / F. Nicolis (eds), Antichi popoli delle Alpi. Sviluppi culturali durante l'età del Ferro nei territori alpine centro-orientali (Trento 2014) 157-181.

2017: R. Roncador, Celti e Reti. Interazioni tra popoli durante la seconda età del Ferro in ambito alpino centro-orientale (Roma 2017).

Roncador/Melini 2010: R. Roncador / R. Melini, Il karnyx celtico di Sanzeno (Val di Non, Trentino): ritrovamento, indagini e ricostruzione. In: M. Carrese / E. Li Castro / M. Martinelli (eds), La musica in Etruria. Atti del convegno internazionale, Tarquinia 18-20 settembre 2009 (Tarquinia 2010) 155-176.

Roncador et al. 2014: R. Roncador / P. Bellintani / E. Silvestri / A. Ervas / P. Piccardo / B. Mille, Karnykes a Sanzeno: dalla ri-scoperta alla ricostruzione sperimentale. In: P. Barral / J.-P. Guillaumet / M.-J. Roulière-Lambert / M. Saracino / D. Vitali (eds), Les Celtes et le Nord de l'Italie (Premier et Second Âges du fer). Actes du XXXVIᵉ colloque international de l'A.F.E.A.F. (Vérone, 17-20 mai 2012). Revue Archéologique de l'Est, Supplément 36 (Dijon 2014) 667-678.

Ronke 1987: J. Ronke, Magistratische Repräsentation im römischen Relief. BAR International Series 370 (Oxford 1987).

Ross 1992: A. Ross, Pagan Celtic Britain: studies in iconography and tradition (revised edition) (London 1992).

Ross 1994: A. Ross, Pottery report. In: Ballin Smith 1994, 236-257.

Rossignani 1975: M. P. Rossignani, La decorazione architettonica romana in Parma. Archaeologica 2 (Roma 1975).

Rossignani/Sacchi 1993: M. P. Rossignani / F. Sacchi, I documenti architettonici de Como romano. In: Novum Comum 2050. Atti del convegno celebrativo della fondazione di Como romana (Como 1993) 85-141.

Rotili 1972: M. Rotili, L'Arco di Traiano a Benevento (Roma 1972).

Russell-White 1995: C. J. Russell-White, The excavation of a Neolithic and Iron Age settlement at Wardend of Durris, Aberdeenshire. Proceedings of the Society of Antiquaries of Scotland 125, 1995, 9-27.

Russo 1981: S. Russo, Fregi d'armi in monumenti funerari romani dell'Abruzzo. Rivista di Archeologia 1981, 30-43.

Rustoiu 2007: A. Rustoiu, Thracian sica and Dacian falx. The history of a »national« weapon. In: S. Nemeti / F. Fodorean / E. Nemeth / S. Cociş / I. Nemeti / M. Pîslaru (eds), Dacia Felix: studia Michaeli Bărbulescu oblate (Cluj-Napoca 2007) 67-82.

2008: A. Rustoiu, Warriors and society in Celtic Transylvania. Studies on the grave with helmet from Ciumeşti (Cluj-Napoca 2008).

Rusu 1969: M. Rusu, Das keltische Fürstengrab von Ciumeşti in Rumänien. Bericht der Römisch-Germanischen Kommission 50, 1969, 267-300.

Rutter 2001: N. K. Rutter (ed.), Historia Numorum: Italy (London 2001).

Ryberg 1955: I. S. Ryberg, Rites of the state religion in Roman art. Memoirs of the American Academy in Rome 22 (Rome 1955).

Rynne 1983: E. Rynne, Some early Iron Age sword-hilts from Ireland and Scotland. In: O'Connor/Clarke 1983, 188-196.

Sachs 1910: C. Sachs, Lituus und Carnyx. In: Festschrift zum 90. Geburtstag Rechus Freihe von Liliencron (Leipzig 1910) 241-246.

1940: C. Sachs, The history of musical instruments (New York 1940).

Saglio 1887: E. Saglio, Carnyx. In: C. Daremberg / E. Saglio (eds), Dictionnaire des antiquités grecques et romaines d'après les textes et les monuments I, 2 (Paris 1887) 925-926.

Salcedo Garces 1983: F. Salcedo Garces, Los relieves de armas del teatro de Mérida. Lucentum 2, 1983, 243-283.

Salway 1981: P. Salway, Roman Britain (Oxford 1981).

Sanader/Tončinić 2009: M. Sanader / D. Tončinić, Das Projekt TILURIUM. Waffendarstellungen auf Steindenkmälern aus Tilurium. In: A. W. Busch / H.-J. Schalles (eds), Waffen in Aktion. Akten der 16. Internationalen Roman Military Equipment Conference (ROMEC). Xanten, 13.-16. Juni 2007. Xantener Berichte 16 (Mainz 2009) 199-202.

2010: M. Sanader / D. Tončinić, Gardun – the ancient Tilurium. In: Radman-Livaja 2010, 33-53.

Sandars 1913: H. Sandars, The weapons of the Iberians. Archaeologia 64, 1912-1913 (1913), 205-294.

Sangster 1995: K. Sangster, George Gordon and Elgin Museum. In: I. Keillar / J. S. Smith (eds), George Gordon: man of science (Aberdeen 1995) 105-115.

Sanz Minguez/Romero Carnicero 2008: C. Sanz Minguez / F. Romero Carnicero, Pintia: fortunes of a pre-Roman city in Hispania. Current World Archaeology 29, 2008, 22-29.

Sarthre 2000: C.-O. Sarthre, L'apport des analyses de monnaies découvertes au Gué-de-Sciaux (Antigny, Vienne) à la compréhension des monnayages pictons. In: I. Bertrand (ed.), Actualité de la recherche sur le mobilier romain non céramique. Association des Publications Chauvinoises: Mémoire 18 (Chauvigny 2000) 263-278.

Sarti 2001: S. Sarti, Giovanni Pietro Campana 1808-1880: the man and his collection. BAR International Series 971 (Oxford 2001).

2002: S. Sarti, The Campana affair. Minerva 13/2, 2002, 42-45.

Sauron 1983: G. Sauron, Les cippes funéraires Gallo-Romains à décor de rinceaux de Nîmes et de sa région. Gallia 41, 1983, 59-110.

Schäfer 1989: T. Schäfer, Die Dakerkriege Trajans auf einer Bronzekanne. Jahrbuch des Deutschen Archäologischen Instituts 104, 1989, 283-317.

Schalles 1994: H.-J. Schalles, Frühkaiserzeitliche Militaria aus einem Altrheinarm bei Xanten-Wardt. Journal of Roman Military Equipment Studies 5, 1994, 155-165.

Schalles/Schreiter 1993: H.-J. Schalles / C. Schreiter (eds), Geschichte aus dem Kies: Neue Funde aus dem Alten Rhein bei Xanten [exhibition catalogue]. Xantener Berichte 3 = Führer des Regionalmuseums Xanten 34 (Köln 1993).

Scheers 1969: S. Scheers, Les monnaies de la Gaule inspirées de celles de la République romaine. Recueil de Travaux d'Histoire et de Philologie Série 5, 6 (Leuven 1969).

1975: S. Scheers, Les monnaies gauloises de la collection A. Danicourt à Péronne (France, Somme). Cercle d'Études Numismatiques: Travaux 7 (Bruxelles 1975).

1978: S. Scheers, Monnaies gauloises de Seine-Maritime (Rouen 1978).

1980: S. Scheers, Enkele niet gekende gallische nabootsingen van romeinse denarii. La Vie Numismatique 30/1, 1980, 125-132.

1983: S. Scheers, La Gaule Belgique: numismatique celtique (Louvain ²1983).

1992a: S. Scheers, Un complément à l'Atlas de Monnaies Gauloises de Henri de La Tour (Paris, Maastricht 1992).

1992b: S. Scheers, Celtic coin types in Britain and their Mediterranean origins. In: Mays 1992, 33-46.

Scheid/Huet 2000: J. Scheid / V. Huet (eds), La colonne Aurélienne: autour de la colonne Aurélienne. Geste et image sur la colonne de Marc Aurèle à Rome. Bibliothèque de l'École des Hautes Études: Section des Sciences Religieuses 108 (Turnhout 2000).

Schleiermacher 1984: M. Schleiermacher, Römische Reitergrabsteine: Die kaiserzeitlichen Reliefs des triumphierenden Reiters. Abhandlungen zur Kunst-, Musik- und Literaturwissenschaft 338 (Bonn 1984).

Schlüter/Platz-Horster/Zazoff 1975: M. Schlüter / G. Platz-Horster / P. Zazoff, Antike Gemmen in Deutschen Sammlungen. IV: Hannover, Kestner-Museum; Hamburg, Museum für Kunst und Gewerbe (Wiesbaden 1975).

Schmuhl 2008: Y. Schmuhl, Römische Siegesmonumente republikanischer Zeit. Untersuchungen zu Ursprüngen, Erscheinungsformen und Denkmalpolitik. Antiquitates 43 (Hamburg 2008).

von Schnurbein 1979: S. von Schnurbein, Eine hölzerne Sica aus dem Römerlager Oberaden. Germania 57, 1979, 117-134.

1986: S. von Schnurbein, Dakisch-thrakische Soldaten im Römerlager Oberaden. Germania 64/2, 1986, 409-431.

Schönfelder 2002: M. Schönfelder, Das spätkeltische Wagengrab von Boé (Dép. Lot-et-Garonne). Studien zu Wagen und Wagengräbern der jüngeren Latènezeit. Monographien des RGZM 54 (Mainz 2002).

2010: M. Schönfelder, Keltische Wanderungen – welche Modelle bleiben bestehen? In: M. Schönfelder (ed.), Kelten! Kelten? Keltische Spuren in Italien. Mosaiksteine – Forschungen am RGZM 7 (Mainz 2010) 46-48.

Schröder 1993: S. Schröder, Katalog der antiken Skulpturen des Museo del Prado in Madrid. 1: Die Porträts (Mainz 1993).

2004: S. Schröder, Katalog der antiken Skulpturen des Museo del Prado in Madrid. 2: Idealplastik (Mainz 2004).

Schröder/García López/Gómez García n.d.: S. Schröder / D. García López / C. Gómez García (eds), La Apoteosis de Claudio. un monumento funerario de la época de Augusto y su fortuna moderna (Madrid no date, c. 2002).

Schulte 1983: B. Schulte, Die Goldprägung der gallischen Kaiser von Postumus bis Tetricus. Typos 4 (Aarau 1983).

Schultz 1997: H.-D. Schultz, Antike Münzen: Bildheft zur Ausstellung des Münzkabinetts in der Antikensammlung im Pergamonmuseum (Berlin 1997).

Schultz 1993: S. Schultz (ed.), Sylloge Nummorum Graecorum, Deutschland. Sammlung der Universitätsbibliothek Leipzig. 1: Autonome griechische Münzen (München 1993).

Schumacher 1935: K. Schumacher, Germanendarstellungen. I: Darstellungen aus dem Altertum (ed. H. Klumbach) (Mainz ⁴1935).

Schutz 1985: H. Schutz, The Romans in central Europe (New Haven 1985).

Score 2011: V. Score, Hoards, hounds and helmets: a conquest-period ritual site at Hallaton, Leicestershire (Leicester 2011).

Scott 1926: H. Scott, Fasti Ecclesiae Scoticanae. 6: Synods of Aberdeen and of Moray (Edinburgh 1926).

Scott 1961: J. G. Scott, The excavation of the chambered cairn at Crarae, Loch Fyneside, mid Argyll. Proceedings of the Society of Antiquaries of Scotland 94, 1960-1961 (1961), 1-27.

Scott/Powell 1969: J. G. Scott / T. G. E. Powell, A bronze horse figurine found near Birkwood, Lesmahagow, Lanarkshire. Antiquaries Journal 49, 1969, 118-126.

Scott 2014: M. Scott, Delphi. A history of the center of the ancient world (Princeton NJ 2014).

Scullard 1970: H. H. Scullard, From the Gracchi to Nero: a history of Rome from 133 B.C. to A.D. 68 (London ³1970).

Sealey 2007: P. R. Sealey, A late Iron Age warrior burial from Kelvedon, Essex. East Anglian Archaeology 118 (Colchester 2007).

Sear 2006: F. Sear, Roman theatres: an architectural study (Oxford 2006).

Segenni 1985: S. Segenni, Amiternum e il suo territorio in èta romana. Biblioteca di Studi Antichi 49 (Pisa 1985).

Sellar 1993: W. D. H. Sellar (ed.), Moray: province and people (Edinburgh 1993).

Servadei 2003: C. Servadei, L'immagine del Celta nella pittura vascolare etrusca. In: Vitali 2003a, 293-306.

Shapland/Armit 2011: F. Shapland / I. Armit, The useful dead: bodies as objects in Iron Age and Norse Atlantic Scotland. European Journal of Archaeology 15/1, 2011, 98-116.

Shaw 2000: J. Shaw, Sanchi and its archaeological landscape: Buddhist monasteries, settlements & irrigation works in Central India. Antiquity 74, 2000, 775-776.

Sheedy 2008: K. Sheedy, Sylloge Nummorum Graecorum, Australia. I: The Gale collection of south Italian coins (Sydney 2008).

Shepherd 1983: I. A. G. Shepherd, Pictish settlement problems in N.E. Scotland. In: Chapman/Mytum 1983, 327-356.

1993: I. A. G. Shepherd, The Picts in Moray. In: Sellar 1993, 75-90.

Shepherd/Greig 1996: I. A. G. Shepherd / M. K. Greig, Grampian's past: its archaeology from the air (Aberdeen 1996).

Shepherd/Shepherd 1978: I. A. G. Shepherd / A. N. Shepherd, An incised Pictish figure and a new symbol stone from Barflat, Rhynie, Gordon District. Proceedings of the Society of Antiquaries of Scotland 109, 1977-1978 (1978), 211-222.

Siebert 2011: A. V. Siebert, Geschichte(n) in Ton: römische Architekturterrakotten. Museum Kestnerianum 16 (Regensburg 2011).

Sieveking 1937: J. Sieveking, Zu den beiden Triumphbogensockeln im Boboligarten. Mitteilungen des Deutschen Archäologischen Instituts, Römische Abteilung 52, 1937, 74-82.

Sievers 2003: S. Sievers, Manching – Die Keltenstadt (Stuttgart 2003).

2009: S. Sievers, Les depots de Manching. In: Honegger et al. 2009, 177-183.

Silberberg-Peirce 1986: S. Silberberg-Peirce, The many faces of the Pax Augusta: images of war and peace in Rome and Gallia Narbonensis. Art History 9/3, 1986, 306-324.

Sills 2000: J. Sills, Review of Creighton 2000. Spink Numismatic Circular, August 2000, 162-163.

2001: J. Sills, A new trumpet type half stater. Chris Rudd List 58, 2001, 4-5.

2013: J. Sills, A new Amminius, an old question: who or what was Sego? Chris Rudd List 132, 2013, 2-3.

Simonett 1947: C. Simonett, Führer durch das Vindonissa-Museum in Brugg (Brugg 1947).

Simpson 1996: D. D. A. Simpson, Excavation of a kerbed funerary monument at Stoneyfield, Raigmore, Inverness, Highland, 1972-3. Proceedings of the Society of Antiquaries of Scotland 126, 1996, 53-86.

Simpson / Simpson 1968: D. D. A. Simpson / M. Simpson, Decorative ring-headed pins in Scotland. Transactions of the Dumfriesshire and Galloway Natural History and Antiquarian Society 45, 1968, 141-146.

Simpson 1968: M. Simpson, Massive armlets in the north British Iron Age. In: Coles / Simpson 1968, 233-254.

1970: M. Simpson, Some Roman-Iron Age finger rings. Proceedings of the Society of Antiquaries of Scotland 102, 1969-1970 (1970), 105-108.

Simpson 1954: W. D. Simpson, Dundarg Castle: a history of the site and a record of the excavations in 1950 and 1951. Aberdeen University Studies 131 (Edinburgh 1954).

Sims-Williams 1998: P. Sims-Williams, Celtomania and Celtoscepticism. Cambrian Medieval Celtic Studies 36, 1998, 1-35.

Sinn 1987: F. Sinn, Stadtrömische Marmorurnen. Beiträge zur Erschließung hellenistischer und kaiserzeitlicher Skulptur und Architektur 8 (Mainz 1987).

Small 1987: A. Small (ed.), The Picts: a new look at old problems (Dundee 1987).

Smellie 1784: W. Smellie, Account of the institution and progress of the Society of Antiquaries of Scotland II (Edinburgh 1784).

Smiles 1877: S. Smiles, Life of a Scotch naturalist: Thomas Edward, Associate of the Linnean Society (London ⁵1877).

Smith 1845: A. Smith, Parish of Banff. New Statistical Account of Scotland 13, 1845, 1-63.

Smith 1904: A. H. Smith, A catalogue of sculpture in the Department of Greek and Roman Antiquities, British Museum III (London 1904).

Smith 1994: C. Smith, Animal bone report. In: Ballin Smith 1994, 139-153.

2000: C. Smith, A grumphie in the sty: an archaeological view of pigs in Scotland, from their earliest domestication to the agricultural revolution. Proceedings of the Society of Antiquaries of Scotland 130, 2000, 705-724.

Smith 1895: J. Smith, Prehistoric man in Ayrshire (London 1895).

1919: J. Smith, Excavation of the forts of Castlehill, Aitnock, and Coalhill, Ayrshire. Proceedings of the Society of Antiquaries of Scotland 53, 1918-1919 (1919), 123-134.

Smith 1868: J. A. Smith, Notice of a remarkable bronze ornament with horns, found in Galloway, now at Abbotsford. Also of a bronze ornament like a »swine's head«, found in Banffshire. Proceedings of the Society of Antiquaries of Scotland 7, 1867-1868 (1868), 334-357.

1881: J. A. Smith, Notice of a massive bronze »late Celtic« armlet and two small objects of bronze (horse-trappings), found with a Roman bronze patella, at Stanhope, Peeblesshire, in 1876; with an account of other bronze or brass armlets found in Scotland. Proceedings of the Society of Antiquaries of Scotland 15, 1880-1881 (1881), 316-361.

1883: J. A. Smith, Notice of a massive bronze armlet, the property of the Right Hon. The Earl of Strathmore. Proceedings of the Society of Antiquaries of Scotland 17, 1882-1883 (1883), 90-92.

Smith 1909: R. A. Smith, A hoard of metal found at Santon Downham, Suffolk. Proceedings of the Cambridge Antiquarian Society 13, 1908-1909 (1909), 146-163.

Smithers 1989: D. L. Smithers, A new look at the historical, linguistic and taxonomic bases for the evolution of lip-blown instruments from Classical antiquity until the end of the middle ages. Historic Brass Society Journal 1, 1989, 3-64.

Snape 1993: M. E. Snape, Roman brooches from north Britain: a classification and a catalogue of brooches from sites on the Stanegate. BAR British Series 235 (Oxford 1993).

Solier 1986: Y. Solier, Narbonne (Aude). Les monuments antiques et médiévaux. Le Musée Archéologique et le Musée Lapidaire (Paris 1986).

Spannagel 1979: M. Spannagel, Wiedergefundene Antiken. Zu vier Dal-Pozzo-Zeichnungen in Windsor Castle. Archäologischer Anzeiger 1979/3, 348-377.

Spânu 2002: D. Spânu, Studien zum Silberschatzfund des 1. Jahrhunderts v. Chr. von Lupu, Rumänien. Prähistorische Zeitschrift 77, 2002, 84-136.

2010: D. Spânu, Semnificații ale tezaurului de la Sălištea. Caiete ARA 1, 2010, 5-24.

2012: D. Spânu, Tezaurele dacice. Creația în metale prețioase din Dacia preromană (București 2012).

Speciale 1979: O. Speciale, Antichità di Albano e di Castel Gandolfo. In: Piranesi: nei luoghi di Piranesi, section »Cori – Palazzetto Luciani: Le antichità del Lazio« (Roma 1979) 75-111.

Speidel 1970: M. Speidel, The captor of Decebalus: a new inscription from Philippi. Journal of Roman Studies 60, 1970, 142-153.

2000: M. Speidel, Commodus and the king of the Quadi. Germania 78/1, 2000, 193-197.

Spinola 1999: G. Spinola, Il Museo Pio-Clementino. Guide Cataloghi dei Musei Vaticani 4 (Città del Vaticano 1999).

Spratling 1981: M. G. Spratling, Enamelled bronze boss. In: M. G. Jarrett / S. Wrathmell, Whitton: an Iron Age and Roman farmstead in South Glamorgan (Cardiff 1981) 180-182.

2007: M. Spratling, Observations on massive armlets [privately circulated, 2007].

Stair 1857: Earl of Stair, Note by the Earl of Stair relative to bronze articles exhibited by his Lordship. Proceedings of the Society of Antiquaries of Scotland 2, 1854-1857 (1857), 237-238.

Stary 1981: P. F. Stary, Ursprung und Ausbreitung der eisenzeitlichen Ovalschilde mit spindelförmigem Schildbuckel. Germania 59/2, 1981, 287-306.

Stead 1965: I. M. Stead, The Celtic chariot. Antiquity 39, 1965, 259-265.

1991a: I. M. Stead, The Snettisham treasure: excavations in 1990. Antiquity 65, 1991, 447-465.

1991b: I. M. Stead, Iron Age cemeteries in East Yorkshire. Excavations at Burton Fleming, Rudston, Garton-on-the-Wolds and Kirkburn. Archaeological Report 22 (London 1991).

1996: I. Stead, Celtic art in Britain before the Roman conquest (London 1996).

1998: I. M. Stead, The Salisbury hoard (Stroud 1998).

2006: I. M. Stead, British Iron Age swords and scabbards (London 2006).

n. d.: I. M. Stead, The Gauls: Celtic antiquities from France [exhibition catalogue] (London no date).

Stead/Rigby 1999: I. M. Stead / V. Rigby, The Morel Collection: Iron Age antiquities from Champagne in the British Museum (London 1999).

Steer 1947: K. A. Steer, An iron implement and other relics from Falla Cairn, Roxburghshire. Proceedings of the Society of Antiquaries of Scotland 81, 1946-1947 (1947), 183-185.

Stefan 2005: A. S. Stefan, Les guerres daciques de Domitien et de Trajan. Architecture militaire, topographie, images et histoire. Collection de l'Ecole Française de Rome 353 (Roma 2005).

Stefanelli 1990: L. P. B. Stefanelli (ed.), Il Bronzo dei Romani: Arredo e Suppellettile (Roma 1990).

Stemmer 1978: K. Stemmer, Untersuchungen zur Typologie, Chronologie und Ikonographie der Panzerstatuen. Archäologische Forschungen 4 (Berlin 1978).

Stevenson 1951: R. B. K. Stevenson, Scotland's ancient treasures from the National Museum of Antiquities of Scotland (Glasgow 1951).

1966: R. B. K. Stevenson, Metal-work and some other objects in Scotland and their cultural affinities. In: Rivet 1966, 17-44.

1967: R. B. K. Stevenson, A Roman-period cache of charms in Aberdeenshire. Antiquity 41, 1967, 143-145.

1976: R. B. K. Stevenson, Romano-British glass bangles. Glasgow Archaeological Journal 4, 1976, 45-54.

1981: R. B. K. Stevenson, The Museum, its beginnings and development. Part II: the National Museum to 1954. In: A. S. Bell (ed.), The Scottish antiquarian tradition. Essays to mark the bicentenary of the Society of Antiquaries of Scotland and its museum, 1780-1980 (Edinburgh 1981) 142-211.

Stevenson/Emery 1964: R. B. K. Stevenson / J. Emery, The Gaulcross hoard of Pictish silver. Proceedings of the Society of Antiquaries of Scotland 97, 1963-1964 (1964), 206-211.

Stewart 1985: M. E. C. Stewart, The excavation of a henge, stone circles and metal working area at Moncreiffe, Perthshire. Proceedings of the Society of Antiquaries of Scotland 115, 1985, 125-150.

Stewart et al. 1999: M. E. C. Stewart / J. Atkinson / G. J. Barclay / A. Cox, Excavations at Allt na Moine Buidhe and Allt Lochan nan Largunn, Perthshire. Tayside and Fife Archaeological Journal 5, 1999, 106-138.

Stewart 2008: P. Stewart, The social history of Roman art (Cambridge 2008).

Stîngă/Pop 2000: I. Stîngă / C. Pop, Trofeul de bronz de la Gârla Mare (Jud. Mehedinți). Drobeta 10, 2000 (Muzeul Regiunii Portilor de Fier), 111-117.

Strachan 1999: R. Strachan, Excavations at Albie Hill, Applegarthtown, Annandale, Dumfries and Galloway. Transactions of the Dumfriesshire and Galloway Natural History and Antiquarian Society 73, 1999, 9-15.

Strack 1931: P. L. Strack, Untersuchungen zur römischen Reichsprägung des zweiten Jahrhunderts. I: Die Reichsprägung zur Zeit des Traian (Stuttgart 1931).

1933: P. L. Strack, Untersuchungen zur römischen Reichsprägung des zweiten Jahrhunderts. II: Die Reichsprägung zur Zeit des Hadrian (Stuttgart 1933).

Strathspey 1983: Lord Strathspey, A history of Clan Grant (Chichester 1983).

Strazzulla 1991: M. J. Strazzulla, Iconografia e propaganda imperiale in età augustea: le lastre Campana. In: E. Herring / R. Whitehouse / J. Wilkins (eds), Papers of the Fourth Conference of Italian Archaeology. I: The Archaeology of Power, part 1 (London 1991) 241-252.

1993: M. J. Strazzulla, L'ultima fase decorativa dei santuari Etrusco-Italici: le lastre »Campana«. In: E. Rystedt / C. Wikander / Ö. Wikander (eds), Deliciae Fictiles. Proceedings of the first international conference on central Italic architectural terracottas at the Swedish Institute in Rome, 10-12 December, 1990. Istituto Svedese di Studi Classici: Skrifter/Kvart 50 (Stockholm 1993) 299-306.

Striewe 1996: K. Striewe, Studien zur Nauheimer Fibel und ähnlichen Formen der Spätlatènezeit. Internationale Archäologie 29 (Espelkamp 1996).

Strobel 2007: K. Strobel, Galatien, die Galater und die Poleis der Galater: Historische Identität und ethnische Tradition. In: H. Birkhan (ed.), Kelten-Einfälle an der Donau. Akten des Vierten Symposiums deutschsprachiger Keltologinnen und Keltologen; philologische, historische, archäologische Evidenzen; Konrad Spindler (1939-2005) zum Gedenken. Österreichische Akademie der Wissenschaften, Philosophisch-Historische Klasse: Denkschriften 345 (Wien 2007) 529-548.

Strong 1961: D. E. Strong, Roman Imperial sculpture (London 1961).

Strong 1928: E. Strong, Art in ancient Rome. I: From the earliest times to the principate of Nero (London 1928; reprinted Connecticut 1970).

Sutherland 1984: C. H. V. Sutherland, The Roman Imperial Coinage. I (revised edition): From 31 BC to AD 69 (= RIC [2]I) (London 1984).

Swan 1999: V. G. Swan, The Twentieth Legion and the history of the Antonine Wall reconsidered. Proceedings of the Society of Antiquaries of Scotland 129, 1999, 399-480.

Sydenham 1952: E. A. Sydenham, The coinage of the Roman Republic (London 1952).

Szabó 1995: M. Szabó, Umbro-Celtica. In: Raftery/Megaw/Rigby 1995, 157-162.

Tamboer/van Vilsteren 1999: A. Tamboer / V. van Vilsteren, Ausgegrabene Klänge: Archäologische Musikinstrumente aus allen Epochen [exhibition catalogue]. Archäologische Mitteilungen aus Nordwestdeutschland, Beiheft 25 (Oldenburg 1999).

2006: A. Tamboer / V. van Vilsteren, Celtic bugle, Roman lituus, or medieval ban horn? An evaluation of cast bronze horns with an upturned bell. In: Hickmann/Both/Eichmann 2006, 221-236.

Tate/Barnes/MacSween n.d.: J. Tate / I. Barnes / A. MacSween, Analyses of massive bronze armlets. In: T. Bryce / J. Tate (eds), The laboratories of the National Museum of Antiquities of Scotland 2 (Edinburgh no date, c. 1982) 89-94.

Taylor 1982: D. B. Taylor, Excavation of a promontory fort, broch and souterrain at Hurly Hawkin, Angus. Proceedings of the Society of Antiquaries of Scotland 112, 215-253.

Taylor 1992: T. Taylor, The Gundestrup cauldron. Scientific American 266/3, 1992, 66-71.

Tempesta 1992: A. Tempesta, I rilievi con armi Cesi: ipotesi di ricomposizione ed interpretazione. Bullettino della Commissione Archeologica Comunale di Roma 94, 1992, 309-340.

Terrer et al. 2003: D. Terrer / R. Lauxerois / R. Robert / V. Gaggadis-Robin / A. Hermary / A. Jockey / H. Lavagne, Nouvel Espérandieu. Recueil général des sculptures sur pierre de la Gaule. I: Vienne (Isère) (Paris 2003).

Thapar 2003: R. Thapar, The Penguin history of early India: from the origins to AD 1300 (London 2003).

Thédenat 1904: H. Thédenat, Liticen. In: C. Daremberg / E. Saglio / E. Pottier (eds), Dictionnaire des Antiquités Grecques et Romaines. III, 2: L-M (Paris 1904) 1268.

Thevenot 1951: E. Thevenot, Le cheval sacré dans la Gaule de l'est. Revue Archéologique de l'Est et du Centre Est 2, 1951, 129-141.

Thomas 1963: C. Thomas, The interpretation of the Pictish symbols. Archaeological Journal 120, 1963, 31-97.

Thomas 2007: J. Thomas, Place and memory. Excavations at the Pict's Knowe, Holywood and Holm Farm, Dumfries and Galloway, 1994-8 (Oxford 2007).

Thompson 1964: D. B. Thompson, Glauke and the goose. In: L. F. Sandler (ed.), Essays in memory of Karl Lehmann. Marsyas, Supplement 1 (New York 1964) 314-322.

Thompson 1889: G. H. Thompson, On vessels found at West Thirston, Northumberland. History of the Berwickshire Naturalists' Club 12, 1887-1889 (1889), 530-531.

Tierney 1960: J. J. Tierney, The Celtic ethnography of Posidonius. Proceedings of the Royal Irish Academy 60C, 1959-1960 (1960), 189-275.

Töpfer 2011: K. M. Töpfer, Signa Militaria. Die römischen Feldzeichen in der Republik und im Principat. Monographien des RGZM 91 (Mainz 2011).

Torelli 2003: M. Torelli, Il fregio d'armi nel Museo di Antichità di Torino. Ipotesi per un monumento di un senatore di epoca Claudia. In: L. Mercando (ed.), Archeologia a Torino. Dall'età preromana all'Alto Medioevo (Torino 2003) 151-169.

Tortorella 1981a: S. Tortorella, Le lastre campana. Problemi di produzione e di iconografia. In: X. Lafon / G. Sauron (eds), L'art décoratif à Rome à la fin de la république et au début du principat. Collection de l'École Française de Rome 55 (Roma 1981) 61-100.

1981b: S. Tortorella, Le lastre campana. In: A. Giardina / A. Schiavone (eds), Società romana e produzione schiavistica. 2: Merci, mercati et scambi nel mediterraneo (Roma 1981) 219-235.

2007: S. Tortorella, Lastre campana dalla villa di Punta Eolo a Ventotene. In: M. Angle / A. Germano (eds), Museo e territorio: atti del V convegno, Velletri, 17-18 novembre 2006 (Roma 2007) 31-42.

2008: S. Tortorella, Processione trionfale e circense sulle lastre Campana. In: Le perle e il filo: a Mario Torelli per i suoi settanta anni (Venosa 2008) 301-321.

Tosi 1992: G. Tosi, Un fregio d'armi Patavino: aspetti topografici e iconografici. Archeologia Veneta 15, 1992, 151-165.

Toynbee 1971: J. M. C. Toynbee, Death and burial in the Roman world (London 1971).

Traversari 1971: G. Traversari, L'Arco dei Sergi. Pubblicazioni dell'Istituto di Archeologia dell'Università di Padova 8 (Padova 1971).

Trillmich 1990: W. Trillmich, Un sacrarium del culto imperial en el teatro de Mérida. Anas 2-3, 1989-1990 (1990), 87-102.

1993: W. Trillmich, Novedades en torno al programa iconográfico del teatro romano de Mérida. In: T. Nogales Basarrate (ed.), Actas de la I reunión sobre escultura romana en Hispania (Mérida 1993) 113-123.

2004: W. Trillmich, Monumentalización del espacio público emeritense como reflejo de la evolución histórica colonial: el ejemplo del teatro emeritense y sus fases. In: T. Nogales Basarrate (ed.), Augusta Emerita: Territorios, Espacios, Imágenes y Gentes en Lusitania Romana. Monografías Emeritenses 8 (Mérida 2004) 275-284.

Trillmich et al. 1993: W. Trillmich / T. Hauschild / M. Blech / H. G. Niemeyer / A. Nünnerich-Asmus / U. Kreilinger, Hispania Antiqua: Denkmäler der Römerzeit (Mainz 1993).

Troxell 1975: H. A. Troxell, Sylloge Nummorum Graecorum. The collection of the American Numismatic Society. 3: Bruttium – Sicily I: Abacaenum-Eryx (New York 1975).

Truckell 1966: A. E. Truckell, The Grierson collection, Thornhill, and its disposal. Transactions of the Dumfriesshire and Galloway Natural History and Antiquarian Society 43, 1966, 65-72.

Tsangari 2007: D. I. Tsangari, Corpus des monnaies d'or, d'argent et de bronze de la confédération étolienne (Athènes 2007).

Turcan 1972: R. Turcan, Les religions de l'Asie dans la vallée du Rhône. Etudes préliminaires aux religions orientales dans l'empire romain 30 (Leiden 1972).

Tusa 1995: V. Tusa, I sarcofagi romani in Sicilia. Bibliotheca Archaeologica 14 (Roma ²1995).

Ulbert 1969: G. Ulbert, Gladii aus Pompeji: Vorarbeiten zu einem Corpus römischer Gladii. Germania 47, 1969, 97-128.

Ungaro 1994: L. Ungaro, Il foro di Traiano: decorazione architettonico scultorea e programma decorativo. In: La ciutat en el món romà – La ciudad en el mundo romano. 2: Comunicacions = Comunicaciones (Tarragona 1994) 410-413.

1995: L. Ungaro, Figure di Daci, un puzzle di armi, »scudi« con ritratti, statue: la lettura dei materiali dopo i recenti restauri. In: E. La Rocca / L. Ungaro / R. Menghini (eds), I luoghi del consenso imperiale. Il Foro di Augusto. Il Foro di Traiano. Introduzione storico-topografico (Roma 1995) 102-108.

Ungaro/Messa 1989: L. Ungaro / L. Messa, Pannelli con rilievi d'armi dal Foro di Traiano: nota preliminare. Archeologia Classica 41, 1989, 215-236.

Ungaro/Milella 1995: L. Ungaro / M. Milella, I luoghi del consenso imperiale. Il Foro di Augusto. Il Foro di Traiano. Catalogo (Roma 1995).

Ungaro/Milella/Lalle 1995: L. Ungaro / M. Milella / A. Lalle, Il Foro di Traiano: i recenti restauri e la decorazione architettonico-scultorea con particolare riferimento ai portico laterali della piazza. Archeologia Laziale XII/1, 1995, 151-161 (= Quaderni di Archeologia Etrusco-Italica 23).

Unz/Deschler-Erb 1997: C. Unz / E. Deschler-Erb, Katalog der Militaria aus Vindonissa: Militärische Funde, Pferdegeschirr und Jochteile bis 1976. Veröffentlichungen der Gesellschaft pro Vindonissa 16 (Vindonissa 1997).

Ure 1793: D. Ure, The history of Rutherglen and East Kilbride (Glasgow 1793).

van der Valk 1987: M. van der Valk, Eustathii Archiepiscopi Thessalonicensis Commentarii ad Homerii Iliadem Pertinentes ad fidem codicis laurentiani editit. 4: Praefationem et commentarios ad libros P-Omega complectens (Leiden 1987).

Van Arsdell 1989: R. D. Van Arsdell, Celtic coinage of Britain (London 1989).

1994: R. D. Van Arsdell, Celtic chicanery IV – the war trumpet. Spink Numismatic Circular, April 1994, 103.

1995: R. D. Van Arsdell, Some recent discoveries. Spink Numismatic Circular, February 1995, 3.

Venclová 1998: N. Venclová, Mšecké Žehrovice in Bohemia: archaeological background to a Celtic hero, 3rd-2nd cent. BC (Sceaux 1998).

Vendries 1995: C. Vendries, A propos d'une exposition d'archéologie musicale: recherches sur le paysage sonore et musical de la Gaule préromaine. In: A. Muller (ed.), Instruments, musiques et musiciens de l'antiquité classique. Ateliers 4 (Lille 1995) 93-105.

1999: C. Vendries, La trompe, le gaulois et le sanglier. Revue des Études Anciennes 101/3-4, 1999, 367-391.

2007: C. Vendries, La trompe de Neuvy. Anatomie d'un objet sonore. In: Gorget/Guillaumet 2007, 120-144.

2017: C. Vendries, Harpes druidiques et trompettes guerrières. La musique des Gaulois dans l'art et l'imagerie populaire du XVIIIe siècle à nos jours. In: Hébert/Péchoux 2017, 53-73.

Venturi 1992: L. Venturi, Gruppo di materiali archeologici conservati nella tenuta di S. Cesareo sulla via Ardeatina. Bullettino della Commissione Archeologica Comunale di Roma 94, 1991-1992 (1992), 428-436.

Veres 2009: J. Veres, The depiction of a carnyx-player from the Carpathian Basin: a study of two Celtic bronze statuettes from eastern Hungary. Archäologisches Korrespondenzblatt 39, 2009, 231-249.

Vermeeren 1993: T. Vermeeren, Prisonniers et trophées dans le monnayage des premiers Sévères. In: T. Hackens / G. Moucharte / C. Courtius / H. Dewitt / V. van Driessche (eds), Actes du XIe Congrès International de Numismatique. II: Monnaies celtiques et romaines (Louvain-la-Neuve 1993) 281-288.

Vermeule 1957: C. C. Vermeule, Herakles crowning himself: new Greek statuary types and their place in Hellenistic and Roman art. Journal of Hellenic Studies 77, 1957, 283-299.

1958: C. C. Vermeule, Aspects of scientific archaeology in the seventeenth century: marble reliefs, Greek vases, manuscripts and minor objects in the Dal Pozzo-Albani drawings of Classical antiquities. Proceedings of the American Philosophical Society 102/2, 1958, 193-214.

1960: C. C. Vermeule, Hellenistic and Roman cuirassed statues: the evidence of paintings and reliefs in the chronological development of cuirass types. Berytus 13, 1959-1960 (1960), 1-82.

1964: C. C. Vermeule, Hellenistic and Roman cuirassed statues: a supplement. Berytus 15, 1964, 95-110.

1966: C. C. Vermeule, Hellenistic and Roman cuirassed statues: second supplement. Berytus 16, 1966, 49-59.

1968: C. C. Vermeule, Roman Imperial art in Greece and Asia Minor (Cambridge MA 1968).

1974: C. C. Vermeule, Cuirassed statues – 1974 supplement. Berytus 23, 1974, 5-26.

Verzár-Bass 2003: M. Verzár-Bass, CSIR Italia. Regio X; II, 1 Trieste (Roma 2003).

Vial 2007: E. Vial, Les figures animals. In: Gorget/Guillaumet 2007, 48-86.

Villaronga 1994: L. Villaronga, Corpus nummum hispaniae ante Augusti aetatem (Madrid 1994).

Vismari 1998: N. Vismari (ed.), Sylloge Nummorum Graecorum, Italia. Milano, Civiche Raccolte Numismatiche. IV: Lucania – Bruttium. 2 Bruttium (Milano 1998).

Vitali 2003a: D. Vitali (ed.), L'immagine tra mondo Celtico e mondo Etrusco-Italico. Aspetti della cultura figurative nell'antichità. Studi e Scavi 20 (Bologna 2003).

2003b: D. Vitali, Un inedito scudo celtico su una kelebe volterrana. In: Vitali 2003a, 75-83.

Vitali/Minarini 2001: D. Vitali / L. Minarini, Tête de jeune homme avec torc. In: L. Flutsch (ed.), Vrac. L'archéologie en 83 trouvailles: hommage collectif à Daniel Paunier [exposition catalogue Vrac] (Lausanne 2001) 168-169.

Vogel 1973: L. Vogel, The column of Antoninus Pius (Cambridge MA 1973).

Vollenweider 1979: M.-L. Vollenweider, Musée d'Art et d'Histoire de Genève. Catalogue raisonné des sceaux, cylindres, intailles et camées. II: Les portraits, les masques de théatre, les symboles politiques; une contribution à l'histoire des civilisations hellénistique et romaine (Mainz 1979).

Vouga 1923: P. Vouga, La Tène. Monographie de la station (Leipzig 1923).

Waddell 2014: J. Waddell, Archaeology and Celtic myth: an exploration (Dublin 2014).

Waddington 2014: K. Waddington, The biography of a settlement: an analysis of Middle Iron Age deposits and houses at Howe, Orkney. Archaeological Journal 171, 2014, 61-96.

Wadsworth 1924: E. L. Wadsworth, Stucco reliefs of the first and second centuries still extant in Rome. Memoirs of the American Academy in Rome 4, 1924, 9-102.

Wainwright 1953: F. T. Wainwright, A souterrain identified in Angus. Antiquaries Journal 33, 1953, 65-71.

1963: F. T. Wainwright, The souterrains of southern Pictland (London 1963).

Walser 1972: G. Walser, Römische und gallische Militärmusik. In: Festschrift Arnold Geering zum siebzigsten Geburtstag: Beiträge zur Zeit und zum Begriff des Humanismus vorwiegend aus dem Bereich der Musik (Bern 1972) 231-239.

Walter 1993: H. Walter, Les barbares de l'occident romain: corpus des Gaules et des provinces de Germanie. Annales littéraires de l'Université de Besançon 494 = Centre de Recherches d'Histoire Ancienne 122 (Paris 1993).

1998: H. Walter, Fragment de manche de patère de Mandeure. In: S. Deyts (ed.), À la rencontre des dieux gaulois: un défi à César [exhibition catalogue Saint-Germain-en-Laye] (Dijon 1998) 51.

Walters 1899: H. B. Walters, Catalogue of the bronzes, Greek, Roman, and Etruscan, in the Department of Greek and Roman Antiquities, British Museum (London 1899).

1903: H. B. Walters, Catalogue of the terracottas in the Department of Greek and Roman Antiquities, British Museum (London 1903).

Warner 1993: R. B. Warner, Irish prehistoric goldwork: a provisional analysis. Archeomaterials 7, 1993, 101-113.

2003: R. Warner, Old letters and new technology – the Ballyrashane gold hoard. In: J. Fenwick (ed.), Lost and found: discovering Ireland's past (Dublin 2003) 151-164.

2004: R. Warner, Irish gold artefacts: observations from Hartmann's analytical data. In: H. Roche / E. Grogan / J. Bradley / J. Coles / B. Raftery (eds), From megaliths to metal: essays in honour of George Eogan (Oxford 2004) 72-82.

Watkin et al. 1996: J. Watkin / I. Stead / D. Hook / S. Palmer, A decorated shield-boss from the River Trent, near Ratcliffe-on-Soar. Antiquaries Journal 76, 1996, 17-30.

Watkins 1980: T. Watkins, Excavation of an Iron Age open settlement at Dalladies, Kincardineshire. Proceedings of the Society of Antiquaries of Scotland 110, 1978-1980 (1980), 122-164.

Watson 1926: W. J. Watson, The history of the Celtic place-names of Scotland (Edinburgh 1926).

Wattenberg 1963: F. Wattenberg, Las ceramicas indigenas de Numancia. Bibliotheca Praehistorica Hispana 4 (Madrid 1963).

Webb 1933: P. H. Webb, The Roman Imperial Coinage. V, II: Probus-Amandus (London 1933).

Weber 1993: C. Weber, Die bronze- und eisenzeitlichen Funde. In: Schalles / Schreiter 1993, 25-31.

Webster 1971: G. A. Webster, A hoard of Roman military equipment from Fremington Hagg. In: R. M. Butler (ed.), Soldier and civilian in Roman Yorkshire. Essays to commemorate the 19th centenary of the foundation of York (Leicester 1971) 107-125.

1985: G. Webster, The Roman imperial army of the first and second centuries AD (London ³1985).

Wegner 1957: M. Wegner, Ornamente kaiserzeitlicher Bauten Roms: Soffitten. Münstersche Forschungen 10 (Köln 1957).

1961: M. Wegner, Kapitelle und Friese vom Bogen der Sergier zu Pola. Bonner Jahrbücher 161, 1961, 263-276.

Wells 1999: P. S. Wells, The barbarians speak: how the conquered peoples shaped Roman Europe (Princeton NJ 1999).

2001: P. S. Wells, Beyond Celts, Germans and Scythians (London 2001).

Wendling 2013: H. Wendling, Manching reconsidered: new perspectives on settlement dynamics and urbanization in Iron Age central Europe. European Journal of Archaeology 16/3, 2013, 459-490.

Werner 1953: J. Werner, Keltisches Pferdegeschirr der Spätlatènezeit. Saalburg-Jahrbuch 12, 1953, 42-52.

Werth 2008: T. J. Werth, Great miracle or lying wonder? Janus-faced romance in Pericles. In: G. Bradshaw / T. Bishop (eds), The Shakespeare International Yearbook. 8: Special section, European Shakespeares (Aldershot 2008) 183-203.

Whimster 1981: R. Whimster, Burial practices in Iron Age Britain. BAR British Series 90 (Oxford 1981).

White 1979: A. White, Antiquities from the River Witham. I: Prehistoric and Roman. Lincolnshire Museums Information Sheet Archaeology Series 12 (Lincoln 1979).

Whitehouse 1997: D. Whitehouse, Roman glass in the Corning Museum of Glass 1 (Corning, New York 1997).

Widemann / Leblanc 1982: F. Widemann / J. Leblanc, Reconstitution de scènes à personnages provenant de monuments élevés en grand appareil de la cité gallo-romaine de Narbonne. Dialogues d'Histoire Ancienne 8, 1982, 339-361.

1985: F. Widemann / J. Leblanc, Dialogue avec M. Janon. Dialogues d'Histoire Ancienne 11, 1985, 783-787.

Wild 1970: J. P. Wild, Button-and-loop fasteners in the Roman provinces. Britannia 1, 1970, 137-155.

Wieland 1996: G. Wieland, Die Spätlatènezeit in Württemberg. Forschungen zur jüngeren Latènekultur zwischen Schwarzwald und Nördlinger Ries. Forschungen und Berichte zur Vor- und Frühgeschichte in Baden-Württemberg 63 (Stuttgart 1996).

2000: Hoops' Reallexikon der Germanischen Altertumskunde 16 (2000) 237-239 s. v. Kappel 2. Bad Buchau-Kappel, Kr. Biberach (G. Wieland).

2012: G. Wieland, Besondere Orte: »Naturheilige« Plätze. In: R. Röber / M. Jansen / S. Rau / C. von Nicolai / I. Frech (eds), Die Welt der Kelten. Zentren der Macht – Kostbarkeiten der Kunst [exhibition catalogue Stuttgart] (Ostfildern 2012) 277-283.

Wilhelm 1974: E. Wilhelm, Pierres sculptées et inscriptions de l'époque romaine (Luxembourg 1974).

Wilkes 1969: J. J. Wilkes, Dalmatia (London 1969).

Willems 1984: W. J. H. Willems, Romans and Batavians. A regional study in the Dutch Eastern River Area, II. Berichten van de Rijksdienst voor het Oudheidkundig Bodemonderzoek 34, 1984, 39-331.

Williams 1998: J. H. C. Williams, Imitation or invention? A new coin of Tasciovanus. Spink Numismatic Circular 106/8, 1998, 350-351.

2001a: J. Williams, Review of Creighton 2000. British Archaeology 57, 2001, 30-31.

2001b: J. H. C. Williams, Beyond the Rubicon: Romans and Gauls in Republican Italy (Oxford 2001).

Wilmott 2001: T. Wilmott, Cohors I Aelia Dacorum: a Dacian unit on Hadrian's Wall. Acta Musei Napocensis 38/1, 2001, 103-122.

Willis 1998: S. Willis, Industrial fired clay objects. In: Main 1998, 371-376.

Wilson 2001: A. Wilson, The Novantae and Romanization in Galloway. Transactions of the Dumfriesshire and Galloway Natural History and Antiquarian Society 75, 2001, 73-131.

2003: A. Wilson, Roman and native in Dumfriesshire. Transactions of the Dumfriesshire and Galloway Natural History and Antiquarian Society 77, 2003, 103-160.

Wilson 1851: D. Wilson, The archaeology and prehistoric annals of Scotland (Edinburgh 1851).

1854: D. Wilson, On the class of stone vessels known in Scotland as druidical paterae. Proceedings of the Society of Antiquaries of Scotland 1, 1851-1854 (1854), 115-118.

1863: D. Wilson, Prehistoric annals of Scotland (London 1863).

Wilson 1980: E. M. Wilson, Excavations at West Mains of Ethie, Angus. Proceedings of the Society of Antiquaries of Scotland 110, 1978-1980 (1980), 114-121.

Wilson 1882: G. Wilson, Notice of a crannog at Barhapple Loch, Glenluce, Wigtownshire. Archaeological Collections relating to the counties of Ayr and Wigton 3, 1882, 52-58.

Wirth 1929: F. Wirth, Römische Wandmalerei vom Untergang Pompejis bis Hadrian. Mitteilungen des Deutschen Archäologischen Instituts, Römische Abteilung 44, 1929, 91-166.

1968: F. Wirth, Römische Wandmalerei vom Untergang Pompejis bis ans Ende des dritten Jahrhunderts (Darmstadt ²1968).

Witteyer 2017: M. Witteyer, Ein Konsolengesims aus dem Theater von Mogontiacum/Mainz. In: A. von Berg / M. Schwab (eds), vorZeiten: 70 Jahre Landesarchäologie Rheinland-Pfalz. Archäologische Schätze an Rhein und Mosel [exhibition catalogue Mainz] (Regensburg 2017) 208-209.

Woelcke 1911: K. Woelcke, Beiträge zur Geschichte des Tropaions. Bonner Jahrbücher 120, 1911, 127-235.

Woimant 1993: G. P. Woimant, Le sanctuaire antique de Champlieu (commune d'Orrouy, Oise). Revue Archéologique de Picardie 1993, 1/2, 63-198.

Woods 2009: D. Woods, Caesar the elephant against Juba the snake. Numismatic Chronicle 2009, 189-192.

Worrell 2008: S. Worrell, Roman Britain in 2007 II. Finds reported under the Portable Antiquities Scheme. Britannia 39, 2008, 337-367.

Woytek 2003: B. Woytek, Arma et nummi. Forschungen zur römischen Finanzgeschichte und Münzprägung der Jahre 49 bis 42

v. Chr. Österreichische Akademie der Wissenschaften, Philosophisch-Historische Klasse: Denkschriften 312 = Veröffentlichungen der Numismatischen Kommission 40 = Veröffentlichungen der Kleinasiatischen Kommission 14 (Wien 2003).

2010: B. Woytek, Die Reichsprägung des Kaisers Traianus (98-117). Moneta Imperii Romani 14 = Veröffentlichungen der Numismatischen Kommission 48 = Österreichische Akademie der Wissenschaften, Philosophisch-Historische Klasse: Denkschriften 387 (Wien 2010).

Woytek/Zawadzka 2016: B. Woytek / A. Zawadzka, Ockham's razor. A structural analysis of the denarii of Coelius Caldus (RRC 437). Numismatic Chronicle 2016, 135-153.

Yates/Bradley 2010: D. Yates / R. Bradley, Still water, hidden depths: the deposition of Bronze Age metalwork in the English Fenland. Antiquity 84, 2010, 405-415.

Zanier 2016: W. Zanier, Der spätlatène- und frühkaiserzeitliche Opferplatz auf dem Döttenbichl südlich von Oberammergau. Münchner Beiträge zur Vor- und Frühgeschichte 62 (München 2016).

Zanker 1988: P. Zanker, The power of images in the age of Augustus. Jerome Lectures 16 (Ann Arbor 1988).

2000: P. Zanker, Die Frauen und Kinder der Barbaren auf der Markussäule. In: Scheid/Huet 2000, 163-174.

2002: P. Zanker, Domitian's palace on the Palatine and the Imperial image. In: A. K. Bowman / H. M. Cotton / M. Goodman / S. Price (eds), Representations of Empire: Rome and the Mediterranean world. Proceedings of the British Academy 114 (Oxford 2002) 105-130.

Zevi 2009: F. Zevi (ed.), Museo Archeologico dei Campi Flegrei. Catalogo Generale. 2: Pozzuoli (Napoli 2009).

Zieglé 2000: A. Zieglé, Le bloc sculpté 5009 découvert place Pey-Berland. In: W. Migeon, Un fragment du rempart romain de Bordeaux. Aquitania 17, 2000, 285-297.

Zieling 1989: N. Zieling, Studien zu germanischen Schilden der Spätlatène- und der römischen Kaiserzeit im freien Germanien. BAR International Series 505 (Oxford 1989).

Zsidi 1995: P. Zsidi (ed.), Gods, soldiers and citizens in Aquincum [exhibition catalogue] (Budapest 1995).